D1237502

Shopping in the Renaissance

Shopping in the Renaissance

CONSUMER CULTURES IN ITALY
1400–1600

YALE UNIVERSITY PRESS ~ NEW HAVEN AND LONDON

2557991

Published with the assistance of the Getty Foundation

Designed by Laura Bolick

Printed in China

Library of Congress Cataloging-in-Publication Data

Welch, Evelyn S., 1959-
Shopping in the Renaissance : consumer cultures in Italy 1400-1600 /
Evelyn Welch.
p. cm.
Includes bibliographical references (p.   ) and index.
ISBN 0-300-10752-8 (cl : alk. paper)
1. Consumers--Italy--History--To 1500. 2. Consumers--Italy--History--16th century. 3. Shopping--Italy-
-History--To 1500. 4. Shopping--Italy--History--16th century.
1. Title.
HC310.C6W45 2005
306.3´0945´09023--dc22
2004024095

A catalogue record for this book is available from the British Library

frontispiece *The Month of June* (detail of Figure 5)

CONTENTS

For the Kids

ACKNOWLEDGEMENTS

This book had its origins during a year as a University of Sussex exchange fellow at the Victoria and Albert Museum in 1996. I owe a great debt to the staff there, particularly to Marta Ajmar, Helen Clifford and John Styles for their encouragement in the early stages of this project. At Sussex, my colleagues, Craig Clunas, Michelle O'Malley and James Shaw read drafts and offered valued advice. Maurice Howard, Nigel Llewellyn, Liz James and Jenny Long have also offered extensive support. I would also like to thank Philippa Jackson, Barbara Furlotti, Fabrizio Nevola and Guido Rebecchini for help with documentary references. At Queen Mary, University of London I am grateful for the discussions I have had with Warren Boutcher, Jerry Brotton and Lisa Jardine. My collaborators on the Arts and Humanities Research Board and the Getty Foundation funded project, 'The Material Renaissance: Costs and Consumption in Italy, 1350-1650' have been the source of many stimulating ideas and suggestions. While it is difficult to pick out specific individuals from this group, Patricia Allerston provided much assistance on the second-hand market in sixteenth and seventeenth century Italy while Reinhold Mueller offered advice on monetary matters. My thanks as well to Jacqueline Musacchio, Patricia Fortini Brown and Deanna Shemek for their help in reading the manuscript in its penultimate stages. As all who work with her know well, to have Gillian Malpass as one's editor is an enormous privilege. I am very grateful to her for her help in shaping this book and to Laura Bolick who has managed its production so ably.

This work depends heavily on material in Italy's archives, both large and small. I would like to thank the staff at the State Archives in Bologna, Florence, Venice, Milan, Mantua and Rome and in the communal archives of Treviso and Prato. In London the staff of the Warburg Institute, The Institute of Historical Research, the British Library and the Conway Library, Courtauld Institute have been unfailing helpful. Ancilla Antonini of Index, Florence provided invaluable assistance with photographs. Funding for the research on this book has come from the Arts and Humanities Research Board of Great Britain and from the Getty Foundation; the work on apothecaries was funded by the Wellcome Trust. I am profoundly grateful for their assistance.

Finally, but far from least, I would like to thank my family for their patience with a mother who hates to go shopping herself but is happy to write about it at length.

A Note on Currency, Weights and Measures

As this book makes clear, Italy had a plethora of different currencies, weights and measures.

Two forms of recording were possible. The first used money of account, a notional form of accounting based on a duodecimal system of lire, soldi and denari (pounds, shillings and pence) with a ratio of 1 lire = 20 soldi = 240 denari. In sixteenth-century Rome and the papal states, however, it should be noted that a decimal system was in place where 1 scudo = 10 giulii = 100 baiocchi. Payments could be made in coins of gold, silver or a mixture of base metals and the ratio between coins and with monies of accounts fluctuated regularly.

Weights and measures were also local. Those referred to here are the braccia, used to measure lengths of cloth or architectural ground plans and the staia, used to measure volume.

Further information can be gained from Peter Spufford, *A Handbook of Medieval Exchange*, London, 1986 and Angelo Martini, *Manuale di metrologia ossia misure, pesi e monete in uso attualmente e anticamente presso tutti i populi*, Turin, 1993 (reprinted Rome, 1976).

1   Michael Landy, *Breakdown*, performance in the disused C&A department store, Oxford Street, London. Car seat on a conveyor belt and shredded remains of Landy's possessions. Commissioned and produced by Artangel, 2001, photograph by Hugo Glendinning.

CHAPTER ONE

Introduction

In February 2001 the British artist Michael Landy took over an empty department store in central London. Before a fascinated and occasionally distraught audience of friends, fellow-artists and strangers drawn in from the streets, he and his assistants placed all his personal possessions on a conveyor belt. Looping round the complex, mechanised route, Landy's furniture, record collection, clothing and even his car were first inventoried and then systematically dismembered, divided and shredded.[1] The work attracted considerable press attention and provoked a powerful public response. Landy's emphasis on destruction was seen as a challenge to the champions of consumerism and as a strong commentary on the seductions of acquisition and ownership. The setting, the bare interior of a store stripped of its lighting, counters and displays, was central to the work's meaning (Figure 1). As shoppers moved on from the performance into the still-functioning department stores and shops nearby, they were invited to reflect on the ultimate purposelessness of their purchases.

Commenting after the event, Landy described his surprise when a number of onlookers equated his actions with those of a holy figure or a saint. Yet the disposal or dispersal of possessions has been a fundamental part of religious asceticism since early Christianity. But unlike the powerful image of Saint Francis of Assisi giving away his cloak to a beggar before stripping off all his clothes in order to refuse his father's wealth, Landy had no intention of forming a new religious order (Figure 2). Landy's attack on human attachment to material possessions was a secular act of artistic performance, a

2   Sassetta, *St Francis of Assisi Giving his Cloak to a Beggar* and *St Francis Renouncing His Earthly Father*, The San Sepolcro Altarpiece, 1444, tempera on panel, The National Gallery of Art, London.

counterpart to contemporary celebrations of affluence and prosperity. As such he was, and is, part of a growing debate. Today, shopping, the process of going out to special sites to exchange earnings for consumable objects, is seen as both a force for good (consumer spending is saving Western domestic economies) and as a danger to society (consumer spending is destroying the environment and local diversity).[2] Given its current importance, such behaviour has been closely scrutinised by anthropologists and sociologists who have often argued that the purchase of mass-produced items is a defining characteristic of modernity.[3] In their turn, economists have looked for rational patterns of consumer spending, while an equally weighty literature has grown up to evaluate the emotive and psychological impulses that lie behind modern consumerism, culminating in a focus on the 'shopaholic' or kleptomaniac, usually a woman who, for complex reasons, is unable to control her desire to either buy or steal from stores.[4]

3   Michael Charles Fichot, *Le Bon Marché Store*, second half of nineteenth century, engraving, Bibliothèques des Arts Decoratifs, Archives Charmet, Paris.

Following in this wake, historians and art historians are using concepts such as the emergence of a public sphere and the agency of the consumer to map out a new narrative linking this changing social behaviour to the development of new architectural spaces.[5] Some have found the origins for contemporary shopping practices in the American malls of the 1930s or in the opening of the first department stores, such as Whiteley's in London in 1863 or the Bon Marché in Paris in 1869 (Figure 3).[6] These purpose-built buildings, with their fixed prices and large body of salaried personnel radically changed the nature of shopping. Buying became a leisure activity as well as a chore, one that women were increasingly able to enjoy. But while some have insisted that this was a distinctive feature of the late nineteenth and twentieth centuries, others have pushed back the transformation to the coffee-houses of eighteenth-century London, the mercers' shops of eighteenth-century Paris, or to the market halls and commercial chambers of seventeenth-century Amsterdam (Figure 4).[7] As new social rituals developed, such as reading the paper, listening to public concerts or discussing scientific innovations, so too did a demand for new products such as coffee, tea, chocolate, porcelain and printed chintzes. Here bow-shaped glass shop windows, with their displays of exotic, imported goods are thought to have tempted buyers, sparking off a capitalist revolution and eventually liberating women from the home.[8]

In the search for the first modern shopping trip, these eighteenth- and nineteenth-century developments are often set against the backdrop of an undifferentiated late medieval past. The story of temporal progression requires more distant periods to be perceived as lacking in sophistication. The pre-industrial world is presented as having had a relatively limited access to a smaller range of regionally produced goods and a

4   An Early London Coffee House, signed A.S., c.1705, watercolour on paper, Department of Prints and Drawings, The British Museum, London.

minimum of disposable income.[9] Most of a family's earnings would have been spent on food. Little was left over for non-essentials, and most goods were produced within the home itself.[10]

These assumptions have meant that while many studies have looked for a growing mass-market for consumer goods in the eighteenth century, Renaissance scholarship has focused on elite patronage or international trade.[11] Recently, however, there has been a tendency to argue that the supposed consumer boom of the enlightenment period started much earlier and that this revolution took place, not in London or Paris, but in fifteenth-century Italy.[12] In 1993, for example, the economic historian Richard Goldthwaite argued that, 'the material culture of the Renaissance generated the very first stirring of the consumerism that was to reach a veritable revolutionary stage in the eighteenth century and eventually to culminate in the extravagant throw-away, fashion-ridden, commodity-culture of our own times'.[13]

But the question arises whether the Italian Renaissance consumerism was really the embryo of contemporary expenditure, a defining moment in the transition from the medieval to the modern.[14] Does the detail from the 1470 Ferrarese frescoes of Palazzo Schifanoia depicting elegant shops with their customers represent a new form of activity or an ongoing tradition (Figure 5)? Is it in any way, however marginal, indicative of, or evidence for, a new form of consumer behaviour? While there will be much in this book that seems familiar, such as the pleasure that teenage girls took in trips to the market, there is a great deal that is very different. Indeed, far from pinpointing the start of 'ourselves' in fifteenth- and sixteenth-century Florence, the experience of the Italian

5   *The Month of June*, detail from lower register showing merchants in their shops, c.1470, fresco, Palazzo Schifanoia, Ferrara.

Renaissance challenges rather than reinforces a sense of linear transfer from past to present. In particular, it threatens some basic assumptions concerning the connections between architecture and consumer behaviour. In the English language the links could not be closer. A standard dictionary defines shopping as, 'the action of visiting a shop or shops for the purpose of inspecting or buying goods'. A shopper is, 'one who frequents a shop or shops for the purpose of inspecting or buying goods'.[15] But this correlation has no parallel in other European languages where there is little, if any, verbal connection between 'the shop' and the activity, 'shopping'.

This is an important distinction because the impact of this assumed association between the architecture of commerce and modernity goes far beyond semantics. Early twentieth-century sociologists and economists who defined concepts of consumption relied on models of social development that considered shopping in stores as a far more sophisticated form of exchange than gift-trade or administered-trade. The latter were only phases that societies went through before finally emerging as fully developed (and hence more effective and efficient) market economies.[16] This was not simply a theory. It was put into practice in countries such as Italy which only became a nation in the 1860s. From that point onwards, defining an Italian city as a modern urban society involved constructing new commercial and social spaces, particularly those modelled on the more seemingly advanced English and French examples. The so-called 'Liberty' or Art Nouveau style was adopted for some shop fronts while glass and iron proved popular for new shopping areas (Figure 6). When in 1864, for example, the city of Florence began demolishing its walls, gates and medieval market centre, it was to mark the town's transformation into the first capital of the new nation (Figures 7 and 8).[17] Florence was not to stop, as one protagonist put it, 'in the lazy contemplation of our past glories but fight gallantly on the road to progress'.[18] In 1865, it was even suggested that the entire market areas of the city centre should be transformed into a glass gallery on the model of the English Great Exhibition Hall before it was agreed to tear it down and rebuild the densely packed centre in a more piecemeal fashion.[19]

Likewise, in 1864, the city of Milan marked its entry into the Italian nation with major urban renewal plans. This included a galleried arcade, whose construction contract was awarded to the British-based 'City of Milan Improvement Company Limited'.[20] As the first King of the united Italy, Vittorio Emanuele II laid the foundation stones of the Galleria, the new glass and iron mall was presented as a symbol of the new country's future prosperity and a rejection of its backwards past (Figure 9).

But these nineteenth-century debates reveal a more complex and contradictory set of attitudes than a simple embrace of British engineering. Photographers using advanced technologies for the period captured the emptied spaces of the old Florentine market while graphic artists produced postcard images of what was to be destroyed. Londoners who had visited the city wrote to *The Times* to decry the destruction of the old town centre and city walls.[21] A sense of the need to preserve an attractive 'local' culture for the tourist market vied with the political desire to be accepted as the equal of the economically advanced countries of Europe and the United States.

The issues raised by the Milanese Galleria and the destruction of Florence's old market centre have resonances that go far beyond the

6 F. Scarlatti Flower Shop, Via Tournabuoni, Florence, 1902, silver salt photograph.

7 (*above left*)   View of the Mercato Vecchio, Florence, with a butcher's shop and other vendors, photograph taken before 1883.

8 (*above right*)   View of the Mercato Vecchio, Florence, following the demolition of central shops and prior to the complete destruction of the market, photograph taken before 1883.

9   Galleria Vittorio Emmanuele II, Milan, 1872–80, albumen photograph. Fratelli Alinari Museum of the History of Photography, Malandrini Collection.

Italian peninsula and the nineteenth century. The competing values of preservation and nostalgia versus modernity and progress continue to have serious consequences today. Planners eager to impose change have tended to describe developing countries as having 'medieval' types of exchange. Open markets in Africa and Asia, systems of barter and supposedly informal networks of credit, have been presented as either backwards, or, conversely, as more romantic and natural than contemporary North American and British supermarkets and shopping malls.[22] As in nineteenth-century Florence, seemingly unregulated and potentially unhygienic markets have been driven from city centres in places such as Hong Kong and Singapore by officials hoping to exclude elements perceived as old-fashioned from their growing economies.[23] In contrast, highly developed urban areas such as New York and London, have re-introduced 'farmer's markets'. These evoke traditional street fairs in order to reassure customers that produce sold from stalls and served up in brown bags is somehow more genuine than shrink-wrapped goods removed from a refrigerated cabinet.

SHOPPING IN THE RENAISSANCE

Given this context, it is difficult to step back and assess how men and women actually went out to shop in the past without falling into a narrative of either progress or decline. This is particularly acute for the Renaissance. During the period between 1400 and 1600, the daily business of buying and selling was an act of embedded social behaviour, not a special moment for considered reflection. While international merchants' manuals do survive both in manuscript and in print, the ordinary consumer's ability to assess value, select goods, bargain, obtain credit and finally to pay, was learnt primarily through observation, practice and experience rather than through any form of written instruction.[24]

This means that any study of Renaissance buying practices, where exchanges were transitory and verbal, has to rely on scattered and often problematic evidence. The images, literary sources, criminal records, statutes, auction and price lists, family accounts and diaries used in this book all had their own original purposes and formats. Their meanings were rarely fixed and the same item might be perceived in different ways in different times and places. For example, a poem such as Antonio Pucci's four-teenth-century description of the Mercato Vecchio in Florence, might carry one meaning for its audience when heard during a time of famine and yet another when read in a period of prosperity. But despite its slippery nature, it is still important to set such 'soft' evidence against the seemingly more stable facts and figures that make up grain prices and daily wage rates.

This book takes, therefore, the approach of a cultural historian in an attempt to gain an insight into the experience of the Renaissance marketplace. While some of the material goes over the immediate boundaries of the title, the book focuses primarily on central and northern Italy between 1400 and 1600. This is, in part, because of the wealth of documentation available for this period and region. Venice, an entrepôt whose retailers served both an international and local clientele, was exceptional in its commercial sophistication and specialisation. But the entire northern and central Italian peninsula, with its multiplicity of large and medium-sized towns and distribution networks of ports, canals and roads that reached far into the countryside, was much more urbanised than the rest of Europe. Unlike England where the inhabitants of villages and hamlets gravitated to larger market towns to buy and sell produce, even the smaller and more isolated of Italy's rural and urban communities housed permanent shops and regular markets.[25] For example, sixteenth-century Altopascio, a Tuscan mountain village with a population of 700 inhabitants had five shoemakers, two grocers and a ceramic seller, a *bottegaio di piatti*, as well as a blacksmith.[26] The slightly larger Tuscan town of Poppi in the Casentino had a population of 1,450. In 1590, its inhabitants benefited from nine grocery stores, two bakeries, two butchers, three drugstores, a mercer's shop, a barber, a tailor and a shoemaker along with workshops for wool, leather and iron as well as kilns producing ceramic wares.[27] These amenities served the wider locality as well as the small town, a relationship noted when the municipal council allowed complete immunity for debtors on market days, 'for the good and benefit and maintenance of Poppi, considering its location on a dry hill and in need of being frequented and visited by other men and people'.[28]

Of equal importance was the diversity and competition between these urban centres, both large and small. Italy's political fragmentation had considerable cultural consequences. By the mid-fifteenth century power on the peninsula was roughly divided between the Kingdom of Naples, the Papal States, the Duchy of Milan and the city-states of Florence and Venice. By the end of the century, however, the fragile balance had been disrupted as the growing powers of France, Spain and the Habsburg empire attempted to gain control. After 1530, Italy's two major territorial states, Lombardy and Naples, were ruled by viceroys who drew on local urban structures but answered to Spain. These multiple boundaries – local, regional and international – allowed for the coexistence of legal systems as well as for the circulation of different forms of currencies, dress, codes of conduct, gesture and language. The diversity had real material meanings. Velvets permitted to butchers' wives in Milan might be forbidden to those in Venice; hats that seemed desirable in Naples may have been rejected in Genoa. Although the costume books from the second half of the sixteenth century such as those of Cesare Vecellio and Pietro Bertelli often exaggerated the differences, the fashions forged in Rome were quite distinct from those in Mantua or Ferrara (Figures 10–12). Even women living under the same jurisdiction, such as those in Vicenza and Venice, might wear different garments (Figures 13–14). This created issues around novelty that were very different from those of nation-states such as France and England where the major contrasts were between a single capital city like Paris or London and the provincial towns and rural communities.

Alongside the political and geographic variations described above, the standard historical narrative points to a period of collapse in population after the Black Death in

Mulier Romana.

28

Nobilis Matrona Mantuana.

Virgo Ferariensis.

10 (*above left*)   Pietro Bertelli, *Diversarum nationum habitus*, Padua, 1594–6, engraving, 'Mulier Romana', Biblioteca Riccardiana, Florence, St.12886, figure 28.

11 (*above right*)   Pietro Bertelli, *Diversarum nationum habitus*, Padua, 1594–6, engraving, 'Nobilis Matrona Mantuana', figure 19, The British Library, London.

12 (*left*)   Pietro Bertelli, *Diversarum nationum habitus*, Padua, 1594–6, engraving, 'Virgo Ferariensis', figure 20, The British Library, London,

13 (*above left*)   Cesare Vecellio, *De gli habiti antichi, et moderni et diverse parti del mondo libri due*, Venice, 1590, engraving, 'Venetiane per casa', Wellcome Library, London.

14 (*above right*)   Cesare Vecellio, *De gli habiti antichi, et moderni et diverse parti del mondo libri due*, Venice, 1590, engraving, 'Vicentina', Wellcome Library, London.

1348 and a resulting increase in living standards as salaries rose. Following a sudden jump in wages in the second half of the fourteenth century, scholars have noted that there was considerable stability for much of the fifteenth century.[29] There was a new wave of population growth beginning in the sixteenth century, one that was partially halted by disease and famine in the 1570s and 1580s before recovering again.[30] This was accompanied by increasing levels of inflation, whose causes remain controversial.[31] Finally, the impact of professional printing which began in the 1460s, the increasing awareness of the Americas and Asia and the Reformation movement are only some of the most dramatic of the many formidable challenges that occurred over this period. In particular, the Catholic response to the religious attacks of Martin Luther and others, as embodied in the Council of Trent (1545–63), had an important impact on civic behaviour. Tridentine regulations, supported by the new inquisitorial and civic groups responsible for preventing heresy, prompted a tightening of social and religious strictures that impacted on everyday behaviour as well as on the Church and its liturgy.[32]

The shifting social and political backdrop of this two-hundred-year period encourages an emphasis on change. Indeed, there were very important signs of innovation in the economy, particularly towards the end of the second half of the sixteenth century. For example, in Venice there was increasing sub-specialisation and the development of new types of shops such as the *vendecolori* who sold pigments to the city's painters.[33] There were also a rising number of patents issued in cities across Italy. These provided monopoly rights to manufacture and distribute a wide range of new products and import substitutes. These included new materials such as the cheaper fabrics that imitated more expensive silks and velvets; glassware that mimicked porcelain; stucco that could simulate bronze; paste gems and pierced pearls that suggested expensive jewels. Hydrolics, milling, the soap and silk industries, and the print trade were only some of the activities that benefited from patents issued in Venice, Florence, Genoa and Mantua during the late sixteenth century.[34] The language used in these documents suggests that producers were increasingly stressing novelty and innovation when appealing to potential buyers. In 1577, the Milanese bookseller Ambrogio Lanfranco was granted a patent giving him a lifetime monopoly on the manufacture and sale of printed fans bearing the emblems of the King of Spain and the Pope along with poems in praise of each, a privilege that was awarded because they were 'new products' that had been devised through Lanfranco's 'ingenuity, industry and expense'.[35]

These designs, which, as these surviving late sixteenth-century and early seventeenth-century versions demonstrate (Figures 15–16), allowed buyers cut out and decorate their own fans, were only one of many novelties that were available to consumers. Inventories and other evidence for ownership similarly suggest an expansion in the number and type of objects owned by householders over the same period. There was more linen in the boxes and chests that orphaned children inherited, more paintings on the walls of the wealthy and moderately well-off families who fought over inheritances, and more maiolica and glassware in the cupboards of widows who took over their husband's estates.[36] The documentation of ownership is reinforced by evidence of importation and regional distribution. For example, the goods arriving at the customs dock in early fifteenth-century Rome were rich both in their number and in the diversity of the items that were unloaded. As an example, a single consignment from one ship arriving at the docks in the mid-fifteenth century contained 58 bone inkwells and caskets, a chessboard, 65 glass vials, a case of coloured crystal glass, 2 barrels of glass rosaries and 5 portable altars. About the same time another Aquilean merchant imported 300 'volti santi', saints' images like the single sheet produced in Florence featuring Saint Catherine of Siena which were sold by licensed picture vendors who had stalls on the Portico of the Vatican (Figure 17).[37] Other imports, particularly by German merchants bringing in small-scale metal wares such as dishes, pins, needles, scissors and glittering gilt

fringes for garments along with paternoster beads and prints are documented for fifteenth-century Bologna and other cities whose custom records have survived for the period.[38]

This evidence could be multiplied while work such as that of the historian Duccio Balestracci indicates that this increase in supply was not limited to the demands of an urban elite but was integrated into rural lifestyles lower down the social scale.[39] The account book of his mid-fifteenth-century Sienese peasant farmer shows that this illiterate sharecropper (he had his clients and suppliers write down his records for him) used a

15 Agostino Carracci, *Sheet for making a Fan*, c.1589–95, engraving, Gabinetto Disegni e Stampe degli Uffizi, Florence, 17010 st.sc. The sheet is inscribed, 'August. Carazza inv e fe'.

16 Macerata, Anonymous artist, c.1625, *Sheet for Making a Fan*, Civica Raccolta delle Stampe A. Bertarelli, Milan, Cassetta Ventole, Artistiche-1. Both images are printed on the reverse with a poem entitled, 'modo per pigliare il santissimo giubileo dell'anno santo in Roma e in Macerata per il Salvioni 1625'.

range of credit arrangements and payments in kind to acquire an expensive bed, red stockings and gold and silver buckles and ornaments. The Florentine sumptuary law of 1475 forbidding peasants who worked the land and their wives and children from wearing any form of silk, velvet or belts that had silver, gold, gems or pearls in them indicates that owning such clothing was considered a possibility.[40] This suggests that the demand for luxuries could cut across social boundaries and that credit was flexible

17 Baccio Baldini (att.), *Saint Catherine of Siena*,
c.1465–75, engraving, Department of Prints and Drawings, The British Museum, London.

enough to permit the satisfaction of both needs and wants. This has been reinforced by recent work on the second-hand trade and the rental market in goods in both Venice and Florence which has shown how important it is to shift attention away from the 'new' to the 'nearly new' in order to fully understand issues of acquisition and demand.[41]

Goldthwaite has suggested that this range of evidence demonstrates a Renaissance consumer revolution, one that prefigured the developments in eighteenth-century London or Paris. But is this really the case? The perspective, of course, depends in part on the evidence involved. Patents will always emphasise innovation while legal statutes were usually anxious to stress tradition. But the past is not simply a shadow of the present and although there was an increase in certain new types of sales, such as lotteries and stage performances by charlatans during this period, most forms of retailing remained remarkably constant. When, for example, major reform campaigns concerning commercial behaviour were initiated in Rome and Bologna in the 1580s, earlier fourteenth-century legislation was revived, often word for word, before being reissued in a new format as a printed leaflet. When offenders came before the magistrates in the late sixteenth century, their excuses similarly mirrored those of two centuries before.

The products they were accused of counterfeiting, adulterating or on which they had failed to pay taxes may have changed, but the language with which buyers, sellers and magistrates described the processes had not. From this perspective, the creation of department stores in late nineteenth-century Florence and Milan becomes more, rather than less challenging to traditional modes of salesmanship in Italy. The new buildings and Art Nouveau shop fronts were exciting and potentially alienating imports, not gradual evolutions from indigenous practices that had slowly changed over time. But at the same time, the stability with which Italian cities managed their consumption practices does not necessarily reflect an impoverished response to transition. Familiar modes and methods could be overlaid with new meanings and adapted to meet changing needs. Selling new goods in 'old-fashioned' ways that relied on personal contact, credit and trust may have made them more, rather than less acceptable to a wider customer base.

Behind the theoretical concerns and interpretations lay practical problems that need investigation. How did men and women of different social classes go out into the street, squares and shops to buy the goods they needed and wanted on a daily, or on a once-in-a-lifetime basis during the Renaissance period? When and where could they shop? Did they send servants, or were deliveries made to their doors? How did they know how much something cost? Could they return items that weren't satisfactory? How did they know when they were getting good value or when they were being cheated?

To answer such basic questions, the book opens by exploring the long-standing metaphors and stereotypes that were to describe the experience of participating in the marketplace. Part Two then looks at the impact these attitudes had on the developing urban geography of Renaissance cities before, in Part Three, turning to the more transient forms of fairs, auctions and lotteries. An examination in Part Four of the consumers themselves allows us to ask how these mental, verbal and visual images shaped the business of buying and selling. Who actually undertook the different types of shopping required by a Renaissance household? How did life cycles, lifestyles and the rhetoric of honour, familial dignity and pride affect the way provisioning and purchasing were undertaken? Finally, the book finishes by exploring two seemingly very different types of commodities: antiquities and indulgences. Despite their diversity, both posed dramatic challenges to contemporary notions of market value and to the concept of commodification itself.

Part One

SEEING SHOPPING

CHAPTER TWO

Markets and Metaphors

One of the clearest descriptions of a Renaissance shopping trip comes from a letter written on 12 April, 1491 by Ludovico Maria Sforza of Milan to his sister-in-law Isabella d'Este in Mantua. Reporting on activities of Isabella's sister, the sixteen-year-old Beatrice d'Este and her young cousin the Duchess of Milan, Isabella of Aragon, he wrote that:

> And now that they are here in Milan, they set off when it was raining yesterday, by foot, on the ground, accompanied by four to six of their ladies, wearing little woollen cloths, or headdresses over their heads, in order to buy those things which are available in the city (*per andare a comparare de le cose che sono per la città*). But since it is not the custom for women to go about with such cloths on their heads here, it seems that some of the women in the street began to make villainous remarks, upon which my wife fired up and began to curse them in return, in such a manner that they expected to come to blows. They then returned home completely muddy and bedraggled, which was a fine sight! I believe that when your Ladyship, who is so spirited, is here, they will go out with even greater spirit, and if any one dares to say villainous things to you, you will defy them all and give those women a real knifing![1]

Isabella replied rapidly in equally jocular terms, prompting Ludovico to write again:

> Your letter in answer to mine concerning the Duchess [Isabella of Aragon] and my illustrious consort having gone about Milan with little woollen headdresses was most pleasing to me. I knew that your sure spirit was ready for such deeds and that you

knew how to behave in such a way that you would not allow anyone to be villain-ous. And when I read your letter, I could almost see you in full spirit, knowing well how to reply to any one who dared to insult you.[2]

The image of the Marchioness of Mantua embroiled in a market brawl is far from the conventional picture of aristocratic female behaviour suggested by Beatrice's demure sculpted bust and Isabella's elegant portrait (Figures 18–19). Nonetheless, there are a number of issues raised by this correspondence that should make us pause. The light-hearted exchange was written in a very specific context: as evidence of a mature man's affection for his much younger wife. When the letter was written, Ludovico's mistress,

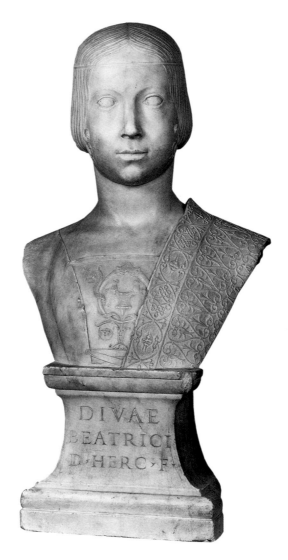

18   Giancristoforo Romano, *Beatrice d'Este*, c.1490, marble bust, Paris, Louvre.

19 Titian, *Portrait of Isabella d'Este*, 1534–6, oil on canvas, Kunsthistorisches Museum, Vienna.

20   Leonardo da Vinci, *Portrait of Cecilia Gallerani,*
'Lady with an Ermine' (detail), c.1495, oil and tempera on
panel, Czartoryski Museum, Cracow.

Cecilia Gallerani, seen in the portrait painted by Leonardo da Vinci, was heavily pregnant. She was living alongside the signorial family in Milan's Castello Sforzesco as she
waited to give birth (Figure 20).[3] The Este had repeatedly complained about this insult
to Beatrice's honour and Ludovico's correspondence was part of a calculated effort to
reassure his sister-in-law of his loyalty. Under pressure for his own sexual misdemeanours, Ludovico could not afford to be seen to criticise his bride. Hence a trip 'to
buy things in the city' was presented as a moment of fun, one that elicited laughter
rather than disapproval.

   As this suggests, the teenage escapade was not part of Beatrice's daily routine. This
was entertainment rather than a chore. But even more mundane marketing was done
by a surprising range of figures. Accustomed to seeing the domestic shopping undertaken almost exclusively by women and servants in London, the early seventeenth-
century writer Thomas Coryate remarked with surprise at the number of Venetian
noblemen who could be seen in the Rialto market:

   I have observed a thing amongst the Venetians that I have not a little wondered at,
   that their Gentlemen and greatest Senators, a man worth perhaps two million of

duckats, will come into the market, and buy their flesh, fish, fruites and other things as are necessary for the maintenance of their family; a token indeed of frugality, which is commendable in all men; but methinkes it not an argument of true generosity, that a noble spirit should deject itself to these petty and base matters, that are fitter to be done by servants than men of a generous parentage.[4]

While Coryate's remarks tell us as much about English practices and his own prejudices as they do about the Venetian marketplace, they are also indicative of the questions that shopping raised among observers concerning the social status and gender of those who frequented the market. Recognising that viewers conceptualised the marketplace as a problematic social space is, therefore, the first step in understanding how they saw themselves and others as active participants.

The Market as Metaphor

To describe the marketplace in the fifteenth or sixteenth centuries was to engage in a series of assumed stereotypes with a long history. Since the early middle ages and probably long before, European commentators had traditionally seen peddlers, markets, shops and vendors as highly charged metaphors with potential meanings.[5] These ran the spectrum from highly positive celebrations of fecundity, abundance and wealth to the most negative views concerning worldliness, sensuality, dirt and disease. The two polarities often co-existed, providing a range of topoi and motifs that could be deployed by writers and artists with the surety that they would be understood by audiences over many generations.

At the more positive end of the spectrum, the standard verbal and visual images employed emphasised the essential role of exchange in enhancing human survival and comfort. To ensure security, a well-managed city, like a well-managed home, had to provide basic sustenance. Urban panegyrics regularly stressed a town's material wealth. From the thirteenth century onwards, writers such as Bonvesin de la Riva on Milan, Giovanni Villani and Benedetto Dei on Florence, or Marin Sanudo and Francesco Sansovino on Venice, drew attention to the number of markets, shops, manufactures and foodstuffs contained within their exemplary cities, providing statistical evidence for urban prosperity. For example, in his *De Magnalibus Mediolani* of 1288, Bonvesin de la Riva celebrated the large number of armourers, and workers of wool, linen, cotton, silk and leather who could be found in the city. In 1338, Villani similarly enumerated the number of bread ovens in Florence that were able to supply its estimated 90,000 inhabitants before going on to list the amount of meat consumed and the manufacturing outlets that flourished within the city walls.[6] In the sixteenth century, Marin Sanudo and Francesco Sansovino both lauded Venice as a series of neighbourhoods that were towns in their own right, each with shops, bakeries and other retail outlets. By carefully and scrupulously managing its territories, this island which had no gardens, Sanudo argued, had more fruit and vegetables and other produce than could possibly be imagined.[7]

Ambrogio Lorenzetti's early fourteenth-century fresco cycle in the council chamber of the Nine in the town hall in Siena was one of the first surviving visualisations of the connection between good governance and material wealth. Here both the captions and the imagery emphasised urban dominion over a fertile countryside.[8] This ensured that peasants would arrive with fat geese, pigs and grain to supply citizens who concentrated on the manufacturing and sales within the shops and stalls of Siena's well-maintained streets (Figures 21–22). The alternative: tyrannical rule by a single individual for selfish purposes, brought destruction, destitution and, above all, starvation for a city that could never be self-sufficient (Figure 23). In the near contemporary manuscript recording grain prices from 1320 to 1359, compiled by the Florentine corn-chandler, Domenico Lenzi, this fundamental contrast between abundance and dearth was depicted in a series of contrasting images (Figure 24).[9] His manuscript was a careful record of the price of basic commodities such as wheat, millet and spelt that were sold in Florence's public grain-market of Orsanmichele. In the first illumination, a depiction of a time of plenty, the harvest had proved bountiful: peasants are seen loading sheaves of high-quality wheat onto their donkeys to take into town. The market itself is shown as replete with well-off, indolent customers who sit on over-stuffed sacks of grain (Figures 25–26). In the background men turn their backs on the merchants who hold out their hands in a gesture of pleading to take their produce. But excess disappears in the next set of illuminations. In an illustration alluding to the poor harvest of 1329, the Tuscan fields are threatened by devils and abandoned by God's angels (Figure 27). Women of all ages are forced to assist at the heavy work of bringing in the small amounts of grain that can be gleaned. In Orsanmichele itself, rioting is quelled only by the intervention of soldiers. While a few able-bodied men are able to carry off limited supplies, the poor, cripples and women are pushed aside (Figure 28). Charity, Lenzi's images suggest, was the first casualty of famine.

This was no abstract fear but one grounded in experience. Throughout the late medieval and Renaissance period, abundance was always a fleeting phenomenon. The prices, types and qualities of foodstuffs were notoriously variable. The time of year, the weather, problems of transport and man-made crises such as warfare or insurrection could result in dramatic fluctuations of costs and supply that individuals often felt helpless to prevent.[10] Florentine diarists writing between the fourteenth and the early seventeenth centuries commonly noted the costs of basic commodities in the marketplace, watching with anxiety as grain prices soared and noting with relief when they returned to levels regarded as normal.[11] Few chroniclers neglected this aspect of civic life or considered it too mundane to record. In 1590, for example, the Florentine Agostino Lapini noted that the peninsula-wide famine was so extensive that, 'they are milling the husks of the grain together with what can be sieved and a small amount of flour. The bakers sell it by weight to poor people at 2 soldi and eight dinari a pound, and this is bread that in any other time would have been given to the dogs, and even then they might not have eaten it.'[12] When 225 carts of wheat arrived in the city later that year, Lapini was more than relieved and wrote that the grain was greeted 'by sounds of trumpets and tambourines'.[13]

21 (*above left*) Ambrogio Lorenzetti, *An Allegory of Good and Bad Government*, 1338, fresco, Palazzo Pubblico, Siena, detail showing shops and schoolmaster in the well-governed commune.

22 (*above right*) Ambrogio Lorenzetti, *An Allegory of Good and Bad Government*, 1338, fresco, Palazzo Pubblico, Siena, detail of peasants entering the well-governed commune with foodstuffs with scenes of manufacture to the rear.

23 (*right*) Ambrogio Lorenzetti, *An Allegory of Good and Bad Government*, 1338, fresco, Palazzo Pubblico, Siena, detail of tyrannical government in the city showing deserted shop.

24 Domenico Lenzi, *Specchio umano*, c.1335, Biblioteca Medicea Laurenziana, Florence, Tempi 3, f. 2, 'The Corn Chandler in his office'.

As this suggests, when the price of basic goods such as bread and flour rose too high, or the quality of a loaf deteriorated beyond a certain point, an unspoken social contract was broken. E. P. Thompson has already suggested this for eighteenth-century England, and it often seemed from early Renaissance comments that being able to buy white bread at a decent price on a daily basis was regarded as a right rather than a privilege.[14] Being given food fit for dogs or for poultry was to be treated as an animal rather than as a human being, a point emphasised during a period of dearth in 1411, when the Florentine textile worker Cola di Maestro Piero railed, 'These traitorous rulers have taken grain from the chickens and fed it to us; By God we shall eat the good [grain] in their houses shortly; we don't deserve to be treated like chickens.'[15]

25 (*above left*)   Domenico Lenzi, *Specchio umano*, c.1335, Biblioteca Medicea Laurenziana, Florence, Tempi 3, f. 6v, 'A Time of Good Harvest'.

26 (*above right*)   Domenico Lenzi, *Specchio umano*, c.1335, Biblioteca Medicea Laurenziana, Florence, Tempi 3, f. 7, 'The Market of Orsanmichele in Florence during a time of Good Harvest'.

When governments were unable to provide for the town in times of famine, there was not only a breakdown of food supply but also a rupture in social stability. Normally expected to remain passive, poorer women took to the streets demanding loaves while workers who depended on daily supplies of grain threatened to take action against their overlords.[16] Thus, the visual reassurance provided by images of fertile fields and bakers' ovens, as in the late fifteenth-century grisaille fresco cycle of the stages involved in bread-making painted for the palace of the unofficial rulers of Bologna, the Bentivoglio, was not simply an attractive landscape view. It provided a message of political stability; the viewers of this cycle would have had few concerns for their own larders, but they would have been very anxious about the wider consequences of famine for their own rulership.[17]

27 (*above left*)   Domenico Lenzi, *Specchio umano*, c.1335, Biblioteca Medicea Laurenziana, Florence, Tempi 3, f. 78v, 'A Time of Poor Harvest'.

28 (*above right*)   Domenico Lenzi, *Specchio umano*, c.1335, Biblioteca Medicea Laurenziana, Florence, Tempi 3, f. 79, 'The Market of Orsanmichele in Florence, during a time of Poor Harvest.'

The constancy of this fear of famine and dearth suggests that families on modest incomes would have found it difficult to move beyond the purchase of bread and other basics to buy more elaborate furnishings and fittings.[18] But such simple equations between daily wages and the cost of consumables do not tell us about alternative methods of acquisition and sale. Nor do they tell us about the more subtle connections between household possessions and the necessities upon which life depended. The very utensils used for cooking, such as those illustrated in Bartolomeo Scappi's 1570 treatise on cookery, often made it possible to buy the food their owners required (Figures 29–30). A ubiquitous system of credit arrangements, both formal and informal, meant that handkerchiefs, tablecloths, aprons, scissors and kitchen pots could all be used as pledges when families needed to pay rent and taxes, have a drink in a tavern, or buy a bushel of grain. In such a system, the linens in the cupboard and plate on the side-board provided a bulwark against famine and ill fortune, one that was as important to survival as the gardens, fields and chicken coops that were regularly cultivated by city dwellers.[19] In their tax returns, for example, Florentines seeking exemption from income tax, stressed their total impoverishment by claiming to own nothing apart from the rags on their backs, saying that these were too tattered to be of any value. This argument carried some weight with tax officials who shared the assumption that even well-worn rags were a form of stored wealth that could be temporarily released when cash was required.[20] This was equally true for the wealthy as for the poor. Expensive clothing, jewels and plate could be mortgaged over and over again, allowing men and women with possessions to spend in ways that far exceeded their immediate means.[21] Here it was not cash but debt secured by material goods that fuelled consumption.

The long-standing connection between the ability to pay for essentials and one's pos-sessions was explored in depth by the late sixteenth- and early seventeenth-century Bolognese poet Giulio Cesare Croce.[22] The son of an ironmonger, Croce constructed a poetic autobiography that emphasised his poverty and his understanding of the plight of the dispossessed. He supposedly taught himself literature by reading the discarded pages of Ovid that were being used to wrap up salami by a local grocer and the popular verse that he both declaimed in the Piazza and distributed in print was embedded with anxi-eties about starvation and financial failure.[23] In 1590, he published a poem on 'rent day' decrying, 'a terrible thing is rent, for those who have pawned their aprons, those their caps, and others their sheets, some their wife's ring, yet others have sold their bed, their gowns, their stockings, their chests, boxes, carriages and dressers'.[24]

Another poem, 'The chatterings on the business and bargains that happen everyday on the Square in Bologna' begins with a description of famine when to save themselves from starvation, the Bolognese:

> . . . have sold everything down to their clothing,
> The beds, the covers, the hangings,
> Chairs, benches and all their furnishings . . .[25]

Only with the return of plenty to the city were these families able to restock, benefit-ing from sales of every type of good in the town's main square:

> From every *Arte*, that makes goods, and every trade
> One hears their cries throughout the day
> And they are a sign of the truth
> To those who wish to inform themselves.
> Go to the Piazza and stand and listen,
> And you will hear shouts:
> O là, who wants to buy a shirt
> That is fully embroidered in patterns?
>
> Who will take, o là, who will buy my stockings?

29 Bartolomeo Scappi, *The Kitchen*, engraving inserted in *Opera di Bartolomeo Scappi, Mastro dell'arte del cucinare*, Venice, 1622, British Library, London.

Who wants to buy a lantern to go about in the dark?
Oh, a beautiful comb,
Oh, here is a pair of socks, and here a lovely doublet
Who wants my chestnut roaster?
For three lira, a dress . . .
A cage for a bird
Who will buy it, oh, who will buy this chandelier?

And then there are those who sell dental powders,
Those selling perfumed pastes, and pendants
Those who sell musk balls and pomanders
Muscat and odiferous angelica
Those who show to the crowd
Papers, drawings, medals and novelties,
Those who have serpents in their hands and tell tales

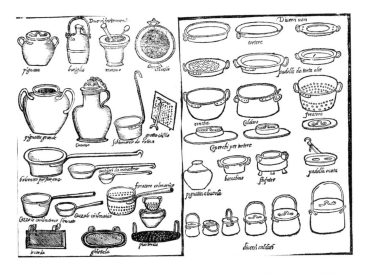

30   Bartolomeo Scappi, *Pentole*, engraving inserted in *Opera di Bartolomeo Scappi, Mastro dell'arte del cucinare*, Venice, 1622, British
Library, London.

> Those who cut purse strings, make gold, play the guitar,
> Those who get dogs to jump, and those with monkeys.
>
> Those who act like Bagolino
> Those who play Master Martin
> Those who sell sweets,
> Those who play Zaffo in the commedies.[26]

In these two poems, Croce placed material goods at the heart of the cycle between
famine and abundance. Yet his lengthy enumeration was not the equivalent of Giovanni
Villani's statistical praise of Florence, or Sansovino's laudatory celebration of Venetian
prosperity. It was a far more ambivalent response to acquisition. As Croce's list grew
longer, his vendors moved from selling honest manufactures – shirts, stockings, lanterns
– to more frivolous items such as drawings and medals, before finishing with sales by
fraudsters and tricksters, such as, 'those who have serpents in their hands', that is, the
charlatans who claimed to be able to prevent snake poisoning by selling special concoctions.[27] Croce pointedly finished the poem with the image of a relatively new arrival
to the urban market scene, the *commedia dell'arte* performers who sold fiction rather
than fact. Far from being a straightforward praise of urban prosperity, Croce warned
that the arrival of plenty might pose as many problems for the unwary as the famine
itself.

Croce's contemporaries shared many of his concerns. In his 1585 publication, entitled the *Piazza universale*, which might be very roughly translated as 'the Universal

Market Square', Croce's near contemporary, the Venetian writer Tomaso Garzoni warned against the social disruptions and degeneration caused by the seductions of the marketplace:

> Amongst the other terrible and detestable occupations is that of the idle . . . which consists in eating, drinking and enjoying oneself. They spend all their time passing through the piazza, and moving from the tavern to the fishmongers and from the Palazzo to the Loggia, doing little all day except wandering from here to there, looking at glassware, mirrors and rattles, that are displayed in the Piazze. Now they move aimlessly through the market in the midst of the peasants, now they stop in some barber-shop to exchange songs and gossip, now they read the news, *nove di banco*, which is simply for the ears of these lazy and negligent men.[28]

Here, in contrast to the industrious and clearly delineated image of Siena's manufacturers as depicted by Ambrogio Lorenzetti in the fourteenth century, Garzoni warned that as the nobility mixed among the peasantry and were distracted by trinkets and news-sheets, the city of Venice was in danger of a decline caused by consumer enjoyments.

SELLING AND SEDUCTION

While it is tempting to interpret the opinions of both Garzoni and Croce as evidence for the development of a new market economy or, potentially as a response to the rising inflation that characterised the last quarter of the sixteenth century, their arguments drEw on numerous precedents. If there was a causal relationship between changing social patterns of shopping in the sixteenth century and the poems and prose that were produced, it was very subtle. Far from being unique to the later period, there was a long-standing conflation between the attractions of the marketplace and its inhabitants, sexual seduction and moral outrage. These are literary tropes as well as contemporary observations

Some of the connections between sexuality and the market were physical as well as metaphorical. In Italy, brothels were often located in, or near, central market areas. Thus, the humanist writer Antonio Beccadelli stressed the link between the Florentine Mercato Vecchio and the town's bordello by focusing on the lower senses of smell and base sexuality in one of the early fifteenth-century passages of his Latin poem the Hermaphroditus: 'Arriving there, take a right; proceeding a little, Stop and ask, oh [my] tired book, for the Mercato Vecchio. Near it is the obelisk, the genial bordello is right there, the place betrays itself by its odour.'[29]

Even respectable shops such as those of the apothecaries could be accused of provoking sensual responses. In 1425, the Sienese preacher and moralist San Bernardino was particularly concerned that boys would be corrupted by the wine in taverns and the sweets available in the apothecaries:

Three things inflame the fire of sodomy: firstly the wood of eating, supping, drinking and gorging. The full purse, gaming . . . capons, crayfish, sturgeons in the tavern lead us on the road to doom and in the hidden places where public whorehouses of boys are kept as public prostitutes. The hotel beds at night when you have your body full of wine bring sodomy to the camp. Wake up citizens, and see that your sons are going to the devil unless you ensure that the taverns are shut at the twenty-fourth hour. You apothecaries, you know well to whom you sell pine-nut biscuits, candies, marzipans and sugar cake and you know who is buying them and why, and your conscience cannot rest easy unless you have no sense of guilt in turning boys bad.[30]

San Bernardino assumed that provoking the flesh through taste, touch and smell would stimulate the passions; to avoid such temptations, another early sixteenth-century humanist, Paolo Cortesi, advised placing a cardinal's palace in a place where the senses would not be aroused, for as he put it, 'gluttony and lust are fostered by perfumers, vendors of delicacies, poultry-sellers, money-vendors and cooks and savoury foods'.[31]

For these moralists any exchange of merchandise for money was potentially tainted; it was not simply an accident of the alphabet that led the fifteenth-century encyclopaedist Polydore Vergil to place *meretrice*, or whore, after, *mercanzia*, or trade, in his discussion of human inventions.[32] Likewise when he wished to damn the impact of printing, the Milanese Dominican friar, Filippo di Strata turned to the same phrase to describe booksellers: 'the city was so full of books that it was hardly possible to walk down the street without finding armfuls of them thrust at you like cats in a bag for two or three coppers . . . printing was a whore'.[33] When the fictive Florentine, the Piovano Arlotto, went out in search of a prostitute, he too described seeking out the 'merchandise', *la mercanzia*, while Pope Pius II insulted Florence by twisting its reputation as a merchant city around to call it a 'whore town', *La città mercatrice, ma che dico, meretrice*.[34]

The mid-fourteenth-century poem on the Florentine Mercato Vecchio by Antonio Pucci who died in 1388 sums up the long-standing problematic inter-relationship between the place, its products and the people who frequented the site.[35] Like Croce, Pucci, who was originally one of Florence's town-criers, was part of an oral culture that was only sporadically captured on the page before the advent of printing. He had already written a lengthy piece on the disaster of the plague of 1348 and brought a jaundiced eye to human desire and behaviour. In his poem on the Mercato Vecchio, Pucci mixed a celebratory note with warning tones. This was a site where peasants from the countryside offered their wares to the serving-women of Florentine families. Respectable men and their wives arrived to watch the scene, dazzled by the seemingly unlimited array of foods and goods on offer. But in Pucci's vision, the market was not only a place of social order but one where petty quarrels could quickly disintegrate into warring factions.[36] Pleasure and danger were available in equal measure:

The Mercato Vecchio feeds the whole world and takes the prize from all other markets . . .

Noble men and ladies stand to one side and often see the female sellers and the gambling hustlers come to blows . . .[37]

As the poem continued, the language grew both more sexualised and troubled. The women selling vegetables were singled out for particular opprobrium:

> For every type of reason there are women [*trecche*] who sell
> I speak of them with harsh words,
> Those who fight throughout the day over two dried chestnuts
> Calling each other whores
> And they are always filling their baskets with fruit to their advantage.
> And other women sell eggs with cheese to make herb omelettes
> And pies and ravioli and the like.[38]

In this passage, Pucci was referring to the *treccole* or *trecche*: saleswomen who moved through the streets and squares selling basic foodstuffs. With baskets on their arms or heads, they offered onions, garlic, fruit and vegetables, eggs, poultry, breads or cooked foods (Figures 31–32). Although ubiquitous, they were highly problematic for Italy's urban communities which generally expected respectable women to either remain indoors or to move through the city with deliberate purpose.[39] Loitering, standing on street corners and deliberately attracting attention to oneself by shouting were not char-

31 Florentine, *El contrasto di carnevale & de la quaresima*, c.1494, woodcut, The British Library, London.

32   Florentine, *Contrasto di carnevale & de la quaresima*, c.1520, woodcut,
The British Library, London.

acteristics of appropriate female decorum. Yet such actions were critical for saleswomen hoping to sell their wares. This meant that customers, above all male customers, who approached these women might be doing so for honest or dishonest reasons; the desire to buy salads might disguise negotiations of a very different type.[40]

The concern that these women evoked over two and a half centuries was remarkable for its continuity. In Croce's late sixteenth-century Bologna, for example, the government statutes of both 1567 and 1588 continued to accuse these women of a combination of sexual misconduct and commercial dishonnesty in terms that would have been very familiar to Antonio Pucci:

And amongst these vendors can be found many women of the type that could not be called honest. They mingle with the women of the market-gardeners who have come to sell their produce in the square, women who are married and live an honest life. Nevertheless these women: sellers of herbs, fruits and vegetables, despite being warned for many years back . . . for some time have disturbed this order and have not wanted to stay in their proper and appropriate places and have occupied and from day to day continue to occupy those places where they mix to the prejudice of this republic, as these vendors sell things at a higher price, and prevent those who

Hortolane.

33 Cesare Vecellio, *De gli habiti antichi, et moderni et diverse parti del mondo libri due*, Venice, 1590, engraving, 'Dell'Hortolane da Chioggia', Wellcome Library, London.

would sell at a better bargain; and often solicit for custom and damage the honour and chastity of those women who are wives and relatives of those market-gardeners.[41]

As a consequence, these Bolognese *treccole* defined as, 'all those who retail fruit, greens, vegetables and their seeds and other things that they have bought in order to sell again which are normally sold by market-gardeners who toil for and cultivate these things themselves', were normally not allowed onto the market square to sell their wares until after the market had officially closed at midday.[42] When they appeared, they were to be visibly separated from the peasant gardeners, the *ortolane*, who were themselves carefully defined as those with market gardens either inside the city walls or from within three miles of the town.

The Venetians also tried to differentiate between the honourable female sellers, the wives of peasants and farmers, from their dishonourable counterparts, the regraters or *rivenditrice*. Costume played a key role in differentiation. Cesare Vecellio described the dress of women who arrived from the Treviso and Chioggia (Figures 33–4) to sell their wares while Pietro Bertelli provided a similar view of the women (and men) who arrived from the Paduan countryside (Figure 35). There were severe punishments for those who to disguise themselves as peasants in order to pretend that they had grown their wares themselves. In addition, those who were retailers were expected to carry a wooden tablet or banner bearing a sign such as the letter 'R' to indicate they were *rivenditrice*. In a final attempt to constrain their behaviour, they were only allowed to buy the goods they would later sell at fixed moments during the day. In early sixteenth-century Florence, for example, a bell was hung on the column that stood in the Mercato Vecchio to sound when the *treccole* could enter the area, usually near closing time. But ironically the bell which controlled the women was placed underneath the now-lost statue by the sculptor Donatello, a figure known as *Dovizia* or Wealth, who must have closely resembled the saleswomen themselves[43] (Figures 36–37). Standing on an antique granite column in the market centre, she was carved as a rounded female figure in classicising drapery.[44] But, while many would have seen the reference to antique figures, she also paralleled the more

34   Cesare Vecellio, *De gli habiti antichi, et moderni et diverse parti del mondo libri due*, Venice, 1590, engraving, 'Contadine della Marca Trivisana' and 'Contadino al Mercato di Venezia', Wellcome Library, London.

troubling fruit and vegetable sellers who gathered below her.[45] The connection was certainly seen by the late fifteenth-century illustrator of the Allegory of Lent who took the *Dovizia*'s pose and used it to depict a vegetable seller (Figure 31) In the Mercato Veccnio, the height at which the figure was displayed must have gone some way to distancing the *Dovizia* and its allegorical meaning from the real women below.[46] But it may be significant that when this figure was redeployed as a small-scale figurine in domestic settings or re-used in pictorial settings, she was shown fully clothed and more clearly labelled as the figuration of *Dovizia*, avoiding any potential misinterpretation (Figure 38).

The multivalent ways in which women who walked through the streets and markets offering goods for sale were perceived and represented was due in part to the key role that they and their male counterparts played in Renaissance urban retail distribution networks. Given their constant presence, they could not be ignored; they could only be contained and controlled. For example, the supply of fruit in fifteenth-century Milan was a complex system of almost exclusively male wholesalers who rented out the produce of specific trees to individual salesmen and women who then sold them throughout the city's streets.[47] Street vendors were also used to distribute the products of farmers, shopkeepers, and even the works of the nuns of San Jacopo a Ripoli who established a printing press in late fifteenth-century Florence.[48] Entire families such as the Vignarchi clan of late sixteenth-century Florence specialised in peddling cloth in

35   Pietro Bertelli, *Diversarum nationum habitus*, Padua, 1594–6, engraving, 'Rustica olitona Patavina and Rusticus recotte venditor Patavinus', figures 17 and 18, The British Library, London.

36   Giovanni Stradano, *The Mercato Vecchio*, c.1560, fresco, Sala di Gualdrada, Palazzo Vecchio, Florence.

37   Giuseppe Moricci, *The Mercato Vecchio of Florence*, 1878, oil on canvas, Museo di Arte Medievale e Moderna, Arezzo.

GLORIA·ET·DIVITIE
IN·DOMO·TVA

38 Giovanni della Robbia, *Dovizia*, c.1494
–1513, glazed terracotta, The William Hood
Dunwoody Fund. The Minneapolis Institute of
Arts.

the Tuscan countryside. With a base in the
city, they kept careful ledgers and were
able to offer credit over a fifty-year
period.[49] Similarly, the many charlatans
based in Siena travelled a well-worn set of
routes throughout northern and southern
Italy, obtaining licences for medications
and potions that were almost identical to
those sold by the more respectable
apothecaries.[50]

But however ubiquitous, mobile
vendors were rarely welcomed or celebrated by legislators. They were often presented as exterior rather than as intrinsic
to the social body of the city-state.[51] As
such they make a useful concluding case-
study of the many, often contradictory
concerns, anxieties and attractions that
buying goods posed during the Renaissance period. It is important, however,
when looking at these mobile salesmen
and women in depth to note that any
intermediary who intervened between
producer and customer was regarded with suspicion.[52] Renaissance economic theory
held that in an ideal society farmers and other small-scale tradesmen should sell wares
directly to their clients. The intervention of a third-party only raised prices and posed
problems of potential deception. Street vendors who re-sold goods that they had bought
at low prices for higher sums were particularly despised. Framed as exotic and troubling, they, and the materials they sold, were thought as seductive and as false as their
sales techniques. In 1418, for example, the Milanese government tried to control the
sale of sweets and cooked apples on the streets because vendors were approaching small
children and asking them to gamble to win a prize.[53] When Canon Pietro Casola com-
mented unfavourably on Venetian women's hairstyles in the 1490s, he noted acerbically,
'The greater part is false hair: and this I know for certain because I saw great quantities of it on poles, sold by peasants in the Piazza San Marco.'[54] Drawing on similar fears,
the Milanese mercers' guild complained about peddlers who were roaming the streets,
'with boxes in order to sell headbands, snoods, ribbons, cloth and other such things'.[55]

They were particularly annoyed by those who bought such fancy goods from shops and then resold them at much higher prices to women, 'How easy it is to deceive women, everyone knows. Because they are vagabonds and do not have a fixed shop in the city . . . they commit frauds and then they cannot be found to be punished and moreover as they have the occasion to enter into anyone's house, under the guise of selling ribbons and caps, they commit other evil deeds.' Even worse, they argued, serving-women, 'moved by vanity' might be tempted to steal in order to buy such frivolities unless peddlers were controlled.[56]

Just as women who sold goods on the streets were often seen as deceivers, women who bought goods were seen as being deceived. Both were the ruination of men. In his play, *Il marescalco*, of 1526–7, Pietro Aretino used the convention of female susceptibility in the third act. The plot revolved around an attempt to marry off a misogynistic courtier, and in an interlude, a Jewish peddler appears. He is a caricature of the dealer in fancy goods, calling, 'To whom will I sell, to whom will I sell these trinkets, these lovely things, my novelties, to whom will I sell?' One of the main characters, the servant Giannico, replies, 'Maybe you have frivolities for brides?' The peddler responds in turn, 'I have nothing else but fans, caps, rouges, waters, bracelets, necklaces, earrings, tooth powders, pendants, girdles and similar ruinations of husbands . . .'[57]

Reinforcing the horror that marriage posed for Aretino's characters, neither the Jewish

peddler nor the potential (and imaginary) bride were supposed to be sympathetic figures in this play. Like the later sixteenth-century print of the Jewish pedlar who sells his goods by crying out in German, 'was welt ihr geben', the salesman is an outsider who cannot be trusted (Figure 39). The implication of these comments was that women were poor judges of quality, both of goods and of people.

Aretino's use of this stock character drew on common assumptions that streetsellers such as Jews and Gypsies were dangerous outsiders who used their charms and the enticements of their calls to gain entry into the home.[58] Indeed, much of the surviving legislation was as much about curbing the sounds of salesmanship

39 Pietro Bertelli, *Diversarum nationum habitus*, Padua, 1594–6, engraving, 'Judeus mercator patavinus' figure 15, The British Library, London.

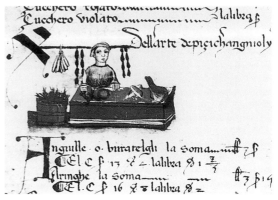

40 (*above left*)   Florentine, Libro delle gabelle, c.1350, f. 25v, 'Treccola'

41 (*above right*)   Florentine, Libro delle gabelle, c.1350, Biblioteca Riccardiana, Florence, Ricc.2526, f.22v, 'Arte dei pizzicagnoli'

42   Florentine, Libro delle gabelle, c.1350, Biblioteca Riccardiana, Florence, Ricc.2526, f. 3v, 'Arti di Por Santa Maria e Orassi' and f. 13v, 'Arte degli speziali'.

as it was about curbing the sales themselves. Thus an early Florentine statute of 1325 stipulated that 'None are to go about the city crying Gold and Silver':

> As infidel youths wander selling fringes, buttons and rings of either gold or silver, or else of old iron or the like, on these occasions they commit many, many thefts in buying and selling the same, and indeed chalices and thuribles, therefore we order that no person should dare or presume to go about the city of Florence and its suburbs shouting or crying out such venal things . . .[59]

Given the long-standing nature of these attacks, it was almost impossible to represent any street seller, whether Christian or infidel, male or female, in a neutral manner. In the polemical terms of the period, markets, particularly those that involved women and food, could be portrayed only as extremes. They were either positive symbols of fertility or dangerous signs of seductive sensuality. This may explain, in part, why, unlike in northern Europe where the genre of market scenes was very popular, so few visual references were made to sellers and selling.[60] Until the late sixteenth century, scenes of salesmanship were confined to a very limited number of fresco cycles and manuscript illuminations depicting orderly government and guild control such as the Florentine guild statutes (Figures 40–42), or the images in the popular *Tacuinum sanitatis*, texts that described the effect of different products on the human body. In the series of illuminated manuscripts dating from the late fourteenth to the beginning of the sixteenth century, *Tacuinum sanitatis* illuminations depicted men and women harvesting or buying the commodities required for human consumption. Here men and women sell

43   Jacob de Bouckelaer, *Market with a Scene of Ecce Homo*, c. 1566, oil on canvas, Galleria degli Uffizi, Florence.

44   Lombard, *Tacuinum sanitatis*, c.1390, Biblioteca Casanatense, Rome, Mss 4182, f. 158, 'Pesces Salati'.

fish from barrels and baskets, carefully weigh out freshly butchered meat or bring milk to the doorstep (Figures 44–46). In all these cases there are few, if any, troubling references to illicit or illegal acts. There is no blood in the butchers' slaughterhouses or any detritus in the shops.

   The sense of idealised order continued in the more prominent public depictions. Lorenzo Lotto, for example, slipped male and female vendors into his fresco cycle of the Life of Saint Barbara in the Oratorio Suardi, Trescore (Figure 47). But these figures were included to encourage a sense of real presence rather than to act as iconographic references. For much of the sixteenth century, picturing the market, peddlers or fairs continued to be a minority activity. There were few visual counterparts to Pucci's poem on the Mercato Vecchio or to the governmental decrees. In the 1580s, however, there was a sudden interest in 'low-life' subject matter, a new attention that may have had as much to do with the popularity and success of northern paintings of these subjects by artists like Bouckelaer as to any indigenous change in Italian pictorial styles (Figure 43). But the demand in Italy was not for the same disturbing, ambiguous ideas that characterised the poems of the period. Instead, most of these visual images which were pro-

Carnes arietū.

lac acetofū.

Natirc 7h.m.j.melioz er cis.anuales pingues uiuamētuz.stoma
co réperato.nocamēti; ɔfueris pau abbominatiocz remotio nocu
mēti . cū brodis stipticis .

Natirc f.q h .meli'er co. qō é mlū qurin uiuamētū .mitigat sirū.
nocumēti gunguis ⁊ dētibɔ .remotio nocumēti . cū gargarismo et
domelys .

45 (*above left*)   Lombard, *Tacuinum sanitatis*, Biblioteca Casanatense, Rome, Mss 4182, f. 138, 'Carnes arietum'.

46 (*above right*)   Lombard, *Tacuinum sanitatis*, Biblioteca Casanatense, Rome, Mss 4182, f. 112, 'Lac acctosum'.

duced before the seventeenth century by artists such as Antonio Campi and Bartolomeo Passerotti, deliberately erased references to disturbing sounds, smells, tastes and textures. Like these images before them, they provided an almost exclusively positive set of market representations (Figures 48–49).

Only in one medium, that of print, is there a similar ambivalence to that shown by legislators, poets and writers described above. The print market had to contend with imports from Germany and the Netherlands where naturalistic or satirical scenes of daily life were more common. A fifteenth-century Florentine niello engraving with a putto urinating in order to oil an itinerant knife-grinder's whetstone may be a response to or even a copy of such examples. [61] Two engravings from the same period depict a drunken pedlar sleeping while his pack is ravaged by monkeys also seem to have a Northern origin, based on a German folk-tale of 'Maestro Pieterlin' (Figure 51).[62] But a number of other early prints took on a different approach, presenting a sympathetic view. Dating to around 1485, one depicts a male milk-seller wearing the tattered clothing associated with beggars (Figure 52). It is inscribed as if he were calling out to women in the home: 'Milk, Ladies, Fresh Milk', 'Late done, late frescha'. The other two prints

47 (*facing page*)   Lorenzo Lotto, *The Martyrdom of Saint Barbara* (detail), 1524, fresco, Oratorio Suardi, Trescore Balneario, detail of village market.

48 (*top*)   Vincenzo Campi, *The Fruitseller*, c.1580, oil on canvas, Pinacoteca di Brera, Milan.

49 (*above*)   Bartolomeo Passerotti, *The Butcher's Stall*, c.1580, oil on canvas, Galleria Nazionale di Arte Antica di Palazzo Barbarini, Rome.

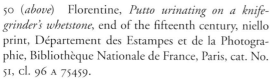

50 (*above*) Florentine, *Putto urinating on a knife-grinder's whetstone*, end of the fifteenth century, niello print, Département des Estampes et de la Photographie, Bibliothèque Nationale de France, Paris, cat. No. 51, cl. 96 A 75459.

51A and B (*above and below right*) *The Monkeys and the Pedlar*, c.1470–90, engravings, top: Hind A. 1. 76, current whereabouts unknown; below: Department of Prints and Drawings, The British Museum, London, 1845-8-25-376. The inscription on the first version of the print offers a warning against imbibing too much wine.

52   Giovan Antonio da Brescia, *Late Done, Late Frescha*, c.1485, engravings, Department of Prints and Drawings, The British Museum, London, F.11.12.

from around the same period, attributed to from either Ferrara or Padua, show male and female peasants whose sticks were laden with goods as if they were on their way to market (Figures 53–54). These images are quite empathetic, emphasising the poverty of the vendors who were undertaking honest labour rather than begging. But these detached, single sheets provoked very different reactions from those the artist intended. Scrawled across the page are words written by several different hands who added proverbs or witty attacks. The image of the peasant woman, for example, is inscribed by one owner as 'La Vilana – la vilanela' and then in a more formal script, 'Villana falsa, maladeta' – false peasant, be cursed'.

The written attacks are an important reminder of just how powerful the attitudes towards peddlers, particularly female peddlers, could be. Even when the artist made no effort, for example by exaggerating Semitic features, to elicit negative feelings, the viewers who left their written remarks responded in a stereotyped manner. It is perhaps unsurprising, therefore, that the first major Italian images of street-sellers were carefully framed to neutralise their protagonists in a manner familiar to earlier artists working in the *Taccuinum sanitatis* tradition. In 1582, the firm run by the descendants of Antoine Lafrery in Rome published a broadsheet by the Milanese artist Ambrogio Brambilla

53 (*above left*)   North Italian, *Female peasant carrying vegetables on a stick*, formerly in the Collection of Count Morosini, Villa Morosini, near Conegliano, current whereabouts unknown (Hind, E.III.26).

54 (*above right*)   North Italian, *Male peasant carrying a rabbit on a stick*, formerly in the Collection of Count Morosini, Villa Morosini, near Conegliano, current whereabouts unknown (Hind, E.III.26).

(Figures 55 and 57). Densely packed, the print measures 39 × 53 centimetres with thumbnail images of over 200 separate figures in distinct boxes. All the vendors were male. Each was underscored with an inscription referring either to the item sold or the cry by which it was sold: paintings on canvas and on wood, fans, paternoster beads, chairs, shoes, glassware and the services they provided such as knife-grinding.[63]

Brambilla's motivations for issuing the print may have been quite complex. He was a member of the now obscure *Accademia Milanese della Val di Bregn*, a society founded in 1560 that was dedicated to composing poetry in the dialect of an almost defunct language of the Val di Blenio valley to the north-east of Bellinzona in Canton Ticino.[64] In 1589, the artist and theorist G. P. Lomazzo published some of Brambilla's works as part of the volume, *Rabish Dra Academiglia da Compa Zavagna. Nabad dra Vall' Bregn*, Milan, 1589.[65] In competition with the Florentine *Accademia della Crusca* that was then trying to construct, regulate and control the language of elite Italians, Brambilla and

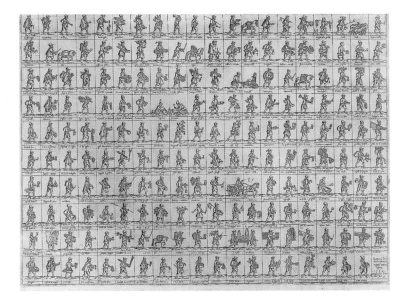

55   Ambrogio Brambilla, *Ritratto de Quelli che vano vendendo et lavorando per Roma con la nova agionta de tutti quelli che nelle altre mancavano sino al presente. Romae, Claudii Ducheti Formis Nepotis Antonii Lafrery*, 1582, etching with some engraving, Department of Prints and Drawings, The British Museum, London, 1947–3–19–26 (173). The inscription has been cut off at the top.

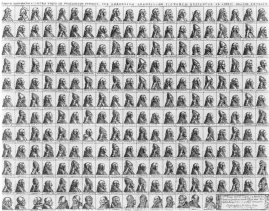

56 (*above left*)   Ambrogio Brambilla, *Portraits of the Popes*, engraving on two plates, Department of Prints and Drawings, The British Museum, London, 1871–8–12–780.

57 (*right*)   *I bei quadri in tavola*, detail of figure 55.

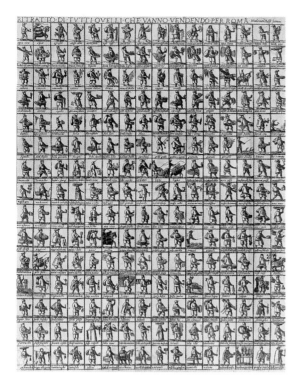

RITRATTO·DI·TVTTI·QVELLI·CHE·VANNO·VENDENDO·PER·ROMA

58 Nicolas Van Aelst, *Ritratto di tutti quelli che vanno vendendo per Roma*, engraving, c.1600, Istituto Nazionale per la Grafica, Rome, inv. F. N. (32149) 39314.

his colleagues, such as Lomazzo and the painter Giovanni Arcimboldo, deliberately used the language of the street and the countryside both in their poetry and in their paintings and prints. Like the images of butchers that the Bolognese painter Bartolomeo Passerotti or the fruit-seller of the Lombard Vincenzo Campi were producing at this point, these were images and ideas that were already common in northern Europe but unusual in an Italian setting (Figures 48–49).[66] Indeed, it is possible that the group was hoping to gain patronage, not within Italy itself, where the Academicians endured a troubled relationship with the Milanese ecclesiastical authorities, but with the Habsburg courts of Madrid and Prague who favoured and bought Dutch and Flemish works.

Yet whatever Brambilla's own reasons for focusing on the vernacular image of street vendors, the print was deliberately designed to appeal to a wide audience. A hint of how it was marketed is evident in the its title, 'A portrait of those who go about selling and working in Rome with a new addition of all those who have been lacking in the others until the present' (*Retratto de Quelli che vano vendendo et lavorando per Roma con la nova agionta de tutti quelli che nelle altre mancavano sino al presente*). But despite the title, there is nothing particularly Roman about the print itself. There is no backdrop, little variety in the clothing the figures wear, and hardly anything characteristic about the range of items for sale. These could be peddlers from any city; only the inscription indicates that they are Roman. The title's claim to be a set of 'portraits' of vendors is similarly misleading for the figures are types rather than individuals. Brambilla was already familiar with this approach to taxonomy having produced a large plate print of 235 portraits of popes from Christ to Pope Gregory XIII which similarly reduced the many individual popes to a single type with a range of minor variations (Figure 56).[67] Thus like the increasing number of illustrated scientific manuals and books of dress and habits being produced in Rome's and Venice's presses, the print tries to pin down and label a generic specimen.[68]

59 (*above left*) *Diverse figure al numero di Ottanta, Disignate di Penna, nell'Hore di Ricreazioni da Annibale Carracci. Intagliate in Rame . . . da Sione Giulino Parigino*, Rome, 1646, f. 71, 'Acoramaglietti', Department of Prints and Drawings, The British Museum, London, 1942.5.14.3 (68).

60 (*above right*) *Diverse figure al numero di Ottanta, Disignate di Penna, nell'Hore di Ricreazioni da Annibale Carracci. Intagliate in Rame . . . da Sione Giulino Parigino*, Rome, 1646, f. 28, 'Hortolana', Department of Prints and Drawings, The British Museum, London, 1942.5.14.3 (29).

The second half of the title, 'a new addition of all those who have been lacking in the others' hints that there were already versions in circulation. This was a marketing ploy in its own right. Buyers were encouraged to believe that they should no longer be satisfied with the earlier version, but needed to acquire another in order to have the 'missing' figures. Deliberately building on a competitive a requirement for a complete set, one of the Lafrery partners, the Belgian, Nicolas van Aelst, reissued the print in a new format five years later (Figure 58). This latest version provided simpler captions that identified what was being sold rather than the seller and put them into alphabetic order. The new scheme allowed buyers to see what they had acquired with ease and significantly added a small number of female vendors to the mix. Other versions quickly followed and it cannot be a coincidence that the Bolognese artist Annibale Carraci produced an extensive series of drawings depicting street vendors while he was in Rome in the 1580s (Figures 59–60). Although the publisher who transformed them into engravings many years later recast them as sketches produced at the artist's leisure, they must have been made with the profitable print market in mind. By the end of the sixteenth century, therefore, the street vendor, who was almost always represented as male in print form, had moved from a transitory, mobile figure to one that could now be pinned down on paper, bound like the figures in costume books into volumes or hung on the wall. As such their individuality and diversity, Christian or Jewish, male or female, was

61   Giovanni di Francesco Toscani, (att.), *Feast of St John*, c.1428–9, cassone chest, Museo del Bargello, Florence, inv. Mobili 161, detail of 'San Paolino' selling antidotes for snakebites by the Baptistery, Florence.

avoided in favour of a common status. As in a collection of scientific specimens, the emphasis was on the type or genus that unified these creatures, not on their differences. The representation of the peddler no longer referred to the person himself, but to a collectable item that could be bought and sold.

'Monte in Banco'

As with Croce's poem and Garzoni's prose, it is tempting to suggest that Brambilla's work and the other popular sixteenth-century prints of street vendors reflected a changing attitude towards salesmanship and the street, a sign of a new consumerism. But, it needs to be stressed, such images were not mirrors of social change. They were products of the change itself. The prints were not about the sudden ubiquity of peddlers on the street; they were concerned with the goods that were for sale, both old and new, of which the picture was one.

62   Girolamo da Pontremola, *Snakehandler*, 1527, fresco, Palazzo del Te, Mantua, Sala dei Venti.

63 *Two mountebanks on a trestle stage*, coloured drawing in a friendship album of Sigmundus Ortelius, 1573–9, British Library, MS Eg.1191, f. 18.

The challenges posed by the easy availability of such a wide range of material objects gave rise to a need to construct a visual and verbal language to contain the marketplace. This can be seen by a final discussion of the most problematic of these mobile salesmen and women. In order to sell a more straightforward image of Rome's prosperity, Brambilla had deliberately excluded not only women but also the most troubling of the figures who dominated Rome's markets and streets: the charlatans or mountebanks.[69] Although they were the source of much comment in the sixteenth century, the presence of figures who claimed to be the descendants of Saint Paul in order to sell the earth of Malta and other concoctions against venom, poison and disease was already well established in Italy.[70] As Katherine Park has noted, an early fifteenth-century Florentine *cassone* depicts an image of one of these *San Paolini* standing by a banner in Florence's baptistery square (Figure 61). This sideshow image of a descendant of Saint Paul selling snake oil or Maltese earth seems morally neutral. The figures in the picture are watching one spectacle, while the main scene concerns a wedding another sight: the wedding itself. Mountebanks also appear in one of the early sixteenth-century roundels of the Palazzo del Te and the corner of the seventeenth-century painting and prints by Jaques Callot of the Fair of Impruneta (Figures 62 and 166). But by that period, these figures were no longer symbols of Pauline purity but metaphors for fraud and deceit. The value, or rather the lack of value of their products made them, like the Jewish peddler or the female fruit-seller, highly suspect. For example, in the Spanish romance-dialogue by Francisco Delicado that was published in Rome in 1528, *El retrato de la Lozana Andaluza*, the protagonist, the courtesan Lozana, is shown the market of Campo dei Fiori and told:

> This is the Campo dei Fiori, the centre of the city. Here are the charlatans, the dentists, the healers of hernias who give potions to peasants and to new arrivals . . . See that radish he has in his hand, he will sell it for a *biacco*, or rather for 4 *quattrini*

and say that it takes away tooth-ache [*sic*]. Watch that one, how he is triumphant for he has a powder against worms, and is in a great hurry to sell it, but his powder is worthless.[71]

As the litany of products suggests the travelling charlatan sold many of the same items as the traditional pharmacist but was differentiated primarily by his performance which often included a combination of special effects. Not all took place in town squares. Luca Landucci described the arrival in sixteenth-century Florence of a charlatan known simply as 'the Spaniard'. To prove the efficacy of the paper prayers he had to sell he performed a so-called miracle, leading his crowd from the market bench in the Mercato Vecchio into a baker's shop. As Landucci explained:

> On arrival at the bakers, he said: give me some uncooked bread! and threw it on the oven to show that it was hot, and then he stripped down to his shirt and dropped his trousers to his knees, and in this way he entered until high up, and stayed there awhile, and picked up the bread and turned around inside. And note, the oven was hot, he brought out the bread and he didn't harm himself at all. When he had got

out of the oven, he was given a torch and he lit it, and lit as it was, he put it in his mouth and kept it there until it was extinguished. And many other times on the bench, over the course of several days he took a handful of lit tapers, and held up his hand for a length of time, and then he put them burning into his mouth so that they went out. And he was seen to do many other things with fire: plunging his hands into a pot of oil that was seen many times by all the people. And thus he sold as many of the prayers as he could make; and I say that among all the things I have ever seen, I have not seen a greater miracle than this, if it is a miracle.[72]

64 Giacomo Franco, *Habiti d'huomeni et donne venetiane con la processione della Ser.ma Signoria et altri particolari, cioè trionfi feste et ceremonie publiche della nobilissima città di Venetia*, 1610, 'Charlatans in Piazza San Marco, Venice', The British Library, London.

Landucci was evidently quite sceptical about the fire-eater's miraculous prayers. His scepticism was widely shared yet the authorities were surprisingly permissive in their attitudes towards these performers. Although often feared and banned as fraudsters and tricksters, they were also eagerly awaited by citizens and visitors alike. They were licensed by the authorities and even worked in tandem with apothecaries. Urban magistrates were very aware of the high level of popularity that these theatrical vendors enjoyed and sought to regulate rather than eliminate their presence.[73] In German Friendship books, for example, popular autograph albums where images were pasted in alongside comments, the figure of the mountebank began to appear with great frequency by the 1530s. Including an image of a charlatan seems to have become evidence that the album's owner had been to Italy, particularly to Venice. They proided a centrepiece for one of Giacomo Franco's 1610 views of the city that were also designed to act as a momento of the visit (Figures 64). Visitors from northern Europe were fascinated by these figures whose ubiquity prompted the Englishman Ffynes Moryson to note that:

> Also not only in Carnavall but all the yeare long, all the market places of great Cittyes are full of Mountebanks or Ciarlatanes, who stand upon tables like stages, and to scll their oyles, waters and salves, draw the people about them by musiche and pleasant discourses like Commedies, having a woman and a masked foole to acte these partes with them.[74]

Thomas Coryate's description of Venice's mountebanks was even more precise:

> The principall place where they act, is the first part of Saint Mark's street that reacheth betwixt the west front of Saint Mark's church and the opposite front of Sain Gemian's church. In which, twice a day, that is in the morning and in the afternoone, you may see five or six severall stages erected for them: those that act upon the ground, even the foresaid ciarlatans being the poorer sort of them, stand most commonly in the second part of Saint Mark's, not far from the gate of the Duke's palace ... the principall things that they sell are oyles, soveraigne waters, amorous songs printed, apothecary drugs and a commonweale of other titles ... Also I have observed this in them, that after they have extolled their wares to the skies, having set a price of ten crownes upon some one of their commodities, they have at last descended so low that they have taken it for four gazets, which is something less than a groat.[75]

These performances are thought to have formed the origins of *commedia dell'arte*, in itself a problematic activity. The masked figures on stage, performing standard comic routines, overturned social and clerical strictures on ensuring that outward appearances conformed to the inner being that God had created. As such, the element of masquerade and performance provided a frisson of illicit activity that authorities tolerated or cracked down on in turn. They were the epitome of sales where buyers had to control

65. Detail of Fig. 64

their own sensory responses, vulnerable to being taken in by the deceit or overcome by the pleasure and excitement that came from the performance of salesmanship.

Conclusion

Mountebanks were associated with the piazza and outdoor performance. During a late sixteenth-century debate in Milan on how to control the large numbers of beggars flocking to spaces such as Piazza Duomo, the Castle, the Ospedale Maggiore and the city gates, it was noted that the indigent were drawn to places where crowds formed to listen to: 'Masters and actors of commodities, herb sellers, charlatans, buffoons, *zanni*, mountebanks and others of similar professions'.[76] But these performers were only one of many displays of oddities or virtuosity that took place in the street, ranging from the display of exotic creatures such as the *mostro* or the Siamese twins that were recorded in Florence in the early sixteenth century, to the 'juggling Turk' who tightroped across the Arno from a rope attached to the top of a church bell-tower.[77] The performances were not only visual but also aural. Sound played a key role in attracting and retaining audiences, including the street poetry of of figures such as Michele del Giogante who gave regular recitations in the squares of fifteenth-century Florence and the sixteenth-century performances of the Florentine poet, known as L'Altissimo, who improvised verse on his visit to Venice and then passed around a sweetbox to collect coins.[78] The street cries of the vendors themselves were part of the aural geography of the city street before eventually being repackaged as sophisticated polyphonic performances.

As these intersections suggest it would be too easy to see charlatans as exclusive to street markets, or as appealing only to an uneducated audience In fact, their interest comes from the way they moved between the public square and the palace interior. L'Altissimo earned his living both from public performances and from the poems that he dedicated to the King of France in return for gifts. When successful, the *commedia dell'arte* performers, like the poets or the Siamese twins, were often invited to enter the palaces and homes of wealthier members of the community and eventually by the sixteenth century they earned an income by selling printed versions of their works or tales that could be more widely disseminated.[79] The famous mountebank Leone Tartaglini of Foiano, 'who sells his wares in public often and is known to all the apothecaries in Venice', had a cabinet of curiosities that attracted visitors from all over Italy and a shop that sold the products for which he was famous.[80] Like street vendors, these jugglers, poets and actors moved between highly permeable boundaries of the private and the public, the street and the household. But in doing so they challenged the distinction between commercial payment and the offering of gifts in exchange for pleasure. On the streets, the shop and in the home, the wise consumer of such fictions, like the wise purchaser of material goods, was expected to understand the distinctions between the real and the illusory, thereby avoiding the deceits that followed seduction. Where labels were potentially untrustworthy, a wary consumer would have to use every skill at his or her disposal to find the truth.

Thus a marketplace excursion was not considered simply a matter of taking a few coins and heading for the city centre. At one level, heavily laden shelves and stalls were supposed to reassure urban dwellers that there was no need to fear for the future. At another, it might provide excitement, diversion and danger as one stopped to watch a performance, buy tempting sweets and savouries, pop into the tavern or hire the services of a prostitute. Information circulated as one acquired a news-sheet or simply heard it passed on as gossip in barber and apothecary shops. How buyers were seen to behave in the face of these temptations would say as much about their social status and moral standing as it did about their wealth. What they thought was 'real' and what was illusory, whether they accepted the libellous gossip of the barbershop, whether they could be palmed off with goat's cheese instead of Parmesan signified far more than a simple credulity. It defined their public identity as wise, informed individuals.

Thus in moving on to examine the regulations that attempted to control contemporary purchasing practices, the aim is not to suddenly uncover 'the realities' that lay behind the rhetorical concerns and ambitions described above. Instead, the interpenetration of ideals and the pragmatics of urban behaviour are the focus for debate, arguing that as communities of all sizes attempted to protect the innocent and unwary from their own desires, they not only constructed the marketplace, they also created their own distinctive urban identities.

CHAPTER THREE

Shopping and Surveillance

Not all shopping was the same in Renaissance Italy. The range of possibilities was vividly depicted in an early sixteenth-century fresco cycle in the courtyard of the castle of Challant in Issogne, located in the border area of the Val d'Aosta, now in northern Italy.[1] At the gateway, the point of transition between the fortified castle and the small surrounding village, an anonymous artist depicted a series of commercial vignettes. The narrative begins with a tavern scene showing men and women drinking and gambling (Figure 66).[2] An extravagantly dressed female figure (suggesting a prostitute) attempts to stab her drinking companion while a male associate intervenes. To stop her violent assault, he smashes a cup on her head. Another more reputably dressed man prevents an unsteady drinker from joining in the fray. The dispute is studiously ignored by the other drinkers whose pained expressions suggest their losses at backgammon and cards; below the table the dogs are similarly indecorous, licking their exposed genitals rather than protecting their surroundings. Despite the weapons on the wall and the soldiers at the table, all are inattentive to their surroundings and ill-prepared for any attack.

If this was a warning to the guards stationed at the entrance to avoid the enticements of drink, gambling and women, further images of misdemeanour lay within. Under the portico that stood in front of the kitchen and the pantry, each lunette featured a different site for sales: a fruit and vegetable market, a pie shop, a grocer's, a draper's shop and a pharmacy (Figures 67–71). Like the tavern scene, the images were moral in their meaning, mingling pleasure in prosperity with concerns about sexuality and security.

66   Anonymous, *Tavern scene*, c.1500, fresco, Castello di Issogne, Val d'Aosta.

67   Anonymous, *Pie Shop*, c.1500, fresco, Castello di Issogne, Val d'Aosta.

68 Anonymous, *Grocer*, c.1500, fresco, Castello di Issogne, Val d'Aosta.

69 Anonymous, *Draper*, c.1500, fresco, Castello di Issogne, Val d'Aosta.

70 Anonymous, *Market scene*, c.1500, fresco, Castello di Issogne, Val d'Aosta.

71 Anonymous, *Apothecary*, c.1500, fresco, Castello di Issogne, Val d'Aosta.

In the pie shop, for example, splayed carcasses hang from the rafters while dogs steal sausages from open baskets. In the market, baskets, barrels and stalls overflow with fruit and vegetables (Figure 70). A range of manufactured goods such as shoes, clogs and stockings are on offer in the background. At first sight, this market seems relatively decorous. But closer examination reveals a more disturbing set of connections. Many of the women have their heads covered. They wear aprons and carry the spindles that suggest the status of respectable housewives and diligent spinners. Yet with few exceptions, they are as available to the male touch and gaze as the goods on offer. Only a small number of figures, those set at the margins of the lunette, concentrate on the fruit itself. In all the other episodes, the fertility and fecundity of the market's produce is deliberately confused with the sexualised contact of buyers and sellers. On the far right, a young man fondles a melon with one hand and points to the belly of the fruit-seller with the other; to the rear of the picture another man seems to be examining figs with his right hand while his left hand reaches out to touch the vendor's breasts. But men were not the only aggressors. On the left a man's attempt to purchase leeks is confused by a young woman's offer of carnations. As their fingers tangle, he seems to have become distracted from his main purpose.

The ambivalent images of abundance and sexual attraction in the Issogne frescoes seem to reinforce the familiar mixed metaphors of fecundity and sensuality already described in Chapter Two. But the remainder of the cycle offers a more nuanced view, suggesting that where shops were ordered, security was possible. For example, in the draper's shop, cloth is carefully stored away in bolts laid out in even rows while the salesmen measure out wares using rulers. Measurement and weighing are also to the fore in the apothecary's shop (Figure 71). Here the long, well-built, wooden counter maintains a crucial separation between the apothecary and his customer. Labelled jars are placed on shelves and to the left, one male figure is seen either writing or keeping accounts. Slightly lower down, the set of scales held by another salesman provides the picture's central focus. In the lowest space of all, a beggar sits wearing a single shoe and ragged clothing. He has been given the menial task of grinding the ingredients, unskilled labour that was often offered as an act of charity rather than as a professional occupation. Finally, a single female figure stands in the central foreground, directly in front of the scales. Although her dress is relatively simple, her high, belted waist and long sleeves suggest she belongs to the urban elite. Only in this site, where arithmetic, measurement, social decorum and charity were all present, could a woman be seen to shop in safety on her own.

Painted between 1496 and 1506, the cycle was probably commissioned under the auspices of the widowed Marguerite de Challant and her cousin-in-law, the regent Georges de Challant, Canon of Lyon and a protonotary apostolic at the papal court.[3] The frescoes discussed above were painted in the portico in front of the castle's kitchen and dining rooms, liminal spaces between the outer areas designed for servants and soldiers and the secure inner courtyard where the family resided. Within the castle's main hall, a very different set of scenes were depicted (Figures 72–3). Here, fictive brocades and

72 Anonymous, Main Hall, c.1500, fresco, Castello di Issogne, Val d'Aosta.

velvets seem to line the walls while faux marble columns and windows frame scenes of the elite pursuits of hunting and falconry.

Read as a sequence from exterior to interior, the two series made reference to concepts of social order. The contrast between the need to buy food and an aristocratic lifestyle based on hunting and hawking was clear. Those living in castles and villas in the countryside were able to obtain the foodstuffs that were most appropriate to their standing such as the game birds that were often forbidden for public sale. The interior images reinforced the message that frequenting shops, either as a buyer or as a seller, was beneath the dignity of the castle's inhabitants. As Tomaso Garzoni put it in a late sixteenth-century rephrasing of Cicero's classical arguments concerning nobility:

> Trading if on a small scale, should be considered a vulgar thing; if, however, it is on a grand scale, importing many things from different parts of the world and distributing them without fraud to all, then it should not be despised. Indeed it seems worthy of praise, if those who undertake it, once they are satisfied with the fortunes they have made retire from the ports to their lands in the countryside.[4]

This distinction, originally outlined in Cicero's *De Officis*, a standard Latin text known to most schoolboys, was a boon to those who wished to retain both patrician status and

73 Anonymous, Main Hall, detail, c.1500, fresco, Castello di Issogne, Val d'Aosta.

commercial success. As long as the business involved the wholesale import and export of exotic high-value items, honour was maintained. It was a particularly familiar topos in Venice, a city that prided itself on a mercantile-based patrician class and ritually lamented the aristocracy's retreat from international commerce in the late sixteenth century.[5] But if wholesale activities were acceptable, retail sales were almost always problematic. In debating an application for entry into the Venetian nobility in the sixteenth century, for example, careful attention was paid to the precise status of the petitioner's ancestry. In one case, it was deemed acceptable that as apothecaries, the applicant's father and grandfather had weighed out wax with their own hands when serving customers. They were admitted, but in another case, the fact that members of the Mueller family had been known to personally serve salami to their clients, counted against their petition.[6] While personal involvement in service might, at a stretch, be appropriate for the elite banking, silk and spice trades, most shop business was supposed to be undertaken by artisans, or by their wives, servants and slaves.[7] When enough profit had been generated, a true gentleman would then leave his business behind and retire to the countryside.

While such conflicts might be expected in international trading centres such as Venice, the anxieties over shopkeeping were not exclusive to this major entrepôt. In encouraging the development of a local elite, for instance, the small Tuscan town of Poppi designed a set of municipal gowns that would demonstrate the standing of their priors and standard-bearers in the mid-sixteenth century. In their regulations they specifically banned the wearing of unseemly garments under the new purple-lined black cloaks and velvet hats, declaring that it was, 'not lawful nor permitted for anyone while wearing the worthy gown to wear openly aprons, smocks or other distinguishing marks of the artisan or the shopkeeper'.[8] In 1593, the Milanese senate took this to its logical extreme, excluding anyone who kept a shop or warehouse from entering the nobility.[9]

If patricians should not be seen behind the counter of a shop as salesmen, could they stand on the other side as customers? Again, like the Issogne frescoes, the classical tradition suggested not. In his mid-fifteenth-century treatise on the family, Leon Battista Alberti outlined an ideal world where the paterfamilias would rely on the produce of his estates rather than on goods purchased from strangers. This was a concept that was further developed by Alberti's contemporary, the Venetian humanist, Francesco Barbaro, who wrote:

> Pericles' custom especially deceives the ignorant and often harms domestic plenty. He sold at one time all the crops he received from his fields and afterwards he bought daily at the market whatever was needed at home. But this daily provisioning with grain, wood, and wine is more proper for a traveller or unsettled soldier than for a citizen and head of a family, for if he did this he would not be splendidly, generously, or comfortably looking after his own wealth.[10]

The surviving accounts of Italy's elite indicate that, as in ancient Rome, a high value was placed on using the produce of one's own estates or smallholding. When Bonaccorso Pitti surveyed his possessions in 1419, for example, he included an inventory of 'all the trees that give fruit in our garden and vineyard, including figs, peaches, plums, cherries, almonds, apples, pears, pomegranates, quince, nuts and olives'.[11] Agricultural tithes or rents on ovens and mills were often paid in foodstuffs rather than in cash while the offering of gifts of homemade or home-grown items or game from one's own lands was an important part of elite exchange.[12] The Marchioness of Mantua, Isabella d'Este sent fish, pickles and other delicacies to family and friends; Cardinal Ippolito d'Este took great pride in giving salami made by his household to distinguished guests and to women whom he hoped to impress.[13]

As letters accompanying gifts of food stressed, home-grown produce was always considered superior to something of unknown origin that had been bought in the marketplace. But while a late fifteenth-century census of the grain stores in private hands in Bologna reveals that the attics and cellars of homes at every social level held sacks of wheat, rice and spelt which were well beyond what the family required for daily sustenance, complete self-sufficiency was rare.[14] Although servants might take out dough to be baked in the local ovens and serve goods grown on the family estate, there was still a need to purchase perishables – vegetables, meats, fish and dairy products – on a regular basis. Moreover, even though a considerable amount of spinning, weaving and sewing took place within even the most superior of households, few estates could provide the diversity of manufactures such as pottery, glassware, textiles and furnishings that were required by Renaissance households. Domestic production and market production need to be understood as complementary rather than as competing forms of provisioning, ensuring that the families of both well-off patricians and artisans alike had to make decisions as to who would take responsibility both for routine shopping and for special purchases.

These decisions were conditioned by the firmly embedded fears and anxieties concerning sexuality, hierarchy and status that were discussed above and in Chapter one. Shopping, even on a small scale, was an activity that required mutual trust, a term rendered by the word *fiducia* in Italian.[15] Buyers had to believe that the goods really matched the description presented by the sellers who, in turn, had to believe that in offering credit facilities or accepting coins that they were not being cheated by someone who would never pay a debt or would do so in debased, clipped or false money.

The easiest way to judge these risks was, of course, for the two participants to negotiate directly, handling and observing both the goods and the coins themselves. But if elite men and women accepted that they had to avoid the lower status areas of the marketplace, someone else would have to make these judgements on their behalf. They then needed reassurance that their servants were not colluding with merchants in order to further defraud them. This in turn meant that the marketplace, particularly the marketplace for foodstuffs, might be dominated by customers who were poor and vulnerable. They too needed protection.

Trust was as problematic in the medieval and Renaissance market as it is today. The assumption that market fraud was the underlying basis of all commercial exchange was a long-standing attitude summed up in an early tenth-century Latin poem:

> There are in the world merchants
> Who, alas, are impostors,
> They buy, or they sell
> Pretending to make a loss,
> They foreswear themselves before God and the saints,
> And care little if they lie . . .
> In weight, number and measure,
> All merchandise by them is infected.
> So that not one is true.[16]

Centuries later, the Franciscan preacher San Bernardino da Siena refashioned these warnings in a sermon on markets and traders delivered in the main square of Siena, the Campo, during the Lenten cycle of 1427. Unlike the anonymous poet, however, San Bernardino made no distinction between honest merchants and dangerous rogues. Everyone's soul was at stake, for as he quoted from the Apocalypse, 'No one can buy or sell unless they have the character of the name of the beast, (the Antichrist)'.[17]

With his use of everyday examples and homely metaphors, San Bernardino's Lenten sermon on the fraudulent nature of the marketplace provided a detailed depiction of minor misdemeanours that would have been familiar to his listeners. After disrespect for God's sacred time, and the sin of usury, the merchant's other misdemeanours focused on deceit, theft and blasphemy. San Bernardino provided a catalogue of misdeeds that could have been lifted from any guild prosecutor's record book:

And he, who sells cloth, shows the top part and says that it is better than it is, selling the cloth with the top sample, without showing the full cloth, and this is false. Then there are those who sell grain and show a sample which is clean and of quality, but it is not that which they give them. These are all falsehoods which are always illicit for in this you are damaging your neighbour . . . He, who sells by measures, must pull the cloth over the ruler . . . Pull it well! And the other who has two measuring rods, one to sell, the other to buy, like those who sell wheat and other grains with a smaller measure to sell than they use to buy . . . The third sin is that of the merchant who sells by measure, he pulls the cloth so hard that it seems it will break. Pull it hard when you have to sell it! I say nothing to you of those who keep the merchandise that is sold by weight damp so that it weighs more . . .[18]

In this example, false weights and measures, fraudulent goods and cheating merchants were assumed to be the norm rather than the exception. To these could be added selling a cheaper piece of meat as a more expensive cut; re-dyeing a second-hand dress and selling it as a new version; using yellow-tin in place of gold leaf; selling fake gems as the real thing; and the multitude of adulterations that appeared in guild and civic prosecutors' lists of possible crimes. But it was not only salesmen who might disguise their products. As sumptuary laws and sermons reminded citizens, in purchasing and using inappropriate goods, buyers might disguise themselves. San Bernardino argued eloquently:

It is vanity when you wear that which does not pertain to you. The merchant who wears a short tunic, that is an offence against God. If he were a brave soldier, then he could wear it, because it is appropriate to him, but not you . . . O merchant, if you wish to appear as a merchant, then wear the garment which is made for you . . .[19]

In San Bernardino's ideal ordered and moral city a butcher's wife would not be confused with the wife of a judge, just as beef would not be sold as veal.[20]

As this suggests, marking an interior identity with an accurate exterior sign was a moral issue. Falsity was as much a sin against God as a crime against the consumer. Clearly labelling both products and people was one solution, and much civic legislation was devoted to making identity visible. In Venice for example, fish-sellers were supposed to wear a circular badge with black letters reading 'Fishmonger'; as discussed in the previous chapter, women who sold goods on behalf of others were to wear a red 'R' for *revenditrice* and no one was to dress as a peasant in order to fool customers into thinking that the produce had been home-grown.[21]

In his sermons, San Bernardino attempted to instil a sense of individual responsibility for mercantile behaviour. But a more common solution was to assume deception on the part of the seller and shift the responsibility onto a seemingly more neutral institutional basis. If a merchant was tempted to cheat, the city in which he lived and worked would identify and punish him. Effective commerce, therefore, depended on effective policing. The establishment of magistracies to oversee basic transactions, such as the Giustizia Vecchia which was set up in Venice around 1173 to regulate the marketplace, demonstrate the importance given to the supervision of petty exchanges from an early stage.[22] But this oversight came at a cost, requiring substantial investments of both time and salaried personnel in order to ensure that the many rules and regulations that were issued, and then reissued, were actually followed. Thus, in fourteenth-century Siena a *guardia segreta* toured the daily market on the Campo to identify fraudulent sales.[23] In early sixteenth-century Bologna, a set of civic officials, the *magistrato dei collegi*, controlled all prices and weights, appointing four senior officials to circulate in the Piazza

Grande to check on what was being sold and to alter prices if they felt they were unfair.[24] During times of tension, the local police force or *milizia* would also maintain a presence.[25] The protection of ecclesiastical bodies could also be invoked. In faction-ridden Pistoia, the job of supervising the marketplace and setting prices was delegated from the fourteenth to the seventeenth century to the charitable institution, the *Opera di San Jacopo*.[26] In Como, the friars of the *Umiliati* order were responsible for ensuring that a merchant's weights could be trusted.

In addition to civic and ecclesiastical institutions, it was common for guilds to join governments in providing additional forms of surveillance. The detailed illumination of the market of Ravegnana in Bologna comes from the 1411 guild statutes of the city's drapers (Figure 74). These regulations were designed to limit the number able to work in the trade and to impose standards such as the use of agreed measurements, as seen in the foreground where a salesman pulls out cloth for a female buyer. Such self-regulation had to be seen to be effective and guildhall officials went through elaborate rituals to reassure consumers. The regulations and sumptuary laws of most cities constantly refer to the need to apply official lead seals, *bolle*, or to provide certificates that authenticated goods or gave permission for their ownership. When the silk guild was estab-

lished in Milan in 1461, for example, the regulations stipulated that all silk cloth sold had to be stamped in the guildhall and that buyers were required to present their purchases within three days of the sale to the guild officials to be checked. If the material was found to be faulty or fraudulent, customers would receive their money back plus a 25 per cent premium.[27] This was common practice. In mid-fifteenth-century Piacenza, three officials were similarly elected to examine all the woollen cloth in the city to determine its quality. Every piece of cloth was to be taken to the *Palacio Merchantie* in order to receive a lead seal as a guarantee of its quality. Piacenza also appointed a goldsmith to visit shops and bankers' tables, 'where gold rings might be found' in order to examine their weight and fineness.[28]

74   *The Market of Porta Ravegnana*, Matricola della Società dei Drappieri, 1411, Museo Civico Medievale, Bologna, ms. Cod. Min. 641, c.1.

The rationale behind this investment of time and effort in was the need to facilitate exports and attract buyers from outside the city walls. The high reputation of goods that were 'bought in Venice' or 'made in Milan' would provide the necessary reassurance of quality and standards. But it was also important to protect local consumers who needed basic commodities. It is unsurprising, therefore, that the most commercial and aggressive mercantile cities invested in a high level of oversight at both ends of the spectrum from luxuries designed primarily for export to daily necessities. In Venice there were over thirty different magistracies responsible for commercial activities, and the patrician writer Francesco Sansovino made a deliberate connection between these regulators and the city's prosperity when describing the Rialto market:

> And from Chioggia there are the fishermen who come to sell their fish here in the *Pescharia*. The names of the fish that are caught and brought here will be named below. There are also oysters in great quantities and as much fish as you could want is brought here daily to sell, and by night time there is nothing left. The reason is that all buy, and live as lords. And here in this land nothing is born at all, of whatever you wish, that is not found in abundance. This is because of the sale of the goods that there are, for everything from every land and every part of the world where there is something to sell, above all to eat, is brought here, and quickly transformed into cash, for all are cash-rich. Here at Rialto it seems a garden; so many greens are brought from nearby, and so many and such a wide variety of fruits at excellent prices that it is a wonderful thing. I will say, as I have heard from one who says, 'where there is garbage, there are goods'. And in the Rialto the prices of some items are limited, so that those who buy are not deceived. The beef sold from the butcher's stall cannot be sold for more than two soldi to the pound and if the weight is light, because there are officials designated to weigh the meat that you have bought, the butcher will be condemned by the Lords who are deputised to do so . . . and so we say, 'weigh justly and sell at a high price'. Other comestibles can be sold at whatever price they can fetch but even so the Giustizia Vecchia has the right to set the price of things to eat at a just price. Thus the land is as well organised as any country can be . . .[29]

Sanudo stressed that Venice's security was based on civic control over both the quality and price of the most basic foods and services. Bargaining was to have little place as most items and services – fish, meat, oil and even a barber's shave – were supervised by designated officials who determined and posted the 'just price' for each item. All types of transactions were meant to be bound by the inscription on the church of San Giacomo di Rialto calling, 'Round about this church may the merchant be equitable, the weights just, and may no fraudulent contract be negotiated.'[30] In sum, Venice was supposed to be a safe place to do business. This was not because of the integrity of the individual merchants involved, but because of the dedicated, unswerving surveillance provided by the city-state.

There were, of course, financial as well as moral incentives involved. A substantial percentage of the government revenues came from the taxes imposed on both the

75 Fifteenth-century painted and gilt casket, The British Museum, London.

importation and sale of basic and luxury goods. Much of the checking at gates, ports and other entry points was designed to stop the flow of contraband rather than to facilitate commerce. This again required a high level of investment in official time and effort. The detailed line-by-line descriptions of the taxes imposed on transport moving in and out of Bologna give some indication of the time that this assessment must have involved. In 1438, for example, one Bolognese-based merchant, Alberto de Alamania, probably a mercer, imported 27 categories of goods, including numerous woollen hats of different qualities and styles, leather gloves, spurs, armoured breast-plates, eyeglasses and boots, paying a total tax of 35 lire.[31] Each item was carefully described, and the appropriate duty recorded. A few days later, another merchant, Bartolomeo Vitalis de Grassis paid 24 lire in taxes on barrels and boxes that were packed with brass candlesticks, basins, cotton thread, gold thread, ivory combs and glass paternoster beads.[32] Other mercers and merchants imported cloth of all types, spun cotton thread, raw wool, gloves, shirts and stockings, buttons, pins, needles, 'scissors for tailors', copper thread, German glass, eyeglasses, copper and tin cups and basins, mirrors and paternoster beads in bone, ivory and glass.[33] The spice trade featured particularly prominently in these records, reflecting perhaps the ease with which items such as cinnamon, ginger and pepper could be carried and the high level of demand for such products.[34] Other goods were imported from specialist purveyors. Florence was obviously renowned for the ready-made caskets and chests that were given to brides similar to that in the illustration from the British Museum (Figure 75) and one merchant, Petenonio de Vidale, imported two containers of such items including 16 round gilt caskets, 4 round caskets with stamped leather coverings and 6 caskets, *da spoxa*, that is, 'for brides'.[35] One of the highest import duties, 6 lire and 13 soldi, was charged to Robin Zudio who had brought in 133 lire's worth of Hebrew books, *litera ebrea* directly from Germany in 1440.[36]

76 Andrea Pisano, *Justice*, c.1336, marble, Museo dell'Opera del Duomo, Florence.

The interest of these toll records is not simply in the scale and diversity of imports; it is also in the efforts made to follow them into the city and to write down, in an excellent notarial hand, every ounce of taxable material that came into Bologna. Officials were not only interested in import taxes; having arrived, the goods might then be subject to additional sales taxes, particularly on basic items such as wine or grain.

Uncovering fraud, seizing faulty, fake or untaxed goods and prosecuting offenders required regular policing and court sittings. In many cases, the work of surveillance was undertaken by a tax farmer, a *daziere*, who had purchased the taxes on produce sold on the square in return for an up-front payment to the city. In places such as Milan and Bologna, he would manage the market, assign sites to different merchants, collect taxes, impose fines and ensure that the area was swept clean on either a weekly or monthly basis. There were other commercial incentives to enforcing urban legislation. In Milan, half the salaries of those who checked the quality and weight of foodstuffs were drawn from the damages that those found guilty had to pay.[37] This obviously caused tensions, and there were frequent accusations that such officials were imposing fines simply in order to increase their own revenue. Finally, those who accused colleagues of misconduct were often given a percentage of the fine that were eventually levied.

Of the multitude of statutory rules and regulations issued by Italy's many towns, the two most crucial themes after taxation were those concerning measurement and money. Traditionally, just measurement was a metaphor for justice itself. The Old Testament language of Leviticus stressed, 'You shall do no unrighteousness in judgement, in metreyard, in weight or in measure. Just balances, just weights, a just *epah*, and a just *hin*, shall you have.'[38] Likewise, the New Testament iconography of the Last Judgement depended on the notion of the weighing of souls. Allegories of civic justice such as the fourteenth-century depiction by Andrea Pisano in Florence or the sixteenth-century image by the Rialto bridge relied on the symbol of the equitable balance, capable of rational and impersonal measurement (Figures 76–7). Indeed, the intimate linking of just calculation and fair judgement was reflected in the emphasis that governments of all complexions placed on managing measurement. Thus, in early fourteenth-century Padua, the *judex victualium*, the judge who considered market crimes, gave judgement in front of a figure of Justice shown holding a steelyard with the inscription, 'and I, by

77 Figure of Justice overlooking the Rialto bridge, Venice.

means of ratio, the mistress of men, regulate actions. I stop crimes involving weight and measure.'[39] Over the centuries the iconography of the good merchant was defined with a set of scales and a yardstick, as in the draper in Jacopo de Cessoli's late four-teenth-century *De ludo schachorum* or in Muscarello's late fifteenth-century Neapolitan treatise on arithmetic. The steelyard, another form of weights, was an equally potent indicator of good measure as in the sixteenth-century frontispiece to Tommasino de'Bianchi de' Lancilloti's *Stadera del formento*. This meant of course, that the measures themselves (as well as the merchants) had to be trustworthy (Figures 78–80).

* * *

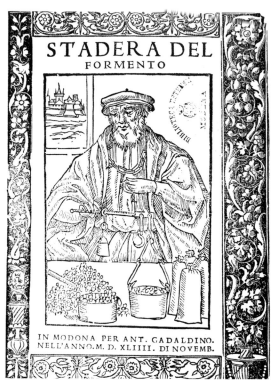

78 (*above left*) Draper with scales and a yard-stick from Jacopo de Cessoli, *De ludo schachorum, volgarizzamento adespoto*, c.1390, Florence, Biblioteca Riccardiana, Ricc.2513, c14v.

79 (*above right*) Tommasino de'Bianchi de'Lancillotti, *Stadera del formento*, Modena, 1544, Biblioteca Estense, Modena 87.C.33 (1), frontispiece.

80 (*right*) Muscarello, *A Treatise on Practical Arithmetic* (Nola, c.1478), Sotheby's Sale, 23 June 1992, Lot 73, f. 100, 'Tailor with three pieces of cloth, scissors and a measuring stick', The Conway Library, Courtauld Institute of Art, London.

Just Measures

This meant, of course, that the measures themselves (as well as the merchants) had to be trustworthy. Publishing and enforcing official measures, whether of currencies, weights, the sizes of bricks and tiles or the clothing that was allowed to butchers' wives, was meant to create a sense of stability and equity based on visible difference. These markers of identity would be guaranteed by the city and its constituent parts such as guilds or religious authorities.[40] In Assisi, the city, like many others determined the standard size for bricks and tiles, inserting a set of measures into the walls of the town hall (Figure 81). In Ferrara, Borso d'Este's ducal seal authenticated the city's weights while in Milan the only cups that could be used in inns were those that had a 30-ounce capacity and were marked with the communal coat of arms (Figure 82).[41] But the converse was also true. Whoever was seen as responsible for these supposedly common standards was also seen to have publicly constituted authority.[42]

Under such circumstances keeping measurements and the acts of measuring in the public domain were crucial to commercial confidence and to urban control. The fourteenth-century statutes of the Florentine oil vendors, grocers and butchers demanded that the guilds' rectors be responsible for:

> Setting up an inquiry against any person who deceives or commits frauds while selling or in buying or in marketing goods or merchandise appertaining to this art and above all acting against those who clearly do not openly set out their measures and market in their shops but keep these measures in hidden spaces.[43]

It was not, however, enough to work in the open. The measures themselves had to be regarded as reliable. The makers of the scales themselves were usually licensed and arrangements were made to provide either public weigh stations, or a set of portable weights that could be carried from shop to shop.[44] This allowed officials to check a store's own weights against the official version. In affixing a lead seal (for which a charge would be made), the veracity of these measurements was then supposed to be assured.

As additional protection, town halls, cathedrals and churches often displayed permanent sets of measures that were made in clay, stone or brass.

Yet while these public displays were common, it is unlikely that individuals actually went to church or town-hall walls to make a final check on the weight or length of their purchases. These were symbols of civic supervision rather than practical aids. As such

81   Official measures for brick and tile sizes, Palazzo del Capitano del Popolo, Assisi.

82   Six weights bearing Borso d'Este's coat of arms, 1452–71, Museo Civico d'Arte, Modena, n.inv.19.

they became powerful signifiers of urban independence. Every town clung to its own weights and measures, even when it made sense to integrate. Despite attempts to impose Florentine measurements throughout his dominions, for example, the Grand Duke of Tuscany was unable to get agreement on a common set of weights. In 1584, his advisor Vincenzo Borghini lamented the consequences of this failure:

> And one can say generally that the nature of weights and measures is both very uncertain and very unstable. They vary from moment to moment, place to place and thing to thing, so much so that to reduce them to a fixed and equivalent term is very difficult, if not impossible. And not only do the measurements vary according to time but maintain the same name, and even at the same moment, vary according to place and country, but the thing that is most strange is that we find different items measured differently so that neither now nor perhaps at any point have all things been measured in the same way.[45]

Borghini's concerns were, of course, motivated by his position at the court of the Grand Duke of Tuscany whose aim was to subsume his territories under Florentine jurisdiction. However sensible his ideas, an agreement on measurements that would have allowed ease of comparison between, for example, Pisan and Sienese cloth, wine, grain or land, would have meant undermining local traditions. No city was willing to take on the measurements of another town voluntarily and, given the Italian peninsula's highly fragmented political structure, this meant that seemingly neutral mathematical or geometric issues such as weights, measures and the exchange rates for different currencies were always highly contested.[46] Buyers ordering from outside their own cities had to use manuals to adjust their orders and it was common practice to send pieces of string or paper giving the outline of the amount desired for fear of getting the amounts wrong.[47] Thus while a multiplicity of diverse measurements allowed for considerable local identity, it encouraged distrust of foreign measurements, even when they were those of a town only a few miles away.

MAKING MONEY

If buyers were suspicious of the qualities and measures of the goods on offer, sellers were equally suspicious of the cash they were paid in return. Around the same time as Vincenzo Borghini was writing on measurements, his compatriot, Bernardo Davanzati was making similar complaints about the changing nature of the money used in exchanges. In his 'Lesson on Money' of 1588, Davanzati pointed out the difficulties of the inconsistent value of the coins that were circulating in Florence and the differences between values agreed in the past and those of the present:

> Difficulties and lawsuits arise from the payment of inheritances, rents, taxes and all forms of debts that were agreed during a period when money was good. The debtor who owes a florin worth 7 lire says: Here is your 7 lire. The creditor replies: You need to give me 10 because, today that is the value of the gold florin that you have to give me or else you have to find me a florin in gold with the lily that was struck at that time. The debtor replies: If I give you a florin worth 7 lire, as the paperwork demands, it is not a minor achievement. If the Prince has reduced the value of the lire, this is a common storm that we share together, and we are all in the same boat. Your lament is with the Prince.[48]

In 1582, the Emilian writer Gasparo Scaruffi produced a treatise addressing this problem, calling for a single world currency that would not vary over time or place. Dedicated to Count Alfonso d'Este Tassoni, the *Giudice de' savi* of Reggio Emilia and *Consigliere secreto* to Duke Alfonso V of Ferrara, it was entitled, *L'Alitinonfo of Messer Gasparo Scaruffi, from Reggio, to bring gold and silver into line so that it can be used universally and against the many abuses of clipping and sweating of coins, as well as to regulate all forms of payment and to reduce the world's currency to a single form of coin* (Figure 83).[49]

Scaruffi argued that reform was needed as, 'every day there arise great problems in making payments, as much within a single city as from one city to the other, and even from one province to the other and things will get even worse if nothing is done'.[50] The solution he argued was one of imperial authority. He called for the creation of a

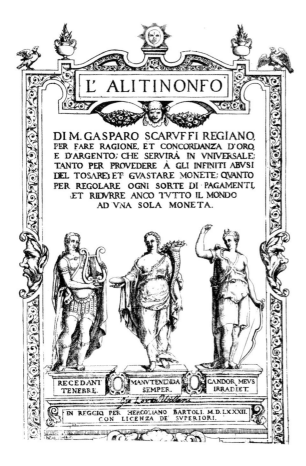

L' ALITINONFO

DI M. GASPARO SCARVFFI REGIANO,
PER FARE RAGIONE, ET CONCORDANZA D'ORO,
E D'ARGENTO; CHE SERVIRÀ IN VNIVERSALE;
TANTO PER PROVEDERE À GLI INFINITI ABVSI
DEL TOSARE, ET GVASTARE MONETE; QVANTO
PER REGOLARE OGNI SORTE DI PAGAMENTI,
ET RIDVRRE ANCO TVTTO IL MONDO
AD VNA SOLA MONETA.

RECEDANT
TENEBRÆ.

MANVTENENDA
SEMPER.

CANDOR MEVS
IRRADIET.

IN REGGIO PER HERCOLIANO BARTOLI. M.D.LXXXII.
CON LICENZA DE' SVPERIORI.

83 Gasparo Scaruffi, *L'Alitinonfo,* Reggio, 1582, frontispiece, The British Library, London.

universal worldwide mint that would issue a *moneta imperiale* that would never vary in value and could be used across the globe.[51]

Scaruffi and Davanzati were writing in a period of widespread concern over inflation and the circulation of myriad currencies was seen as one of the main problems. Unlike England which operated a Royal mint, or France where licensed mints issued a limited range of coins such as the *livres tournois,* Italy had competing mints operating across the politically fragmented peninsula. The refusal to move over to a common currency was, like the refusal to use common measurements, a sign of political independence.

This was because coins had very strong visual identities; they were not simply pieces of metal, they were symbols of authority, and the close identification of rulership and coinage was confirmed by nicknames they were often given. The Venetian silver shilling of the fourteenth century was known as the *cenoglello* or 'little knee' after the kneeling figure of the Doge.[52] When Teddeo Pepoli, the Lord of Bologna began issuing double shillings in 1338, they were immediately known as *pepolese* and in the sixteenth century, when the first Florentine scudo was minted in 1530, it was known as the *Alessandrino* after Duke Alessandro de' Medici. Its successor was likewise called a 'Cosimo' after the new duke. The most popular silver coin of the sixteenth century, the Roman scudo was known either as a *Giulio* after Pope Julius II or a *Paolo* when it bore Paul III's features (Figure 84).

Such portrait-based coins, known as *testoni,* or 'big heads', created particularly strong links between coins and rulers as is evident in the gold ducat of Ferdinand of Aragon, king of Naples, or the ducat of the young duke of Milan, Gian Galeazzo Sforza (Figures 84–5). This close identification with signorial power meant that Doge Nicolas Tron's issuing of his own features on a Venetian lire in 1472 was greeted with horror in the republic. In 1479, a Piacentine chronicler found it worth noting when Bona Sforza issued new coins, *grossi* worth 20 soldi each, containing both her features and those of

84 Gold ducat of king Ferdinand of Aragon, c.1470, Gabinetto numismatico, Milan.

her young son, for whom she was acting as regent. He was shocked as this was the first time he had ever seen a woman's face on a coin (Figure 86).[53] When Bona was deposed in 1480 her features were quickly exchanged for those of the new regent, Ludovico Maria Sforza (Figure 87).

Because of this association between political authority and legal tender, it was equally common to ban the coins of political opponents or outlaw untrustworthy foreign issues. Here again, such controls required constant surveillance. Duke Ferdinando dei Medici set up a much-hated police force whose primary duty was to search homes, shops, stalls and people's pockets for illegal currency. The monies seized would be taken to the mint to be melted down, with half the profit going to the official responsible for the seizure.[54] The punishments for counterfeiting and altering coins were severe and unlike many other statutes, these were implemented with great alacrity. Those making and passing false coins were put to death, along with those thought to have aided and abetted them. But those found guilty in the mid-sixteenth century were almost always of minor status and often foreign to the city, suggesting that the magistrates were only scratching the surface of a highly lucrative business.[55]

Coins had to be accepted by their users as well as by the governments that issued them. In mid-sixteenth-century Milan, there were over forty types of coins in circulation, a situation which was not uncommon.[56] To reduce the confusion, written records were usually kept in so-called monies of account, that is in lire, soldi and denari (pounds, shillings and pence) that had little relationship to the 'real money' in people's pockets. The use of monies of account disguises the fluctuating value of the pounds and pence which depended, in part, on the exchange rates between gold, silver and the debased mixed metal billon and copper coins. Gold was supposed to be the most reliable form of exchange and in the fourteenth and fifteenth centuries, the dominant gold coins used for international trading were those of the major Italian cities: the Florentine florin and the Venetian, Milanese and Genoese ducats or *zecchini*. But by the beginning of the sixteenth century, the French *écu* had became the European standard and most Italian cities had begun producing similar coins known as *scudi*.[57] At the end of the century, the light, almost gossamer-thin gold coins were themselves under threat from the heavy, finely produced silver coins that were issued in the north and by the new imperial power of Spain: guilders, thalers and Spanish *reales de a ocho*, or 'pieces of eight'.

85 (*top*)   Silver *testone* of Gian Galeazzo Maria Sforza, Duke of Milan, c.1480, Gabinetto numismatico, Milan.

86A and B (*middle*)   Coin bearing portraits of Bona Sforza and her son Gian Galeazzo Maria Sforza, 1479, Gabinetto numismatico, Milan.

87A and B (*bottom*)   Coin bearing portraits of Ludovico Maria Sforza and his nephew Gian Galeazzo Maria Sforza, 1480, Gabinetto numismatico, Milan.

Generally, however, the silver coins were highly volatile in comparison with gold, suffering constant inflation, while the billon or copper coins that were used in small-scale transactions had only a token value. As new coins were issued and old ones withdrawn it was important to establish a common understanding of their face value, one that was always less than their intrinsic metallic worth. Regular announcements were made by town criers or circulated as printed *bande* identifying what was and what was not legal tender and the relationship of different coins to the monies of account. Diarists and chroniclers as well as accountants regularly noted the changes and reassessed the value of their savings often with anger and dismay.

Thus with the exception of the highest value coins, money was often less trustworthy than other forms of exchange. Not only did buyers and sellers alike need to pay attention to what different governments were willing to accept, they also had to ensure that the coins they accepted had not been clipped, faked or sweated (a practice that involved putting coins into a purse with mercury to draw off a proportion of the metallic content). Given the variations and sudden changes in value, barter must have been as safe, if not safer than offering cash.

PRICE AND VALUE

Bartering two different types of good still required a consensus on their respective values and here too, governments and guilds would intervene. Just as there was a genuine label, so too was there an honest price. Although the laws of supply and demand were well understood, establishing and policing pricing was a mechanism for protecting the poorest members of society from the most rapacious. As James Shaw and others have shown, capitalist assumptions about supply and demand were complicated by an assumption that the market could be easily manipulated by deceptive merchants.[58] It was widely agreed that one of the most shocking aspects about the way that mountebanks sold their goods was the wide spread of prices that they were willing to accept, suggesting that there was no intrinsic value to their goods. Thomas Coryate's description of these Venetian sellers quoted earlier emphasised that:

> I have observed this in them, that after they have extolled their wares to the skies, having set a price of ten crownes upon some one of their commodities, they have at last descended so low that they have taken it for four gazets, which is something less than a groat.[59]

Yet it was also accepted that prices might vary for other reasons. When the printer Giunti wrote to Vincenzo Borghini concerning the purchase of prints in Rome, he made it clear that the cost of the item would vary dramatically according to how and when it was sold:

> Ordinarily they are sold at 20 soldi a sheet especially when they are not left-overs. And although sometimes they can be bought from certain people on feast days for

a *carlino*, they can also be sold for three *giulii* so that with one thing and another, 15 soldi is best.[60]

The advice was sensible. On a feast day where many vendors might be attempting to undercut each other by selling the same print, the price might be very low, but on other occasions the same item might be found for almost three times the price. The right price to pay was somewhere in the middle.

Because of these multiple variations, estimating value was regarded as one of the highest forms of consumer skill and in large mercantile cities there were quite formal mechanisms for assessing the potential value of an item. For legal purposes such as inventories or debt collections, professional valuers might be called upon to assist. Second-hand dealers regularly fulfilled this function for institutions and individuals alike. Likewise, when disputes occurred over valuations, guild officials might be called upon to adjudicate. With highly specialised goods, such as gems, gold and silverware and antiquities, elite purchasers usually turned to unofficial as well as official experts, asking those regarded as having special expertise for their opinions. For example, goldsmiths and painters were often approached for their opinions on antiquities. A knowledge of the 'going rate' for books is certainly suggested by the inventory of the manuscripts compiled by Francesco Sassetti in the 1470s as was the list of prices indicated under the drawings of the hardstone vases from the Medici collection that were put up for sale by a consortium of merchants in Florence in 1502.[61]

If price variations were common, they were also regarded with suspicion. When prices for basic commodities changed dramatically, the assumption was that greed was as much to blame as bad weather. Again, this was based on a long tradition. The late Roman legal theorist Gratian had argued:

> Whoever at time of harvest or vintage, not because of necessity but because of cupidity, buys grain or wine, for instance buys a measure for two pennies and keeps it until it is sold for four pennies, or six, or more we say that such (a one acquires) filthy gain.[62]

Hoarding was one reason that prices might change but the social relationships between buyers and sellers also had an impact. In 1427, San Bernardino of Siena was scathing about these variations, 'I say to you that it is absolutely not licit to sell the same thing at a higher price to one person than another person; you have to sell in exactly the same manner to those whom you know as you would as if you didn't know them at all.'[63] He reiterated this in another sermon, arguing against lowering prices when the buyer was either richer or more powerful:

> You must not sell the same merchandise at a higher price to one person than to another, but sell them both equally to both the poor and the rich. The money of the poor is the same as that of the rich and powerful; and it is not licit to fool the poor person who does not understand commerce and who trusts in you.[64]

The need to protect the poor and the unwary was usually the stated aim behind government interventions in the setting of prices for many basic goods and services. One of the earliest surviving price lists dates from 1173 when Doge Sebastiano Ziani set the maximum prices that could be charged in Venice for basic commodities and established the weights and measures that were to be used for such sales.[65] Further lists continued to be disseminated well into the late eighteenth century for products as diverse as university textbooks, shoes, wood, oil, meat and fish. Bread, which varied by weight rather than price, was given the greatest attention. In Milan, for example, 6 officials were paid 5 florins per month in 1385 to set bread prices and weights and were empowered to impose immediate fines of 10 soldi if they found badly baked or overpriced loaves.[66] Among the many later versions of such controls, the Duke of Mantua issued a long and complex set of rules on bread production in 1555. He was trying to prevent the sale of 'fancy' breads in odd shapes or with additional ingredients that might disguise the lack of an appropriate quantity or quality of flour. The edict stressed that:

> The bread seller is to keep a list of prices that will be given to them on a weekly basis . . . in every place where they will either sell or have sold bread. This is to be written and posted in such a way that it can be seen and understood by both the wise and the idiots; the people will be able to very easily see from this list and divisions of the price list which will be printed the following sections with different prices from two lire up to 31 lire and 18 soldi and to know how many ounces of bread they will get for every two soldi.[67]

The key point in this statement was the public nature of the information that had to be laid out in a way that 'it can be seen and understood' by all. Most basic commodities were subject to similar controls. In sixteenth-century Piacenza, for example, meat prices were set twice a year, dividing the year into a pre- and post-Easter period running until September.[68] By 1572 the prior and the city's main magistracy, the Anziani, were distributing printed *listini dei prezzi*, price lists which were supposed to be publicly displayed on *tavolette* each morning outside the butchers' stalls. One of the earliest printed edicts from Bologna, issued on 21 January 1539, was a similar list: *La provisione et limitatione sopra il precio delle carni*. Like the Mantuan bread weights, the prices set in this sheet were supposed to be openly displayed, 'above the stalls, fixed onto tablets and they must be printed'.[69]

Displaying prices was not, of course, the same as selling at these prices. Most Jewish communities had agreements with the cities in which they were allowed to reside concerning kosher meat. But they regularly found that they were charged more than was permitted, prompting demands for intervention by urban officials.[70] Holding back goods and only offering them 'under the counter' to those willing to pay more was another practice that officials were keen to stamp out. In Rome, a decree was issued in 1588 threatening butchers and other food-sellers with a 25 scudi fine and three lashes if they did not sell at the prices published in the official *bandi*.[71] But given the range of goods that the city tried to police, it could not have been easy to enforce. For example, a printed edict of 1598 identified 60 goods and services that were subject to price controls in Rome (Figure 88). The majority were foodstuffs beginning with the four-penny white loaf. This was followed by good-quality flour, wine, different cuts of meats, candles, raisins, dried prunes, capers, fish and cheese. The list finished with a set of services: the price of shoeing a horse or a mule (differentiated according to whether or not both the shoe and the nails were replaced or only the shoe) and the cost of hostel services which varied according to the number of meals that were taken and the stabling costs involved.[72] The long document ended with the current exchange rate between the gold scudo and the silver *paolino* and again between the *paolino* and the four-penny piece, the *quattrino*. Finally across the bottom came the strongly worded warning:

> The Most Reverend Lordships command that all the vendors of the above goods must always keep their displays full and sell to every person in whatever quantity at the established prices and that they must keep the present tariff fixed in a place where it can be seen by everyone at a penalty of three lashes.[73]

The attempts to control food prices and the cost of a stay in an inn were understandable given Rome's large itinerant population. In Jubilee years, the city officials had to

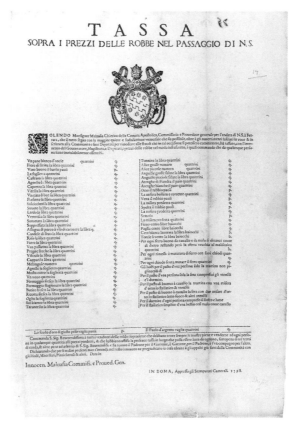

88 *Tassa sopra i prezzi delle robbe nel passaggio di N. S.*, 1598, print, The British Library, London. The actual prices and exchange rates have been left blank.

make special efforts to ensure that visitors were not defrauded or overcharged. But they were not unique to the city. The ease and low cost of printing meant that official hand-outs and pamphlets informing the populations of Bologna, Milan, Florence and Venice of new rules and edicts proliferated from the mid-sixteenth century onwards. Posted on walls, gates and poles, they created a visual sense of the unease that governments felt concerning the market and its members as well as educating the wider public and visitors of the 'correct' price for commodities.

It was not only food that came under official scrutiny. In early fifteenth-century Milan, for example, prices were set for different types of shoes and stockings by the *Ufficio di Provvisione*. They varied according to the material used for the upper – silk was the most expensive – and by style, colour of leather and according to the age of the wearer, children's shoes being much cheaper than adults'.[74] But after sudden protests by the shoemakers' guild who argued that this was, 'against common practice', vendors were suddenly permitted to return to their usual practice of selling, 'leather and other goods at the most convenient price possible'.[75] This was subsequently overturned, sug-gesting a struggle between city and guilds for control over merchandising.

The Milanese example took place against the backdrop of severe political and mili-tary unrest in 1410. Why then spend the energy on defining the prices for shoes? The correlation between imposing authority and imposing values, financial or otherwise, on goods, was clear. But not all motives were 'top-down'. In many instances, the guilds themselves might intervene in an attempt to limit dangerous competition. Undercut-ting was prevented by setting prices for basic items of clothing such as shoes and stock-ings, including luxury versions of these goods. Thus in Florence, the tailors' guild tried to establish fixed prices for 78 different types of garments in 1415, ranging from elabo-rate cloaks to burial shrouds.[76] In 1504, the guild again set out the standard prices at which items should be sold by its members and others, an edict that was reissued thirty years later under ducal rule with higher prices.[77] Similar lists were issued in Milan in 1534 and included thirty-one garment types and their prices.[78]

In all these circumstances, the point was less whether goods were actually sold at offi-cial prices or not, and more that such lists of prices provided a visible marker of legal-ity and communal constraints; they allowed participants to decide whether they were part of a commonly instituted and accepted basis for sales, or whether they were oper-ating on the edge of social order. In enforcing prices and in punishing miscreants, gov-ernment officials established their own political and moral right to control the city. Under such circumstances refusing to sell at these prices was a dangerous act of defi-ance as well as a commercial decision. In 1471, for example, the Milanese butchers went on strike, collectively refusing to open their shops until prices were raised to a prof-itable level.[79] It is unsurprising, therefore, to see that a flurry of edicts concerning price and quality of basic commodities often accompanied a change in government or a time of particular political tension. With a long tradition of civic surveillance, accepting the official value of what was being sold was an important element of confidence in the government itself.

Credit

For many buyers and sellers the price that was set was only the beginning of negotiations over how it would be paid. But while the use of credit in the highest levels of international banking and business has received considerable scholarly attention, the levels of mutual indebtedness at local level are only now being addressed. Many transactions, even the most minor ones using pennies, involved some element of credit, and a number of studies on northern Italy have shown, 'the degree to which sales concluded not with a payment but with a promise to pay'.[80]

Buyers made their promises in different ways. Many were verbal and can only be traced in wills that asked heirs to make the appropriate repayments. Others were based on very formal arrangements, involving notaries and the appointment of guarantors, so-called *fideiussores*, who promised to pay what was owed if the debtor failed to do so. Still others made arrangements to pay by bank transfers. The first surviving chit of this type was handed over to pay for the cleaning of a cess-pit in early fifteenth-century Florence.[81] The accounts of shopkeepers were continually dominated by credit arrangements, The tax records of Florentine merchants such as the apothecary Matteo Palmieri listed those who owed money in great detail, dividing them into those of whom they had some hope of repayment, and those in whom they had given up any hope at all: 'I find all these debtors, between the good and the sad, the miserable, the bankrupt and the dead, and in great part I have been already taxed on them, and have never received the payment . . .'.[82]

Palmieri's comments were designed to impress the officials with his potential poverty. His insistence that he would never be paid may have been rhetorical and is contradicted by Richard Marshall's study of almost thirty account books from Prato between the late thirteenth and early fourteenth century. He too has shown the high levels of credit offered by merchants such as cheesemongers, second-hand dealers, apothecaries and shoemakers. Customers either kept a running total, left pledges behind as surety or traded debts as a means of payment. In order to avoid the sin of usury, the interest charged was often disguised by varying the price paid according to the credit terms that were agreed. Although the periods of time between sale and payment might be extensive, Marshall's diverse community of shopkeepers had an almost 95 per cent success rate in eventually reclaiming the debts that they were owed.[83] Indeed, Marshall's merchants and the Pratese cheesemonger studied by Paola Pinelli acted as much as small-scale bankers and money changers as they did as retail tradesmen.[84]

It may be that in a relatively small community such as Prato, with a population of fewer than 10,000, mutual indebtedness was a relatively straightforward affair. Easy credit was an important part of encouraging repeat custom. Failure to pay in full could be mitigated by a range of informal arrangements concerning an exchange of services or goods in kind. Here barter might merge with credit and arithmetical treatises, such as those of Filippo Calandri, explained how to exchange cloth for grain instead of cash (Figure 89). But credit arrangements were just as important in large towns as in small villages. The sixteenth-century account books of the Roman second-hand dealer

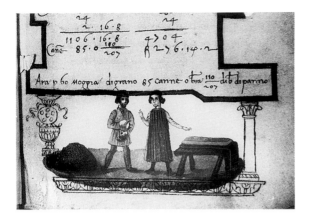

89 Filippo Calandri, *Trattato di aritmetica*, Florence, c. 1490, Biblioteca Riccardiana, Ricc. 2669, c56v, 'Bartering 60 *moggia* of grain for 85 *canne* of cloth'.

Benedetto di Segni show a similar pattern to those of the fourteenth-century Pratese accounts described above.[85] For example, the Neapolitan printer Gabriele Richetto bought an apron of new black cloth for 13 scudi and arranged to pay for it at a rate of 4 scudi per month. But before he had paid that debt, he went on to buy a pair of stockings and other basic items of clothing. Benedetto di Segni also acted as a banker, loaning the binder Domenico Albertini 9 scudi on the basis of pawned clothing. He mixed the two types of services, selling a pair of black stockings on credit and making a cash loan to one Domenico Contarini, bringing the latter's total debt to 11 scudi.[86] The arrangements could be quite complex but were almost always based on material goods. When he took out a loan from di Segni, the Roman printer Paolo Graziani used the following items (that actually belonged to someone else) as pledges:

> Two silver cups of twenty ounces each, two rubies and a diamond, in the coffin shape, and four copper plates for prints; a gilt-brass clock, and a silver assay stick; a gilt glass clock and various small copper plates for prints.[87]

Di Segni's accounts are commonplace. There are few, if any, shopkeeper's records that suggest a fully monetarised set of cash transactions and it may be that only the most minor of street vendors took payment in coin on a regular basis.[88]

In places such as Rome, anonymity and transience made the situation more problematic. Punishments for lack of payment, whether physical or financial, could not guarantee that funds would be forthcoming. How did sellers find ways to trust customers who were either unknown or risky? In Venice, insolvent debtors were forbidden to enter the Rialto and in late sixteenth-century Rome officials tried to force those who were known to be in substantial debt to wear a green beret in public.[89] It was not only the poor who owed money. More often, impoverished artisans had to petition to be paid in order to make payments in turn and there was widespread recognition of the social inequalities involved in credit relationships. An imbalance in status might mean that the very wealthy would be allowed generous credit terms while those who could least afford it might have to wait a long time to be paid by their superiors. With their official bailiffs, governments could seize goods in ways that were difficult for poorer clients to imitate. When powerful figures required funds, they might similarly squeeze their debtors. In recognition of this imbalance, Roman regulations concerning bankruptcies and debts insisted that the poorest creditors be reimbursed first, the *miserabiles* who would become dependent on charity if they were not paid.[90] There was a particular concern that those who owed money might be forced into theft or prostitution, an anxiety that was particularly directed at innkeepers who were suspected of running brothels. There were regular decrees in Rome forbidding inn and tavern keepers from offering more than six days' credit; hotel managers were not allowed to provide more than two months' credit. If they did so, they lost the right to collect the said debt.[91] There was also a recognition of the civil consequences of debt. In 1513, for example, Rome's governor issued a decree forbidding landlords from evicting tenants until the rent had not been paid for at least a year.[92]

Debtors' prisons were the final destination for those unwilling or unable to pay or for those who had stood surety for absent creditors. A list of those housed in the Milanese prison of the *Malastalla* in 1461 gives the names of forty-five men placed there at their respective creditors' behest.[93] The amounts they owed varied, ranging from the sums of around 350 lire that Giovanni da Garbara owed to a business partner to the 55 lire that Aluisino da Sarono owed his miller or the 10 lire that Tomasso Piffero owed for his bread. The list was presented to the Duke of Milan as part of a request for clemency. Even though in most cases their debts had been forgiven, the prisoners were unable to leave because they were being charged for their room and board. Lacking any possessions or security, they were unable to either pay or pledge payment.

The story of the cycle of debt and credit remained common throughout the fifteenth and sixteenth centuries. It has been estimated that approximately 6 per cent of Rome's population had been through the city's debtors' prison in the late sixteenth century.[94] The establishment of what would become Italy's banking system, the *Monte di Pietà*, was formulated by Franciscan preachers in the 1470s against this background of concern over debt and the consequent poverty. Their aim was to provide assistance to the poorest members of society and prevent them from falling into the clutches of the Jewish community. Yet by the mid-sixteenth century, buying the jewels, gold and silver that had been deposited in these new institutions was already being recommended as a safe form of investment for those who wanted to preserve a noble lifestyle.[95] As Massimo Fornasari has pointed out, there was considerable irony in the way an institution designed to support the poor developed into a strategy to ensure that wealth remained within the aristocratic elite.[96]

For many, whatever their status, indebtedness was a way of life rather than a threat, one where final repayment would only come after death. At that point, creditors would look to take what they could of the inheritance and force the estate to make a full or partial repayment. The city's bailiffs would be sent in to seize movable assets and goods which had once been private possessions would appear on the streets as auctioneers and dealers assessed their value. Only the dowries of widows were exempt. Personal appearance and household possessions were, therefore, not only signals about social standing and prestige. As Craig Muldrew has shown for early modern King's Lynne, they were also key indicators of credit-worthiness. These objects, added to the personal relationships that bound buyers and sellers, made this economy of credit and debt function effectively and surprisingly efficiently.

CONCLUSION

It would be easy to dismiss the constant legislative attempts to control the marketplaces, measurements and monies of Renaissance Italy as irrelevant. Laws were issued but not enforced. Prices were set but then private deals were done to pay above or below the official rate. Mint masters might make false coins in their own time; magistrates and officials responsible for investigating weights and measures might be corrupted and those assessing the quality of bread or wine were often related to those making the actual sales. Officials might be more interested in collected fines than in actually catching genuine miscreants.

Certainly, the constant repetition of similar orders, decrees and punishments between 1400 and 1600 is more an indication of a continuity of anxiety than a sign of an increasing ability to impose order. The long list of prosecutions by the magistracy of the Giustizia Vecchia in Venice on which fines were reduced between 1507 and 1563 included a wide range of misdemeanours concerning the sale of contraband goods including rice, grapes, figs, brocades, silks, wax, velvets, saffron, cheese, wine, oil, salami, fruit and vegetables, nails and knitwear.[97] There were also prosecutions against those selling leather that hadn't been stamped by guild officials, falsifying weights while selling cheese, opening shops on holy days, selling tin or yellow silk as gold in caps and cloth. Magistrates imposed justice on those importing forbidden items such as Mantuan berets or maiolica from Ravenna.[98] But the Giustizia Vecchia only had twenty men in its police force. In mid-sixteenth-century Cremona, there were only nineteen men available to monitor the activities of the over 35,000 men and women in the town and its territories.[99] Although local governors and judges, such as the podestà, did have soldiers at their disposal there were few police forces, apart perhaps from that of the Inquisition established in the mid-sixteenth century, that were powerful enough to ensure that social behaviour matched the ideals of the relevant rules and regulations.

To be successful, therefore, the commune required the surveillance not simply of its appointed officials but of the wider community as a whole. In the main, denunciations came from neighbours, rivals or observers on the streets (often sparked by the promise of a percentage of the eventual fine or a personal grudge). Unless the sin was serious, such as coining false money, the fines imposed in places like Venice were minor but exemplary: a small sum and the donation of a candle to the Giustizia Vecchia's chapel. For more serious crimes, the use of whippings, the removal of the hands of thieves and the public pillorying of debtors and fraudsters, were designed to spread fear as well as act as an aid to prevention. This meant that the legislation could only function against a backdrop of a broad acceptance of its moral underpinnings. There were few arguments in favour of a 'free market' for all goods, and the lifting of restrictions, taxation and price controls was normally a sign of desperation rather than a stimulus to enterprise. This had considerable consequences for the visibility of exchange. Only when transactions were out in the open could there be confidence that the rules were being implemented by both parties. It had to be kept literally 'over the counter' and 'above board'. Yet keeping commerce on display had a considerable impact on the urban environment. If successful, the behaviour of buyers and sellers would be open to constant comment, limiting those who might be willing to be seen. Where and when commerce took place, how and when it was literally seen and heard, was not a casual matter but one that demonstrated the very viability of a government's ability to secure the trust of its consumers.

Part Two

THE GEOGRAPHY OF EXPENDITURE

CHAPTER FOUR

Time

The previous chapter established that visibility was a crucial factor in defining urban authority and providing reassurance for consumers. But in a society where transactions might start on the street, mature in a tavern and finish with a vow in the local church what was public and what was private?

In answering this question it is important to recognise that boundaries took many forms. Physical barriers – walls, gates, doors and windows – were only one means of separating activities and were not necessarily the most important features. In commercial and legal contexts, the home could be as public as the banker's table. The presence of witnesses created public space rather than a specific location. As long as a notary was present to record the transaction, sales, both large and small, could take place anywhere. This was particularly true when the act of signing the contract and taking delivery of the goods remained two separate activities. But even when this was possible it was not always desirable. Notaries charged fees, and were rarely used for small-scale exchanges. While a shopkeeper's written accounts were also legal documents, it was not enough to refer to this paperwork when disputes arose.[1] Instead, when problems occurred, witnesses, reputation and rumour were all invoked in an attempt to receive justice. Paradoxically, this meant that the smaller the transaction or the more informal the exchange, the more important it was to keep it out in the open.

The traditional spatial organisation of Italian city centres was designed to enhance this visibility. From the fourteenth through to the sixteenth centuries the system of open markets and shops where the customer stood in the street while the shopkeeper stood on the other side of the trestle or counter, allowed for regular surveillance. As suggested by both the *Taciunum Sanitatis* image of the sale of the compound drug, theriac, from the 1390s, and the panel celebrating the cobblers' guild from Turin over a century later, the boundary between both shop and street was defined yet permeable (Figures 90–91). To all onlookers it was clear who was taking part, what was being purchased and by whom. This supervision was considered particularly essential for basic items such as bread. In 1483, the Milanese government noted the close relationship between honest merchandising and the place and time that goods were sold, noting that, 'following the great laments that have come to the Duke concerning the abuses that are being committed in provisioning, bringing dearth and a rise in prices . . . it is prohibited to buy or to have bought foodstuffs anywhere apart from the designated sites and during the

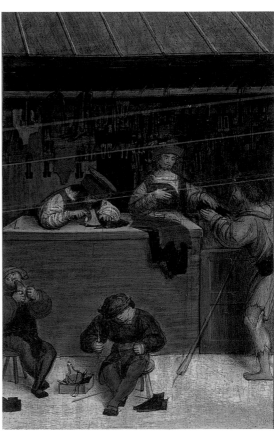

90 (*left*)   Lombard *Tacuinum sanitatis*, late fourteenth century, Codex Vindobonensis, series Nova 2644, Oesterreicheische, Nationalbibliotek, Vienna, f. 53v, 'Preparation and Sale of Theriac'.

91 (*right*)   Giovanni Martino Spanzotti and Defendente Ferrari, *The Cobbler's Shop*, panel from the shutters of the Altarpiece of the Compagnia dei Calzolai, Chapel of SS. Crispino and Crispiniano, Cathedral of Turin.

designated hours'.[2] But even elite activities such as banking had to take place in public; in cities such as Venice trust in monetary exchange was only possible when it took place out in the open in the squares of Rialto and San Marco.

Keeping commerce visible meant enforcing spatial order. There was a common assumption that trades should be clustered on specific streets and neighbourhoods. It was a source of pride when a city could be read as if it were a set of chapters in an encyclopaedia. When describing Naples in 1464, for example, one commentator noted that:

> The noble merchants in Naples are located where one enters from the gate into the Mercato and then in the *contrada* of San Allo and San Zuane where the mercers are sited, as it would be in Venice on the road between Rialto and San Marco. Then one comes to the *contrade* of the sellers of cotton, who offer quilts, textiles and cottons, and then there is the tax office and the contrada of the Florentines; that of the Genoese and the *contrada* of the bankers and the goldsmiths; then one finds the *contrada* of the armourers where those who make arms and those who sell them are located . . . and the contrada of the Scallescia where cloth is sold. The *contrada* of the Sellaria where the masters who make wonderfully beautiful saddles are located is lovely . . . All these said *contrade* of the merchants are right next to each other so that it seems, when walking, to all be a single neighbourhood.[3]

But despite the desire for such a co-location of vendors in large cities, there were always overlaps and disagreements. Each generation thought that they would be able to succeed where others had failed. In Milan, the city's Spanish governor, the Count of Fuentes was still trying to impose order in 1610, when he was praised because, 'by his command with great prudence the Arts have been placed separately in each *contrade*. Each one is now inhabited by the same profession so that one shop cannot be confused with another' (Figure 92).[4]

Yet even if it was never fully enforced, the assumption that a good city demonstrated order and discipline by systems of zoning remained a constant for many centuries. The

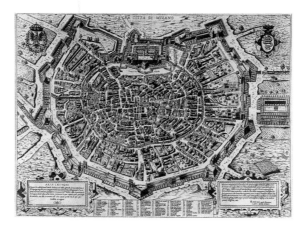

92   Antoine Lafrery, Map of Milan, 1573, engraving,
Civica Racolta delle Stampe A. Berterelli, Milan.

increasingly large number of maps produced in the sixteenth century, such as that of the city of Milan, suggested that streets and squares could be neatly arranged and labelled according to their different purposes. It may be that the very ubiquity of this belief limited the theoretical attention given to commerce and commercial spaces in the burgeoning literature on urban design. When they were discussed, the ideas proposed were usually very generic. In his writings on architecture, for example, Leon Battista Alberti argued that an ideal city was circular in format, with radial zoning:

> The best means of dividing a city is to build a wall through it. This wall . . . should form a kind of circle within a circle. For the wealthy citizens are happier in more spacious surrounding and would readily accept being excluded by an inner wall and would not unwillingly leave the stalls and the town-centre workshops to the marketplace traders; and that rabble . . . of poulterers, butchers and cooks, and so on, will be less of a risk and less of a nuisance if they do not mix with the important citizens.[5]

Once these wealthy residential suburbs had been isolated from the smells and bustle of commerce, the inner commercial centre could then be properly subdivided:

> The charms of a city will be very much enhanced if the various workshops are allocated to distinct and well-chosen zones. The silversmiths, painters and jewellers should be on the forum, then next to them, spice shops, clothes shops, and in short, all those that might be thought more respectable. Anything foul or offensive (especially the stinking tanners) should be kept well away in the outskirts to the North . . . Some might prefer the residential quarters of the gentry to be quite free of any contamination from the common people. Others would have every district in the city so well equipped that each would contain all its essential requirements; thus it would be quite acceptable to have common retailers and other shops mixed in with the houses of the most important citizens . . . Clearly utility demands one thing, and dignity another.[6]

Alberti was reflecting a language that was common for the period. In 1452, for example, the governors of Siena had attempted to shift the butchers from the city centre and define the trades that could be seen in the most public of areas along the Campo and the main street, the Strada Romana (Figure 93). The rationale was phrased both in terms of the decorum referred to above and the importance of a central location:

> it would be much more useful, honourable and beautiful if the more noble and appropriate trades, especially for foreigners, were located in sites that are more public and hallowed in the city, and more frequented by foreigners to the city, particularly those travelling to and from Rome, which are an infinite number . . . so that seeing these various wares they may be encouraged to buy, but not seeing them, they do not even think of doing so.[7]

The fifteenth-century Sienese architect and theorist, Francesco di Giorgio Martini, was even more specific in his advice:

93 Francesco Vanni, *Sena Vetus Civitas Virginis*, 1599, etching, Biblioteca Communale di Siena. The Strada Romana runs through the centre of the town.

> The Silk Guild should be sited in that street [the Strada Romana], as the principal ornament of the city, because it is most used by foreigners and citizens . . . the pharmacies, tailors and mercers should be regularly distributed around the streets for the usefulness of private citizens . . . the metalworkers and butchers should be off the principle roads while being near to them.[8]

The comments given above and below all assume that the urban centre should be the focus for commerce rather than the periphery. A higher level of valuable and valued trades should be concentrated where they were both an ornament to the city and easily seen by visitors intent on making purchases. Most theorists left the matter here, rarely considering the issue further or providing any additional details. One of the rare expositions on the marketplace and its shops was written in the 1460s by Antonio Averlino, known as il Filarete, in his treatise *Sforzinda*, dedicated to the new Duke of Milan, Francesco Sforza (Figures 94–5). Like Alberti and Francesco di Giorgio, Filarete was anxious to maintain hierarchy and order within his new city. He suggested using a series of separate squares to do just this:

> The hall of civic justice [is] in the middle of the piazza; it occupies one-quarter of the whole. It is completely on piers. I do this so the merchants can carry on merchandising and their other business here. As I said, it is all on square piers below. It is all vaulted and supported by these piers . . . On each side of the piazza, that is in front of and behind the Palazzo della Ragione there will be small piazzas 40 braccia square with a small church in each. Because of their continuous services they will be useful and sufficient for the merchants and other persons who are located around these two piazzas. In one piazza there will be the jewelers, those who work in gold, and in the other there will be exchange banks. . . .[9]

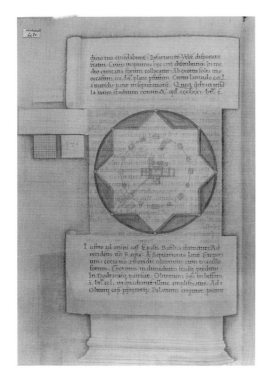

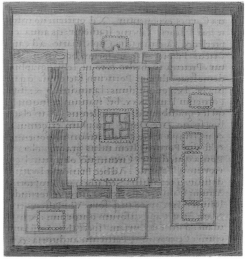

94 (*left*) Filarete, *The Ideal City of Sforzinda*, c.1464, Venice, Biblioteca Marciana, MS. Lat. VIII.2 (2796), f. 49v, 'Outline of Ideal City', The Conway Library, Courtauld Institute of Art, London.

95 (*right*) Filarete, *The Marketplace of Sforzinda*, c.1464, Venice, Biblioteca Marciana, MS. Lat, VIII.2 (2796), f. 83, 'The Macellum', The Conway Library, Courtauld Institute of Art, London.

The combined 'Hall of Justice' and the merchant's palace was already in place in Milan, where the Broletto served both functions (Figure 96). But in addition to recommending the siting of high-value shops in the city centre, Filarete was unusual in his recognition of the need to consider the sales of more mundane essentials. He went on to provide suggestions for innovative types of butchers' and fishmongers' stalls before concentrating on where such sales should be located:

> First of all I will surround it with a portico 10 braccia wide and [supported] on columns. The butchers will be located in the full length of the Northern part. It will be in this form. The portico will be twenty braccia wide and ten braccia of it will be walled up, that is [there will be] a wall in the middle . . . Behind the piazza will be [a place] for slaughtering animals with a canal along the portico to carry away all the refuse. This is in the centre of its entire portico. Over the canal there will be a bridge . . . meat of various kinds will be sold on one side. As I have said this wall that divides the portico will have doors. These will open on the part behind the portico where they can store meat when they have some left over. In front of the row will be the blocks where they cut up the meat. The Western part . . . will be the fish market.

96   Milan, view of the Broletto in the town centre.

The canal could perhaps pass close to it. In the Southern part will be markets for the sale of fowl, and of cheese, sausage and such things. The bakeries will be at the eastern end . . . in the remaining space we will build a church. On the summit of this church will be placed a figure of the goddess, *Copia*. The fruit-sellers can stand under the portico and on the steps when it rains. In the space left over at the other end of the piazza vegetables will be sold and at the other end things will be sold, either wood or second-hand goods of any sort.[10]

Filarete's manuscript was written, in part, as a contribution to his campaign to gain patronage both in Milan and, later, in Medicean Florence. But despite working for Francesco Sforza for almost two decades, he did not succeed in implementing many of his ideas. In presenting the new duke with a way of reforming his city, Filarete was both drawing on and embedding a language of civic beautification and urban order with an important tradition in fourteenth- and fifteenth-century Italy. If the first quotation referred to Filarete's Milanese experience of the Broletto, the second reference to the figure of *Copia* (which must suggest Donatello's figure of the *Dovizia*) points to the theorist's home town of Florence which also kept its butchers' market in the city's centre. In siting the fishmongers' stalls by a canal, he made further reference to his Florentine experience where fish was sold by the Arno river.

    In cities such as Milan, Rome, Florence and Venice, there were well-established magistracies with names like the *magistrati delle strade* or the *magistratura per l'ornamento* which were responsible for street paving, street cleaning and building permissions. The rules and regulations issued by these magistracies are a good indication of the tensions that a central location for sales created within the Renaissance city. Although it was widely agreed that the sale of basic commodities such as foodstuffs had to be kept under careful observation, this requirement often clashed with an equally powerful instinct to marginalise activities that were seen as either undignified or unhygienic. Butchers, fish-mongers, poultry-sellers, cheesemongers, and vendors of fruits and vegetables, money-lenders and their customers were all expected to submit to urban oversight. But at the same time the blood, animal odours, droppings, dirt and, indeed, the people such activities attracted were all a potential embarrassment to an increasingly self-aware civic patriciate. Thus while the desire for surveillance pointed to a central location, the anxiety over potential contamination and confusion suggested a more appropriate placement on the urban periphery. Despite the clarity of the advice given by Alberti and his contemporaries above, cities continually struggled with the dilemma of how to control and discipline commerce within their walls and gates. Even in the late sixteenth century, when innovative architects such as Bartolomeo Ammanati presented new plans for central markets, they continued to deploy traditional formulae prescribing rows of carefully ordered stalls laid out in a rectilinear pattern in the urban centre. (Figure 97).[11]

Achieving this ideal was often elusive. Although a number of towns, such as Florence with its Mercato Vecchio and Piazza del Grano or Venice with its concentrations of butchers and fishmongers in the Rialto and Piazza San Marco, did have specifically demarcated areas for the sale of foodstuffs, it was as, if not more, common to use a centrally located open space for multiple purposes. The Campo in Siena, for example, could house the city's market, religious and civic processions and events such as its annual bullfights and horse races (Figure 98). This meant that squares adjacent to or in front of cathedrals, town halls and palaces, would be filled with a market at one moment and cleared for another type of activity at the next. Wheeled carts, such as those shown in the market in Bologna, billowing, tent-like sheets fixed to poles, collapsing trestle tables, baskets and folding trays all provided the portable infrastructure that transformed empty squares into commercial centres for buying and selling and then returned or turned it to new purposes (Figure 99). This meant that the

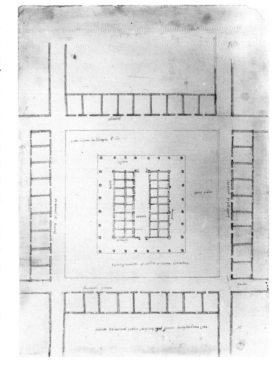

97 Bartolomeo Ammannati, *Plan for an ideal public market*, pen and ink drawing, 1550–84, Florence, Gabinetto dei Disegni, Uffizi, Florence 3399A.

98 Vincenzo Rustici, *Bull Hunt in the Campo of Siena*, c.1600, oil on canvas, Monte dei Paschi Collection, Siena.

boundaries were auditory and transitory rather than permanent and fixed. During the day, the long, high sounds of trumpets or bagpipes demanded attention for announcements while the melodic songs of professional street-sellers and the short, sharp outcries of the public auctioneers provided the information that shoppers needed about the products and prices on offer.[12] When bells tolled at midday or in the evening, the visual efflorescence of goods and people in the city centre was supposed to vanish. Here time and sound, not architectural design, provided the framework for buying and selling.

DIVIDING THE YEAR

While such transient boundaries provided admirable flexibility they were not without their own problems. When Venice's Piazza San Marco, Milan's Piazza del Duomo or Bologna's Piazza Grande were equally able to shelter markets, civic processions and religious preaching, how were the very different types of behaviour expected in each type of space enforced? If an infrastructure of civic and sacred authorities was required to

99   Archivio di Stato, Bologna, Insignia degli Anziani, 1705, vol. xi, cc.63–4, 'Piazza Maggiore in Bologna with the mobile stalls of the market'. Note the trapeze artists in the foreground.

police the days and hours, how did bell-ringers, trumpeters and callers know what type of time to sound?[13]

The answer is complicated by the multiplicity of times available in the Renaissance period. Astronomical time: the rising and setting of the sun; the waxing and waning of the moon; the appearance of the stars; and the agricultural seasons, had the comfort of a seeming immutability. The calendar scenes in the frescoes of the Torre d'Aquila celebrated the universality of such cyclical moments (Figure 100).[14] With peasants in the field and the nobility on horseback or at play, the routines of the harvest or the hunt reinforced an inevitability of social stratification. These were not abstract concepts. As Ottavia Niccoli has shown, although sixteenth- and seventeenth-century witnesses in Bolognese court cases could be precise about moments relating to the agricultural cycle – sowing, ploughing, reaping – they often found it difficult to relate these to precise months or days.[15] These speakers presented a sense of time that was very much shaped by seasonality and its associated activities.

But even in the countryside, time, or rather its measurement, was never a purely natural phenomenon. Instead it was a symbol of allegiance to a chosen social community, a public matter with private nuances. If few could calculate their birth-date with

100   *Month of April*, c.1400, fresco, Torre d'Aquila, Castello del Buonconsiglio, Trent.

precision, bankers, notaries, legal courts and the Church kept close track of the year, an important issue when determining an anniversary, or the end of a period of credit and the recouping of an investment. Until 1582, when a major calendar reform took place under Pope Gregory XIII, the majority of Italians on the peninsula, like their counterparts across Europe, identified years in roughly similar ways (although their Jewish compatriots would have calculated these differently). But even here there were variations. For Italian Christians, Orthodox and Catholic, there were six potential starts to any year: 1 January, 1 or 25 March, Easter, 1 September or 25 December.[16] Months were derived from earlier Roman divisions and these, at least, rarely shifted. Nonetheless their days had three potential reference points: using a numerical date (the first of the month), a saint's day (such as the feast of Saint Catherine) or among those with humanist aspirations, by using the ancient Roman system of Kalends (the first day of the month), Ides (the thirteenth day except in March, July and October when it fell on the fifteenth day), and Nones (eight days before Ides). Under such circumstances, it is perhaps unsurprising that among the first prints issued in Florence was a perpetual cal-

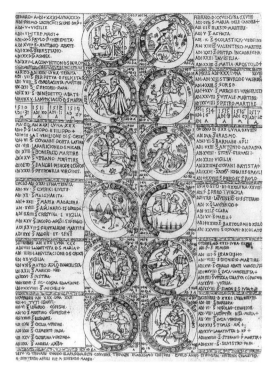

101 Florentine School, *Calendar*, 1465, Department of Prints and Drawings, The British Museum, London, V.1–74.

endar, while a book describing how to calculate annual dates, first published in Venice in 1476, proved to be almost an instant bestseller (Figure 101).[17]

On top of this layering of Christian, arithmetical and classical divisions came astrological and humoral meanings, ensuring that goods might be considered particularly suitable for use in months when one sign was in the ascendant or when the weather was hot or cold, wet or dry. A set of late fifteenth-century prints illustrating the months of the year emphasises the products and activities that were appropriate to consume or carry out in times such as October and November, advice that would have been familiar from health manuals such as the *Tacuinum santitatis* (Figures 102–03).[18] The twice-yearly trade wind sailings from ports such as Venice and Genoa could also affect the seasonal supplies with the availability of spices, cotton and dyes dependent on these bi-annual movements. Merchants' manuals from the fourteenth century onwards provided clear advice on how to design an itinerary that took advantage of the relevant dates of fairs and the availability of different products.[19]

Liturgical rhythms were as important as seasonal variations, since what one could buy or sell at certain points of the year was closely linked to the Church's dictates.[20] Items forbidden at one moment might be permitted at another and vice versa, and vendors were consistently asking for special licences because of the nature of the Christian calendar. In preparation for Easter, Christmas and Carnival, for example, the Venetians completely freed the sale of foodstuffs for the three days leading up to these festivals on the squares of San Marco and Rialto to ensure adequate supplies.[21] Similarly, the credit ledger of the Florentine bookseller Piero di Giuliano Morosi indicates that the rhythm of binding work in his shop varied according to the liturgical season, with a large demand for devotional works during Lent and Easter and for gift-giving at Christmas.[22]

These Catholic reference points were complicated by the Church's mixture of movable and immovable feasts. Easter was the most complex. It had to fall on the first Sunday following the first full moon after 21 March, a date determined according to a tortured set of lunar calculations. To avoid errors, permanent Paschal calendars such as

102 (*left*)   (?)Ferrarese, *March*, 1470–80, engraving, Department of Prints and Drawings, The British Museum, London, E.III.14.

103 (*right*)   (?)Ferrarese, *October*, 1470–80, engraving, Department of Prints and Drawings, The British Museum, London, E. III.15.

that of San Vitale in Rimini were sited in major churches while portable tables such as the 1461 Florentine printed version were circulated in an attempt to ensure synchronisation across the Latin Roman Catholic Church (Figure 104). For laymen and women, breviaries and prayer books often began with a similar, often personalised calendar that allowed them to fix the date and the day with precision.[23] Again, some of the earliest printed broadsheets and engravings provided instructions on how to make these calculations oneself, and the embroiderer Andrea di Domenico della Stufa carefully filled his private *zibaldone* with lunar tables and 'the tables for the days of Carnival and for Lent'.[24]

Dating Easter Sunday determined the commencement of Carnival and Lent, events with a considerable impact on a community's consumer possibilities. The start of Carnival, with its requirements for masking, sweet foods and nuptial celebrations could prove quite flexible. From 26 December, Saint Stephen's Day, until Ash Wednesday, different groups of revellers would either ask the permission of a civic or signorial

authority to start the masking or simply begin the festivities at their own initiative. This was a period for weddings, theatrical performances in both the home and the street and a large-scale investment in lavish clothing and high-quality foods. The start of Lent, in contrast, had no such variability. It was clearly fixed as forty days before Easter and had to shift in line with the celebration of Christ's Resurrection. Its commencement, Ash Wednesday, was meant to mark a very visible change in behaviour from one phase to the other. For the next forty days, the types of food that one could eat were supposed to be very different from those on offer during the

104 Florentine School, *Easter Tables*, c.1461, Department of Prints and Drawings, The British Museum, London, 1895.6–17.43.

rest of the year. Fats and flesh were forbidden, ensuring that fish prices were carefully controlled for the forty-day period in question and that meat sales were restricted. In his poem, Antonio Pucci stressed the shift in the goods available in Florence's Mercato Vecchio. On Ash Wednesday, the capons and chickens of Carnival would be replaced by the garlic and onions that were more suitable for Lent, *sì come a Santa Chiesa piaque*.[25] For Pucci, the arrival of Easter was then marked by the sudden reappearance of a market full of plenty, with items ranging from once-forbidden meat to song-birds, mousing cats and household goods for the upcoming festivities that would have been unseemly in the previous Lenten season.

The Catholic Church had a deep investment in controlling the calendar. The Counter-Reformation movement saw an increasing tightening of days and dates both inside and outside the Lenten season. Under such circumstances, determining Easter was as much a sign of ecclesiastical authority as it was of natural astronomical rhythms. By the sixteenth century, the tables for calculating its annual date no longer synchronised with the lunar cycle and in 1582, Pope Gregory XIII signed a papal bull designed to reconcile the discrepancies. He celebrated his control over the calendar by issuing a medal proclaiming the return to the 'true year' and issuing new calendars and edicts asserting the Church's control over time (Figures 105). But in cancelling ten days in October of that year he put late sixteenth-century Italy and other Catholic countries out of step with Protestant and Orthodox countries which continued to follow the old-style Julian calendar (England only shifted in 1752, Russia in 1918 and Greece in 1923).[26]

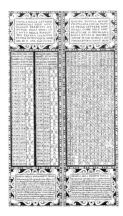
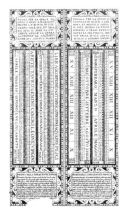

105   Perpetual calendar using new dates of Gregory XIII, 1582, engraving, Civica Racolta delle Stampe A. Berterelli, Milan.

The new Gregorian calendar made it clear that accepting a way of judging the date was a matter of accepting papal supremacy.

Yet even in Italy Catholic time was neither universal nor consistent. For example, Christians may have held Sunday in esteem, but this was not true of local Jewish communities. Instead, Saturday, often the busiest market day of the week, was held as sacred; Sunday was simply an ordinary working day. When relations were good, compromise was possible. Jewish charters almost always referred to their rights to close businesses and avoid being called to court on Saturdays and Jewish holy days such as Passover, or the autumn feast of Tabernacles.[27] They were still willing to serve Christians on Saturdays, but only after a fashion. In 1417, for example, a Christian buyer from Perugia bought a mattress and a blanket from a Jewish dealer and needed to pay for his purchases. As the client testified, he went to the Jew Deodato's home, because 'it was their feast day, when they do not handle money; he was in his aforesaid house, so he had me put two florin coins in a small copper box with a lid which was standing on a shelf'.[28]

Such willingness to come to arrangements over the conflicting nature of Jewish and Christian time came under great strain during the Easter Holy Week when energetic anti-Semitic preaching was common. In mid-fifteenth-century Foligno, for example, the town council insisted that, 'Jews shall be obliged to be confined to their houses during Holy week from Thursday evening until the bells sound on Saturday night.'[29] This confinement, of course, was made fiercer in the sixteenth century when curfews imposed on a daily basis in major cities such as Florence and Venice, meant that the evening bell had a fiercer meaning for Jews as they rushed to return to their walled ghettos than it did for Christians.[30]

*   *   *

Holy Days/Holidays

Ecclesiastical control was visible on a daily as well as an annual basis. Each of the seven days of the week had its distinct purpose. By the fifteenth century, Sunday was supposed to be a day of rest for Christians when all work was to cease. But this was neither automatic nor universal. For many generations, Sunday markets had been designed to benefit workers who came into towns and villages to both worship and to stock up for the coming week. Their increasing repression in the fourteenth century was resisted, particularly in the countryside, and, despite clerical campaigns, examples of monthly Sunday markets could still be found in late fifteenth-century Umbria.[31] The conflict was a powerful one. As popular images of the 'Sunday Christ' – which showed Christ attacked by implements of those who worked on Sunday – indicate, any work undertaken on this day could be seen as an attack on Jesus himself.[32] Yet poverty or political expediency might allow for exemptions. Thus the recently installed Duchess of Milan, Bianca Maria Sforza, accepted the petition of one Pietro de Morettis, *calderaio*, 'to keep in his shop vases, finished and unfinished, despite the fact the statutes forbade it, and to carry them about the city and to the fairs and markets, even on *giorni festivi*'.[33] A real crisis might call for the waiving of all restrictions. In 1447, for example, the new Ambrosian republic, facing total financial and political disaster following the death of the last Visconti ruler of Milan, demanded that Milan's mills work overtime even during forbidden holiday periods and at night in order to guarantee bread supplies.[34]

Sunday was not the only day of the week to come under the Church's scrutiny. For observant Catholics, Wednesdays and above all Fridays were supposed to be set aside for abstinence from both sexual activity and from the consumption of meat and fats; thus in Rome butchers were not supposed to operate in the markets on Tuesdays or Thursdays to prevent meat and fat being eaten the following day.[35] Some decisions were less than official. To gain an additional day of rest, the popular so-called 'Holy Monday' meant that artisans might unilaterally declare the need to stay at home instead of returning to work.

In addition to these weekly fixed points, the Christian liturgical calendar was filled with other holy days, *giorni festivi* that commemorated the lives of the Virgin and Christ and chosen saints. If the seven days of the week provided a superficial communality of time across Christian Europe, it was difficult to prevent further fragmentation as towns made an increasing number of individual days special for a range of secular and sacred reasons. Even after the Tridentine reform of the breviary in the late sixteenth century, the major feast days stipulated by the Roman Church were still outnumbered by many more obscure local feasts that only had a special resonance for particular individuals or were politically inspired memorials. There were all sorts of reasons to decree a holiday. The birth of male heirs to princes, the deaths of important persons within and without the city, declarations of both war and peace or the announcement of military victories could all prompt a sudden declaration that shops had to shut. For example, the Medici's success in retaking Florence in 1513 meant that 27 September, the feast of the family's patron saints, Cosmos and Damian, became a new feast for the Florentines, 'as if it were a Sunday'.[36] As observances multiplied, the chances of mistakes increased. Merchants such as the bookseller Francesco de Madi took to listing those days on which they would be fined if they were found open, weighing up the economic costs of doing business against the moral and social damage that would incur.[37] The enforced inactivity was not always unwelcome. The sculptor and courtier Antico, who served one of the minor Gonzaga courts, was well known for refusing to work on holidays.[38]

Giorni festivi were not necessarily specific to a day of the week but to a date in the calendar and pragmatic guilds often suggested celebrating the feast at a different moment if it fell during their city's main market day. Other forms of compromise were also possible. For example, the statutes of Florence's butchers demanded respect for the feasts of Easter, Santo Spirito, the Annunciation, Christmas, the Birth of the Virgin, and Anthony Abbot, their patron saint. But given how vulnerable meat was to putrefaction, work that aided distribution could still take place as long as it did not involve sales and most importantly, was not seen to take place. Their statutes declared:

> On those days no one in the guild should by any means keep their shop open, nor open their shutters or doors that lead into them, nor in any way or under any circumstances sell meat or anything else appertaining to their guild, neither from shops, windows, doors of the house or slaughterhouses; but that they can only for the service of the public slaughter in their shops, but with their doors shut and when the twenty-third hour sounds then they can receive the dead cattle, but then they must immediately close the door of their shop and only open it during the act of receiving it and this only for as long as it takes to bring it in and no longer, closing it immediately as described above. They can then consign wholesale meat to the grocers once 23 hours has sounded, giving the buyer that which appertains to him, such as feet and hooves, all however must be undertaken with the door shut with the exceptions of the feast of Easter, of the Resurrection and of the birth of Christ when no one under any circumstances or pretence is able to work, nor to do anything related to this work.[39]

Medical emergencies could similarly override religious considerations. The accounts for the Florentine apothecary, the Speziale al Giglio, indicate that the shop made sales every day of the year, including Sundays, Christmas, Easter and the town's major feast day of San Giovanni. This may not be surprising. Apothecaries, such as the Giglio, were often exceptions to the ordinary rules about closure. Such sales were, however, usually taken in rotation. In 1444, for example, the Venetian government ordered:

> That the apothecaries on the street that goes from Rialto to San Marco must not open their shops on feast days, with the exception of a single shop that must not show what they have on display except for medications. They should keep their balconies open with carpets, and not show or sell anything except that which pertains to medicine and amongst these we intend to include all those apothecaries who are in the neighbourhood.[40]

The regularity with which reference was made to the rapid closure of doors and shutters suggests how important the appearance of the silent, shut commercial sector was to the image of the good city during religious festivals. But unlike Protestant reformers who emphasised complete abstinence from anything that could have been defined as work on Sundays, Catholics could prove more flexible. While artisans could not actually open their shutters on a day of rest, they were far from inactive.[41] Although a Roman saddler might not be creating a new saddle in his workshop, he felt no shame in delivering it; in one case he was stopped during his delivery and the conversation on the street led to another order. Thus the actual opening of the shop shutters was only one, perhaps relatively minor, aspect of doing business. But seeing shop windows filled with merchandise was such an obvious violation of civic decorum that it had to be stopped while other, more discreet modes of commercial engagement were tolerated. This was particularly true when the objects that were themselves for sale undermined ecclesiastical norms. In 1565, the Venetian Giustizia Vecchia threatened to fine those who displayed indecent or shameful images in the shopping area of the *merceria* or in the portico of San Marco on either Sundays or holidays. Although sales were permitted, only images of saints and devout or decent subjects were considered licit:[42]

> On the *merzeria* truly one can only keep *santi* and sheets of drawings or paintings with devout and honest subjects and not things that are dishonest and shameful, and this is also true under the portico of San Marco.[43]

In this case it was not commerce that was the problem, it was the product. Even as preachers fulminated against the sin of working on feast days, civic authorities recognised that it was often imperative to do so. Even following the Council of Trent's new strictures on the calendar in the late Cinquecento, most cities tried to regulate Sunday working rather than ban it all together. When more rigorous action was taken it was regarded as an unusual event. In 1574, for example, the Florentine Bastiano Arditi recorded how one Sunday was the start of a new period of serious enforcement:

> On 20 June 1574, on Sunday morning, we started to observe an announcement that was issued about eight days ago that described an infinite number of types of work that were being carried out on days on which work was prohibited. And so that one no longer sees these tasks being carried out in the city on the said feast days, something that would be too long to explain. And we see that this has been caused by the recent Synod that has finished.[44]

Arditi never went on to discuss the ban's long-term success, and just how complex controlling time could prove to be is clear from a slightly earlier attempt to enforce shop closure in Modena in 1566. As the published *gride* related:

> It has come to the attention of Her Highness, Barbara, Duchess of Ferrara and of the Illustrious and Reverend Cardinal of Ferrara that there is little reverence and honour paid to God and his saints in honouring the obligatory feast days in this

blessed city of Modena and that with little fear, shops are kept open most dishonestly on these days and people buy without making any difference between one day and the next. And so, by this public announcement, we order, wish, establish and command that from now on no one, whether merchant or artisan, should dare to keep their shop, warehouse, stall or habitation of any sort, neither in part nor in their entirety open during the days of Sunday and those of the Apostles and of all the solemn feasts at a fine of ten lire marchesan for each time they disobey . . . prohibiting again to each and every person named above to work on these days under the same penalty . . . with the exception of those to whom it is permitted to sell greens and fruits of all sorts on the piazza every day and to the *hortolane* in their usual places; likewise the medicinal apothecaries, *speciale di medicine*, may keep their door and the shutter of their shop open. And likewise the cowmen can sell butter; the bakers can sell bread on the piazza, from their ovens and from their stalls on these days, keeping the door and the bottom shutter open. And again, the butchers who in those days may sell early in the morning and after lunch until the start of vespers, except on those days when the feast falls on a Saturday when they may sell throughout the entire day. And to the barbers it is permitted to keep open the door and the shutters of their shop in order to medicate, cup or bleed and for no other purpose. And similarly, one cannot bring into the city, any goods at all using carts or wagons without a licence from a judge in cases of necessity.[45]

The Modenese law is instructive in that it suggests that even during the Tridentine period when ecclesiastical oversight grew more rigorous, it was still common practice to ignore the liturgical calendar or make exceptions for goods such as vegetables, meat, medicines and medical services. Modenese merchants offering other goods or services simply had to weigh up the damage of a relatively insubstantial ten lire fine and then decide how carefully they needed to follow the law. This is important: while many economic historians have taken the number of holidays as a given, subtracting Sundays and feast days from the working year, there were clearly numerous exceptions to this practice. Although payment records indicate that although building workers did stop construction on the day of rest, much of the city may have gone about its business as normal. Shop windows may have stayed shut, but work, sales and manufacture carried on behind closed doors.

The key point, however, is not the precise number of days that workers and artisans tended their shops or provided services, but the fact that the need to maintain Catholic norms of behaviour was never openly questioned. When arguing for leniency or claiming innocence, those who had been found working on holy days never argued that there were too many holidays; they merely claimed ignorance, poverty or special exemption.

When the cheesemonger Piero dal Gallo opened his shop in the Rialto on a Saturday in 1542, the feast day of San Simione, he simply argued that he did not know that his guild held this as a sacred festival. He had, he testified, always opened his shop on this day and saw no reason why he should stop:

Piero dal Gallo in his defence said that it was true that he had opened his shop, and that for almost fifty-five years, he had always opened his shop on feast days apart from those of Christmas, Saint Stephen's Day, the birth of the Virgin and the feast of Saint John the Baptist . . .[46]

Piero dal Gallo may have suspected that the sudden enforcement of San Simione's holy day was prompted by more than religious zeal. In Pavia in 1545, the mercers' guild protested following a crackdown by the *giudici delle strade* on illegal trading on holy days that were outside the main Catholic calendar as stipulated in the breviary. They argued that:

> Since 1499 the mercers of this city had been vexed by the *iudici de le stratte et victualie* for keeping their shops open and selling their goods on the feast days that were not prohibited by the Holy Church, but only prohibited and forbidden by some ancient statutes and ordinances . . . And considering that this prohibition on sales on the said feast days that were not commanded was neither to the profit nor honour at all of the city but only for the utility of the said judges who for any reason conceded licences to sell and open shops on the said feast days, despite the said statutes and ordinances and wishing to deal with these inconveniences and extortions, these Signori allowed the said guild of the mercers full licence to keep their shops open, and sell their wares and keep tables, stands . . . outside their shops as needed for their business on those days that were not prohibited by the Holy Church without the need for any further licence . . . therefore now the *iudici de le stratte et victualie* of Pavia have not ceased to molest them, forcing them to defend themselves and fining them.[47]

As this case suggests, controlling the calendar was a struggle for identity and authority as well as for income. Here two authorities, a powerful guild and a civic magistracy, came into conflict over the definition of holy days, a situation that was only partly resolved when the Church itself redefined its breviary as part of the Council of Trent's new regulations of religious behaviour.

SATURDAY SHOPPING

Urban and ecclesiastical officials were not always interested in closing down trading. They were also concerned to encourage it. If some days called for abstinence, others called for increased consumption and expenditure. Towns, both small and large, hired trumpeters and criers to announce special shopping opportunities to the widest possible public. Most communities had a dedicated market day or days, often including a Saturday. This day's importance for marketing was invoked when guilds asked to waive their observance of feast days that fell on a Saturday. In fourteenth- and fifteenth-century Venice, peddlers were only permitted into the Rialto from the top of the church of San Giacomo to the stairs known as 'of the Tuscans' on that day and the normally forbidden sale of shoes was also allowed.[48] The right to a space for a Saturday market was highly desirable and attempts to acquire pitches in Piazza San Marco suggest that considerable profits could be made.[49] Because competition was high and sites were limited, numerous strategies were devised to ensure a semblance of equity. Guilds marked out spaces and then assigned them by lot. For example, in Venice, the early fourteenth-century shoemakers' statutes resolved that:

> Because, it used to be the case that on Saturdays in Piazza San Marco, those selling clogs and those selling shoes were all mixed together, something which always gave rise to noise and quarrels amongst them when they had to take their posts, to stop the arguments and fights and to avoid the dangers which could befall, from this time forward, on Saturdays in the said square, the clog-sellers must be separated from the other artisans, towards San Geminiano, twenty tables further than them in whatever road; and just as the head of the guild drew lots for the spots on the square in the middle of the year, from now on these areas must be sorted by lot once a month, that is at the beginning of the month.[50]

This type of dispute was very common but it could be argued that as permanent shops expanded, Saturday markets became more of a chore than an opportunity. If this were true, open markets should have declined in favour of permanent shops. But this ignores the multiplicity of reasons for holding public markets. They did not simply offer profits, they were also ways of forcing shopkeepers out into the open so that their products could be sampled, compared and above all, taxed. They also brought income for the authorities who controlled the public market site and allowed those without shops to benefit from a wide customer base. Thus in fifteenth-century Rome, it was forbidden to open any *bottega* while the Campidoglio market was under way on Saturdays.[51] The same provision, it is worth noting, was issued for Jewish merchants who also had to shut their shops on Fridays and sell their produce in the Roman marketplace of the Mercatello.[52] A similar decree was issued in mid-sixteenth-century Bologna insisting that all the shops surrounding the Piazza Grande also close from vespers on Friday evening to midday on Saturday.[53]

The focus on an official market day had other important dimensions, providing a crucial time and arena for the dissemination of official and unofficial information. Public announcements and changes to legislation were announced in the market; a study of sixteenth-century Bologna has shown that public justice, including whipping and hangings, primarily took place on the main square by San Petronio on Saturdays when the market was at its height.[54] Here alongside sale of fruit and vegetables, second-hand clothes, glassware and pottery, those found guilty of blasphemy were supposed to have a nail driven through their tongue and then be placed, 'publicly in chains for four continuous hours with a mitre on their head at the door of San Petronio'.[55] Although major punishments were carried out under the sign of the wolf at the Lateran, the Saturday market on Rome's Capitoline hill, selling everything from grain, fruit and vegetables, shoes, clogs, clothing, mercery and ceramic wares, was also the site where minor transgressors were placed on an ancient marble lion. There they stood with a mitre on their heads and a placard describing their crime.[56] In Milan, the market was the site for more severe justice as prisoners were both jailed and punished in the Broletto. A number of men were burnt there on the order of the Holy Inquisition in 1558 and one Giovanni Angelo Lombardi known as il Buffone was hanged, drawn and quartered in 1559.[57]

Governments were all too aware, however, that while there were advantages of bringing large crowds together, such assemblies were not always passive. In 1353 in Rome, for example, on a Saturday in Lent during a period of famine, 'a voice went up in the market in Rome: "Puopolo, puopolo!" at which voice, the Romans ran here and there like demons ignited by the worst furore', eventually stoning one of the Orsini responsible for running the city who was accused of exporting grain for his own profit.[58] Thus while there were obvious advantages to the provision of a defined moment when people could come together to exchange goods, ideas and gossip, it clearly also created potential problems of control. A market crowd could quickly become a mob and needed to be treated with care.

SHOPPING HOURS

Towns and the Church were not only interested in controlling the days of the week, they were also interested in the hours of the day. In 1376, the merchants of Lucca provided a detailed definition of when different categories of shops were allowed to open:

> Thus it is allowed that the shutters of the said shops can be honestly opened to sell from within the shop except on Sundays and on feast days from the feast of Santa Regola to that of Easter . . . and again it is licit to open on all feast days except for Holy Friday, which should be observed until nones. The apothecaries are allowed to keep the shutters of their shops open and to sell with honesty until terza is sounded and from terza until vespers they must keep their shutters closed and only sell under licence. After vespers they can open their shutters again and sell legally. And it is licit for shoemakers, hosemakers and drapers to keep the shutters of their shops open until terza . . . and to hand over finished work to their clients, but not to take any new orders.[59]

In this highly nuanced notion of what was permitted to whom, when and where, the hours of the day, referred to here as nones, terce and vespers, were as important as the day itself. But, like the start and length of the year, hours were a concept that stood somewhere between nature and culture. In Italy, as elsewhere in Europe, the day was divided either by marking the movements of the sun and the moon, by following a specific liturgical rhythm of prayers and invocations or by using a water- or sand-clock or some other mechanical device to generate regular intervals which could be measured. Even where there was a division into hours, not all hours were the same. For example, although some notaries used a twelve-hour day that began at midnight, for many others a new day began at sunset. Noon, the moment when the sun passed the meridian, could happen up to eighteen hours later.[60] Over a full year, the hour shifted gradually as the final hour of dusk became the twenty-fourth hour and sundown marked the beginning of the new day, or the first hour. Thus when regulations indicated that the city gates were closed at the third hour, this usually implied three hours after sunset rather than three o'clock in the afternoon. This meant that most towns with urban clocks had to employ timekeepers to reset their mechanisms every five to ten days according to agreed tables. Although complex, this method of telling time was common well into the eighteenth century. In his *Italian Journey*, Goethe describes how he had to learn this new way of telling time, one he regarded as 'an entertaining occupation' once he entered into the Italian peninsula. He noted that each new day began at nightfall when the clocks struck one. Between February and May, this hour occurred later and later in the day. In June and July, 'time stood still' and in August the process was reversed until 'time stood still' again in December and January.[61]

While the historian Jacques Le Goff has argued that 'merchant's time' replaced 'sacred time' during the Renaissance, these measured hours of the clock joined rather than displaced the bells that called out both the so-called six 'canonical hours' and the eight 'hours of the Virgin'.[62] By the fourteenth century most Italian cities regularly mixed all of the forms of time-telling described above. The liturgical moments that roughly divided the monastic day and night were closely connected to the rising and setting of the sun. Matins (sunrise), lauds, prime (the first hour), terce or terza (the third hour or around 9am), sext or sesta (midday), nones (the ninth hour or around 3pm), vespers (the evening mass) and compline (sunset) all referred to different times of day and of worship. As the bells rang to call clerics, friars, monks and nuns to their devotions, towns and villages could follow their progress allowing the wider community to divide their days and nights accordingly. The bells that were added for civic purposes joined rather than displaced their monastic or church partners. As early as 1314, for example, the commune of Treviso approved a statute that allowed employers to deduct a third of the wages of employees who did not show up by the first communal bell and from those who left before the sounding of the Ave Maria bell in the evening.[63] The latter, the bell which signalled when vespers were said at dusk, was a particularly important punctuation mark between day and night. It almost always fixed the moment that commerce was supposed to cease, and from 1318 onwards, anyone who stopped and said this prayer to the Virgin gained a swift indulgence when they heard the bell.[64] Like calling the faithful to prayer in an Islamic city, this meant that the Ave Maria bell was much more than a simple time-telling device; it prompted a very specific form of religious, non-commercial behaviour.[65]

Almost all of the injunctions about the opening and closing of markets and shop shutters discussed above referred to sound, above all to the sound of bells. These were usually linked to urban clocks that were often of very impressive construction. Yet however dramatic, the clocks themselves would have had little effect on anyone but their immediate viewers. By the late fourteenth century, therefore, Italy's major clocks were usually tied into a system of bells that informed the community within its auditory zone of the time of day and the various activities expected of its listeners.[66] Certainly by the early fourteenth century, sound provided one of the most important boundaries for behaviour. Among the earliest examples of bell-clocks was that recorded in Orvieto in 1308. The innovation was next registered in Modena and Parma, where the clock 'which signalled the hours' was used to announce periods of work and specified moments of rest for day-labourers.[67] By the end of the fourteenth century there were bell-towers with clocks in Milan, Padua, Vicenza, Trieste, Genoa, Bologna, Siena and Florence. Some, like those of Bologna and Venice, eventually acquired elaborate automata mixing visual delights that attracted attention with the sounds that conveyed information (Figure 106). The formulae could be quite complex, relying on shifts in tone and the number of bells to pass on specific meanings. Although the highly prescriptive tolling of Venice's bells is best known, use of sound to create communal order was not a new concept. For example, in Opicino de Canestris's description of the city of Pavia in 1320, he noted that there were different bells for different purposes: the town council was summoned by one sound, the citizens by another while yet a further tone preceded civic proclamations. There were bells for funerals, one to announce the evening closing of all businesses and a later bell, 'the wine bell' to shut the taverns.[68] In Treviso, at about the same time, communal officials were expected to be at their post by the time the first bell finished tolling to mark sunrise. At the third hour, they could leave again but would be expected to come back an hour later and work until vespers.[69]

Given the importance of hearing these bells, it was important to invest in a heavy and sonorous sound and those on Treviso's periphery petitioned to have an additional bell added to ensure that they too were kept informed of the expected rhythm of their working lives.[70]

Listening to bells meant accepting civic authority and conforming to public notions of appropriate behaviour. The sounding of time was regarded as a mark of civilised life, one that worked with, rather than against, the inevitability of nightfall. Walled towns had regular routines and systems for opening and shutting their gates at dawn and dusk. Goods could not enter until a certain hour, leading

106　The Torre dell'Orologio, 1495–9, Piazza San Marco, Venice.

to queues of suppliers from the countryside on market days. There were regulations about the precise moments when trading could start and when it had to finish, rules designed to ensure equity among purchasers and to prevent the cornering of a market in any single product. These moments could shift according to the seasons and the amount of daylight available. It was, however, not so much the specific time when purchasing began, as the internalised sense of order that an agreed external commencement and finish provided. In 1523, the statutes of the small Tuscan village of Diacceto in Ponte a Sieve lamented the lack of respect for the bell that opened their weekly market:

> Wishing that this market should have a good order and should grow to the utility and benefit of the men and the people of this podesteria, and considering how many statutes up to this point have stated that the market should be held in the castle on Monday and that sales should start at the sound of the bell; and because it is an inhuman thing that a market of this distinction should not have a style and order as do other similar markets, now we order that for the future no one can, in any way under any pretext, sell or buy anything until the bell sounds.[71]

The phrase, 'cosa inhumana' or 'inhuman thing' is a striking one. Higher-level rationality and discipline came from listening to a formal sound and responding appropriately. Only animals and the disorderly would do otherwise. Like a whistle in a playground today, the bell invoked controlled behaviour that demonstrated civilised society.

Bells and hours were not simply used to mark opening and shutting times; they also provided subdivisions within the day itself. Although there is little evidence to suggest a formal lunch hour, magistrates, judges and other civic officials certainly did stop work at around noon, and some form of pause amongst retailers is also plausible. In the early seventeenth century, Thomas Coryate noted of Piazza San Marco that, 'The frequency of people being so great twice a day, between six of the clock in the morning and eleven, and again between five in the afternoon and eight', again suggesting a clear demarcation into morning and afternoon sessions.[72] In the 1588 sumptuary laws issued under the Medici, the government tried to regulate dress on an hourly basis for its male citizens who were required to wear a fifteenth-century style of dress, the *lucco*, a long woollen tunic, when acting in a public capacity. The section on how this was enforced, as recorded in a contemporary diary, began:

> As Florence is founded on the guilds and on mercantile traffic, citizens can more easily look after their business, shops and trade and lead a healthy life and move around if they wear a black cloak and the apron, which comes down just below the knee. This they can wear during their workdays in the morning until the bell of the Uffizi. But after the bell they must wear the *lucco* until they go back home for lunch. After the noon bell and until the evening bell of the Ave Maria in winter they must wear the *lucco*.[73]

Apart from the extraordinary attempt to force Florentine men to wear a garment that had been out of use for almost a century, the legislation also tried to differentiate between different moments of the day and the different types of behaviour expected of each. Some were public, and others, such as midday lunchtimes, were more private. These different temporal subdivisions created additional boundaries among the goods that could be sold as well as between the types of buyers and sellers that were permitted in the squares. In fourteenth-century Pistoia, for example, the sale of flesh and fish took place in the morning, while that of less perishable items such as grain, vegetables and nuts was only permitted in the afternoon after the sounding of nones.[74] In many towns the prostitutes in civic brothels were only supposed to sell their services from the first bell of the morning until 'two hours into the evening', while the wine bell was supposed to stop public drinking.[75] The ability of regraters, that is those who resold produce, to access the market place was similarly dependent on the specific hour of the day.

CONCLUSION

Sixteenth-century maps, like that of Milan, offered an ideal of the geometry and order that officials craved by clearing the streets of people and presenting the *piazze* as empty spaces. But the figures who came back to buy and sell on a daily, monthly, or even annual basis often gained a sense of entitlement over the spaces they regularly occupied.[76] By 1580, for example, the Milanese officials fulminated against those, 'who make themselves owners of the Piazza',[77] and in Bologna there were complaints against those who tried:

To sell on the ground of this piazza or to erect poles or sloping beams against the walls or on the columns or pilasters or in any place that they wish to above or around these, as do the many who occupy these same spaces with seats or benches, tables, boxes or chests, tents, jalopies, stretched out mats, shops of wood . . . so that they occupy the space of this square.[78]

Maintaining transience required constant vigilance. As city governments such as those of Venice, Milan, Vicenza and Brescia invested in expensive architectural façades for their town halls and cathedrals, the relationship between the permanent structures and the temporary, time-based activities became tenser and more strained. Signs and decrees went up in sites like Arezzo's Loggia, ordering that:

No one is to dare to play ball or any other game, however minimal. There is to be no market, nor can anyone sell anything to eat . . . except in the case of rain. Nor can anyone who is a harlot or a scabrous person stop under any circumstances. And so that this loggia is kept neat and clean . . . no one is to dare draw signs or scribbles or other things with charcoal or similar things on the walls.[79]

Even today, seventeenth- and eighteenth-century sculpted versions of these regulations survive, such as that inscribed on the church of San Paolo in Venice outlawing ball games, blasphemy and sales in the vicinity (Figure 107). Such visible signs of regulation are not indications that this policing succeeded in sanitising the urban centre, but signs of its impossibility. The relationship between shifting markets, peddlers and performers and the permanent backdrop against which they moved might change over time, but as long as shopping needed to remain out in the open and under observation the tensions could not be avoided.

107 Plaque forbidding ball games and sales from the church of San Paolo, Campo San Paolo, Venice. The inscription reads, 'MDCXI ADI X Agosto. Sono prohibiti tuti i giochi quali si siano et anco del vender robba, metter bottege intorno a questa chiesa per deliberatione delli ecc. esecutori contra la biasema con penna di pregione e alla bando et anco lire trecento de piccoli.'

CHAPTER FIVE

Place

Previous chapters have stressed the role of sound in defining commerce. Pedlars' cries marked transient moments for purchasing; official bells opened and closed markets. But silence was also a precious commodity. In Renaissance urban spaces, quiet and stillness were demonstrations of restraint and self-control. They acted as a sign of elite commerce that was distinct from the noise of the everyday market. Thus, the fourteenth-century statutes of the Florentine grocers' guild forbade its members to call over customers who were browsing in other shops.[1] The bread-sellers who stood at their stalls in Piazza San Marco and Rialto were told they were not to 'shout and thrust bread at clients, they must stand with composure behind their *bancone*', while a Venetian decree of 29 October 1507 prohibited the vendors of berets and hats from leaving their stalls, 'to call out to anyone, or to grab them by the hand or by their clothing'.[2]

The purchase of valuable or rare items was, above all, supposed to be undertaken in silence. In 1502, the Venetian chronicler Sabellico tried to emphasise the superior nature of the international trade that took place in the Rialto by stressing that it was transacted in whispers.[3] When Venetian customers wanted to compare the best silks before making a major purchase, the relevant guild would organise a viewing known as a *paragon*.[4] Those merchants with the best reputation for high-quality goods would be invited to present their material for scrutiny. Experts from the guild would inspect and guarantee the cloth, sealing both ends of the bolt as a sign that it could be admitted to the *paragon*. These were then numbered and displayed without any indication as to their origins. A list of the numbers and shop names was copied onto a paper or a wooden

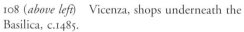

108 (*above left*)   Vicenza, shops underneath the Basilica, c.1485.

109 (*above right*)   Vicenza, shops underneath the Basilica, c.1485.

110 (*right*)   Vicenza, detail of shop front, c.1485.

tablet but the identities of the sellers were only revealed once the final choice had been made. Then, and only then, could negotiation over price take place. Explicit instructions were given to the merchants involved that they were to stand silently beside their wares and not to call out or draw attention to themselves. But as Luca Mola has shown, in 1511 the Venetian government was forced to intervene to prevent silk merchants and their assistants from shouting out. The magistrates stressed their 'shameful behaviour' in volubly trying to attract the attention of would-be buyers.[5]

Yet shifting from the street market to shops was not a simple matter of moving from sound to silence or from exterior to interior spaces, and it was often difficult to distinguish between the permanent and the ephemeral sites for sales. In 1446, for example, the statutes of the Venetian mercers' guild lamented, 'for some time now many foreigners from various countries have begun to stock and sell mercery, on the Rialto bridge, on the Piazza San Marco and throughout the city, on stalls, on stands, and on the ground and from makeshift shops, either on working days or on holidays'.[6] In 1534, Venetian legislators were trying to ban 'false shops' by forbidding beret-sellers from 'daring to put out berets to sell on top of false shops, or rather on stalls or on the ground, or in any other sort of place that you can imagine, rather than in the usual shops with walls, which are true and natural'.[7]

What then was this 'usual shop with walls, which is true and natural' to which the legislators referred? In his 1471 treatise on architecture, Leon Battista Alberti described his ideal version of a *bottega*:

> Within the city, the shop that lies beneath the house and provides the owner with his livelihood should be better fitted out than his dining room, as it should appear more in keeping with his hopes and ambitions. If at a junction, it should occupy the corner position, if in a forum, it should lie on one of the sides, and if on a military road, at a conspicuous bend; almost the sole concern should be to entice customers by the goods on display. For internal construction it would not be unseemly to use unbaked brick, wicker-work, clay, a straw-bound mud, or timber; on the outside though, it must be taken into account that neighbours may not always be honest and polite; accordingly the wall should be reinforced against the assault of both man and weather.[8]

Crucially, Alberti assumed that the shop was typically connected to a domestic dwelling and that location rather than any distinct architectural feature was the key feature for commercial success.[9] This meant that a well-sited shop with a tempting display required only a basic interior constructed of very simple materials such as wickerwork or mud.

It is not easy to flesh out Alberti's short description. Few Renaissance commercial environments have survived unchanged. Those that do exist are usually connected to public buildings that were valued for other reasons such as churches, town halls or palaces. There are, for example, late fifteenth-century shops underneath the transformed Palladian Basilica in Vicenza (Figures 108–10) and sixteenth-century shops designed by Giorgio Vasari for the new Loggia of the Misericordia in Arezzo (Figures 111–13).[10] Both

111 (*above left*)   Arezzo, Shop front in the Loggia of the Misericordia, Piazza Grande, c. 1573–93.

112 (*above right*)   Giorgio Vasari, *Wooden Model of the Loggia of the Misericordia,* Arezzo, Museo di Casa Vasari, Arezzo, 1570–3.

113 (*right*)   Giorgio Vasari, *Drawing for a shop front,* c. 1570, Vasari Sketchbook, p. 121, The Conway Library, Courtauld Institute of Art.

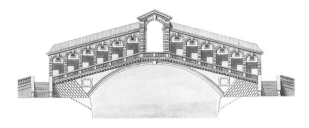

114 Antonio Visentini, *The Rialto Bridge*, c.1760, drawing, The Royal Collection, Windsor Castle.

115 View of the shops in the Rialto bridge, c.1900, photograph.

a model and a drawing survive for the latter demonstrating the care with which alternative openings were considered for these commercial spaces. The sixteenth-century Venetian purpose-built shops, the *Drapperie* and those integrated into the Rialto bridge as part of its reconstruction in the 1550s are also still standing as are a number of commercial sites inserted into the very walls of San Giacomo al Rialto (Figures 114–19).[11] Despite their different locations, these buildings shared many characteristics. They were generally small, single-vaulted spaces with mezzanine areas lit by a window above. Cellars provided additional storage areas and might be lit by a low-level window. This format can be seen in images and plans such as those for the new loggia in Imola dating from the end of the fifteenth century (Figure 120), designs for a shop on the Piazza Piccola in Pavia in 1585 (Figure 121), and images of the archbishop's palace in Florence as redesigned by Giovanni Antonio Dosio in 1574 (Figures 122–4).[12]

Diversity lay, therefore, not in the design but in how items were displayed. Alberti was deliberately vague about what type of goods his ideal shop would have either sold or manufactured. Indeed, one of the difficulties of comparing Italian commercial design with that of, for example, England, lies in the fact that today the English language increasingly separates a place of sale, 'the shop', from that of production, 'the workshop'. But in Italian and Latin, a *bottega* or an *apotecha* could be both. Indeed, in the case of some crafts, such as those of goldsmiths or shoemakers, it was often obligatory to combine the two. Quality was only assured if the customer could actually see the object ordered being made; guild statutes usually demanded that any items that were 'bought in' had to be clearly marked to differentiate them from the maker's own wares.

116　Venice, View of the *Drapperie* from the Rialto bridge.

117　Gabriel Bella, *Bancogiro di Rialto*, 1779–92, oil on canvas, Fondazione Querini Stampalia, Venice.

118   View of a shop embedded in the church of
San Giacomo in Rialto, Venice.

119   Canaletto, *Piazza San Giacomo in Rialto*, c. 1740–60, National Gallery of Canada, Ottawa.

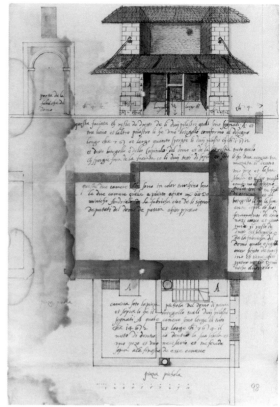

120 (*above*)   Design for the Palazzo Riario, Biblioteca Communale, Imola.

121 (*right*)   Drawing of a shop, Archivio di stato, Pavia, notarile, filza 4474, Gargani, Giovan Alberto, 20 November 1585.

By contrast, in other businesses, such as woollen or silk industry, it was explicitly forbidden for workers to sell their wares from their place of manufacture.[13]

Between these two extremes lay a wide range of possibilities. In a few instances, such as glass manufacture in Venice, there were complex rules dividing those items such as *cristallo* that could be sold only by makers themselves in Murano and cheaper wares that could be sold by dedicated glass retailers located in the main city.[14] Similarly, mercers, pharmacists and grocers bought in supplies that had been made by others, but also made their own products for public sale at both wholesale and retail levels. Thus the term, *bottega*, referring as it does to almost any form of commercial or working environment, makes it difficult to identify a shop's distinguishing features with precision.

SIGNING SHOPS

One way of defining the shop lay in its differentiation from other public structures. A true *bottega* was neither a temporary fixture such as a market stall, nor was it meant to be a large wholesale outlet. Yet many Renaissance shopkeepers found it difficult to main-

122 (*above left*)   Francesco Morandi, called 'Il Poppi', *Portrait of Cardinal Alessandro di Ottaviano dei Medici*, Archiepiscopal Palace, Florence.

123 (*above right*)   Detail of Figure 122.

124 (*left*)   Giovanni Antonio Dosio, *Designs for the new Florentine Arcivescovado*, 1574, Florence, Florence Uffizi, Gabinetto Disegni e Stampe 3255/A.

tain these distinctions and had wholesale and retail aspects to their businesses. Thus the wealthy merchant Francesco di Marco Datini, who exported cloth throughout Europe sold small amounts of fabric from his shop in Prato in the late fourteenth century.[15] He even had some of his material made up into stockings for ready sale to the local community. In practice, therefore, the main difference between a warehouse and a shop was that a wholesaler's stock was usually much larger than that of his retail counter-part. When the Milanese Canon Pietro Casola wanted to praise Venice's *botteghe* in the late fifteenth century, he deliberately confused them with the city's warehouses, writing:

> who could count the many shops so well furnished that they almost seem warehouses, with so many cloths of every make – tapestry, brocades and hangings of every design, carpets of every sort, camlets of every colour and texture, silks of every kind; and so many warehouses full of spices, groceries and drugs and so much beautiful wax! These things stupefy the beholder.[16]

In suggesting that the city's shops seemed like warehouses, Casola was clearly thinking of Venice's best-known site, the Fondaco dei Tedeschi, which was eventually rebuilt even more sumptuously in the sixteenth century as an impressive building with rich marble decorations, allegorical frescoes by Titian and Giorgione on the exterior and a range of storage and living spaces within the interior (Figure 125).[17] This Fondaco, a term derived from the Arab *fonduq*, was a site where professional resellers or retailers were supposed to be able to buy in bulk for export. In this form of 'bonded warehouse', which was part lodging and part storage site, imported or luxury items were to be purchased only under strict controls.[18] Designated officials were assigned to each merchant by lot. These intermediaries were supposed to accompany and guide their clients throughout the city both to ensure that business was conducted purely for export purposes and that all Venetian taxes and regulations were obeyed. The purpose of such an arrangement was more than fiscal. Although Venice was a major producer and importer of luxury items such as silks, lace, high-value wool cloths, gold and silverwares, the Senate was anxious to prevent its own citizens from acquiring and displaying this wealth. Keen to avoid waste and to sustain the illusion of a common senatorial class who did not compete in terms of dress and display on an aristocratic level, officials stipulated that these goods were supposed to move in and out of the city without passing into the homes of respectable Venetians.[19]

Although it had unique concerns and anxieties, Venice was not unusual in having such warehouses. In other towns, they ranged from the public, state-owned sites designed to ensure appropriate taxation and security, such as the Fondaco built by the Da Carrara family in Padua for wool cloth, to the much smaller repositories, *magazz-ini*, which private owners kept to store their own goods.[20] But whatever its scale or function, the Fondaco was only supposed to act as the first stage in moving goods into the retail market. The restriction on the type of customer who was permitted to enter, and the emphasis on export rather than local circulation had considerable implications. Thus when small amounts were sold, *al minuto*, to the wider public from the Fondaco

125　Venice, Fondaco dei Tedeschi, 1505–8.

dei Tedeschi, there was generally an outcry at the damage that such sales were doing to local shops.[21] This was the case in 1466 when the Venetian mercers attacked the behaviour of German exporters based in the Fondaco:

> And since for some time, contrary to our orders . . . a habit most damaging to all our mercers and shopkeepers who sustain the taxation for our city has been introduced that in their rooms in the warehouse they keep merceries and sell retail and make shelves just as they do in the shops of the mercers.[22]

This complaint suggests that canny buyers knew that they got the best deals by trying to buy directly from the warehouse itself rather than from their local shops, both obtaining high-quality goods at better prices and potentially evading Venetian taxes.

At the other end of the spectrum were the concerns raised by potential confusion between commercial and domestic spaces. As previously discussed, notarised business transactions using witnesses regularly took place within the home. Mercers, grocers and other merchants expected to bring goods to their customers' dwellings or to send out samples for inspection. But if buying within the home was accepted, selling was not. Although houses might contain shops, particularly on the ground floor, they were usually treated as separate areas and often had separate entrances. When it was necessary to use the same door for both purposes, legislators became anxious about the clarity of determining when a shop was open or shut.[23] Indeed, as has already been suggested the domestic sales of unregulated goods came close to what would today be called the black market and both civic and guild statutes usually limited or outlawed such activities.

Such bans, of course, suggest that overlaps were more common than officials would wish and that there were many shades of grey in this black market. The difficulties of sustaining an exclusively commercial environment were complicated by the fact that many Italian artisans lived above the shop, and a small number actually lived in the shop itself. It was very easy to add on a commercial space to a domestic dwelling. In 1477, for example, Gabriele Calznis, an apothecary in Porta Romana in Milan, was given permission to construct four columns next to his house and put up a 'board or a table between them to set out merchandise to sell'.[24] Such arrangements may have been particularly convenient in circumstances where wives or other female relatives served at the counter or where the family could save on the expense of renting an additional space. Thus the 1427 Florentine tax records, the Catasto, reveal that approximately 26 per cent of the city's householders lived above the *bottega*, a number that, though still significant, had diminished to 18 per cent by the end of the century.[25] It needs, however, to be stressed that while the two fifteenth-century tax surveys or *catasti* and the later Grand Ducal tax survey, the *decima* of 1561, both demonstrated a continuing conjunction between the domestic and the commercial, they also indicated that this intersection was almost non-existent in the wealthier parts of the city centre. If bankers and silk or wool merchants negotiated from their homes, they did not sell products to the wider public from their palaces.[26] Using one's own home as a retail outlet or a site of manufacture seems to have been a sign of poverty rather than one of convenience.[27]

This conclusion is confirmed by other sources. For example, after Francesco Sforza's conquest of Milan in 1450, he awarded a growing number of signorial licences allowing retail sales of low-value goods such as flour from private homes due to the poverty of their inhabitants.[28] But following an outcry from local guilds, the new duke was forced to rescind these permits. The anxieties expressed over the rupture of guild regulations were more than economic. In legal terms, the baker's oven was a public amenity, not a private kitchen. The prostitute's bed was a place of business, not one of matrimonial legitimacy. Business was meant to take place in a *bottega* precisely because, unlike the home, the shop was potentially open to all. It could be inspected and transactions that took place elsewhere were described as dark, *occulto* or as transgressive.

This did not mean, of course, that shops were completely separate from homes, merely that the homeowner was not necessarily the same person as the shopkeeper who worked below. Although the most expensive new palaces that were constructed in the fifteenth and sixteenth centuries in cities such as Siena, Florence and Milan deliberately avoided inserting commercial spaces on their ground floors, the requirement for rental income meant that many families and institutions continued to include shops in their new palaces. This seems to have been particularly the case in Rome. When Raphael designed a palace for the papal courtier, Giovan Battista Branconio dell'Aquila in 1518, he included a series of simple shops within the elegantly constructed bays, designed, it has been suggested, on the model of the market of Trajan in Rome (Figures 126–7).[29] The awnings, counters and trestle tables displayed in a later drawing depicting the palace suggest that little concession was made to the grandeur of the location by the shopkeepers in question. Sixteenth-century engravings by Antoine Lafrery and early twentieth-century photographs show that the ground floors of the Alberini and Caprini palaces and the Palazzetto Turci in Rome were similarly occupied by commercial outlets (Figures 128–30). Even the sides of Cardinal Riario's palace, now known as the Palazzo della Cancelleria, were studded with shops (Figure 131). Clearly, despite the elite nature of these palaces, the income derived from these *botteghe* was too important to refuse.[30]

This was also true of small as well as large towns: in Treviso, a property survey from 1567 shows that many householders gained a substantial income from renting parts of their dwellings to others. For example, the wealthy merchant Luca Fassadoni rented out one shop on the ground floor of his house to two artisans and an adjacent building to an innkeeper (who in turn sub-let part of the ground floor to a saddle-maker and a tailor), provide a very substantial annual income of 400 lire.[31] In another instance, the

126 Antoine Lafrery, *Speculum Romanae magnificentiae*, 1549, engraving, Palazzo Branconio dell'Aquila, The Conway Library, Courtauld Institute of Art, London.

127 Giovan Battista Naldini, view of Palazzo Branconio dell' Aquila on Borgo Nuovo, c. 1560, Gabinetto Disegni e Stampe, Uffizi, Florence, n.239 Ar.

128 (*above left*) Antoine Lafrery, *Speculum Romanae magnificentiae*, 1549, engraving, Alberini Palace, Rome, The Conway Library, Courtauld Institute of Art, London.

129 (*above right*) Antoine Lafrery, *Speculum Romanae magnificentiae*, Rome, 1549, engraving, Palazzo Caprini, Rome, The Conway Library, Courtauld Institute of Art, London.

130 (*right*) Palazzetto Turci, Rome, c.1880–1900, photograph, view of palace with shops on the ground floor.

131 Piranesi, *Varie vedute di Roma*, Rome, 1748, Palazzo della Cancelleria, The Conway Library, Courtauld Institute of Art, London.

widow of a tailor survived by renting out part of her house to a perfumer, Magistro Silvestro da Napoli.[32] This was a common strategy for women who rented out rooms, often to other women, in order to share expenses.[33] But whatever their status, many other owners, even the wealthy, rented out sections of their basements, attics and sheds as manufacturing sites, storage areas or stabling to provide for a steady income. In fact, the Treviso survey, which describes each building in detail on a street-by-street basis, suggests that it was very rare to have only one activity taking place within a single dwelling, particularly in the poorer outskirts.

Given the ease with which the distinctions between the domestic and the commercial were blurred, a critical factor in sustaining differentiation was the use of a visible marker: a sign. San Bernardino da Siena emphasised this aspect when discussing the close correlation between external appearance and appropriate status in his 1427 Sienese Lenten sermons:

> By what do we know the shops, eh? By their signs . . . thus we know the shop of that wool merchant by his sign. So too, the merchant knows his shop by its sign . . . How do we know who makes usurious loans? By the sign of the balance and balls. How do we know who sells wine? Simply by the sign. Similarly, how do we recognise a hotel? Simply by its sign. When you go to the tavern to get wine, because you see the sign, you say, 'Give me wine', isn't that so?[34]

As the preacher emphasised, these symbols informed potential clients of the availability of certain types of products and the identity of the retailer. Nonetheless, while merchants used quite specific signs to identify shops and products, these were usually generic images – crowns, Moors' heads, angels, suns or moons – rather than any specific reference to the wares in question (Figure 132). In Antonio Tempesta's engraving of the month of December an innkeeper salutes his customers under the sign of the crown (Figure 133); to the rear of Lorenzo Lotto's painting of the martyrdom of Saint Barbara in Trescore, a drinker reclines on a bridge by a tavern sign that simply bore a symbol of a wineglass (Figure 134). More exotic names, such as at the sign of the

132   Shop sign with the symbol of the quarter of Santa Maria Novella, from above a shop in Via Calimala, Florence. Museo di San Marco, Florence.

'Saracen' or at the sign of the 'Moor' did not necessarily indicate foreign products but made a memorable symbol (Figure 135).[35]

Very few of these images have survived and there are no early Italian counterparts to the famed French sign painted for a Parisian dealer Gersaint by Watteau or the English signs by Hogarth.[36] But even if they were not produced by well-known artists there is evidence of their importance in Italy. Increasingly, manufacturers took over the shop sign as a symbol for their own manufactures. Printers' marks, for example, were almost always indicated as 'at the sign of' while apothecaries marketed their medicines as having been produced again, 'at the sign of the Dolphin' or 'at the sign of the Lily'.

133 Antonio Tempesta, *December: Village Scene with Inn,* c. 1610, etching, Los Angeles County Museum, Los Angeles.

134 Lorenzo Lotto, *The Martyrdom of Saint Barbara,* 1524, Oratorio Suardi, Trescore Balneario, detail of tavern sign.

Like merchant's or goldsmiths' marks, they became symbols of quality as well as of location and by the sixteenth century such symbols were bought and sold as products in their own right.[37] Eventually the right to use the term, 'at the sign of the Angel' became a commodity protected by copyright that could be inherited or traded.

The conjunction of quality and imagery was understandable because these symbols had a long history of acting as civic or merchants' guarantees. From the fourteenth century onwards Florentine bakers were required to place the city's symbol of the fleur-de-lis over their doors. In Pistoia, bakers were obliged to seal each loaf of bread with the same symbol to guarantee that it was of sufficient weight and quality.[38] Similarly, individual goldsmith's marks had to be registered while silk merchants had to ensure that their marks were woven into the selvage of the cloth and that lead seals issued by the relevant guilds were attached to their bolts.[39] This meant that controlling signs was a means of controlling shops and shopkeepers. Thus, by the late sixteenth century, any Venetian planning to open a shop was required to register their sign with the city government while the magistracy of the Giustizia Vecchia controlled printers' marks.[40] The book of Venetian shop signs, which runs from 1560 to 1597, shows that 517 new *botteghe* registered during the almost forty-year period. Although this sounds like a high number, in fact it is a relatively small turnover for a city with a population of almost 100,000. The majority of these new shops were selling high-value goods for which Venice was famous, with mercers or haberdashers taking pride of place with 29 per cent of new openings. Apothecaries followed closely behind at 16 per cent while goldsmiths, booksellers and grocers were also setting up shops on a regular basis. These new licences were not, therefore, necessarily evidence of a shift from exterior markets to interior shops. Instead, the register highlights the continued attempts by the Venetian authorities to keep a close watch over their most valuable and highly regulated enterprises.

In Florence there was a similar increase in shops during the fifteenth century, rising from 1,540 shops recorded in 1427 to 1,660 in 1480. Given the expansion in population, this is unsurprising. Of greater interest is the significant rise in the proportion of retail outlets in comparison with dedicated sites of production.[41] For example, the number of apothecaries rose from forty-four to fifty-two and many were now selling a wide range of goods such as cosmetics and perfumes alongside their more traditional offerings of spices, and simple and compound medicines. The census of 1561 showed yet a further rise in the number of shops to a total of 2,172, the majority of which were concentrated on the south side of the Arno river with the greatest intensity in the parish of Santa Croce.[42]

These records demonstrate another important fact. Most shops were rental properties that were often owned by institutions rather than by individuals. The income they generated was used to support the salaries of officials and the lifestyles of those who would or could not work either because of their social or religious status. In Venice, the city itself owned the entire Rialto area while the 1427 Florentine *catasto* shows that over 20 per cent of all the shops were owned by the Church and other charitable organisations. The Hospital of Santa Maria Nuova was one of the largest owners of shops, closely followed by the Hospital of San Giovanni Battista and the guilds themselves.

For valuable properties with excellent locations, a would-be renter might have to pay a non-returnable deposit, known as an *entratura*, either to the previous occupant or the owner. Once rented, Tuscan guild regulations were adamant that the shop could not be offered to anyone else until its current occupant left.[43] This meant that one factor limiting design change was that shops were rarely owned by the retailers themselves. If shopkeepers made minor improvements they did so at their own expense; if they made major alterations, they could only do so with the permission of their landlord and usually had to put up the capital themselves, although they might be able to reduce their rental payments accordingly.[44]

Further constraints on shop development were enforced by guild statutes which were often concerned to restrict the number or scale of the shops that any single owner could operate. Here although expansion was an obvious way of increasing sales capacity, it was perceived as unfair competition or, even worse, as the creation of a potentially dangerous monopoly. There was, therefore, limited incentive to make permanent alterations to the physical infrastructure. While some businessmen did consolidate a series of shops into one large space, it was as common to find entrepreneurial shopkeepers investing in alternative businesses, moving into exports or setting up new *botteghe* in other cities rather than expanding their original premises.

Avoiding investment in fixed structures made sense for there was a high rate of mobility among shopkeepers. Although these were stock complaints designed to reduce tax assessments, the ritual laments about tenants (both retail and domestic) leaving without paying their rents at the end of the year seem to have had some basis in fact. The goldsmith and sculptor Benvenuto Cellini regularly moved to different premises in sixteenth-century Rome according to his economic circumstances while even someone as successful as the apothecary Luca Landucci in Florence moved through three different locations during his career. Likewise, a Venetian survey taken in 1582 found that, for example, a building in the parish of San Giacomo Crisostomo by the Canal Grande was 'almost entirely occupied by stores that were rented for very short periods of time, sometimes for only a day or at the most a month'.[45]

The eventual impact of all these factors was to remove the focus of attention from the permanent shop structures to the portable products. Given the importance of stock over the setting, two further potentially contradictory concepts had to be addressed: visibility and security. Exclusively residential buildings usually limited the number of windows on the ground floor and provided a clear differentiation between interior and exterior spaces. In contrast, *botteghe* used large unglazed openings, such as those seen in the photograph of the Palazzetto Turci, that deliberately erased the distinction. Some images, as suggested by the details of shops in Siena's Good Government and the drawing of the Palazzo Branconio indicate that merchants used curtains to provide shelter from the heat and dust and that doors formed only a nominal divide between the shop and the road in which clients walked past. In northern Italy, this border was often further confused by the covered *portici* that allowed shopkeepers to put their wares out into the street regardless of the weather. Here manufacture and display often spilled out onto the street, much to the dismay of local legislators and magistracies responsible for policing the state of the roads (Figure 136).

But openness did not necessarily lead to accessibility. Although customers might be able to see inside with ease, they could not enter at will, nor was everything on display. Although hidden from view, storage areas in attics, back rooms and basements were an important part of the overall structure. There were usually round or square windows above lighting the attics while the Alberini palace engraving shows the grated windows that provided light for the cellar inserted into the counters themselves.

Of the many applications for building permission presented in mid-sixteenth-century Mantua, a high proportion were requests to extend and illuminate similar basement areas.[46] By the 1530s, the constant attempts to excavate for storage purposes had turned

136 Masuccio Salernitano, *Novellino*, Venice, 1492, woodcut, 'The Cobbler's Shop', The British Library, London.

the city centre around the Mantuan Broletto into a warren of cellars and street openings. With both passers-by and horses falling into these open holes, the city magistrates ordered that everyone had to put up gratings over their basements to prevent further accidents.[47]

These storage areas did not allow customers to enter and browse the full stock. Instead, the space between buyer and seller was usually blocked by some sort of counter. When customers wanted to come inside they came through a simple gap at the side as shown in the shops depicted in both Palladio and Vasari's drawings for shop entrances from the sixteenth century (Figure 137). This was the scheme proposed for Imola and used on the Rialto bridge.[48] Another common type of shop entrance, as evidenced by a number of surviving examples from the Aretine loggia to shops in Pistoia (Figures 138–9), used a central gap with stone counters to either side. Such a system can also be seen in Giovanni Stradano's painting of the Via Calimala in the Mercato Vecchio from the mid-sixteenth century (Figure 140). The base of these low walls seems to have become a site for displaying goods. A fifteenth-century image of a fruit-seller indicates that his products were placed here (Figure 141). A late sixteenth-century drawing of a glass-shop in Pistoia demonstrates how little had changed. Despite the very different nature of the products and a transition period of almost one hundred years, shop architecture remained remarkably constant, with the new, highly fashionable Venetian glassware laid out on the simple shelves on the roadside (Figure 142).[49]

Such openness was often insisted on by guild statutes that demanded that all manufacture take place under the public gaze to ensure quality, decrying any covering that might obscure the shop's interior.[50] But accessibility also posed problems. Tempting merchandise might invite theft. The baskets of coins and jewellery held on the tables

137 Palladio, drawing for a palace with ground floor shops, RIBA drawing, Palladio XIV/II. The Conway Library, Courtauld Institute of Art, London.

138 (*above*)   Pistoia, shops with central openings.

139 (*right*)   Pistoia, detail of shop front.

140 (*facing page*)   Giovanni Stradano, *The Mercato Vecchio*, (detail), fresco, 1561, Palazzo Vecchio.

of the bankers and money-changers in Piazza San Marco and Piazza San Giacomo in Rialto in Venice prompted regular and almost always unsuccessful attempts to grab and run before vigilant observers captured the thief.[51] But while such rapid reactions were possible during the day, protection was also required at night. Any vulnerable area might be accessed by a determined thief.[52] One of the prisoners housed in Milan in 1471 was 'Petro da Bergamo who used a hammer at night to break into the balcony of the shop of Giovanni da Brenano, and to steal, between goods and cash, more than 250 lire from the shop'.[53] It was not even enough to use sturdy locks. In 1595, the Milanese Francesco Busso, called 'of the Keys', and his accomplice Pagano Pagani were put to death for 'having made keys that could open houses and shops without making a sound'.[54]

Crimes against property were taken very seriously and dealt with harshly. Because it was so difficult to stop burglaries, governments reacted powerfully when thieves were caught. In 1575, the break-in that took place in the shop of Luca Landucci (the grandson of the earlier diarist) in Florence was the subject of considerable comment and dire retribution:

On the fifth of April, Luca Landucci, apothecary at the loggia of the Tornaquinci was robbed and his shop was emptied of sugar, wax and all that he had. A few days later, Niccolo di Bastiano, a rider was found guilty of this and other thefts that fol-

141 Filippo Calandri, *Trattato di aritmetica*, Florence, c. 1490, Biblioteca Riccardiana, Ricc. 2669, c.100v, 'A Fruit and Vegetable Shop'.

142 Drawing of a shop selling glass, Pistoia, Archivio di stato, Spedale Riuniti. Il Ceppo, n.1885, c.5.

lowed . . . he was hanged from the windows of the Bargello and the two artisans who helped him melt down the goods were put to the rope.[55]

Alongside theft, fire and other natural disasters were the great fears for merchants with fixed premises. In 1505, a major conflagration broke out in the Fondaco dei Tedeschi destroying the entire building. In January 1514 an even greater disaster occurred when a fire broke out in a shop in one of Venice's major commercial streets, the *Corderia*, and spread throughout the commercial area of the Rialto. With typical hyperbole, Marin Sanudo compared it to the sack of Troy and estimated that at least 35,000 ducats, representing a year's worth of rental income, had been lost along with the merchandise.[56] Such events were all too common. In 1551, for example, the Florentine chronicler Marucelli noted how in February of that year:

In our city in the Mercato Vecchio, I know not whether through negligence or because of the anger of our eternal God, fire broke out in five shops: four grocers and one apothecary that was called the *Spetiale del Sole*, with damages of between 12 and 14,000 scudi without considering the site itself . . .[57]

As Marucelli noted, the disaster lay not simply in the loss of the building, but in the loss of rental income and, above all, in the loss of the stock. Even celebratory events could bring disaster. When rumours circulated concerning the possible birth of a male heir to Duke Francesco de' Medici in 1575, the Florentine shopkeepers' primary response was to rush and close their shutters, 'because of their worries that the plebians would act according to their custom and put the goods in shops to the sack'.[58]

FIXTURES AND FITTINGS

The care taken to prevent fire, burglaries and other forms of losses emphasises the large amounts of material goods that were made for a speculative market rather than simply to order. For mercers and apothecaries, the large capital investments in the stock contained within their shops made these spaces more like storehouses or treasure-chests than open areas for browsing. Shutter mechanisms, which can be seen in a mid-fifteenth-century image of a goldsmith's shop, in Girolamo Genga's 1528 drawing of Florentine *botteghe* and in a 1920 view of the Ponte Vecchio, were simple but effective. The open shutters provided shade and a bottom counter, but could then be locked together at night for security (Figures 143–5). At night and on holidays, the closed shop exteriors, with complex locks and heavy barred wooden shutters, suggested that something worth stealing lay within (Figure 146).

As has been described above, shops may have been defined more by their contents than by the elegance of their permanent architectural fittings. This was particularly true during temporary ritual occasions when shop displays were an important element of the overall spectacle. During the King of Denmark's entry into Mantua in 1474, for example, the chronicler Andrea Schivenoglia recorded how:

> On the 23rd of March the most beautiful shops in Mantua were created that had ever been made and in front of them were set out almost 5,000 woollen cloths and this was done to show the wealth of this city to the Germans.[59]

The Venetians also used their shops to display their wealth. In a letter written to the Sforza secretary Cicco Simonetta concerning a visit by the Holy Roman Emperor, Frederick III to Venice in 1469, the writer was frank about the *Serenissima*'s motivations in taking their distinguished visitor down the shopping street of the merceria:

> And then we went along the *marzaria* . . . and they had had all the shops and stalls filled and they did everything to make him, and those who were with him and all who looked on, understand that they (the Venetians) were rich and powerful and great lords and nothing was lacking in this effort. Tomorrow they will show him the Arsenal.[60]

143 (*top left*) Jewellers' shops, Ponte Vecchio, Florence, gelatin and silver salt photograph, c.1920 Alinari. Note that the shutter mechanisms are similar to those in Figure 145.

144 (*above*) Girolamo Genga's *Mythological Pageant*, 1528/29, drawing, Leonora Hall Gurley Memorial Collection, 1922.825, The Art Institute, Chicago, detail of shops and their shutters.

145 (*right*) Baccio Baldini (att.), *The Planet of Mercury and His Children*, c.1460–5, engraving, Florence, Department of Prints and Drawings, The British Museum, London, detail of goldsmith's shop showing shutter mechanism.

146   Two views of locked shops in the Rialto, Venice.

Showing shops, followed by a display of naval ships, was a far from subtle hint of Venetian international prowess. The Florentines took a similar pride in their *botteghe*, displaying their contents as part of an annual festival in honour of their patron saint Saint John the Baptist. On this occasion, even items that had already been sold or made to commission for others might be put on show. Thus in both 1491 and in 1513, the *cartolaio* or stationer who had provided parchment to the cathedral of Florence borrowed two of the Duomo's most elaborate liturgical manuscripts during the festival when the citizens, as one commentator put it:

> ostentatiously show their things in the more frequented places of the city. For almost all the artisans and those with warehouses who do business in such places put whatever precious things they have outside if they have such things . . . In the greater honour of the city and perhaps for greater profit . . .[61]

Honour and profit made an important combination, and the festival was controlled by officials, *festaiuoli*, who used their authority to manage both the finances and the effect of the eventual display. They wanted to be discriminating in what elements of Florentine manufacture were on show, focusing on the most elite elements and charging others for the privilege of participating. As a concerned Luca Landucci noted:

And on the 19th of June 1510, the *festiuoli* of San Giovanni issued a decree that no artisan was permitted to open his shop from the 20th until the feast of San Giovanni without their permit, at a penalty of 25 lire. And to obtain this permit cost some 2 grossi, others 3 and some up to 4. And this was a great blow to the poor because the decree said that this did not refer to the wool merchants, nor the silk merchant nor the bankers; and it was considered to be an unjust, defamatory and vile thing to make the artisans pay for the feast of San Giovanni.[62]

The 1510 festival referred to above was undertaken in a period when Florence was attempting to regain its status as an independent republic. But even when the city was under princely rule, the ritual retained its importance. A description from 1588 is highly evocative of the elaborately staged effect as merchants displayed wares that were normally inaccessible to prying eyes and, as suggested by stringent sumptuary laws, supposedly forbidden to the city's own inhabitants:

And even the shops of the silk merchants were open, and inside these from the shutters they had made around the whole of the shop, rich cloths, some of them were in bolts, some were hung down, still others attached to the walls of the shops, which made a rich display. And by the shutters outside stood two boys with peacocks feathers in their hands or fans of cloth with long handles and they continuously drove away the flies, but they could not stop the dust. Around these shutters sat the masters on chairs of leather and cloth with great pomp, showing their friends the beauty of their cloths. As to their richness and variety, one sees such workmanship and craft that has never been seen before in Florence, neither in the churches, nor during weddings, nor for any other use, because such cloths are almost always exported.[63]

Another chronicler informs the reader that this display was carefully contrived. Far from being a show of the enterprise of individual merchants, much of the fabric on display actually belonged to Duke Ferdinando dei Medici.[64] As with the Mantuan and Venetian examples described above, little would be left to chance in demonstrating urban wealth and prosperity.

By the late sixteenth century, artisans, such as one Roman candymaker who borrowed tapestries to decorate his shop interior during the Christmas period, were concerned to present a luxurious interior. But under ordinary circumstances daily displays of merchandise had very different purposes from these public events.[65] Keeping goods out of sight or out of reach might be as important as an extravagant show of opulence. To get some sense of how stock was regularly shown to customers requires a more careful use both of inventories (which often concentrate on what was in the shop rather than on how it was shown) and of visual records such as the Issogne frescoes. In looking at shop displays, however, it is also important to remember that (despite guild regulations suggesting otherwise) many vendors sold a wide range of products that were outside their immediate competency. The early fifteenth-century records of a cheesemonger's shop from Prato show that he sold far more than cheese, offering both salted and fresh foods as well as sewing materials such as needles, thread and buttons. Other goods in his shop included glassware and bottles, ironware including handles for agricultural implements, candles and pens.[66] Although there was increasing specialisation, particularly in cities such as Venice where the sale of pigments was specifically exercised by *vendecolori*, a multiplicity of products was still preferred by most salesmen.[67] New small-scale products like prints, fans or stucco ornaments, could be easily added to the stock of a wide range of vendors without requiring any investment in new shop furnishings. In the early sixteenth century, for example, Alessandro di Francesco Roselli, son of an engraver and cartographer, sold his father's prints from his mercer's shop in Florence.[68]

With such overlap it is difficult to argue that there were very different infrastructural requirements for different types of commercial enterprises. Even the most elite and established activities such as the sale of valuable fabrics or banking had surprisingly minimal physical requirements. These included basic tables, desks for writing, shelving and money boxes. In 1372, a member of the Florentine Corsini family noted the expenses for setting up two shops, one wholesale woollen cloth shop and one retail outlet. He would:

> pay for a desk for writing and a chest to keep money in which are in the main shop of Via Maggio for 4 soldi di piccioli, and for a table to display the cloth and for a writing desk with shelves to the rear which is in the smaller shop on Via Maggio, three gold florins, and we bought these things from Antonio di Niccolò di Cione.[69]

In Venice, a carpet laid out on the window, as shown in Carpaccio's image of the money-changer Saint Matthew, was usually the sign that banks were open for business (Figure 147). The counter was often formed from the shutters themselves as illustrated above in the fifteenth-century Florentine image of the children of the planet Mercury (Figure 143). Storage shelves and boxes were additional basic elements. Simple shelving systems placed to the rear of a shop were usually supplemented by hanging items on hooks, strings and rods and by putting goods outside on trestle tables, barrels and boxes. This arrangement was used to signify shop interiors in Milanese illuminations of the influence of Mercury and Jupiter but the format was not unique to Italy (Figures 148–9). It seems to have been traditional across Europe as evidenced by depictions of shops and stalls in France and the Netherlands (Figure 150). Additional furnishings were only required for more specialised activities. Bookshops, for example, might have lecterns displaying copies of volumes that could be ordered. Printed books were often sold unbound, and customers could choose how they wanted their editions collated.[70]

Containers, baskets, vials and barrels in straw, wood, metal, glass and pottery, were an important part of a shop's stock. The shop that invested the highest amount in its packaging was, without doubt, that of the higher-end apothecary or *speziale*. These sites sold a wide range of products, ranging from wax, sugar and sauces to the ingredients for the most elaborate medications. But many of the ingredients that were sold by the apothecary for medicinal purposes were far from impressive in their own right. They were either simples, composed of single ingredients usually taken from plant or mineral substances, or compounds made up of numerous items combined according to a

147   Vittore Carpaccio, *The Calling of Saint Matthew*, 1502, tempera on canvas, Scuola di San Giorgio degli Schiavoni, Venice.

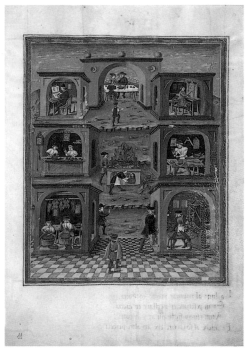

148 (*left*) Lombard, c.1460, *De Sphaera*, Modena, Biblioteca Estense, ms. Alpha.x.2.14, c.11r, 'The activities under the influence of Jupiter'.

149 (*right*) Lombard, c.1460, *De Sphaera*, Modena, Biblioteca Estense, ms. Alpha.x.2.14, c.6v, 'The activities under the influence of Mercury'.

doctor's recipe. It was important to be able to label these goods so that they were easily identifiable. Such labelling was also key to consumer confidence. If the herbs emerged from a ceramic jar marked 'borage', there was an acceptance that that was indeed what was being purchased. But the investment went well beyond lettering. The illuminations from a mid-fifteenth-century version of *Tacuinum sanitatis* laid great emphasis on the glass and maiolica jars and vessels lining the shelves to the rear of each vendor (Figures 151–5). Apothecaries were acutely aware of the need to create a strong up-to-date visual presence. The almost 238 surviving containers commissioned by an apothecary in Messina, from the Patanazzi workshop in Urbino, give an idea of how impressive the effect must have been on visitors. Now housed in a seventeenth-century pharmacy in the small Sicilian town of Roccavaldina, row upon row of elaborately decorated jars bearing the intial pharmacy's sign of the dove suggested a major investment in display (Figures 156–9).

   In addition to the containers, pharmacists bought purpose-built counters and shelving that would display these containers to best effect. In 1462, for example, the Flo-

150   French, fifteenth century, 'A Street with shops and the arms of Robert Stuart, Marshall of
Aubigny', Paris, Bibliothèque de L'Arsenal, ms. 5062, f. 149v.

151 (*above left*)   Paduan, 1450–60, *Tacuinum sanitatis*, Sotheby's Sale, 17 December 1991, Lot 50, The Conway Library, Courtauld Institute of Art, London, 'Oleum amigdalarum'.

152 (*above right*)   Paduan, 1450–60, *Tacuinum sanitatis*, Sotheby's Sale, 17 December 1991, Lot 50, The Conway Library, Courtauld Institute of Art, London, 'Zucharum'.

153 (*below left*)   Paduan, 1450–60, *Tacuinum sanitatis*, Sotheby's Sale, 17 December 1991, Lot 50, The Conway Library, Courtauld Institute of Art, London, 'Muschus'.

154 (*below right*)   Paduan, 1450–60, *Tacuinum sanitatis*, Sotheby's Sale, 17 December 1991, Lot 50, The Conway Library, Courtauld Institute of Art, London, 'Sirupus acetosus'.

rentine apothecary and diarist Luca Landucci, described with a mixture of pride and concern the cost of his first outlet:

And on the fourth of September 1462, I took my leave of Francesco di Francesco, apothecary at the Sun, who gave me a sixth of my annual salary, 50 florins, and I set up in partnership with Ispinello di Lorenzo and in the hope of a greater good I gave up a certain one. And we first opened the apothecary of the King in the Mercato Vecchio, which had first been a second-hand clothes dealers' shop, which had a low roof. And we raised the building and spent a fortune, even though such an expense was against my wishes, we did every thing without thrift. The cupboard alone cost fifty gold florins.[71]

The image of the apothecary's shop in Issogne in chapter three reinforces Landucci's stress on the physical investments made in the shop. The counter was an elaborate, long wooden structure that was purpose built for the space. The shelves were carefully arranged and, above all, the packaging of the ingredients was expensive: maiolica, glass and wooden boxes. The late fifteenth-century inventory of the Speziale al Giglio in Florence included an image of the Virgin Mary, over 200 *albarelli* jars of different sizes, 44 syrup jars, 30 ceramic oil flasks and 58 glass flasks for distilled waters. There were 40 boxes of dried herbs, and pills were held in small boxes. At the heart of the shop was the *descho da vendere in botegga*, a counter that was approximately 10 *braccia* long and 2 *braccia* wide, and included cupboards with 15 drawers. To the side were additional cupboards with drawers that held ingredients, recipe books as well as boxes and vials for dispensing goods. Mortars, bronze basins and weights were all on display at the front of the shop while the specialist items needed for the shop's main business of candle-making were kept in the kitchen to the rear.[72]

The inventory taken almost a century later of a *speziale* shop in Venice, the 'Two Towers', which was run by Francesco, shows a similar range of goods.[73] The first item was the requisite image of the Madonna and Child with a lamp hanging beneath it followed by the shop sign itself, *Lo insegna delle 2 torre usade*. The stamp showing the same sign was presumably used to mark products that left the shop such as wax candles guaranteeing both their origin and quality.

156 (*above left*)   Roccavaldina, (Messina), View of pharmacy exterior.

157 (*above right*)   Roccavaldina, (Messina), View of pharmacy interior.

158 (*below left*)   Roccavaldina, Detail of shelving.

159 (*below right*)   Roccavaldina, Detail of maiolica from 1580.

The comparatively high level of investment in the infrastructure was prompted, in part, by the need to prove to both customers and the supervisory authorities, such as the sixteenth-century *Protomedicato* officials who made annual inspections, that these pharmacies had the appropriate effective ingredients. The imperative to provide evidence and information about the apothecary's intellectual credentials led to the creation of some of the first collections of the marvels of natural history. Above the shop of the late sixteenth-century Veronese apothecary, Francesco Calzolari (1521–1600), were three rooms with the dual function of exhibiting rare specimens and of proving the efficacy and purity of the ingredients used in his internationally famous and widely exported theriac, a drug used against snake poison that was made up of more than ninety separate ingredients.[74] The first room had a cabinet containing 'legitimate' theriac and mithridatum ingredients, while the next two chambers had books, manuscripts and distillation equipment, and the final room contained portraits of famous naturalists.[75] In 1584, a catalogue was published which, as Paula Findlen has shown, illustrated, 'the breadth of the pharmacopeia that Calzolari had amassed, [it] was an advertisement for his trade' (Figure 160).[76]

With its specialist containers, labels, drawers and equipment, the apothecary's shop and its proto-museums and botanical gardens lay at one end of the spectrum of shop display. There were few other spaces of this type in the Renaissance. Although goldsmiths were similarly concerned with demonstrating the quality of their ingredients, the items that were often on show in their shops were so small that they may not have required special storage areas or containers. For example, the 1528 inventory of the Sienese goldsmith Giovanni Francesco contained at least 131 pieces, all of which were small-scale items available for immediate sale. There was no record of any boxes, bags or containers. It may simply be that the compilers were only interested in listing the jewellery. The inventory suggests a good stock; customers would have been able to purchase gold rings with gems of different values and sizes ranging from the most expensive, a 164-lire ruby ring, to more modest silver buttons, pieces of coral, brass chains (worth 5 lire), silver pendants and tableware such as flasks and vases.[77] The shop also had two chests containing eyeglasses but it is unclear whether these were for sale or for the artisan's personal use. Giovanni Francesco also owned a great deal of broken fragments of gold and silver, undoubtedly destined to be melted down and transformed into new pieces. His working equipment included a set of weights, a box with drawings and models, and a range of hammers, chisels and other tools for working metal and maintaining the small kiln. Illumination was important. The shop had several chandeliers and lamps, presumably for lighting the shop rather than for sale. Finally, the devotional aspects of the day's work would have been aided by a large brass figure of the crucified Christ which was valued at 2 lire and another wooden crucifix worth 10 soldi.

In general a goldsmith's products and tools did not take up much room. In contrast, the shops of second-hand dealers such as that of Antonio de Ludovisi in Bologna reveal a space literally stuffed with goods and textiles. In 1509, the Bolognese dealer's inven-

160 Musaeum Fran. Calceolari iun. Veronensis a Benedicto Ceruto medico incaeptum . . . in quo multa ad naturalem, moarlemque philosophia[m] spectantia, non pauca ad rem medicam pertinentia erudite proponuntur & explicantur; non sine magna rerum exoticarum supellectile, quae artifici plane manu in aes incisae, studiosis exhibentur, Verona, apud Angelaum tamum, MDCXXII. Preliminary half-title leaf, The British Library, London, 462.1.16

tory included 47 different pairs of stockings for his customers to choose from, including those in the livery colours of different families and political factions.[78] It would have taken a brave client to chose *calze Sforzesche* in the year in which Ludovico Maria Sforza had died in a French prison cell, but the others were less controversial. In addition to stockings, his shop had 33 doublets on offer ranging from those suitable for a small boy, *da puto* at 15 soldi, to an elegant black taffeta top costing 5 lire. There was also a small selection of women's clothing including a corset, a *guardacuore* in blue cloth for 5 lire and a torn Flemish dress at 1 lire and 10 soldi. Some of the items such as a pair of detachable sleeves in silver cloth that could have been bought for 3 lire seem remarkable bargains. In addition to the second-hand garments, Antonio de Ludovisi also had a large collection of basic textiles in different colours and qualities that he sold by measure as well as a small number of items that had been left to him as pledges, such as 'a Spanish style *cappa monachina*'. The shop of the Venetian second-hand dealer Antonio Rosatti near San Marco in 1556 seems to have had a more valuable range of specialised goods than his Bolognese counterpart. Venetian second-hand dealers often fitted out entire wardrobes and households, and Rosatti could have provided his clients with anything from a velvet doublet to woollen tunics. Garments that might have been rented out for special occasions such as the 68 carnival masks 'with beards' and 25 'women's masks' were stored in a room in his house rather than kept on display in his shop.[79]

Rosatti presumably stored his carnival costumes at home because the demand for such items was highly seasonal. None of the above inventories makes it clear exactly how this stock was shown to customers. Antonio de Ludovisi's Bolognese inventory mentions 'the shop's display case', (*la mostra de la butegha*), a table, a table for writing with its dresser, a box and another box for money. The list of goods in the 1500 inventory of the Milanese shop of the Porro brothers, dealers in 'cloth of silk, gold and silver', is only somewhat more forthcoming. It reveals a remarkably lavish stock in their Porta Vercellina store. Each bolt was carefully numbered and valued, and included long lengths of gold and silver brocade, Spanish cremesine velvets, damasks, flat and raised velvets in different colours, numerous black velvets and Venetian satins and tabbies.[80] The 1537 inventory of the Venetian silk merchant, Pasquale Niccolo de Bracchis, *a serico posite in Rivoalto*, was similar, containing 26 lengths of approximately 70 *braccia* each of red, purple and black velvets.[81] There were an additional total of 25 bolts of velvet and damasks as well as tabbies and other types, including imported clothes and linings from Spain and the Morea. But despite the value of the stock, the only shop furnishings that were listed were a set of weights and measures.

Numbering bolts and then keeping them well out of reach aided security. But the distance between such goods and potential customers had an additional purpose, forcing contact between shopkeeper and buyer. Clients could not touch or examine goods without asking first. This initial engagement immediately set up an expectation – an obligation to carry on to the next stages, which was to ask for the price, begin bargaining and conclude the sale. Moreover, the relatively small space available for display suggested that the selection was at the discretion of the merchant rather than the customer. He or she might not supply the precise wares on display but pack up a similar item taken from the stockroom. It is also possible that only favoured customers might be shown the higher quality or higher value items stored away behind the counter. The salesman or saleswoman might have to go through some considerable effort to retrieve the items, further reinforcing the need to finalise the purchase in order to justify the imposition.

But while the salesman had control over what was shown, it is important to stress that consumption did not always involve a purchase and that browsing was also possible. In cities that relied on the custom of transient visitors, it was possible to enter a shop or workshop without an invitation or obligation. In Venice, for example, Thomas Coryate noted the range of paintings that he was able to see in a painter's *bottega* near Piazza San Marco:

> For I saw two things in a painter's shop in Saint Marks, which I did not a little admire; the one was the picture of a hinde quarter of veal hanged up in his shop which a stranger would imagine to be natural and the true quarter of veal, but it wasn't . . . The other was the picture of a gentlewoman whose eies were contrived with the singularitie of cunning that they moved up and down of themselves . . . Also I observed another thing in the shop . . . the picture of famous Cassandra . . .'[82]

These are the only pictures that Coryat mentions in his account of Venice, and suggests that workshops could have been as important in forming a painter's reputation as the churches and palaces where his work was displayed. There are other examples casual observation of goods that were being produced for elite consumers and patrons. In 1495, for example, the Sforza courtier noted how he had dropped into the goldsmith Caradosso's workshop to find him working on a jewelled collar with which he hoped to tempt the duke.[83] On 2 June 1531, Marin Sanudo noted that while passing through the street of the jewellers, the *ruga de zoielieri*, he had seen a jeweller with 'a gold ring with a most beautiful clock, on which he was working, which both showed the hours and sounded, which he wanted to send to sell in Constantinople'.[84]

The casual nature of these interchanges generates the conundrum that while window displays were designed to keep shopping out in the street and under the gaze of the authorities, shop interiors offered seclusion and security. Normally, these back rooms were used for storage, preparation of materials or as a retreat for the shopkeepers themselves. In 1590, the bookshop of a Florentine printer had, 'a large shop counter with a little chest under the counter' with a small room off to the side. Here the inventory records a bed, a table, two paintings, two pictures of the virgin, 'attaccate al muro in foglio', a table on which to 'bind books' and a chest full of papers.[85] Some shopkeepers used these areas to keep specialised goods that would have been of interest only to specific clients. When he visited the shop of a French second-hand dealer, referred to simply as 'Francesco ragatherius' in Rome in 1551, the Bolognese naturalist Ulisse Aldrovandi recorded that he went, 'in a room behind . . . the shop where one sees an almost infinite number of beautiful antique statues'.[86] But whatever their immediate purpose interior shop spaces could stand somewhere between the public and the domestic, providing sites for gossip and gambling as well as for commerce. Arithmetical treatises used dice as a method of teaching probability but many different games were played on these sites (Figures 161–2). For example, a fourteenth-century Florentine grocer was accused of holding illegal cardgames in his shop; customers sat on the large drums of *parmigiano* and other cheeses as they placed their bets. Barbershops were also well-known sites for sociability. In 1433, a group of elite men were surprised while gambling at the barber's by the Ponte Vecchio, and the Milanese barbers' statutes emphasised that it was only licit to play draughts (which did not involve gambling) and outlawed other games within the shop.[87] Taking bets on the sex of unborn children was another popular pastime with books being opened in shops; in 1533, Puccio Pucci placed a bet with the apothecary Matteo *speziale* on the number of fetuses that his wife was carrying. He lost when she delivered the five infants that Matteo had predicted. Pucci did not declare whether they or the mother survived, merely that he had to hand over 7 lire to the *speziale*.[88]

The privacy afforded by such places could be a cause for concern for more serious reasons. In 1565, Samuel known as Ventura, a Jew from Perosa, was accused of printing and circulating libellous accusations against another member of the Venetian Jewish community.[89] Among the many witnesses called was Gabriel Mengatti of Gubbio, 'apothecary at the Sign of the Jew'. When asked whether he knew the accused, the apothecary responded that, 'yes, Samuel and the painter, Licinio had come to speak together in his shop'. On one occasion, they had retreated into 'my small room', *una mia cameretta*. In his testimony, the shopkeeper claimed that he had not actually allowed this to happen. Clearly nervous of being implicated, he swore that he had only found

161 (*left*) Filippo Calandri, c. 1490, *Trattato di arit-metica*, Florence, Biblioteca Riccardiana Ricc.2669, c.105v, 'Gambling with Dice'.

162 (*above*) 'Gambling with Dice', Muscarello, *A Treatise on Practical Arithmetic* (Nola, c.1478), Sotheby's Sale, 23 June 1992, Lot, 73, f. 78v, The Conway Library, Courtauld Institute of Art, London.

them there on his return from the Rialto. When he asked them what they were doing, he had been told that Samuel was hiding from his accuser and had begged to be allowed to stay.[90] The apothecary was obviously emphasising his lack of participation in the conversation in order to avoid accusations of aiding a criminal. But the use of such interior spaces for potentially conspiratorial purposes was so common that in the late sixteenth century, the Venetian government often stationed its spies outside major apothecary shops as a means of identifying slanderers or those speaking against the state.[91]

CONCLUSION

It is often assumed that the shift from the open market to the comfort of the shop interior is a key aspect of the transition between the late medieval and the early modern, a shift that would have taken much of the theatricality out of the streets and replaced it with much greater solemnity, safety and intimacy. But as discussed, the two arenas were not necessarily antagonistic. Shopkeepers were also vendors in the marketplace; peddlers often acted as agents for shopkeepers, becoming reliable visitors whose return could be anticipated. One form of marketing did not replace the other. Instead, each was seen as having different aspects, both positive and negative. The open market allowed visibility, comparison, price controls and guarantees of quality as well as a common agreement on value. The potentially more private negotiations that took place within the *bottega* allowed a better sense of decorum for those who could not be easily seen in the public market, reassurance that the vendor could be found again, and the chance to establish long-term credit relations.

The contrasts may have been outweighed by their inter-connections. They were the normative, routine sites that provided the backdrop against which the alternatives of transient excitements such as fairs took place. The latter may have been equally predictable and common, but they relied on being seen as different from the everyday. The next section, therefore, shifts from a framework designed primarily to reinforce security to those, such as fairs, auctions and lotteries, which increasingly sought to add notions of excitement, risk and opportunity.

Part Three

ACQUISITION AND EXCITEMENT

CHAPTER SIX

Fairs

Between the two extremes of the daily marketplace with its chatter, noise and smells and the supposedly dimly lit, silent interior of the mercer's or apothecary's shop lay many other forms of opportunities for buying and selling. Yet although they all had the same basic commercial purpose, some forms were thought more exciting than others. In his early sixteenth-century description of Venice, Marin Sanudo boasted that his city's weekly markets were the equivalent of other towns' annual fairs:

> San Polo is the fifth sestier, called by the name of its church, because here there is the church of San Polo with a very large, wide and beautiful square where every Wednesday morning a market is held full of all the things one could want, which because it happens so often, is not esteemed by our citizens. Nonetheless in any other city and town, if it happened once a year, it would be considered a most rich and beautiful fair. And on Saturday, a market is held in Piazza San Marco which is even more beautiful than this.[1]

In Sanudo's view, it was the very regularity of his city's major shopping moments that rendered them so mundane, a notion that has given rise to the suggestion that Venice was a 'perpetual fair'.[2] Certainly, Sanudo's perceived sense of *ennui* contrasts sharply with the comments of Obadiah da Bertinoro, a Jewish merchant from the Marches, when writing of his excitement as the twice yearly fair of Recanati approached:

> In the midst of my sorrows, I am consoled by the thought that the time of abundance and the remission of debts is upon us – the Recanati fair, where the redemption of the earth will be proclaimed . . . and we shall be able to select good-quality goods.[3]

The association of a fair with a time of redemption may seem an exaggeration but it forcibly conveys the anticipation that such moments could generate. As Sanudo suggests, fairs were supposed to be special events, times outside the banality of the everyday, a moment when a much wider and more diverse range of goods was suddenly available. At their best, fairs brought together buyers and sellers from far away for purchases of rare and specialist goods. This seems to have been an idea that was widely understood and San Bernardino tried to urge his listeners to compete with each other for proper confessions just as they did when they went to the fair:

> Many people go to the fair, buying merchandise in competition with one another. And so do you during Lent, seeing one another go to confess, so much more willingly you do good, competing all the more.[4]

In his turn, Leonardo da Vinci was able to use the image of the fair as a metaphor for the poet who:

> may be compared to those merchants at fairs who stock varied items made by different manufacturers. The poet does this when he borrows from other sciences, such as those of the orator, philosopher, cosmographer and suchlike, whose sciences are completely separate from that of the poet. Thus the poet becomes a broker, who gathers various persons together to conclude a deal.[5]

On a less elevated level, Pietro Aretino's prostitute heroine, Nanna, could similarly describe herself as worthy of Italy's most famous fairs, 'I would not disgrace Lanciano, Recanati and as many fairs as there are in the world'.[6]

Although San Bernardino, Leonardo and Aretino were using analogies that would have been familiar to their contemporaries, surprisingly little is known about Italian fairs. Indeed in comparison with France and the circuit of fairs in twelfth and thirteenth-century Champagne, Italy played a very minor role in the international system of credit and distribution of goods north and south of the Alps. While Italian merchants were major players abroad, relatively few important events were held on the peninsula itself. The international story is one of places such as Frankfurt with its fifteenth-century book fair or Lyons with its major centres of exchange for silk, wool, books and prints. But even if they were only a minor element of the European-wide system, the Italian fairs did have crucial social and economic functions in the peninsula's internal distribution network.[7] Large consignments arriving at the ports of Venice or Genoa were broken down into smaller parcels which merchants could then distribute either by sea or by land using the fair system.[8] Purchases made at major fairs could then be sold further inland, allowing even rare goods to arrive in the peninsula's hinterlands. Such arrangements enabled merchants to avoid creating a glut on their local market and enhanced the range of their potential clientele. For example, the Florentine, Benvenuto di Francesco Nuti, who worked in partnership with the silk firm of Andrea Bianchi, specialised in selling ribbons, belts, ecclesiastical vestments and altarcloths at the fairs in the Abruzzi and in the Marche such as Castel di Sangro, Lanciano, Sulmona and Recanati, using the profits to purchase the raw silk that he sent back to

Florence.[9] Fairs were also important in moving goods inland to less accessible areas. Buyers at the fair of Recanati on the Adriatic coastline, such as the representative for the hospital of the inland town of Macerata, would purchase spices and drugs from Venetian merchants.[10] The hospital pharmacy, in turn, would sell these goods on to its customers further inland, making a visit to Venice itself unnecessary. For example, the painter Lorenzo Lotto noted that he had purchased pigments from 'Maestro Durante pictor da Caldarola'. Maestro Durante had bought the colours from the apothecary messer Quintiliano dal Monte de L'Olmo in Ancona, who had earlier obtained them from the fairs of Recanati and Ancona.[11] As Lotto was based in the same area, he obviously found it easier to rely on these professionals rather than attend the fairs himself.

Traditionally, fairs were supposed to be special events, moments that were worth the wait. But the annual or bi-annual fairs were not sales as the shopper understands them today, with cut-price bargains.[12] Although they did offer potential savings, their attractions lay elsewhere: in credit arrangements, potential tax concessions and most importantly in waivers on bans against foreigners and foreign goods.[13] Only during fair periods could those from outside the community sell goods without joining the appropriate local guild. The licence to hold the fair of Senigallia in the Marche issued by Pope Leo x in 1519 sums up the most common of these privileges:

> That according to the custom of the city, on the day of Saint Francis, for the entire month of October, the city of Senigallia is permitted to celebrate a fair, safely and securely, to which all type of merchandise can be brought in and removed, without any tax, and every man can come and stay freely and securely whatever debt or crime he may have committed, apart from homicide or rebellion against our Lordship and the Holy Roman church.[14]

Given their unique nature, fairs were only supposed to last nine days but, as the licence described above suggests, they usually lasted much longer, between fifteen and thirty days and occurred with regularity in almost every region across Italy, with a particular concentration in the summer and autumn months. A fair might have a link to a site of pilgrimage and overlap with a saint's respective festival. This combination of attractions swelled numbers, increasing custom and providing a spiritual backdrop to commercial transactions. Thus Recanati built on the reputation of the church of the Madonna of Loreto; the Florentine fair of Impruneta on its miracle-working image; the Umbrian fair of Senigallia on its relics of Mary Magdalene.[15] That these connections were not negligible is indicated by the fact that the town of Aquila shifted the dates of its annual saffron market to re-dedicate it to San Bernardino of Siena after the town's sudden acquisition of his body in the mid-fifteenth century.[16]

But while fairs might take advantage of pilgrims, they were not dependent on them. Although pictorial images of fairs such as those of the Bassano brothers or Jacques Challot from the late sixteenth and early seventeenth centuries suggested that they were spread across country fields in a random fashion, Italian fairs were not informal events (Figures 163–7). In Challot's print, the snake-handlers and charlatans mixed with vendors of fine wares. They were scattered amid those administering public punishment of criminals in an organic, unstructured series of events. But if the artists wanted to render these fairs as accessible, rural affairs open to all comers, this was not how they were perceived by urban authorities. Fairs such as Impruneta were instituted and managed by civic and ecclesiastic authorities for very precise economic and political purposes and remained highly controlled. Fairs gave localities a status that was highly desirable in its own right. Thus, in 1432, Filippo Maria Visconti awarded the small Lombard town of Chiavenna a concession to hold a fair as recognition for its fidelity during the war with Venice.[17] Likewise when Francesco Sforza wished to reward his loyal secretary Cicco Simonetta, he made him lord of the village of Sartirana and allowed him to organise a weekly market and fair in order to increase the revenue from his holdings.[18]

Sforza's concession made sense because fairs were perceived as a catalyst for economic regeneration. In 1426, when, following years of warfare, Reggio Calabria was reduced from a population of 1,300 hearths to one of merely 200, Alfonso of Aragon accepted

163   Francesco Bassano il Giovane, *The Great Market*, c. 1582, oil on canvas, Galleria Sabauda, Turin.

164 Leandro Bassano, *Market scene*, oil on canvas, Galleria Sabauda, Turin.

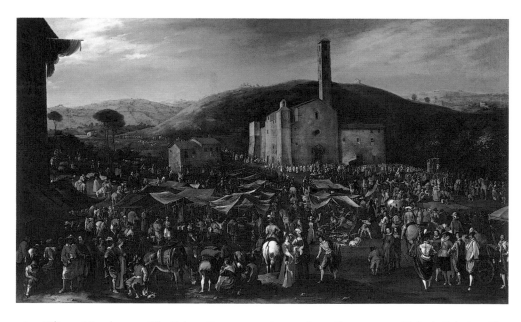

165 Filippo Napoletano, *The Fair at Impruneta*, 1600–c.1640, oil on canvas, Galleria Palatina, Florence.

166 Jacques Callot, *The Fair at Impruneta*, 1620, etching, National Gallery of Art, Washington, D.C., R.L. Baufeld Collection, 1969.15.60.

the town's petition and allowed them to hold a new fair on the feast of San Marco.[19] In 1434, Gian Francesco Gonzaga was similarly advised to institute one or even several fairs a year as a means of stimulating trade in Mantua.[20] As local merchants pointed out, the Gonzaga would not lose revenue. These fairs were not entirely tax-free: they merely allowed special arrangements for those goods that hadn't been sold. Sellers (and sometimes buyers) would not be taxed on exports. The merchants who made these suggestions stressed that the increased volume of trade would more than make up for any loss on transit taxes.

But if the examples above suggest that new fairs were started as local initiatives, promoters were aware that they would only succeed if they were part of a larger regional network. Fairs required considerable trust, and the recurrent nature of interconnected events allowed for flexible credit arrangements. For example, two merchants from southern Italy buying four pieces of cloth from a Brescian merchant promised to pay their debt on demand the following August in any one of sixteen fairs located between Lanciano in the south and Recanati and Venice in the north.[21] They expected to see each other at these events, meaning that while the location changed, the players often remained familiar.

167 Detail of Figure 166.

Sellers worked their way from fair to fair, choosing their targets carefully. In Pegolotti's early fourteenth-century *Pratica della mercatura*, he noted how, 'the fairs of Apulia begin in this order', advising his readers which he thought were worth attending. For example, he recommended the fairs of Ascoli and Taranto but warned against those of Manfredonia and Foggia.[22] It was key, therefore, to insert any new event within the existing structures. In 1585, the city of Aquila tried to get taxation privileges for its fair from the royal court in Spain arguing that:

> In the papal states there are many fairs, such as there are in the city of Foligno, which is held in the month of April about sixty miles from Aquila, the fair of Farfa, fifty miles from Aquila and which takes place in September, like that of Recanati, which is held in November and is about one hundred miles away and that of Terni, fifty miles away and which takes place in January. All the merchants who are going with their merchandise to buy and to sell in these fairs could come, with great ease to the fair of Aquila in May and August and from Aquila go on to Lanciano.[23]

The citizens of Lanciano begged to differ and immediately petitioned the court to stop Aquila's new status from undermining the special nature of their event:

> the multiplicity of fairs is damaging to merchants and destroys the fairs first, and the fewer fairs which take place, and the more distance there is between them, the greater the traffic and profit. Because the fairs of Foligno and Farfa bring great damage to the fairs of Lanciano, it is important that they should take place at different times and at a great distance the one from the other . . . and because of the prolongation of all these fairs often one damages the other as the fair of Lanciano damages that of Salerno.[24]

Yet competition was not always problematic for many fairs were quite specialised. Some, like the saffron fair in Aquila or the horse fairs in Bellinzona in the north, dealt only in a single commodity and usually involved auctions among a small community of buyers and sellers.[25] Others offered a much wider range of goods and services and were open to the general public. In Salerno, for example, tumblers, musicians and gamblers vied for customers among the booths selling needles, pins, rope and haberdashery, spices, medicines and velvets.[26] The bi-annual fair of Recanati in the Marche that had inspired such enthusiasm from Obadiah was a crucial centre for the distribution of spices and medical supplies. Lanciano, described by Pope Leo x in the sixteenth century as, 'the emporium of the entire kingdom', sold the widest possible range of goods: books, glassware, slaves, pottery, textiles and metalware of all types.[27]

These were all, however, primarily wholesale events. For example, over a seven day period during the fair at Salerno, a Neapolitan notary, Ser Petruccio Pisano, recorded 102 transactions.[28] These included the sale to a German merchant by two Frenchmen resident in Naples of 5,000 hair combs. They also sold 25 dozen scissors and 50,000 pins to a Genoese merchant living in Cosenza.[29] Not all the merchandise sold was of low value. At the same event the Florentine Battista Pandolfini sold another Genoese merchant from Cosenza 12 pieces of fine silk for 700 ducats.[30]

The twice-yearly fairs of Lanciano referred to above were key moments in the movement of goods from wholesale to retail distribution, so much so that Venetian merchants often kept warehouses in town in order to supply their booths with ease, ensuring that Venetian products and imports made their way across Italy and into the rest of Europe. In 1545, for example, Matteo Gallian di Capua, 'glassmaker', bought four cases of crystal from the Venetian Giacomo di Battaglia da Venezia, promising to repay him next August in either Lanciano or in Venice itself.[31] Matteo repeated his order annually over the next two years.[32] Clearly the orders were not transactions between total strangers. Nonetheless, the idea of the fair as a meeting of alien peoples who put aside difference to exchange goods remained a very powerful concept. The Hiermonymite friar, Cornelio Guasconi, praised the much smaller fair of the Assumption in his local town of Cesena in the Marche in 1525 by deliberately stressing the interactions of nations and religions that were usually opposed to one another:

> The day then of the Holy Assumption
> Which comes in August, a great fair is held.
> Fifteen days of great consolation.
> Always there are merchants arriving from every port
> Considerable cash can be seen, and many people.
> Greeks, Turks and Christians of every type.[33]

But despite the boast, studies of both the fairs of Cesena and Lanciano have shown that they were essentially regional events, with few Muslim or Orthodox traders in sight. Similarly other supposedly 'international' fairs were mainly composed of local traders. For example, of the nineteen merchants who took communal stands at the fair of Senigallia in 1580, all came from the duchy of Urbino. Of the seventy-three names listed seventeen years later, those whose origins were identified were again from the immediate locality. Those who came from furthest afield arrived from Venice, Ferrara and Ravenna.[34] In southern Italy the picture was very similar. Even Lanciano rarely hosted merchants who had travelled great distances. Studies of notarial contracts executed at other fairs have shown equivalent results. For example, of the 286 merchants documented in the notarial records of a week's activity at the fair of Salerno in 1478, the vast majority, 211, were from the local area.[35] An examination of contracts made during the fair of the town of Como in northern Italy in 1436 reveals that again around 84 per cent of deals were arranged between vendors and purchasers from the town and its immediate locality. Of the non-Comasque, the major group were the nearby Milanese while many of the seemingly foreign merchants referred to as *alamanni*, or Germans, were actually resident in Lombardy.[36]

But if the people were from the local region, the goods were not, and the arrival of both strangers and strange things brought anxiety as well as opportunities. Disease was one of the major fears and outbreaks of plague would prompt the cancellation of fairs and markets. In 1463, for example, King Ferrante of Naples ordered the suspension of all fairs in his kingdom whenever there was a danger of contagion from merchants arriving from the East.[37] In 1468, the citizens of Trani complained that the archbishop's representative often refused to allow the city to suspend its fair in times of plague, 'threatening protests and excommunication because of the great utility which it brought to the Archbishop himself'.[38] During the plague of 1576, all markets in the district of Milan were suspended, 'considering . . . the grave danger that occurs in permitting markets where a large number of people congregate which could easily bring serious danger to the public as there is suspicion of plague in many of the surrounding areas'.[39]

The metaphor of the spread of disease could be used to define the need to quarantine dangerous ideas and products as well as illnesses. A late sixteenth-century letter from an anxious archbishop to the citizens of Lanciano in southern Italy exemplifies how problematic the ease of distribution proved for ecclesiastical authorities during the Counter-Reformation period:

> I ask that you give every assistance to my vicar, who is acting in my name, in order to ensure that, if necessary he can take the appropriate steps to make sure that the purity of your city is not infected. I do not say this because I fear anyone from your town itself, but because I know that during fairs, a great multitude arrive, amongst whom the devil himself may have a few of his ministers. I will particularly give orders that the said vicar should look over all the books which are being brought to the fair, and that he confiscate all those which are prohibited, so that they are not sold, nor spread through the Regno.[40]

As such orders indicate, fairs needed as much oversight as any other type of market. The 1374 statutes of the small Tuscan village of Borgo San Lorenzo di Mugello suggest the discipline involved in organising what was essentially a minor local event. Because it was held on the Feast of Saint John the Baptist, a day celebrated with competing fairs by other Tuscan towns, the town council was particularly anxious to ensure attendance:

> How and when the fair at Borgo San Lorenzo should be held:
> The fair at Borgo is always held on the day of Saint John the Baptist . . . it should be run by the podestà or the notary of the said league together with the *gonfaloniere* and with the consuls of the commune of Borgo. It should be announced that same month, fifteen days before the feast and fair, and at all the markets of the Mugello and at Prato, Empoli, Feghine, Firenzuola, Marradi and Palazuolo, according to the oath that they have sworn that it should be enough as it will only last for the day of the said feast, and one day before and one day after. And the said feast should be held at the expense of the commune of Borgo . . . and no one who comes to the fair should be confined or troubled, in either person or property, during the said days of the fair and no artisan from the league of Borgo can go to any other market or fair on the day of the feast of the said fair, on a pain of one hundred soldi against those who do go. And every artisan accustomed to go to market at the appropriate time, that is when the day-bell sounds, must go on the morning of the said festival and stay in the market of Borgo with their merchandise.[41]

The citizens of Borgo San Lorenzo were clearly concerned that the appointed officials, such as the podestà, might not pay for the trumpeters required to circle the considerable distances of the Tuscan countryside announcing the fair. The presence of the citizens of other towns was a sign of political allegiance. Anyone who profited from the weekly market could not slip away to sell their goods at other fairs which might overlap with that of Borgo San Lorenzo. Similar regulations can be found elsewhere. In the small town of Penne in southern Italy, for example, all those who owned shops facing onto the main square were forced to shut them and take a stall at the fair.[42] On occasion, the city might enforce the closure of all its shops and force the removal of shopkeepers to the fairground, as in the case of San Severo in southern Italy.[43]

Thus fairs, like regular markets, were not the result of individual entrepreneurship but of careful urban control. Major events required long-term planning and organisation. The roads into town needed to be secure enough to reassure those travelling with valuable goods that they would not be easy prey, and major fairs sent out armed troops to guard passes and trade-routes in order to provide a safe passage for their visitors.[44] If substantial numbers were expected, arrangements for housing, food supplies and security had to be put into place. Fairs were not, therefore, spontaneous carnivalesque events, as suggested by the representations of the Bassano brothers or of Jacques Callot, but carefully managed annual routines. Subject to their own parallel legislation, they mirrored the forms of surveillance that the city effected on a daily basis. Even in the smaller events, a designated master or captain of the fair was usually elected on a rotating basis to provide supervision. In Puglia, for example, the nomination was made either by the archbishop, the chapter of the cathedral or the king. Elsewhere in southern Italy the city magistrates elected these officials; barons might also hold rights of appointment to important positions in the fair. In most areas, the candidate had to be a local. A salary was often attached to the job along with considerable responsibility for the careful and secure functioning of the event. The fair's overseers kept records of all transactions, settled disputes and, as in the case of the sixteenth-century Perugian Fiera dei Morti, even published the prices at which goods could be sold.[45]

As it grew in importance during the sixteenth century, the Umbrian fair of Senigallia developed an elaborate bureaucracy with a special magistracy, one that eventually superseded that of the ordinary municipality. A captain of the fair, drawn by lot from the noblemen sitting on the city council, maintained order and intervened in commercial disputes.[46] In Trani in southern Italy, the archbishop appointed a master of the market while in Lanciano, where the investiture of the masters of the fair was a major performance, the officials were chosen by the guilds themselves.[47] Like podestà or judges, they were supposed to be impartial figures selected from outside the community. The Thursday before the opening of the twice-yearly event, once in May and again in August, the committee members responsible for supervising the fair were sworn into office accompanied by representatives of the subject guilds, 'in decent trappings, with barded horses'. The official opening occurred when the masters took possession of the tribunal from which they would ensure that justice was done.[48]

The location of fairs further indicated their status as somewhere between the permanent and the temporary. In Salerno and Perugia, for example, fairs were spread throughout the city, with temporary booths nestled in church squares, on the streets, and in the fields outside the city. The arrangements often mimicked the hierarchies that were more difficult to impose within the city's permanent structures. Thus by Salerno's Porta Nova on the urban edge there were sites for gymnasts and jugglers and spaces to play games of chance; next to these were temporary booths selling pins, needles, thimbles and other types of dry goods along with taverns and wine stores. By the more elegant site of the church of Saint Peter, there were stalls for the druggists, spice-sellers, goldsmiths and jewellers. Along the beach and by the port, fresh and salted meat and fish products were sold while on the plain of San Lorenzo outside the town the large-scale merchandising of valuable cloths, particularly velvets, took place.[49]

Major fairs such as those of Recanati and Lanciano quickly outgrew the cities to which they were attached. They were distinguished by the construction of ephemeral architecture outside the city walls with temporary shops, stalls and stands that stood in parallel next to the urban community that supported the fair. Thus Senigallia's fair was just outside the city walls near the artificial canal and port through which its products arrived and left and was only included within the town once new city walls were erected by Duke Guidobaldo II della Rovere in 1546.

But even when a fair stood outside the city walls, it still needed the full range of urban facilities. Although constructed as temporary accommodation, the imitation of permanent places such as loggias, taverns and shops gave the combined illusion of stability with the attraction of a special moment. A plethora of stalls and other forms of shopping spaces might be thrown up in wood and canvas in the hopes of profiting from rentals. In Senigallia, for example, the town council and private entrepreneurs arranged for the construction of the wooden stalls which were rented out to merchants attending the fair. In 1563, a declaration was passed that 'the merchants of the city cannot rent out their *botteghe* until the community has managed to rent out its own shops'.[50] The Church was as eager to benefit from its control over space as were the civic authorities. For example, the tiny village of Quercia outside Rome was dwarfed by the structures built by the Dominicans who ran the town's bi-annual fair. In Gonzaga, the stalls designed to house the food-sellers who supplied provisions to pilgrims coming to Santa Maria delle Grazie soon became permanent fixtures, again providing an income to the Church itself.[51] The canons of the cathedral of Bari rented out stalls and stands to merchants as did the Archbishop of Salerno.[52] The documentation for the investment in temporary stalls required for the fair of the small Umbrian town of Senise in 1488 illustrates some of the organisation, expense and types of buildings required in setting up a mid-sized fair:

For the forty-one stalls built to be rented at one ducat per stall to the merchants . . . 41 ducats.
For the thirty stalls covered with tents to be rented at 5 carlini each to the merchants . . . 15.2.10 ducats.

For the seven stalls covered with wood which are smaller than those above to be rented out at one and a half and one tarì to the mercers in the fair . . . 2 ducats.

For the forty taverns made for the fair, to be rented at one tarì each as is usual . . . 8 ducats.[53]

The fairs discussed above were major events with a distinctive wholesale purpose. In addition, cities celebrated important feast days by encouraging or enforcing the use of fairs within their town walls that were designed to appeal to a wider buying public. Florence, for example, held its annual fair on the Via dei Servi while Milan celebrated the Feast of Saint Ambrose in the central area of the Broletto. The most impressive urban fair in Italy, one that attracted elite visitors over at least three centuries, was intimately associated with the feast day of the Ascension in Venice, known as *La Sensa*. The fifteen-day event was part of the wider celebration of the marriage of the city's Doge with the sea, a maritime fertility ritual which had formed a part of Venetian self-promotion since the thirteenth century.[54] The Doge boarded a gilded boat, the *Bucintoro*, from which he tossed a ring into the waters (Figure 168). The nuptial theme was extended in a number of important ways during the days preceding and following the festival. For example, only women were shown the relics in the Treasury of San Marco on the eve of the Ascension Day ceremony itself. As importantly, the feast was marked by a fifteen-day trade fair in Piazza San Marco, one very much associated with the purchase of goods for nuptial trousseaux. Vecellio's printed image of *La sposa in Sensa* stresses the lavishness with which brides were expected to dress during this period (Figure 170). Another print shows, 'Peasant women from the surrounding countryside in Venice, who can be seen in Venice on the day of the Ascension of our Lord, the feast of the Fair of Venice' (Figure 169). This was indeed a period where women, particularly those from the lower social groups, were expected and indeed encouraged to purchase goods. Thus masters often gave cash advances to their servants at this time; for example, Agostino Spinelli gave Gironima da Gorizia four lire *per spender andar in Sensa*; in her will dated 1508, Catarina da Scutari, a servant of Giacomo Morosini, asked that a dress 'bought at this Ascension' be given to a poor woman of her choosing.[55]

During this two-week period, Venetian shopkeepers were required to shut their doors and take stalls in the square, an obligation which was not always welcome. Like the more permanent sites on Piazza San Marco, the right to sell

168 Caneletto, *Ascension Day Festival at Venice*, 1766, pen and brown ink with grey wash, heightened with white, over graphite on laid paper, National Gallery of Art, Washington, D.C., Samuel H. Kress Collection 1963.15.5.

169 (*above left*)   Cesare Vecellio, *De gli habiti antichi, et moderni et diverse parti del mondo libri due*, Venice, 1590, 'Contadine di terre circonvicine', Wellcome Library, London.

170 (*above right*)   Cesare Vecellio, *De gli habiti antichi, et moderni et diverse parti del mondo libri due*, Venice, 1590, 'Spose nel tempo della Ascensione, o Sensa in Venetia', Wellcome Library, London.

from a Sensa stall was assigned by lotteries held by the guilds. But if the lotteries started as a means of selecting from those anxious to participate, by the sixteenth century the process had become a format for forcing unwilling members to take up places. In 1585, the mercers' guild noted that of the thirty members who were supposed to sell wares during the fair, only nine had come forward voluntarily. This unwillingness to participate threatened 'the honour and ornament of the city' and the guild's official, the Gastaldo, ordered that 60 names be placed in a bag. The 21 that were drawn would have to commit themselves to two weeks on the Piazza on pain of a fine.[56] Mercers such as Francesco 'da Tre Anzoli' who sub-let their stalls were similarly punished.[57]

The mercers seem to have been unhappy about leaving their permanent shops in order to take up temporary residence in the often poorly constructed wooden shelters that were erected in rows in Piazza San Marco. But the relationship between the stall and the shop was not always oppositional. The construction of the *Sensa* site was supervised by the guilds themselves. Although the image may have been deliberately simplified to stress the innovative nature of the new oval-shaped, gas-lit construction of the late eighteenth century, the booths must have resembled those still depicted in the *Old Fair of the Sensa* by Gabriel Bella in the eighteenth century (Figures 172–3). They were available in different sizes and were meant to mimic rather than replace shops, with shelving to the rear and locks for security. For example, in 1593, the mercer's guild employed messer Bruno delle Tre Pigne to build 'shops for their mercers, both big and small . . . that will be completely furnished with shelves, locks, shutters, keys and other things . . .'[58] The roofs were to be completely leak-proof. The difficulties of providing high-quality temporary accommodation, however, are emphasised in the list of repairs that were already needed when the fair was at its height in late May. Many of the fifteen booths occupied by the mercers were missing shelving or the benches were broken. One didn't have seating, others lacked locks, shelves or shutters.[59] The effect could hardly have been impressive.

But despite this, the language of ornament and honour was consistently used when debating who should participate in the *Sensa* fair. The fact that the alabaster- and perfume-sellers had 'most beautiful *botteghe* that are a great ornament to the square' was used to argue for their presence on the Piazza in 1544.[60] An undated 'note of the professions and arts which must be present in *Sensa*' probably from the late sixteenth or early seventeenth centuries lists goldsmiths, mercers, perfumers, the sellers of combs and paternoster beads, needles, swords and knives, coppersmiths, tinsmiths, carpenters, glassmakers, mirror-makers and shoemakers, groups who were also listed in a drawing showing the position of their booths in Piazza San Marco (Figure 171).[61] Vendors of religious images of the Virgin who were not painters themselves were permitted to sell their wares, while non-Venetian artists also took advantage of the lifted restrictions to send their pictures to market.[62] For example, when Lorenzo Lotto was working in the Marche, he arranged for the sale of his paintings during the Ascension Day fair as did artists such as Tintoretto later in the century. Although there are few records of the precise types

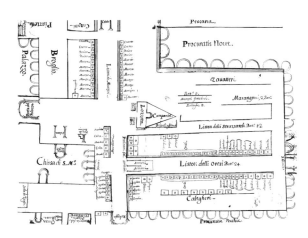

171   *The Arrangements of Stalls at the Sensa Fair*, Venice, Archivio di Satato, Procuratori di San Marco di Supra, Chiesa, B.53 and ASV, Miscellanea Mappe 1396.

172   Gabriel Bella, *The Old Fair of the Sensa in Venice*, 1779–92, oil on canvas, Fondazione Querini Stampalia, Venice.

173   Gabriel Bella, *The New Fair of the Sensa in Venice*, 1779–92, oil on canvas, Fondazione Querini Stampalia, Venice.

of images that were on sale, Michael Bury has noted that in a case brought by Donna Cecilia before the Venetian inquisition in 1585, she accused a Perugian captain of having bought obscene pictures, 'in Piazza San Marco, la festa della Sensa'.[63] The late fifteenth-century account book of the Venetian bookseller, Francesco de Madi, indicates that he too sold a distinctly different type of product from his stall in Piazza San Marco than he did from his permanent shop. Whereas the latter carried a large stock of expensive, but slow-selling items, the fair required cheaper items and images which permitted a high turnover with low margins.[64]

Yet not all the items were aimed at those of lower economic status. The spectacle appealed to buyers at all levels and while there were opportunities to purchase inexpensive, portable items on impulse, there were also more valuable items for sale. Silk, whose use was regulated by sumptuary law in Venice, was excluded from the fair but other specialities were put on display. The glass manufacturers in particular used this annual event to encourage purchases of new fashions and styles (Figures 174–6). In 1510, the crystal glassmakers of Murano issued the following edict designed to prevent anyone else from showing the highest quality, pure glass for which they were famous at the Sensa fair. Only the makers from Murano were permitted to take stalls during this period:

> No glass shop or stall should sell crystal glass either at the time of the *Sensa* or in other periods of the year here on the Piazza di San Marco, at Rialto, or in other places or markets . . . The crystal glassmakers of Murano can sell freely in the city of Venice, and where they wish according to our statutes which affirm that our predecessors prohibited the sale of the said crystal glass in this city by anyone apart from the glassmakers of Murano at the time of the Ascenscion day festival . . . And neither in the period of the *Sensa* nor in any other period, can they make a pact with the owners or workers of the shops of Murano to set up a shop or stall of any sort in the Piazza San Marco or Rialto or any other place in Venice what so ever. And similarly, those of Murano may not sell nor have sold crystal glass in this city except in the period of the *Sensa*.[65]

Sophisticated customers recognised that new styles would be available at this time of year and arranged to make their purchases either during the fair or after it had taken place. On 2 May 1529, for example, Isabella d'Este wrote to Jacopo Malatesta in Venice:

> Being persuaded that some beautiful new vases will be in the shops of the glassmakers this Ascension tide, be content to find up to ten or twelve drinking vessels that are different in style, cups and glasses that have thin white filaments without gold. And we desire that in buying them you should take Alfonso Facino (the Marchioness's carver) as your companion as he is in Venice, so that the two of you together, by advising each other, could be more diligent in satisfying our intentions.[66]

At the end of the century, Tomaso Garzoni similarly noted the extravagant glass he had seen during the fair:

174 (*top left*) Goblets, c.1500, glass, Venice (Murano), The British Museum, London.

175 (*top right*) A jug and footed bowl, c.1500, 'chalcedony' glass, Venice (Murano), The British Museum, London.

176 (*above*) Pitchers and goblets, c.1550, Venice (Murano), The British Museum.

And today this art is at its height in Murano. There is nothing imaginable in the world that is not made into glass or crystal, there have even been castles with towers, bastions, cannons and walls as we saw once during the *Ascensa* in Venice.[67]

As Garzoni suggests, he could see this extraordinary glasswork without having to buy it. The *Sensa* fair was as much about viewing, touching, tasting and hearing as it was about making a profit, and complaints about limited spending were common. In 1518, the Venetian diarist Marin Sanudo noted that, 'In the *Sensa* fair there were many foreigners, but they spent little money.'[68] Ludovico Ariosto's caricature of the indecisive buyer at the Ascension Day fair in Venice provides another view of the chance to examine elite items without being intimidated:

> As one who is slow to part with his money
> Nor takes pleasure in any purchase
> Circles the *Sensa* three times or more
> And goes about looking at all sides and stays silent
> He finally stops where one finds an immense abundance
> of all the goods that one could need
> And he wants this or that or that thing
> he tries a hundred and still cannot decide
> he puts this to one side, and leaves the other
> And that which he has discarded he picks up again.[69]

It was not only fabrics, prints and glassware that were on view; the customers and visitors themselves were under observation. Beatrice d'Este finished her description of her visit to San Marco in 1493 by describing the dazzling sights of the Ascension Day fair. She was in Venice, supposedly on a private trip, but in reality her presence was part of a plan to reconcile the Republic with her husband's increasing ambition to control the Milanese state. She wrote home daily, deliberately describing her outings in terms designed to reassure:

> this morning my illustrious mother, Don Alfonso, Madonna Anna and I, with all our company, set out for San Marco, where the Doge had invited both us and our singers to assist at mass and see the Treasury. But before reaching San Marco, we landed at the Rialto and went on foot up those streets which are called the Merceria, where we saw the shops of spices and silks and other merchandise, all in good order and in great quality and quantity of the most diverse goods. And of other crafts there was also an excellent display, so much so that we often lingered to look now at one thing, now at another and nothing displeased us all the way to San Marco . . . After mass we were taken by the Doge to see the Treasury . . . we saw everything piece by piece, which was a great pleasure, for there was an infinite quantity of most beautiful jewels and some magnificent cups and chalices. When we came out of the Treasury, we went on the Piazza of San Marco, among the shops of the Ascension tide fair which is still going on, and found such a magnificent show of beautiful glass, that we were fairly bewildered and were obliged to remain there for a long time . . .'[70]

Beatrice finished the letter by describing the dress and jewellery she had worn that day, an embroidered red gown and rubies that had attracted such attention that viewers had practically put their eyes up against her chest to see them better. However rhetorical, the overall description suggests a very contrived form of viewing. The Venetian government traditionally organised a visit to the merceria for its visitors, asking shopkeepers to lay out their best pieces for a spectacular showing. But while Beatrice looked, she did not shop. She admired the things that were for sale, but she was not seen to either make a selection or to bargain. In San Marco, she was shown the valuables in the church treasury, items that were not supposed to be regarded as commodities, before being led out into the square where yet more of Venice's high-quality goods, the glassware of Murano, could be seen in the *Sensa* stalls. At the same time, however, the young woman was aware of constantly being under scrutiny herself. Just as she was looking at the wealth of the Venetian state, her headdress and indeed her breast were being examined for signs of her wealth and the standing of the Milanese state. But at the same time as being examined by the crowd, she revealed neither her wants nor her needs. Just as the Venetian state used its wares to emphasise its ability to stimulate desire for its wealth and exotic objects from viewers, so too elite visitors could demonstrate their ability to control their desires.

CONCLUSION

The care with which Beatrice's valuables were assessed was a common part of Renaissance correspondence in which writers often mention what they thought the owner must have spent on his or her clothing and jewellery. What was unusual about this event was the highly public nature of the excursion. In attending the Ascension Day fair, Beatrice inevitably mingled with the wider social groups of Venetian society, both viewing and being viewed. This meant that information about her wardrobe was disseminated and discussed by a larger number of people than one would normally expect. But fairs were not the only periodic opportunities for such observations. In turning to auctions and lotteries, further opportunities for acquisition could be found. The crucial aspect of all these events was that they provided a chance to see, and sometimes to touch or taste new goods. They allowed those who might never buy elegant glassware or expensive silks a chance to discuss their price, quality and design. In doing so, they generated a social as well as commercial community that had a shared understanding of how value should be assigned and a shared language for praise and condemnation of Renaissance material culture.

CHAPTER SEVEN

Bidding and Gambling

If fairs were exciting events, they were also predictable. The very continuity of annual meetings generated trust among the regular participants. But fairs were not the only way of acquiring exotic or unusual goods. There were a number of other less predictable and far riskier ways of making acquisitions. Some systems, such as auctions, were expanded forms of traditional civic sales; others, such as lotteries, were suspiciously new and dangerously enticing. What they shared was the fact that, unlike the fairs which thrived on long-term credit, these sales were restricted to cash buyers. Only those who could pay rapidly and in coin could participate. But far from acting as a barrier to participation, this stipulation made such moments more democratic than many other forms of purchasing. In theory, any bidder with money to hand, no matter what their origin or status, could acquire a piece of furniture at auction or buy a lottery ticket. The only risk might be to their reputations.

COUNTING DOWN

Known as *incanti*, auctions had been common across Italy since at least the thirteenth century and probably long pre-date the first available references.[1] Although the term comes from the word 'enchantment' suggesting their potentially mesmerising qualities, they were perceived as the most transparent of all forms of salesmanship and were used to sell almost every type of service or goods. There were, for example, highly specialised wholesale auctions for fish or base metals in Venice and auctions for the rights to manage galleys sailing to the Levant in Venice and to Flanders in Florence; there were also sales for the right to collect taxes, and even, in sites such as Treviso, to provide stationery for town halls (Figure 177).[2] Similarly, auctions were used in Italy as elsewhere in Europe to sell second-hand goods, running the gamut from furniture, mattresses and clothing to books, paintings and sculpture and even, occasionally, slaves (Figure 178).[3]

Using the term 'auction' to translate *incanto* can prove misleading. Although there were some similarities to today's events, the Renaissance versions were undertaken for very different motives. Some were more akin to a system of tendering, ensuring that the best value was achieved for public goods and services. Others were designed to act either as a form of charity or to obtain payments for creditors. Generally, their main purpose was to rapidly release funds from a family's store of material wealth. It was widely held that the public nature of the enterprise was essential to its fairness and success. To ensure a good crowd, these auctions were supposed to take place in a central location. Town trumpeters or criers would be sent into the streets and to nearby villages to announce upcoming sales. For example, in the town of Recanati in the Marche,

177 Gabriel Bella, *The Auction of Galleys in Piazzetta San Marco*, 1779–92, oil on canvas, Fondazione Querini Stampalia, Venice.

178 *Sale by Town Crier*, after a woodcut in Joos de Damhouder, *Praxis Rerum Civilium*, Antwerp, 1557.

announcements were made concerning pawn auctions by the *banditori del commune* (at a cost of two *bolognini* per announcement paid for by the money-lender trying to redeem his pawns).[4]

The auctions themselves were noisy. They involved shouting out bids and accepting the highest price once a set time had passed. In Verona, the sale of rebels' possessions in 1442 was announced by trumpet blasts from the town hall. In Treviso, civic officials wearing red hats, known as *precone*, were responsible for acting both as town criers and as public auctioneers selling off goods in the weekly main market.[5] The distinctive garb was similar to that used by the auctioneers, the *comandadori*, in Venice. They too were professional funtionaries who acted as both the bailiffs who seized the goods of debtors and as the town criers who sold them off (Figure 179).[6]

Given the oral, ephemeral nature of these events, it is often difficult to get a clear sense of how they actually operated. Rules and regulations do survive but they were often circumvented. Inventories and records of completed transactions add to this picture as do the often astonished comments of contemporaries concerning what was being sold. Taken together, they suggest a series of stages to an Italian auction. The most common pattern was a preliminary valuation of the goods in question. For example, in 1500 Marin Sanudo noted that before the valuables of those who owed money to state officials could be sold in Piazza San Marco, they had to be valued by two 'estimators of movable goods'.[7] Once a value had been set, it acted as the basis for the auctioneer's cry. Bidders either shouted out the sum proposed or offered a higher amount. When the time was up, as judged either by the length of a burning candle or by the ringing of an official bell, the successful bidder could take away his or her new possession following full payment. This usually included a small set sum that was paid directly to the auctioneer. In some cases, if the valuation was not achieved, the goods were re-auctioned rather than being undersold. In others, the successful bidder might have to wait for up to eight days to see if someone else would offer a higher price.[8]

Auction records survive in a number of formats. Among the earliest are those of the cathedral of Milan. In 1386, the Fabbrica del Duomo, the magistracy responsible for the cathedral's reconstruction, embarked on a major campaign to raise the cash needed to pay for workers and materials. As they began demolishing the surrounding area and laying the new foundations, they organised theatrical events, sent out petitions, put up offering boxes in workshops and encouraged legacies and donations at the altar. Many of the donors who responded, however, did not, or could not, leave cash. Instead, they offered clothing, jewellery, household items and even livestock.

The new institution needed coins with which to pay its workers, not clothing or chickens. By 1390, the Fabbrica had appointed an official auctioneer to sell off these donated goods. On Sundays, a time when the church would be well attended, this dealer would hold an auction by the church door.[9] These were charitable events, providing opportunities for spiritual salvation as well as bargains. Thus among the first items sold were linen and clothing given by Maddalena Trecchi, goods that were immediately bought back by her husband, Ambrogio, who was himself an official of the cathedral Fabbrica, for 16 lire.[10] When a fur coat was auctioned, five bids were put forward, and it was sold, again to a member of the cathedral Fabbrica, for 44 lire. Even inexpensive items might generate considerable excitement. A nearly new garment with buttons and a gilt fringe in the Venetian style attracted five bids and an eventual price of 6.8 lire.

But while charity was a factor, profit was also involved. By the early fifteenth century, goods were selling quickly for very reasonable prices. A piece of silk, 'on a blue base worked in damascene with white and red silk' was donated on 2 August and was put up for sale a week later when it realised 22 lire.[11] As a comparison, 4 *braccia* of linen sold for 9 soldi on the same day. There were some real opportunities to be had. In 1402, for example, Giovanni Conti paid 25 soldi for a gilt-silver goblet that had been given to Santa Maria Maggiore by the deceased Archbishop of Milan.[12] Conti was also a member of the Fabbrica, and there have to be some suspicions of insider-trading. Nonetheless, the aim was to raise as much money as possible, and the identity of the eventual buyer was not a major consideration. The auctioneers were sensitive to different markets, dividing garments into separate lots if they would fetch a better price overall. Thus a cloak with enamelled buttons was split into its constituent parts with the cloth selling for just over 7 lire while the buttons fetched the much higher price of 15 lire. Unsurprisingly, dealers became increasingly involved as wholesale purchasers; goldsmiths usually bid for large lots of jewellery and metalware. In March 1402, for example, 1,369 lire's worth of buttons were purchased by a single goldsmith.[13]

The register from 1437 to 1452, a period of considerable political and military unrest, saw a steady series of sales of both major and minor items. In 1437, for instance, a buyer picked up a red velvet gown with gold fringes and a waistband embroidered with gold lettering for the substantial sum of 62.10 lire.[14] In 1451, auctions included ebony combs valued at 1 lire and painted boxes, knives and little forks in a black leather case for 6 lire.[15] Books such as the paper edition of a treatise on the Virtues and Vices sold for 1 lire and 12 soldi.[16] The registers from the 1450s indicate that armour was regularly on sale, presumably as soldiers or their families made donations following their deaths or offerings as thanks for survival. From the second half of the century, the auctions were combined with what might be described as a 'company shop' as goods were increasingly sold directly to cathedral workers. This meant that the auction ceased to be a special one-off event and that sales were far more regular. For example, the donations of linen and flax that were left at the altar on Sundays were immediately weighed and made available during the week when they were almost always bought by stonecutters and stonemasons.[17] Higher value items were sent on consignment to established second-hand dealers who contracted with the Fabbrica to take over the sale of such donations.[18]

These auctions, with their mixture of charitable opportunities and bargain hunting, were unusual but not exceptional. The Milanese could also attend auction sales of the goods seized for non-payment of taxes, the possessions of rebels, or pledges on loans that had not been repaid. A detailed explanation of how this was done survives from the period of the short-lived Ambrosian republic that governed Milan from 1447 to 1449. This was a period when the city of Milan attempted to institute a communal form of government after almost a century and a half of signorial rule. The need for a regularised system of auction sales was primarily due to the new government's desperate need for cash to pay its mercenary armies. Everything that could be sold was put up for auction. This included the personal possessions of the deceased Visconti Duke, such as his jewellery as well as the tiles and bricks of his fortress, and the lands once under his control. The property and effects of those who had been declared as rebels were also auctioned off with great speed. In addition the system was designed to be used by the increasingly indigent population who were being pressed to pay taxes and debts. In defining the purposes of their public auctions, the Republican magistrates stated that, 'Auctions were honourable, decent, honest and useful to the greatest benefit and help for the poor, the wealthy, artisans, merchants and nobles and all of whatever their standing, be it great, medium or small.'[19] All goods, private or public, requiring a rapid sale were now, the commune ordered, to be sold under the auspices of its official vendors, the de Busti brothers, who alone were responsible for 'auctioning, delivering, selling and alienating all types of goods'.[20] They were to hold the sales at the town hall, the Broletto, every Monday, Wednesday and Saturday just after dinner, *post prandium*, unless it was a feast day (in which case it would take place on the following non-festal day or be cancelled). The goods to be sold would be stored in the Broletto itself. The sum that was raised from the sale was meant to go to the lender or to the original owner of the item, and the de Busti's profits were restricted to a small cash sum dependent on the value of the item being sold. The de Busti's contract gives a good description of how the sale itself was to be organised. To begin the auction:

> The crier or trumpeter must, with a high and sonorous voice, announce to all those around in such a way that they can clearly understand, that whatever goods will be auctioned will be given to the highest bidder. And then three times he should announce the item, the price at which it was being auctioned, and then he should

say these words, 'The first, the second, the third, done'. He should do this for as many times as it takes to say the entire *Pater Noster* as clearly as possible. And then if he has not reached the price for the auctioned item, he should return it to the said officials . . .[21]

The public nature of the announcement of the price, the use of the 'Our Father', that is, the *Pater Noster* prayer to time the auction and the final acceptance of the bid with the word 'done' suggest a condensing of time which was characteristic of most auctions. In the excitement, potential buyers would not have time to bargain or negotiate. They would have to make rapid decisions and be prepared to make immediate payment. But the speed of the event was potentially undermined by the final provision. If the estimated value was not achieved, the price was not lowered. Instead, the goods went back to the de Busti brothers to be re-auctioned. The assumption was that someone would eventually want to pay the estimated price, not that the item was over-valued.

The Milanese officials were undoubtedly drawing on a set of long-standing practices. Governments always needed cash and regularly refused to take goods in kind as payments towards taxes. As Reinhold Mueller has shown, debt auctions were held almost every day in Venice during the fourteenth-century Chioggia wars. The regulations imposed on the small Tuscan village of Sovicelle in 1383 by the Sienese government indicate how widespread the use of auctions already was by the late fourteenth century:

> Since many people are taxed and then pretend that they are not who they are, and because they don't pay the commune they grow greatly indebted, and their pawns are held for taxes or loans at the request of the vicar or camerlengo or because of a fine. According to the statutes, we must collect pledges from all those who are named within twenty days and from that point onwards, the camerlengo and the vicar should to sell them at auction within eight days on pain of a ten lire fine for the said camerlengo . . . and they must be auctioned off on two different feast days and announcements must be made so that everyone will come to the auction of the pawn-pledges in front of the house of the vicar, or if the said camerlengo wants to bring them to sell in Siena without a licence, or by request when twenty days have passed with the licence of the vicar. But he should rather have them auctioned off for the maintenance of the poor, and this is his decision. The amount is credited to the revenues of the camerlengo, in compensation for the amount owed by the owner of the pledge, except for the expense of transport and other reasonable expenses.[22]

The need to reiterate this legislation, however, suggests a pattern of resistance rather than a smooth system of tax payments. Sovicelle citizens were being forced to sell their goods in order to pay taxes to the Sienese government, then in a period of disarray. The local townsfolk were not coming forward with either their names or their dues. In a small community, it might be difficult to find anyone who would be willing to collaborate by buying the goods of tax defaulters, hence the need eventually to send the pledges to Siena to be sold.

Larger cities had the advantage of anonymity but even here supposedly public auctions might be fixed so that the outcome was already predetermined. For example, the records survive of an unusual slave auction that took place in Genoa in 1457. As part of the sale of the estate of the patrician Raffaele Lomellini, his domestic servant Magdalena was brought into the city's commercial centre, the Piazza Banchi, over an eight-day period to be auctioned. The highest bid was made by a male member of the Lomellini family who was acting for the widow of her original owner, because 'he had offered more than the others'.[23] We do not know if this was a genuine competition but in instructing his executors to sell his books after his death, the Milanese canon, Francesco della Croce, tried to set out the parameters defining who could bid for his estate. Although they were to be sold by auction, firstly Milanese citizens and then those in religious orders were to take precedence as buyers.[24] Only once these two categories had had a chance to bid could the books be offered more widely. There are many other cases where buyers actually proved to be close friends, relatives or even the original owners of the items that were being sold at auction, evidence that suggests there were few genuinely impersonal markets in formation through the auction system.[25]

Venice was undoubtedly the city with the widest range of auctions. Patricia Allerston has shown the complexities of its networks for second-hand sales. Professional criers working under the jurisdiction of the Giustizia Vecchia sold off household goods by the so-called *pietre delle bande* in the squares of Piazza San Marco and the Rialto (Figures 179–83). A further magistracy controlled the auctions of pledges held by the Jews.[26] In addition to pawn redemption, these same officials were ordered to fulfil testamentary bequests and hold *incanti di particolari persone* for those who needed to sell goods rapidly in order to raise cash.

The purposes behind the different auctions determined how rapidly they were executed. While, as demonstrated below, pawn pledge auctions could be delayed for up to a year, a family's need to satisfy creditors or the state might call for an immediate sale. The 1602 Venetian auction regulations reiterated a

179 Matteo Pagan, *Procession of the Doge and Patriarch of Venice*, 1599, woodblock print, Department of Prints and Drawings, The British Museum, London, 1860-4-14-16, detail showing the *comandadori*.

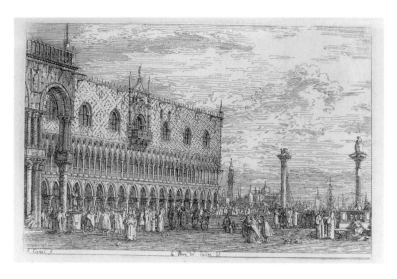

180 Canaletto, *Piazza San Marco*, 1741, National Gallery of Canada, Ottowa, Ontario, inv. N. 6641d.

much earlier notion that auctions were of benefit to the indigent because, 'it often happens that the poor have a sudden need to sell some of their belongings at auction . . . because they cannot afford to wait for any length of time'.[27] Regarding such events as acts of Christian charity rather than commercial moments, the Venetian government allowed such sales even on holidays (although Jews were not allowed to buy during Christian festivities).[28]

Given the urgency, these sales were carried out with great rapidity, and the evidence from a case brought against a Venetian crier gives a good picture of how they took place in this city. In 1583, Francesco della Vedova protested that he had been falsely accused of holding an unlicensed sale of a pair of black damask breeches that he had auctioned on behalf of the nobleman, Nicolò Saitor. He pointed out that it was his obligation to raise the highest price possible and that he had cried out, 'For five ducats, for five ducats' as required.[29] Della Vedova needed to avoid the accusation of carrying out an unlicensed auction because official supervision was regarded as key to his probity. Auctioneers were assigned by lot to ensure that there was no collusion between the crier and either the seller or the buyer. The mid-seventeenth-century reiteration of how *comandadori* were to undertake their business is, despite its late date, worth reporting in full for the detailed picture it gives of what the ideal auction should have looked like:

> The auctions which are carried out in Rialto, San Marco and other places must occur with the good form, rule and order that have been practised at different times with the authority of the Senate . . .
> Whoever has occasion to sell furnishings of whatever sort at auction must present the magistrate with an inventory containing the quality, quantity and colour of the

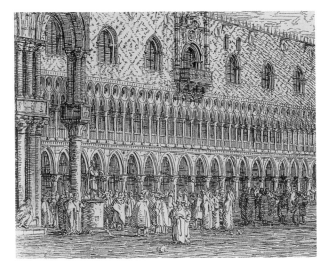

181   Detail of Fig. 180 showing the *comandadori* standing on the pietro delle bande in Piazza San Marco.

goods and must swear that they are their own property and have not been bought for resale. Having done this an auctioneer will be selected by lot and given a licence allowing him to sell the said furnishings at auction in public places, and he must be assisted personally by the vendor or some other person in his place . . .

Likewise as a service for the poor and for those who want to sell items worth ten ducats or less, twelve auctioneers will be selected by lot on a weekly basis and they will assist for six days continuously on the Piazza of the Rialto in order to receive and sell goods. The name of the said auctioneers will be posted on a tablet in the offices of the Giustizia Vecchia . . .[30]

The paperwork required to operate this system was relentless, and much of what is known about Venetian auctions comes from the bureaucracy generated by these regulations. For example, the sale of the goods of the Venetian official Salustio Gnechi in 1599 was caused by a dispute over his inheritance.[31] The appropriate authorities, the Giudici di Petizion, who were responsible for properties worth more than 50 ducats, intervened to sell the estate and divide the proceeds among the competing heirs. This process generated two inventories: the first recording the household goods in Gnechi's estate, the second listing the items that were eventually put up for public sale by auction. In the latter document, the over 500 items were grouped into lots, usually by type and perhaps by quality. There were 75 men's shirts, 140 pieces of white maiolica and Gnechi's crimson robes of office. The auction itself took place in Piazza San Marco over eight days and raised a total of 10,000 lire. Tellingly, the most valuable pieces were not sold in the square. Instead, the gold and silver, including numerous personal items such as signet rings and cups with the Gnechi family arms, were taken to the Rialto to be sold. Purchasers were primarily goldsmiths who paid by weight and then refashioned the items for resale.

The Venetian state kept control over this important form of salesmanship through its own magistrates, but in other republics, such as those of Florence or Siena, household auctions were managed by charitable institutions. In Florence sales were held in the baptistery square under the jurisdiction of the Office of Wards and Orphans, the Magistrato dei Pupilli.[32] The charity inventoried the households of widows and orphans, arranged for the sale of goods and the eventual investment of the proceeds to ensure a

decent income for the fatherless family. To ensure a good crowd of potential bidders, the auction sales were supposed to be widely announced, not just in Florence itself, but also in the *contado* and in nearby towns and villages. The sales became increasingly important after 1555 when Duke Cosimo dei Medici insisted that the Pupilli manage all second-hand sales, not just those of designated orphans and their families. As in Venice, there seems to have been an important period before the actual auction took place when items could be viewed either *in situ* in the family home or in a central part of the city. This was common in Rome as well, and Michele de Montaigne described viewing an Orsini cardinal's valuables prior to their sale in Rome in 1581:

After dinner, the French ambassador sent a footman to tell me that if I wished, he was coming to pick me up in his coach to take me to see the furniture of Cardinal Orsini, which was being sold, since he had died this summer in Naples and had left as heir to all his vast property a niece of his, a little girl. Among other rare things was a taffeta coverlet lined with swans' down. In Siena you see a good many of these swan's skins complete with features and I was asked no more than a crown and a half for one, all prepared. They are the size of a sheepskin, a few of them would be enough to make a coverlet of this sort. I saw an ostrich egg, decorated all over and painted with pretty pictures. Also a square box to put jewels in that contained a certain quantity of them; but since the box was most artfully arranged with mirrors all around, when it was opened it appeared much wider and deeper in every direction, and seemed to hold ten times as many jewels as were in it, since one and the same thing were seen many times by the reflection of the mirror and the mirrors were not easy to detect.[33]

The Orsini auction was taking place under classic circumstances. The cardinal's heir was a minor who required cash investments for her dowry rather than coverlets and jewel boxes. These valuables, once designed for a specific individual's use, were now more widely available at a price to new owners for whom they might have new mean-

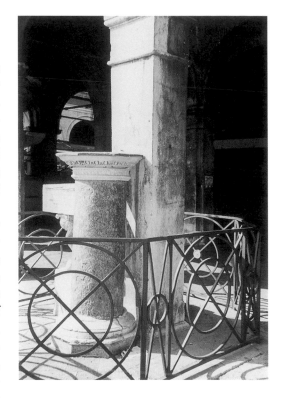

ings. Crucially, neither Montaigne nor the French ambassador seemed to have had any intention of making a purchase themselves. They were merely there to enjoy the spectacle. As a careful observer, Montaigne was also able to reflect on what he had already learned about the cost of swans' down and on this basis evaluate the asking price of the Orsini coverlet.

It is unclear from Montaigne's commentary precisely where the viewing took place or whether he would have gained access to the auction if he had not been led there by the French ambassador. Although common, these sales were not without their problems of public reputation. They represented failure, either of familial continuity or of financial solvency. When the aristocrat was a foreigner, such as the Spanish ambassador whose possessions were sold at public auction in Genoa in 1569, or someone without any direct heir, there seems to have been little concern about the open nature of the event.[34] At other times, however, the auctioning of a nobleman's goods was perceived as a deliberate act of public shaming. The sale of the Medici goods in 1495 in the central site of Orsanmichele by the *Ufficiali dei Ribelli* in order to satisfy their creditors was a very deliberate insult to the once powerful family.[35] As Jacqueline Musacchio has shown, the event was followed with fascination by contemporary Florentines. Luca Landucci mentioned it three times in his *zibaldone*, seeing the loss of the Medici velvet and gold-embroidered bed coverings and paintings such as Lorenzo dei Medici's own birth salver as symbols of the transience of *fortuna* and as God's punishment for excessive pride.[36] When the Venetian Francesco Sansovino described the sale of a Venetian rebel's goods, he too drew a moral meaning, noting, 'I saw the household goods of a noble man condemned for some sinister occurrence sold at auction. They would have been too many and too much for any Duke of Italy.'[37]

But the auction was not only a place where viewers assessed the contents of family homes and the value of individual items; it was also a moment to observe the behaviour of bidders. A letter, from one Scipione de Licio in Venice to Isabella d'Este in 1534, suggests the level of competitiveness that auctions could generate:

I found myself, my most excellent patron, on the day, at a good time in the Piazza of San Bartolomeo in Rialto where there was an auction under way of many lovely things and jewels. And amongst these things was a most beautiful piece of coral that was being bid for by many buyers, and almost everyone said that it was one of the most beautiful pieces of coral that had been seen in over one hundred years and that the jewel should land in the hands of every great master. And I, knowing that no one there who was bidding would have been able to obtain it for the greatest master, who would have been myself in the name of your Ladyship, my patron, it seemed to me that I should not stop bidding until the very end. In this way I convinced all the other bidders that the coral should stay in my hands, and I am sending it to your Ladyship, praying that you deign to accept it with this agreement that when your sublime Ladyship gets up in the morning, that you should look into it, which will bring your highness a happy and sweet heart, one worthy of a demi-goddess.[38]

In his letter Scipione was depicting himself as a victor. He wanted his achievement to be seen as a triumph for his skill rather than simply the ability to pay a higher sum than his competitors. There was no charge made to Isabella for the coral; as in a chivalric tale, she was the recipient of his trophy rather than a customer. But the Marchioness understood the business of Venetian auctions very well and would have known that her role was to offer her admirer a gift in return, either hiring him to set the coral appropriately or sending a monetary token of her affection.

PAWNS AND PLEDGE AUCTIONS

The auctions described above were those that the authorities actively encouraged. There were others, however, where the actual sale of the item was almost a fictional end-point to a long and protracted credit arrangement. One of the major differences between the Renaissance period and the twentieth century was the role that objects, even those of the most minimal quality, played as stores of value. Today it would be impossible to bring a tea-towel into a tavern and ask for a drink or pay your taxes with a set of handkerchiefs. But this would have been relatively common in a period when there were few items that could not be offered as pledges. When Bolognese citizens found themselves unable to pay the salt or other taxes at the beginning of the fifteenth century, for example, they left a wide range of items with the town's *Massarolo dei pegni* until they could return with the small amounts that were due.[39] Everyday items were mixed with more valuable pledges. On one day in mid-January 1420, a butcher left behind his weights while another offered an old towel as pledges against their respective milling taxes of 1 lire and 15 soldi. A few days later, it was the turn of a second-hand dealer who left a barrel, while another debtor (whose profession was unstated) presented a pair of gloves as his pledge.[40] Others who owed money left old hoes, hammers, cooking pots, a brass cup, a pair of scissors, or in one case, a single white stocking.[41] Some artisans were probably offering shop stock rather than personal possessions. The many pieces of old linen left by second-hand dealers were likely to have been part of their inventories.[42] Similarly, Giovanni Tasetto *spadaro* left an old sword against a 4 soldi debt, while the shoemaker, Lorenzo *chalzolaro* left a pair of women's clogs for his 2 soldi debt.[43] There was a surchage made for such payments and a debt of 4 soldi, for example, had to be paid back with 4 soldi and 4 denari. Crucially, the majority of items were rapidly redeemed (the word *rescosso* was then written next to the account). In some cases, however, such as that of the shoemaker, the owner never returned, and the item, however new or worn, would be put up for public auction.

These auctions were usually organised by city officials who acted on behalf of private creditors as well as for the city. This was necessary since pledges were also the basis on which money was lent by pawnbrokers, shopkeepers, innkeepers and even by friends and relatives. Typically, the lender offered a percentage of the total value of the item in question at a set interest rate for a fixed period. If the debtor was unable to return the capital and interest within that time frame, the creditor claimed the item as his own and could then, following an additional set amount of time, sell it on. In many cities, the profit was limited to the return of the capitol and interest with any additional funds being returned to the original owner.[44]

Pawns ran the full gamut of material possessions and those taking out and accepting loans ranged from the most elite figures of the nobility to the very poorest. The early fifteenth-century inventory of a Milanese nobleman included items that he held as pawns for small-scale loans that he had made, while at the death of a sixteenth-century Sienese innkeeper the list of his possessions included numerous pawned items from very valuable cloaks and caps to minor pieces of linen.[45] Anything could be used as a pawn; even coins could be treated as pawnable objects rather than as currency.[46] On 28 November 1459, for example, one of Francesco Castellani's servants took out a loan, pledging a gold coin, a *fiorino largo* for the much smaller sum of 7 soldi that he needed to pay in silver money for hay that day.

Studies of individual pawnbrokers have shown that the most common type of pledges were household goods. These sat alongside workers' tools and the occasional items of higher value, such as spoons, rings and other metalware. The truncated inventory of a Pistoiese Christian pawnbroker's shop in 1417 indicated, for example, that he held 80 items at his death, 79 of which had been pawned by men. Customers were merchants, artisans, weavers, goldsmiths and brokers who brought in low-value goods, primarily clothing, some suits of armour, belts, underwear and stockings. The most expensive items included a silver fork with an ivory handle which came in on 9 May 1417 and left the next day.[47] But other accounts show that the range of customers who borrowed money in this way was not restricted to the poor. For example, listed among the forty-four Sienese who left books as pawn at the *Monte di Pietà* between 1483 and 1511 were patricians, tailors, priests, lawyers and eleven women (for whom their books of devotion may have been one of their most valuable possessions) (Figure 184).[48] Despite many strictures against usury, even the clergy were involved. For example, the Jewish pawnbroker, Manno da Pavia, was forced to return a book that had been pledged by the Bishop of Novara, *Il Ducato*, as it actually belonged to the ducal library in Pavia.[49]

Even the most distinguished individuals were regularly forced to pawn goods. When, for example, the Duke of Urbino Federigo da Montefeltro could not afford to redeem

184　Late sixteenth century, list of pawns, Siena,
Archivio di stato, Monte di Pietà, n. 7, c. 45.

the jewels that he had pawned in Florence for 4,000 gold ducats, Francesco Sforza intervened to ask that they be sold to him rather than auctioned in public.[50] Sforza was
himself a heavy user of pawnbrokers. In the early stages of his career, he had borrowed
2,000 florins from Rica, the widow of Benedetto of Ancona in Pesaro, in 1447, and had
to turn to Venetian bankers to borrow again in order pay off the interest for fear that
she would sell his gold brocade robes.[51]

Sforza was charged 14 per cent interest against the security of lavish items such as:

> A garment of red silk velvet lined with marten fur with open sleeves
> A short green mantle of silver brocaded silk lined with marten fur
> A garment of silver red silk with open sleeves lined with marten fur
> A garment of silvered blue silk velvet lined with marten fur.[52]

Using clothing and other goods as pledges was a common strategy even when a family
had liquid capital at their disposal. Despite his wealth and possessions, the Gonzaga's
chief artist and architect Giulio Romano left a wide range of goods, 'pawned with the
Jews' at his death. His daughter told those inventorying his estate that she knew only

of the items that he had deposited with four different bankers in order to raise a total of over 230 scudi. These included:

A large carpet, 20 gold scudi; another 9 carpets, not very good and 4 pieces of torn wall hangings at the bank of the Grasini, 100 lire. Messer Vitta has 10 silver gilt spoons, a gilt silver cup with its foot, and a most beautiful string of coral, but I don't know how much it was pawned for. A hanging of Cambrai cloth with cords of red silk, in the Milanese fashion, pawned for 10 gold scudi, but I don't know where. A necklace of jewels pawned at Governolo for 130 gold scudi. A necklace of lapis touched with gold, I believe for 10 gold scudi. A doublet of dark red silk pawned for 50 scudi. A jacket and a pair of sleeves at Grasini's, 9 scudi; 48 pieces of fur which have been pawned twice . . . in the house of Benedusi. A piece of ormesine silk from Florence given to the banker at Governolo for interest, red and yellow.[53]

Giulio Romano should have had pawn slips for each of his items, but the fact that his daughter, Virginia, could not remember either where the items were or how much they had been valued at explains why communities were anxious to make sure that the original owners were always informed once the time of their loan had come to an end when their goods were at risk of being sold.

Thus, unlike civic or charitable auctions which were supposed to turn material wealth into cash as fast as possible, pawn pledge auctions were regulated in ways designed to forestall the eventual sale. The 1327 statutes of Verona, for example, insisted that at least three public announcements were made by the pawnbroker, including a visit to the debtor's home, before the *pegni* could be sold in the town's main square.[54] In Milan pawned goods could only be sold after a year had passed, and after a public announcement of their sale had been made in the public marketplace. A further month's delay was required before the sale could then take place.[55]

The lengthy delays made it hard to realise the capital that had been lent. In 1439, the Jewish community of Recanati petitioned:

That after one year it should be legal to sell the pledges of foreigners and after eighteen months those of citizens without any penalty or the involvement of the interested parties, because our experience has been that the owners of these pledges oppose those who sell at auction and in public and it is therefore impossible to regain the money lent as is just.[56]

This seemingly reasonable request was refused. Instead it was reiterated that pledge sales had to take place in the presence of the moneylender, a notary and four citizens elected by the commune in the main square of the city. The money which remained after the loan and the interest had been repaid was to be returned to the owner. If it could not be sold, the owner was given yet another month's grace and then and only then, could the item be considered the property of the pawnbroker. By 1456, Jewish moneylenders were again complaining of intimidation in the square and they finally received permission to sell the items two months following their announcements. But even then such speed was only possible for items of very low value. If the amount in question was over three ducats they were expected to bring the buyer before a magistrate to swear to the price that had been paid and to arrange for any excess profit to return to the original owner.

The question of selling pledges or pawns was not only of interest to professional lenders. As suggested above, almost every *bottega*, inn and even individuals accepted pledges as guarantees against future payments; it was regarded as licit to charge a higher price for items bought on credit than those paid for with cash. But this was still seen as problematic and the anxieties over loans and usury were at their most acute when considering the Jewish community. Although not all pawnbrokers and bankers taking pledges were Jewish, money-lending was often tarred with anti-Semitism. Giulio Romano's daughter, for example, prefaced the list of her father's pawns by simply saying that they were 'with the Jews'. Towns such as Mantua and Ferrara signed contracts with Jewish families and communities promising protection for their religious freedom in return for such commercial aid but never felt completely comfortable with the arrangements. In 1454, for example, following complaints that Jewish money-lenders were acting irresponsibly with their securities and sending goods outside of the city, Pavian lenders were told they could sell only at public auction within civic jurisdiction, returning any profit to the debtor.[57] Similar reforms undertaken in Bologna in 1473 demanded that all unredeemed goods were to be taken from Jewish pawnbrokers, placed in a publicly maintained warehouse and then sold at auction by communal officials. Again, any profit above and beyond the actual debt was to be returned to the original owner.[58] Finally, in Venice, the Jewish community in Mestre was required to bring their pawns to the Serenissima to be sold under the jurisdiction of the Sopraconsoli and the magistracy of the Piovego. The former were to inspect items left as collateral every two months to ensure that they were not being damaged (some clauses demanded that money-lenders keep cats in order to control the rats).[59] Only in 1512 were Jews allowed into the city itself. They then found themselves very rapidly confined to a single area, the Ghetto.

The anti-Semitism that became increasingly vociferous in the late fifteenth century made the role of Jewish money lenders and pawnbrokers ever more contentious. A number of Franciscan preachers decided that the dangers of using Jews outweighed the dangers of potential usury and called for the establishment of charitable loan schemes known as the *Monte di Pietà* (Figure 185). The creation of these *Monti* was often the trigger for an expulsion of the local Jewish community but in other cases they joined rather than displaced the existing networks of bankers. Certainly, the format that was established was very similar to that used by traditional pawnbrokers. In Milan after 1496, for instance, loans by the new *Monte di Pietà* were made on up to two-thirds of the value of the metallic content and half the value of textiles or other goods. Because of these similarities, the *Monte di Pietà* had to work hard to construct an image that was in opposition to that of the Jewish pawn-dealer. The sixteenth-century banner of the *Monte di Pietà* in Faenza provided an idealised vision of its operation (Figure 186).

Depicted are respectable matrons with aprons and staffs. Black-gowned widows and hard-working men bringing in household linens, belts, chains and pots and pans. These are carefully recorded and stored and in return the needy receive the coins required to pay their loans, bills and taxes. Yet, despite this ideal, fraud was still possible, as in the case of Massimiliano *stimatore al Monte della Pietà* in Florence in 1573, who took off the tickets from items he had valued in order to pawn them himself.[60] Naturally, these new organisations stressed their probity and charitable nature (as opposed to the greed of pawnbrokers). In the 1590 poem on 'rent days', referred to in Chapter Two, Giulio Cesare Croce advised his readers to trust Bologna's *Monte*. Instead of selling their possessions to pay their rents, he advised taking out a loan:

> Note well, what I will teach you
> Take first a pledge
> That is of such importance

185   Marco da Montegallo, *Tabula della Salute*, 1494, engraving, Biblioteca Nazionale, Florence, inv. B.6 18.B.

That you will gain the substance
And with a happy face
Take it straight to the Monte
Where they will take pity on you.
A terrible thing is rent

When your pledge has been accepted
And you have received your cash

186   Giovanni Battista Bertucci, Monte di Pietà banner, late sixteenth century, oil on canvas, Banca di Romagna, Faenza.

Take hold of your pawn-slip
And head off with your pennies
The landlord salutes you
And gives you your receipt
For this is a good solution
A terrible thing is rent.[61]

But while Croce and others saw the new *Monti* as positive alternatives, these institutions were actually more rigorous in collecting their debts than the traditional pawnbrokers. In Milan, unredeemed items were auctioned off after only a fifteen-day period of grace instead of the year that Jews had to put up with.[62] The *Monte* may have removed some of the contact between Christians and Jews but it did not slow down the dispersal of family goods. Nor did it remove the shame of financial failure. The Milanese *Monte di Pietà* decreed that when pawn pledges were eventually sold off at auction, they would be shown to potential buyers, 'laid out on a bench so that they can be seen by everyone, but for the honour of those who have pawned the goods, the pawn slip will be covered over'.[63] This was more than an observance of proud sensibilities. If a family lost its reputation for an ability to repay a loan, it lost the ability to borrow. Exclusion from the delicate system of credits and deficits that made up the Italian urban economy made it almost impossible to break out of poverty.

LOTTERIES

Selling a debtor's possessions at auction condensed the moment of sale and ensured that payment would be made in cash. But it only functioned when there were enough potential buyers who were prepared to be seen to compete in public or could arrange for proxies to bid on their behalf. Although auctions remained an important mechanism for anxious creditors, in the sixteenth century governments and ambitious entrepreneurs alike increasingly turned to a new form of salesmanship to raise money from the sale of household and other goods: the lottery (Figures 187–8).

Lotteries had been popular in the southern Netherlands throughout the fifteenth century and their initial reinvention in Italy was prompted by financial desperation.[64] As a further means of raising the money needed to pay their armies, the Milanese Ambrosian Republic offered lottery prizes drawn from the *borsis ventura* or 'bag of fortune' of up to 200 ducats in 1448.[65] Buyers purchased tickets on which they wrote their names. If these tickets were drawn, they won the prize. This simple system was eventually adopted by entrepreneurial second-hand dealers elsewhere later in the century. The ever-observant Venetian Marin Sanudo noted in his diaries that:

In Rialto there has arisen a new mode of gaming, by placing a small amount in trust to fortune. It started off as a low-level thing by the second-hand dealer, Girolamo

Bambarara, and has now grown. First anyone who wanted gave 20 soldi, then 3 lire and then a ducat. They put up prizes: carpets, wall hangings and other things. Now they are putting up silver worth about 200 ducats, and others have put up gold, charging a ducat per name. And it is done in this way: whosoever wants to participate writes on a piece of paper and hands over their money. Everyone gathers in a certain shop chosen for this purpose, where there are two bags with as many slips as have been deposited. The second bag has slips with the name of the prize and slips that say patience, *patientia*. When everyone is gathered, they call in a small boy and having mixed the slips well in the said sacks, the youth takes out a name from the first sack and then goes to the second. If he pulls out a slip with 'prize', the person wins; if he pulls out the slip that says 'patience' he gains nothing and has lost; thus every day in Rialto there is someone doing this.[66]

Sanudo's description suggests that the formula adopted owed much to the way political responsibilities were assigned in Republican states. The drawing of lots was done by a young boy who would pull out the name of an office from one leather bag and then the name of the potential office-holder from another.[67] This was perceived as less susceptible to bribery or corruption. Indeed, it was used in any situation where chance was seen as the fairest form of selection. In the case of Fra Sabba da Castiglione, his will of 1546 bequeathed funds to dower five poor maidens from his parish in his home town of Faenza. The names of all eligible girls were to be placed in a purse and the slips extracted by a boy of seven. The first name to emerge would have a dowry of 24 lire bolognese, the remaining four girls would be given 20 lire.[68]

But while chance made such draws seem more equitable, the element of *fortuna* involved made them equally akin to gambling. As magistrates quickly recognised, these lotteries were simply new forms of games of chance. Gambling, as opposed to gaming, did not involve skill, and was as widely practised as it was condemned. It seems that well before the eighteenth century, when the Venetians developed their well-known public gaming den, the *Ridotto*, bets were being taken by specialist agents in the Rialto. Most of the information concerning betting, of course, comes from attempts to outlaw it. In 1578, for example, Florentine and Roman edicts prohibited the betting, *a maschio e femmina*, which involved placing bets on the sex of an unborn child while another set of decrees issued in 1587 and 1569 prohibited bets on the creation of cardinals.[69] In Venice, it was common to gamble on the outcome of Senatorial elections, a practice that gave rise to fears of office 'fixing', not for political reasons, but in order to win large bets.[70]

In a period when the Rialto bridge area housed a number of public gaming tables it is not surprising to see merchants using the same techniques to generate sales. Initially, a disapproving Venetian government responded by trying to ban private lotteries. In 1522, a decree was issued by the Council of Ten clearly stating that:

Under no circumstances will we tolerate this new game that has begun for some days to take money from him or her which is called, Lotto, with such universal murmurings on the destruction of all its participants as well as because of the inconveniences and disorders that come from these so that it is necessary to take provisions against it. On the authority of this council tomorrow morning we will publish on the steps of the Rialto and in San Marco an edict declaring that no one may start another lottery in our city on pain of two years in our prisons and a 500 ducat fine . . . And from this day and for all of March during Carnival . . . you cannot put in or take out any tickets according to the said penalty. And if due to the said days of Carnival there are not the said lotteries, and the placing of tickets are not closed, those to whom they have been sold must have their money refunded . . .[71]

Sanudo noted that this attempt was generally ignored and that the Rialto remained full of lotteries despite the threat of the confiscation of all the prizes.[72] Eventually the Council of Ten had a change of heart, and the scheme was deemed suitable for public purposes. To control this new form of salesmanship the Venetian government sent observers to witness the drawing of lots and soon began using it to raise funds for its own purposes.[73] On 5 March 1522, for example, the Venetian government sold jewels and silk cloth from Cyprus by lottery, and the following year, the woods of Lignago in the Terra Ferma were allocated in the same way. By the late 1520s, Venice's taxes on wine and sugar, the butchers' and fishmongers' stalls, and even, in the latter part of the century, the new shops in the Rialto were all sold off using lottery tickets.[74] The system was enormously popular, and despite many announcements it proved difficult to stop individuals from holding unauthorised lotteries. In 1525, those without special licences were warned that they faced fines of up to 200 ducats or six months in prison if they did not desist. In Rome, edicts were issued forbidding any type of 'lotteria o ventura' on any object without a licence.[75] In smaller towns however there seems to have been less regulation. Lorenzo Lotto, for example, organised a lottery in Ancona in 1550, offering 30 intarsia cartoons and sixteen paintings as prizes.[76] He was even able to buy cloth the following year using lottery tickets that were worth half a giulio each as payment. The summary that he provided in his account book in July 1551, suggests that he had sold a remarkable 884 tickets. He then held a draw for seven of the paintings and raised a total of 44 scudi and 4 bolognini. The cost of the whole operation had been relatively small, 4 scudi and 44 bolognini providing a profit of almost 40 scudi.[77]

The vogue for lotteries was satirised by Pietro Aretino in a letter written in 1537 to Giovanni Manenti, the author of plays performed by the Venetian Company of the 'triumphanti'.[78] Its bite comes from the recognisable description of gullible types and the human frailty that gaming encouraged:

This new game is really the invention of Lady Luck, who's a mare and of Mistress Hope, who's a cow. It's they who devised this fiendish torment to make people abjure their faith and hang themselves . . . I think it must be the best thing in Italy, since it takes the fancy of a whole host of people all at once; even the whores fall for it, and it attracts both the common people and men of culture.

As soon as it makes its appearance on the public square, along trot the twelve thousand chosen . . . The skinflint first spreads out his cups, rings, chains and coins,

and then starts his banter with the crowd that has gathered to see the show . . .
Another goes to stretch out his hand and imagines himself grasping one of the jewels
or the necklaces and placing it on his finger or round his neck. And others still set
about handling the beakers and the bowls thinking of the display they would make
on the sideboard. One sets his heart on getting money, another land and another
houses.

I see swarms of people in this delirious state, suffocating and trampling on each
other as they jostle for their tickets . . . All this is trifling as regards those who can
afford to throw money away. But it is tragic when the poor and defenceless get ine-
briated too. Some poor wretch has sold the very bed he lies on, just to get two goes
in the game . . . A peasant, having chanced along to see the draw and hearing that
six *marcelli* were enough to win, sold his cloak and bellowed that he would never
touch a spade again, even if it were the one Christ used when he appeared as a gar-
dener . . . How many servant girls squander their wages in this way? How many
harlots lose all they've earned from their screwing? How many families pawn their
best shoes for a chance in the lottery? . . . Grief itself would burst its sides laughing
at the humour of a book one might write about the ineffable thoughts of those antic-
ipating that they'll win a share of the lottery's six thousand gold pieces. One man is
thinking about decorating the apartments of his house; another embroiders cloth;
another buys horses . . . It's all good fun, save when one gives away the lucky tickets
and keeps the worthless one . . . But what is the state of mind of those who have
achieved their goal? Well, they crowd around the stand, which is raised high up and
which is so lavishly decorated that you would think Lord Lottery had taken a wife
or that Dame Fortune was celebrating her wedding. And now the boy assistant has
plunged his hands into the urn that is filled with tickets, causing all the onlookers'
hearts to beat faster as they stand there transfixed with eyes and ears riveted on the
fellow with a smiling face and loud voice who first reads what's on the ticket and
then shouts out: 'White'. And no sooner is a prize handed out than the voices of a
thousand dejected people fade away . . . and when the top prize is drawn, with a '*leva
eius*' treacherous Hope abandons the mob . . .'[79]

Aretino was vicious in his attack on the damage that the lottery did to the vulnerable
and the deluded. But there was also an element of anxiety about the damage that such
events did to social order. If they were honestly run, all participants regardless of status
and gender had a chance, however small, of winning. Sanudo, for example, noted that
lotteries were particularly popular with women, writing, 'many women have put money
in the said lottery, so that all run to put in a little in order to have a lot, because they
see that with one ducat they can win 100 gold ducats and those pearls that are worth
180 ducats'.[80] Patrician women in particular were attracted by the lottery's anonymity.
If they were lucky and won something, all that was needed to collect the prize was a
receipt with the same name as the ticket. Thus participants often put in either false or
fanciful names or joined together as consortia with names such as, 'Felix concordia' or
'Dio me manda bona ventura.' Patrician women were extensively represented among

the 100 winners of one lottery drawn in Venice in 1521 whose first prize of 1,000 ducats was won by Marco Aurelio di ser Nicolo, the illegitimate adolescent son of a member of the Council of Ten. Thus, although the chances of winning must have been limited, there were enough stories of individual successes to ensure the lottery's continued popularity. In 1587, the tale spread of a poor widow who had won a diamond worth 6,000 scudi in a lottery organised to sell the estate of the Marchese of Cassano. Overcome by the shock of her good fortune, she 'died of happiness', leaving her two daughters with her new-found wealth.[81]

By the mid-sixteenth century there was a veritable explosion of lotteries, particularly in major cities such as Genoa, Venice and Rome. To prevent fraud, Roman legislation made it obligatory to show the public the jewels, gold and silver that might be won.[82] Tickets would be sold until the organiser announced a date for the 'closing' when prizes would be drawn. Because ticket-holders were not always present when the draw was made, additional auctions were organised to sell off uncollected prizes. As there could be considerable delays between the moment of sale and the draw, the tickets or *bollettini* had a value in their own right, being used as parts of inheritances and as pledges against loans. The 1535 accounts of the Venetian patrician Francesco Priuli indicate that he bought numerous tickets (*bolletini*) both in his own name and as part of several consortia who obviously agreed to divide the winnings. He carefully noted the number assigned to each ticket, its respective cost and the name of the group he had joined, such as that of the 'Bon compagni'.[83]

One late sixteenth-century lottery can be followed with some precision through the surviving advertisement for the goods on offer. In December 1570, the Venetian Magistracy of the *Provedidori del Comune* arranged to sell the valuables of the Banco Dolfin, probably following a bankruptcy claim. Despite their elite status, the Dolfin family's jewellery, silver and gold plate, furniture, houses and textiles were all priced, and a printed inventory was issued. A copy survives in the Mantuan archives where it had been sent to Duke Guglielmo Gonzaga by his representative in Venice, Alessandro Capilupi. As the ambassador explained:

> I am sending your excellency the printed inventory of all of the goods that will be put into the lottery of the Dolfini. I don't know when they are going to organise the draw. But now they are starting to pull in money and it is thought that the draw will happen shortly because there are many creditors who are owed a good sum of money and to get some back some of them would be willing to lose up to one thousand or even two thousand scudi . . .[84]

The inventory was highly tempting, with over 800 lots and a total estimated value of 100,000 ducats.[85] Divided into categories such as jewels, gold and silver, furnishings and clothing, tapestries, property, silk cloths and woollen cloth, winners might gain a house in Udine worth 2,400 ducats or a tapestry with a woodland scene valued at 698 ducats. There were also numerous silver basins, ewers and cups, all with the Dolfin coat of arms as well as carved gilded chairs with red velvet cushions, a cradle, and paintings such as an image of Our Lady or one of Mars and Venus (valued at 54 and 53 ducats

187   Giovanni Michele Graneri, *Drawing of the Lottery, Piazza delle Erbe, Turin*, 1756, oil on canvas, The John and Mabel Ringling Museum of Art, The State Art Museum of Florida, SN 195.

respectively). The cost of tickets was not printed, but potential winners were warned that they would have to pay 3 per cent of the item's value if they won. In the case of some of the most expensive items such as a large diamond valued at 7,500 ducats, this would have amounted to 225 ducats, itself a sum well beyond the means of most Venetians. But the women's embroidered shirts and the ducal robes were much more affordable, while the Dolfin family silver was valued at prices ranging from 12 ducats to 121 ducats, meaning that the winner would have had to pay between 3 ducats and only a few soldi if they had won a cup with a distinguished coat of arms.

CONCLUSION

Venice was not unique in its use of lotteries. By the end of the sixteenth century they had become a major form of salesmanship in Rome and in Genoa, cities where the drama of the Piazza and the excitement of fortunes won and lost was at its peak.[86] The

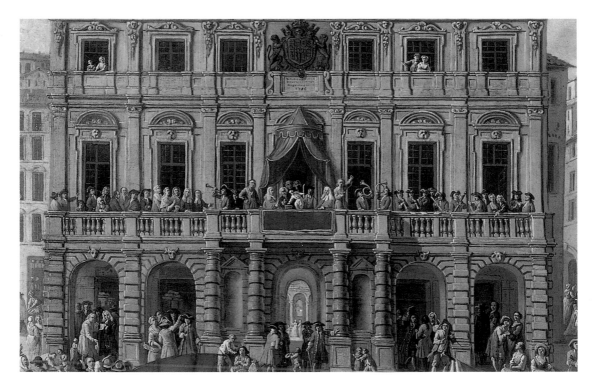

188   Detail of Figure 187.

lottery lists, like the auction prices described above, made the business of buying and selling, winning and losing into a very public piece of theatre. In demanding the viewer's attention, they served not only to shift household goods, gold and silver, but also to provide a moral message. As buyers and potential buyers witnessed the acquisition of second-hand carpets, clothing or buttons, they could learn the lesson of the transience of wealth as well as the price of old breeches, coral or gilt cups. Watching the Dolfin silver disappear was a key lesson in *fortuna* as well as in consumption.

Part Four

RENAISSANCE
CONSUMERS

CHAPTER EIGHT

Men in the Marketplace

Previous sections of this book have explored the metaphors of abundance and anxiety as well as the regulations that framed contemporary concepts of the marketplace and its inhabitants. Other chapters have discussed when and where shopping took place, looking at the alternative mechanisms that were available for making acquisitions such as fairs, auctions and lotteries. In the penultimate section the book turns to the some of most difficult questions of all: who went out to buy goods and how?

The answer seems to depend, in part, on what was being bought and why. The circumstances surrounding the purchase of furniture or velvets were deliberately framed in ways that were supposed to be quite distinct from buying bread or garlic. But given the common use of bargaining and credit, the many overlapping elements made such distinctions difficult to sustain for very long. No matter how elevated, every transaction involved an element of social contact, verbal exchange, gain or loss.

Most descriptions of these transactions, however, focused on the lower end of the scale, suggesting that only peasants bargained. Thus, despite his mixed audience of elite and plebian listeners, San Bernardino's imitation of the activities that took place in Siena's markets only emphasised the inelegant banter involved in minor exchanges (Figure 189):

> First let us consider the lies which are used in selling. I say that I know so many that it seems that he has sworn to never buy or sell anything, unless he has told you at least a dozen lies. I can tell you of one who wants to buy a pair of slippers. He goes to the shoemaker who says – 'What do you want with those slippers – I will give

189 Neroccio de Landi, *San Bernardino Preaching in the Campo*, c. 1474, Siena, Palazzo Pubblico.

them to you for twenty soldi' – 'By the Evangelist I will not give them to you.' 'Go on, take them for I promise you that they are perfect, in truth (and he's lying by the throat) – What do you want them for less? – I don't have any for less.' 'By the Evangelist, I don't have eighteen soldi (You have just sworn something which isn't true) – You want fifteen.' 'No I promise you that you won't find better slippers in this city than these.' 'I will not give you more than fifteen soldi.' (Now, you are lying too.) 'Okay, in good time, give me eighteen soldi, as I have already paid for this many times – By the Evangelists, I will not give you more.' 'By the Evangelists, you will not have them.' And then in the end, he gives them to you and you take them for seventeen soldi, after everyone has sworn and lied many times.[1]

In another anecdote drawn from the same sermon, the preacher continued his attack on blasphemous language by presenting an argument between a buyer and seller where the issue was not the price, but how it was to be paid:

Are there none of those that sell garlic and onions? They won't sell unless they swear: I want my money in cash – I don't want to give you cash – By the Evangelist, I will not give it to you – By the Evangelist, you will give it to me – By the Evangelist, I will not – Oh my, don't you see what you do: you deny God for a head of garlic.[2]

While San Bernardino's anxieties were over blasphemy, the haggling over price and arrangements over payment he portrays can be confirmed from legal records such as a case brought in Perugia in April 1470. In this episode a woman from the Umbrian countryside, Donna Agnese described how she had gone into the city to make, what was for her, a major purchase. The court records showed that:

In the month of July of this year, Donna Agnese went to Sabatuccio's shop to buy a bodice. Among the numerous items he had in stock and on show, Sabatuccio showed her a beautiful red doublet. She tried it on and found it fitted perfectly, in both length and breadth. Seeing that it became her so well, she asked Sabatuccio how much he wanted for it. After lengthy haggling and much talk, they agreed on a price of 12 lire.[3]

The lengthy negotiations had reduced the price to 12 lire, a relatively reasonable amount. Perhaps regretting the bargain, Sabatuccio, a Jewish second-hand dealer based on one

190   Eighteenth-century engraving of the Pantheon and the Piazza della Rotonda with vendors in the foreground, The Conway Library, Courtauld Institute of Art, London.

of Perugia's main streets, the Via Vecchia, failed to deliver the doublet, forcing Agnese's lawsuit. Despite this, the overall impression is of an intimate encounter between a Christian woman from the countryside and a Jewish man in the city, one that included a least one episode of dressing and undressing as Agnese tried the doublet on (inviting the question of where she did so).

The verbal nature of these exchanges allowed for communication about reputation as well as about price and credit. When, for example, the wealthy Pratese merchant Francesco di Marco Datini wanted to buy fresh meat from Florence, he advised his correspondent to, 'Go to the stall where you see the most people gathered and say, "Give me some good veal for that gentleman of Prato – and be sure to give him the best." '[4] In shopping for Datini, therefore, the Florentine friend would have emphasised his connections to a wealthy patron as he purchased some veal. Such interactions were not always positive. While waiting in an apothecary's shop, the *Aromatario della Luna*, in the Mercato Vecchio in early fifteenth-century Florence, the prostitute Maddalena of Ragusa hit the daughter of one of the servants of the Florentine signoria over the head with her clog, resulting in a 3-florin fine and a florin to be paid in compensation to the victim.[5] In 1472, a number of women who sold vegetables by the Pantheon in the Piazza Rotondo in Rome were arrested for similarly aggressive interactions with their patrician clients (Figure 190). On one occasion, a slave known as Caterina who sold greens by the Pantheon insulted a member of the Roman aristocracy, Paolo di Cecco di Massimo. She owed him both the capital and the interest on a loan, and according to witnesses publicly insulted him with the following words, 'you lie through your teeth . . . you idiot, half of you is still in your mother's body', an engagement which ended with Paolo hitting her over the head with a pumpkin.[6] In another instance, a vendor by the Pantheon, Lucia Ramundi, traded insults with a member of the baronial Porcari family, Cornelio di Battista, resulting in a fight during which she threw him to the ground.[7]

The tussles could become very serious. The records of a much later Bolognese case describe the death that occurred when a fourteen-year-old boy attempted to buy cheese. The court was told that the cheese-monger had:

> said that he wanted five *quattrini*, and the boy said that he wanted to give him three, and then the boy saw amongst the show of cheeses, another piece of sheep's cheese, and asked what type of piece that was, and the vendor replied that it was sheep and that it was worth more, saying, 'this is from sheep, and this is from cow', but then the boy replied, 'but which of these cows is your mother?'[8]

Unfortunately for the young buyer, the insult prompted the cheese-monger to draw his knife and slit the boy's throat.

These episodes generally involved men and women of lower status. It was unusual for Italy's elite families to end up in court over minor market disputes even when they ended in violence. Thus haggling or higgling are terms that were usually reserved for minor purchases. But it was not simply the lower social classes who bargained. Purchasers of spices, silk or woollen cloth, antiquities, books or furnishings were just as if not more likely to negotiate as those buying basic foodstuffs whose prices were often fixed.

But if, as suggested, bargaining took place at all levels, how could patricians be seen to discuss prices publicly? Could they openly interact with social inferiors or express their needs and desires before an audience? When the Holy Roman Emperor Frederick III came to Venice in February 1469, for example, his behaviour in the city's shops caused considerable shock. As part of his formal entertainment, he was accompanied to the central Venetian shopping district, the Merceria. The Milanese ambassadors, who had little love for the emperor who was then refusing to recognise the legitimacy of the Sforza claim to Lombardy, described Frederick III's behaviour in scandalised terms:

> At the twenty-first hour, we left the palace walking down the Merceria with quite a few of the Signoria, looking most exquisitely at the shops, with the emperor often asking the price of the goods himself. Even though Lords Domenico Moro and Zaccaria Balbo each said: 'Sacred Majesty, all us to have the said goods carried home', nonetheless it seemed to him worthy to call out like a merchant, and without a doubt, familiarly as a good merchant would. At the apothecaries, he lingered as well, asking the prices and occasionally taking sweets in his hand and eating them publicly and domestically, giving them to his retinue with his fist. He wished to see the silk warehouse. The Tuscans showed him a considerable number of fabrics, most exquisitely, and again he often called for the price. The Signoria said to these Tuscans that they were to send those things which pleased him most to the house.[9]

Even given the Milanese dislike for the Holy Roman Emperor, the letter suggests that the overtly mercantile behaviour of the most aristocratic figure in Christendom violated a number of accepted norms. Eating in public, using his own hands to take and pass around sweets, seemingly bargaining with the merchants themselves by asking the price, were all 'domestic' activities that aristocrats undertook discretely, not as part of a public ritual. Moreover, as the Venetian Senate typically subsidised these shopping expeditions, when Frederick III called for the prices he reduced an event intended as a form of gift-giving into an overtly commercial exchange.

This and other episodes suggest that openly negotiating in even superior shops such as those of silk merchants and apothecaries was best avoided by the patrician elite. There were, of course, many exceptions. During the late sixteenth century the Duke of Mantua, Guglielmo Gonzaga, spent much of his leisure time in Venice in the shop of the mercer, Bonifacio Bontempelli.[10] But it is not known whether Guglielmo mixed with other customers. Moreover, Bontempelli was an exceptional figure of great wealth and stature within the Serenissima; his shop was more a showcase for Venice's wealth and prestige than a simple set of counters and shelves. For those who were more concerned about being seen in such spaces, there was a range of alternatives. Goods could be first observed in shops and their eventual purchase negotiated in the privacy of the home as a mid-sixteenth-century case against a Venetian mercer suggests. In 1545, the salesman Batista who had 'San Hieronymo' as his shop sign, brought a silk and gilt snood to the home of *magnifico messer* Lorenzo Rimondo who purchased it as a head-dress of pure gold. Accused of misleading his client, the mercer argued that the snood in question was of 'the type that are regularly sold in the Merzeria and in the Ghetto and in other places'.[11] His implication was that the buyer should have been fully aware of the varying qualities and prices and that it was Rimondo's fault for not examining it closely enough. Although the mercer was found guilty, the guild accepted his evidence to the extent of reducing his fine. Clearly, if buyers who stayed at home were to chose wisely, they needed to know what was available on the street. But the episode also indicates that where there was enough social disparity, the more elite buyer could force the seller to come to his home. In this way, the home could become an extension of the negotiating space, an arena where the buyer's authority might outweigh that of the seller.

Picking how and where to shop was not, therefore, a straightforward decision for those with a social position to protect. Bargaining in public might compromise one's reputation, particularly if one lost during the negotiations; but buying from the home reduced market knowledge and choice. For some, of course, there was simply no alternative. For those women who were either single or the head of the household (a category that accounted for almost 16 per cent of homes in mid-sixteenth-century Milan), a reticence about bargaining in public was a luxury that they could ill afford.[12] For others, it was physically impossible to go out onto the street. The increasing numbers of women who belonged to religious orders in the fifteenth and sixteenth centuries faced special constraints. Although nuns might be extensively involved in the commercial world both as suppliers and consumers, it was difficult if not impossible for them to conduct their transactions in the open. This did not stop them from making purchases

Ceſtaruoḷi

191   Cesare Vecellio, *De gli habiti antichi, et moderni et diverse parti del mondo libri due*, Venice, 1590, 'Cestarolo', Wellcome Library, London.

but it meant that they did need to use special arrangements. For example, numerous nuns owed money to the Florentine apothecary Matteo Palmieri in the 1430s, while 84 out of the 98 women who owed money to the Florentine bookseller Piero di Giuliano Morosi between 1589 and 1608 were women in convents who had used intermediaries to make their purchases.[13] Attracted to the specialised bindings and illustrations that decorated the standard devotional works for which Morosi was known, the nuns were able to see what their fellow sisters had received and make their selections known via friends and relations.

Involving intermediaries was a solution used by those in the secular as well as in the sacred world. At one level, purchasers got market boys (*cestaroli*) to take their groceries home for them so they would not be burdened in the street (Figure 191). At another level, professional brokers, known either as a *sensale*, *mezzano* or *messetto*, abounded in Renaissance cities. They were used to arrange marriages, to locate unusual items or to facilitate the distribution of large quantities of produce on behalf of civic guilds.[14] Their involvement was often obligatory for wholesale investments or for transactions of very high value, such as the purchase of a horse at auction or a piece of expensive silk cloth. In Venice, for example, the use of brokers was required for foreign merchants staying in the city's Fondaci.[15]

Most local families and individuals would only have had to use a *sensale* on an occasional basis. Their presence would have been particularly common during moments of major expenditure such as weddings. More commonly, householders could ask friends, relatives or servants to make their choices on their behalf, particularly when the items were of low value. But even here, there were concerns. Could servants be trusted to chose wisely or would they steal the money they had been given for the daily shopping or collude with suppliers? The late sixteenth-century Venetian satirist Tomaso Garzoni provided a suitably ironic vision of the household 'factor' that did his master's shopping. His description, which sums up a wealth of long-standing concerns, is worth quoting at length. In this profession of housekeeper, he wrote, 'is needed faithfulness, diligence, solicitude, skill, prudence, experience, correctness, charity, goodness and courtesy'.[16] But all too often:

> In buying goods, for the most part they are used to spending little and to saving more . . . You see them lurking about the piazza for . . . two white endives, attaching themselves to a basket for a whole day before buying a pumpkin to put in vinegar . . . They circle the square a thousand times before negotiating over a penny's worth of eggs to make an omelette or six shrimp to honour a visitor, nor are they ever exhausted by running around the shops to see if some old caviar has been thrown out to the cats, or some rancid butter has been thrown at the dogs, being their profession to want salt with worms and to buy onions for fennel . . . If they were saving on behalf of their master, I would stay silent, but . . . they are a cancer in the household goods of their master . . .'[17]

Despite the exaggerated nature of this portrayal, it does sum up much of what was feared about domestic slaves and servants, who were sometimes seen as enemies within.[18] Two contemporary sixteenth-century Venetian dialogues, *Dialogo del patron, et del Zane* and the *L'ultima licenza della buona massara dalla cattiva patrona*, revolve around similarly deep-rooted worries that servants were innately greedy or lazy unless they were placed under careful supervision and that masters were deliberately cruel and unreasonable to their staff, prompting their defection.[19]

A decision as to whether to send an employee or to go into the market oneself was not, therefore, always an easy one. In England and the Netherlands, the task of daily shopping was usually delegated to the most senior woman in the home, the wife and/or mother. But this was not always possible in many Italian cities where respectable women were, by preference, expected to keep a low profile in public. The contrast was noted by numerous visitors. When the Venetian ambassador Alessandro Magno went to London in the late sixteenth century, he was astonished by the number of women who could be seen in London's markets and streets: 'The Englishwomen have great freedom to go out of the house without menfolk . . . many of these women serve in the shops. Many of the young women gather outside Moorgate and play with young lads, even though they do not know them . . .'[20]

These remarks were echoed by other contemporaries such as Coryate, as mentioned in Chapter Two, and by Ffynes Moryson, who noted in 1593 that in Venice, 'only the men, and the masters of the family, go into the market and buy the victuals, for servants are never sent to that purpose, much less women'.[21] The presence of elite men in the marketplace is confirmed by the special facilities developed to ensure that senators and patricians would be able to chose produce but did not have to carry it home. Moryson noted in Rome that, 'there were . . . little boys who attend in the market place with baskets, who for a soll will carry home the meat you buy; and dare not deceive you though you goe not with them'.[22] In Venice, Cesare Vecellio depicted a similar type of servant, the market *cestarolo* who also ensured that the shopping arrived at home with ease (Figure 191).

The presence of elite Venetian senators in the Rialto fish and fruit markets (which were, of course, only a few paces away from the elite mercantile areas reserved for international trade) does suggest that even routine grocery shopping was an activity that could have been carried out by a wide range of social groups.

There were some general principles: women and servants, particularly female servants, tended to do the low-scale daily buying of groceries; men usually bought the more valuable items. But even here, practice seems to have been much more complex than this gendered division would suggest. If poorer families and single individuals had limited choices as to who did the shopping, the possibilities open to well-to-do household in a large city were multiple. The paterfamilias could make the purchases himself, or he could delegate the task to his servants, to his wife or to other female relatives. Sellers could come to the door or even into the house; friends could be asked to pick up items or professionals could be employed.

The account books of local merchants that survive in Prato, Florence and Milan indicate that all these techniques might be used within a single shop. The shopkeepers studied by Richard Marshall in fourteenth-century Prato – shoemakers, cheesemongers, second-hand dealers and apothecaries – served a wide clientele including women, but it is not always clear whether they actually came into the shop themselves or sent servants. The late fifteenth-century accounts of the apothecary, the Speziale al Giglio in Florence, do demonstrate that although the bulk of the clientele were male, a small percentage of women, mainly widows, were able to come into the shop on their own and contract debts in their own names. Social status was a major factor in how the transaction was actually achieved. In 1493, for example, one male head of household came into the shop on a daily basis to pick up emetics and syrups for a female servant who was ill at home. But when an order was placed by members of Florence's patrician families, the apothecary sent his own servant to deliver the medication to the clients' homes or even attended himself.[23]

Location may have been a significant factor in determining who could come into a shop or market. A respectable woman may have been able to go out into a local market in her immediate neighbourhood without fear of losing her reputation. The late sixteenth-century accounts of the operator of a Florentine bread oven recorded the trays of unbaked loaves that he was given by different families.[24] Although the lists were organised according to the name of the male householder, the dough baked for local artisan families was generally brought by women: wives, daughters, sisters, aunts and mothers-in-law. Families of higher status sent male servants rather than female relatives. This suggests a more mixed social environment where the male servants of elite families would gossip with the women from the surrounding streets as they waited for the loaves to emerge from the oven. This provided an ideal opportunity to exchange information across social boundaries, ensuring that the neighbourhood felt fully qualified to comment on the behaviour of families hidden behind palace walls.

In contrast, the accounts of a hosier supplying underwear, stockings, shifts and other basic garments from late fifteenth-century Milan records an exclusively male clientele.[25]

Although the name of the shopkeeper is missing, he was clearly well connected to the court, for the majority of his clients were members of the Milanese aristocracy who served the Sforza. Duke Ludovico Sforza's main secretaries and counsellors such as Filippo Feruffino and Giovanni Matteo Bottigella ordered stockings in livery colours for themselves and their households in large quantities along with other basic under-garments. It is worth noting that despite their standing, these men did not have in-house tailors who made these essentials for them, nor did the hosier come to their palaces. Instead, the names of those who placed the order in the shop, collected the garments and paid for them show that there was a regular stream of men of different ranks who came through the door. Sometimes the orders were given by the gentlemen themselves, more often their male servants put in their requests. The clients were not always aristocrats. A falconer dropped by to get a pair of Sforza stockings in white and red colours and to have his tunic repaired.[26] A painter stopped to pick up bleach or whitewash, *biancha da imbiancare* and bought a pair of stockings for ten soldi.[27] The male customers asked for stockings and underwear for their wives and children as well as for themselves. Thus an order for *pano turche per fare calze per una spoxa* to make stockings for a bride was set against the account of Luchino da Massino in 1485 while Feruffino ordered 'sleeves to give to the ladies of Giovanni Stefano da Castiglione'.[28] But even when the account was held directly in the name of a woman, such as that of domina Lucia da Tolentino who had stockings made in the Tolentino livery colours for her household in 1486, the order was placed, paid for and collected by a male member of the household, in this case her household factor, *lo Danexe*.[29]

ACCOUNTING FOR EXPENDITURE

Without a large-scale study of all of these account books, it is difficult to suggest a sta-tistically significant pattern to shopping choices that might be due to place, type of good sold or change over time, much less the motivation behind the choices involved. Family records need to be explored in greater depth and detail, looking at documents where Latin poetry might be mixed with references to births, deaths and weddings, as well as to the prices paid for fruit and vegetables.

In the private and public libraries and archives of Florence lie hundreds of such family records, diaries and accounts sometimes termed *zibaldone* or *ricordanze*, as well as books that simply recorded income and expenditure.[30] Using handwriting ranging from the finest humanist script to a barely legible scribble, men and widowed women noted the cost of melons, pumpkins, lettuces, onions, garlic, chickpeas, meat, poultry, fish, flour and wine. They recorded repairs made to shoes and stockings and the purchases of new gloves, hats, swords and carpets. If these books were more substantive, they noted the outlays for land, property, expensive clothing and furnishings as well as births, deaths and events of historical significance.

Today, this paperwork appears as an often fragile and almost always doomed attempt to control a shifting world of material possessions. Jewellery was loaned out to friends or relations, only to return lighter or missing its gems and pearls. Clothing, manuscripts and furniture were borrowed and never returned. Linen disappeared at the laundry, dresses were stolen by servants and goods destroyed by fire or simply lost through care-lessness. Accounting did not stop these disasters from happening but it did ensure that the owner knew what had happened and who had been responsible, even if it was simply God himself. The writer could then either take action or accept with resignation and good grace that the damage caused by fighting with friends and neighbours would prove worse than the loss itself.[31]

There have been many explanations for this enduring pattern of Florentine family books. A supposedly mercantilist mentality, high levels of literacy, training in arith-metic, a desire to prove ownership, or the need to position one's own family within the civic tradition of Republican office-holding have all been suggested. To this should be added the interrelationship between household and public practice. When patrician men held office as priors, they knew that their daily expenses were being carefully recorded on a daily basis. For example, accounts of the foodstuffs purchased for the Florentine priors' table survive from the early part of the fourteenth century. The expec-tation of such oversight may then have been translated into domestic practice or at least have reinforced the habit of keeping family accounts.[32] But it is also important to stress that these documents are not unique to Florence. The account book of Venetian patri-cian Francesco Priuli discussed below, like that of the painter Lorenzo Lotto, are rare survivors from northern Italy.[33] The archives of the Milanese cathedral also contain frag-ments of patrician scrawls noting down the pawning of jewellery and the purchasing of underwear and furniture.[34] These suggest a much more widespread activity than has hitherto been suspected. Yet the Tuscan accounts are unusual in carrying on over many centuries, providing a sense of the longevity of domestic practices in a changing social environment. For even as sixteenth-century Florentines acquired titles, knighthoods, court roles and responsibilities, they still carefully noted their tailor's receipts and weighed their vegetables, cheeses and salami.

These books are, of course, far from neutral records. Neither exclusively double-entry book-keeping systems nor purely literary memorials, they are often a curious mixture. It is not always clear for whom they were designed. Although accounts were admitted in court as legal records, they were also very personal writings. Occasionally, they seem to have been designed primarily for the writer's own benefit, and for that of his or her descendants. One fact, however, is clear: unless the protagonist was a widow, the writer was always male.[35] This means that whatever their actual role was within the house-hold, wives, daughters and female servants were transformed into passive ciphers, the recipients of petty sums to pay for minor items rather than buyers in their own right.

This was very much in accordance with the conventional understanding of how the domestic economy was supposed to function. When he wrote on feminine virtue in 1580, the poet Torquato Tasso used a long-standing metaphor to equate the well-run city with the well-run household:

That which is said concerning the government of the city, one sees equally in domes-tic management or of the household, as we wish to call it. Being composed of acquisition and preservation, it is well ordered that the offices would be distinguished from each other and that the office of acquiring should be attributed to the man and that of preserving to the woman. The man struggles to acquire and carries out farming or operates in commerce in the city . . . but the woman looks after that which has been acquired and her virtues are employed inside the house, just as the man demonstrates his outside.[36]

While much work has shown the influential roles that women held in Florentine society, Tasso's ideal seems to have been the accepted model of decorum over many generations. Even second-hand sales, which in England attracted primarily female buyers, were dominated by men in Florence. This was true even when the items were destined for women. For example, the accounts of Lapo di Giovanni Niccolini Siringatti show that in 1384 he was able to pick up a wide range of high-quality second-hand household linen from dealers, including garments designed for pregnant women, for a total of just over 12 florins.[37] In 1417, he bought a range of domestic goods from his son-in-law Ugo Altoviti's estate. In this case he had the covers and quilts brought to his own house where he had them valued by three second-hand dealers. He then bought a writing desk with four shelves for his study from the dealers who had bought the remainder of the estate themselves.[38] This was a transaction prompted by the fact that Siringatti's daughter and three grand-daughters had returned to live with him. Clearly he needed more furniture for his suddenly expanding family and with the help of a second-hand dealer, a *rigattiere*, Siringatti went on to purchase andirons, fire-tongs and a bed from another estate.[39]

The acquisition of such goods by male householders was pronounced across all sectors of Florentine society. A more modest artisan, the fifteenth-century Florentine bronze-caster Maso di Bartolomeo, noted in his *zibaldone* in January 1450 how he had bought a second-hand green dress for his sister-in-law from the wife of master Andrea Tedescho, a garment whose value he had had estimated by two tailors.[40] That same month he bought linen for undergarments, paid for stockings and slippers, arranged for the mending of his wife Ginevera's dress or *cioppa*, and purchased light-blue woollen cloth for a *giornea* for his daughter Tommasa. In a similar fashion, when Giovanni and Niccolaio Niccolini raised their two nieces in the mid-fifteenth century, they personally bought the items needed for the girls' clothing, including minor items such as ribbons, threads and fasteners, rather than using female servants or relations.[41] In fact, as numerous scholars have shown, the items that are shown in the images of decorous Florentine girls were almost always bought by their male relatives rather than by themselves.[42]

What these accounts do not record, however, were the negotiations that took place within the household before or after these purchases were made. Did Maso ask his daughter or wife what type of garment they wanted or did he assume that they would be pleased with his purchases? Did Lapo Siringatti consult his wife as to whether the bed was a suitable addition to their possessions? Did he allow her to look at the goods in advance, or did he simply make all the decisions himself?

The letters of elite women such as Lucrezia Tornabuoni, wife of Piero dei Medici and mother of Lorenzo, help to answer some of these questions. Lucrezia was a very powerful figure in her own right and as a widow she kept her own accounts. Her correspondence during her husband's lifetime, like that of her mother-in-law, Contessina, primarily concerned maintaining the family's possessions, particularly their clothing. She sent items back and forth to family members and arranged for repairs and modifications. But while she concentrated on looking after the goods the family already had, her letters also indicate that she was well aware of what was available both at home and abroad, thanking those who sent her items or acted as her agents.[43] She similarly corresponded directly with the nuns of the convent of San Piero in Lucca to whom she sent linen to be embroidered.[44]

The surviving account book kept by the Medici bank in Pisa for her expenses dates towards the end of her lifetime from 1474 to 1477. Here, the widowed Lucrezia managed a series of farms and their produce, and purchased ticking for featherbeds, sugar and cloth, including basic linens which were sent as a gift to the nuns of Sant'Agostino.[45] The widow Alessandra Strozzi undoubtedly kept similar accounts for her household in Florence. She too relied on her sons in Naples to send her regular consignments of flax (which she like so many other women of the period spun for household linen), almonds, capers and sweetmeats. In her letters, she passed on requests from her daughter Caterina, who wanted soap and waters from Naples, 'to make her beautiful'.[46]

The first entry in another Strozzi widow's account book from 1486, indicates that she too rapidly took over running the home at her husband's death.[47] Although it may have been kept by a male relative or household servant, it is noteworthy that she emphasised that it was 'my book' when setting out the opening page. It is very unlikely that these women only learned how to keep household records at their husband's deaths, or that the widows who acted as procurators for the under-age children suddenly ceased to occupy themselves with family matters when their boys came of age. In his mid-sixteenth-century *ricordanza*, for example, the Florentine Pier Berardi acknowledged this ability by praising a relative, Mona Orsina, saying that, 'in the affairs of women she was not inferior to the most able; she knew well how to keep accounts and writings, she was a very good housewife and greatly increased her sons' goods with her earnings, after the death of her husband . . . .'[48]

Yet while it is right to be suspicious of the concept of the monolithic patriarchal buyer, it is clear that at all levels in Florence the head of the household was expected to keep close oversight of the family's income and expenses. In some cases, such as that of wedding garments bought in late fourteenth-century Florence, the whole family might be involved but payments still had to be approved by the male householder.[49] Major expenditure such as buying land, horses, jewellery, clothing or household furnishings would almost always come under his jurisdiction but he would also expect to know where his money was going on a daily basis. For example, among thousands of mercantile records regarding the international trade of Francesco di Marco Datini of Prato are a series of small *libri di spese*, domestic account books for his households in both Florence and Prato.[50] Datini was a major figure in the trade of raw and finished materials with an extensive business network that spanned the Mediterranean and the Atlantic routes. His main residence was in Prato, where he built and decorated a major new palazzo while his business often took him to Florence where he kept a second home. Unlike many other figures of his wealth and standing, Datini maintained a relatively small household, living with his wife Margarita, his illegitimate daughter Ginevra, and his mother. Despite the presence of these women, his household servants and shop assistants, Datini kept, or rather had kept, a record of even his most minor personal transactions. These surviving *libri di spese* record the daily expenses of visiting the market, sending out the laundry or going to the barber. They could be quite emotional as well as arithmetical. In 1399, for example, Datini left a lengthy account of his passionate engagement with the group known as the *Bianchi*, a movement of white-clad pilgrims who travelled across Europe in search of millenarian salvation. Following an evocative description of his pilgrimage, he noted the prosaic costs of this spiritual event. In order to go on the procession in Florence, Datini had spent 3 lire on bread, 2 lire on a pendant for his paternoster beads as well as buying a new pair of shoes, rope for a belt, eggs, figs and peaches, wine, fodder for his animals and new shoes for his horses and mules. In total, the excursion cost 35 lire, 1 soldo and 11 denari piccolo, and he was careful to note it all.[51]

But these *libri di spese* were not simply about new things or special events, they were also places to record repairs, loans and even the washing. In 1400, Datini noted the value of each item sent from Prato to Florence to be professionally laundered, cross-checking to make sure that it had been returned. For example, on 26 July 1400, Datini sent out sheets, towels, table linen, his nightcaps and his daughter's shirts to be washed by a professional male launderer in Florence. They were returned two days later.[52]

Laundry was only one of the many tasks that required professional intervention and service. Running several households was a complex business and from these *libri di spese* and other records, it seems the Datini household in Florence was run primarily an extension of his business. It was composed of male workers who used a young boy, a *fante*, to do their daily shopping. On one day, Friday, 16 December 1385, the boy Salimbene di Niccolò di Dono was sent out to the market to buy eggs. On that same trip he bought goods that would have usually come from a grocer: salted tuna, wine, Parmesan cheese, capers and candles, all of which came to the surprisingly large total of 50 soldi and 7 denarii.[53] The largest amounts, 19 soldi and 7 denari and 16 soldi respectively, were spent on half a round of Parmesan cheese and on two pounds of wax candles. This was large-scale shopping. The next day, the same household gave 5 soldi to the poor and bought 3 pounds of fish, yet more tuna, 5 pounds of veal, 26 eggs, garlic, leeks, and paid for the use of an oven to bake their bread. Despite all the strictures against Sunday shopping, payments were made on the next day for yet more candles and sausages.[54]

While the Florentine records make exclusive reference to male employees as buyers, the accounts of the Datini household in Prato provide a much more complex set of domestic arrangements. Here Francesco gave his most senior household servant, Cristo-foro de Ferrara, regular sums of between 12 and 30 lire for household expenses, sug-gesting that Cristoforo rather than Margarita Datini did much of the daily provisioning.[55] But Datini was not too proud to frequent the market himself. For example, Datini's records note that on Saturday, 16 February 1408, 3 staia of corn were purchased, 'bought by Francesco from a worker in the market'.[56] On the same day, he personally bought 7 and a quarter staia of barley, 6 staia of spelt, 2 bunches of mint and 4 bunches of leeks from different market stalls before finishing off the morning with a trip to the barbershop where presumably he had a shave.[57]

These Saturday outings were regular occurrences. For example, on another Saturday in March of that year the *libro di spese* noted that another Datini servant, Cecco, bought the leeks and bread while the merchant dropped into the barbershop again. The deci-sion to go to a public location rather than be shaved at home may have been prompted by political and social conditions. Gossip, information and male sociability may have been important aspects of these activities. Despite his wealth, Datini still needed to forge relationships with other men from Prato. Appearing in the marketplace was one method of reinforcing his reputation as a citizen and as a member of the community.

Francesco's visits to Prato's Saturday market were probably more symbolic than sub-stantial. Cristoforo da Ferrara seems to have done most of the marketing while Mar-garita Datini played a more minor role. Margarita's surviving letters make it clear that once she was considered mature enough, she too was allowed to handle the small sums of money required to pay small-scale expenses.[58] Accordingly, in 1408, Francesco noted that he gave his wife 1.2 lire to pay a woman who had turned up with a sheep and to pay for other transactions made at the door of their house.

This proved to be a consistent pattern. Where evidence survives, it does seem that wives, particularly after a few years of marriage, were allowed and expected to make the small-scale daily decisions about items that needed to be paid either in the market or at the door. For example, the fifteenth-century accounts of members of the dei Rossi and Castiglionchio families in Florence show that mothers in both homes were given limited sums of around 4 lire to buy stockings for their sons.[59] While Margarita Datini, Lucrezia Tournabuoni and Alessandra Strozzi were far from typical Tuscan women of the fourteenth and fifteenth centuries, their ability to place orders with male relatives, obtain high-quality items from suppliers at home and abroad and judge the quality and standards of the goods they received may have been more common than we have assumed. But they did not interact with the suppliers themselves; instead they worked through trusted male relatives. They avoided dishonour and never needed to engage in the face-to-face negotiations that women lower on the social scale confronted on a regular basis.

*   *   *

THE CASTELLANI FAMILY IN FLORENCE

Inevitably, the historical record prioritises written transactions, emphasising orders that were made through intermediaries rather than the purchases paid for in the market with coins. But even where traces of the latter exist, they too suggest that buying involved multiple stages and a range of social connections. In looking at another Florentine case, it is evident that for men as well as for women, shopping was a series of relationships rather than a simple exchange of money for material goods.

Francesco di Matteo Castellani, a mid-fifteenth-century Florentine, left behind two very detailed *zibaldone*, a combination of domestic accounts and familial diaries.[60] Originally published by Giovanni Ciapelli, they have been used by a number of scholars who have been interested in Castellani's clothing purchases, his relationships with humanists and the book-trade, and his acquisition of second-hand goods.[61] Examined as a whole, however, they also provide a great deal of information about the ways in which material possessions were bought, sold and used to forge connections of credit and friendship.

Francesco was born on 4 March 1418 to two of Florence's most elite families. His father was Matteo Castellani and his mother was Giovanna di Giovanni di Rinieri Peruzzi.[62] Like the Datini of Prato, both the Castellani and Peruzzi families had prospered from international trade. They had been prominent members of the Guelph party since the early fourteenth century, an alliance that brought them knightly status, an unusual position in communal Florence. Castellani grew up in a very wealthy household, with ten domestic servants.[63] In 1427, the Florentine tax estimate listed the family as one of the richest in the city. But at Matteo's death in September 1429, when Francesco was only twelve, the inheritance proved a troubled one. The Castellani found themselves on the losing side against the victorious Medici faction after 1434, and much of the family was sent into exile. Francesco was protected by his relative youth. At the same time he found that his knightly status meant that he continued to take on ceremonial roles. Nonetheless, he would never hold political office during his lifetime and found himself subject to constant punitive taxation. Thus, unlike many of the exiles, such as the Strozzi who left Florence to make a new fortune in Naples, Castellani remained in his home town. But he paid for this privilege with the gradual erosion of his once-large patrimony.

From the very first entries in the *zibaldone*, the tensions caused by the duality of Castellani's knightly status and his political exclusion are evident. Although his landed estates provided grain, wine and game for his table, and his rental property in Florence made it possible to raise the cash needed to pay off debts, he had to regularly raid his investments in the city's dowry fund, the *monte delle dote* to satisfy regular tax demands. In 1460, he only narrowly avoided imprisonment and the confiscation of his property over his non-payment of an increasingly onerous tax burden.[64] Yet at other points he can be found paying for elaborate garments in order to represent the same government on ritual occasions, clothing allowed only to Florence's knights. In a republic where appearance was scrutinised at every level, Castellani was forced to maintain his stature by a high level of consumption. Until his death at the age of seventy-seven in December 1494, his political and social credit depended in the most literal sense on what he and his family wore, ate and gave as gifts to friends and potential allies.

Because of Francesco's youth, his mother managed his affairs until he reached maturity in 1436. He then took over managing the accounts himself.[65] It is unlikely that Giovanna Peruzzi, known as Nanna, ceased to be involved with her son's affairs, but at this point she was written out of his documentation. From this moment, the records note the bargains that he found on the street and the necessity to protect and indeed recoup items lost to the family. For example, among his first annotations was a reminder to find out how a Jewish pawnbroker had managed to sell one of his family heirlooms to a second-hand dealer, followed by a record of his purchase of a Hungarian sword from a passing peddler for which he planned to get a new pommel.[66] But this *ricordanza* was not a *libro di spese minute* like that of Datini household. Instead, Castellani simply lumped together payments for food and household costs that were probably itemised elsewhere. What can be seen from his accounts, however, is that many of his household needs: wine, cheese, poultry and the flax that was spun for the household linen were not obtained in the market but from his farm in Antella. The estate's products also acted as a form of barter, and Castellani was able to settle his apothecary bill in bushels of grain. In addition, he owned a number of ovens in Florence and it is likely that he had his servants make up the dough that provided the household's bread. But even these items of domestic production required expenditure. To bottle his wine, Castellani had to buy substantial numbers of glass containers; to get the flour to make his bread, he had to enter into an arrangement with the local miller. There was little that was exclusively homemade about these goods.[67]

Francesco di Matteo Castellani's household was probably much smaller than that of his parents. In 1436, he married a member of another anti-Medicean family, Ginevra di Palla Strozzi. His wife, who brought him a dowry of 2,000 florins, was only thirteen when she came to live with him and she died childless at the age of twenty-one in October 1444. Her status as an adolescent who had yet to produce an heir may explain why she made so little impact on the Castellani accounts. She appears primarily as someone requiring medical care, and during her last illness there was a sudden increase in expenditure as she journeyed to the baths at Pontremoli, accompanied by her brother and a woman hired specifically for that purpose.[68]

The cure was a failure. Four years after Ginevra's death, Castellani married again. This time Cosimo dei Medici himself brokered a dowry of 1,700 florins, and the wedding with Lena di Francesco di Piero Alamanni took place in 1448, a hopeful sign of potential political reconciliation.[69] The wedding changed Francesco's lifestyle much more radically than his previous marriage as the sixteen-year-old Lena became pregnant almost immediately. Castellani already had two illegitimate sons, Niccolò and Bartolomeo, born to one *monna* Gentile, and his wife eventually produced three further daughters and a son who died in infancy in 1453. With these offspring came the associated costs of nursing, clothing and dowries. It is very noticeable that the expenditure on lavish clothing for the adults declined as the costs of servants needed to help raise these children rose, and the status of the parents shifted from bride and groom to that of mature parents of a growing family.

To help with their household, the Castellani employed, housed, clothed and fed an ever-shifting number of retainers. In 1459, for example, Francesco had a manservant, Giovan Piccino, whom he termed *mio famiglio*, who was paid 7.10 lire per month, plus clothing and expenses, such as his barber's bill. It would be Giovan Piccino who would go out to market on a regular basis. At times he was joined for specific purposes by the stable master, Giovanni di Tedesco (who was briefly replaced by his son, Giovanni di Giovan Tedesco despite the fact that, 'for the moment he does not speak a word of our language and is pretty useless'). Additional male retainers came and went with regularity. Although they make less impact on the registers, the Castellani also employed female servants, particularly after the birth of Lena's daughters. When Lena went to take the waters at Bagno a Morbo near Volterra, Francesco noted that she was accompanied by her brother, and an unnamed widow.[71] A wet nurse was then employed for two years to look after Francesco's illegitimate son Niccolò, and another was hired in 1460 to care for the newborn Giovanna.[71] In 1459, there was a reference to Caterina, 'mia serva' and, as the family increased, Giuliana, 'nostra serva', appears in the accounts of 1460. By this year, following Lena's many pregnancies and illnesses, they seem to have taken on a housekeeper, *monna* Lena di Vanni. In addition, specialists were sought for specific occasions. A midwife, *monna* Filippa, was paid 5 lire and 8 soldi for helping Lena during Giovanna's birth, and Lena personally paid a piper, Bernardo de Sancti Piffero, a gold florin each time he came to the house to teach her two older daughters, Maria and Margherita, to dance.[72] But while Castellani's illegitimate son, Niccolò was sent to the abacus school behind the Mercato Nuovo to learn basic skills of arithmetic, there is no indication that the girls received any other formal education.[73]

Because of their differing structures and purposes, the records dating before 1459 tell more about Castellani's major expenses while those written after that date tell more of the household's day-to-day running costs. Both indicate that purchases were often complex, particularly those involving clothing. For example, in August 1442, Castellani bought 6 *braccia* of red velvet for the large sum of 67 lire from the weaver Nofri d'Angelo, using the services of two intermediaries, one of whom was a silk merchant.[74] A few days later he took the material along with cheaper cloths intended for the lining to be made into a doublet, a close-fitting padded upper garment that was becoming increasingly fashionable in Florence. He handed the material over to Antonio, known as *el Tatta farsettaio*, a figure with whom he developed a regular commercial relationship. He used Tatta again in 1448, when he took black satin velvet worth 2 *braccia* to be made up into another doublet. This time, the artisan supplied the sleeves for the same doublet from a second-hand set that he had bought from a member of the Pucci family as part payment for yet another doublet.[75] The fabric made up the bulk of the cost of the garment. Tatta himself was only paid 15 grossi or just over 4 lire for his tailoring while his assistant received a single silver grosso as a tip, *per benvestita*.[76]

As these discrepancies between the high value of the materials and the much more modest cost of the manufacture suggest, cloth retained its value over time. In 1449, Francesco decided to use up some fabric that he had purchased almost eleven years earlier and bought a set of ready-made fur-lined sleeves to make up the standard Florentine male patrician dress, the *luccho*. The work was done by a tailor, Andrea da Bibiena, whose worker, like that of Tatta, Francesco again tipped, *per benvestita*. But this was not the end of the job. The *luccho* then had to be given to a furrier, Francesco *vaiaio*, to be fully lined.

When Francesco ordered elaborate clothing for his new wife as part of her counter-dowry, the gifts given to the bride in 1448, the number of figures involved grew even greater. As Carol Frick has shown, at least five different professions were used in the construction of sixteen-year-old Lena Castellani's new dress. Work on the garment went on over a four-year period involving mercers, tailors, the jewellers who supplied the many pearls required, the embroiderer who designed and constructed the elaborate decoration on the surface of the dress and even an accountant who kept track of the agreements that were reached.[77] The initial discussion over this dress occupied almost five folios of the *ricordanza*. Francesco, who had already designed embroidered sleeves with mottoes for himself during his first marriage, gave precise instructions as to the gown's appearance, with patterns constructed in gold and silver thread and pearls along the bodice and the sleeves that may have been similar to the pearl insets in the garment worn by a

woman of the Este family in a contemporary portrait by Pisanello (Figure 192). He seems to have personally gathered the valuable materials involved in the garment and delivered them to the embroidery firm of Maestro Giovanni Gilberto where a contract concerning its production was negotiated with some difficulty. But due to the delays in its delivery and Castellani's increasing debts, the dress was never worn. The embroiderer eventually died leaving the garment unfinished; in 1452, Castellani sent an agent to settle his account. In the end the dress was taken apart and its constituent parts were sold.[78] Over the years, other expensive garments that had once belonged to Lena were also sent to pawnbrokers to pay for family taxes.[79]

192 Pisanello, *Portrait of Ginevra* or *Margarita d'Este*, c.1434, tempera on panel, Musèe du Louvre, Paris.

Lena's feelings on this matter are unrecorded. In fact, the few references to her household activities show only her carrying out domestic tasks similar to those undertaken by Margarita Datini. Thus she received one *fiorino largo* in September 1452 for 'her expenses' and in August 1459, Francesco noted that his wife had bought a quantity of fennel from a female vendor, *monna* Mea dalla Porta, whose name 'of the door' suggests that she was probably a peddlar.[80] When one of Castellani's tenants paid her rent in pennies, *quattrini*, he handed the coins over to his wife, *per spese*.[81] But by 1461, with the birth of several children, her increasing maturity (she would have been almost thirty by this time) meant that she was making more important purchases in her own right such as a piece of cloth worth 64 lire and a worked headdress.[82] She was also paying the household servants and the women who wove linen for her with the money that Francesco gave her.[83]

If there was a need for closer supervision over family purchases, Francesco went out into the market personally. When friends came to dinner he ordered the provisions that were required; in 1459, he bought fish 'and other things from the apothecary' before entertaining members of the Pucci family.[84] Likewise, he personally chose gifts for friends and relations, even when these were destined for women. In 1442, for example, he had some of his old silver melted down so that he could send two silver salt cellars to Alessandra Strozzi, his first wife's sister-in-law, then in exile in Padua, to celebrate the birth of a son.[85] In October 1447 he chose twelve small silver forks 'in the Venetian style' from the goldsmith *orafo* Cosme as a wedding gift for the daughter of Carlo Federighi and in 1448 he sent damask cloth and a box of gilded candies to the wife of Piero da Iesi who had given birth to a boy.[86] If he made the arrangements himself, price was not always discussed directly. In 1442, for example, he bought, from a Strozzi relative, a small amount of basic cloth to make stockings, writing that 'we didn't make a price, but as I will give him some money, I am making a note here'.[87] Face-to-face negotiations brought other benefits in terms of flexibility. He was able to make arrangements that might have been more difficult for his servants to achieve. Accordingly, when (in 1447) Castellani bought 11 *braccia* of black velvet from Piero di Peterini's silk company for 23 florins, he noted that he had arranged for payment in kind, exchanging the cloth for wine, grain and flour.[88]

In addition to overseeing purchases that were important either in terms of expense or of honour, Castellani also sought out items of scholarly interest. Although not a humanist himself, he was closely connected to a group of scholars and intellectuals who were associated with the burgeoning interest in classical texts. Thus on 5 July 1447 at the estate sale of the deceased Antonio Bellaci he bought two manuscripts of Justinian and Suetonius for 4 florins. This was a private, rather than a public sale, and when he made the payment, it did not go through a procurator or an institution such as the Pupilli. Instead he sent the cash to Bellaci's widow directly, sending a female servant, *mona Guida nostra serva* to deliver the cash rather than using the male servants that he typically employed.[89] It is possible that it was easier and more discreet for another woman to enter a widow's home without causing comment. His book purchases increased extensively during the late 1450s and 1460s when his political and financial fortunes were at their lowest ebb. While it is important not to underestimate Castellani's own passion for the classics, it could appear that his tenuous ties to those who were closer to the Medici faction were heavily reinforced by a common interest in Latin and Greek texts.

These examples suggest that Francesco Castellani, like Francesco Datini before him, took a close personal interest in the Florentine marketplace and its many opportunities. Yet his accounts also show that while he insisted on handling high-value goods or those where a documented intellectual or social interest existed, he was far more reticent about other types of public appearances in the city centre. He relied heavily on third parties in his transactions. Sometimes the need for an intermediary was prompted by a requirement for specialist advice; at other times the arrangements were more casual. Having met a linen-dealer socially in the house of Daniele Alberti, he handed over a woollen cloak since, as he noted, the latter said he could sell it off to Castellani's advantage.[90] Informal contacts were important on other occasions. In 1442, for example, he bought a horse for 18 florins using Neri Pitti, a mutual friend, as his intermediary.[91] But professionals were also involved in Castellani's purchases and sales: on 3 December 1444, he sold a bay horse with a star on its forehead to a soldier in Florence's horse market, the 'mercato del cavallo' for the substantial sum of 29 florins. He used as his *mezo*, or middleman, one Maestro Ambrogio.[92] Two weeks later Francesco bought cloth for almost the same amount from the warehouse of the wool merchant Luigi Bartoli. Despite the high value of this purchase and the fact that he almost certainly knew Bartoli personally, he still used an intermediary, the *sensale* Fruosino Ciucci.[93] The use of a broker who would register the transaction with the guild may, in fact, have been a requirement for the sale's validity.

Credit was very dependent on personal reputation, but whenever the issue involved debt, Castellani was always very careful to disguise his presence through a third party. Almost any action that might suggest that he was in personal financial need was hidden behind a layer of male servants or by a range of other male friends, relations and professional intermediaries. He used these friends and servants to drop off his belts at the pawnbrokers, to take jewellery out of town to obtain further loans, or to place his clothing on consignment with second-hand dealers.[94] For example, the first entry for 1459 records that he pawned 'a pretty belt with a round gilt clip in the Parisian style worked with foliage in relief and with seven large studs on a piece of black cloth, old and rotten'.[95] He sent the belt via a dyer, pawning not only the belt but also pearls, rings, a fur-lined cloak and a hat at the lender known as the *presto di Sancta Trinita* for six fiorni larghi.[96] Another pawn, this time of four silver spoons, was made in a similar fashion in July, again in the name of a family servant. Shortly afterwards, the same servant went on to redeem goods that had been pawned by Castellani in Pistoia, a town he had stopped off at while trying to sell grain in Empoli.[97]

The *zibaldone* provides interesting insights into the rationale behind each episode. The pledges were almost always connected to an immediate need for cash, either to pay

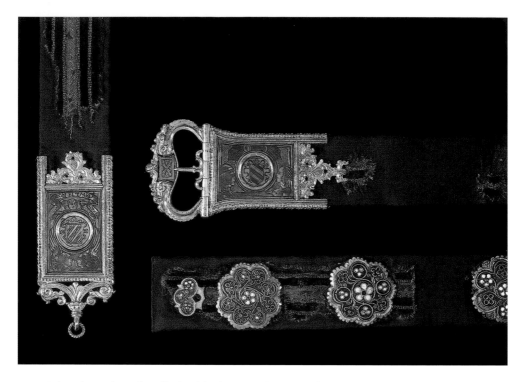

193 Belt, silver gilt and niello buckles bearing the arms of the Malatesta of Rimini and Cesena, c.1450, The British Museum, London.

the taxes that had to be met in high-quality gold and silver coins, or to pay for small-scale purchases and salaries. Pawning often seemed better value than actually selling the goods. At one point in 1459, for example, Castellani clearly considered disposing of some of his valuables and had his belts estimated by a number of goldsmiths in Florence's Mercato Nuovo. The metal element of these belts, which may have resembled the examples from the British Museum, provided their monetary worth (Figure 193). But when he was only offered a valuation of 26 grossi, he decided that it was more advantageous to pawn them.[98] Another time when Castellani decided to literally divest himself of eight shirts by placing them on consignment with a second-hand dealer on 17 October 1459, the linen was taken to the shop by his servant Giovan Piccino and his friend, the human-ist poet Luigi Pulci. They were enjoined, the writer recorded, to obtain the best price pos-sible.[99] However, less than three weeks later, it was clear to all concerned that the price at which they could be sold was too low to be viable. On 6 November 1459, the servant Giovan Piccino picked up the shirts and took them to one of Lena's relatives, Jacopo di Boccaccino Allamanni, to offer as exchange for a loan.

Castellani's constant, sometimes even desperate need for cash meant that he often had to use multiple sources from different social communities at the same time. In one week in 1450, he borrowed 150 ducats from a banker in Florence, Bono di Giovani Boni; he then deposited a pearl collar and a diamond ring with a jeweller in the hope of a sale on consignment and borrowed a substantial 25 florins from a shoemaker. At the same time he asked for a total of 51 florins from Strozzi relatives, offering his newly made *luccho* and other garments as security.[100] He carefully noted that they had his full permission to sell these items if he could not return the cash.[101] Sometimes he over-stretched himself. In October 1459, Castellani could not afford to redeem his pawns in full, and sent money to Manuello di Bonaventura Ebreo to cover his interest, along with a diamond worth 18 florins as security for a further loan of 6 florins.[102]

The use of multiple friends, professional associates and relatives to obtain cash as well as credit extended to his suppliers as well as to his peers. Richard Marshall has shown how minor retailers acted effectively as bankers and this was true for Castellani who relied on many individuals for such small-scale loans.[103] His tailor, grocer, butcher and shoemaker knew him well and provided credit over many years. Sometimes these were for purchases, but often they were simply loans for unstated purposes. A shoe-maker, Bartolomeo da Cioffoli from Incisa, where the family had property, was partic-ularly important in sustaining Castellani's cash flow.[104] The relationship between the two men in the countryside, where Castellani was the landlord of a large estate, may have been quite different from that between the Florentine and his artisan neighbours in the city. But Castellani also borrowed extensively from Florentine shopkeepers, often using very casual arrangements. He took a *fiorino largo* from his local grocer, Perugino Pizzicagnolo al Ponte Vecchio, to pay his servants' wages and to redeem items that one of his retainers had pawned.[105] This grocer again often loaned Castellani money and acted as a moneychanger providing the small silver coins that were needed for daily transactions in exchange for gold coins.[106] Finally, other artisans were also important lenders, either of goods offered on credit or simply for cash loans. In 1459, for example, Castellani sent Giannozzo to redeem a belt that the glassmaker, Nicolao, had had since 1457 as security against a minor debt for the purchase of 60 flasks for wine.[107] Both Castellani and the glassmaker had simply forgotten about the debt, suggesting that such arrangements were relatively common. In another instance earlier in 1450, Castellani had borrowed the much larger sum of 100 florins from a doublet-maker. In this instance he used a friend, the pro-Medicean Florentine official, Ser Giovanni Cafferecci da Voltero, *capitano de' fanti*, or captain of the guard, as his intermediary, offering two rings as security for the loan.[108] Cafferecci, it should be stressed, was not a minor figure in the city. He had been in service to the Medici family since 1429, and had acted as tutor to Cosimo dei Medici's second son, Giovanni. Cafferecci and his wife and daugh-ter went with Lena Castellani to the baths of Bagno a Morbo near Volterra in 1459. In noting that the captain was his 'compare' or fellow godparent, Castellani was record-ing his increasing acceptance into the Medici orbit.[109]

As these transactions suggest, Castellani's accounts tell us as much about the inter-relationships between buying and selling, owning and loaning as they do about pur-chasing. We can see the major role an investment in objects played in sustaining his lines of credit. He used material goods – valuables such as belts, cloaks, silver spoons and cloth hangings – as surety for loans and as a means of favouring relations. One gilt cup alone, inscribed with reliefs of deer and foliage and the arms of his mother's family, the Peruzzi, went in and out of pawnshops, banks and friend's homes on so many occasions that Castellani stopped describing it in detail. By 1460, many of the family's most prized possessions were in the hands of others. The extravagant clothing that Lena had once been given or hoped to receive had been carefully wrapped in linen cloth and sent out to the Jewish money-lender, Manuele, so that Francesco could pay back Cafferacci, the captain referred to above. But at the same time, in order to preserve public appearances, Castellani borrowed: 'a large pearl set in gold and enamel or rather black niello, a diamond set in gold enamelled in the Parisian style with white and red flowers and green foliage, and a ruby set in gold and attached to buttons without any enamelling', so that Lena could wear them to the wedding of a member of the Benizzi family in January 1460.[110] The public appearance of wealth obtained through this particular loan disguised the private indebtedness.

While these examples suggest that Castellani was almost always the debtor or the figure pleading to pay with agricultural products rather than cash, this was not the case. He was also at the other end of such relationships, accepting his rents in kind and making small-scale loans to his own friends and relations. For example, a doublet-maker rented space from Castellani, providing clothing for four male servants in return.[111] When a baker couldn't pay his rent for one of Castellani's ovens, he offered one and a half *braccia* of cloth instead. Although the patrician wrote disdainfully of its quality and condition, he had it assessed by a number of second-hand dealers and a *sensale* and finally accepted it as payment.[112] In addition, Castellani lent his clothing, sword and armour to blacksmiths and other artisans when they needed to put on events for particular feast days and when they were given offices by the government that required special garments.

Castellani's accounts demonstrate how material goods also forged connections horizontally with family and friends as well as vertically with social superiors and inferiors. Francesco's second entry notes that he had loaned the Peruzzi cup and four cloth hangings with his family arms to one Falcone di Nicola Falconi when the friend married his sister to yet another Florentine patrician, Domenico di Filippo Lenzi. His next recorded loan was to the mathematician, Domenico dal Pozzo Toscanelli, to whom he sent a 'large world map with inscriptions'. Andrea Boccaccini Alamanni borrowed the newest edition of the letters of Cicero, and accepted in writing that they were worth 25 florins as he promised their safe return.[113] In December of that same year, Castellani loaned Ser Clemente, the schoolmaster in the house of his friend Cafferacci, 'his newly acquired Justinian and Suetonius' and then later sent over a copy of 'the rules of Quirino Veronese'.[114]

These loans were made without financial remuneration, deliberately removing them from market values. As Castellani noted sadly when a pearl necklace was returned seemingly lighter than it had left, the loss was not worth complaining over.[115] Just as he did not want to turn family ties into purely financial relationships, so too he avoided turning credit arrangements with artisans into connections of friendship. While his valuables moved from his own home to those of grocers, doublet-makers and pawnbrokers, he did not invite them to his table nor did he sit at theirs. The links were supposed to be very different, reinforcing rather than breaking down social stratifications. While Castellani might owe his grocer money, he was still a knight. Yet at the same time there was a strong sense of mutual reliance. Unlike a member of the Medici family, Castellani did not have the political authority to force his creditors to wait for his payment or to make friends and relations provide him with loans. There had to be far more negotiation and understanding. Castellani's suppliers hoped for his solvency and relied on his custom, in some cases presumably for prestige and in others possibly for profit. He, in turn, could not have functioned without their cash, credit and provisions. Under these circumstances, the running of errands, buying, selling, borrowing and lending were not impersonal acts but connections that bound different levels of society together in mutual interdependencies.

THE PRIULI FAMILY IN VENICE

The connections forged by shopping and other forms of exchange come across equally powerfully in the accounts of Venetian patricians. But here the geography of the city and its particular social structure made for a very different set of arrangements. Again, it is not possible to do statistical analysis or comparison because of the limitations of Venetian evidence, where far fewer account books survive. Those that can be found are often associated with the legal need to prove probity. In the early fourteenth century, for example, the executors responsible for the estate of the deceased Niccolò Moresini kept a careful account of the monies they had spent maintaining his household until his children came of age.[116] This was not a personal record but a means of proving that the inheritance had not been squandered. Bernardo Morosini's 1343 *libro di spese minute* recorded daily outings and major purchases. From the book it can be seen that vegetables such as cabbages or lettuces were purchased almost every morning and evening; meat and wine were bought approximately every three days. By February, the family was buying beans and peas, and eventually as spring emerged, figs, almonds and other fruits. Honey and sugar were relatively rare items while one single purchase of oranges quadrupled the price of the daily shopping trip. As was common in Florence, the bread was made at home and then sent out to be baked in the neighbourhood bakery while additional loaves were bought from the local grocer. Cheese, oil, drinking water and wood were the family's other major regular purchases.

But if this early record is a rare example, it does suggest that Venetians were interested in tracking their expenses in ways that were quite similar to their Florentine counterparts. For example, the painter Lorenzo Lotto kept a highly detailed record of his income and expenditure. The accounts from 1535 to 1537 that survive for one branch of the noble Priuli family on which this section will focus make it clear that this book is merely a continuation of one begun much earlier in 1512.[117] The writer who tracked his daily expenses for over twenty-three years was Francesco Priuli, a member of one of the most prominent Senatorial families in Venice and related through his mother, Orsa, to another key clan, the Malipiero.[118] His immediate household seems to have consisted of his wife, Zizilia or Cecilia, the daughter of Jacopo Marin. In 1535, his father-in-law made the final payment of 300 ducats towards Cecilia's dowry, and a reference to the first dowry payments that had been made earlier that year suggests that the marriage had been a relatively recent one.[119] The eldest child referred to in the accounts, Camillo, must have either been a child by a first marriage or an illegitimate son. Camillo had been under the care of the schoolmaster Jacomo Adriaticho since 1531 when 'he began to go to school', suggesting that he must have been about ten at the time the accounts began.[120] The purchase of a copy of Burchiello's sonnets and Cicero's letters on his behalf in 1535 reinforces the assumption as this would have been an age to move on to more difficult Latin reading; in 1536, Priuli bought a printed edition of Virgil for his son and in 1537, bought him a Greek textbook, suggesting the boy had moved into adolescence.[121]

The other son who appears in the accounts, Domenico, seems to have been a much younger child by Francesco's wife, Cecilia. During the period the accounts were kept, a third child was born, a daughter, but the infant died shortly after birth. The family was an extended one and while it is unclear precisely where they lived, Priuli made purchases on behalf of his sisters, Juana and Cecilia (who, despite sharing the same name with his wife Cecilia, is always clearly noted as his sister in the text). He also supported his mother who was actively engaged in spending household monies on her son's behalf.[122]

In comparison with the Florentine household studied earlier, the Priuli kept a relatively small number of servants, far more of whom were female. The most important figure was the female housekeeper or *massara*. They initially employed Lucrezia who was replaced in 1436 by Lucia. Both women were paid around 12 soldi a month and received an additional allowance for clothing and shoes. The family followed fashion to the extent of housing at least one dwarf, Orsola *nana*, while the infant Domenico was looked after by a woman known as Vendramina who may also have been a dwarf. In addition, there were at least two other servants over the period in question, a maid, Paula, and a young boy, Marco Antonio.

There was no secretary to keep the accounts, which were double-entry summaries of what must have been much more detailed individual *libri di spese* like those of Datini. The handwriting was consistent over this whole period and regular references to *mi* or myself when describing purchases suggest that the scribe was indeed Priuli. Accountancy was clearly as important to the Venetian as it had been to his Florentine counterparts. Indeed the first recorded payment in the new account book was for the book itself, 14 soldi, a sum that was immediately followed by payments for salads at the same price. But the fascination of this record is not simply in what Priuli bought but also in the range of different ways and sites from which he and his family made their purchases. His notes show him buying indulgences, lottery tickets and church masses as well as food, wine, fuel, clothing and transportation. As with Castellani, these activities forged connections across the many social divides of Venetian society.

Income and Expenditure

While the Castellani family had relied on landed estates, rents and *monte* shares, the Priuli family income is harder to assess. Overall, the record suggests the significant prosperity and financial confidence that came with political prominence in sixteenth-century Venice. Francesco loaned money out to friends and relations rather than relying on credit himself. Although he did borrow small sums regularly, leaving jewellery or plate as a pledge, he was comparatively free of long-term obligations. His income, however, is very difficult to follow from this account book. There was money from rents on houses in the city itself and from arrangements made to take grain in lieu of rent on property in the Terraferma.[123] Lottery tickets seem to have been a remarkably effective means of generating cash. In 1537, Priuli went into partnership with at least four other friends and family members to obtain tickets, paying only 7 ducats for the privilege of joining a range of syndicates. The following year, he was able to record a profit of just over 134 ducats.[124] This success suggests that far from being a form of wild gambling, purchasing lottery tickets was a sensible financial strategy.

Perhaps with an eye towards tax officials, Priuli ensured that his expenditure was easier to track than his income. In the first half of the book, he kept a running total of what his household had spent on a weekly, monthly and annual basis. In his final annual account he divided the expenses between those 'of the mouth', *da bocca*, and those that were 'extraordinary', *da vestire*, which included clothing and special purchases. In the second part of the book he kept double-entry accounts against the names of each of his creditors and debtors. This format makes it simple to track his expenses over the year.

The major fluctuations over the three-year period which went from 398 lire to 265 lire the following year were not in the more basic expenses of feeding the household, the *spese di boccha* but in the additional extraordinary expenses such as clothing. Although there was a greater amount spent on luxury items for festivities in 1535, it is not always easy to explain the annual discrepancies. There was more that was consistent from year to year. October, for example, was a month when winter clothing was organised, a practice that often involved orders for new garments and fresh linings for existing items.[125] In November, a pig was usually slaughtered and the cost of the spices required for sausage-making helped to lift the amounts spent that month, as did the payments made for masses for the feast of All Souls.[126] Christmas does not seem to have prompted much attention but in early January of each year, Francesco had to give each member of his household a small tip, usually a gold or silver coin, *per bon anno*.[127] In 1535, the carnival that followed was celebrated by the family in some style. The couple decorated their main hall, the *portego*, for a party and paid out further small sums to their servants in tips.[128] Dona Orsola *nana* was tipped *per festa* while Antonio *regazo* got cash, *per spender in Carneval*.[129] Every year, Lent and Easter brought the associated costs of religious devotions. Although Francesco made small donations to the church on a regular basis througout the year, they rose considerably at this point. He paid for his wife and household servants' confessions in March 1535. In 1536, he purchased inexpensive books of prayers for himself and his mother during Holy Week (at a cost of 16 denari each) and made additional donations on Maundy Thursday.[130] The state of his family's spiritual health was as important as their material welfare, and in June 1535, he spent several soldi for the confession that Cecilia had made in order to benefit from a plenary indulgence.[131]

After these liturgical festivities and religious obligations came the celebrations that formed the Ascension Day fair in mid-May. Attending the *Sensa* fair was a major occasion for the whole family. Priuli had to keep a separate (now lost) account book of the amounts given to his family and retainers as tips, a task he delegated to his wife who actually handed out the cash *per pagare la Sensa*, a total of just over six ducats.[132] He placed coins in Cecilia's purse as she left for the fair herself.[133] Her purchases were not itemised, but in 1535, Francesco repaid her brother, Ser Polo Manin, *mio cugnado* just over 15 lire for the things that he had acquired *in Senza* including rash cloth, *rassa*, of different colours, plain white cloth for shirts and a hat for Camillo.[134] In 1536, Francesco went to the Sensa himself and took advantage of the unveiling of new glassware to buy, 'a salt cellar for the table in glass' for the very reasonable price of just 5 soldi.[135]

While these routine expenses could be generally planned and predicted, sudden unexpected costs could raise the family's outgoings especially since minor but costly health problems were common. For example, one of Priuli's sisters suffered eye trouble in 1536, prompting the purchase of medicines and the repair of her eyeglasses.[136] This cost only 3 soldi but when an illness required a doctor the amounts were elevated as these professionals expected to be paid immediately in gold coin. Thus when Messer Maffeo de Mapleci *medico* came to see Cecilia in 1535, Francesco immediately handed over a single gold scudo in return for the visit.[137] The prescription for her recovery included the common request that she should eat poultry and the next payment was for 2-lire's worth of chickens and capons. She was obviously expecting in the winter 1536–7 and delivered a baby girl soon after over the Easter weekend.[138] As the 1.1.3 lire paid for the costs of calling godparents to witness the baptism indicates, she lived long enough for the important ritual of baptism. But the costs of the burial that followed soon after, 3.3 ducats, were surprisingly high.[139] The whole event had clearly been traumatic for Francesco's wife and he purchased her a special chair for her to sit on and delicate food such as poultry to aid her recovery.[140]

Unlike Castellani, Francesco was not always forthcoming as to who actually carried out his household tasks and much of what follows has to be gleaned by cross-referencing. It is certainly possible that all the shopping was done by others and that Priuli only recorded their expenses without referring to the actual purchaser. But this seems unlikely. Priuli was always careful to note when he gave money to others for particular types of expenditure. For example, his mother paid for many household expenses, as did his housekeeper, and he always noted when Cecilia was given funds 'for her expenses'. The other servants rarely received money to spend on their master's behalf and were only reimbursed when they bought the clothing that formed part of their own annual salaries. By 1537, his son Camillo was increasingly trusted to run errands. Thus while it is dangerous to infer from silence, it was probably Priuli who made the other purchases in person. If true, Priuli looked after both major and minor tasks. He paid a poulterer for the chicken bones that Cecilia would make into needles and the silk merchants for fine velvets for himself, his wife and children.[141] He had a range of different strategies for making these purchases. He relied on a small number of regular suppliers for basic household items, using a single grocer, Zuan Paulo Sumariva, for products ranging from salted cheese, oil, writing paper, salt and inexpensive cloth.[142] In 1536, the goods listed in as expenses under Sumariva's name totalled 20 ducats.[143] He

also seems to have gambled regularly in the grocer's company, presumably in the shop itself. In addition to these contacts, Francesco went to the Merceria to buy the cotton and silk threads that were used to sew caps, shirts and stockings for the household. When it came to buying women's clothing, Priuli, like Castellani, made the arrangements to buy both the fabrics and to organise the tailoring. This was true for shoes as well as for major garments. Priuli bought Cecilia's elegant clogs that had uppers of white silk and cost 1.4 lire. Even his little son Domenico's shoes were in white silk and cost 8 soldi.[144] Fashionable items remained a priority over all three years. In 1537, for example, Francesco bought his wife the very desirable fox furs with full heads as illustrated in the Veronese portrait of Countess Livia da Porto Thiene and her daughter and in Lorenzo Lotto's portrait of Lucina Brembati (Figures 194–6). The costs of the

194 Paolo Veronese, *Countess Livia da Porto Thiene with Her Daughter, Porzia*, 1555, oil on canvas, The Walters Art Museum, Baltimore.

195 Lorenzo Lotto, *Lucina Brembati*, c.1518, oil on canvas, Accademia Carrara di Belle Arte, Bergamo.

'white fox with its head to carry in her hand for Zizilia, and for its box' were high at just over 14 lire.[145]

At the same time as relying on a series of regular suppliers, Priuli also took advantage of the sudden opportunities for bargains, regularly frequenting auctions and buying lottery tickets. When Castellani was writing his account books in Florence, the second-hand Pupilli auctions had been restricted to professional dealers. He had to turn to professional dealers to get the items he wanted. But in sixteenth-century Venice, an elite male figure such as Priuli saw no need to use intermediaries to buy even the most banal items at auction. Thus in 1535 he bought a 'cap of rough red wool' for his boy-servant, for 4.4 lire, paying 1 soldo to the *comandadore* as his fee.[146] He also furnished his servant's rooms this way. He bought a table carpet, and another 'old carpet' and in 1537, he bought a bed with feather cushions for his housekeeper at a cost of 2 ducats and 11 soldi, a sum that included the cost of the *commandadore*'s charges and the necessary transport.[147] But these were not merely moments to buy cheap goods appropriate for servants. Many of his luxury items were also purchased at auction. He bought a set of buttons in the Ghetto at the auction of the Jews, *l'incanto dei hebrei*, and at the same

196 Detail of Fig. 195 showing marten head.

site purchased a pearl necklace and bracelet on another occasion (this time paying the substantial sum of 19 soldi as the auctioneer's charge).[148] All these items, he noted, were for his wife. Other items purchased at auction included a gilt set of paternoster beads, for which he had to pay additional sums to both the auctioneer and the guild's senior official.[149] Having made these purchases he might then go on to modify them. For instance, the jewels he bought from the Ghetto auction in May of 1535 were later turned into a pendant for Cecilia by a goldsmith at the cost of an additional 2 ducats.[150]

In bidding, Francesco Priuli was supposed to be participating in an open market where only one's ability to pay in cash determined participation. But the personal relationship that the family had with one of the Venetian auctioneers suggests that this ideal of anonymity was more complex. On the evidence of this account book, one crier known as Francesco *comandadore* had a long-standing relationship with the Priuli family. This manifested itself in September 1536 when the auctioneer loaned Francesco Priuli 5 ducats. The ostensible motive was to subsidise a trip to see the patrician's brother-in-law in the town of Este.[151] The debt was quickly redeemed and soon afterwards, Priuli himself paid Francesco *commandadore* a commission, a 'sensaria', for finding and purchasing a diamond worth 50 ducats on his behalf.[152] When the family wanted to sell off unwanted items, they again turned to the same auctioneer to act on their behalf. In 1536, for example, the *commandadore* sold a table carpet at auction for 13 ducats.[153] Some deals were done more privately. On 22 February 1535, Priuli arranged for Francesco *comandadore* to sell a black velvet fur-lined piece of cloth on behalf of Bernardina, the daughter of the goldsmith Magistro Almoro, who had given it to him as a pawn pledge.[154]

This second Francesco probably had a relatively modest social status in Venice, acting as a bailiff, as discussed in chapter seven, town crier and official auctioneer. He would have had a uniform, including a characteristic red cap, and was able to march in official processions. It is not, therefore, completely surprising to find a relationship of service and loyalty between Venice's most elite patricians and these servants. They frequented the same public spaces, the Rialto and Piazza San Marco, and were able to do services for each other that facilitated both their lives and careers.

It was more difficult, but not impossible, for other family members to forge these types of relationships. Francesco's mother Orsa Malpiero and his housekeeper seem to have generally kept his home in order and paid for items that were delivered to the door. His wife Cecilia used her own funds to make small-scale purchases and was then repaid. For example, when she took a delivery of fresh eggs at the door, Priuli specified the coins that he gave her as reimbursement 'in bagatini' or small, low-grade coins.[155] When Cecilia went out to see friends in Campo San Piero, by contrast, he handed over much higher-grade silver 'mocenigo' coins.[156] Items where it is known that Cecilia made the purchase directly herself were relatively minor, up to a maximum of 18 soldi, and included a set of string laces for their son, Domenico (perhaps to tie up his trousers), money to pay Orsola *nana* for spinning thread for shirts, and cash for the purchase of candles.[157]

But despite her relative lack of involvement in family finances, Cecilia was far more mobile than her Florentine female counterparts and was able to actively participate both in the city's religious life and its more secular pleasures. She attended confession regularly, went to the Sensa fair annually and went by boat to the homes of friends and relatives. Her husband provided her with coins to do her shopping at the Sensa fair and small sums to gamble with, coins *per zuogar*. Cecilia's movements are known because Priuli paid the gondolier who moved his wife about the city, noting her destinations.[158] Over the three years between 1535 and 1537, his wife visited relatives and friends in the noble houses of Ca' Zana, Ca' Foscari and Ca' Malpiero. In late November 1535, she went to Ca' Martello to offer her condolences for a family death.[159] At Christmas she moved about Venice by boat, taking numerous trips, including one to Ca' Foscari for her entertainment, *per alegrarsi*.[160] The following year after Easter she went to a wedding of a member of the Venier family and on other occasions she went out as far as Murano.[161]

Cecilia's recorded visits were almost exclusively by water, a means of transport that like the increasingly popular enclosed carriages on land afforded relative privacy. Although the family did not employ its own gondolier, Priuli almost always used the same rower for Cecilia, the oarsman Stefano Barcarola. The list of payments for 1535 for services rendered by Stefano record that the money was paid directly to his wife, Dona Ruosa. The payments included rowing Cecilia to the Malipiero family palace in Sant'Apostoli and returning to fetch her in the evening (a trip that cost 6 soldi), taking her on another occasion to the Dolfin family home, delivering wood, wine from Marghera, and building materials, as well as taking Francesco himself to 'La Fusina' and to a party at the palace of the Orio family.[162] In September 1535, for example, Priuli noted that he had paid 4 soldi to take a boat to see the *festa dei pugni*, the famed Venetian festival where young men contended for possession of Venice's bridges.[163] He also travelled to the Terraferma where his brother-in-law managed estates near the town of Este that provided the family with much of its agricultural produce. These trips must have provided opportunities for social contact and the accounts show that Priuli knew both the gondolier and his wife extremely well. Priuli was godfather to one of the couple's sons while Dona Ruosa acted as wetnurse to his younger son Domenico during a serious illness.[164] Priuli specifically cited her help during this difficult period as his reason for paying for the education of the couple's children, arranging for them to be taught to read by his son Camillo's own schoolmaster.[165] In March 1536, he accepted one of Dona Ruosa's dresses as a pledge against a loan for her daughter Paula's dowry, eventually writing off the loan as an act of charity as well as making a further loan to allow Stefano to mend his boat.[166]

CONCLUSION

Because direct operations in the public marketplace carried their own problems for elites, the use of intermediaries was essential. The ties of trust had to go through multiple layers rather than form a single, temporary transaction between buyer and seller. The favours, loans and errands that resulted were acts that formed long-term ties of clientship, strengthened by a language of friendship and service.

The ease with which he moved in different marketplaces made Priuli resemble the late fourteenth-century merchant of Prato, Francesco di Marco Datini, far more than the knightly Castellani of fifteenth-century Florence. But just as Castellani's debts to his grocer did not lower his social superiority, Priuli's relationships with his boatman, grocer and auctioneer did not raise them to the Senatorial elite. Instead, these links reinforced distinctions, while providing the social cohesion that was so important to the successful image of Republican Florence and Venice.

CHAPTER NINE

Shopping with Isabella d'Este

The previous chapter suggested that the roles women played as consumers in Renaissance Florence and Venice were often hidden in family records. Although there are glimpses of their participation in the marketplace, women emerged from the shadows of their husbands' paperwork only when widowed. But in turning to the Italian Renaissance courts, wives, mothers, daughters and sisters suddenly appear with far greater clarity. As figures that might eventually substitute for their husbands, consorts such as Eleanora of Aragon, shown in a contemporary treatise holding the *bacchetta* of command, or her daughters Isabella and Beatrice, cultivated a public reputation that would allow them to rule if and when it became necessary (Figure 197).[1] Death, warfare, illness, exile, imprisonment or even an extensive hunting trip might suddenly catapult them into the position of regent. Yet even as obedient spouses, these women had incomes that allowed for considerable independence. They did not have to wait for widowhood to act as powerful figures in their own right. With more cash in hand than many patrician men, they were powerful purchasers who were able to make a significant impact on the Renaissance marketplace.[2]

THE BUREAUCRACY OF BUYING

To understand how court women, and in particular the exemplary figure of Isabella d'Este operated as consumers requires an understanding of the structures in which their

Detail of Fig. 19

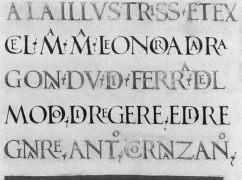

197 Cosmè Tura, *Portrait of Eleanora of Aragon*, 1478–9, The Pierpont Morgan Library, New York, MS M.731, f. 2v.

buying took place not only in Mantua but in most, if not all, Italian courts. Court consumption was a profoundly different business from the forms of purchasing used by even the most wealthy Republican families such as the Priuli or the Medici. Like other institutions such as monasteries and hospitals, courts were communities with predictable needs. There was a consistent demand for basic foodstuffs and essential items of clothing such as shoes, stockings, underwear, fuel and transport. While some of this, such as linen, sausages or salami, was made in-house, much more was purchased from outside sources.

The expense and difficulty of simply providing enough to eat for the court can be seen from a letter from the Marquis of Mantua's majordomo on 16 July 1488:

Your lordship writes of your surprise at the lack of foodstuffs [*vivere*] in the house. It is true that we have done everything possible and have not been lacking in diligence . . . Your Excellency should know that we have 500 mouths to feed on ordinary wages and with the expense of forage for the horses, of whom your lordship has more than 650. We have seen that for the said 500 mouths we need 770 lire a week of ordinary expenses, not including bread and wine which must also be purchased. Then there are the remainder who fall outside of this on whom we spend about a third more . . . According to the *spenditore* the 770 lire that are assigned to the ordinary expenses are simply not there and it is for this reason that there are problems and that often we lack the things that we need at court.[3]

Almost forty years later in 1521, another official, the court treasurer Girolamo Arcario was still trying to keep some control over basic expenditure, writing:

Your lordship knows that it is necessary to keep to a limit of one-hundred and ninety-two mouths who have bread, wine and meat and twenty-eight charitable cases as well as seventy-four hounds and one hundred and thirty horses, thus there is unhappiness on the part of many.[4]

These and other attempts at frugality were similarly without effect; in 1540, Federico II's widow, Margarita Paleologo, had to again issue a public announcement limiting the number of courtiers and servants who would be paid from the signorial purse.

Feeding, housing and clothing courtiers, stabling the horses and maintaining the dogs, falcons and other members of the menagerie required constant control and vigilance. The key problem centred on the fact that court appointments were not made on the basis of practical need, but for political purposes. Maintaining a group of loyal (or potentially disloyal) men and women was not a luxury that could be avoided. It was a necessary part of controlling urban and territorial communities. Although there were complaints about the constraints that acting as courtier placed on one's freedom, obtaining a court position was a much sought-after sinecure. This meant that jobs were multiplied and subdivided in order to offer employment. For example, a letter from the court doctor to the Duchess of Milan explained why her six-year-old son Galeazzo Maria needed a full complement of servants:

> Three chamberlains will never suffice in dressing our lord: two are needed to hold him when he is being buttoned, one needs to hold the stockings, another the shoes and another the dress. And Gentile is always used in the morning to bring in and hold the undergarments in which he is dressed. It would not be fair to take his usual office from him and indeed from messer Gaspare and the others who will be excluded. They are *camerieri da camera* and as such will not stand for it.[5]

As this suggests, those organising the household did not, therefore, always have control over the potential exponential increase in demand for pay and positions.

The situation in many court communities was further complicated by the existence of multiple households and sub-courts. As the letter above indicates, the six-year-old heir Galeazzo Maria had his own servants who formed a separate court from that of his parents. Thus most major signorial courts need to be seen as a set of interconnected and often competing households, rather than as a single family unit. The primary or central court served the ruler; other members of the family had their own, usually smaller, retinue. Each of these generated accounts, contracts and bills. In 1517, for example, Isabella and Francesco Gonzaga's seventeen-year-old son Federico had a travelling court of approximately fifty different servants including secretaries, a bishop, a chaplain, a tailor, a household manager or *spenditore*, a barber, a cook, servants for the table, a blacksmith and stable hands.[6] Isabella herself was responsible for feeding and housing almost one hundred different courtiers and servants, both male and female. When she went to the Lago di Garda for a spring outing in 1514, her basic travelling court consisted of ninety-three mouths to feed, and a further eighty horses who all needed lodging and stabling.[7]

Controlling the expenses of these courts, both major and minor, involved a multi-layered set of officials who generated a detailed set of forms that had to be filled in before any payment could be made. There were a number of different ways of doing this. Annual contracts or even lifetime contracts were issued for the regular supply of perishable foodstuffs, for the provision of hose, underwear, tunics and doublets for servants, or for the lining of garments with warm furs. In Milan, for example, the rights to sell fruit and vegetables, fish and poultry throughout the city were offered by the Visconti and Sforza in return for supplying the court first at an agreed price.[8] The appointment of court suppliers was traditionally made by the duchess rather than the duke and was often made in return for political services that had been rendered to the family rather than on the basis of best value or cost. In this fashion, the Milanese duchesses often gave their midwives, ladies-in-waiting or other servants, lucrative bakeries or vegetable stalls, or placed them in charge of bread supplies in the city. Those who received such privileges sub-let them in turn, creating a multi-tiered set of taxes on the eventual holder of the position.

The contracts that were issued by the Milanese court constantly stressed that certain privileges or liberties afforded to these suppliers would only be permitted once the court had been fully serviced. This was true both for perishables and for dry goods such as the expensive cloth that was a key element of both status and reward. A courtier or servant who lived with the ruling family would expect to receive a basic wardrobe on an annual basis as well as gifts of fabric and cast-offs from the signorial wardrobe. The consistent demand for high-quality cloth meant that each court either stockpiled textiles in their dispensary to be released on presentation of a chit, or placed regular orders with appropriate manufacturers (as happened under Filippo Maria Visconti in Milan). In Naples, for example, Alfonso of Aragon had a *guardaroba* within the palace as well as a *botiga dela cort*, also known as the *botiga del S. Rey* close to the palace in Castel Nuovo. The latter held imported wools, cottons and linens as well as some velvets and silks.[9] The internal *guardaroba* was managed by a senior courtier with the assistance of twelve black slaves and a cat who was responsible for keeping the site free of mice and rats.[10] Isabella's personal wardrobe in Mantua had enough brocades and damasks to inspire a request from her son that he should be allowed to use them to make six long gowns for the Turkish ambassador. It is worth noting that she had the material to hand while the mercer's shops in Mantua did not.[11]

The pressure to show largesse while, at the same time, controlling spiralling expenses, meant that there was a constant oversight and that the rulers themselves might be rather distanced from these regular and basic purchases. A sense of the paperwork involved is made evident in a decree of 1524 concerning who could sign chits for Isabella's provisions:

By the authority of the present decree, we desire and order our accountants and our master of the books, that every year you must accept every expense of whatever type of amount that the Honourable Girolamo Bressanino, our *spenditore*, has incurred and will incur for our needs and that of our court by way of *mandati* or slips, *bollette*, or *filze* that have or will be signed in our name by one of the following, that is the honourable Giovanni Maria Capilipo, our butler, Carlo Ghisi, the master of our wardrobe, Girolamo Andrea Sio, our stablemaster and Francesco Cusatio, our factor general or their successors.[12]

All this implies that buying at court was done in bulk by appointed officials. This meant that purchasing was increasingly systematised By the late sixteenth century many courts, such as those of Modena, Parma and Turin, used books of prices, *libri dei prezzi*, in which the different *spenditore* established the maximum prices that the court would pay for different goods ranging from nails to gold thread.[13] Consumption had become an institutional as well as an individual concern.

But while the court had both the scale of demand and the political weight to distort the marketplace, its members generally worked with suppliers rather than against them. Despite the supposed social discrepancies between commercial and aristocratic behaviour, there were very close connections linking the signorial court and their merchants and suppliers. The Sforza's *spenditore* in Milan, Gottardo da Panigarola, saw no conflict in establishing his own companies to manufacture the luxury goods, particularly the valuable textiles that he was responsible for ordering himself.[14] In sixteenth-century Florence and Ferrara, these connections were formalised when Duke Cosimo I and Alfonso II both set up dedicated manufacturing operations designed to guarantee regular supplies of luxury items such as tapestries and porcelains.[15]

The Gonzaga family in Mantua used some of these same techniques but took a slightly different approach. There were patents and licences issued to encourage the establishment of new skills and industries in the city: in the second half of the Quattrocento, Marquis Ludovico Gonzaga invested in the local wool trade and gave permission to a Brescian to set up a manufacturing unit to make white soap. This failed, however, and despite repeated attempts the business of soap-making was not put on a stable footing until 1552.[16]

Instead of developing local luxury production, the Mantuan elite and the Gonzaga family in particular relied on the consumer goods available in their much larger neighbouring city-states, becoming sophisticated international consumers. Thus while local Mantuan retailers did have long-standing arrangements for the supply of candles, oil, basic cloth and linens, making arrangements to bill the court annually or bi-annually, the court tended to use the urban centres of Venice, Milan and Florence for their luxury purchases rather than support indigenous manufactures. These major cities were easily accessible through the canal routes, and the court could waive, or arrange to have waived, the taxes that normally increased the costs of such imports. The excellent transport links meant that the turn-around time between request and delivery could be remarkably rapid. For example, on 28 March 1501, Isabella wrote to Lorenzo da Pavia asking for forty ostrich feathers, two-thirds of which Lorenzo was able to ship five days later on 2 April.[17]

The household economy of a Renaissance court such as the Gonzaga, therefore, was quite different in both scale and organisation from that of the patrician household. The detailed running of the large-scale needs could be delegated to officials, while the signorial family feigned a general ignorance of their financial situation. From her account books from the early fifteenth century it appears that the first Marchioness of Mantua, Paola Malatesta Gonzaga, usually borrowed money from her ladies-in-waiting when she wanted to give coins to beggars in the street or make a donation in church.[18] Refusing to carry her own purse may have been a symbol of her status as an aristocratic spouse. Nonetheless, Paola's financial records demonstrate clearly that she was a *buon massara*, a good housewife who kept a very close eye on where money came from and where it went.

Paola combined her household management with a religious fervour that led to her eventual beatification. Her great-granddaughter-in-law Isabella d'Este followed in the tradition of careful financial oversight, without however seeking a fully religious role. As such she provides an illuminating case-study of elite female consumption. Although it was never sufficient, Isabella did have money of her own and throughout her lifetime she shopped with enthusiasm. In April 1491, she wrote to Girolamo Zigliolo, a member of the Ferrarese court who was just about to leave for France. Zigliolo knew Isabella well, and his understanding of her demands would have been conditioned by his earlier years of living with the young girl and her sister, Beatrice. He was well accustomed to meeting the requirements of court women. Isabella's mother Eleanora had been a demanding customer and later, her sister-in-law Anna Sforza also used Zigliolo to buy her textiles and accessories.[19]

In her letter, the seventeen-year-old Marchioness of Mantua gave a series of excited commands:

> I am sending you a hundred ducats and wish you to understand that you are not to return the money if any of it is left, after buying the things that I want, but are to spend it in buying some gold chain or anything else that is new and elegant. And if more is required, spend that too, for I had rather be in your debt so long as you bring me the latest novelties. But these are the kind of things that I wish to have – engraved amethysts, rosaries of black, amber and gold, blue cloth for a *camora*, black cloth for a mantle, such as shall be without a rival in the world, even if it costs ten ducats a yard; as long as it is of real excellence, never mind! If it is only as good as those which I see other people wear, I had rather be without it![20]

At first sight, this letter seems to be an artless list of items. The ebullience comes from the fact that, as a new bride, Isabella could afford to buy such luxuries and that, as her father's daughter, she could find someone trustworthy to purchase such things in Paris. The emphasis on extravagance, however, was deliberate. In her first years as marchioness, she often used language that implied a disinterest in cost. That same year, for example, she told the poet and courtier Niccolò da Correggio to spare no expense or speed in buying luxuries on her behalf when he went too to France, 'Since we are by nature full of appetite [*appetitose*], goods are more dear to us the faster that we can have them.'[21] A decade later, Isabella would similarly write of her 'insatiable desire for antiquities' and how, as she wrote in 1504 to Lorenzo da Pavia, goods had to be obtained at any cost, 'because our appetite has no concern about the expense'.[22] Words related to bodily consumption such as appetite and desire were a regular feature in Isabella's correspondence and in disdaining discussion of cost, Isabella may have been trying to distinguish herself from a mere merchant who would have been more concerned with his finances.

Isabella was trying to show herself as someone who was above detailed monetary discussions and unconcerned with self-restraint. But a closer analysis shows how carefully this young woman constructed her requests. First, she sent cash: 100 ducats in gold coins that would have been easily negotiable in France. Second, she was willing to go over budget and to place herself in debt to Zigliolo (regardless of whether he wanted to become her banker). In return she was looking for special products that were difficult to obtain in either Mantua or Ferrara: the highest quality cloth, particularly black and blue velvets whose popularity at the French court was renowned. She was also looking for engraved gems and amber rosaries, specialities of Parisian goldsmiths. Even more interesting, however, was Isabella's expression of her understanding of quality. In part this was a question of price. But novelty and competition were equally important criteria. In contrast to the attempts to enforce conformity on the urban women of Florence and Venice through sumptuary legislation, Isabella very deliberately did not want to blend in. She wanted to stand out. Only the highest quality would do; as she told one correspondent when requesting tabby silks in 1492, she would only consider, 'that which is excellent in every respect, if it is not the most beautiful it is not worth anything'.[23]

Even within her family, Isabella's insistence on quality and novelty was exceptional. Her reputation for high standards and innovative design would become one of the most important defining characteristics of how she was perceived throughout her career. For example, towards the end of the marchioness's life, Bona Sforza, Queen of Poland, wrote a letter concerning Isabella's headdresses and hairstyles on 15 June 1523:

> Via the nephew of the Royal barber we have had a letter from your ladyship and six silk and gold snoods in the latest fashion . . . we pray Your Ladyship to let us know when some new style of binding the head happens and to send us something that is pretty and pleases you, for we are sure you never miss anything as Your Ladyship is the source and origin of all of the loveliest fashions in Italy.[24]

Even discounting Bona Sforza's hyperbole, Isabella maintained her seriousness as a skilled and passionate purchaser throughout her almost fifty years as Marchioness of Mantua. While life-cycle changes, particularly her marriage in 1490, the birth of her son in 1510 and the death of her husband in 1519, were key moments of transition, each prompted the need for new spending rather than a restriction in her habits of acquisition. Thus her first pregnancy prompted a gift from her husband that allowed her to buy everything that was needed for before and after the birth, a remarkable 640 *braccia* of dark tabby silks and velvets and unspecified clothes of 'different colours', silk threads for sewing and 1,000 pieces of fur for lining along with 20 fox skins.[25] As she matured and her family grew, she needed to ensure that her children's needs were met as well as her own. Finally, as a widow, Isabella did not retreat into black or retire to a convent. When her son requisitioned her apartments for his own use, she simply set about devising a completely new and even more elaborately decorated set of private rooms for herself.

198   Gian Cristoforo Romano, portrait medal of Isabella d'Este (obverse),
cast and chased gold in enamelled frame set with precious stones, c.
1498–1507, Kunsthistorisches Museum, Vienna.

Thus while Isabella restrained her expenditure when external events such as warfare, plague or political disorder were pressing, making purchases for herself, her family and friends was a key part of her daily routine. When funds were almost non-existent, she found other ways of financing her growing reputation for stylish innovation. But if the marchioness's approach to the purchase of antiquities and to pictorial patronage has been treated with scholarly respect, her work with artisans and suppliers to develop new forms of perfuming gloves, caps, hair-bands and toothpicks has received comparatively little attention. But these were not peripheral or marginal activities. As discussed below, these items, which were often sent out as gifts, were an integral part of Mantua's inter-national reputation. Moreover, in making her purchases in Mantua itself, as well as in Venice, Genoa, Milan, Florence and Rome, Isabella's impact on the market for luxury goods should not be underestimated.

While it is sometimes tempting to see Isabella as an aberration, indeed as someone almost in the grip of a compulsive shopping disorder, this would be anachronistic. Comparisons with both her predecessors and successors suggest that the Marchioness was using a long-established and widely disseminated set of parameters for court expenditure. In acquiring antiquities, Isabella bought very different kinds of goods than many of her female contemporaries. But she operated in ways that both her grandmother and granddaughters would have recognised. These strategies included using dedicated allowances, constructing an image of a mother spending on her family, and deploying male, and to a lesser extent female, intermediaries to make purchases on her behalf.

But if Isabella d'Este was not alone in wanting to obtain valuable goods; she was almost unique in terms of the survival of her letters. Those written to her were carefully stored; the letters she sent out were scrupulously copied into *copialettere* books by her secretaries.[26] Since the late nineteenth century, this extensive body of material has been closely scrutinised for references to artists such as Leonardo da Vinci and Giovanni Bellini.[27] But in Isabella's correspondence all forms of manufacture were treated with the same seriousness, concern for quality and authenticity. For example, a single letter sent by the instrument-maker Lorenzo da Pavia on 31 August 1502, dealt with his search in Venice for a master capable of making a marble pavement for the floor of Isabella's *studiolo* and the carving of ebony and jasper stones. He also reported on the work under way on an elaborate stuccoed bed that Isabella was having constructed in Venice as well as describing the slow progress of Giovanni Bellini who was proving resistant to taking on new work. He finished by suggesting that Perugino, who was based in Florence, would be an appropriate substitute and that the 25 ducats that should have gone to Bellini would be better spent on the bed.[28]

ISABELLA'S INCOME

Where did Isabella find the money to fund this expenditure? For several generations, the Gonzaga family wealth had been based on a range of sources including indirect taxes, loans (forced and voluntary), agricultural wealth and the salaries paid to its signore as military condottiere working for either Milan or Venice. While Gonzaga women had access to only a small percentage of these funds, the amounts involved were still substantial and far exceeded those of their Republican counterparts. Isabella's dowry came to approximately 30,000 ducats, including jewels and other valuables. Although this allocation was far smaller than the 150,000 ducats that her new sister-in-law Anna Sforza had brought to Ferrara, it was considerably higher than the average Venetian dowry of about 1,500 ducats or the 500 ducats that an illegitimate Gonzaga daughter might receive. Her mother, Eleanora of Aragon, had undertaken the negotiations, stressing that, *la dotte è la segurezza de la donna* that is, 'the dowry is a woman's security'.[29] According to the Mantuan ambassador with whom Eleanora was liaising, Isabella would leave Ferrara in 1490 with:

> 8,000 ducats worth of good quality, lovely jewels, a dinner set of silver that was worth more than two thousand and the release of the jewels that are in the hands of

Francesco Baldi in Venice and the ruby that Lorenzo has in Florence which are worth 7,000 ducats in cash to us and the 3,000 that she will bring with her which will make up much of the 25,000. The list of the other things on top of the dowry that Madama wishes to give to the Marchioness I estimate to be worth between 8 and 10 thousand ducats.[30]

The 9,000 ducats' worth of gifts from her family would include: 'many gowns of different coloured silks as well as those of gold and silver most beautifully worked, along with ornate clothes and chests, coffers and trunks, both gilded and un-gilded, and numerous ornaments and gifts of diverse types and conditions to a price and value of nine thousand gold ducats in total'.[31]

These goods would become a key part of Isabella's income, enabling her, like any other wealthy Italian, to turn material wealth into ready cash. But rather than buy new gems for the young bride's dowry, the Este family planned to redeem Gonzaga jewels that were already held as pledges by two bankers. The new marchioness would then be able to wear Gonzaga family gems and eventually use them as collateral for further loans herself. She would not, however, be able to give them away, leave them to others in her will, or sell them without her husband's permission.

Isabella had not only material goods and financial connections, she also had cash. On her arrival in Mantua in 1490, she was assigned an allowance composed of the revenues that accrued from a series of taxes and farms. Thus at the moment of her marriage Isabella went from being an adolescent with little experience of the financial management to being a woman of means in her own right. It is perhaps not surprising, therefore, to find that her early letters, written between the ages of sixteen and nineteen, stressed her excitement over the new luxuries and delicacies that were now available to her. But at the same time, she and her staff were aware of the importance of enhancing her income and balancing her books.

While the day-to-day management of Isabella's income was in the care of a male treasurer, there was a strong tradition in the north Italian courts of regular financial oversight by female consorts and regents. When, for example, Ippolita Maria Sforza, the daughter of the Duke of Milan and the wife of Alfonso, Duke of Calabria, was kept short of cash by her husband, she was able to turn to a range of financiers for help.[32] Her creditors included Jewish money-lenders, Roman bankers, and rulers such as Lorenzo dei Medici and Federico da Montefeltro, who gained political as well as financial leverage by providing such assistance. Isabella was more wary of such strategies, preferring where possible to separate out clear lines of credit with professional bankers rather than find herself with uncomfortable political obligations. But she too regularly turned to male counterparts throughout northern Italy when she needed to make a purchase that she could not immediately afford or when the family as a whole needed to raise cash. In addition, Isabella used the leverage of her social position to encourage gifts, and offered goods in kind rather than cash payments. Thus an attempt to purchase some of the antiquities of the Medici collection in 1502 foundered on an inability to agree on the value of the Mantuan cloth that Isabella was offering as payment.[33]

In a letter of 18 May 1502, Isabella laid out her overall financial position to her father:

My most illustrious father,
When I first came to this illustrious house I was assigned an allowance of 6,000 gold ducats a year for my wardrobe and that of my women and from which I had to marry my ladies and provide for all the servants and women of my company and for two gentlemen and above this I had to pay the expenses of one hundred mouths to feed. Then when I had greater liberty in terms of adding and subtracting from my retinue in my own style, my husband voluntarily, at the persuasion of his accountants, assigned a further 2,000 ducats for my expenses to remove all this weight from my shoulders, including the expense of my company which was assigned to me in this way: the 6,000 of my allowance came from the tax on milling, 1,000 from another tax, and for the final 1,000 I was given the court and land of Letepaludani, which in total came to 8,000 ducats. It is true that thanks to the industry of myself and my servants I have been able to increase the income derived from the said lands by approximately 1,0000 ducats and from this profit I have acquired the court of Castiglion Mantovano and of Bondenzo in such a way that I now have about 2,500 a year in income. But at the same time about 50 mouths have been assigned to this money. Thus it is true that my lord has given me other lands for my entertainment such as Saccheta and Porto, but the income from these does not cover the great expense, indeed sometimes I spend even more, having to keep them in good repair. . . .[34]

Isabella was conducting a delicate balancing act in this letter, presenting herself as a good manager but one who despite her efforts had little cash left over and was still in need of help from her father. The managerial techniques she used were very similar to those deployed by previous Mantuan marchionesses since the early fifteenth century. For example, the farm of Letepaludani (now Palidano) was probably a traditional dower property for it had belonged to Barbara Hohenzollern in the 1460s.[35] Isabella, like her predecessors, took an active interest in her farms and in the sale of their products. She was keen to develop rice cultivation which was proving an increasingly successful cash crop. Following a particularly good harvest in 1530, she wrote, for example, to Angelo Trotto in Ferrara:

I find myself with about 1,500 weight of rice to sell, and because I think it will be easy to sell them in Ferrara, either for the needs of the territory or through some merchant, I wanted to let Your Magnificence know and send you a sample, so that you can decide if this rice can be sold there and I will send it off even if it can't be paid for as I will then send it on to Venice by that route.[36]

Using family contacts to sell her produce in Ferrara had the advantage of being able to negotiate the tax-free shipments and sales that Isabella would have found difficult in Venice. But despite this and other documentary evidence that the marchioness was able to raise considerable sums of money, she was always anxious to emphasise the limitations of her budget. In the letter to her father, she stressed that her fixed expenses had grown ever larger. But while many scholars have accepted Isabella's complaints at face value, she was actually being quite elusive. Although she claimed to have little spare income because of rising staff costs, it was very common among many courts to avoid paying salaries until absolutely required to do so, or to only pay them in arrears. Moreover, these were often paid in kind rather than in cash.[37]

In part, Isabella needed to emphasise her poverty because of the many demands made on her funds by male relatives. Although her husband and father had far greater incomes, she, like her mother before her, was regularly called upon to support larger family enterprises. It is important to stress that in a court society, matrimony did not mean a blurring of boundaries between the goods that belonged to husband and wife; exchanges between their wardrobes, or between their wardrobes and those of their children were recorded as carefully as those that took place with recipients outside the court itself. Indeed, one of the reasons for our in-depth knowledge of the movement of goods is because each time an item was handed out or returned, a marginal note was written in the relevant inventory. The lady-in-waiting or courtier who received the dress or plate from the wardrobe for the use of their lord or lady was held personally responsible for its safe return, finding their salary or privileges docked in cases of loss, theft or damage.

This means that family strategies where each Gonzaga member contributed to the dynasty's needs must be differentiated from those designed to protect the reputation and wealth of the individual concerned. When, for example, Isabella could see the benefits of her husband's large-scale expenditure, such as the attempt to raise his brother Sigismondo to a cardinalship in Rome in 1494, she immediately mobilised her own funds and valuables towards the effort.[38] Again, in 1506, when Francesco demanded that Isabella use her jewellery to raise money to subsidise grain purchases during a period of plague she was equally forthcoming but, by this stage, she began to express concerns that they were not managing their debts more carefully:

> I marvel that your Excellency wishes to take advantage of our jewellery, you have asked me for 1,000 ducats worth with much respect and excuses concerning your needs. All that I have is yours . . . and if on some occasions I have shown reluctance it has been when you have wished to lend them to others or to pawn them without making arrangements to redeem them for people like us should not keep jewels except as a storehouse to serve our needs. Thus willingly I send your Excellency that which you have requested so that, in this time of crucial need due to plague, you can use them at your will. In encouraging you to keep your goods at home I am doing my duty. I will now perform your wishes. Il Cusatro will give you two jewels estimated by master Giovanni Francesco and master Niccolò at 1,450 gold florins.[39]

As was usual, Isabella's correspondence was carefully phrased. She pointed out the fact that there really was a good reason for using the jewellery to raise money: the plague. She then reminded her husband of the need to make arrangements to ensure that they didn't actually lose the gems, much less those that they had already pawned. Finally, she noted with precision what the agreed value of the gems had been at the time of writing.

While Isabella considered her material wealth such as her gold, diamond and enamelled medal (Figure 198) as 'a storehouse to serve for our needs', she was very anxious that her husband's profligacy might mean that they lost these valuables to the open market. If they could not repay their debts, there was every danger that their bankers might try and sell them at auction, a result that the marchioness had already wanted to avoid in 1499 because, 'the shame would be worse than the damage to their finances'.[40] In an even earlier incident in 1496, she had written to Francesco II in similar terms:

> I am of course, always ready to obey Your Excellency's command in everything, but perhaps you have forgotten that my jewels are at present in pawn at Venice, not only those which you have given me, but those which I brought when I came as a bride to Mantua or have bought myself since my marriage. I say this, not because I want to make any difference between what is yours and what is mine, but to ensure you are aware that I only have four jewels left in the house along with the large balas ruby which you gave me when my first child was born, my large diamond, my 'favorito', and the last one which you recently gave me. If I pledge these, I shall be left entirely without jewels and shall be obliged to wear black, because to appear in coloured silks and brocades without jewels would be ridiculous. Your Excellency will understand that I only say this out of regard for your honour and mine.[41]

Along with providing subventions for her husband, Isabella had considerable responsibilities for her children's expenditure. By 1507, she had seven children, including her beloved sons, the heir, Federico II and two other boys, Sigismondo and Ercole. While she was criticised by her relatives for her lack of interest in her daughters, her rapport with Federico II was intense. In his youth Isabella seems to have regarded the boy as an extension of herself. Writing a letter in 1515 from Rome, she addressed her fifteen-year-old Federico, *mia anima* (my soul), and opened her greetings with:

> My Federico. I send you a thousand blessings and as many kisses . . . Be happy since without fail I will leave here on the first Monday following Lent. You do very well to take such good care of me, because I love you more than anyone else in the world, nor do I have any other valuable except you . . . Recommend me to your father and I send you one more kiss. In Rome on 7 February from your mother who loves you as much as she loves herself.[42]

It is, therefore, understandable to find that she made loans, provided financial support and purchases to Federico with a generosity and willingness that only started to show its limits when he himself became duke in 1519. During these last decades as a widow, Isabella returned to her earlier strategies of protecting her income from her male relatives. In 1531, when Isabella inherited her lady-in-waiting Margarita Cantelma's estates, she replied evasively to a request from her son for money:

> If I did not see that you evidently share the popular fallacy that Signora Cantelma's bequest has greatly enriched me, I should be extremely surprised at your boldness in daring to ask me for 3,000 ducats. You know that it has never been my habit to hoard money . . .[43]

The emphasis on the fact that 'it has never been my habit to hoard money' is an important one. Isabella did not save cash but, as noted money spent on jewels, antiquities and valuable cloth was the equivalent of investing in a bank account. These goods could be used as pledges against the borrowing of substantial sums. This meant that when Isabella needed to raise 400 ducats rapidly in order to participate in an auction of antiquities in 1502, she was able to do so with ease.

Such loans were not impossible for other patrician women. But what differentiates court women such as Isabella or her friend the Marchioness of Cantelma from their Republican counterparts is that as long as they were seen as actively supporting their husbands and sons, they could spend their own income with considerable freedom. Isabella did not need to ask the marquis's permission before spending substantial sums of money. As long as the funds came from her treasury and could be justified as decorous expenditure that would bring lustre or benefit to the family as a whole, Isabella was free to spend according to what she herself termed, her 'insatiable desires'.[44]

SEEING AND SHOPPING

Isabella's letters were constantly concerned with making purchases, arranging for items to arrive, debating the quality of the said items, and then organising either for their return or the purchase of yet more of the same. How then did she know what was available on these different Italian and international markets, how could she assess their value and quality? What was the relationship between her sometimes constrained ability to negotiate in the public arena of the markets and shops and the purchases she made behind the scenes?

In the late fifteenth and early sixteenth centuries, Mantua was a reasonably sized town of between seventeen and twenty thousand inhabitants. Surrounded on all sides by the river Mincio, its main industries were agricultural, the production of wool cloth, and increasingly the manufacture of berets, knitted stockings and other forms of innovative clothing.[45] Mantuan merchants were active and kept supplies of luxury goods in stock. When a list of goods stolen from a shop by the church of Sant'Andrea was announced in 1461, for example, it included silks and ermine furs as well as sugar, boxes of coloured candies, veils, silver buttons, coral paternosters, gems and rings.[46]

Although Gonzaga financial records are limited, a number of registers do survive from the first half of the fifteenth century, including annual contracts with local suppliers who expected to be reimbursed on a six-monthly basis.[47] They provided essential provisions and services such as the lining of all the court's clothing for the winter months.[48] But, as has been suggested, Mantuan manufacturing could never fully compete with its much larger neighbours such as Venice, Milan, Bologna, Florence, Genoa and Rome, each of which provided the court with luxury goods. In 1430, Mantuan merchants specifically asked that most expenditure be undertaken locally, and that the court only send to Venice for the most exotic of items that could not be obtained at home.[49] But this advice was rarely heeded and the Gonzaga continued to be some of the Serenissima's best customers. To make a selection from the widest possible choice meant, therefore, leaving Mantua. This was not a simple task for an elite figure such as Isabella. Any excursion, however small, had potential political consequences and could involve considerable cost. During her husband's lifetime, Isabella needed Francesco's permission to leave home, an acquiescence that was not always forthcoming.

In looking at Isabella's ability to shop publicly, her excursions can be divided into three overlapping categories: family visits, state visits and visits for personal reasons. The marriage between the Gonzaga and the Este had been designed to cement a long-standing alliance between the two courts and Isabella went back and forth to Ferrara with considerable regularity. The slightest illness on the part of relatives might prompt such a trip, but most of her journeys were taken for less dramatic reasons. This meant that she continued to maintain close contact with Ferrarese courtiers such as Zigliolo and his brother, and it also meant that she knew the work of Ferrarese craftsmen and suppliers well and was able to turn to them with great regularity. For example, Isabella seems to have been particularly fond of the sweets and biscuits made by the Ferrarese apothecary, Vincenzo, ordering *confetti* and other sugar items from him in large quantities.[50]

Family ties made other areas similarly accessible, providing the marchioness with both hospitality and a legitimate reason for travelling abroad. From 1491 until 1497, the presence of her sister Beatrice in Milan made that city and the ducal territories of Lombardy important Gonzaga destinations. Isabella went to Milan on at least six occasions during her lifetime, first in 1490 for her sister's wedding. She then joined her father in Milan in 1491 and returned in 1495 for the birth of Beatrice's second son. Her visits were more sporadic after the Sforza's fall from power in 1500, but she retained important contacts among silk suppliers and mercers and most critically with aristocratic intermediaries who could serve her needs long after her sister's death and her brother-in-law's demise. Her sisters-in-law provided additional links to other major courts such as those of Urbino and Rome. Isabella and the Duchess of Urbino, Elisabetta Gonzaga, became very close friends and tried to see each other often. Isabella's relationship with her brother's second wife Lucrezia Borgia was more frosty, but she kept up a keen correspondence and was always willing to send gifts to other Borgia relatives.[51]

In using her family ties as a means to travel, Isabella resembles Cecilia Priuli who similarly moved about Venice visiting relations. The Este trips were simply on a grander scale. When Isabella wanted to go to places where she had no immediate blood relatives, she used a different range of excuses to justify her mobility. Acceptable reasons for women of all social ranks included the requirements of her health, both physical and spiritual. As she grew older the need to take the waters in a range of baths allowed Isabella to move considerable distances. Religious vows were also powerful motivations for leaving Mantua. For example, following the successful birth of her first child, Isabella went to Loreto in the Marche in 1494 and returned there in 1520. In 1506, she fulfilled a vow to visit the Gonzaga-financed shrine of Santissima Annunziata in Florence; that she was unable to conduct negotiations in person. Her understanding of the Venetian market for scents, for example, allowed her to reject the notion that little of what she was looking for was available that year. Instead, she assumed that her correspondent, the ambassador Taddeo Albano, had simply misunderstood her needs. With greater clarity, he would be able to fulfil her wishes. She wrote:

> Concerning the amber, we have decided not to undertake that expense for the moment. In terms of the Damscene water that you say is unavailable in Venice, we doubt that we understand each other, because this type of water is usually available in Venice at all times. And so that you understand our concept better, they are waters that are sold in the Levant and that are stored in little flasks covered in straw.[60]

By seeing the full range of options in the shops herself, by getting to know private collections that might come up for sale and by identifying people on whom she could rely, Isabella could maintain a high degree of control even when she could not shop herself.

MAIL ORDER

By their very nature, Isabella's oral discussions with merchants and artisans were ephemeral. While she did write directly to her suppliers her correspondence reveals her careful use of third parties to ensure that she was able to obtain the finest quality items, even when she could not choose them herself.

Although the term 'agent' is often used for convenience when describing Isabella's intermediaries, this term confuses the nature of the relationship. It was not a professional arrangement made for profit. No commission was ever charged. For example, though one might have expected her to turn to the suppliers such as goldsmiths, mercers and apothecaries whom she patronised during her travels, she rarely seems to have done so directly. For their part, though Mantuan merchants were used to transport goods, they too were rarely asked to act as intermediaries in their own right. Thus while Isabella wanted a Mantuan apothecary to bring items back and forth from Venice on his barge or carriage, she did not want him to act as her wholesaler. Instead, when she wanted to place an order Isabella turned to men with either a certain standing at court or to elite artisans in whose good judgement she placed her trust.

There was nothing unusual about such arrangements. Shopping was an act of clientage. As such it was taken very seriously by ambassadors stationed abroad. The mid-fifteenth-century correspondence between Barbara Gonzaga and the men sent to represent the Mantuan court in Milan is replete with requests for silks, brocades and other speciality goods from the city.[61] The later correspondence between the same two cities demonstrates that ambassadors continued to play this role well into the sixteenth century.[62]

There were great benefits to this system. The officials would normally use their own funds to make the necessary purchases. They could be reimbursed back home in either local currency or with favours and privileges. As their standing at court depended on their connections with their overlord, ambassadors could be expected to make every effort to please. In using official Mantuan representatives in Venice, such as Taddeo Albano or Benedetto Agnello, Isabella was following in this venerable tradition. But unlike Barbara Gonzaga who worked almost exclusively through the Mantuans, Isabella cast her net much wider. For example, when she wanted a particular item, she might ask several people to try and find it rather than rely on a single source. As one case shows, in 1491 she asked Girolamo Stanga, a member of the Cremonese aristocracy serving her sister in Milan, to contact his brother in Genoa to buy Spanish-style mantles, the *sbernie* that had been recently popularised by the new duchess of Milan, Isabella of Aragon. She wanted, 'a dark red mantle, plus one in black and another in some strange colour'.[63] On the same day she contacted a Mantuan, Giorgio Brognolo, in Venice and asked him for the same items in more or less the same terms, 'a mantle of dark *leonato*, one in black and another in some strange colour that is most beautiful'.[64] By asking both for the same item, she was doubling her chances of success.

Having said this, it is unclear how either Stanga or Brognolo were to know what she meant by the strange colour (*stranio collore*) that the young marchioness was requesting, and at times Isabella's language seems more of an exhortation than a precise order. In the early stages of her career, she often used cost as a measure of quality. In 1496, for example, Brognolo was told to find fur linings and a furpiece with its head intact (one that may have been similar to that of Cecilia Priuli):

> Try to find a good fur lining for a cape; we wish you to buy eighty that are excellent and beautiful in every way, even if you have to search all of Venice, and see that you find one which I can carry in my hand that has the skull intact. Even if it costs as much as ten ducats, I will give the money gladly as long as it is really a fine fur. And beyond this, we wish you to send eight *braccia* of the best crimson satin which you can find in Venice, and it should be from the *paragon*, because we want to use it to make the said cape, and by the Lord, use all your accustomed diligence, for nothing will give us greater pleasure.[65]

But such imprecision caused problems. It was not always easy to get colour, sizing and style right by correspondence. Hats were too large, gloves of the wrong quality, and colours were inappropriate. Many of her correspondents anticipated their patron's potential displeasure by suggesting that they themselves were not fully pleased with the material they were passing on, but were doing so in the hope that she would decide for herself. In 1496, Isabella described the type of linen that she was looking for to Giorgio Brognolo in terms that would have been difficult to follow with accuracy:

> We wish to have six to eight *braccia* of Rhenish linen that is so fine and beautiful that it is beyond comparison because we already have a good quantity of the ordinary type. We wish you to search all of the warehouses in Venice to find the most beautiful and have it shown to your wife who will understand these things better than you. If you cannot find this amount of excellent material, send out a left-over

the price of an ebony mirror cover that he was making to her design he gallantly claimed:

> God would not wish that I should seek anything for it beyond the fact that it gives you pleasure, and on my account, I should like to make you a present of it but, seeing that I have to earn my bread, I am forced to be a villain (*sono constreto a eser vilan*).[73]

Although highly contrived, the letter is honest. If he had been able to avoid charging, Lorenzo would have benefited in other ways, moving beyond the category of those who made money out of their activities to that of the nobility who did not engage in trade. Isabella would have then been expected to eventually repay him in some other way, either through a 'gift' of gold coins or some other benefit.

The rewards of such service were often subtler than salaries or direct profits. Having a public affiliation with one's social superior was an important element of reputation. Isabella was able to intervene with clerics and the papacy to obtain benefices for Lorenzo and his family. During a period of dearth in Venice, Lorenzo da Pavia asked Isabella to send him 500 sacks of Mantuan grain. This was not simply to subsidise his household but also to show his ability to gain favour and connections. The gift would, Lorenzo wrote, 'demonstrate to those of Venice that I have the grace of your Excellency'.[74]

As part of this strategy it was very common for artisans to offer desirable items as a donation in the expectation of a gift of even higher value in return. For example, on her receipt of a bronze copy of the *spinario* or 'thorn-puller' from the sculptor Antico who was then serving the court of her brother-in-law, Bishop Ludovico Gonzaga of Guastalla, Isabella deliberately avoided sending a cash payment in return. Instead, she sent one of her velvet dresses to his wife, stressing that this was not a *premio* or reward but a sign of her affection. Although this has often been read as a method of cheating Antico out of his just due, quite the opposite was the case. As shall be explained in the next chapter, Antico was not only a sculptor, he was also a courtier with high social aspirations. The gift of velvet was a way of acknowledging his status, not a substitute for the money that he was owed.[75]

As this suggests, the relationship between Isabella, her intermediaries and the marketplace was a complex one that had to account for mutual honour as well as for mutual profit. It took considerable time and effort to satisfy Isabella's discerning tastes, and her friends worked hard to please her. In Milan the marchioness would normally turn to a local patrician, Giovan Angelo Vismara. He arranged loans, made purchases of silks, spices, perfumes as well as thread, buttons and needles. Isabella, like many women of the period, had a constant need for sewing materials. In a letter of 1494, the marchioness explained why she was asking him, rather than a professional merchant, to undertake these tasks:

> We have received the *aqua ninfa*, which has pleased us. We are expecting the other things which are still to be sent, above all the collar when it is finished. We would be pleased if you would send us six full *braccia* of black velvet with a long pile of the type that you

had made last year, and if you can't find some already made, have it made immediately, but with the obligation that we can have it here five days before Carnival.

The needles were attached to your letter. We are returning some of them to you as a sample for the others, that is four for sewing, of which please send half a thousand-weight of each type, but of the long type for mending I want them to be a bit longer. [. . .]

If we use you in these women's matters, (*cose da dona*), do not marvel for it is our custom that when we find someone we can trust, we place all our business indifferently in their hands, but you can give the bother to your women who may understand our meaning better than you can.[76]

The phrase, 'it is our custom that when we find someone we can trust, we place all our business indifferently in their hands', is key to understanding what was expected. Isabella saw her agents as extensions of herself, as men who were able to see her needs, wants and desires and to ensure that they were satisfied. She work with those such as Lorenzo who were 'of the same mind' as her.

Nonetheless, even as Isabella developed a sophisticated form of long-distance purveying, her frustration at not being able to make a direct selection herself, or worse at being treated as an ignorant consumer, could easily spill over into anger. Her correspondence concerning a set of leather gloves is very revealing about the tensions of doing business at a distance. On 13 August 1506, she wrote to Floramonte Brognolo who was then in Rome:

We understand that a shipment from Spain of a great quantity of gloves from Ocagna (a town specialising in leather products near Toledo) has arrived, of which we have need. But we want them to be of the best quality and of the type from Valencia which yellow inside and worn with the inside leather folded over. We ask you to examine them carefully and to have them examined by others, above all by someone Spanish who will understand and know their quality and how they should be made for use by women. And if they are appropriate for our needs, spend two ducats on them and send them to us by the first means possible, and tell us whom we need to pay.[77]

Isabella's request was quite detailed. The gloves with cuffs that she wanted were of the most fashionable type similar to those seen in a portrait that was once considered to be of Isabella herself (Figure 199). It was important to get just the right quality and however trustworthy she considered Brognolo, he was to find an expert connoisseur, a Spaniard who would understand their special nature. The precision with which she made her order may have been due to her poor experiences of glove sales in the past. In 1494, Isabella d'Este had asked a Ferrarese courtier to buy Spanish gloves on her behalf. When they arrived, however, she was livid. As she explained to Bernardino Prospero:

We gave ten ducats to Sanzio to buy as many gloves of d'Ocagna for our use when he went to Spain, and being in Ferrara we spoke to him that he should serve us well.

199   Francesco Torbido, *Portrait of a Woman with a Glove*, oil on canvas, Isabella Stewart Gardner Museum, Boston. (Acquired in 1896 as a portrait of Isabella d'Este).

It has now been many days since his return, and since then he has sent us twelve dozen of the saddest gloves that had he searched all of Spain in order to find such poor quality I don't believe he could have found as many. In Rome, Genoa and Florence there are better ones without comparison and using some diligence in Ferrara itself he could have found some that were as good and perhaps even better. Therefore we have decided to return them so that you do not think that we have such little judgement in gloves that we would think that these were good enough to give to our ladies-in-waiting and to some of our friends. We would be ashamed to give them to people whom we love and they would never wear them. Can you please send them back and tell him how badly we have been served . . .[78]

Isabella's imperious tone disguised the care with which she mustered her arguments. Although she did not go to the markets of these cities herself, and had never been to Spain, she emphasised her understanding of fine leather. This was to impress on Prospero that she should not be fooled. She knew where the best imported versions could be found: Rome, Genoa and Florence. She was concerned that 'her judgement' might be thought wanting if she merely accepted them without complaint, much less sent them out as gifts.

The connection between careful selection and gift-giving was critical. Isabella's purchases were part of an economy of friendship that was designed to protect both herself and her family from political harm in the turbulent decades of the first half of the sixteenth century. Mantua was a small territorial state that had to tread a very careful path in the competition between the growing powers of France, Spain, the Habsburg Empire and Venice. While her husband Francesco II used his reputation as a horse-breeder, card-player and soldier to make connections amongst the elite male aristocrats in the international courts of Francis I and Charles v, his wife created a similarly high reputation for herself.[79] She became known as a deviser of new fashions and as an expert perfumer, obtaining and mixing scented waters and musk from civet cats and applying them to a range of different objects that could be carried or used by men and women alike. This was an important combination of a commercial economy – the leather gloves and the scents were imported items that had to be purchased and were not always easy to obtain – and the domestic economy where they were personalised by elite individuals. Her skills were much in demand. When her son Federico went to the French court as a hostage in March 1516 he wrote back to his mother, asking her to send 'perfumes in large quantities to give to these ladies . . . and enough gloves, and a jar of soap for the hand that is large enough to give to many women and again, oils, powders and waters'.[80] Four years later, the Mantuan ambassador was able to report that the gloves had been an enormous success with the French queen and strongly urged Isabella to make more. He described how he had been chatting and:

Turning to talk of gloves, Her Majesty showed me those that she had in her hand. It was a feast day, Sunday, and she told me that these were the gloves that had been given to her by your Ladyship and by the Signor Marchese her cousin when he was in France and that she had preserved them so that she still had another pair. And so that they would last longer she only wore them on feast days while they were new and then she would wear them every day but take them off at night and put on another pair in order to be thrifty. And this she did because she had no other pair of gloves of any type that pleased her as much as these ones and that she had been sent an infinite number by different people in Italy and Spain, but these were her favourites saying that she did not know what in the world she would do when they were finished . . .[81]

Isabella had a series of techniques for softening and perfuming her gloves, and the queen specifically requested cedar oil scent (if the marchioness wished to send her some more). Isabella was quick to take the hint but she needed to ensure that her role as a purveyor of gloves did not diminish her elite standing. This was a dilemma with which she was familiar. Earlier, in a letter dated 18 May 1516 to Federico at the French court that was accompanied by three jars of hand cream, Isabella had used language that identified her as a professional perfumer with her own shop or *bottega*:

> We are sending a small box in which there are three ointment jars, one in crystal covered in gold for the Queen, those in horn, one is for the Queen Mother and the other for the Duchess of Lansone, her sister. As we have reminded you present them in our name adding in whatever words seem appropriate to you. We are sure that they will please her, because in our opinion we have never made any better. And we would be pleased if you would say to Her Majesty that we are delighted to be able to serve her Highness in something that pleases her and that we know we can do this as concerning odours we will not cede place to the best perfumer in the world. And we entreat Her Majesty not to change shop, but to give us enough time so that we can serve her . . . We are pleased to supply the said Queen and Madam with our recipe, but to tell the truth we do not wish to undertake this for the other women.[82]

The phrase Isabella used here, 'not to change shop', *non cambiare la bottega* is revealing. Rather than see the provisioning of French women with scent and soaps as a menial task unworthy of a marchioness, Isabella was playing with the terms of shopkeeping and service. But the role of perfumer was one she would only undertake as part of a witty conceit and for political alliance, not for monetary profit. To start sending her products out to all the women at the French court, regardless of their status, would have indeed placed Isabella in the position of provisioner rather than one of petitioner.

CONCLUSION

One of the most fascinating aspects of Isabella's correspondence was her ability to turn the metaphors and concepts that were traditionally usually used to attack women to her own benefit. Following the fall of the Sforza, for example, she wanted to retrieve a clavichord that had once belonged to her sister Beatrice. As part of this campaign, she wrote to the new owner, the nobleman Galeazzo Pallavicino, and explained that, 'since we are a woman and full of appetite, there is less blame in our asking and greater excuse than there would be in a man'.[83] Similarly, when Ludovico Cannossa joked that Isabella was becoming a *mercatante* or a dealer in antiquities, he was using terms that would have normally been considered insulting if addressed to an elite male.[84] In this way, Isabella and her correspondents were able to manipulate and play with language. Isabella could ask the Queen of France to 'not to change shop' because there was no danger that she might be mistaken for a shopkeeper. But, as suggested above, if she had started to supply the whole French court this distinction might have been lost. As Isabella played at being a glove-maker and perfumer to the Queen of France, she was careful not to charge her social superior for the services she provided. In this play on words, the exchange would be one of favours and affection, not of Mantuan *quattrini* or French *livres tournois*.

One final episode illustrates Isabella's ability to slide between the competing rhetorics of profit, value and friendship. In 1506, Michele Vianello, the Venetian citizen who had acted as Isabella d'Este's intermediary in her negotiations with the painter Giovanni Bellini and shown her the amber paternoster beads, died. He left considerable debts and a number of determined creditors.[85] Lorenzo da Pavia had been living with Vianello and Isabella asked him to contact the heirs and negotiate a price for two objects she had noted in his collection on an earlier visit to the city: an agate vase and a painting by Jan Van Eyck of *Pharaoh drowning in the Red Sea*. At the same time, she used other prestigious contacts such as Pietro Bembo, in case there was a need for 'the authority of a gentleman' to prevent these items joining those being 'auctioned off by others'.[86]

Isabella's hopes of a rapid private sale were quickly dashed. Vianello's creditors had made a collective decision to realise the highest possible price by putting his goods up for auction at the Rialto. Lorenzo da Pavia wrote back to Isabella and sent a colleague to Mantua to discuss further action. He noted that there had already been a great deal of preliminary discussion about the prices certain objects would fetch:

> And the canvas of the Pharaoh, and of the organ, these two items will be higher in price than anything else; for the agate vase there will not be so many buyers, and everything is to be sold at auction and friendship will not matter, because this morning I have understood that they wish to sell them at auction with the following conditions: that if within eight days they can find someone who wishes to pay more than it was sold at, it shall be his and if they can't find anyone else, the original buyer will retain it. And this they are doing in order to take every precaution. Up to now it seems that there are numerous buyers but we shall see when it comes to actual cash what actually happens . . .[87]

Similarly, Isabella's Venetian correspondent Zuan Francesco Valier also noted that the painting had aroused considerable interest and that there was already an offer of 100 ducats on the table. He finished by saying that, 'I think it will sell for much more.'[88] The Vianello sale clearly had generated a great deal of public comment and speculation prior to the auction. Although the format was conventional, the quality of the items for sale and the status of potential buyers meant that the prices were far greater than those realised in an ordinary household sale. While the evidence is limited, the correspondence suggests that the second-hand dealers accustomed to paying a few lire for a picture or a set of leather hangings would have been excluded by the amounts involved. Instead, given the antiquities, oil paintings and musical instruments that were suddenly available that the clientele was unusually well informed and highly competitive. Isabella would have had to move rapidly if she was going to succeed. An auction purchase required a cash payment, and she made appropriate arrangements to borrow the necessary funds, negotiating a loan of 400 ducats with a Ferrarese banker. When the auction finally took place, Lorenzo and the Mantuan ambassador had little trouble in obtaining the agate vase for 105 ducats. But the much-desired painting went to the Doge's brother Andrea Loredan, at 115 ducats, 15 ducats above the price Isabella had authorised her bidders to offer. The officials, realising that there was even greater profit to be had, then tried to change the rules. Traditionally, buyers had been able to offer higher bids up to eight days following the final bid. Now, they tried to extend this to thirty days. This was clearly no ordinary auction.

Having failed to obtain the painting by bidding, Isabella changed tactics. The public moment was over and she reverted to private negotiations. She refused to agree to the thirty-day extension over her prized agate vase and used contacts and political alliances to release it from storage before moving on to obtain her much-desired picture. For Isabella, the public framework of the auction had been problematic. Even had she been able to get to Venice, she could not have appeared in the Rialto to bid against her male counterparts. But now friendship did matter and she used her diplomatic skills to secure a sale. Instead of publicly challenging Loredan by offering the sellers a higher price under the post-auction extension, she wrote directly to the buyer himself. In her letter, Isabella offered him a profit of 25 ducats as well as his expenses. At the same time, she sent emissaries, including Lorenzo da Pavia, to persuade Loredan to accede to her request. Her letter mixed concepts of commercial profit with altruistic friendship to good effect:

> And knowing Your Magnificence to be of the most noble heart . . . we have taken heart because of the great desire which we hold to have this painting, to beg you that you might out of courtesy and kindness give us this picture as we will willingly repay your money with whatever profit you so wish. In doing this, you will gain, not only the money, but also our person, with the obligation to be forever in your debt and prompt to gratify you in all your needs.[89]

Loredan proved amenable to such persuasion, reselling the picture and insisting that the marchioness also take and reimburse him for other items he had bought at the same auction, an eighteen-piece porcelain set and 'a portrait of that master Jan of Bruges who had made the Submersion'. With the additional cost of the case for the picture, and expenses for the auctioneers (suggesting that buyers as well as sellers had to pay a commission) and the expense of transport, the entire sale came to 137 ducats.[90] Despite paying 37 ducats more than she had originally anticipated, Isabella was delighted. She wrote in thanks reminding Loredan that, 'the greater your liberality, the greater our obligation to you will be'. Loredan's reply was transmitted by Lorenzo da Pavia who warned that the negotiations had to be 'kept as secret as possible.[91] He does not wish it to be known that he has sold it for nothing but if asked he wants to say that he gave it as a gift.'[92] It is impossible to judge Loredan's motivations with precision. Was he regretting his enthusiastic purchasing at auction or merely taking advantage of the diplomatic contacts this exchange provided? But what is clear is that by the end of this transaction the public scenes of commercial exchange had merged with the seemingly private world of gift-giving, personal debt and obligation.[93]

CONCLUSION

Detail of Fig. 200

CHAPTER TEN

Priceless

At her death in 1529 Isabella d'Este had acquired a reputation for shrewd purchasing. Her antiquities, precious objects and paintings, kept first in her private study or *studiolo* and then during her period as widow in her so-called grotto, were known throughout Europe. As the visitors who asked to see the rooms were aware, the statues, cameos and ancient medals that were arranged in these rooms were impressive not only in terms of their quality but also for their ever-increasing financial value. Over time, the items that she had struggled to obtain either as purchases or gifts became worth thousands of ducats to a cash-strapped duchy. But this rising value brought a dilemma to the fore by the end of the sixteenth century. Were these symbols of Gonzaga prestige that, like the palace itself, had to be preserved for future generations? Or were they, as Isabella had once said of her jewellery, 'a storehouse to serve the family's needs'? In 1571, the questions became real. Deeply in debt, the Gonzaga heirs, Guglielmo and his younger brother Ludovico, were locked in dispute over the collection's future. While the latter pushed for a sale, Guglielmo argued against it on two seemingly contradictory grounds. He noted, that 'the Grotto is made up of antiquities, and is adorned with vases and lovely things that if kept together bring reputation to our house'.[1] Yet at the same time, he wrote that it was unlikely the grotto's contents would really raise the suggested 50,000 ducats because their value was so volatile 'they did not have an ordinary price because they are estimated more or less according to the desire and delectation of the person involved'.[2] In his mind, the risk of losing family honour was greater than the opportunity for financial reward. For the moment, the collection remained intact.

Detail of Fig. 211

In studying the role of the antique in Renaissance culture, scholars have often focused on Guglielmo Gonzaga's first point – the issue of reputation – but have ignored the second, the highly subjective nature of the market for antiquities that developed in late fifteenth- and sixteenth-century Italy. The appreciation of Greco-Roman civilisation and its monuments is traditionally studied as the response of academically minded scholars and intellectuals to the past, not as a new set of consumer demands. But in taking this elevated approach, there is a danger of overlooking just how dramatic a shift took place in terms of fashion and taste. This was not an issue reserved for the wealthy elite. While the market in antiquities remained a very specialised one, the changing concept of what constituted a valuable piece of statuary had a broader impact. The shift helped to transform concepts of public and private property and in terms of what could be seen as for sale and what was literally 'beyond price'.

Buying the Past

The physical remains of Roman culture had long littered the Italian peninsula. But before the late fourteenth and early fifteenth centuries, there was only a limited demand for these objects. Many could be obtained for almost nothing. Until about the 1440s, the coins and small bronzes were usually discovered rather than deliberately excavated. They were then exchanged among a small group of passionate enthusiasts. At the most, they made their way into the shops of professionals such as goldsmiths who would then transform them into more marketable commodities like rings and seals. Occasionally, more impressive items could also be had through the offices of the same metalworkers. When, for example, the Trevisan notary Oliviero Forzetta compiled a short list of tasks to complete in Venice in 1335, he jotted down where he expected to find select manuscripts, antiquities and drawings.[3] He reminded himself that there were bronze busts in the shop of the goldsmith, 'Giovanni the German', and marble heads in the shop of

another goldsmith, Ognibeni *aurificis*. He noted that there were statues in convents and churches, such as the figures of putti from the throne of Saturn which were then in San Vitale in Ravenna (Figure 200). In addition, he was aware that classical texts could be had from the stationers' shops and that a number of drawings by the painters Paolo and

200 *Putti from the Throne of Saturn*, Marble, 1st–2nd century AD, Museo Archeologico, Venice.

Marco Veneziano, whom he may have known in Treviso, were being held as pledges with moneylenders.

Forzetta, who had lived in Venice, knew the city well and the list has been used to demonstrate the early interest in the Veneto for the collecting of antiquities. What it also demonstrates is the difficulty of making such purchases. If Forzetta had planned to acquire, rather than simply admire, the items that were listed, he would have had to negotiate directly with a wide range of different individuals: church officials, stationers, goldsmiths and pawnbrokers. A century later, in the early fifteenth century, the situation was very similar. The acquisition of classical remains was still confined to a small number of buyers and sellers most of whom knew each other and had a personal knowledge of what was available. There was only a very limited broader market for anything but the most complete figurative pieces, or for jewel-like cameos and hard-stone vases. This was in part due to the fact that despite the many literary laments over Rome's impoverishment, there was no automatic veneration for its monuments.[4] Marble had many uses, only one of which was for display and study. With undecorated Roman stones, their value lay not in their preservation, but in their reuse as mortar for new construction.[5] In 1426, for example, when the humanist movement dedicated to the revival of classical Ciceronian Latin and the collecting of Greek manuscripts was building momentum, Roman officials sold the rights to excavate the plain Tavertine stones from the Basilica Giulia to a consortium of lime-burners.[6] The same fate awaited the Colosseum, the Circus Maximus and other Roman monuments whose remains were all employed in the building of Saint Peter's cathedral, and the new palaces of the elite Roman cardinals. As late as 1456, the marble merchant, Pellegrino *marmorario* supplied 760 cannon balls made out of ancient stones while Pope Pius II, a humanist scholar in his own right, authorised the use of the stones of the Colosseum to build the piazza and steps of Saint Peter's.[7] Even those stones that carried inscriptions and ornamentation were put to mundane uses on a regular basis. The Greek scholar Manuel Chrysoloras denounced the fact that statues were used as blocks from which to mount horses, embedded in house foundations, or used to provide mangers in stables.[8]

The drawings and prints produced by visitors to Rome such as Martin Van Heemskerk and Etienne Dupérac stressed this sense of neglect and abuse of the city's classical past (Figures 201–03). Showing a depopulated and desolate landscape, the drawings suggested a random assortment of antiquities littering the city rather than a carefully considered arrangement or collection. Even private collections such as that of the Galli family were depicted as a random set of gathered marbles (Figure 204). This vision implies a lack of appreciation by the indigenous Roman population that seemed to justify the appropriation of these monuments by those who truly knew their worth. But by the time Van Heemskerk arrived in Rome in the 1530s, this message was more his own construction than a reality. By this stage, the worth of these antiquities was much more widely understood. While the buildings themselves continued to be used and adapted for new purposes (one plan involved transforming the Colosseum into a wool-manufacturing centre), the collectable materials that such sites yielded had taken

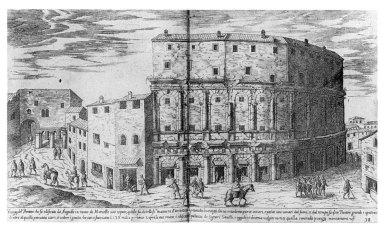

201 *Circo Massimo e Palazzi imperiali del Palatino*, Etienne Dupérac, *I vestigi dell'antichita di Roma*, Rome, 1575, f. 3, The British Library, London.

202 *Vestigi del Theatro che fu edificato da Augusto in nome di Marcello*, Etienne Dupérac, *I vestigi dell'anti-chita di Roma*, Rome, 1575, f. 38, The British Library, London.

203 Marten Van Heemskerk, *View of the Forum Nervae with Temple of Minerva*, c. 1532–6, Kunstbibliothek, Berlin, Skizzenbuch, 1, f. 37r.

204   Martin Van Heemskeerk, *Antiquities from the Galli Garden*,
c.1532–6, Kunstbibliothek, Berlin, Skizzenbuch, 1, f. 27.

on a high monetary value. From being remains that were of interest only to scholars
and a small number of collectors, the marbles, bronzes, coins and cameos that emerged
from the ground provided the basis for potential fortunes. For example, between the
two assessments made in 1465 and 1492, the value of the expensive cameo of the Ark
of Noah which had passed from the collection of Paul II to that of the Venetian jeweller Domenico di Piero before finishing in the hands of Lorenzo dei Medici had risen
almost six-fold from 330 florins to 2,000 florins.[9] The increase can be partly explained
by the object's increasingly distinguished provenance. But the classic economic explanations of high demand and a limited supply were also at play as Lorenzo competed
with cardinals, princes and bankers for the remains of Rome's past.

With wealthy patrons willing to pay large sums for even minor antiquities, digging
in the city of Rome and its surroundings became the sixteenth-century equivalent of
prospecting for gold or oil. If a large-scale statue was found intact, the rewards could
be immense. In 1514, for example, Filippo Strozzi explained how Piero di Lorenzo dei
Medici's wife, Alfonsina Orsini, had paid for the construction of a basement in a
convent in Rome. During the excavation, they had found five classical figures. Now
identified as a series of Roman copies of statues from the Athenian Acropolis, the statues
were remarkably well preserved[10] (Figures 205–06). This meant that they were indeed
highly prized and as Strozzi put it, 'she [Alfonsina] is the most fortunate woman that
ever was, for the money that she gave to God has rendered her more than if she had
lent it out at a usurious interest'.[11] By the early sixteenth century, the papacy began
allocating areas for digs to cardinals, and professional excavators began sub-letting plots
in which to dig and make discoveries.[12] Increasingly, a set of intermediaries emerged

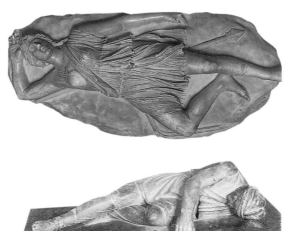

205 (*top*)   *Dying Amazon*, Roman copy of Hellenistic original, Museo Nazionale Archeologico, Naples.

206 (*above*)   *Dying Persian*, Roman copy of Hellenistic original, Museo Nazionale Archeologico, Naples.

who were able to put those who found such objects in touch with those who wanted to buy them. There was no longer any need to negotiate as Forzetta had done on an individual basis in different sites and shops. By the early sixteenth century there were figures who had enough of a reputation for specialist dealings to be given nicknames such as 'Domenico of the Cameos' or 'Antonietto of the Medals' (a dealer who was also referred to as 'Antonio Antiquario').[13] The latter rented land for the specific purpose of excavating for antiques that he sold from his shop in Rome, sharing his profits with the owners when discoveries were made.[14] Entrepreneurs increasingly joined forces to set up partnerships in the sale of antiquities. Thus in 1560, the hatmaker Giuseppe della Porta invested funds in a company with the goldsmith Vincenzo Mantovano. The former provided the capital, the latter, the expertise. The two were to divide the profits equally. But when they purchased a head of Vespasian that Michelangelo had praised, raising its value to 500 scudi, the two men fell out and the case ended up in court.[15]

As with oil fields or gold mines, the developing market provoked a debate on the concept of public ownership and private profit. Were things that were discovered underground the property of the finder, the landowner, the local ruler, or even 'the people'? By 1495, rental agreements acknowledged the possibility of shared ownership of potential finds and provided for the eventual division of the sale of any coins or statues. In renting three pieces of land on Monte Siccus, for example, the tenant agreed to split any profit he made on the 'metal, tavertine, marble or stone objects' that he might find there with the owner.[16] By the sixteenth century, this was a common clause in most contracts dealing with Roman property where the mutual interests and rights of both the tenant and the owner over treasure-trove discoveries were acknowledged. This was not, however, a completely free market. Those with a high level of political or religious authority could commandeer the best finds. Thus in 1455, Carlo dei Medici had been prevented by the intervention of Pietro Barbo, the future Pope Paul II from obtaining medals that he had already reserved to send to Florence. In another letter, Carlo noted that, as the artist Pisanello lay dying, a long line of contenders stood outside his chambers negotiating for his collection of coins and medals with his servants.[17] Again, Pietro Barbo had used his position to ensure that he was the successful contender. Whoever the incumbent, the pope always had the greatest political authority and when the Laocoon was uncovered in 1506, it was already clear that the Vatican would become its next resting place (Figure 207). This acquisition was not, however, uncontested. A letter written by Bonsignore Bonsignori that year described the conflict between the Pope who wanted the statue for his own residence and 'li Romani' who wanted to place it on the Capitoline hill. The situation was only resolved when the original owner of the land, Felice de' Fredis, was given generous papal rewards: the taxes arising from entry into the gate of San Giovanni and an appointment as curial *scriptor*.[18]

Papal oversight and cupidity only served to make these finds more desirable and more difficult to obtain for other collectors. The personal interest of Rome's popes in the city's antique past varied from incumbent to incumbent but most established their priority over the most important finds and tried to monitor and control exports. In 1471, for example, instructions were issued to the papal castellan of the port of Ostia forbidding exports of antiquities without Sixtus IV's permission.[19] Sixtus IV himself, however, declined to incorporate such statuary into the Vatican palace. Instead, a plaque on the Capitoline hill celebrated the transfer in 1471 of some of Rome's most prominent ancient remains to the Roman people themselves

207 *Laocoon*, Roman copy after Hellenistic original, 1st century AD, Vatican Museums, Vatican City.

·SIXTVS IIII·PONT MAX·
OB IMMENSAM BENIGNITA
TEM·AENEAS INSINGNES STA
TVAS·PRISCAE EXCELLENTIAE
VIRTVTISQVE MONVMEN
TVM·ROMANO PO PVLO
VNDE EXORTE FVERE·RESTI
TVENDAS CONDONANDAS
QVE CENSVIT·
LATINO DE VRSINIS CARDINA
LI CAMERARIO ADMINISTRA
NTE ET·IOHANNE ALPERINO·
PHIL· PALO SCIO·NICOLAO PI
NCIARONIO VRBIS CONSER
VATORIBVS PROCVRATIBVS
ANO SALVTIS NOSTRE·M·CCCC
LXXI·XVIII·RL· IANVAR·

208 Plaque recording the donation of sculptures by Sixtus IV to the Roman People, 1471, Musei Capitolini, Rome.

(Figure 208).[20] But further efforts to prevent private ownership were often simply restricted to controlling the traffic in antiquities. In the early sixteenth century, Isabella d'Este noted that the magistrates who controlled Rome, the Conservatori, were seeking to prevent exports, and she investigated a range of ways to smuggle marbles from the city. In 1515, Leo x issued an order demanding that any marbles that were uncovered within the city limits be brought to the painter Raphael. Despite the document's rhetorical accusations against stonecutters who destroyed reliefs with valuable inscriptions, the motivation seems to have been centred on the need to ensure a regular supply of building material for the new basilica of Saint Peter's. The bull specifically stated that the Pope was determined, 'that the City's ruins suffice as an ample source for this material, and that stones of every kind are dug up here and there by practically everyone who in Rome, or near Rome, undertakes to build or simply to turn the earth'.[21]

Although it may not have prevented further depredations, Raphael's appointment was an important public recognition of the many roles, official and unofficial, that painters, goldsmiths and sculptors played in establishing and controlling this new market for the antique.[22] Crucially, it was widely recognised that genuinely new entries to this market could not be created; they had to be excavated and then authenticated. How to value and price such goods, how to recognise fraudulent or poor quality pieces, became key questions. So too did the most basic issue of whether they should be bought and sold at all. For many commentators, these were the records of an ancient civilisation that should be emulated not marketed. They should have been preserved for posterity rather than bought and sold.

Although the market for antiquities was a new one, the issues around it had a much longer history. There were considerable precedents in previous controversies over the trade in classical texts. While the small circle of humanists who undertook lengthy excursions in the late fourteenth and early fifteenth century to unearth rare Greek and Latin texts had made a virtue of the value of free exchange, the manuscripts they found and copied commanded high prices.[23] In their ideal world, they acted as generous colleagues, making and distributing rare texts for little if any reward beyond the immediate costs of their endeavour. The search for books was supposed to be a search for knowledge, not one undertaken for monetary speculation. For example, the humanist chancellor of Florence, Poggio Bracciolini, who collected ancient manuscripts, epigraphs and antiquities, wrote to his friend Niccolo Niccoli in 1425: 'Now please if you come across any books which you think are worthy of me, either buy them or take an option on them until you let me know. Now that I have begun, I want to collect myself this property that will be worth more in every age than monetary savings.'[24] But when he found himself in debt a few months later, he considered auctioning off the books he had already bought.[25] When Niccolo Niccoli himself had been forced to sell his household goods in the early 1420s, Bracciolini framed this as a non-commercial act – 'I praise you for having held an auction in order to be freer.'[26] But other humanists, Bruni and Guarino in particular, accused Niccoli of having a purely monetary interest in his texts and antiquities.[27]

Acquiring manuscripts in order to trade them, rather than for a supposedly pure intellectual interest, immediately downgraded the scholar and devalued his goods. When, for example, the would-be humanist Enoch of Ascoli arrived in Rome in 1456 with a collection of new treatises that he had discovered in places such as Zeeland in northern Europe, Carlo dei Medici wrote to his half-brother Giovanni dei Medici in Florence to discuss their availability and price:

> It is true that Enoch has brought certain new things, as you will see from the inventory that I am sending you, but in truth they are worth more for their novelty than for their utility. Up until now he has not wanted to make copies for anyone, unless some great master does not worthily remunerate him, and he has hopes of at least two or three hundred florins, but see whether you want to throw away so much money for things that the Latin language could do well without, and in the opinion of the many wise men who have seen them, apart from the four that are starred, the rest aren't worth a bean. Nonetheless I will keep you advised. Concerning the medals, I am using every diligence, but as I have already written, there is a marvellous famine thanks to that Monsignore di San Marco (Pietro Barbo).[28]

Enoch of Ascoli was using a series of techniques that would become standard in the trading of sculpture as well as of manuscripts. An inventory had been drawn up and was being circulated in order to attract attention. Samples were being shown to generate interest. He was hoping that his collection would bring his reputation to the attention of a major patron (such as Giovanni dei Medici) who would then be able to reward him handsomely in return for a 'gift' of the manuscripts.

The d'Ascoli manuscripts may not have made it to Florence, but the writer's last remark is worthy of attention. As Carlo dei Medici pointed out, the act of a single buyer such as Pietro Barbo could dramatically change the market for antiquities of all types. This was true for other types of classical material, and it is unsurprising to find that the debate that dominated the trade in manuscripts shifted easily to the market for antiquities. The connection between collecting manuscripts and collecting the medallic or sculpted images of the men and women to whom the texts referred had been popularised by earlier humanists such as Petrarch.[29] The early fifteenth-century Florentine humanist and chancellor Poggio Bracciolini referred to above was similarly proud of both the inscriptions he had collected from marbles and the ancient heads that he kept in his bedroom.[30] But he was already sensitive to the deceits of the trade, writing in 1421 of how he had commissioned a friend to look for Greek statuary during his travels in the Aegean:

> I gave some errands to Master Franciscus of Pistoia when he left us. Among them the most important was to look for any marble statue, even if it were broken, or any unusual head which he could bring back to me with him. Yesterday I received letters from him written from Chios in which he informed me that he was holding in my name three marble heads by Polycleitus and Praxitiles. I do not know what to say about the names of the sculptors, as you know the Greeks are very wordy and perhaps they have made up the names in order to sell the heads more dearly. I hope that I am wrong to suspect this.[31]

The early humanists such as Bracciolini were rarely wealthy men. They financed their own acquisitions by selling parts of their own collections or acting on behalf of others. Laurie Fusco and Gino Corti have shown how the Roman humanist Giovanni Ciampolini played a pivotal role in the creation of famous collections of statuary.[32] For example, in 1489, the intermediary that Lorenzo dei Medici was using in his negotiations with Ciampolini wrote concerning a head of the Emperor Nerva that was up for sale: 'It is just beautiful, but it seems to me that Ciampolini estimates it beyond what it is worth and is demanding an insane sum for it. Since I have heard that he has better objects that he does not want to show, I think it would be good to let him be and to pretend not to crave after it so much because eventually he will not find better terms than ours.'[33]

The classic negotiating technique of pretending indifference was matched by Ciampolini's own sales tactics. When the Roman sold Lorenzo a statue of three fauns, he was adamant that he was lowering its price because of their friendship: 'he let me know that they cost 50 ducats and that if he were to give them to others and not to me, he would ask 100 ducats'.[34] Lorenzo, used to bargaining fiercely, was insistent that Ciampolini throw in an antique vase without extra charge before concluding the bargain.

Much of the dealing that took place was mediated with a fine sense of decorum. The two men never discussed prices directly. When the deal was concluded, it was agreed that Ciampolini's vase would be a gift to Lorenzo. Detaching the collector from the actual process of purchasing was an important part in creating the division between 'virtuous riches' and those which were simply valued for their material wealth. Increasingly, the language of gift-giving became central to such transactions. In March 1528, for example, the Mantuan ambassador in Rome, Francesco Gonzaga, announced that he had located a collection of seven marble heads owned by Raphael's pupil Giovanni Francesco Penni. In his instructions on how to proceed the Marquis of Mantua, Federico Gonzaga, wrote:

We have received the note that you sent concerning the ancient heads that that painter has here in Rome, and we have seen its contents and the price that the painter is asking for them, which is 80 ducats. Although he has offered to give them to us, we have decided that we want them in every respect, and therefore we want you to accept them as a gift in our name, and send them to us as quickly as possible, and then from the first quarter's allowance that we have give the said painter 60 ducats, because we have spoken with people who have seen the said heads, and they have said that that was the price that he paid. But to him say that we have accepted his heads as a gift and that we wish him to accept this money as a gift, for it is as a gift that we offer it.[35]

The anthropological literature on gift-giving is rich in such examples of exchange, but here the relationship was mixed between the commercial and the non-commercial. Although he was offering his sculptures as gifts, Giovanni Francesco Penni made the sum that he expected in exchange very clear. The amount paid as such a gift was expected to reflect the status of the patron as much as the value of the antiquities. For his part, Gonzaga obtained market information about Penni's costs. In ensuring that the painter was repaid rather than reaping a profit, he re-balanced the relationship. Penni now benefited from his new social connection with the Marquis of Mantua, not from the 20 ducats that he might have expected to gain from the bargain. If 60 ducats was a 'gift' as Gonzaga emphasised over and over again, there could be no further negotiations.[36] The later sixteenth-century correspondence published by Clifford Brown between Gerolamo Garimberto and Cesare Gonzaga is similarly full of references to the appropriate 'gift' to make to men, and occasionally women, who provided the latter with antiquities. For example, it was suggested that the collector, Paolo del Buffalo, who had given Gonzaga a piece of alabaster for his *studiolo*, should be given a pair of dogs or a horse rather than money in return.[37]

Whether gift or commodity, the letter concerning Penni's collection and del Buffalo's statues also reveals the complexities of actually establishing precise monetary value. Although gold could be weighed, and cameos treated as gems, objects such as marble had only a very limited intrinsic value as either building material or, when burnt, as quicklime. It was widely recognised that the market for antiquities, as in any market, was driven by demand. But price was also affected by the perceived condition of the item in question. Separating high-quality items from those that were indifferent or inauthentic required specialist knowledge. In the early stages of the fifteenth century, the authentication and valuing of antiques were primarily undertaken by the self-same community of collectors working alongside goldsmiths, painters and sculptors who established a reputation for skilful judgement. In many cases it was this ability that brought artists into daily discussions with their patrons, rather than their expertise with a brush or pen. For example, in 1538 Giulio Romano apologised to the Duke of Mantua for a delay in some negotiations over a number of Flemish pictures that he was selecting on the latter's behalf. He had been busy with the duke's mother Isabella, meeting a jeweller who had brought cameos to the castle. He was, in his words, 'being used as the middleman' (*a mezzo*) in order to settle the price of the five antique gems that she had chosen.[38] Giulio was also willing to help other members of the court. A letter of 28 March 1523 from the courtier and writer Baldessare Castiglione to his agent in Rome, Andrea Piperio, gives some insight into the key role that Giulio played in determining what was, and was not, worth buying:

> Giovan Francesco wrote to me a few days ago saying that he has found me some antiquities (*anticaglie*) and that they will cost 10 ducats. As I thought that the whole thing had been arranged with Giulio's involvement and consent I therefore wrote to you saying that you should give him the 10 ducats. Now I understand that in Giulio's opinion these are not great things, and that I have paid too much, so if you haven't paid him, don't, excusing yourself in whatever way you think best, saying that you have no more of my money in your hands, or some other thing that you can think of. This is above all because Giulio has had sent to me a fabulous cameo, which he says he has seen. It is an extremely beautiful thing, and he can get it at a good price, so I have decided to take this with the intention of not buying any more antiquities this year, unless some great opportunity comes up in either price or quality. Giulio says that the owner wants 100 ducats for it but that he can get it down to 40 or 50, which still seems to me to be too much, particularly since I have little money at the moment, but if he can get it for 25 or 30 ducats I want him to get it . . . I would much rather have one excellent thing than have 50 which are mediocre. I also want the painting by Master Antonio da San Marino, this cameo and that torso for my bust that Giulio wrote to me about, and then I won't get anything more this year.[39]

The friendship that grew between Giulio Romano and the distinguished writer and courtier Castiglione was only one of many new relationships that the desire for antiquities was able to forge across social boundaries. There are many examples of goldsmiths, painters and sculptors who were able to employ their techniques of connoisseurship in order to become important intermediaries in this new marketplace. When demand outstripped supply for originals, they were then able to insert their own productions as substitutes.

There has been a considerable debate over the issue of antique fakes and forgeries in the sixteenth century, particularly of ancient coins, by sculptors such as the Paduan Giovanni Cavino.[40] But reproductions had their own value. Produced in print, in gesso, in sulphur medals and in wax, they provided a relatively inexpensive way of participating in this culture of *all'antica* decoration. That many artisans responded to this growing demand is suggested by the contract to make eleven reproductions of the River Gods in the Vatican Belvedere which was agreed in 1545.[41] The number of surviving sixteenth-century versions of the Laocoon and the *Spinario* (Figure 210) in different materials and sizes is a similar testimony to the trend towards the making of such reproductions.

The market for antiquities and for *all'antica* emulations inspired a diverse range of marketing strategies. While some, like the print-seller Antoine Lafrery, who sold engravings of ancient monuments in Rome, sought to broaden their customer base through catalogue sales, others tried to make their works as exclusive as possible (Figure 209).[42] One of the most dramatic examples of the latter strategy is provided by the sculptor Pier Jacopo Alari-Bonacolsi, better known by his nickname, 'L'Antico'. Pier Jacopo's father, Antonio, was a butcher who ran a stall in Mantua's main meat market.[43] The circumstances under which the young man was educated are unknown, but his work suggests initial training as a goldsmith. He first appeared in the 1490s in the service of a cadet branch of the Gonzaga family based in Bozzolo. He was part of the entourage of Gianfrancesco Gonzaga and his wife, the Neapolitan princess Antonia del Balzo. He was referred to as *mio famiglio* by del Balzo when the latter had him carry a belt to Mantua as a gift to Francesco II Gonzaga.[44] Antico lived in the castle of Bozzolo itself and in 1501 was listed as one of six salaried chamberlains. By 1516, the courtier-sculptor had established his right to use the name of one of Mantua's most elite families, that of the Bonacolsi. A decade later, he was formally styled as *nobile*.[45] His place among Mantua's elite was publicly confirmed when, following the intervention of Isabella d'Este, his daughter Delia married a member of the court, Galeotto Nuvoloni in 1518.[46] In their turn his sons, Federico and Alessandro, became courtiers to Federico II in 1525.[47]

Mantua was a particularly fluid social environment and earlier examples of the rising status of the artist at the Gonzaga court included Pisanello, Andrea Mantegna and Giulio Romano. But Antico was unusual in that he neither acted as a court artist to the main branch of the Gonzaga itself, nor provided the wide range of services that would have been expected from the typical artistic retainer. Unlike the other three painters mentioned above, he did not create frescoes or altarpieces. Nor did he organise spectacles or provide drawings for tapestries, cushions, embroideries and metalware. Instead, he was known specifically for his understanding of ancient statuary and for his ability to restore and to emulate objects from the past. Antico produced highly polished, almost jewel-like works in bronze. Some were direct copies from famous antiquities such as the *Spinario* (Figure 211). Others were emulations rather than imitations. They did not reproduce any known ancient model, but appealed to the same sense of small-scale elegance generated by the cameos and gems that were in such demand. His nickname, 'The Antique', was a genuine tribute to his singular skill in creating something that was both contemporary and at the same time carried the aura of the classical past.

Antico also provided opinions on statues that his patrons and friends were considering as purchases. His expertise was regularly sought whenever the marquis or marchioness considered acquiring antiquities. In 1507, for example, Isabella sent a dealer to show the sculptor the items offered for sale, asking for Antico's advice as to their originality and price. His ability to repair goods once they had been purchased was also celebrated. He had spent considerable periods in Rome and his name survives on one of the restored horses of Montecavallo. In February 1525, Federico II Gonzaga told his ambassador in Rome to find whatever statuary he could, 'and do not stop at any price to get them, even if they are mutilated in part, either in the nose, eye or in any other

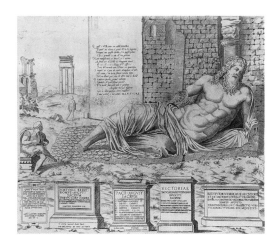

209 (*left*)   *Marforio*, engraving made for Antoine Lafrery, *Speculum Romanae magnificentiae*, Rome, 1546, British Museum, London.

210 (*below left*)   *The Spinario*, first century BC, bronze, Palazzo dei Conservatori, Musei Capitolini, Rome.

211 (*below right*)   Antico, *The Spinario*, gilt bronze, c. 1501, Private Collection, New York. Photograph, The Metropolitan Museum.

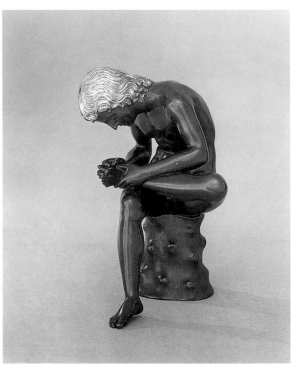

place, still buy it because l'Antico will be able to repair them in such a way that they will be fine'.[48]

Like his contemporary Antonio Riccio in Padua who supplied large numbers of figurines to that city's scholars and collectors, Antico could have created a production line that made multiple versions of these statuettes, distributing them in a range of different formats and prices. There is evidence that on a number of occasions he was willing to make such copies. In 1499, for example, Bishop Ludovico Gonzaga sent Antico's version of the *Spinario* to the sculptor, Gian Marco Cavalli. The statuette was to act as a model for a bronze copy that the cleric had promised to send to the Venetian Marcantonio Morosini. When Antico then personally undertook the casting and chasing, this was specifically referred to as an added bonus. Yet despite the ease with which Antico could have disseminated his work to a wider market, he chose to emphasise the exclusivity of his clientele. When, for example, he agreed to make versions of his works for Isabella d'Este in 1519, this was done as a special favour for an elite patron and not as the start of a new business enterprise. Indeed, he had already had the bishop's chaplain imprisoned for making unauthorised copies of his works.[49]

Such tight control was necessary if Antico was to profit from the rise in his personal social status. There were considerable monetary rewards involved as Antico was paid up to 30 ducats for each of the bronzes that he produced for the Gonzaga and received a monthly salary for his role as chamberlain. The connections brought important additional benefits. In 1504, for example, Antico and Isabella came to an agreement by which his family's ownership of a stall in the meat market of Mantua would remain outside the general system of public auctioning. In return, he sent the marchioness the gold statute of Saint John the Baptist that she had been pressing him to finish for some time. Even more lucrative favours were possible. Antico eventually became the officer responsible for the ports and mills of Mantua, a post that generated substantial tax revenues.[50]

Antico's repositioning of himself as a courtier rather than an artisan was a deliberate form of self-definition. His entrepreneurial ability was devoted to developing strategic relationships rather than identifying a broad market for his new products. His elegant bronzes, his role as restorer and his ability to judge value and price in the market for antiquities were the special skills that made possible his family's transition from butchers to courtiers. His sons and daughter would not work with their hands, but live off the family reputation and social connections that their father's abilities had created.

Because of his limited high-quality output, Antico did not seek customers. Instead, his clients solicited his works themselves. Direct discussions of money were rare; many of his payments were in kind rather than in cash. This disassociation between the product, the producer and the market economy was an increasingly important element in the market for antiquities. For just as the prices of marbles, coins and cameos rose to unprecedented levels in the sixteenth century, so too many collectors made significant efforts to remove their objects from the vulnerabilities of the marketplace. As the acquisition of antique statuary, coins and medals grew in popularity the question of their eventual dispersal centred on whether they were simply household valuables that, like tapestries, furnishings and linens, could be sold to pay off debts or provide for the needs of heirs or whether they were somehow singular and in need of special treatment.

The two extremes can be seen in the testament and codicil of the Venetian patrician and prelate Giovanni Grimani whose first will of 1592 originally suggested an ambivalent attitude towards his collection:

> I declare that, having perhaps offended God by collecting medals made of gold, silver and other metals, cameos and intaglios, both antique and modern, and having spent on such vanities a great amount of money which could have been applied to works of charity, now after humbly beseeching God through Jesus Christ to pardon me, I declare and state that all the above mentioned antiquities should be sold for a good price.[51]

But in a complex and emotive change to his will six months later Grimani specifically revoked this order. He requested that the cameos and medals remain as part of the contents of his *studiolo* and be given to his nephew, 'for the honour of our house of the Grimani'.[52]

The language of family honour would become increasingly popular as testators urged their heirs to respect the integrity of their collections. To achieve this end, they had to convince sons, nephews and other relations that there was greater value in continued ownership than in the money raised by an immediate sale. The Roman collector Marcantonio Altieri had emphasised in his will of 1511 that if his son tried to sell the family sculpture collection, the Roman Conservators were authorised to seize the works for public display.[53] A letter from Paulo Manuzio to the Doge Andrea Loredan from the same period similarly insisted that:

> You could never leave your sons any land, palace or treasure which could equal the value and excellence of these antiquities of yours. These are not material goods, which one may acquire with simple labour; the collection is not a gem which one may obtain at a price; these are virtuous riches, which do not fall to the lot of the uneducated, which one may only collect with judgement, with infinite knowledge over a long period of time . . .[54]

To the notion that Loredan's antiquities were 'virtuous riches' that demonstrated the owner's taste and intellectual standing was attached a strong sense of family obligation. In his will, for example, Cardinal Pietro Bembo asked that his son should, 'not sell, pawn, or give away for any reason whatsoever any of my antiquities, whether of stone, copper, silver or gold . . . but to keep them on account of his honour and my memory'.[55]

In 1548, the Venetian patrician Gabriel Vendramin similarly pleaded with his heirs, providing a careful argument as to why they should not sell his collection of drawings, prints, antiquities, vases, medals and *naturalia*:

> I declare that all the things that are found in this small room, which are worth many hundreds of ducats . . . would bring in more than they cost, and that this expenditure has not deprived our family of a single ducat; rather I can say that it has brought it profit, and it remains for me to explain why. I cannot refrain from declaring that

all these things, both for their high quality and because of the many years' hard work taken to acquire them, and most of all because they have brought a [. . .] peace and quiet to my soul during the many labours of mind and body that I have endured in conducting the family business, they are so pleasing and dear to me that I must pray and beseech those who inherit them to treat them with such care that they shall not perish. And . . . I order that none of these things shall be sold, or pawned, or loaned, either in whole or in part or in any conceivable way . . .[56]

To ensure that no such sale would take place after his death, Vendramin asked that this *camerino delle anticaglie* be sealed until an heir who would maintain it could be located.

The reason for inserting such requests into last wills and testaments was, of course, the common practice of settling debts and dividing the estate after death. Most Renaissance collections had been made possible by financial, political or familial failures. Paul II's collection of cameos, coins and medals was immediately sold after his death in 1471 by his successor, Sixtus IV. Lorenzo dei Medici's treasures were similarly dispersed following his family's exile in 1494. Some collectors, aware of their debts, tried to plan for a more orderly disposal. In his will, Cardinal Francesco Gonzaga asked that his cameos and sculptures be sold to satisfy his creditors, while the Venetian jeweller Domenico di Piero listed the types of goods in his home and stipulated the prices at which his valuable antiques should be offered to potential purchasers.[57]

Even where relatives wanted to preserve a family collection, they might be forced into a sale by impatient creditors. When Cardinal Marino Grimani died in 1546, for example, his brother Giovanni, the wealthy Patriarch of Aquileia, could not stop the former's collection from being put on the market. Despite his authority and prestige, he was forced to pay 3,000 scudi to recover the coins, medals, gemstones and 200 cameos.[58] Faced with the real possibility of dispersal and disposal, a number of collectors tried to stop this cycle of sale and resale by attaching their own identities, those of their family and even the reputation of their city to the objects in question. When the Patriarch, Giovanni Grimani, referred to above, prepared his own will he was understandably sceptical about his own family's willingness to preserve his collection. He eventually left treasures (apart from his cameos and medals) to the city of Venice into whose abstract, institutional care he bequeathed his collection.

Such donations had a long pre-history, particularly in gifts of libraries. Humanists or other collectors who had amassed important classical or religious texts were accustomed to leaving their books to monastic institutions rather than to their immediate family. Despite having heirs, Oliviero Forzetta divided his library between the convents of Santa Margarita and San Francesco in Treviso in the early fourteenth century. In the 1440s, Cosimo dei Medici constructed and furnished the Dominican convent of San Marco with a library that would be open to scholars.[59] By the mid-fifteenth century, the city itself was seen as a potential repository for such initiatives. In the 1470s, the Greek prelate and scholar Cardinal Bessarion left his manuscripts to the Venetian state.[60] In explaining his decision, he provided an emotive account of preserving a heritage that needed to be saved from destruction:

From almost the earliest years of my boyhood I strove with all my might, main, effort and concentration to assemble as many books as possible as I could on every sort of subject . . . For I feared, indeed I was consumed with terror – lest all these wonderful books . . . should be brought to danger and destruction in an instant . . . Finally, I reflected that my dream would not have been fully realised if I failed to make sure that my books which I had assembled with such care and effort were so disposed in my lifetime that they could not be dispersed and scattered after my death. They must be preserved in a place that is both safe and accessible, for the general good of all readers, be they Greek or Latin.[61]

The notion that such items were part of the 'general good' that needed to be protected for future sale had obvious links with the wealth of church treasuries. One might have expected Bessarion to follow an earlier tradition and donate his library to a monastic institution. But as part of his strategy to encourage the Serenissima to fight the Ottoman Empire that had invaded his homeland, Bessarion chose Venice, rather than the Church as the repository for his treasures. In the 1470s it remained a relatively unusual concept to choose the city, rather than one's own family, to be as caretakers of personal memory. But it rapidly took on a wider acceptance by the end of the century. The eventual construction of the library of San Marco by the sculptor and architect Jacopo Sansovino in the sixteenth century provided a space for storing not only books, but also the antiquities that scholars expected to examine alongside their texts within their *studioli*. In 1532, for example, the Venetian Senate commanded Jacopo Sansovino to remove the putti holding the Throne of Saturn from a house that was being demolished (figures that had originally attracted Oliviero Forzetta's attention) and to place the panels in the library of San Marco.[62]

Originally, however, donations of antiquities to Venice had been less concerned with public access and more with preserving memory. In 1523, another member of the Grimani family, Cardinal Domenico left a collection of Flemish paintings and classical statuary to the city on the condition that the goods were kept together in the benefactor's name, a condition that was honoured by placing the items in the Palazzo Ducale with appropriate inscriptions.[63] This was not, it should be stressed, a donation to the Venetian people or one intended for public display. The room chosen was a chamber that the Doge passed through when moving from his private quarters to the Collegio, not one that was open to a wide range of Venetians. But when, as discussed above, in 1587, the Patriarch of Aquileia, Giovanni Grimani, the last remaining nephew of Domenico Grimani, offered to donate his own collection to the Venetian state, he imposed a number of new conditions. First, the city would have to provide an appropriate setting for the collection, one that would allow foreigners and visitors to see the antiquities, 'so that they can see as a notable thing, these antiques which will have been placed in a public place'. His uncle Domenico's collection, hidden within the Palazzo Ducale, was to join his own works in the ante-chamber of the Biblioteca Marcianai to create a 'noble sight'.[64]

The Grimani collection did not spark off a complete revolution in the relationship between private collecting and public institutions. But it did offer new possibilities to those concerned for posterity. The city-state and its magistrates, rather than one's immediate heirs, friends and neighbours, could be trusted to look after one's prized possessions. In 1605, therefore, the apothecary and naturalist Ulisse Aldrovandi left the contents of his studio to the city of Bologna to form the basis of a civic museum at his death.[65] Indeed, the practice was becoming common enough that a number of collectors were forced to specifically exclude their home towns as recipients of their inheritance. In 1604, another apothecary, Francesco Calzolari from Verona, asked that the local government be forbidden from taking over his rooms filled with specimens of natural history, designating his nephew as his heir instead.[66]

These proto-museums were caused by the failure of inheritance and a distrust of future generations. In Venice, in particular, there was a sense that familial or individual memory had a greater chance of survival if entrusted to the city rather than to heirs whose financial circumstances might change. The development of a successful market in antiquities had succeeded in generating a parallel space where trade was not possible. Pricing became irrelevant since these goods were now never again be for sale. Yet the rhetoric of 'pricelessness' had little meaning unless a price could be attached. Together they formed a set of boundaries, stated and unstated, that profoundly shaped how men and women conceptualised and explained values, intellectual, spiritual or monetary.

BUYING HEAVEN

When the Venetian government built the library of San Marco in the heart of the city the building joined other repositories of state goods, including the Treasury of San Marco. Taken as booty, or deliberately stolen from the East as *sacra furta*, the relics, holy vessels and vestments in the Treasury were usually shown to visitors following their visit to the town's shopping centre. The contrast was a deliberate one. Distinguished guests could price, purchase or be given the fabrics and delicacies of the *merceria*, but the treasures of the Venetian state were not for sale.

But like the antiquities described above, the cyclical process of commodification, de-commodification and re-commodification was as common among religious items as it was among their secular equivalents. Although donations to the Church were meant to deliberately remove spiritually valuable goods that were encased in gold, silver and gems from the earthly marketplace, they remained vulnerable to sale or other forms of disposal. One example is the trade in relics, where it was widely accepted that theft or purchase were acceptable modes of obtaining the remnants of saints and martyrs (which were then often known as 'sacred pawns' or *sacra pignora*). The Ospedale della Scala in Siena, for instance, provided an important provenance for its version of the sacred nail from Christ's cross by pointing to its purchase at an auction held in 1359 at the Loggia dei Veneziani in Constantinople on behalf of the Emperor John VI Cantacuzeno who was then in grave financial difficulties.[67] Had he been successful, the Florentine goldsmith Antonio Averlino's attempts to steal the head of Saint John the Baptist (his city's patron saint) from Rome in 1455 would have gained him high rewards rather than a jail sentence.[68] In 1599, threatening a perpetual banishment to the galleys, the vicar general of Rome outlawed entry into the city's catacombs to prevent the theft of early Christian relics.[69]

Once having arrived at their rightful destination in a church treasury, these scraps of bone, teeth and textiles were immediately removed from any future sale. But, as institutional investors in relics knew well, they still provided monetary rewards. Their presence sanctified the city and brought pilgrims who came seeking redemption. In buying candles, paying for masses and purchasing official indulgences associated with a particular shrine or relic, penitents would have to pay in cash. These were either to be used for the benefit of worshippers in the form of candles or oil that would be burnt before the altar or stored away until they were required for liturgical purposes. Church treasuries and sacristies, with their relics and reliquaries, valuable vestments and the equipment needed for services and the mass, were supposed to be absolutely free of commercial interest. But the clergy and their monastic counterparts were as liable to financial difficulties as their lay relations and given the intrinsic worth of the metal in these objects, the temptation to sell or pawn was very great. Most cities tried to curtail the pawning of religious items, in part to prevent them from falling into the hands of Jewish pawnbrokers. In Florence, for example, regulations stated that no loans could be made against 'altar cloths, chalices, crucifixes, missals and breviaries of churches' without special authorisation. In Mantua similar bans were made against the pawning of 'sacred clothing and cloths and other objects that are used in the Christian church'. These laws imply, of course, that such practices were common.[70] In 1460, the serving girl of Nicolo di Iacopo de' Giugni in Florence was accused of pawning 'two books that could have been used for saying the divine office'. She was eventually excused because they were *diurni et non brevarii*, that is, daybooks rather than breviaries.[71] Finally, in 1481 in Florence the rules were modified to allow crucifixes, *croci* or *crocelliere* or other things which were not actually in use to be pawned. In practice, this meant that it was almost impossible to differentiate between what could and could not be legitimately pawned or sold from a church sacristy.[72]

The Church authorities themselves could not always be trusted to look after ecclesiastical property. In 1550, the governor of Rome was forced to issue a decree threatening the servants of the deceased Paul III with excommunication if they did not return all of the vases, silver, ornaments and money that they had removed from the Vatican following the pope's death.[73] In 1555, however, the vicar general was still threatening the same punishment for those holding the 'precious objects' that belonged to the Holy See.[74] Finally in 1560, Pius IV listed the jewels, gems, manuscripts, horses, paintings and furnishings that had been stolen from the apostolic palace during the illness and death of the previous Pope.[75]

The relationship of the Catholic Church to material wealth is a complex note on which to conclude. But it is important to recognise that behind the practices of secular merchants and buyers who sought to distinguish between goods that were for sale and those that were 'beyond price' lay a long and vexed religious tradition. Like the antiquities given to the Roman or Venetian people, goods given to the Church for ecclesiastical purposes were, despite their high level of material value, supposed to stand outside commercial exchange.[76] One of the most profound schisms of the sixteenth century, the Lutheran reform, took place precisely because the Catholic Church in Italy was seen to have blurred these boundaries beyond redemption.

The indulgence controversy that began in 1517 forced a confrontation with what was, and what was not, acceptable to sell in public. An indulgence could be obtained in a number of ways either by undertaking an act, such as visiting a church or relic or by purchasing a certificate from an authorised vendor. Indulgence peddlers, or pardoners as they were known in England, developed highly sophisticated sales techniques. Like insurance salesmen or financial advisors today, they first had to convince their buyers that they needed this benefit. What then were they selling? How did they generate a demand?

By the mid-thirteenth century, the bifurcation between heaven and hell had been complicated with the development of the concept of a midway point, purgatory.[77] The number and severity of one's sins determined one's place in purgatory following death. To ensure forgiveness, a system of confession and penitence had been put in place and indulgences were essentially variations on the penances that were applied by a priest to sinners. Traditional penitence took place over a long period of time: the expiation of even a minor sin might require up to a decade of fasting. Thus, instead of asking his flock to undertake such an onerous act, the early Church had allowed priests to commute the punishment to something more feasible, such as giving alms, saying prayers and, by the thirteenth century, obtaining an indulgence. A forty-day indulgence, known as a quaratine, would be the equivalent of fasting on bread and water for forty days while a plenary indulgence would erase the whole of the punishments that were due to sin both on earth and crucially, in purgatory itself. The purchase of an indulgence involved the enactment of a ritual of confession and forgiveness.[78] But there was often a tangible piece of paper involved, and printed indulgences usually left a blank space for the buyer's name to be inserted as in the German example of around 1480 (Figure 212). In England there are records of men and women dying with trunks filled with these papers as a form of 'spiritual insurance'.[79]

For their proponents the benefits were enormous. Available to both the living and the dead, indulgences provided relief from spiritual suffering and from the fear of punishment in purgatory. The income that they raised supported crusades, the construction of churches and cathedrals and even the building of bridges, dams and roads.[80] Like many major enterprises, the cathedral and hospital of Milan were constructed almost entirely on the back of forty-day remissions that could be purchased both on site itself and from travelling preachers who took a percentage of the profits.[81] Although they were supposed to be sold for a limited period only, these indulgences were crucial

212   German printed Indulgence, c.1480, with
space left blank for purchaser to fill in his or her
name. The British Library, London, IA.6432.

to the finances of building projects and were regularly renewed. In 1390, for example,
the Lord of Milan Gian Galeazzo Visconti announced that he would press the pope for
a share of the Jubilee indulgence, arguing that since many could not get to Rome from
the north due to the wars that he was then waging they should get it if they visited
Milan's major churches instead.[82] The Jubilee indulgences were so popular that rather
than being issued every century, they were repeated at regular intervals. In 1526, for
example, the papal chamberlain Pietro Armellini was in negotiations with Venice over
the benefits of proclaiming a jubilee to raise money for the building of Saint Peter and
investments in the Venetian Arsenal to provide ships to send against the Turks.[83] Only
a year later, in May 1527, Clement VII issued a plenary indulgence to anyone who took
up arms against the invading Imperial army.[84]

Although the Church constantly stressed that it was only true repentance and confession that made an indulgence effective, the activities and certificates associated with
the practice became desirable ends in their own right. Once the concept of making a
cash purchase of forgiveness and redemption became widely accepted, worshipping
relics, attending mass at a designated site, going on a pilgrimage, or buying a piece of
paper in lieu of such activities became an active consumer choice with competing sites
of salvation.[85]

Indulgences could be issued by archbishops but the most powerful remissions were
reserved to the pope himself. In some cases, their purchasers had to visit the holy location, make a full confession and take mass, before they acquired the full benefit. But
given the difficulties of travel, most papal or episcopal indulgences organised teams of
friars to move out into the countryside on a European-wide basis, preaching, blessing
and selling at fixed rates (on which the friar gained a percentage) the religious benefits
involved. Already by 1287, the synod of Liège had to remind priests to tell their parish-
ioners about the benefits of an indulgence, 'without fraud', to sell them only in church
or in the square and not go selling the parchments door-to-door.[86] In the debates against
Luther during the first quarter of the sixteenth century, Catholic apologists continued

to defend the practice but admitted that they had been handled 'scandalously and very foolishly'.[87]

The most controversial indulgence, the one that prompted Luther's revolt, was associated with the decision to rebuild the Basilica of Saint Peter's in Rome. In February 1507, the bull, *Salvator Noster*, was published by Julius II authorising the award of indulgences at a minimum donation of 10 silver grossi each to aid the construction of the new church.[88] This was a major investment and purchasers could expect dramatic benefits in return: full plenary remission of all their sins absolving them of the pain they might expect to suffer in purgatory. As importantly, they could purchase absolution for all those souls who were already in purgatory. Additionally, one could purchase a confessional letter that allowed the buyer to select a confessor who could both absolve them of all their sins (even those that technically required the intervention of the highest authorities such as the pope) and commute vows such as those to undertake pilgrimage into more easily executed acts of piety. Finally, preachers were expected to argue that the purchase of such a letter enabled buyers to participate in the universal good of the entire Church.[89] If this were not enough encouragement, in issuing the indulgence for Saint Peter's the pope also gave it monopolistic privileges. When the benefits of supporting the new basilica were being pronounced in any one town, no other indulgence could be sold.

Given that this was an international exercise, the papal curia organised a very careful set of criteria for indulgence sales. In places such as Germany, the minimum tariff to purchase an indulgence was set at 10 grossi but a sliding scale was then provided as a guideline (much in the way that voluntary museum donations are set today). The confessor was expected to encourage payment according to the gravity of both the donor's sins and their status. Suggested payments were fixed at 25 gold florins for royalty, 10 gold florins for abbots, prelates, counts and barons and their wives, 6 gold florins for those with an annual income of 500 florins, 3 florins for those with an income of 200 florins down to between a single and a half a florin for salaried labourers.[90]

Both France and England refused to participate in the indulgence campaign for Saint Peter's and the pope and his advisors were keenly aware of the accusations of profiteering. In Germany, where the rights to hold the indulgence were effectively sub-contracted to Archbishop Albert of Mainz, the Petrine indulgence sales were supposed to be organised with great care in order to make a clearer differentiation between salesmanship and salvation. A set of instructions, complete with mock sermons, was provided to preachers and the task of their sale outside Rome, 'in all the lands and in all possible places', was given to the Observant Franciscans, a group long regarded as most antagonistic to monetary profit. But while the formats used by indulgence-sellers were supposed to create a clear boundary between the spiritual and the commercial, there were many overlaps. Both preacher and quack salesmen used theatrical techniques of sight and sound to draw a crowd and both offered pieces of paper with certificates and seals testifying to their efficacy.

There was a long tradition to such efforts. When, for example, the city of Berne obtained an indulgence for the completion of their cathedral of Saint Vincent, guaranteeing the same remission of sins as a Jubilee visit to Rome, they had one thousand copies of the document printed for distribution. They then hired a preacher who gave sermons on the bull's benefits twice daily; fifty confessors were employed who encouraged public as well as private penitence.[91] Two-thirds of the cash raised was to go to the rebuilding and the remainder was remitted to Rome, 'for resistance to the Turks and other unbelievers'. Alongside such careful organisation lay the ceremony and spectacle that were so key to successful sales. In Germany, the friars arrived in towns, as one commentator noted, 'bearing the bull of the indulgence on a cloth embroidered in gold and met with all the priests, monks, city counsellors, schoolmasters and students, men and women, with chants, candles, and processions'. According to the official instructions, preaching was then supposed to take place inside the main church, although it might spill out onto the square. Enough priests had to be in place in order to allow for the full confessions that enabled the indulgences' efficacy. All other masses throughout the city were to be halted, and all local indulgences were suspended. Once listeners had been made aware of its benefits, a sermon was given stressing how essential it was to make a purchase. The crowd was then encouraged to confess and make their payments in return for a certificate in which they could insert their name. The paper stated that they had been given a significant period of remission from their time in purgatory but did not record the payment that had been made. Strong visual metaphors were used to encourage participation. During the sermon those listening were encouraged to imagine that they were in the new Basilica of Saint Peter's itself. The fact that they did not actually have to go to Rome in order to benefit from the indulgence was also stressed. The official instructions to the Franciscans who were preaching told them to emphasise that:

> Buying a confessional letter is always a bargain. Imagine if you were obliged to go to Rome or to some other dangerous place, you would be obliged to put your money in the bank and pay 5, 6 or even 10% in order to find it safely in Rome . . . And here for a quarter of a florin you can receive these letters, by whose efficacy you will find secure, not money, but a divine and immortal soul in the celestial homeland.[92]

During the sermon, the friars were expected to lead a rosary chant of 'Our Father' and 'Hail Maries' for those sinners who had refused to buy indulgences, or worse, impugned the business, referring to it literally as *negotium*.[93]

Although the indulgence was only supposed to last a year, its profitability and popularity meant that it was regularly renewed. In 1515, for example, Leo X put out a new bull, *Sacrosanctis salvatoris*, that opened with the suggestion that the faithful could use this new indulgence as a literal 'stairway to heaven', *scalas ad aulae coelestis*.[94] But given the long tradition of anti-clerical polemics against avaricious friars and priests, this was an uncomfortable conjunction. Only a small part of the funds raised found its way to the construction site.[95] Preachers were accused of offering indulgences as payment for their beds and meals in taverns and indeed for the sexual services of prostitutes.[96] As suggested above, the venality of indulgence-sellers in Germany was often held responsible for provoking the backlash that led to Luther's initiation of what would become the Protestant Reformation. His sermons of 1517 prompted by the preaching of the Dominican monk Johann Tetzel who was responsible for selling indulgences to raise money for Archbishop Albert of Mainz. In the sermons delivered a year later in 1518 Luther argued that giving directly to the poor was far better than building a church, much less buying an indulgence. While this underestimates the complexity of the attack, he and his anti-papal reformers issued broadsheets and polemics that emphasised the monetary, rather than the spiritual side of the transaction. In their descriptions, the passing over of silver and gold coins in exchange for salvation was not a sideline, it was central to the purchasing of an indulgence. The print produced by Philp Melanchton, for example, deliberately compared the money-changers in the Temple whom Christ had evicted to the papal sale of indulgences. In his, and many other Protestants' view, this was literally buying one's way into heaven, rather than trusting in God's judgement (Figure 213).

But while Reformation scholars have explored the consequences of the indulgence controversy as Protestant beliefs spread north of the Alps, there has been little if any questioning as to why the same practices raised so little concern in Italy itself. Despite its centrality to Luther's attack on the established Church, the Council of Trent devoted only minimal time and attention to indulgences. There were no calls to limit or ban their use, much less to impose any major reform. When the Council published its decree on indulgences on 4 December 1563, the document merely stressed the antiquity of the practice and as in the past, warned against abuses.[97] In Italy, at least, the overlap between commercial and sacred practices would continue.

CONCLUSION

It could be that in Italy purchasing indulgences was more of an activity than a product. Italians visited churches and shrines as well as buying pieces of paper. But the answer is undoubtedly complex and may be tied up in a greater acceptance of ambiguity. As the discussion on antiquities has suggested, things could both have a price, and at the same time, be too valuable to be sold. Contracting with God, contracting with one's family, neighbours and friends produced spiritual, emotional and social obligations as well as legal and financial agreements. The one did not preclude the other.

Moreover in Italy, as elsewhere in Catholic Europe, merchants and preachers contended for the same audiences. But while they competed, they also used each other's techniques and resources. Clerics published the stories of miracles achieved through votive offerings, friars sold indulgences at a set of sliding prices while the mountebank passed out sheets with tales of cures and healing and then bargained over the eventual cost of his medications. Prelates did not deny the attraction of the mountebank's theatre; they simply argued that the remedies they proposed were more effective than a quack's elixers. The co-existence lasted well beyond the Council of Trent. Thus as late as early eighteenth-century Naples, one preacher drew his audience away from the mountebank

ANTICHRISTVS.

Hic fedet Antichriftus in teplo Dei, oftendens fe tanquã fit Deus,
Sicut Paulus p̃dixit.ij.ad Theffa.ij.Comutat & fubuertit omes diuinas
conftitutiones,queadmodũ Daniel dicit.Opprimit facram fcripturam
v̄edit difpenfatiões,indulgentias,pallia,ep̃atus,b̃ñficia,tollit thefauros
fçculi,diffoluit matrimonia,grauat fuis legibus cõfcientias,fancit iura
& rurfum eadē p̃ pecunia refcindit,refert in nũerũ diuorũ fanctos,fuu
Canonizat,b̃ndicit & maledicit in quarta gn̄atione,& p̃cipit fuã vocī
audiri tã quã vocē dei.c.fic omñs.dift.xix.Et nemini ē p̃miffũ de fedi
Apftice iudicio iudicare vel retractare,xvij.dift.iiij.c,Nemini.

CHRISTVS.

Inuenit in templo vendentes oues & boues & columbas & nũmur-
larios fedentes, Et cũ feciffet quafi flagellum de funiculis, omnes eiecit
de templo,oues quoꝗ & boues & nũmulariorum effudit ęs,& menfas
fubuertit.Et his qui columbas vendebãt,dixit.Auferte ifta hinc,& nos-
lite facere domũ patris mei,domũ negationis.Iohã.ij.Gratis accepiftis,

213   Philip Melanchton, *Antithesis figurate vitae Christi et Anthichristi*, J. Grunenberg, Wittenberg, 1521, Department of Prints and Drawings, The British Museum, London 1851-8-2-2 (23 and 24).

troupe by shouting and showing his crucifix, 'The true Pulcinella . . . the really great Pulcinella, here he is.'[98] On another occasion in the same period, Camillo de Lellis, from the Abruzzi, came into the square of his home town on a Sunday to say that he 'had resolved to come into the square to find you and be a spiritual mountebank for your salvation . . . just as the other mountebanks always sell something useless to the people at the end of their patter, so at the end of my talk I would like not to sell, but to give you a pious and blessed thing'.[99]

In making their pleas, these southern Italian preachers were appealing to the same notion of consumer knowledge that merchants prized: the skill of being able to distinguish between true and false goods and to assess price and value. Yet as has been discussed the ability to see goods as both having a carefully negotiated price and at the same time, as having characteristics of the priceless, was key to the success of both the preachers' request for offerings and the merchants' sale of specialist goods such as antiquities. The open ambiguity of what was valuable on this earth, and what had a value for all eternity, provided an opportunity for fluidity rather than a challenge to clerical authority.

As this suggests, the habits gained by buying, selling and reselling had an impact that went well beyond furnishing homes or stocking larders and wardrobes. The emphasis throughout these chapters has been on the argument that Renaissance shopping, whether undertaken as a regular outing or as a special occasion, was not a simple act. It was a key moment that brought people of different status, religion and sex together. Behind the seemingly routine activities of displaying goods for sale, selecting objects for purchase, negotiating a price and taking delivery lay a multi-layered set of deeply embedded assumptions and beliefs. The very everyday nature of the connections that were made provided an extremely powerful reinforcement to social order. Far from being a fixed event tied to a single space, 'the shop', Renaissance buying practices were a multiplicity of interconnected events and acts, dependent as much on time, trust, social relations and networks as on the seemingly impersonal issues of price, production and demand.

Notes

CHAPTER 1

1   M. Landy, *Breakdown*, London, 2001.
2   N. Kline, *No Logo: Taking Aim at the Brand Bullies*, New York, 2000. See also J. Daunton and M. Hilton, eds, *The Politics of Consumption: Material Culture and Citizenship in Europe and America*, Oxford, 2001.
3   D. Miller, *A Theory of Shopping*, Cambridge, 1998 and J. G. Carrier, *Gifts and Commodities: Exchange and Western Capitalism since 1700*, London, 1995. M. L. Roberts, 'Gender, Consumption, and Commodity Culture', *American Historical Review*, 103 (1998), 817–44, provides an essential overview.
4   M. R. Solomon, G. Bamossy and S. Askegaard, *Consumer Behaviour: A European Perspective*, Harlow, 2002; G. McCracken, *Culture and Consumption: New Approaches to the Symbolic Character of Consumer Goods and Activities*, Indianapolis, 1986. On compulsive shopping see A. L. Benson, ed., *I Shop Therefore I Am: Compulsive Buying and the Search for Self*, London, 2000, and for a broad perspective on the contemporary social psychology of material goods see H. Dittmar, *The Social Psychology of Material Possessions: To Have is to Be*, Hemel Hempstead, 1992. See also R. Bowlby, *Just Looking: Consumer Cultures in Dreiser, Gissing and Zola*, London, 1985 and 'The Ultimate Shopper', *Women: A Cultural Review*, 11 (2000), 109–17.
5   See M. de Certeau, 'Practices of Space', in Marshall Blonsky, ed. *On Signs*, Baltimore, 1985, 122–45, and *The Practice of Everyday Life*, Berkeley, 1984 (first published in French in 1974). See also S. Buck-Morss, *The Dialectics of Seeing: Walter Benjamin and the Arcades Project*, Cambridge, Mass., 1989. For the perspective of a cultural geographer see E. W. Soja, *Postmodern Geographies: The Reassertion of Space in Critical Social Theory*, London, 1989; M. Ogborn, *Spaces of Modernity: London's Geographies, 1680–1780*, New York, 1998;

and P. Osborne, 'Modernity is a Qualitative, Not a Chronological Category', *New Left Review*, 192 (1992), 65–84. A sophisticated overview of some of the strengths and weaknesses of this approach can be found in L. Nead, *Victorian Babylon: People, Streets and Images in Nineteenth-Century London*, New Haven, 2000.

6 There is a substantial literature on the development of the department store. See, for example, E. D. Rappaport, '"The Halls of Temptation": Gender, Politics and the Construction of the Department Store in Late Victorian London', *Journal of British Studies*, 35 (1996), 58–83; A. Adburgham, *Shops and Shopping, 1800–1914*, London, 1981; S. P. Benson, *Counter Cultures: Saleswomen, Managers and Customers in American Department Stores, 1890–1940*, Urbana, Ill. 1986; W. Hamish Fraser, *The Coming of the Mass Market, 1850–1914*, London, 1981; C. Gardner and J. Shepherd, *Consuming Passion: The Rise of Retail Culture*, London, 1989; W. Severini Kowinski, *The Malling of America: An Inside Look at the Great Consumer Paradise*, New York, 1985; M. B. Miller, *The Bon Marché: Bourgeois Culture and the Department Store, 1869–1920*, Princeton, 1981; L. Mui and H. Mui, *Shops and Shopkeeping in Eighteenth-Century England*, London, 1989; R. Williams, *Dream Worlds: Mass Consumption in Late Nineteenth-Century France*, Berkeley, 1982; and J. Stobart, 'Shopping Streets as Social Space: Leisure, Consumerism and Improvement in an Eighteenth-Century County Town', *Urban History*, 25 (1998), 3–21.

7 C. Sargentson, *Merchants and Luxury Markets: The Marchands Merciers of Eighteenth-Century Paris*, Los Angeles, 1996; S. Schama, *The Embarrassment of Riches: An Interpretation of Dutch Culture in the Golden Age*, New York, 1987; and E. Honig, *Painting and the Market in Early Modern Antwerp*, New Haven, 1999.

8 For a critical overview see M. Finn, 'Sex and the City: Metropolitan Modernities in English History', *Victorian Studies*, 44, (2001), 25–32. A further critique of the Eurocentric nature of many consumption studies can be found in C. Clunas, 'Modernity, Global and Local: Consumption and the Rise of the West', *American Historical Review*, 104 (1999), 1497–1511.

9 See, for example, N. McKendrick, J. Brewer and J. H. Plumb, *The Birth of a Consumer Society in Early Modern England*, Bloomington, Ind., 1982. A significant exception to this trend is C. Shammas, *The Pre-Industrial Consumer in England and America*, Oxford, 1990.

10 See the arguments and counter-arguments in J. de Vries, 'Between Purchasing Power and the World of Goods: Understanding the Household Economy in Early Modern Europe', in J. Brewer and R. Porter, eds, *Consumption and the World of Goods*, London, 1993, 85–132.

11 An exception is the excellent study by R. K. Marshall, *The Local Merchants of Prato: Small Entrepreneurs in the Late Medieval Economy*, Baltimore, 1999.

12 R. Goldthwaite, *Wealth and the Demand for Art in Italy, 1300–1600*, Baltimore, 1993. For such arguments concerning early modern England and America see Shammas, 1990; M. Spufford, *The Great Reclothing of Rural England*, London, 1984; and J. Thirsk, *Economic Policy and Projects: The Development of a Consumer Society in Early Modern England*, Oxford, 1978.

13 Goldthwaite, 1993, 31. For a useful critique see L. Martines, 'The Renaissance and the Birth of a Consumer Society', *Renaissance Quarterly*, 51 (1998), 193–203. See also the comments concerning contemporary approaches to the market in R. Friedland and A. Robertson, *Beyond the Marketplace*, New York, 1990.

14 Similar arguments concerning consumption can made for much earlier periods. There is an extensive literature on Greco-Roman markets. See, for example, J. M. Redfield, 'The Development of the Market in Archaic Greece', in B. L. Anderson and

A. J. H. Latham, eds, *The Market in History*, London, 1986, 9–28; N. Boymel Kampen, *Image and Status: Roman Working Women in Ostia*, Berlin, 1981; and *idem*, 'Social Status and Gender in Roman Art: The Case of the Saleswoman' in N. Broude and M. D. Garrard, eds, *Feminism and Art History: Questioning the Litany*, New York, 1982, 63–78. See also S. Faroqhi, *Towns and Townsmen of Ottoman Anatolia: Trade, Crafts, and Food Production in an Urban Setting, 1520–1650*, Cambridge, 1984; and the anthropological model suggested by C. Geertz, 'Suq: the Bazaar Economy in Sefrou', in *idem*, *Meaning and Order in Moroccan Society: Three Essays in Cultural Analysis*, Cambridge, 1979, 123–244.

15 *The Shorter Oxford English Dictionary*, 3rd edition, Oxford, 1973, 1979–80.

16 The work of theorists such as Karl Polanyi and George Dalton has been critical in this debate. See A. J. H. Latham, 'Markets and Development in Africa and Asia', in B. L. Anderson and A. J. H. Latham, eds, *The Market in History*, London, 1986, 201–20.

17 E. Detti, *Firenze scomparsa*, Florence, 1970. Florence was the capital of the new Italian nation from 1864 until 1870. See also F. Borsi, *La capitale a Firenze e l'opera di G. Poggi*, Florence, 1970.

18 Borsi, 1970, 82.

19 Commissione storico-archeologica comunale, *Studi storici sul centro di Firenze*, Florence, 1889, 10.

20 A. Grandi, 'Le trasformazioni di Piazza del Duomo nella storia' in A. B. Belgiojoso, A. Grandi, D. Rodella and A. Tosi, eds, *Piazza del Duomo a Milano: storia, problemi, progetti*, Milan, 1982, 55.

21 V. de Grazia, *Irresistible Empire: America's Advance Through the Twentieth Century*, Cambridge, Mass., forthcoming. See also E. Scarpellini, *Comprare all'Americana: le origini della rivoluzione commerciale in Italia, 1945–1971*, Bologna, 2001.

22 This is a point already made much earlier by R. Hodges in *Primitive and Peasant Markets*, Oxford, 1988, 155, who stresses, 'We must convey to politicians the point that like medieval markets, those in the Third World are not "congealed in aspic" forever. We need the benefit of long run, wide-angle vision – of an anthropological vision – to avert the catastrophes of our making.' See also R. A. Schneider's comparison of contemporary Los Angeles to early modern urban centres, 'The Postmodern City from an Early Modern Perspective', *American Historical Review*, 105 (2001), 1668–75.

23 D. Dewar and V. Watson, *Urban Markets: Developing Informal Retailing*, London, 1990; and A. M. Findlay, R. Paddison and J. A. Dawson, *Retailing Environments in Developing Countries*, London, 1990. For an overview of the impact of shopping centres in the USA see K. J. Jackson, 'All the World's a Mall: Reflections on the Social and Economic Consequences of the American Shopping Center', *American Historical Review*, 101 (1996), 111–21.

24 On merchants' manuals see the extensive survey in J. Hoock, P. Jeannin and W. Kaiser, eds, *Ars Mercatoria: Handbücher und Traktate für den Gebrauch des Kauffmans, 1470–1820*, 3 vols, Paderborn, 1991–2002. Abacus schools specialising in basic arithmetic and arithmetic manuals provided basic instruction in currency conversions, estimates of weight and volume and other essential techniques for commerce. See R. Goldthwaite, 'Schools and Teachers of Commercial Arithmetic in Renaissance Florence', *Journal of European Economic History*, 1 (1972), 418–33.

25 For a discussion of the range of urban and rural spaces see G. Chittolini, *La formazione dello stato regionale e le istituzioni del contado secoli XIV e XV*, Turin, 1979 and *idem*, 'Quasi-città: borghi e terre in area lombarda nel tardo medioevo', *Società e storia*, 47 (1990), 3–26.

26 F. McArdle, *Altopascio: A Sudy in Tuscan Rural Society, 1587–1784*, Cambridge, 1978.

27 G. Benadusi, *A Provincial Elite in Early*

Modern Tuscany: Family and Power in the Creation of the State, Baltimore, 1996, 18.

28 Benadusi, 1996, 26.

29 See the useful overview in C. M. Cipolla, *Before the Industrial Revolution: European Society and Economy, 1000–1700*, London, 1993.

30 J. de Vries, 'Population' in T. A. Brady Jr, H. A. Oberman and J. D. Tracy, eds, *Handbook of European History* (Grand Rapids, Mich., 1994), 1, 1–50 and J. de Vries, *European Urbanization, 1500–1800*, London, 1984.

31 A. de Maddalena, *Moneta e mercati nel '500: la rivoluzione dei prezzi*, Florence, 1973 and B. Pullan, 'Wage-Earners and the Venetian Economy, 1550–1630,' *Economic History Review*, 16 (1964), 407–26.

32 This is a point made by O. Niccoli, 'Rituals of Youth: Love, Play and Violence in Tridentine Bologna', in Konrad Eisenblicher, ed., *The Premodern Teenager: Youth in Society*, 1150–1650, Toronto, 2002, 74–94.

33 L. C. Matthew, ' "Vendecolori a Venezia": The Reconstruction of a Profession', *Burlington Magazine*, 144 (2002), 680–6.

34 Much of the literature on patents has focused on the printing trade. See, for example, C. L. C. E. Witcombe, *Copyright in the Renaissance: Prints and the 'Privilegio' in Sixteenth-Century Venice and Rome*, Leiden, 2004. For discussions on patenting inventions see L. Mola, *The Silk Industry in Renaissance Venice*, Baltimore, 2000, 186–9 and P. O. Long, 'Invention, Authorship, "Intellectual Property" and the Origin of Patents. Notes towards a Conceptual History,' *Technology and Culture*, 32 (1991), 846–84.

35 The concession given to Lanfranco is published in K. M. Stevens and P. F. Gehl, 'The Eye of Commerce: Visual Literacy Among the Makers of Books in Italy', in M. Fantoni, L. C. Matthew and S. Matthews-Grieco, eds, *The Art Market in Italy: Fifteenth to Seventeenth Centuries*, Modena, 2003, 277. For another example

of a patent see the 15-year concession granted on July 15 1588 to the 'ebreo M. Maggino di Gabriele' to make new types of medicines and to create a 'mistura' for fine crystal and 'vetri tondi' in *Regesti di bandi, editti, notificazioni e provvedimenti diversi relativi alla città di Roma ed allo stato pontificio*, Rome, 1920, 1, 92.

36 Goldthwaite 1993 and L. Jardine, *Worldly Goods: A New History of the Renaissance*, London, 1998.

37 A. Esch, 'Roman Customs Registers, 1470–1480: Items of Interest to Historians of Art and Material Culture', *Journal of the Warburg and Courtauld Institutes*, 58 (1995), 83.

38 In Bologna, customs records show that German merchants were importing from metalware, such as scissors, needles and pins, to glass and bone paternoster beads as well as spices. See Archivio di Stato, Bologna, Soprastante ai dazi: introiti per mercanzie entrate in città, b. 92, October 1443 where Zohanne d'Alegmagna, 'dedano per lo infrascripte cose extrate de le sue baule de merce conduit da Ferrara' The goods that were taxed included: 'spicchi de legno, scodarole, stagno lavorado, cofaneti de legno, bacili, candelieri, occhiali, paternostii d'osso, aghochie da sarto, forbexine de fero'. In April he was back with many of the same products but was also importing: 'tremolanti, paternostii de vedio and campanelle de ottone'. From Tuscany other merchants were importing, 'lavoro de terra de magiolica', eyeglasses and cases of 'cofanetti da sposa' and 'confanetti argentadi'. See the more detailed discussion in Chapter seven.

39 D. Balestracci, *The Renaissance in the Fields: Family Memoirs of a Fifteenth-Century Tuscan Peasant*, University Park, Pa., 1999. On artisan ownership in Venice see, I. Palumbo Fossati, 'L'interno della casa dell'artigiano e dell'artista nella Venezia del cinquecento', *Studi veneziani*, n. s. 8 (1984), 109–53; and P. Pavanini, 'Abitazioni popolari e borghesi nella

Venezia cinquecentesca', *Studi veneziani*, 5 (1981), 63–126. For the problem of economic capacity for consumption see De Vries, 1993.

40   C. Mazzi, ed., *Provvisioni suntuarie fiorentine (29 novembre 1464–29 febbraio 1471)*, Florence, 1908, 10. See also V. Pinchera, 'Vestire la vita, vestire la morte: abiti per matrimoni e funerali, XIV–XVII secolo', in C. M. Belfanti and F. Guisberti, eds, *Storia d'Italia; la moda*, 19, Turin, 2003, 232 and M. S. Mazzi and S. Raveggi, *Gli uomini e le cose nelle campagne fiorentine*, Florence, 1983. P. Malanima, *Il lusso dei contadini: consumi e industrie nelle campagne toscane del sei e settecento*, Bologna, 1990, is useful even though it covers a slightly later period.

41   See the essays by P. Allerston and A. Matchette, in M. O'Malley and E. Welch, eds, *The Material Renaissance*, Cambridge University Press, forthcoming.

CHAPTER 2

1   A. Luzio and R. Renier, 'Delle relazioni di Isabella d'Este Gonzaga con Ludovico e Beatrice d'Este', *Archivio storico lombardo*, anno 17, series 2, 7 (1890), 110–11: 'Io non potria explicare la milesima parte de le cose che fanno et de li piaceri che se pigliano la Illustrissima Duchessa de Milano et la prefata mia consorte . . . et essendo hora qui a Milano, se missseno heri che pioveva ad andare loro due cum quattro o sei donne per la terra a piede cum li panicelli, sive sugacapi, in testa per andare a comprare de le cose che sono per la città; et non essendo la consuetudine qui de andare cum li panicelli, pare che per alcune done gli volesse esser ditto villania, et per la prefata mia consorte se azuffò et cominciò a dirli villania a loro, per modo che se credeteno de venire a le mani. Ritornorono poi a casa tutte sguazate et strache, che facevano uno bello vedere. Credo che quando la signoria vostra serà de qua gli

andarano cum megliore animo perchè haverano lei apresso, quale è animosa, et se li serà alcuna che ardisca de dirli villania la Signoria Vostra le defenderà tutte et gli darà una cortellata.'

2   Luzio and Renier, 1890, 111: 'La lettera de la signoria vostra responsive a la mia circa l'andare de la Illustrissima Duchessa de Milano et de la Illustrissima consorte mia per Milano col panicello mi è stato gratissima, sentendo el bon animo suo a simile offitio et de saperse melio deportare a non lassarsi dir villania: che leggendo la lettera sua mi pareva vederla tuta animosa et sapere ben rispondere a qualuncha motto li fose facto.'

3   Ludovico had agreed to marry off his young mistress as part of the conditions of his marriage. But on 13 February 1491 she was still in the Castello Sforzesco. The Ferrarese ambassador, Giacomo Trotti, reported to Ercole d'Este that Ludovico, 'voleva andare in Rocha a fare quello facto a Cicilia e a stare cum epsa in piacere . . . ogni nocte il dorme con lei e il dì due volte la visita e la sera avanti cena. Scio che madona nostra (Beatrice) pigliaria qualche molestia . . .' Archivio di Stato, Modena, Ambasciatori, Milano, busta 6, 13 February 1491. Cecilia's son was born on 9 May 1491. A year later, Ludovico was still promising to arrange her marriage or to make her a nun, see busta 7, 14 February 1492. For further information on Cecilia see J. Shell and G. Sironi, 'Cecilia Gallerani: Leonardo's Lady with an Ermine', *Artibus et historiae*, 25 (1992), 67–84.

4   Thomas Coryate, *Coryat's Crudities* (1611), M. Schutte, ed, London, 1978, 268.

5   This is a European-wide phenomenon. For example, the 1531 rhyming description of Nuremberg described that city's marketplace in very positive terms: 'When through the Lindgasse you've been led, You'll see the market place ahead. Where wool is sold and textiles rare; velvet and silk and camel's hair. Dealers in herbs and apothecaries here have their shops; and

peas and cherries and cheese and cabbage are for sale; And pubs despense fine white wine and ale.' See A. Cowan, *Urban Europe, 1500–1700*, London, 1998, 3.

6 E. Fiumi, 'Economia e vita privata dei Fiorentini nelle rilevazioni statistiche di Giovanni Villani', in C. M. Cipolla, ed., *Storia dell'economia italiana: saggi di storia economica*, Turin, 1959, I, 325. See also D. Degrassi, *L'economia artigiana nell'Italia medievale*, Rome, 1996, 211–12.

7 M. Sanudo, *De origine, situ et magistratibus urbis Venetae ovvero la città di Venetia (1493–1530)*, ed. A. Caracciolo Aricò, Milan, 1980, 30–1; and F. Sansovino, *Venetia: città nobilissima et singolare*, Venice, 1581.

8 There is extensive literature on this fresco cycle. See, for example, E. Castelnuovo, ed., *Ambrogio Lorenzetti: il Buon Governo*, Milan, 1995; and Q. Skinner, 'Ambrogio Lorenzetti's Buon Governo Frescoes: Two Old Questions, Two New Answers', *Journal of the Warburg and Courtauld Institutes*, 62 (1999), 1–28.

9 On the text see G. Pinto, *Il libro del biadaiolo: carestie e annona a Firenze della metà del '200 al 1348*, Florence, 1978. For the illustrations see S. Partsch, *Profane Buchmalerei der bürgerlichen Gesellschaft im Spätmittelalterlichen Florenz. Der Specchio Umano des Getreidenhändlers Domenico Lenzi*, Worms, 1981.

10 For fluctuations of prices and wages see G. Vigo, 'Real Wages of the Working Class in Italy: Building Workers' Wages (Fourteenth to Eighteenth Century)', *Journal of European Economic History*, 3 (1974), 378–99. See also, D. Zanetti, *Problemi alimentari di una economia pre-industriale*, Turin, 1964.

11 M. Montanari, *La fame e l'abbondanza: storia dell'alimentazione in Europa*, Rome, 1999, 127. The theme of famine in sixteenth- and seventeenth-century Italian literature has been extensively discussed by P. Camporesi, *Il paese della fame*, Bologna, 1978; and *idem*, *Il pane selvaggio*, Bologna,

1980. For grain prices in Florence see R. Goldthwaite, 'I prezzi del grano a Firenze dal XIV al XVI secolo', in *idem*, *Banks, Palaces and Entrepreneurs in Renaissance Florence*, Aldershot, 1995, VI, 5–37.

12 G. Corazzini, ed., *Diario fiorentino di Agostino Lapini dal 252 al 1596, ora per la prima volta publicato*, Florence, 1900, 311: 'Qui in Firenze si macinorno le crusche del grano, et insieme con la stacciatura et un poca di farina, se ne faceva pane; e li fornai lo vendevano a peso soldi 2 denari 8 la libra alle povere persone, che era pane che per altri tempi si sarebbe dato ai cani, e forse non l'arebbono mangiato.'

13 Corazzini, 1900, 317.

14 The concept of a moral economy was developed in E. P. Thompson, 'The Moral Economy of the English Crowd in the Eighteenth-Century', *Past and Present*, 50 (1971), 76–131.

15 G. A. Brucker, *The Civic World of Early Renaissance Florence,* Princeton, 1977, 325–30.

16 The riot that took place during the Florentine famine of 1496 is discussed in C. Carnesecchi, 'Un tumulto di donne', *Miscellanea fiorentina di erudizione e storia*, 2 (1895), 45–7 and briefly by F. W. Kent, 'Be Rather Loved Than Feared: Class Relations in Quattrocento Florence', in W. J. Connell, ed., *Society and Individual in Renaissance Florence*, Berkeley, 2000, 25. On grain supplies more generally see S. Tognetti, 'Problemi di vettovagliamento cittadino e misure di politica annonaria a Firenze nel XV secolo', *Archivio storico italiano*, 157 (1999), 419–52; and A. Brown, 'Lorenzo and Public Opinion in Florence', in G. C. Garfagnini, ed., *Lorenzo il Magnifico e il suo mondo*, Florence, 1994, 61–85.

17 The fresco cycle which is difficult to access and reproduce is illustrated in V. Sgarbi, *Antonio da Crevalcore e la pittura ferrarese del quattrocento a Bologna*, Milan, 1985, 21.

18 This is the argument made, for example, by R. E. Spear, 'Scrambling for *scudi*: Notes on Painters' Earnings in Early

Baroque Rome', *Art Bulletin,* 85 (2003), 312. On the cost of food in Rome see J. Revel, 'A Capitol City's Privileges: Food Supplies in Early Modern Rome', in R. Foster and O. Ranum, eds, *Food and Drink in History,* Baltimore, 1979, 37–49.

19 A similar point is made by R. C. Davies, *Shipbuilders of the Venetian Arsenal: Workers and Workplace in the Preindustrial City,* Baltimore, 1991, 102.

20 See G. Brucker, 'Florentine Voices from the Catasto, 1427–1480', *I Tatti Studies,* 5 (1993), 11–32. Those who claimed exemption from the 1427 Florentine taxes, the *catasto* as miserabiles stressed that they had literally only the clothes on their back such as the fifty-five-year-old widow, Monna Santa, who noted that even these were *cativi e triste.* Others emphasised their poverty by saying that they had been forced to 'sell or pawn everything that I possessed in this world'.

21 See, for example, the private loan made in 1496 by Francesco di Angelo Gaddi of 18 gold ducats on the pledge of 'Uno nappo d'ariento dorato con historie di San Giovanni Batista il quale hebbi da Tomaso Saxetti e li passai 18 d'oro in oro e mi disse detto nappo essere di Giovanbatista Guasconi mio cognato in sul quale lo haveva sovvenuto di decti danari e quando me li pagasse li rendessi il nappo.' Cited in C. Bologna, *Inventario de' mobili di Francesco di Angelo Gaddi, 1496,* Florence, 1883, 19. For a similar situation in seventeenth-century Rome see R. Ago, 'Il linguaggio del corpo', in C. M. Belfanti and F. Guisberti, eds, *Storia d'Italia: la moda,* 19, Turin, 2003, 126–7. Credit arrangements and pawn pledges are discussed in greater detail in Chapters three and seven.

22 D. Shemek, 'Books at Banquet: Commodities, Canon and Culture in Giulio Cesare Croce's Convito Universale', *Annali d'Italianistica,* 16 (1998), 85–101.

23 P. B. Bellettini, R. Campioni and Z. Zanardi, eds, *Una città in piazza: comunicazione e vita quotidiana a Bologna tra*

cinque e seicento, Bologna, 2000, 117. On Croce see P. Camporesi, *Il palazzo e il cantimbanco Giulio Cesare Croce,* Milan, 1994. Croce's poetry was published in expensive and inexpensive versions suggesting that he was actively seeking a range of different markets for his work.

24 G. C. Croce, *Lamento de poveretti. I quali stanno à casa a piggione, & la convengono pagare. Composta per il Piascentino in Mantova per Benedetto Osanna, stampatore ducale,* 1590, ff. 1v–2:

> Mala cosa è la piggione,
> Chi impegnato il ferraiuolo, chi la cappa, e chi un lenzuolo.
> Chi l'anel della mogliera, che ha venduto la lettiera, chi il giuppone, e la calcette, con le banche, e le casette, le carieghe, e il crendenzone.
> Mala cosa è la piggione

On Croce see M. Rouch, *Storia di vita populare nelle canzoni di piazza di G. C. Croce: fame, fatica e mascherate nel '500,* Bologna, 1982. See also *idem,* 'Diffusion orale, fefuilles volantes, ecrits populaires au XVI siècle: Le cas de Giulio Cesare Croce a Bologna', in *Autres Italies: La culture intermediares en Italie: Les auteurs et leur publique,* Talence, 1994, 31–53.

25 G. C. Croce, *Chiacciaramenti sopra tutti li traffichi e negoccii che si fanno ogni giorno sù la Piazza di Bologna. Composti da Giulio Cesare Croce, Opera da ridere. In Bologna per gli Heredi del Cochi,* 1625, f. 1v:

> Il tempo stretto, e la gran carestia, le passate miserie, e gli accidenti.
> Han fatto fare un'habito a le genti, che non credo mai più si levi via,
> Qual'è, che per salvarsi dalla ria Fame, han venduto fin'ài vestimenti,
> I letti, le coperte, e i paramenti, Sedie, banzole, e ogni masseria. . . .

26 Croce, 1625, f.1v,

> Sopra ogn'arte, che fanno, e ogni mestiero

S'odono i gridi tutto il giorno intiero
E per segnal del vero,
Chi brama di volersene informare
In Piazza vada, e pongasi ascoltare,
Che sentirà gridare
O là, chi vol comprare una camisa,
Ch'é tutta ricamata à la divisa?
Al feraiol di frissa,
Ch'al tol, ò la, chi compra un calzadur,
Ch'vol un lanternin d'andar al bur?
O al bel petenadur,
Aihò quì un par de calz, e un bel
zippon,
Chi vol una padella da marun?
Per tre lir un saion . . .
La gabbia per l'usel
Chi la compra, ò la? chi tol st'candlier?

f. 4v
V'è poi chi vende polvere da denti,
Chi profumi di pasta, chi pendenti,
Chi vende varii unguenti,
E chi palle muschiate, e chi pomata
Chi moscardin, chi angèlica odorata,
Chi mostra à la brigata
Carte, e disegni, medaglie, e novelle,
Chi ha serpi in man, chi fa le bagatelle;
Chi taglia le scarselle,
Chi fa l'orbo, chi suona il chitarrino,
Chi fa saltar' il can, chi il babuino;
Chi fà da Bagolino
Chi da mastro Martin, chi da trastullo,
Chi da Zaffo in comedia, chi dà bulo,
Ogn'un si dà trastullo,
Ogn'un sguazza, ogn'un gode in questi
rivi
A la barba di quei che son corrivi.

27 On the snake handlers see K. Park, 'Country Medicine in the City Marketplace: Snake Handlers as Itinerant Healers', *Renaissance Studies*, 15 (2001), 104–20.

28 T. Garzoni, *La piazza universale di tutte le professioni del mondo*, ed. P. Cherchi and B. Collina, Turin, 1996, II, 1294: 'Fra l'altre professioni vitiose et detestabili, si pone quella ancora degli oziosi, che fanno il mestiero di Michelazzo, che consiste in mangiare, bevere, e andare a solazzo, et spendono tutto il tempo di lor vita in passegiar per piazza, e andar dall'ostaria in pescaria, et dal palazzo alla loggia, non facendo altro tutto il giorno che girar di qua e di là or a sentendo canta in banchi, or a guardando il toro che passa, e ora mirando i bicchieri, i specchi, et sonagli, che in piazza sono distesi; ora vagando per il mercato in mezo de'villani vanamente, ora posando in qualche barberia a contar frottole e fanfalucche, hora leggendo le nove di banco, che sono proprio per l'orrechie di gente ociosa, et negligente.'

29 A. W. B. Randolph, *Engaging Symbols: Gender, Politics, and Public Art in Fifteenth-Century Florence*, New Haven, 2002, 57. On the bordello see M. S. Mazzi, *Prostitute e lenoni nella Firenze del quattrocento*, Milan, 1991, 249.

30 San Bernardino da Siena, *Le prediche volgari (Florence, 1425)*, ed. C. Cannarozzi, Florence, 1934, 2, 100; 5, 38: 'Tre cose fanno crescere il fuoco della sodomia: prima le molte legne del mangiare, del pappare, del bere e inzeppare. La borsa piena, giuocare, istarne, capponi, lamprede, istorioni a taverne di corso di malvegge e ne'luoghi risposti ove si tiene publico bordello de'garzoni come di pubbliche meretrici, i letti per albergare la notte quando anno pieno il corpo di vino, la lussaria sodomita in campo. Insensati cittadini che vedete i vostri figliuoli che diventano indemoniati e non vi provvedete a fare sererare le taverne alle ventiquattro ore. Voi ispeziali sapete bene a cui le vendete i pinnocchiati, la zuccata e il marzapane e le torte inzuccherate, e sapete bene a cui le vendete e per che cagione, e non ve ne pare essere tenuti a coscienza si siete bene, perchè non ai un poco di coscienza a fare diventare giovani cattive.'

31 K. Weil-Garris and J. F. D'Amico, *The Renaissance Cardinal's Ideal Palace: A Chapter from Cortesi's* De Cardinalatu', Rome 1980, 73.

32 B. Weiss and L. C. Pérez, *Beginnings and Discoveries: Polydore Vergil's 'De inven-*

toribus rerum', Nieuwkoop, 1997, 236–42.

33 M. Lowry, *The World of Aldus Manutius: Business and Scholarship in Renaissance Venice*, Oxford, 1976, 26.

34 Mazzi, 1991, 370, n. 9. See also R. C. Trexler, *Power and Dependence in Renaissance Florence: The Women of Renaissance Florence*, 2, Binghamton, N.Y., 1993, 31–65.

35 A. Pucci, 'Proprietà di mercato vecchio', in N. Sapegno, ed., *Poeti minori del trecento*, Milan, 1952, 403–07, translation adapted from T. Dean, ed., *The Towns of Italy in the Later Middle Ages*, Manchester, 2000, 122–4. See also G. Cherubini, 'Rilegendo Antonio Pucci: il "mercato vecchio" di Firenze', in *Cultura e società nell'Italia medievale: studi per Paolo Brezzi*, Rome, 1988, 1, 197–216.

36 Cherubini, 1988, 1, 198.

37 Pucci, 1952, 406:
> Gentili uomini e donne v'ha da lato,
> che spesso veggion venire a le mani
> le trecche e'barattier ch'hanno giucato.

38 Pucci, 1952, 404:
> Sempre di più ragion vi stanno trecche:
>
> diciam di quelle con parole brutte,
> che tutto il dì per due castagne secche
> garraono insieme chiamandosi putte:
> e sempre son fornite di vantaggio,
> secondo il tempo, lor panier di frutte.
> Ed altre vendono uova con formaggio
> per far de gli erbolati e de le torte o rav-
> iuoli o altro di paragio.

39 In late sixteenth-century Bologna the government tried to make a clearer set of differentiations by insisting that *treccole* who were acting as agents for local farmers were able to appear in the market as if they were peasant women while those acting on their own behalf had to display an 'R' on either a wooden tablet or from a banner, which stood for *rivenditrice*. See D. Mancini, 'Storia di uno spazio: la vita economica e sociale di Piazza Maggiore di Bologna del secolo XVI al secolo XVIII', Tesi di Laurea, Università degli studi di Bologna. Faccoltà

di Scienze Politiche, 1983/4, 71–4. In Venice from 1546, regraters were supposed to 'wear a sign, that is for the men a "C" of red cloth and the women, likewise, have to be without an apron'. See Biblioteca Marciana, Venice, MS It VII 1572, f. 40: 'portar il segno, cioè un C di panno rosso li uomini, et le donne star debbano senza farriuolo'. For some of the difficulties of actually distinguishing prostitutes, see A. Camerano, 'Donne oneste o meretrici? Incertezza dell'identità fra testamento e diritto di proprietà a Roma', *Quaderni storici*, 99 (1998), 637–66.

40 For a comparative discussion see A. J. Adams, 'Money and the Regulation of Desire: The Prostitute and the Marketplace in Seventeenth-Century Holland', in P. Fumerton and S. Hunt, eds, *Renaissance Culture and the Everyday*, Philadelphia, 1999, 229–53.

41 Mancini 1983/4, 74–5: 'che fra dette rivenditori si trovano molte donne di tal qualità, che non conviene all'honestà che si habbino da mescolarsi fra le donne di detti hortolani, che portano detti beni a vendere in piazza, le quali donne sono maritate e d'honesta vita. Nondimeno queste persone rivenditrici di herbino e vettogaglie suddette for monetate da alcuni anni in qua da favori de nobili e alle volte ancora da famigliari pro tempore d'essi signori presidente al governo di detta città perturbando detto ordine e non volendo stare nelli suoi proprii, et debiti luoghi hanno già preoccupato e di giorno in giorno preoccupano i luoghi . . . fra quelli si mischiano in pregiuditio della republica essendo che tali revenditori over rivenditrici quelle medesime cose vendono a più caro pretio, e impediscono quelli che la venderano a miglior mercato, e spesse volte sollecitano, e insidiano all'honore e pudicitia di dette donne che sono moglie e delle famiglie di essi hortolani.' Additional confusion was caused by the fact that the *treccole* often sold goods on behalf of the *ortolani*. This was solved visually by attempting to force

them to announce their identity. They were to have a sign, 'con lettere T. overo P. overo R. in una tavoletta di legno largno non meno di quattro once attaccato ad un bastone nella quale sia chiaramente designato e formato da tutte e due le bande il detto solito e conveniento loro segno alto da terra . . . in modo che sia facilmente veduto.' See Mancini, 1983/4, 71.

42 Mancini, 1983/4, 52: 'tutti quelli i quali rivendono frutti, herbaggi, hortami, semenze di essi e altre cose da loro prima comprate per rivendere, le quali vendono gli hortolani di propri lavoreri e coltura.'

43 For the most recent discussion of this statue see Randolph, 2002, chapter one.

44 B. A. Bennet and D. G. Wilkins, *Donatello*, Oxford, 1984, 71. See also the article by D. Wilkins, 'Donatello's Lost *Dovizia* for the Mercato Vecchio: Wealth and Charity as Florentine Civic Virtues', *Art Bulletin*, 65 (1983), 401–23.

45 Much more work on these female sellers has been done for northern Europe than for Italy. See, for example, M. Wiesner Wood, 'Paltry Peddlers or Essential Merchants? Women in the Distributive Trades in Early Modern Nuremberg', *Sixteenth-Century Journal*, 12 (1981), 3–14.

46 The column was a site for a range of physical punishments. In 1477, for example, the Jew Aliuccio di Ceno di Mirandola was condemned to pay a fine of 25 florins or he would be taken to the 'colonna del mercato vecchio' for two hours 'con la lingua fuori dela bocca e con un chiodo infisso nella lingua'. See M. Ciardini, *I banchieri ebrei in Firenze nel secolo xv e il Monte di Pietà fondato da Girolamo Savonarola*, Borgo San Lorenzo, 1907, 69. The connection between corporal punishment and marketplace was quite common. The gibbet in Bologna was erected on the steps of San Petronio on Saturdays during the weekly market. See Mancini 1983/4, 107.

47 M. P. Zanoboni, 'Frutta e fruttaroli nella Milano Sforzesca', *Archivio storico lombardo*, anno 123, series 12, 4 (1997), 117–51.

48 The San Jacopo press recorded that a charlatan, a '*cerretano* who called himself "Antonio the Lombardo" left 35 soldi as payment for 500 of the Sunday epistles'. See M. A. Rouse and R. H. Rouse, *Cartolai, Illuminators and Printers in Fifteenth-Century Italy: The Evidence of the Ripoli Press*, Los Angeles, 1988, 37. There are records of at least six more *cerretani* commissioning prints from the press.

49 Archivio di Stato, Florence, Libri di commercio e di famiglia, 5127, 5128, 5130, 5132, 5133.

50 D. Gentilcore, '"Tutti i modi che adoprano i ceretani per far bezzi": Towards a Database of Italian Charlatans', *Ludica*, 5–6 (2000), 201–15.

51 See, for example, the statistics in S. Favalier, 'Le attività lavorative in una parrochia del centro di Venezia (San Polo – secolo XVI), *Studi veneziani*, n. s. 9 (1985), 187–97; and R. MacKenney, 'The Guilds of Venice: State and Society in the Longue Duree', *Studi veneziani*, n. s. 34 (1997), 15–44. For a study of salesmen and women in Brescia see G. Bonfiglio-Dosio, *Il commercio degli alimentari a Brescia nel primo quattrocento*, Brescia, 1979, 93. She calculates that of the 58 *rivenditori* in the city, 21 were female of whom only 2 were widows.

52 J. Shaw, 'Retail, Monopoly, and Privilege: The Dissolution of the Fishmonger's Guild of Venice, 1599', *Journal of Early Modern History*, 6 (2002), 407.

53 Santoro, 1929, 557: 'considerando i viziosi costumi sono indotti i fanciulli dei nobili e dei cittadini di Milano dai venditori di dolciumi, deliberano che nessuno deve fare e vendere leccabono ossia mele cotte e nussun venditore di offelle e simili dolciumi deve adescare giovanni minori di 20 anni a giuocare a vincere un premio e molto meno a giuocare con cartine, dadi e simili.' My thanks to Trevor Dean for this reference.

54 M. Margaret Newett, *Canon Pietro Casola's Pilgrimage to Jerusalem in the Year 1494*, Manchester, 1907, 144.

55 G. Lira, 'Il controllo e la repressione degli "oziosi e vagabondi": la legislazione in età spagnola', in D. Zardin, ed., *La città e i poveri. Milano e le terre lombarde dal rinascimento all'età spagnola*, Milan, 1995, 307

56 Lira, 1995, 307.

57 P. Aretino, *Tutte le commedie*, ed. G. B. de Sanctis, Milan, 1968, 69.

58 In mid-sixteenth-century legislation imposed by the Spanish governors in Milan, Gypsies were forbidden to enter the city on pain of expulsion from the state or years of galley service. See G. Lira, 'Aspetti dell'applicazione della pena di morte a Milano in epoca spagnola', *Archivio storico lombardo*, anno 115, series 11, 6 (1989), 155–6.

59 R. Caggese, ed., *Statuti della repubblica fiorentina*, Florence, 1921, 11 432: 'Quod nullus vadat [per] civitatem clamando aurum et argentum – Cum quidam iuvenes infideles vadant per civitatem clamando et petendo ad vedendum fregios et bottones et anullos aureos vel argenteos, es vel ferrum vetus aut similia, quorum occasione multa et multa furta commictuntur in emendo et vendendo predicta et etiam calices et turribulos, quandoque statutum et ordinatum est quod nulla persona audeat vel presummat ire per civitatem Florentie vel burgos aut suburgos gridando vel clamando talia venalia . . .'

60 E. Honig, *Painting and the Market in Early Modern Antwerp*, New Haven, 1999 and *idem*, 'Desire and the Domestic Economy', *Art Bulletin*, 83 (2001), 294–315.

61 On the European phenomena of such images see V. Milliot, *Les cris de Paris ou le peuple travesti: Les représentations des petits métiers parisiens (XVIe–XVIIIe siècles)*, Paris, 1995. See also D. Miller, *Street Criers and Itinerant Tradesmen in European Prints*, Stanford, Calif., 1970 and most recently, S. Shesgreen, *Images of the Outcast: The Urban Poor in the Cries of London*, Manchester, 2002.

62 G. Lambert, *Les premières gravures itali-* ennes, quattrocento–début du cinquecento: *Inventaire de la collection du département des estampes et de la photographie*, Paris, 1999, 17.

63 A. Petrucci, 'Aspetti della vecchia Roma: i venditori ambulanti in una stampa antica', *Capitolium*, 8 (1932), 436.

64 *Rabisch: il grottesco nell'arte del cinquecento: l''accademia della Val di Blenio, Lomazzo e l'ambiente milanese*, Milan, 1998.

65 C. Alberici, 'Ambrogio Brambilla', *Dizionario biografico degli italiani*, 13, Rome, 1971, 729–30. For the edition see G. P. Lomazzo, *Rabisch: Giovan Paolo Lomazzo i facchini della Val di Blenio*, ed. D. Isella, Turin, 1993.

66 *Rabisch*, 1998, 200.

67 M. Bury, *The Print in Italy, 1550–1620*, London, 2001, 153–4.

68 On costume books see J. Guerin dalle Mese, *L'occhio di Cesare Vecellio: abiti e costumi exotici nel' 500*, Alessandria, 1988 and J. A. Olian, 'Sixteenth-Century Costume Books', *Dress*, 3 (1977), 20–48. For the Carracci prints, see S. McTighe, 'Perfect Deformity, Ideal Beauty, and the "Imaginaire" of Work: The Reception of Annibale Carracci's "Arte di Bologna" in 1646', *Oxford Art Journal*, 16 (1993), 75–91.

69 R. Tessari, *Commedia dell'arte: la maschera e l'ombra*, Milan, 1984. See also K. Gill, 'Women and Performance: The Development of Improvisation by the Sixteenth-Century "Commedia dell'Arte"', *Theatre Journal*, 43 (1991), 59–69. On the image of the mountebank see M. A. Katrizky, 'Italian Comedians in Renaissance Prints', *Print Quarterly*, 4 (1987), 236–54. For a discussion of the philosophical intersections between the market and the theatre in Renaissance England see J. C. Agnew, *Worlds Apart: The Market and the Theatre in Anglo-American Thought, 1550–1750*, Cambridge, 1986.

70 M. A. Katrizky, 'Marketing Medicine: the Image of the Early Modern Mountebank', *Renaissance Studies*, 15 (2001), 121–53. For a study of mountebanks in England see R.

Porter, *Health for Sale: Quackery in England, 1550–1850*, Manchester, 1989.

71 A. Modigliani, *Mercati, botteghe e spazi di commercio a Roma tra medioevo et età moderna*, Rome, 1998, 189: 'Questo è Campo de Fiori, il centro della città. Quelli sono ciarlatani, cavadenti, ripositori d'ernia, che la danno a bere ai contadini e ai nuovi arrivati . . . Guardate la radice che ha in mano quel tale; la vende per un baiocco, ossia per quattro quattrini, e dice che toglie il mal di denti . . . E guardate quell'altro, come è tronfio; dice che ha una polvere contro i vermi, e ha una gran fretta di venderla, ma la sua polvere non vale nulla . . .'

72 L. Landucci, *Diario fiorentino, dal 1450 al 1516*, ed. I. del Badia, Florence, 1883, 299–300.

73 Gentilcore, 2000.

74 K. Richards and L. Richards, *The Commedia dell'Arte: A Documentary History*, London, 1990, 22.

75 Richards and Richards, 1990, 26–7.

76 Lira, 1995, 304–5: 'Maestri e recitatori di comedie, herborari, zaralatani, buffoni, zanni, canta in banchi et alre persone di simil professione.'

77 Landucci, 1883, 343.

78 In Florence those who 'canta in panca', performed outside the church of San Martino al Vescovo on Sundays and feast days. For a comprehensive discussion see D. Kent, 'Michele del Giogante's House of Memory', in W. F. Connell, ed., *Society and Individual in Renaissance Florence*, Berkeley, 2000, 110–36. Marin Sanudo recorded how, 'In questo zorno, in Terra nuova, dove si leze *publice*, uno fiorentino poeta venuto in questa terra a la Sensa, chiamato lo Altissimo, ma il nome proprio è [. . .] montò in cariega facendo adunar gran numero di auditori, tra li qual io Marin Sanudo vi andai con domino Gasparo di la Vedova; il qual recita versi a l'improvisa, uno sona la lira e lui li recita. Comenzò prima voler con dir in laude di questa terra: poi entrò con dir li era stà

posto una poliza su la scuola dovesse dir di anima, et cussì intrò a dir di anima, ma *judicio meo* fu cossa fata a man e composta a Fiorenza, perchè disse bene. Poi mandò una confetiera atorno zerchando danaro, e trovò certo numero, dicendo un'altra fiata, diria a l'improvisa.' See M. Sanudo, *I diarii di Marino Sanudo*, ed. R. Fulin et al., Venice, 1889, 25, col. 391. On L'Altissimo see R. Renier, ed. *Strambotti e sonetti dell'Altissimo*, Turin, 1886.

79 E. Coppi, ed., *Cronaca Fiorentina, 1537–1555*, Florence, 2000, 66–7.

80 P. Findlen, 'Inventing Nature: Commerce, Art and Science in the Early Modern Cabinet of Curiosities' in P. Smith and P. Findlen, eds, *Merchants and Marvels: Commerce, Science, and Art in Early Modern Europe*, New York, 2002, 297–323 and 304.

CHAPTER 3

1 S. Barberi, ed., *Il Castello di Issogne in Valle D'Aosta: diciotto secoli di storia e quarant'anni di storicismo*, Turin, 1999; M. Leva Pistoi, Aosta, eds, *Costumi a Issogne: aspetti del '400 quotidiano nelle lunette del castello di Issogne*, 1985; N. Gabrielli, *Rappresentazioni sacre e profane nel castello di Issogne e la pittura nella Valle d'Aosta alla fine del quattrocento*, Turin, 1959.

2 On taverns and their role in the marketplace see G. Cherubini, *Il lavoro, la taverna, la strada*, Naples, 1997.

3 For discussion of Challant's patronage in terms of manuscript illumination see A. Vallet, *Il miniatore di Giorgio di Challant: l'arte e la vita di un'artista itinerante nella regione alpina occidentale alla fine del medioevo*, Aosta, 1999.

4 T. Garzoni, *La piazza universale di tutte le professioni del mondo*, ed. P. Cherchi and B. Collina, Turin, 1996, ii, 875. See also the discussion in U. Tucci, *The Psychology of the Venetian Merchant in the Sixteenth-Century*, in J. Hale, ed., *Renaissance Venice*, London, 1974, 346–78.

5   Interestingly, late fifteenth-century Florentine men seemed to have been more interested in a total detachment from
commerce than is often assumed. Gene
Brucker has estimated that perhaps as
many as one-third of Florentine elite
familes lived exclusively off their investments, reporting in their *catasto* returns
that the head of the household claimed to
have no profession or occupation, 'non fa
nulla'. See G. Brucker, 'Florentine Voices
from the Catasto, 1427–1480', *I Tatti
Studies*, 5 (1993), 22.

6   The petitions are discussed in A. Cowan,
'Love, Honour and the Avogaria di
Comun', *Archivio veneto*, 5th series, 179
(1995), 5–19.

7   In Venice in 1414, women were banned
from serving in the city's area for bread
sales, the 'paneteria' unless they were
slaves. There was concern, however, about
slaves acting as merchants in their own
right. In 1478, for example, the Genoese
guild of the 'pollaioli e rivenditori di frutta'
petitioned to have a law reinforced
banning slaves from running stalls in their
own right. See D. Gioffrè, *Il mercato degli
schiavi a Genova nel secolo XV*, Genoa, 1971,
92.

8   G. Benadusi, *A Provincial Elite in Early
Modern Tuscany: Family and Power in the
Creation of the State*, Baltimore, 1996, 68.

9   E. Verga, 'Le leggi suntuarie e la decadenza
dell'industria in Milano, 1565–1750',
Archivio storico lombardo, anno 27, series 3,
13 (1900), 67.

10 F. Barbaro, '*On Wifely Duties*', in B. Kohl
and R. G. Witt, eds, *In This Most Earthly
Paradise: Italian Humanists on Government
and Society*, Manchester, 1978, 217.

11 A. Bacchi della Lega, ed., *Cronica di Bon-
naccorso Pitti*, Bologna, 1905, 208.

12 Among many examples see Martelli,
Ugolino di Niccolò, *Ricordanze dal 1433 al
1483*, ed. F. Pezzarossa, Rome, 1989, 89,
Martelli's mill was rented annually in
return for 20 *staia* of flour. He also lists the
agricultural products received from two

farms in 1433 on 104–5. For rents paid in
grain see, G. Corazzol, *Fitti e livelli a
grano: un aspetto del credito rurale nel
Veneto del '500*, Milan, 1979; and *idem*,
Livelli stipulati a Venezia nel 1591, Pisa,
1986.

13 For Isabella see D. Shemek 'In Continuous Expectation: Isabella d'Este's Epistolary Desire', in D. Looney and D. Shemek,
eds, *Phaethon's Children: The Este Court
and its Culture in Early Modern Italy*,
Tempe, Ariz., forthcoming. On Ippolito
d'Este see M. Hollingsworth, 'Coins,
Candlesticks and Cavalli: The Economics
of Extravagence', in M. O'Malley and E.
Welch, *The Material Renaissance*, forthcoming.

14 S. Luig, 'The Quarter of Porta Procula:
Space and Ritual in Renaissance Bologna',
Ph.D. diss., University of Sussex, 2001,
76–7.

15 The most influential discussion of early
modern credit relations remains that of C.
Muldrew, *The Economy of Obligation: The
Culture of Credit and Social Relations in
Early Modern England*, Basingstoke, 1998.
For Italy see the useful discussion by W.
Panciera, *Fiducia e affari nella società
veneziano del settecento*, Padua, 2000; and
the work by P. Allerston and A. Matchette
in O'Malley and Welch, forthcoming.

16 E. Du Meril, *Poesies populaires latines du
Moyen Age*, Paris, 1847, 142: 'Item mundi
mercatores,/ Quid sunt, heu: quam truffa
tores?/ Sive emunt, sive vendeunt,/ Semper
fallere praetendunt,/ Deum sanctosque
perjurant,/ Et mentiri parum curant,/
Pondus, numerus, mensura,/ Sivi omnis
mercatura,/ Sic per ipsos sunt infectae,/
Quod vir unus agit recte.'

17 Bernardino da Siena, *Prediche volgari sul
Campo di Siena: 1427*, ed. C. Delcorno,
Milan, 1989, II, 113: 'Niuno non può comprare o vendare, se non quello che ha la
caratere del nome de la bestia. E'l nome
de la bestia è l'Antecristo'. On San
Bernardino as a preacher see C. L. Polecritti, 'In the Shop of the Lord: Bernardino

of Siena and Popular Devotion', in P. Findlen, M. M. Fontaine and D. J. Osheim, eds, *Beyond Florence: The Contours of Medieval and Early Modern Italy*, Stanford, Calif., 2003, 147–59.

18 Bernardino da Siena, 1989, II, 1116–17: 'E colui che vende il panno, mostra la testa e falla migliore che non è il panno, e vende el panno col barragone de la testa, e non riesce il panno; e questa è falsità. Così di colui che vende il grano, e mostra il saggio e mondalo e nettalo; e non è così fatto quello che poi gli dà. Tutti questi modi e simili so falsità, e mai non t'è lecito, però che tu vidi qui el danno del prossimo . . . Così di colui che vende a misura, che tira il panno in su la canna . . . tiral bene! E l'altro che ha due canne, l'una da vendere, l'altra da comprare. Similemente dico di colui che vende el grano e l'altra biada, che ha lo staio minore da vendare, che da comprare . . . Terza circonstanzia di peccato è quella di colui che vende a misura; ché tirarà tanto il panno, che talvolta è per istracciarlo. Tiralo forte, quando tu l'hai a vendare! . . . Non ti dico nulla di coloro che tengono le mercantile all'umido, quando le vende a peso, perché pesino più.'

19 Bernardino da Siena, 1989, II, 1069–70: 'ed è vanità quando tu porti quello che non apartiene a te. El mercatante che porta la giornea, quella è offensione di Dio. Se fusse uno soldato virile, elli te la torrebbe, però che quella s'ada a lui, non a te . . . O mercatante, vuoi tu parere mercatante? Or porta l'abito per modo che si confacci a te.'

20 San Bernardino's concepts were also expressed in legal terms. There is an extensive literature summarised in C. Kovesi Killerby, *Sumptuary Law in Italy, 1200–1500*, Oxford, 2002.

21 J. Shaw, 'Retail, Monopoly, and Privilege: The Dissolution of the Fishmonger's Guild of Venice, 1599', *Journal of Early Modern History*, 6 (2002), 409, n. 35.

22 G. Marangoni, *Associazioni di mestiere nella repubblica veneta (vittuaria–farmacia–medicina)*, Venice, 1974, 21.

23 M. Tuliani, 'Il campo di Siena: un mercato cittadino in epoca comunale', *Quaderni medievali*, 46 (1998), 83.

24 D. Mancini, 'Storia di uno spazio: La vita economica e sociale di Piazza Maggiore di Bologna del secolo XVI al secolo XVIII', Tesi di Laurea, Università degli studi di Bologna. Facoltà di Scienze Politiche, anno academico 1983/4, 42.

25 A. Modigliani, *Mercati, botteghe e spazi di commercio a Roma tra medioevo et età moderna*, Rome, 1998.

26 In Florence, measures were first under the control of the Calimala guild, then in 1415 they were handed over to the Uffizio della Torre. In 1422 the responsibility passed to the Uffizio del Monte Comune and in 1496 to the Parte Guelfa. See D. Finiello Zervas, 'The Florentine Braccio da Panno', *Architectura: Zeitschrift für Geschichte der Baukunst, Journal of the History of Architecture*, 9 (1979), 6–10. For Pistoia see 'Appunti di metrologia pistoiese', *Bulletino storico pistoiese*, 3rd series, 10 (1975), 3–47.

27 C. Santoro, *I registri delle lettere ducali del periodo sforzesco*, Milan, 1961, 88–9.

28 E. Nasalli Rocca, ed., *Statuti di corporazioni artigiane piacentine*, Milan, 1955, 342–3.

29 M. Sanudo, *De origine, situ et magistratibus urbis Venetae ovvero la città di Venetia (1493–1530)*, ed. A. Caracciolo Aricò, Milan, 1980, 30–1: 'et anche di Chioza ne stanno peschatori i quali vieneno co'l suo pesse a vender quivi in Pescharia. La nome delli pessi che si piglia qui intorno, et portasi, qui di sotto sarà descripti; ancora ostreghe ne sono in grandissima quantità, et portassi quanto pesse si voglia al zorno qui per vender, come è la sera più non vi è. La cagione prociede che tutti compra, et viveno da signori; et qui in questa Terra non vi nasse alcuna cossa, *tamen* di tutto – e sia qual si voglia – se ne trova abbondantemente; et questo è per il spazamento della robba che vi è; perchè di ogni cossa, et di ogni terra, et parte del mondo che possa vegnir roba – massime da manzar –

qui vi viene, et presto si chata danari; questo è per esser tutti danarosi. Quivi par a Rialto un horto, tante herbe dalli lochi vicini portate vi viene; et tanti, et varii frutti, et bon mercado che è cossa mirabile, ma dirò come intesi da uno, che disse, 'dove è il spazamento, ivi è la robba'. È in Rialto limitadi li pretii di alcune cosse, acciò non siano ingannadi coloro che comprano. La carne di manzo si vende in Beccharia, non si puol vender più di soldi do la lira, et si fusse scarsso peso, però che vi sono deputati officiali che pesano poi comprate le carne, sarebbe li beccheri condannati dalli Signori ivi deputati. Quella di agnello soldi . . . di vedello soldi . . . la lira del oio non puol valer più de soldi 4 la lira, le candele di sedo soldi 4 la lira, el barbier per conzadura è il consueto soldi 4, il caro delle legne non puol ecceder di ogni tempo soldi 28, et sono deputati carrizadori di Commun acciò sia fatto giustitia, et il dover a cadauno; et si dice cussì in le altre cosse: 'pesa zusto, et vendi caro'. Dalle altre cose da manzar si vendeno como loro voleno, *tamen* la Giustizia Vecchia – che sono Signori deputati – hanno libertà di metter le cosse da manzar a zusto precio. Sì che questa Terra è tanto benissimo ordinata quanto terra che fusse, nè sia mai al mondo; hanno in tutto ordine, et questo è quello la si mantiene et augmenta. Quivi a Rialto sotto alcune hostarie è il loco publico della Terra dove stanno meretrice, benché in varii luoghi ancor ne sia, come è a San Marco, a San Luca, et a San Cassano in Carampane . . .'

30 R. Mueller, *Money and Banking in Medieval and Renaissance Venice. ii. The Venetian Money Market: Banks, Panics, and the Public Debt, 1200–1500*, Baltimore, 1997, 14.

31 Archivio di Stato, Bologna, Soprastante ai dazi: introiti per mercanzie entrate in città, b. 92, f. 147, 3 January 1438.

32 Archivio di Stato, Bologna, Soprastante ai dazi: introiti per mercanzie entrate in città, b. 92, f. 131, 4 January 1438. The same account is listed in Archivio di Stato, Bologna, Soprastante ai dazi: dazio delle mercanzie e sigillino, b.105, 1431, f. 197.

33 Archivio di Stato, Bologna, Soprastante ai dazi: introiti per mercanzie entrate in città, b. 92, f. 126. Many of the merchants cited were called, 'd'Alemania', although it is not clear whether they are from Germany or Bolognese citizens of German origin.

34 Goods were usually listed as coming on the canal routes from either Mantua or Ferrara. Often the recipient was recorded as a *speziale* or apothecary. But it is not always easy to tell if Bologna was merely an intermediate stage or the final destination of these items.

35 Archivio di Stato, Bologna, Soprastante ai dazi: introiti per mercanzie entrate in città, b. 92, f. 67. De Vidale obviously specialised in fancy goods. He shows up regularly as an importer, and later brought in a number of goods via Modena including metallic decorations for garments such as 'tremolante' and three 'berete da lana et una in grana' via Ferrara. In May he imported a further '18 cofaneti da spoxe arzentada tondi'.

36 Archivio di Stato, Bologna, Soprastante ai Dazi: introiti per mercanzie entrate in città, b. 92, f. 67.

37 Santoro, 1961, 106.

38 W. Kula, *Measures and Man*, Princeton, 1986, 9.

39 E. Frojmovič, 'Giotto's Allegories of Justice and the Commune in the Palazzo della Ragione in Padua: A Reconstruction', *Journal of the Warburg and Courtauld Institutes*, 59 (1996), 35.

40 On measurements see A. Martini, *Manuale di metrologia, ossia misure, pesi e monete in uso attualmente e anticamente presso tutti i popoli*, Turin, 1883. See also G. Uzielli, *Le misure lineari medioevali e l'effigie di Christo*, Florence, 1899.

41 C. Santoro, ed., *I registri dell'ufficio di provvisione e dell'ufficio dei sindaci sotto la dominazione viscontea*, Milan, 1929, 463.

42 B. Krosch, *Scales and Weights: A Historical*

43 F. Morandini, ed., *Statuti delle arti degli oliandoli e pizzicagnoli e dei beccai di Firenze (1318–1346)*, Florence, 1961, 55: 'statuimo che rettori di questa arte . . . siano tenuti sollicitamente inquirere contra ogni persona, la quale inganno, o frode commettesse in vendere, o comperare, o in mercatare le cose e de le cose e mercatantie a questa arte apertegnenti e maximamente contra coloro, i quali non palesemente ne le loro boteghe, ma in cose oculte e riposte tengono le misure e fanno varie mercatantie, overo per luoghi diversi de la città con loro non buone misure . . .'

Outline, New Haven, 1965, 140. For a discussion of the Netherlands see P. Arnade, M. Howell and W. Simons, 'Fertile Spaces: The Productivity of Urban Space in Northern Europe', *The Journal of Interdisciplinary History*, 32 (2002), 547.

44 In sixteenth-century Piacenza, for example, the Anziani made arrangement in 1557 to allow all meat to be reweighed in the prior's own office. See C. Zilocchi, *I tormenti della carne: beccai, beccarie, macelli a Piacenza*, Piacenza, 1993, 29–31. More generally see U. Tucci, 'Pesi e misure nella storia della società', *Storia d'Italia: documenti*, 5, Turin, 1973, 581–612.

45 Zervas, 1979, 6: 'E si può dire generalmente la cosa delle misure, e de' pesi incertissima; ed instabilissima, e da non potersi se non tempo per tempo, luogo per luogo, e cosa per cosa determinare; e che ridurla a un termine fisso' ed uguale, sia molto difficile, se non impossibile.' The quote continues in note 2: 'E non solamente secondo i tempi sono variate le misure mantendosi i nomi, nè pure secondo i luoghi, e paesi sono ne' medesimi tempi state diversissime; ma che può parere strano, si veggono nel medesimo tempo, e luogo varie, secondo la diversità delle materie, che si misurano, che nè ora, nè forse anche allora in tutte le cose si adoperavano le medesime.'

46 See B. di Pasi, *Tariffa de pesi e misure*, Venice, 1557. This was first published in 1503. See also J. Day, *The Medieval Market Economy*, Oxford, 1987, 4.

47 R. Goldthwaite, 'Schools and Teachers of Commercial Arithmetic in Renaissance Florence', *Journal of European Economic History*, 1 (1972), 418–33.

48 B. Davanzati, *Lezione delle monete di Bernardo Davanzati fiorentino con note scelte dell'autore e di Antonio Maria Salvini*, ed. P. Custodi, Milan, 1804, 42: 'Ne' pagamenti adunque de'lasci, livelli, censi, ritratti e d'ogni debito nato nel tempo che la moneta era buona, nascon difficultà e litigi. Il debitore di un fiorin d'oro di 7 lire dice: eccoti 7 lire. Risponde il creditore: tu me ne darai pur 10, perchè tante oggi ne vale il fiorin dell'oro che tu mi dei dare, o tu mi trov'e dà esso fiorino d'oro in oro giliato, e battuto di quel tempo. Replica il debitore: se io ti dò un fiorino di 7 lire, come la carta canta, io non fo poco; se'l principe ha le lire peggiorate, quest'è tempesta commune, e tutti siam nella stessa barca; duolti del principe.'

49 The work was accompanied by an explanatory treatise, *Breve instruttione sopra il discorso fatto dal Mag. M. Gasparo Scaruffi per regolare le cose delli danari. In Reggio per Hercolano Bartoli*, 1582.

50 Gasparo Scaruffi, *L'alitinonfo di M. Gasparo Scaruffi Regiano per fare ragione e concordanza d'oro e d'argento che servira in universale tanto per provedere a gli infiniti abusi del tosare et guastare monete, quanto per regolare ogni sorte di pagamenti, et ridure anco tutto il mondo ad una sola moneta, In Reggio per Hercolano Bartoli*, 1582, f. 1v: 'tutto dì nascono così gran disordini, nel far pagamenti, tanto in un'istessa Città, & da una Città all'altra, quanto anco da una Provincia all'altra; & ne nasceranno de'maggiori, se non vi si provede'. See also the short discussion in L. Bellocchi, *Le monete di Bologna*, Bologna, 1987, 27–8.

51 Scaruffi, 1582, f. 30v.

52 A. Stahl, *Zecca: The Mint of Venice in the Middle Ages*, Baltimore, 2000, 44.

53 G. Agazzari, *Chronica Civitatis Placentiaea*, ed. A. F. Villa, Parma, 1862, 74: 'Eodem anno 1478, prefata D. Ducissa fecit fieri

grossos a solidis 20. Super quos fecit sculpire suam imaginem naturalem quod a secundo nunquam auditum est mulierem taliter sculpiri et similiter pro ea fecit aureos a duobus ducatis cum tali imagine et cum imagine filiii sui Johannis Galeaz ducis Mediolani.'

54 Carlo M. Cipolla, *La moneta a Firenze nel cinquecento*, Bologna, 1987, 65.

55 G. Lira, 'Aspetti dell'applicazione della pena di morte a Milano in epoca spagnola', *Archivio storico lombardo*, anno 115, series 11, (1989), 165–6.

56 G. de Luca, *Commercio del denaro e crescita economica a Milano tra cinquecento e seicento*, Milan, 1996.

57 R. A. Goldthwaite and G. Mandich, *Studi sulla moneta fiorentina*, Florence, 1994, 11.

58 Shaw, 2002.

59 O. Langholm, *The Legacy of Scholasticism in Economic Thought: Antecedents of Choice and Power*, Cambridge, 1998, 26–7 and *The Merchant in the Confessional: Trade and Price in Pre-Reformation Penitential Handbooks*, Leiden, 2003.

60 M. Bury, *The Print in Italy, 1550–1620*, London, 2001, 45.

61 A. de la Mare, 'The Library of Francesco Sassetti (1421–1490)', in Cecil H. Clough, ed., *Cultural Aspects of the Renaissance. Essays in Honour of Paul Oskar Kristeller*, Manchester, 1976, 160–201. For the Medici hard stone vases see C. M. Brown, *'Per dare qualche splendore a la gloriosa città di Mantua': Documents for the Antiquarian Collection of Isabella d'Este*, Rome, 2002, 149. The agent negotiating on behalf of Francesco II Gonzaga emphasised that once he knew what the marquis was willing to pay, 'li tirarò più basso che porò'.

62 Langholm, 1998, 88.

63 San Bernardino, 1989, II, 1131: 'E io vi dicò che per niuno modo v'è lecito di vendare più a uno che a un altro la medesima cosa; tanto la debbi vendare a chi la cognosce, quanto a chi non la cognosce'.

64 D. Degrassi, *L'economia artigiana nell' Italia medievale*, Rome 1996, 207: 'Non

che debbi vendere una medesima mercatanzia più a uno che a un altro, ma mandare di pari el povero e'l ricco; ché così sono e denari de'poveri come quegli de'ricchi e potenti; ché non t'è lecito ingannare el poveretto che non s'intende della mercatanzia e che si fida di te.'

65 G. Marangoni, *Associazioni di mestiere nella repubblica veneta (vittuaria–farmacia–medicina)*, Venice, 1974, 63.

66 Santoro, 1929, 438.

67 G. Malacarne, *Sulla mensa del principe: alimentazione e banchetti alla corte dei Gonzaga*, Modena, 2000, 265: 'Ordine et capitoli sopra la fabbrica del pane et sopra il vender farina alla piazza, col compartito di esso pane, secondo il solito calmero del prezzo del formento e con un nuovo calmero della semola . . . Poi obligandosi anchora essi Condottori a tener in ogni luogo dove venderanno o faranno vendere pane, una lista del compartito del Calmero che sarà lor dato di settimana in settimana dal Massaro et Savi della città, scritta et posta per modo che, et dalli dotti et dagli idioti possa essere vista et intesa; il popolo potrà da quella lista e dal compartito del Calmero che sarà stampata in fine de i seguenti capitoli con diversi prezzi cioè da due lire fino a trent'una e soldi dicotto, vedere et conoscere facilissimamente quante oncie di pane haverà d'havere scere d'havere per ogni due soldi, e se il peso del pane sarà stato giustamente compartito sopra il prezzo del formento et sopra le spesse et guadagno limitato secondo il solito in essi capitoli, o pure se i Condottori haverranno alterata la lista predetta per fare il pane di manco peso dal dato loro come di sopra.'

68 Zilocchi, 1993, 16.

69 P. B. Belletini, R. Campioni and Z. Zanardi, eds, *Una città in piazza: comunicazione e vita quotidiana a Bologna tra cinque e seicento*, Bologna, 2000, 112: 'sopra delle banche affisse nelle tavolette, et che siano stampati'. In Siena, the city statutes of 1545 insisted that that meat and fish

prices were publicly displayed. See M. Aschieri, ed., *L'ultimo statuto della Republica di Siena (1545)*, Siena, 1993, 405–6.

70 L. Allegra, 'Avuto reguardo al maggior prezzo, che dagli ebrei si pagano li viveri: confetti e consumi alimentary nei ghetti piemontesi', *Zakhor: Rivista di storia degli ebrei d'Italia*, 4 (2000), 127–58.

71 *Regesti di bandi, editti, notificazioni e provvedimenti diversi relativi alla città di Roma ed allo stato pontificio*, Rome, 1920, I, 27.

72 *Tassa sopra i prezzi delle robbe nel passaggio di N. S. In Roma appresso gli Stampatori Camerali, 1598*, British Library, London, 1897.66.2 (17).

73 Ibid., 1598: 'Commanda S. Sig. Reverendissima à tutti i venditori delle robbe sopradete che debbano tener sempre le mostre piene e venderne ad ogni persona in qualunque quantita alli prezzi predetti et che habbiano affissa la presente tassa in luogo che possa essere letta da ognuno, sotto pena di tre tratti di corda . . .'

74 P. Venturelli, 'Vigevano e la calzatura tra il XIV e il XIX secolo', in *Dalla parte della scarpa: le calzature a Vigevano dal 1400 al 1940*, Vigevano, 1992, 26.

75 Santoro, 1929, I, 264 and 267.

76 *Statuta populi et communis florentiae publica auctoritate collecta castigata et praeposita anno salutis MCCCCXV*, Fribourg, 1778, II, 218–23.

77 C. C. Frick, *Dressing Renaissance Florence: Families, Fortunes and Fine Clothing*, Baltimore, 2002, 29.

78 E. Currie, 'The Fashions of the Florentine Court: Wearing, Making and Buying Clothing, 1560–1620', Ph.D. diss., University of Sussex, 2004, 320–5.

79 'A proposito di scioperi', *Archivio storico lombardo*, anno 28, series 3, v. 16 (1901), 453–4.

80 J. S. Grubb, *Provincial Families of the Renaissance: Private and Public Life in the Veneto*, Baltimore, 1996, 116. For comparative work on debt and credit see C. Muldrew, *The Economy of Obligation: The Culture of Credit and Social Relations in Early Modern England*, Basingstoke, 1998, and 'Credit and the Courts: Debt Litigation in a Seventeenth-Century Urban Community', *Economic History Review*, n. s. 46(1993), 23–38.

81 M. Spallanzani, 'A Note on Florentine Banking in the Renaissance: Orders of Payment and Cheques', *Journal of Economic History*, 7 (1978), 145–65.

82 E. Conti, ed., *Matteo Palmieri: ricordi fiscali (1427–1474)*, Rome, 1983, 34.

83 R. K. Marshall, *The Local Merchants of Prato: Small Entrepreneurs in the Late Medieval Economy*, Baltimore, 1999.

84 P. Pinelli, *Le attività molteplici di un caciaiolo pratese alla fine del Trecento*, Florence, 1994, chapter 3. Between 1403 and 1411, the cheesemonger Paolo di ser Ambrogio made 316 loans. Given the large number of loans and deposits, Pinelli sensibly asks whether Paolo di ser Ambrogio should really be regarded as a small-scale banker as well as a vendor of foodstuffs.

85 G. L. Masetti Zannini, *Stampatori e librai a Roma nella seconda metà del cinquecento: documenti inediti*, Rome, 1980, 16.

86 Masetti Zannini, 1980, 17.

87 Masetti Zannini, 1980, 17: 'Due bicchieri d'argento di once venti: doi rubini et un diamante fatti a sepoltura et quattro stampe di rame; un horologio d'ottone indorato et un saggio d'argento; un horologgio di vetro indorato et diverse stampe di rame picchole.'

88 P. F. Gehl, 'Day-by-Day on Credit: Binders and Booksellers in Cinquecento Florence', *La bibliofilia*, 100 (1998), 391–409. See *idem*, 'Credit Sales Strategies in the Late Cinquecento Book Trade', in *Libri, tipografi, biblioteche: ricerche storiche dedicate a Luigi Balsamo*, Florence, 1997, 193–206.

89 On Venice see D. Calabi and P. Morachiello, *Rialto: le fabbriche e il ponte, 1514–1591*, Turin, 1987, 15. For Rome see *Regesti di bandi*, Rome, 1920, I, 32.

90 *Regesti di bandi*, 1920, I, 59.

91 *Regesti di bandi*, 1920, I, 5.

92 *Regesti di bandi*, 1920, I, 7.

93 Archivio di Stato, Milan, Comuni 53, MCC-CCLXI *Lista carceratorum Malestale Mediolani.*

94 J. Delumeau, *Vie économique et sociale de Rome dans la seconde moitié du XVI siècle*, Paris, 1957–9.

95 M. Fornasari, *Il 'thesoro' della città: il Monte di Pietà e l'economia bolognese nei secoli XV e XVI*, Bologna, 1993.

96 Fornasari, 1993, 9.

97 Archivio di Stato, Venice, *Governatori delle pubbliche entrate*, 465, fascicolo 468.

98 Archivio di Stato, Venice, *Governatori delle pubbliche entrate*, 465, fascicolo 469 and 470.

99 Lira, 1989, 152–3, n. 11.

CHAPTER 4

1 When the painter Domenico Puligo complained that he hadn't been paid for two pictures that he had delivered to Jacopo *fornaciaio* in 1524 he produced his account book as evidence for the transaction. See L. A. Waldman, 'Puligo and Jacopo di Filippo *Fornaciaio:* Two Unrecorded Paintings of 1524', *Source: Notes in the History of Art*, 18 (1999), 25.

2 C. Santoro, *I registri delle lettere ducali*, Milan, 1961, 217: 'a seguito delle grandissime lamentele pervenute al Duca sugli abusi che si commettono nelle vettovaglie, provvocando carestia e aumento dei prezzi . . . proibisce a chiunque di comprare o far comprare vettovaglie se non nei luoghi e nelle ore stabilite . . .'

3 C. Foucard, 'Fonti di storia napoletana nell'archivio di stato di Modena: descrizione della città di Napoli e statistica del regno nel 1444', *Archivio storico per la provincie napoletane*, 2 (1877), 733: 'La nobiltà de merchadanti come saria a Venezia la ruga tra Rialto e Sammarco. Così a Napoli si intra per la porta delo Mercato, e intrase in la contrata di S. Allo

e de San Zuane dove sono li merzari; poy se trova la contrada deli bambaxi, dove vende coltre, telle, bambasi, poy se trova la contada de la doana e la contrada deli fiorentini; deli zenoysi, la contrada de li banchieri e argentarii; da poy la contrada deli armaroli dove stanno quilli fanno le arme e quelle vende . . . e niun altro. Item la contrada dela Scalexia dove se vende li drappe. Da poy se trova la contrada de la Sellaria dove stanno li maistri che fanno selle belle e polite . . . siche tutte le predicte contrade de mercadanti è contigua l'una a l'altra, siche pare andando per quella essere tutta una contrata.'

4 P. Venturelli, *Vestire e apparire: il sistema vestimentario femminile nella Milano spagnola (1539–1679)*, Rome, 1999, 69.

5 L. B. Alberti, *De Re Aedificatoria. On the Art of Building in Ten Books*, trans. Joseph Rykwert, Neil Leach and Robert Tavernor, Cambridge, 1988, 118.

6 Alberti, 1988, 192.

7 F. J. D. Nevola, ' "Per ornato della città": Siena's Strada Romana and Fifteenth-Century Urban Renewal', *Art Bulletin*, 82 (2000), 31. See also *idem*, ' "Lieto e triomphante per la città": Experiencing a Mid-Fifteenth-Century Imperial Triumph along Siena's Strada Romana', *Renaissance Studies*, 17 (2003) 581–606.

8 Francesco di Giorgio Martini, *Trattati di architettura, ingegneria e arte militare*, ed. C. Maltese, Milan 1967, II, 364–5 (Book III): 'L'Arte della seta in qualla strada sia locata che più fusse ai forestieri e ai cittadini usata; come principale ornamento della città; . . . gli speziali, sarti e merciai siano per le strade distribuiti per commodità dei privati . . . [fabbri, i beccai..] fuori dalle strade principali: vicini però a quelle.' I would like to thank Fabrizio Nevola for this reference.

9 *Filarete's Treatise on Architecture*, trans. and ed. R. Spencer, New Haven 1965, II, 126.

10 Ibid., 1965, II, 127–8.

11 M. Kiene, *Bartolomeo Ammannati*, Milan, 1995, 199.

12 For a discussion of the importance and methods of public announcements in sixteenth- and seventeenth-century Venice see F. de Vivo, 'Dall'imposizione del silenzio alla "guerra delle scritture": le pubblicazioni ufficiali durante l'interdetto del 1606–1607', *Studi veneziani*, n. s. XLI (2001), 179–213. For an important study of early modern sound culture see B. Smith, *The Acoustic World of Early Modern England*, Chicago, 1999.

13 Issues connecting space to mentalities and daily behaviour have been the focal point of considerable work in the social sciences and cultural geography. The classic text is H. Lefebvre, *The Production of Space*, trans. D. Nicholson-Smith, Cambridge, Mass., 1991. See most recently P. Arnade, M. Howell and W. Simons, 'Fertile Spaces: The Productivity of Urban Space in Northern Europe', *The Journal of Interdisciplinary History*, 32 (2002), 515–48. For a specific discussion of market spaces see E. Griffin, 'Sports and Celebrations in English Market Towns, 1660–1750', *Historical Research*, 75 (2002) 188–208.

14 K. Lippincott, *The Story of Time*, London, 2000. A very useful summary of the ways in which time was calculated in Italy can be found in E. S. Cohen and T. S. Cohen, *Daily Life in Renaissance Italy*, Westport, Conn., 2001, 163–76. For comparative work see G. T. Moran, 'Conceptions of Time in Early Modern France: An Approach to the History of Collective Mentalities', *Sixteenth-Century Journal*, 12 (1981), 3–19.

15 O. Niccoli, *Storie di ogni giorno in una città del seicento*, Rome, 2000, 6–15.

16 Lippincott, 2000, 51.

17 M. Quinlan-McRath, 'The Villa Farnesina, Time-Telling Conventions and Renaissance Astrological Practice', *Journal of the Warburg and Courtauld Institutes*, 58 (1995), 53–71.

18 K. Albala, *Eating Right in the Renaissance*, Berkeley, 2002.

19 J. Hoock, P. Jeannin and W. Kaiser, eds, *Ars Mercatoria: Handbücher und Traktate für den Gebrauch des Kaufmanns, 1470–1820*, Paderborn, 3 vols, c.1991–2001.

20 See the discussion regarding the shift from the Catholic to the Protestant calendar in D. Cressy, *Bonfire and Bells: National Memory and the Protestant Calendar in Elizabethan and Stuart England*, Berkeley, 1989.

21 Venice, Biblioteca Marciana, Mss It. VII 1572 (7642): Sommario: capitolare antico della Giustizia Vecchia, f. 212v: 1578.

22 P. F. Gehl, 'Day-by-Day on Credit: Binders and Booksellers in Cinquecento Florence', *La bibliofilia*, 100 (1998), 396.

23 F. Maiello, *Storia del calendario: la misurazione del tempo, 1450–1800*, Turin, 1994.

24 G. Ciapelli, *Carnevale e quaresima: comportamenti sociali e cultura a Firenze nel rinascimento*, Rome, 1997, 26.

25 G. Cherubini, 'Rilegendo Antonio Pucci: il "mercato vecchio", in *Cultura e società nell'Italia medievale: studi per Paolo Brezzi*, 2 vols, Rome, 1988, I, 205.

26 Maiello, 1994. For a discussion of the new calendar see N. Courtright, *The Papacy and the Art of Reform in Sixteenth-Century Rome: Gregory XIII's Tower of the Winds in the Vatican*, Cambridge, 2003, 33–40.

27 A. Toaff, *Love, Work and Death: Jewish Life in Medieval Umbria*, London, 1996, 99.

28 Toaff, 1996, 98.

29 Toaff, 1996, 183.

30 B. David, 'Curfew Time in the Ghetto of Venice', in E. E. Kitell and T. F. Madden, eds, *Medieval and Renaissance Venice*, Urbana, Ill. 1999, 237–75.

31 Toaff, 1996, 122, provides an example of a Jewish peddler, 'Abramo da Camerino who was licenced to wheel his handcart, selling rags and second-hand clothes through the small Sunday market of Santa Maria delle Lacrime at Trevi since 1475'. For medieval Sunday markets in England see P. Sawyer, 'Early Fairs and Markets in England and Scandanavia' in B. L. Anderson and Latham, eds, *The Market in History*, London, 1986, 65–6 and 71.

32 For reproductions of Italian wall paintings

and manuscripts of the Sunday Christ see the comparative discussion in A. Reiss, *The Sunday Christ: Sabbatarianism in English Medieval Wall Painting*, Oxford, 2000, 11. On debates over the Sabbath see S. Bacchiocchi, *From Sabbath to Sunday: A Historical Investigation of the Rise of Sunday Observance in Early Christianity*, Rome, 1977.

33 C. Santoro, *I registri delle lettere ducali*, Milan, 1961, 23.

34 Natale, 1987.

35 Ciapelli 1996, 37 and A. Modigliani, *Mercati, botteghe e spazi di commercio a Roma tra medioevo et età moderna*, Rome, 1998, 77.

36 L. Landucci, *Diario fiorentino dal 1450 al 1516*, ed. I. del Badia, Florence 1883, 342.

37 H. F. Brown, *The Venetian Printing Press: An Historical Study*, London, 1891, 39: 'Qui si notarono le feste nele quale si ten serate le botege a Rialto e preza et quelle harono signata la * se tene aperto a mezo et non si mete fora roba in la balcone.'

38 A. H. Allison, 'The bronzes of Pier Jacopo Alari-Bonacolsi, called Antico', *Jahrbuch der Kunsthistorisches Sammlungen in Wien*, 89/90 (1993–4), 280–1.

39 A. Zagli, F. Mineccia and A.Giuntini, *Maladetti beccari: storia dei macelli fiorentini dal cinquecento al duemila*, Florence, 2000, 29–30.

40 Biblioteca Marciana, Venice, MS VII 1572 (7642), f. 219–219v: 'Che li specieri di Rialto sino a San Marco venendo con la ditta via non possano in giorno di festa tener aperte le loro botteghe, eccettuato una bottega solo che vadi ver essere in ora di prendere tutto quello che avrà in mostra non compresi li specier di medecine, li quali deveno tener li balchoni aperti con tapedi, non tenendo alcuna cosa in mostra, ne vendeno cosa che non spetti a medicina ne meno in questi s'intendono compresi li specier delle contrade.'

41 Cohen and Cohen, 2001, 163–76.

42 M. Bury, *The Print in Italy, 1550–1620*, London, 2001, 177.

43 Bury 2001, 180. See also Brown, 1891.

44 B. Arditi, *Diario di Firenze e di altre parti della cristianità (1574–1579)*, ed. Roberto Cantagalli, Florence, 1970, 2: 'A dì 20 di giugno 1574, in domenica mattina, si comincio a osservare un bando, mandato inanzi otto giorni, qual conteneva che una infinita di mestieri quali si esercitavono i giorni festivi come il giorno di lavoro erano proibiti. E così non si vedevano più esercitarsi per la città in detti giorni festivi, quale sarebbe cosa lunga el narragli. E si vedeva che era cosa causata dal sinodo già fatto.'

45 *Gride ducali, provisioni, gratie et ragioni della citta di Modena et da osservarsi in essa nuovamente date in luce*, Modena, 1575, 30–1: 'Essendo pervenuto a notitia della Serenissima Barbara duchessa di Ferrara et dell'Illustrissimo et Reverendissimo Cardinale di Ferrara, la poca riverentia & honore che si fa et porta a Iddio, et alli suoi Santi nell'honorare le feste commandate in questa sua inclita città di Modena, anzi che con poco timore in tali giorni inhonestissimamente si tengono aperte le boteghe et si vende, et si compra senza alcuna differenza di un giorno ad un'altro. Per tanto, per questa lor publica grida, ordinano, vogliono, statuiscono et commandano, che per l'avenire non ardisca alcuno, ne mercante, ne artigiano di qual grado et conditione si voglia, in questa città di Modena tenere aperte le boteghe loro, fondachi, stationi et habitatione di qualunque sorte, nè in tutto, nè in parte, dove si facciano, o vendono alcune sorte nelli giorni delle domeniche, et degli Apostoli et di tutte le feste solenni, sotto pena di lire dieci marchesani per ciascheduna volta che contrafaranno . . . proibendo ancora ad ogni et qualunque persona sopranominata il lavorare in detti giorni sotto la medesima pena . . . eccetuando però dalla presente grida, che sia lecito ad ogni uno in tali giorni vendere herbe comestibile e frutti di qualunque sorte sopra le piazze e alle Hortolane alli suoi soliti luochi et simil-

mente alli Speciali di medicine tenere l'uscio et il scassetino delle lor boteghe aperto solamente. Et parimente al li Vaccari, sia lecito in tali giorni vendere pouine e butero. Et ancora alli Fornari che possano vendere pane supra le piazze et alli lor forni et poste in detti giorni, tenendo però l'uscio aperto e la scassa di sotto. Ancora alli Beccari, che in tali giorni possano vendere la mattina a buon hora et dopo il desinare fina alla prima di vespro, eccetto però, che se tali feste venissero di Sabbato, s'intendano di potere vendere tutto il giorno. Et alli Barbieri sia lecito tenere aperto il suo uscio e il scassetino delle lor botege per medicare, ventosare, salassare et non altrimenti. Et similmente, che non si possa condurre in tali giorni nella città cosa alcuna con carri, ne con carrette, senza licenza di esso giudice in caso di necessitade, sotto la medesima pena.'

46 Archivio di Stato, Venice, Governatori delle pubbliche entrate, busta 465, f. 12a, 19: 'Laudo di sentenza della giustizia vecchia contro Piero dal Gallo e altri casar-ioli di S. S . . . che hanno tenuto bottega aperta di sabato, 1542-x-31 to 1542-1-9. Die 31 Octobre 1542.

47 L. Giordano, 'Il disegno per una bottega per Piazza Piccola', *Bollettino della società pavese di storia patria*, n. s. 48 (1996), 184, n. 8: Sino di lo anno 1499 li marzari di questa cita vexati da li iudici de le stratte et victualie per tenere le loro apoteche aperte et vendere le loro merce in le feste non prohibite da la sancta matre Ecclesia ma solum prohibite et ferriate per vigore de alcuni antiqui statuti et ordini . . . li quali considerando tale prohibitione di vendere in le dete feste non comandate utsupra non cedere al comodo ne honor alcuno di essa cita ma solum ad utilitade di essi iudici quali a tuti per alcuni rispeti concedevano licentie di potere vendere et stationare in le dete feste, non obstante li statuti et ordini predetti et vollendo provedere a talli inconvenienti et extor-

sioni, essi signori deputati concessono al detto paratico de li marzari ampla licentia di potere tenere le lor apotece aperte et vendere le lor merce et tener fora de le lor apotece li deschi sive tavole, scamni et rastelli al lor exercicio necessarii in detti giorni di feste non prohibito da la sancta matre Ecclesia come di sopra senza altra licentia che si habii de havere da detti iudici . . . tamen li moderni iudici de le strate et victualie di Pavia non cessano molestarli, dandoli de le defexe, et facendo de le condemnatione indebite contra di loro.'

48 D. Davanzo Poli, *I mestieri della moda a Venezia nei sec. xiii–xviii: documenti*, Mestre, 1986, 1, 16: Calegheri non possino vender in Rialto se non il Sabato.

49 Davanzo Poli, 1986, 1, 12: 'Così ordiniamo e stabiliamo che nessun calzolaio . . . osi né presuma comperare calzature né qualunque altro lavoro pertinente quest'arte, al mercato in San Marco o a Rivoalto, nel giorno di sabato o negli altri giorni in cui si fa mercato nei luoghi pre-detti, lavorato e fatto a Venezia, per rivenderlo.'

50 Davanzo Poli, 1986, 1, 15: '1306 . . . poichè una volta nei giorni di sabato in piazza S. Marco zocolari e ciabattini vendevano stando mescolati e ciò provocava sempre rumore e questioni tra loro quando dove-vano prendersi il posto, per far cessare liti ed alterchi ed evitare quei mali che pote-vano accadere, d'ora in avanti il sabato in detta piazza tutti gli zoccolari debbano rimanere separati dagli altri artigiani verso S. Geminiano, 20 tavole più lontani da quelli in qualunque ruga; e come una volta il ga-staldo di quest'arte sorteggiava i luoghi di piazza a metà dell'anno, così d'ora in poi detti luoghi debbano essere sorteggiati una volta al mese, cioè all'inizio di ogni mese . . .'

51 Modigliani, 1998, 117.

52 Modigliani, 1998, 57.

53 D. Mancini, 'Storia di uno spazio: la vita economica e sociale di Piazza Maggiore di

Bologna del secolo XVI al secolo XVIII', Tesi di Laurea, Università degli studi di Bologna. Faccoltà di Scienze Politiche, 1983/4, 42.

54 In her analysis of sixteenth-century Bolognese court records, Mancini found that 343 judicial executions took place on Saturdays; 57 took place on Wednesdays (which was also considered a more important market day than others). See Mancini, 1983/4, 120. On justice in the marketplace see also D. Postles, 'The Marketplace as Space in Early Modern England', *Social History*, 29 (2004) 41–58.

55 Mancini, 1983/4, 120.

56 Modigliani, 1998, 38–9.

57 G. Lira, 'Aspetti dell'applicazione della pena di morte a Milano in epoca spagnola', *Archivio storico lombardo*, anno 115 series 11, 6 (1989), 164 and 167. On public punishment see also, G. Panico, *Il carnefice e la piazza: crudeltà di stato e violenza popolare a Napoli in età moderna*, Naples, 1985.

58 Modigliani, 1998, 12.

59 D. Corsi, ed., *Statuti urbanistici medievali di Lucca : gli statuti delle vie e de' pubblici di Lucca nei secoli XII–XIV: curia del fondaco: statuto del 1371*, Venice, 1960.

60 Lippincott, 2000, 129.

61 J. W. von Goethe, *Italian Journey*, Princeton, 1989, 42–5. See H. Gay, 'Clock Synchrony, Time Distribution, and Electrical Timekeeping in Britain, 1880–1925', *Past and Present*, 181 (2003), 108.

62 J. Le Goff, 'Merchant's Time and Church's Time in the Middle Ages', in *idem*, ed., *Time, Work and Culture in the Middle Ages*, London, 1980, 29–42.

63 A. Marchesan, *Treviso medievale: istituzioni, usi, costumi, aneddoti, curiosità*, ed. L. Gargan, Bologna, 1990, 1, 112.

64 On the Ave Maria bell see F. Novati, *Tre postille dantesche: Come Manfredi sè salvato. La 'squilla di lontano' è quella dell'Ave Maria. La vipera che'l melanese accampa*, Milan, 1898.

65 Cohen and Cohen, 2001, 167. In 1456 Pope Calixtus III hoped to build on this habit by introducing a midday bell, at which men and women were also supposed to again stop and recite a prayer against the Turks and in favour of a potential crusade.

66 The use of bells in the countryside in France as the primary means of communication continued until the beginning of the twentieth century. See A. Corbin, *Village Bells: Sound and Meaning in the Nineteenth-Century French Countryside*, New York, 1998.

67 G. Dohrn-van Rossum, *History of the Hour: Clocks and Modern Temporal Orders*, Chicago, 1996, 129.

68 Dohrn-van Rossum, 1996, 204.

69 Marchesan, 1990, 1, 118.

70 Marchesan, 1990, 1, 119.

71 G. C. Romby and M. Tarassi, eds, *Vivere nel contado al tempo di Lorenzo*, Florence, 1992: 'volendo ch'l decto mercato habbia buono ordine et aumentisi in utile et bene degli huomini et persone di decta potestaria, et considerato quanti statuti insino a oggi in decta pot estaria facti del mercato che el lunedi si fa in decto castello et del vendere inanzi al suono della campana et altri inanzi; et perchè ell'e cosa inhumana che uno mercato di qualla qualità non habbia modo et ordine come gli altri mercati simili, et però si provede che nessuno per lo advenire possa o debba in alcun modo nì sotto alcuno quesito colore vendere o comperare inanzi al suono della campana sotto pena che di sotto si dirà'.

72 T. Coryate, *Coryat's Crudities*, Glasgow, 1905, 314.

73 G. O. Corazzini, ed., *Diario fiorentino di Agostino Lapini dal 252 al 1596*, Florence, 1900, 273: 'E perché Fiorenza è fondata in su l'arte e traffichi mercantili, acciocché li cittadini possino andare piú speditamente a rivedere i loro maneggi, botteghe e lavori, e procurare insieme la sanità, si eccettuano parimente i giorni di lavoro, l'ore della mattina fino al mezzo della campana delli uffizii, nel qual tempo possino andare in cappa, o in ferraiuolo nero lungo che passi sotto il ginocchio. Ma dopo il sopra detto

termine di mezzo della campana delli uffizii, si continui il medesimo abito civile, per ripigliarlo dopo desinare al mezzo il suono della campana dopo mezzo giorno. E perché nelli giorni festivi non suona la campana della quale si possa pigliare il termino certo; però si debba prendere e regolare da questa ora, che sonerebbe la mattina la detta campana delli uffizii se fussine giorno di lavoro; e dopo mezzo giorno sia l'altro termine il secondo tocco di vespro.' See also L. Cantini, *Legislazione toscana*, Florence, 1800–8, v. 12, 118. On Tuscan sumptuary legislation see C. Carnesecchi, *Donne e lusso a Firenze nel secolo XVI: Cosimo I e la sua legge suntuaria del 1562*, Florence, 1902 and C. Kovesi Killerby, *Sumptuary Law in Italy, 1200–1500*, Oxford, 2002.

74 G. Cherubini, ed., *Storia di Pistoia. II. L'età del libero comune: dall'inizio del XII alla metà del XIV secolo*, Florence, 1998, 399.

75 Cherubini, 1998, II, 405.

76 D. Zocchi, 'Milano: XVI–XVII secolo: il problema dei "siti" e delle piazze', in D. Calabi, ed., *Fabbriche, piazze, mercati: la città italiana nel rinascimento*, Milan, 1996, 76–101.

77 Zocchi, 1996, 80.

78 Mancini, 1983/4, 27: 'Da vendere sopra il suolo di esse piazze o le tengono assise over pendenti ai muri, o alle colonne o a pilastri o in altro qual si voglia modo sopra o d'interno a quelle, e come fanno molte che occupano luoghi nelle medesime con banchi, o banchetti, tavole, casse o cassoni, tende, trabocche, stuore distese, botteghe di asse e altri tutti i quali con qual'altra si voglia casa e in qualunque modo vogliano occupare del spatio di esse piazze.'

79 C. Conforti, *Giorgio Vasari: architetto*, Milan, 1993, 255, n. 26: 'Nessuno ardisca giocare alla palla né a qualsivoglia altro gioco benchè minimo. Non vi si faccia il mercato, né vi si tenga alcuna cosa da mangiare per vendere ... se non in caso di pioggia. Né mai vi si possano fermare o

stare arlotti o persone scabbrose ... Et acciò che essa loggia si mantenga pulita e netta ... nessuno ardisca far caratteri, scarabozzi o altro con carbone e cose simili sui muri ...'

CHAPTER 5

1 F. Morandini, ed., *Statuti delle arti degli oliandoli e pizzicagnoli e dei beccai di Firenze (1318–1346)*, Florence, 1961, 55.

2 For bread sales see M. della Valentina, 'I mestieri, del pane a Venezia tra '600 e '700', *Atti del istituto veneto di scienza, lettere ed arti*, 150 (1991–2), 113–217; on beret-sellers see D. Davanzo Poli, *I mestieri della moda a Venezia nei sec. XIII–XVIII: documenti*, Mestre, 1986, I, 126.

3 D. Howard, *Venice and the East*, New Haven, 2000, 113, citing Marc'Antonio Sabellico, *Del sito di Venezia città (1502)*, ed. G. Meneghetti, Venice, 1957, 17.

4 L. Mola, *The Silk Industry of Renaissance Venice*, Baltimore, 2000, 97–103.

5 Mola, 2000, 102.

6 D. Chambers and B. Pullan, eds, *Venice: A Documentary History, 1450–1630*, Oxford, 1992, 281.

7 Davanzo Poli, 1986, I, 125–6: 17 febbraio 1534: nessun beretter ... ardisca metter fuora berrette per vender sopra botteghe posticie finte, overo sopra scagni, stuore o in terra nec etiam in ogni altro luogo che imaginar si possa salvo che nelle solite botteghe aperte vere e natural.

8 L. B. Alberti, *De Re Aedificatoria: On the Art of Building in Ten Books*, trans. J. Rykwert, N. Leach and R. Tavernor, Cambridge, 1988, 152.

9 For an example of investment in retailing see K. Lowe, 'A Florentine Prelate's Real Estate in Rome between 1480 and 1524: The Residential and Speculative Properties of Cardinal Francesco Soderini', *Papers of the British School of Rome*, 59 (1991), 259–82.

10 For Vicenza see S. Moretti, 'Vicenza: XV–XVII secolo: tra volontà di riscatto e

"normalizzazione" ', in D. Calabi, ed., *Fabbriche, piazze, mercati: la città italiana nel rinascimento*, Rome, 1997, 233. F. Barbieri, *La basilica palladiana*, Vicenza, 1968, 186–7, n. 4, notes that in 1485–6 shops with storage space above were constructed 'verso la piazza grande'. In 1495, a number of these were demolished and replaced.

11 D. Calabi and P. Morachiello, *Rialto: le fabbriche e il ponte, 1514–1591*, Turin, 1987.

12 For Imola see S. Zaggia, 'Imola: 1474–1499: La costruzione della piazza maggiore durante la signoria Riario', in D. Calabi, *Fabbriche, piazze, mercati: la città italiana nel rinascimento*, Rome, 1997, 389–407. For Pavia see L. Giordano, 'Il disegno di una bottega per Piazza Piccola', *Bollettino della società pavese di storia patria*, n. s., 36 (1984), 181–7. On the episcopal palace in Florence see, M. C. Miller, 'The Medici Renovation of the Florentine Arcivescovado', *I Tatti Studies: Essays in the Renaissance*, 9 (2001), 92.

13 Mola, 2000, xiv.

14 F. Trivellato, *Fondamento dei vetrai: lavoro, technologia e mercato a Venezia tra sei e settecento*, Rome, 2000.

15 F. Melis, *Aspetti della vita economica medievale: studi nell'archivio Datini di Prato*, Siena, 1962, 502–03, 618–19.

16 Chambers and Pullan, 1992, 167.

17 G. M. Thomas, *Capitolare dei visdomini del Fontego dei Todeschi in Venezia*, Berlin, 1874. The major study of Venice's *fondaci* is that of E. Concina, *Fondaci: architettura, arte e mercatura tra Levante, Venezia e Alemagna*, Venice, 1997. See also Howard, 2000, 126–31 who summarises the relevant bibliography.

18 O. R. Constable, *Housing the Stranger in the Mediterranean World: Lodging, Trade, and Travel in Late Antiquity and the Middle Ages*, Cambridge, 2003, 306–61.

19 On sumptuary laws in Venice see M. Margaret Newett, 'The Sumptuary Laws of Venice in the Fourteenth and Fifteenth Centuries', in T. F. Tout and J. Tait, eds, *Historical Essays by Members of the Owens College, Manchester, Published in Commemoration of its Jubilee*, New York, 1902, 245–78. For a recent discussion of Venetian material culture see P. Fortini Brown, 'Behind the Walls: The Material Culture of Venetian Elites', in J. Martin and D. Romano, eds, *Venice Reconsidered: The History and Civilization of an Italian City-State*, Baltimore, 2000, 295–338.

20 B. Kohl, *Padua under the Carrara, 1318–1405*, Baltimore, 1998, 141.

21 Thomas, 1874, 220.

22 Thomas, 1874, 220 and 229: 'E perchè da uno certo tempo in qua in contra la forma di ordeni nostri . . . et sta introducta una consuetudine damnosa a tutti i marzari et botigeri nostri che sostien le gravezze de la terra per la terra: che ne le sue camere del fontego se tien marzarie et vende a menudo et se fa scanzie come se fano in le botege di marzari.'

23 Biblioteca Marciana, Venice, Capitolare antico della Giustizia Vecchia, MS It VII 1572, f. 38v.

24 C. Santoro, ed., *I registri delle lettere ducali del periodo sforzesco*, Milan, 1961, 360.

25 M. L. Bianchi and M. L. Grossi, 'Botteghe, economia e spazio urbano', in F. Franceschi and G. Fossi, eds, *Arti fiorentine: la grande storia dell'artigianato*. II. *Il Quattrocento*, Florence, 1999, 34. For a comparative case of the shift from mixed commercial and domestic space to a greater separation in fifteenth-century Rome see the discussion of the decision by a member of the Cenci family to move away from the piazza Giudea where he had his business see M. Bevilaqua, *Il Monte dei Cenci: una famiglia romana e il suo insediamento urbano tra medioevo ed età barocca*, Reggio Calabria, 1998, 30.

26 For example, the partnership agreement between the two Roman print-sellers Petrus Spranghers and Pietro de Nobili nearly broke down in 1584 when the latter insisted that he wanted to sleep in their jointly owned *bottega* in the Parione district. De Nobili argued that he was con-

cerned for the security of the stock, a long list of prints that he had provided for the enterprise. See E. Lincoln, *The Invention of the Italian Renaissance Printmaker*, New Haven, 2000, 186.

27   M. L. Bianchi, 'Le botteghe fiorentine nel catasto del 1480', *Ricerche storiche*, 30 (2000), 29 and P. Battara, 'Botteghe e pigioni nella Firenze del '500', *Archivio storico italiano*, 95 (1937), 10–11.

28   Santoro, 1961, 106, Antonio da Fontana was given the right to sell, 'farina ai frumento, miglio, segale e mistura nella sua abitazione in Porta Cumano, paroccia San Carpoforo anche se gli statuti stabiliscono che i fornai debbano vendere la loro merce presso il Broletto'. Francesco Sforza made similar concessions. See ibid., 108. The revocation of these rights only took place in 1469, see ibid., 122.

29   P. N. Pagliara, 'Palazzo Branconio', in C. L. Fommel, S. Ray and M. Tafuri, eds, *Raffaello architetto*, Milan, 1984, 197–204.

30   For the engraving see R. Lanciani, *Storia degli scavi di Roma e notizie intorno le collezioni romane di antichità*, Rome, 1989–2002 (reprint), I, 129.

31   Treviso, Archivio communale, Commune 355: *Descrizione case e parrochie di Treviso, 1518–72*, 1567, f. I–IV. Quartieri della Madona, die iovis 30 Januari 1567.

32   Treviso, Archivio communale, Commune 355, f. 3.

33   M. Chojnaka, *Working Women of Early Modern Venice*, Baltimore, 2001, 16 and 'Women, Men and Residential Patterns in Early Modern Venice', *Journal of Family History*, 25 (2000), 1–25.

34   Bernardino da Siena, *Prediche volgari sul campo di Siena, 1427*, ed. C. Delcorno, Milan, 1989, II, 1070: A che si cognoscono le buttighe, eh? A le insegne . . . così si cognosce la bottiga di quello lanaiuolo al suo segno. Così il mercatante si cognosce la sua bottiga al segno [. . .]; ibid., 1091: 'A che si cognosce dove si presta a usura? Al segno de la tenduccia. A che cognosci dove si vende il vino. Pure al segno. Simile, a che si cognosce uno albergo? Pure al segno suo.

O se tu vai al taverniere per aver del vino perché tu vedi il segno tu li dici: "Dami del vino": non è così?.'

35   For a discussion of pharmacy signs see A. Astorri, 'Appunti sull'esercito dello speziale a Firenze nel Quattrocento', *Archivio storico italiano*, 147 (1989), 49–50.

36   On French and English shop signs see R. Wrigley, 'Between the Street and the Salon: Parisian Shop Signs and the Spaces of Professionalism in the Eighteenth and Early Nineteenth Centuries', *Oxford Art Journal*, 21 (1998), 43–68; A. McClellan, 'Watteau's *Enseigne de Gersaint*: Gersaint and the Marketing of Art in Eighteenth-Century Paris', *Art Bulletin*,78 (1996), 439–53; D. Garrioch, 'House Names, Shop Signs and Social Organization in Western European Cities, 1500–1900', *Urban History*, 21 (1994), 20–48; and J. Stobart, 'Shopping Streets as Social Space: Leisure, Consumerism and Improvement in an Eighteenth-Century County Town', *Urban History*, 25 (1998), 3–21.

37   K. M. Stevens and P. F. Gehl, '"The Eye of Commerce": Visual Literacy Among the Makers of Books in Italy', in M. Fantoni, L. C. Matthew and S. F. Matthews-Grieco, eds, *The Art Market in Italy: Fifteenth to Seventeenth Centuries*, Modena, 2003, 273–81.

38   G. Masi, ed., *Statutum bladi republicae florentiae (1348)*, Milan 1934: 'Quod fornacii et panacterii, tam masculi quam femine, et qui et que faciunt panem ad vendendum, seu vendunt panem venalem de grano vel blado debeant ponere et retinere ante domum in qua habitant tabulam pictam ad lilium publicam ita quod per omnes sciatur quod faciunt seu vendeunt panem venaleum.' On Pistoia see G. Cherubini, *Storia di Pistoia: L'età del libero commune: dall'inizio del XII alla metà del XIV secolo*, Florence, 1998, II, 1136.

39   Mola, 2000, 163–4, 173–6.

40   R. MacKenney, *Tradesmen and Traders: The World of the Guilds in Venice and Europe, c.1250–c.1650*, London, 1987. On printer's marks and shop signs see G.

Moro, 'Insegne librarie e marche tipografiche in un registro veneziano del' 500', *La bibliofilia*, 91 (1989), 51–80.

41 Bianchi, 2000.

42 Battara, 1937, 6.

43 Bianchi, 2000, 149.

44 A. Sapori, 'Case e bottege a Firenze nel trecento', in *idem*, *Studi di storia economica (secoli xiii–xiv–xv)* 3 vols, Florence, 1955, 1, 312.

45 E. Concina, 'Trasformazioni della struttura urbana attraverso fonti d'archivio: Analasi e restituzione grafica delle fonte locali descrittive per la città di Venezia', in E. Molteni, ed., *Estimi e catasticazioni, descrittive, cartografia storica, innovazioni catalografiche*, Treviso, 2001, 114.

46 Ferrari, D., ed., *Giulio Romano: repetorio di fonti documentarie*, Rome, 1992, 11, 971 and 1013.

47 M. Romani, *Una città in forma di palazzo: potere signorile e forma urbana nella Mantova medievale e moderna*, Mantua, 1995, 136.

48 S. Folds McCullagh and L. M. Giles, *Italian Drawings before 1600 in the Art Institute of Chicago*, Chicago 1997, 114–15.

49 D. Heikamp, 'Zur Mediceischen Glaskunst, Archivalien, Entwurfs Zeichnungen, Gläser und Scherben', *Mitteilungen des Kunsthistorisches Institutes in Florenz*, 3 (1986), 39.

50 Grossi, 2000, 7.

51 R. Mueller, *Money and Banking in Medieval and Renaissance Venice*. 11. *The Venetian Money Market: Banks, Panics, and the Public Debt, 1200–1500*, Baltimore, 1997, 74.

52 For the problem of theft in late thirteenth- and fourteenth-century Venice see S. Piasentini, *'Alla luce della luna': i furti a Venezia, 1270–1403*, Venice, 1992.

53 Archivio di Stato, Milano, Sforzesco, Communi 53, 1471: 'Infrascripti sono quilli liqualli al presente se ritrovano in le presone e forteze del magnifico d. Capitano de Iusticia de Milano . . . Petro ad Bergamo sostenuto adì xviii de febraro passato per havere con una tinnella de note tempo forato e rotto al balchono dela botega de Zoanne da Bregnano e dapoy furatoli dela decta botega tra dinari et robba per più de ccl libre . . .'

54 G. Lira, 'Aspetti dell'applicazione della pena di morte a Milano in epoca spagnola', *Archivio storico lombardo*, anno 115 series 11, 6 (1989) 166.

55 G. Sapori, ed., *Giuliano de' Ricci: cronaca (1532–1606)*, Milan, 1972, 146, 1575: 'Addì 5 d'Aprile fu rubato Luca Landucci speziale alla loggia de' Tornaquinci e vòtali la bottega di zuccheri, cere et di ciò che vi havea. Trovossi pochi giorni doppo colpevole in questo furto Niccolò di Bastiano Cavalcanti . . . et fu preso et addì x d'ottobre fu impiccato alle finestre del Bargello, et dato della fune a duoi artefici che gli aiutavano smaltire le robe.'

56 R. Cessi and A. Alberti, *Rialto: l'isola, il ponte, il mercato*, Bologna, 1934, 86–91.

57 E. Coppi, ed., *Cronaca fiorentina, 1537–1555*, Florence, 2000, 127: 'Apresso, addì 29 di febraio 15551 occorse nella nostra città di Firenze in Mercato Vecchio, non so se per trascurataggine o vero per ira del sommo et eterno Iddio, s'attaccò fuoco in cinque botteghe, quattro pizzicagnoli et uno speziale, che si chiamava lo speziale del Sole, con danno di 12 o 14 mila scudi senza i siti . . .'

58 B. Arditi, *Diario di Firenze e di altre parti della cristianità (1574–1579)*, ed. R. Cantagalli, Florence, 1970, 42: 'Levossi la voce che era mastio e andò e' rumore per tutta la città et seravasi le botteghe pensando e dubitando della furia della plebe che non facessino secondo il costume loro, l'opere senza discorso e mettessino a sacco le robe de bottegai.'

59 Carlo d'Arco, trans. and ed., *Cronoca di Mantova di Andrea Schivenoglia dal mcccxlv al mccccxxxiv. Raccolta di cronisti e documenti di storia lombarda*. 11. Milan, 1856, 178: 'Adì 23 de marzo foe fato le piu belii boteghii per Mantoa che mai foxeno fate et foe mexe fora denanze dei garzarii panni intreghii de lana cerca 5,000 ma questo foe fato per mostrare la richeza de la tera a questi todeschi.'

60 P. Ghinzoni, 'Federico III Imperatore a Venezia (7 al 19 Febbraio 1469)', *Archivio veneto*, 37 (1889), 137: 'Poj andò per Marzaria. El duse vene insino a cavo della Piaza, poi tornò perchè non po più . . . Avevano facto fornire tute le botige, banchi et fano tuto el suo perforzo per farli intendere a luj et chi e con lui et a chi vede che sonno riche, potente et che sono gran segnore, et qui non lassano mancare niente per farli intendere questo. Domane li mostrarano l'arsena.'

61 M. S. Tacconi, 'Appropriating the Instruments of Worship: The 1512 Medici Restoration and the Florentine Cathedral Choirbooks', *Renaissance Quarterly*, 56 (2003), 7. On the festival as a whole see G. Mancini, 'Il bel San Giovanni', *Rivista d'arte*, 6 (1909), 185–227.

62 Landucci, 1883, 302: 'E a dì 19 giugno 1510, e festaiuoli di San Giovanni mandorono un bando che non fussi niuno artefice ch'aprissi botteghe da dì 20 detto insino fatto San Giovanni, a pena di lire 25, senza loro segno; e chi aveva el segno costava a chi due grossi e chi tre e chi quattro. E feciono grande avenìe a'poveri, perochè'l bando disse non s'intendeva per'lanaiuoli, nè setaiuoli, nè banchi; che fu tenuta una ingiusta e infamatoria cosa e vile a far fare la festa di San Giovanni agli artefici.'

63 Franceschi, 1999, 167: 'Erano pertanto le botteghe di detti setaioli tutte aperte e dentro di quelle, dallo sportello, era fatto un palco pendente e largho quanto tutta la larghezza della bottegha il quale dolcemente saliva sino presso al palco di ciaschuna bottegha, e sopra a detto palco che pendeva erano accomodati i ricchi drappi, alcuni di quelli a falde, alcuni altri distesi, altri avvolti a' subbi e parte appiccati alle mura delle botteghe, i quali facevano un ricco paramento. E in su lo sportello di fuori stavano due fattorini con reste di penne di pavone in mano o ventiere di drappo con aste lunghe e cacciavano continuamente le mosche, ma dalla polvere non si potevano difendere. Intorno a' detti sportelli stavano i maestri a sedere sopra seggiole di cuoio e di drappo con molto fasto, mostrando a' loro amici la bellezza de' loro drappi. Quanto alla loro ricchezza e varietà si vedeva tal opera e tal lavoro che in Firenze non vi se né vede mai, né per le chiese, ne alle spose, né per uso alcuno, perché simili drappi si spacciavano tutti fuori . . .'

64 See G. O. Corazzini, ed., *Diario fiorentino di Agostino Lapini dal 252 al 1596 ora per la prima volta pubblicato*, Florence, 1900, 270, where the description in the diary of makes it clear that many of the fabrics on display in 1588 were the personal property of Duke Ferdinando dei' Medici.

65 Oral communication from Elizabeth Cohen.

66 P. Pinelli, *Le attività molteplici di un caciaiolo pratese alla fine del Trecento*, Florence, 1996, 15–28.

67 L. Matthew, ' "Vendecolori a Venezia": The Reconstruction of a Profession', *Burlington Magazine*, 144 (2002), 680–6.

68 E. Carrara and S. Gregory, 'Borghini's Print Purchases from Giunti', *Print Quarterly*, 17 (2000), 4.

69 A. Petrucci, ed., *Il libro di ricordanze dei Corsini (1362–1457)*, Rome, 1965, 37: 'E chosone per uno desco da scrivere e una chassa da tenere danari, la quale è nella bottega magiore di via Magio, soldi xv di piccioli e per una mostra di panni e uno desco da scrivere con l'asito di dietro, la quale è nela bothega minore di via Magio, fiorini tre d'oro, le dete cose conperamo da Antonio di Nicolò di Cione.

70 C. Bec, 'Une librairie florentine de la fin du xve siècle', *Bibliothèque d'humanisme et renaissance*, 31 (1969), 321–32. The inventory of Zanobi di Mariano had 80 manuscripts and 141 printed books including 30 unbound copies of Josephus, *De bello iudaico*.

71 Landucci, 1883, 3–4: 'E a dì 4 di settembre 1462, mi parti da Francesco di Francesco speziale al Sole che mi dette il sezzo anno, di salario, fiorini 50, e feci conpagnia con

Ispinello di Lorenzo, e la speranza del maggiore bene mi fece perdere el ben certo. E aprimo lo speziale del Re in Mercato vecchio, ch'era prima un rigattiere, ch'erano tetti bassi; e alzamo la casa e spendemo un tesoro, benchè fussi contro a mia voglia lo spendere tanto, fecemo ogni cosa sanza masserizia: uno armario che costò 50 fiorini d'oro.'

72 This will be discussed in more detail in J. Shaw and E. Welch's forthcoming book on the Speziale al Giglio.

73 Archivio di Stato, Venice, Giudici di Petizioni, Inventari, 1592: 'adì 14 marzo in Venetia: Inventario delle robbe consegnate per me Fabricio Foresto che erano nella botega delle 2 torre a me Mario Vitalle medicinalle come ut simili et robbe vive'.

74 P. Findlen, *Possessing Nature: Museums, Collecting, and Scientific Culture in Early Modern Italy*, Berkeley, 1994, 273–7. The museum was part of a debate between the different makers of theriac within Verona itself. Calzolari had prided himself on his re-creation of the original galenic version of the compound, having published 'A letter on certain Lies and Calumnies Made Against his Theriac' in response to an attack by an apprentice at the *Spetieria dall'Angelo* in Verona, Ercolano Scalcina. The latter was accused of being someone who made, 'recipes for smelly fats, pomades . . . fragile balsams and quintessences that deafen the piazzas daily in the mouths of charlatans'.

75 Findlen, 1994, 66.

76 Findlen, 1994, 37.

77 Archivio di Stato, Siena, Notarile 1898: Apoteca Giovanni Francesci aurificis, 1528, 26 March. I am very grateful to Philippa Jackson who provided me with a copy of this inventory.

78 L. Frati, *La vita privata di Bologna dal secolo XIII al XVII*, Bologna, 1900, 242–7.

79 P. Allerston, 'The Market in Second-Hand Clothes and Furnishings in Venice, c.1500–c.1650', Ph.D. diss., European University Institute, Florence, 1996, 26.

80 Archivio della Veneranda Fabbrica del Duomo di Milano, Milan, Heredità 97, n. 21: Ambrogio Porro.

81 P. Molmenti, *La storia di Venezia nella vita privata dale origini all caduta della republica*, Bergamo, 1905, II, 623–3.

82 T. Coryate, *Coryat's Crudities*, Glasgow, 1905, 393.

83 E. Welch, *Art and Authority in Renaissance Milan*, New Haven, 1995, 243.

84 Molmenti, 1905, II, 156: 'Noto. Vidi questa matina in ruga de zoielieri in man di sier Francesco Zen di sier Piero, baylo a constantinopoli uno anello d'oro, sopra il qual è uno horologio bellissimo, qual lavora, dimostra le ore et sona, et quello vol mandar a vender a Constantinopoli . . .' It is worth noting that the sons of Petro Zen had formed a company to invest in goldsmiths' work to sell to the sultan Suliman II.

85 G. L. Masetti Zannini, *Stampatori e librai a Roma nella seconda metà del cinquecento: documenti inediti*, Rome, 1980, 290–1.

86 Lanciani, 1990, III, 278.

87 F. Franceschi, 'La bottega come spazio di sociabilità', in F. Franceschi and G. Fossi, eds, *Arti fiorentine: la grande storia dell'artigianato. II. Il Quattrocento*, Florence, 1999, 77–8 and Santoro, 1961, 169–70.

88 Archivio di Stato, Florence, Libri di commercio e di famiglia, 4180: *Questo giornale è di Puccio di Rinaldo di Bernardo Pucci*, 1533, f. 2.

89 P. Cesare Ioly Zorattini, ed., *Processi del S. Ufficio di Venezia contro ebrei e giudaizzanti (1561–1570)*, Florence, 1982, 49.

90 Ioly Zorattini, 1982, 62.

91 Personal communication from Dr Filippo di Vivo. On apothecary shops as sites for sedition, see R. Palmer, 'Pharmacy in the Republic of Venice in the Sixteenth-Century', in A. Wear, R. K. French and I. M. Lonie, eds, *The Medical Renaissance of the Sixteenth Century*, Cambridge, 1985, 100–31.

CHAPTER 6

1 M. Sanudo, *De origine, situ et magistratibus urbis Venetae ovvero la città di Venetia (1493–1530)*, ed. A. Caracciolo Aricò, Milan, 1980, 27: San Pollo è'l quinto sestier, chiamato a *nomine ecclesiae*, però che ivi è una chiesa di 'San Pollo con un campo molto grande e largo e bellissimo, dove di Mercore da mattina ivi si faun mercado di ogni cossa che si vuol, il qual per esser cussì spesso, da nostri non si stima. *Tamen* in ogni città, et castello, altro sarebbe, s'il vi fusse pur una volta all'anno, bellissima et ricca fiera; ancor di Sabbato si fa mercado, sopra la piazza di San Marco che è molto più bello di questo.'

2 G. Luzzatto, *Studi di storia economica veneziana*, Padua, 1954, 201–10.

3 A. Toaff, *Love, Work and Death: Jewish Life in Medieval Umbria*, London, 1996, 203.

4 C. L. Polecritti, 'In the Shop of the Lord. Bernardino of Siena and Popular Devotion', in P. Findlen, M. M. Fontaine and D. J. Osheim (eds), *Beyond Florence: The Contours of Medieval and Early Modern Italy*, Stanford, Calif., 2003, 159.

5 P. Elmer, N. Webb and R. Wood, *The Renaissance in Europe: An Anthology*, New Haven and London, 2000, 185.

6 Cited in A. Nuovo, *Il commercio librario a Ferrara tra XV e XVI secolo: la bottega di Domenico Sivieri*, Florence, 1998, 91.

7 See the helpful discussion in S. R. Epstein, 'Regional Fairs, Institutional Innovation, and Economic Growth in Late Medieval Europe', *Economic History Review*, 47 (1994), 459–82.

8 P. D. Curtin, *Cross-Cultural Trade in World History*, Cambridge, 1984.

9 F. Edler de Roover, 'Andrea Bianchi, Florentine Silk Manufacturer and Merchant in the Fifteenth Century', *Studies in Medieval and Renaissance History*, 3 (1966), 233.

10 L. Zdekauer, 'Per una storia delle fiere di Recanati (1384–1473)', *Atti e memorie della reale deputazione di storia patria per le provincie delle marche*, series 3, 2 (1918), 245–65.

11 L. Lotto, *Libro di spese diverse (1538–1556)*, ed. P. Zampetti, Venice, 1969, 40–1. On Lotto see M. Firpo, *Artisti, gioiellieri, eretici: il mondo di Lorenzo Lotto tra riforma e controriforma*, Rome, 2001.

12 Epstein, 1994, 459–82.

13 G. Cherubini, 'Foires et marchés dans les campagnes italiennes au Moyen Age,' in C. Desplat, ed., *Foires et marché dans les campagnes de l'Europe médiévale et moderne*, Toulouse, 1996, 71–84.

14 R. Marcucci, 'La fiera di Senigallia', *Atti e memorie della reale deputazione di storia patria per le provincie delle marche*, n. s., 8, 1912, 266: 'Item quod, secundum consuetudinem dicte civitatis, a die sancti Francisci per totum mensem octobrem quotannis in civitate senogalliensi possint celebrari nundine salve et secure, ad quas omne genus mercium portari et exinde extrahi possit, sine aliqua solutione alicuius gabelle, et quilibet homo venire et stare libere et secure a debito et quocumque maleficio possit, exceptis homicidis et sanctissimi domini nostri et sancte romane ecclesie aut ipsius communitatis rebellibus.'

15 Marcucci, 1912, 247–526.

16 A. Grohmann, *Le fiere del regno di Napoli in età aragonese*, Naples, 1969, 83.

17 G. Mira, *Le fiere lombarde nei secoli XIV–SVI: prime indagini*, Como, 1955, 118.

18 Mira 1955, 152, n. 36.

19 Grohmann, 1969, 186.

20 M.A. Grignani, ed., *Mantova 1430: pareri a Gian Francesco Gonzaga per il governo*, Manuta, 1990, 131.

21 Grohmann, 1969, 64.

22 Grohmann, 1969, 62–3, n. 45.

23 Grohmann, 1969, 85–6: 'Facendosi nello Stato ecclesiastico molte fiere, come sono nella città di Foligno, che si esercita nel mese di aprile e è discosto dall'Aquila 60 miglia circa, la feria di Farfa, lontano dall'Aquila miglia 50 e si esercitano nel mese di settembre; quella di Recanati, nel mese di novembre, discosto dall'Aquila milia cento et quella di Terni, discosto dall'Aquila cinquanta milia e si esercita di

genaro, potriano tutti li mercanti che concorrono con le loro mercantie per comprare et vendere in dette ferie venire con molto loro comodità alle ferie dell'Aquila di maggio e d'agosto et dall'Aquila andarsene poi a Lanciano.'

24 Grohmann, 1969, 86: 'il moltiplicarsi delle ferie è danno alli mercanti et destructione delle ferie prima et che quanto manco sono le ferie et più distanti tra di loro tanto maggiori li trafichi et guadagni. Perché le ferie di Foligno et di Farfa fanno grandissimo danno alle ferie di Lanciano, ancorché si faccino in diversi tempi et che siano molto lontano tra di loro ... per la lunghezza che si è causata in tutte le ferie, molte volte una guasta l'altra come la feria di Lanciano guasta quella di Salerno ...'.

25 Mira, 1955, 98.

26 Grohmann, 1969, 214.

27 Grohmann, 1969, 91.

28 A. Sapori, 'Una fiera in Italia alla fine del quattrocento', in *idem, Studi di storia economica (secoli XIII–XIV–XV)*, I, Florence, 1955, 445.

29 Sapori, 1955, 457.

30 Sapori, 1955, 461.

31 C. Marciani, 'Il commercio dei cristalli alle fiere di Lanciano nel secolo XVI', *Archivio storico per le provincie napoletane*, n. s. 39 (1960), 320.

32 Marciani, 1960, 320–1.

33 A. I. Pini, 'La fiera d'agosto a Cesena dalla sua istituzione alla definitiva relogamentazione (1380–1509)', *Nuova rivista storica*, 68 (1984), 175:

El giorno poi del la Santa Assumptione che vien d'agosto, se fa una gran fiera quindese dì con gran consolatione. Sempre mercanti vien d'ogni riviera dinar assai si vede, e assai persone grechi, turchi e christian d'ogni maniera.

34 Marcucci, 1912.

35 Sapori, 1955, 448.

36 Mira, 1955, 103 and erratum at the end of the volume.

37 Grohmann, 1969, 130.

38 Grohmann, 1969, 130.

39 *I cinque libri degl'avvertimenti, ordini, gride, et editti fatti, et osservati in Milano ne' tempi sospettosi della peste negli anni MDLXXVI et LXXVII*, Venice, 1579, 47: 'considerando ... il pericolo grande, che s'incorre a permettere il fare mercati, ove concorrono gran numeri di gente, che facilmente potriano causare gran danno al publico, stando i sospetti della peste in diverse parti circonstanti'.

40 C. Marciani, 'Il commercio librario alle fiere di Lanciano nel' 500', *Rivista storica italiana*, 70 (1958), 421: 'Vi prego di dare ogni favore al Signor Vicario che resta in luogo mio, occorrendo in caso, acciò provveda opportunamente che la purità della città vostra non venga ad infettarsi. Nè dico questo perchè io tema d'alcuno della città, ma perchè so che nelle fiere concorre gran moltitudine tra la quale potrebbe il demonio avere alcuno dei suoi ministri. Darò ancora ordine all'istesso Vicario che riveda i libri che si portano alle fiere, e che si pigli tutti i proibiti, acciò non si vendano, nè si spargano per il Regno.'

41 G.C. Romby and M. Tarassi, eds, *Vivere nel contado al tempo di Lorenzo*, Florence, 1992, 64: 'Come et quando si dè fare la fiera al Borgo a San Lorenzo: La fiera dal Borgo continuamente si faccia il dì di San Johanni dicollato ch'è sempre a dì XXVIIII d'agosto, la qual per lo podestà o notaio della decta lega e'l gonfaloniere insieme co'consoli del comune dal Borgo sien tenuti e debbano farla bandire del decto mese xv dì inanzi alla decta festa e fiera, per tutti i mercati del Mugello e a Prato et a Empoli, a Feghine et a Firenzuola et a Marradi et a Palazuolo, sotto vincolo di loro giuramento come ella debba bastare el dì della decta festa e uno dì inanzi et un dì indietro. Et la decta festa si de' guardare a le spese del comune dal Borgo et niuno che venga alla decta festa possa esser offeso anzi sia difeso da la decta lega a le spese della decta lega. Et che niuno debitore d'altrui, salvo che del comune di Firenze,

possa esser costretto o gravato, in persona, o, avere, durante la fiera predecta co'decti dì. Et che niuno artefice della lega dal Borgo il dì della festa della decta fiera possa né debba andare ad alcuno altro mercato o fiera, a la pena di soldi C a chiunche v'andasse. Et che ogni artefice usato ad andare a' mercati la mattina a buon'ora, cioè a la campana del di, cioè la mattina della decta festa, a la pena di soldi XL, colla sua mercatantia debba andare in sul mercato del Borgo.'

42 Grohmann, 1969, 249.

43 Grohmann, 1969, 147–8, n. 54.

44 Grohmann, 1969, 243.

45 C. Cutini, 'La disciplina giuridica della fiera di Ognisanti', in *La fiera dei morti di Perugia*, Perugia, 1980, 39.

46 Marcucci, 1912, 270.

47 Grohmann, 1969, 132.

48 Grohmann, 1969, 240.

49 Grohmann, 1969, 214.

50 Marcucci, 1912, 275.

51 E. Castelli, *Storia dell'antichissima fiera delle grazie dal 1425 ad oggi*, Mantua, 1979, 29.

52 Grohmann, 1969, 237.

53 Grohmann, 1969, 238:

> Per logie fabricate quaranta una locate per ducati uno la logia a li mercanti, secundo è solito. duc. 41.0.0
>
> Per logie trenta una coperte da tende locate ad carlini cinque l'una a li mercanti, secundo è solito . . . duc. 15.2.10
>
> Per logie septe coperte de frasche più pizule de le sopra dicte locate sey ad tarì uno et mezo l'una et una per tarì uno a li merzari foro in la fiera duc. 2.0.0
>
> Per taverne quaranta facte in dicta fiera, locate ad tarì uno l'una secundo è solito . . . duc. 8.0.0

54 L. Padoan Urban, 'La festa della "Sensa" nelle arti e nell'iconografia', *Studi veneziani*, 10 (1968), 291–353. See also G. Luzzatto, *Studi di storia economica veneziana*, Padua, 1954, 202–4, and D.

Romano, *Housecraft and Statecraft: Domestic Service in Renaissance Venice, 1400–1600*, Baltimore, 1996, 177 and E. Muir, *Civic Ritual in Renaissance Venice*, Venice, 1981, 131–2.

55 Romano, 1996, 177.

56 Archivio di Stato, Venice, Arti 354, Sensa, Register Z, f. 27, 12 April 1585.

57 Archivio di Stato, Venice, Arti 354, Sensa, Register Z, f. 46, 16 July 1563.

58 Archivio di Stato, Venice, Arti 354, Sensa, Register Z, f. 3, 24 March 1593.

59 Archivio di Stato, Venice, Arti 354, Sensa, Register Z, f. 35, 25 May 1593, *Notta delle Botteghe quale fano bisogno da esser accomodatte et notta dela quale deli concieri che li hanno bisogno come giù sotto*.

60 Archivio di Stato, Venice, Arti 354, Sensa, Register Z, f. 56.

61 Archivio di Stato, Venice, Procuratori di San Marco, de supra (Chiesa), b. 50, proc. 99, 2. This is discussed in Luzzatto, 1954, 203–4 and in P. Allerston, 'The Market in Second-Hand Clothes and Furnishings in Venice, c.1500–c.1650', Ph.D. diss., European University Institute, Florence, 1996, 218.

62 L. Padoan Urban, 1968. 331, n. 185: '1322, Indicion sexta die primo octub. ordenado e fermado fo per misier Pietro Veniero e per misier Marco da Mula Iustixieri vieri, lo terzo compagno vacante. Ordenado fo che da mo in avanti alguna persona si Venedega come Forestiera non osa vender in Veniexia alguna anchona impenta. Salvo da la Sensa, che alora sia licito a saschun de vender anchone infin ch'l durerà la festa . . .'

63 M. Bury, *The Print in Italy, 1550–1620*, London, 2001, 177.

64 A. Nuovo, *Il commercio librario nell'Italia del rinascimento*, Milan, 1998 (1998b).

65 Archivio di Stato, Venice, Arti 725: 1510, 27 May.

66 A. Luzio and R. Renier, 'Il lusso di Isabella d'Este, Marchesa di Mantova: l''arredo degli appartamenti', *Nuova antologia*, n. s. 4, 63 (1896) (1896c), 278–9: 'Persuadendoni che alle apoteche delli vitriari a questa

Ascensa appariranno qualche belli vasi novi, siati contento de ritrovarne sino a diece o dodici vasi da bevere che siino varii di foggie, taze e bichieri et che habbino li fili bianchi schietti senza oro. Et vi piacia che in capparli conducati con voi per compagno Alphonso Faccino, qual è li in Venetia, perchè ambidui insieme l'uno col parere de l'altro sarete più atti a satisfare a l'intento nostro. Li potreti poi consignari a Joan Bono Andreasio exhibator presente, al quale havimo dato special carico de farceli havere. Et dil costo vi saranno poi rimessi li denari. See also the discussion in G. Malacarne, *Sulla mensa del principe: alimentazione e banchetti alla corte dei Gonzaga*, Modena, 2000, 60.

67 T. Garzoni, *La piazza universale di tutte le professioni del mondo*, ed. P. Cherchi and B. Collina, Turin, 1996, ii, 871: 'E oggidì è tanto in colmo a Murano quest'arte che non è cosa imaginabile al mondo che col vetro e col cristallo non si operi, essendosi fatto fino ai castelli con torri, bastioni, bombarde e muraglie, come nell'Ascensa di Venezia tal volta s'è visto.'

68 Padoan Urban, 1968, 331, n. 188: 'Et la Sensa si fa: vi è molti forestieri, ma pochi danari si spende.'

69 L. Ariosto, *Cinque canti*, ed. L. Firpo, Turin, 1963, i, 34, cited in Padoan Urban, 1968, 332, n. 190:

> Come chi tardi i suo'denar dispensa,
> nè ogni compra tosto si compiace,
> cerca tre volte e più tutta la Sensa,
> e va mirando in ogni lato, e tace;
> si ferma alfin dove ritrova immensa
> copia di quel ch'al suo bisogno face,
> e quivi or questa or quella cosa volve,
> cento ne piglia, e ancor non si risolve;
> questa mette da parte e quella lassa,
> e quella che lasciò di nuovo piglia;
> Poi la rifiuta e ad un'altra passa;
> Muta e rimuta, e ad una alfin s'appiglia

70 P. Molmenti, *La storia di Venezia nella vita privata dale origini alla caduta della republica*, Bergamo, 1905, ii, 628: Beatrice d'Este

to Ludovico Maria Sforza, 30 May, 1493: 'questa matina la Illustrissima madona mia matre, el signore Don Alphonso, Madonna Anna ed io cum tuta la compagnia se ponessimo a camino per andare ad oldire la messa a Santo Marco, dove el principe ne haveva invitati cum li nostri cantori et per monstrarne el thesoro: ma inante giongessimo a Santo Marco, smontassimo in terra a Realto et a pede ne andassimo per queste strade, che sono marzarie, dove trovassimo le boteche de spiciaria, de setta tute ben in ordine et per qualità et per quantità grandissima de diverse cose et così de le altre arte che facevano uno gran bel vedere, per modo che ne facevano sovenzo demorare per vedere hora una cosa hora un'altra, e non ce rincresceti niente fin a Santo Marco, dove gionti che fussimo sonando li trombeti nostri sopra la chiesa ad una logia denante trovassimo el principe che ce venete in contra presso la porta de Santo Marco . . . Fornita la messa se aviassimo pur col principe al loco del thesoro, nel quale loco per la grande multitudine del populo che era concorso come era anchora per le strate, durassimo la magior fatica del mundo a intrare non valendo che se facesse ogni cosa per fare dare loco cridando fin al principe, el quale principe per la gran spinta fu forza ne abandonasse et ne lassasse intrare nui cum pochi che fui poi anchora cum gran faticha. Intrati vedessimo a cosa per cosa el thesoro, che ne fu de gran piacere et per esserli infinite et belle gioje cum alcuni dignissimi vasi. Usciti andassimo per la piazza de Santo Marco sopra le boteche de la fera, dove trovassimo tanta copia de vetri belli che l'hera uno stupore, et qui ne fu forza demorare gran pezo et vedendo che l'hora se faceva tarda se aviassimo a casa a disnare che erano xvii horo. Io era vestita de la veste de panno morello recamato cum li pecti reversati che havevano el caduceo: haveva el vezo de perle a collo et lo robino in pecto ale quali gioie, et in ispetie al rubino, se guardava tanto et si parlava cum dire, 'quello ha posto l'uno dì, non ha posto l'altro', che ce fu de quelli che mi missano quasi l'ochi fin sopra el pecto per guardarlo, et vedendo tanta anxietà, io li disse dovessino venire in casa che gli lo monstraria voluntera . . .'

CHAPTER 7

1 The literature on Italian auctions has developed substantially in recent years. See the articles by P. Allerston, 'The Second-Hand Trade in the Arts in Early Modern Italy'; J. M. Musacchio, 'The Medici Sale of 1495 and the Second-Hand Market in Late Fifteenth-Century Florence'; and E. Welch, 'From Retail to Resale: Artistic Value and the Second-Hand Market in Italy (1400–1550)', in M. Fantoni, L. C. Matthew and S. F. Matthews-Grieco, eds, *The Art Market in Italy: Fifteenth to Seventeenth Centuries*, Modena, 2003, 301–12, 313–24 and 283–300 respectively.

2 For gold, silver and copper auctions in Venice see G. M. Thomas, *Capitolare dei visdomini del fontego dei todeschi in Venezia*, Berlin, 1874, 24 and 41. In 1333 there were twelve auctioneers responsible for the sale of copper. They were expected to know Latin and German and to start the auction when the 'prima campana de li officiali' ceased to toll and carry on until all the materials had been sold. On the Venetian and Florentine galley auctions see D. Stöckley, *Le système de l'incanto des galées du marché à Venise (fin XIIIe–milieu XVe siècles)*, Leiden, 1995; and M. E. Mallett, *The Florentine Galleys in the Fifteenth Century*, Oxford, 1967 40–2. Every five years, Trevigian officials auctioned off the rights to supply stationery to the bidder who could provide the best price. See A. Marchesan, *Treviso medievale: istituzioni, usi, costumi, aneddoti, curiosità*, ed. L. Gargan, Bologna, 1990, 1, 187.

3 For a comparison with Dutch auctions see J. M. Montias, *Art at Auction in Seventeenth-Century Amsterdam*, Amsterdam, 2002 and N. De Marchi, 'The Role of Dutch Auctions and Lotteries in Shaping the Art Market(s) of Seventeenth-Century Holland', *Journal of Economic Behaviour and Organization*, 28 (1995), 203–21.

4 B. Ghetti, 'Gli ebrei e il Monte di Pietà in Recanti nei secoli XV e XVI', *Atti e memorie della reale deputazione di storia patria per le provincie delle marche*, n. s. 9 (1913), 377–434.

5 Marchesan, 1990, 1, 161.

6 Allerston, 2003, 305.

7 M. Sanudo, *I diarii di Marino Sanudo*, ed. R. Fulin et al., Venice, 1880, 3, col. 94: 'Fu posto, per el principe, consieri, cai di 40, e tutto il colegio, una parte aricordata, come intisi, per sier Lunardo Grimani, savio da tera ferma: che tuti li debitori di la Signoria nostra, zoè cazude, governadori e raxon nuove, debino pagar per tuto il mexe di fevrer senza pena, poi, in termine di do mexi, siano tolti per la Signoria nostra per el quinto mancho, e posti in San Marco, sì beni mobeli come stabeli; et siano facti do stimadori di mobeli et do di stabeli, et siano venduti; et poi venduti, quelli de chi serano li beni, habi 4 mexi di tempo da rescuoderli; qualli passadi, non possi haver più gratia.'

8 C. M. Brown with A. M. Lorenzoni, 'An Art Auction in Venice in 1506', *L'Arte*, 18–19/20 (1972), 126–36.

9 Archivio della Veneranda Fabbrica del Duomo di Milano (AVFDM), Register 11, front cover: 'In principio huius libri adsunt ordinis facti . . . pro rebus mobilibus parte fabrice oblatus ad publicum incantum vendendis.'

10 AVFDM, Register 11, f. 2, 4 January 1402.

11 AVFDM, Register 11, f. 21: in campo azuro laborata al dalmaschino de seta alba et rubea.

12 AVFDM, Register 533, f. 8.

13 AVFDM, Register 533, f. 37.

14 AVFDM, Register 201, f. 280.

15 AVFDM, Register 201, f. 284.

16 AVFDM, Register 201, f. 289.

17 AVFDM, Register 676 (1490).

18 AVFDM, Register 676 (1490).

19 A. R. Natale, ed., *Acta libertatis mediolani. I registri n. 5 e n. 6 dell'archivio dell'ufficio degli Statuti di Milano* (*Repubblica Ambrosiana, 1447–1450*), Milan, 1987, 50.

20 Natale, 1987, 50: 'officialium ad incantandum, deliverandum, vendendum et alienandum omnes res'.

21 Natale, 1987, 53: 'quod preco seu tubator debeat, tunc, alta et sonora voce, prenuntiare et circumstantes omnes, ita ut plene intelligant, premonere quod eiusmodi res incantata delivrari vult, ipso istanti, plus offerenti; et, subsequenter, tribus vicibus, altissima voce declarando rem, que et pretium, quo incantata est, exprimat et dicat hec verba: 'La prima, la seconda, la terza', faciendo et interponendo moram, a prima vice ad secundam, et a secunda ad tertiam, per tanti temporis intervallum, quo tota *Pater noster* oratio dici distincte potuerit et, postmodum, si non erit qui pretium augeat, debeat eiusmodi res incantata ei qui plus obtulisset per dictum Offitialem delivrari cum virga in eius manu per dictum Offitialem ponenda et, deinde, per incantatorem eidem Offitiali restituenda; hacque servata et adimpleta solemnitate et not aliter intelligatur et sit eiusmodi res delivrata plenius et in incantotoris jus et arbitrium omnino translata.'

22 For the impact of the Chioggia wars see R. Mueller, 'Effetti della guerra di Chioggia (1378–81) sulla vita economica e sociale di Venezia', *Ateneo veneto*, n.s., 19 (1981), 27–41. The Sovicelle pronouncement is published in G. Prunai, ed., *Statuti dei Comuni di Monastero S. Eugenio (1352), Monteriggioni (1380) e Sovicille (1383)*, Florence, 1961, 141: 'Ancho providero perché molti sono gravati e fanno vista di non essere loro e perché non si paga el comune ne viene in debito grande, ch'e pegni pegnorati per datii o preste a petitione del vicaro e camarlengo o per condemnagioni secondo forma di statuto, si debba ricogliere per colui di cui sono o a suo nome fra vinti dì, e da ini i'la el camarlengo e'l vicaro sieno tenuti di vendargli a l'oncanto fra octo dì a la pena a esso camarlengo di diece lire, e chi più ne da colui l'abbi, e debbasi incantare due diversi dì di festa e mandare el bando che ognuno venga a l'oncanto de'pegni denanzi a la casa del vicaro, o vuole esso camarlengo portargli a vendere a Siena senza licenzia o vero richesta di colui cui sono, passati vinti dì, co'licentia del vicaro, ma più tosto farlo incantare a mantenimento de la povera gente, e questo sia in suo arbitrio, e ciò che se n'à si metta a entrata al camarlengo, a posta di colui cui è el pegno, excepto le spese del messo e altre spese che vi fussoro facte ragionevoli.'

23 J. Heers, *Esclaves et domestiques au Moyen Age dans le monde méditeranéen*, Paris, 1981, 186.

24 M. Pedralli, *Novo, grande, coverto e ferrato: gli inventari di biblioteca e la cultura a Milano nel quattrocento*, Milan, 2002, 189.

25 The first surviving record of a pawn sale for the Florentine Monte de Pietà in 1504 shows the debtor's mother, Monna Piera de' Baroncelli, redeeming her son's clothing and domestic objects such as a tablecloth and a knife. Her son had pawned eleven items between 1503 and 1504, the most expensive of which was a lined gown. See C. Bresnehan Menning, *Charity and State in Late Renaissance Italy: The Monte di Pietà of Florence*, Ithaca, N.Y., 1993, 93.

26 M. Sanudo, *De origine, situ et magistrativus urbis Venetae ovvero la città di Venezia (1493–1530)*, ed. A. Caracciolo Aricò, Milan, 1980, 135–6.

27 P. Allerston, 'The Market in Second-Hand Clothes and Furnishings in Venice, c.1500–c.1650', Ph.D. diss., European University Institute, Florence, 1996, 239: occorre spesse volte che le povere persone, che hanno momentaneo bisogna di vender alcuna sua robba all'incanto . . . et acciocchè non habbino ad havere dilatione di tempo . . .

28 Allerston, 1996a, 236.

29 Archivio di Stato, Venice, Giustizia Vecchia 76: 1583, 19 December: 'Querela ala Avogaria de Comun di Francesco della Vedova comandador di dui depositione giurate come false: Questo dico io Francesco dalla Vedova comandaro recito essendomi sta dato uno paro de braghesse de damasco negro a scachetti da magnifico Nicolo Saitor in Realto fin sotto li 5 luglio prossimo passato per dover quelle incantar et vender quel maggior pretio fusse stato possibile; et havendo io quelle portate sopra el Rialto scessero li fanti dell'officio della Giustizia Vecchia e pensando che io non havese licentia a mi tolsero decte braghesse et quelle portorno al sudetto officio et demandatomi el contrafattio delle leggi fecero essaminar diversi testimonii fra li quale sono stato essaminato uno Hieronymo strazzaruol in S. Cassiano e uno Marin strazzaruol ai Frari li quali sono stati cosi arditi che poco curando l'amine loro et per rasone della robba et insieme dell'honor et vita mia gli ha vassato l'animo in tal caso deponer il falso deponendo lui Hieronymo che mi vide incantar de braghesse gridando a cinque ducati, a cinque ducati et Marino che io havendo accetate de braghesse per pretio de ducati cinque dal sartor et me le havea cussì giurate et come più diffusamente nelle loro depositione a compare testificatione in tutto false e contrario al vero et da horo ditte modo altro fine se non per ruinarmi dalla robba et vita et gli andava ad effeto se la maestre del Signore domino Dio nostro non agiusticava facendose dir la verita in luce tolte la giustizia me ha assolto et et li denuntiate condanati nele spese per il che vedendo io la perversita loro et anco per discargo dell'honor mio accio de loro s'assegnino da cometter tal falsità. . . .'

30 Archivio di Stato, Venice, Giustizia Vecchia 76: 23 August 1656: Il Serenissimo Principe permessi fa saper di ordine delli illustrissimi signorie essendo forma e risoluta volontà di sue signorie illustrissime che l'incanti che vengono fatti in Rialto,

San Marcho et altri luochi passono con quelle buone forme e regole et ordini che sono praticati in diversi tempi con la auctorità dell'illustrissimo Senato a comandamento de venditori et compratori anno vero con il presente e publico proclamo voluto portare a notitia universale quanto in dettà materia si dovera osservare.

Chi occorra vender mobili de qualle si sia sorte sopra gli'incanti dovera presentar nell' magistrato di sue signorie illustrissime con l'inventario destinto con la qualità, quantità e colori delle robbe che doveva esser giurate che stano di sua propria ragione ne fatte ne comprate per rivendere, il che seguito dall'illustrissimo cassier di detto officio quando sarà cavato un comandadore a sorte e dattagli licenza che da quello siano ney publici luochi vendere detti mobili al' incanto sopra il quale doverà assistere personalmente detto venditore overo altra persona in suo luocho che dovera esser datta in scritta da lui al magistro al tempo della presentatione dell'inventario detto tutte le penne instruite delle legi.

Come parimente per servitio delle povere gente e de quelli che vorane far vender robbe da ducati dieci in giù sarano dall'illustrissimo cassier di settimana in settimana estratti a sorte dodeci comandadori dall numero de tutti che doverano assistere per lo spatio di giorni sei all continuo nella piazza di Rialto per dover ricever et vender le predette robbe.

Li nomi delli predetti comandadori sarano affisi in luogho publico sopra una tavoletta nell' officio di Giustizia Vecchia per debita notitia tanto de essi comandadori quanto de venditori.

Siano tenuti et obligati detti comandadori a qualli sara tratta la vendita delle robbe quella esercitar personalmente dovendo decti comandadori tenir l'inventario publicamente ch'ogni uno lo possi vedere et nella vendita di detti mobili essistenti sopra quello inventarii per bolettine sia tenutto dispenar di volta in volta gl' cai (incanti?) di robba secondo anderano vendendo.

Ressi . . . ad essi comandadori prohibito il poter ricever robbe di altra sorte sotto qual si sia prestesto vicendo sopra essi incanti oltre la notatte sopra gli'inventarii o bolettini dell' magistrato come nei posciano et ancho quelli che farano fare gli'incanti agionger ad essi mobili oltre li descritti come sopra in penna a detti a detti comandadori che in alcuna cossa del presente proclama trasgredisce ducati 50 perder li beretta et esser bandito di Rialto giusto le leggi.

Non potendo parimente li marangoni, indoradori ne altri artesani della cita porre sopra essi tavolini, casse, littiere ne altre robbe di qualsiasi voglia sorte nove overo acconciate in penna de fiorini 25 et perder la robba debbano li comandadori essercitar legalmente il suo ministerio senza fraude d'inganno . . .

Siano incaricati li gastaldo e compagni dell'arte de strazaruol di andar almeno quatro volte all'anno sopra gli'incanti per veder se vengono comessi in quelli trasgressioni in pena de fiorini 50 in cadauno in esso che mancassero a quanto di sopra per il qual offitio potereno seco condurre uno o più fanti del magnifici Giustizia Vecchia illustrissimi per far le debite esecution . . .'

31 J. Hinton, 'By Sale, By Gift: Aspects of the Resale and Bequest of Goods in Late Sixteenth-Century Venice', *Journal of Design History*, 15 (2002), 245–62.

32 For the Pupilli regulations in Florence see F. Morandini, 'Statuti e ordinamenti dell'ufficio dei pupilli et adulti nel periodo della repubblica Fiorentina (1388–1535)', *Archivio storico italiano*, 113 (1955), 520–51; 114 (1956), 92–117; 115 (1957), 87–104. See also Musacchio, 2003, 313 and A. Matchette, Unbound Possessions: The Circulation of Used Goods in Florence, c. 1450–1600', Ph.D. diss., University of Sussex, 2005.

33 D. Thornton, *The Scholar in his Study:*

Ownership and Experience in Renaissance Italy, New Haven, 1998, 25.

34 C. M. Belfanti and F. Guisberti, 'Introduzione', in *idem*, eds, *Storia d'Italia: la moda*, 19, Turin, 2003, XXII. See also M. Cataldi Gallo, 'Il commercio degli abiti usati a Genova nel XXII secolo', in *Per una storia della moda pronta*, Florence, 1991, 102.

35 Musacchio, 2003, 312.

36 Musacchio, 2003, 315.

37 F. Sansovino, *Venetia: città nobilissima et singolare*, Venice, 1663, 385 and I. Palumbo-Fossati, 'L'interno della casa dell'artigiano e dell'artista nella Venezia del cinquecento', *Studi veneziani*, n. s. 8 (1984), III.

38 Archivio di Stato, Mantua, Archivio Gonzaga, b. 1469, Scipione de Licio to Isabella d'Este, 9 January 1534: 'Trovandomi patrona excellentissima del dì de bona mano in piaza de San Bartolomeo de Rialto dove se feva uno incanto de multe belle cose et zoye et tra le altre era un bellectissimo corallo il quale da multi era incantato et quasi ogniun diceva che tal corallo era de belli che mai se avesse visto cent'anni fa et che tal zoyecta stareve ben in mano de ogni gran maestro et per avere io cogniosciuto che nissun de quelli li quali erano per incantare seriano stati boni de torlu per maior maestro che seria stato io in nome de vostra excellencia et mia patrona per tanto a me parse de non cessare may de incantare per fin al fine. Ita che tucti concorrenti o convinti el corallo e restato alle mey mani el qual mando a vostra illustrissima signoria pregando quella piaza dignarsi de aceptarlo con questi pacti che quando vostra sublimità se lieva el matino piaza in quello mirarsi dentro el quale ferà in vostra signoria el core elgre et jocundo quasi de una semidea.'

39 Archivio di Stato, Bologna (ASBo), Massarolo dei pegni, b. 17, 1410–29. This magistracy had a long history, and some of the earliest records date back to the second half of the fourteenth century see Massarolo

dei pegni, b.16, f. 86v which illustrates the major effect that the salt tax had on citizens who were unable to make the compulsory purchase of a pound of salt per year.

40 ASBo, Massarolo dei pegni, b.17, f. 3.
41 ASBo, Massarolo dei pegni, b.17, f. 3v.
42 ASBo, Massarolo dei pegni, b.17, f. 5v.
43 ASBo, Massarolo dei pegni, b.17, f. 30v.
44 For an example of a contested introduction of pawnbroking in a Tuscan town see G. P. Scharf, 'Fra economia urbana e circuiti intercittadini: il ruolo degli ebrei a Borgo San Sepolcro a meta del quattrocento', *Archivio storico italiano*, 156 (1998), 447–77.
45 R. A. Goldthwaite and G. Mandich, *Studi sulla moneta fiorentina: secoli XIII–XVI*, Florence, 1994, 40.
46 P. Hohti, 'The Innkeeper's Goods: The Acquisition and Use of Household Property in Sixteenth-Century Siena', in M. O'Malley and E. Welch, eds, *The Material Renaissance*, forthcoming.
47 L. Zdekauer, 'L'interno d'un banco di pegno nel 1417 con documenti inediti', *Archivio storico italiano*, series 5, 17 (1896), 63.
48 C. Bresnehan Menning 1993, 94.
49 S. Simonsohn, *The Jews in the Duchy of Milan*, 4 vols, Jerusalem, 1982, 1, 252.
50 Goldthwaite and Mandich 1994, 335.
51 Simonsohn, 1982, 1, 36 and 51.
52 Simonsohn, 1982, 1, 29: 'uno vestito de zettano cremosi raso argentato foderato de martori con maniche averte; Una mantellina verde de zettano brochato d'argento foderato de martori con la bramatura . . . Uno vestito de zettano cremosi argentato con maniche averte foderato de martori; Uno vestito de zettano azuro raso argentato con maniche averte foderato de martori . . .'
53 D. Ferrari, ed., *Giulio Romano: repetorio di fonti documentarie*, Rome, 1992, II, 1204: 'Di più sodetta signora tutrice dice esser in pegno presso l'Hebrei i beni et altre robbe de'quali in una lista di mano di sua signoria del tenore sottoscritto, che comincia:

Impegnato al banco di Nuvoloni un tapedo grande, scudi 20 d'oro; altri tapedi 9 non tropo boni, e 4 pezi de spalere rotte; al bancho de Grasini, lire 100. Messer Vitta cuchiari numero 10 d'argento indorati, una taza d'argento con il piede, indorata e una filza de corali belissimi, ma non so per quanto siano in pegno. Un sparaviero di cambraglia con corde di seta cremesina, alla milanese, impegnato, ma non so dove, scudi 10 d'oro. Una colana de gioie impegnata a Governolo, per scudi 130 d'oro. Una colana de lapis segnata di oro, mi chredo scudi 10 d'oro. Una trabacha de dobeleto de seda morella e ranza inpegnata scudi 50. Un zaco e un par de maniche a Grasini, scudi 9; peltro impegnato in due volte pezi 48, pesa pezi 7, libre 10, in casa di Benedusi. Una trabaccha de oremesino di Fiorenza, datta al banchereo di Governolo per l'interessi, cheremesina e giala.'
54 S. A. Bianchi and R. Granuzzo, eds, *Statuti di Verona del 1327*, 2 vols, Rome 1992, 1, 348.
55 Simonsohn 1982 1, 14. For examples of announcements see *idem*, 1, 217.
56 B. Ghetti, 'Gli ebrei e il Monte di Pietà in Recanati nei secoli XV e XVI', *Atti e memorie della reale deputazione di storia patria per le provincie delle marche*, n. s. 9 (1913), 377–434: 'che fosse lecito vendere dopo un'anno i pegni dei forestieri e dopo diciotto mesi quelli dei cittadini senza alcun bando e senza citazione della parte interessata, perchè per esperienza ormai era nota che i padroni dei pegni si opponevano a che questi si vendessero all'asta ed in pubblico; onde ad essi riusciva impossibile recuperare il denaro mutuato secundum debitum iustitie'.
57 Simonsohn, 1982, 1, 145.
58 M. Fornasari, *Il 'thesoro della città': il Monte di Pietà e l'economia bolognese nei secoli XV e XVI*, Bologna, 1993, 42–3.
59 R. Mueller, *The Procuratori di San Marco and the Venetian Credit Market*, New York, 1977, 220 and 352–3.
60 G. De'Ricci, *Cronaca (1532–1606)*, ed. G.

Sapori, Milan, 1972, 76–7: 'Passomi di leggieri la gratia fatta dal serenissimo principe a un . . . di Massimiliano stimatore al Monte della pietà che usava di spiccare le polize da i pegni che si impegnavono et poi farli rimpegnare, et lui si ripigliava i danari rimettendovi le medexime polize.'

61 G. C. Croce, *Lamento de poveretti: i quali stanno à casa a piggione, & la convengono pagare. Composta per il Piasentino in Mantova per Benedetto Osanna, stampatore ducale*, 1590, ff. 3v–4: Nota ben, quel ch'io insegno

> Primamente piglia un pegno
> Che sia tanto d'importanza
> Quanto monta la sustanza
> E poivi con lieta fronte
> A portarlo tosto al Monte
> Che t'haverane compassione
> Mala cosa è la piggione.
> Come il pegno sia accettato,
> El danar haurai tirato
> Recipe il tuo scrittarino,
> E poi và con il quattrino
> Il patron tosto saluta
> E fatti far la ricevuta,
> Perchè questa è buon untione
> Mala cosa è la piggione.

62 P. Campostella, *Il Monte di Pietà di Milano*, 3 vols, Milan, 1966–73, I, 71.

63 Campostella, 1966, I, 71–2: 'distesi sopra un banco a ciò se vedano per caduno, et per honore di quelle persone che li harano impegnati se copri el boletino cum qualche peza o altramente in sino che sarano venduti. Et venduti che sarano sia levato el boletino'.

64 L. Campbell, 'The Art Market in the Southern Netherlands in the Fifteenth Century', *Burlington Magazine*, 118 (1976), 195–6; and De Marchi, 1995, 203–21. The only major discussion of Renaissance lotteries is the piece by L. C. Matthew, 'Were There Open Markets for Pictures in Renaissance Venice?' in M. Fantoni, L. C. Matthew and S. F. Mathews-Greco, eds, *The Art Market in Italy: Fifteenth to Seven-*

teenth Centuries, Modena, 2003, 253–61.

65 Natale, 1987, 292–4.

66 M. Sanudo, *I diarii di Marino Sanudo*, ed. R. Fulin et al., Bologna, 1903, 32, cols 467–8: 'In Rialto è sussita uno novo modo di vadagnar metando poco cavedal a fortuna, e fu comenzà in cosse base, auctor Hieronimo Bambarara strazaruol, poi è venuto più in grosso. Prima' cadaun che voleva dava soldi 20, poi viene a lire 3, poi a ducati uno, e si meteva li precii, tapedi, spaliere e altre cose; hor è venuto arzenti per zercha ducati 200, et altri ha messo una peza de restagno d'oro dando ducati uno per nome. Et si fa a questo modo: chi vol esser si nota sopra uno sfoio di carta e dà contadi fuori li denari . . . tutti chi ha messo si reduseno in certe botege a questo deputade, dove in do sacheti e tanti boletini quanti quelli hanno depostà in uno sacheto et in l'altro tanti boletini scriti che dirà et tal precio; chi dise patientia. Et cussi reduti tutti, sei chiama uno putin et si fa ben messedar li boletini in ditti sacheti, poi cava fuora il nome dil primo sacheto et va al secondo, se vien precio quelo li tocho èsuo: se vien il boletin ch' è scritto *pacientia*, non vadagna nulla et è so disaventura; sichè ogni dì in Rialto si sta su queste pratiche.' See also *idem*, vol. 52, cols 504–7, 1530, for a detailed description of the complexities of determining how prizes would be allocated.

67 S. Chojnacki, 'Political Adulthood in Fifteenth-Century Venice', *American Historical Review*, 91 (1986), 802.

68 S. Cortesi, *I due testamenti di Fra Sabba da Castiglione*, Faenza, 2000, 11 and 151.

69 *Regesti di Bandi, editti, notificazioni e provvedimenti diversi relativi alla città di Roma ed allo stato pontificio*, Rome, 1920, I, 65 and 67 and G. O. Corazzini, ed., *Diario fiorentino di Agostino Lapini dal 252 al 1596 ora per la prima volta pubblicato*, Florence, 1900, 294.

70 J. Walker, 'Gambling and Venetian Noblemen c.1500–1700', *Past and Present*, 162 (1999), 31.

71 G. Dolcetti, *Le bische e il giuoco d'azzardo a Venezia, 1172–1807*, Venice, 1903, 219: 'Non essendo per alcun modo da tollerar questo nuovo Zuogo da alcuni Zorni in qua trovato da Trazer denari da questo, et da quell'altro chiamato lotho cum tanta murmuration universalmente de tutti si per li desviamenti de zaschedun de le sue facende come etiam per li inconvenienti et disordini che de facili potriano seguir per causa de quello, l'è al tutto necessario de farne provitione però. L'andera parte che per autorita de questo Conseio sia preso che doman da mattina pubblicar se debbi sopra le Scalle de Rialto et San Marco, che non se possi modo aliquo principiar più alcuno in questa città nostra sotto pena a quello over quelli contravenisse a questo ordine et deliberatione nostra de star anni doi ne le preson nostre seradi et pagar ducati 500 ... Quelli veramente fossero fin questo Zorno za principati fenir per tutto Marti proximo dì de Carneval, et non più, qual passado, non se possi per alcuno modo buttar, ne cavar bollettino alcuno, sotto la pena predicta. Et se per caso per detto dì de Carnevale non fossero dicti Lothi Serradi, ne butati li bollettini quelli che hanno tochato i denari siano obbligati restituirli a quelli de chi fossero, sotto la pena sopra scritta.'

72 Sanudo, 1903, 32, col. 505.

73 It is worth noting that this is a common shift. In Rome, for example, they established an 'ufficio dei sensali delle scommesse' in 1588 who provided licences for gambling on the sex of unborn children. See *Regesti di bandi*, 1920, I, 92–3, 1588. Thirty *sensali* were licensed to take bets on the creation of cardinals, ibid., I, 95. They were finally banned outright in 1589.

74 Dolcetti, 1903. See the printed announcement concerning lottery sales of houses, taverns and jewels held in Venice in April 1526 which Sanudo copied into his diary: Sanudo, 1894, 41, cols, 205–6.

75 *Regesti*, 1920, I, 79 for the norms for running lotteries.

76 Matthew, 2003, 257. For a seventeenth-century sale of pictures by lottery see A. Segarizzi, 'Una lotteria di quadri nel secolo xvii', *Nuovo archivio veneto*, n. s. 28, (1914), 172–87.

77 L. Lotto, *Il libro di spese diverse (1538–1556)*, ed. P. Zampetti, Venice, 1969, 129.

78 For Giovanni Manenti as the author of the play, *Philargio, Trebia and Fidel*, which was performed on 9 February 1525 see D. S. Chambers and B. Pullan, eds, *Venice: A Documentary History, 1450–1630*, Oxford, 1992, 380.

79 P. Aretino, *Selected Letters*, trans. and ed. G. Bull, London, 1976, 133–7.

80 Sanudo, 1903, 32, cols 501–4: Molte donne ha posto danaro in ditto lotho; sichè tutti core a meter poco per aver assai, perchè si vede tal con un ducato averli tochà 100 d'oro, e tal perle che val ducati 180 e via discorendo ...

81 B. Furlotti, ed., *Le collezioni Gonzaga: il carteggio tra Roma e Mantova (1587–1612)*, Milan, 2002, 138.

82 *Regesti*, 1920, I, 102, 2 January 1590: 'Grazie uscite al primo e secondo lotto fatto in Roma l'anno 1582; *Regesti*, 1920, II, 123 and 127.

83 See Chapter eight for a more detailed discussion.

84 D. Sogliani, ed., *Le collezioni Gonzaga: il carteggio tra Venezia e Mantova (1563–1587)*, Milan, 2002, 137: ... mando qui alligato a vostra eccellenza in stampa l'inventario di tutte le robbe che si hanno a porre al lotto de'Dolfini, il quale non so quando si caverà. Ma hora si è dato principio a torne denari e si guidica però in brieve sia in termine da poterse cavare, perchè molti rimangono creditori loro di bona soma di danari e per rihaverli si sarebbero contentati di perdere tal uno d'essi mille e duo milla scudi.

85 Archivio di stato, Mantua, Archivio Gonzaga, b. 1502, f. II, cc. 661–664, *Gratie del lotto del banco Dolfin in virtù della parte dell'illustrissimo Collegio de' X et Gionta, sotto di VI settembre M.D.L.XX.*

86 See, for example, 'Grazie uscite al primo e secondo lotto fatto in Roma l'anno 1582' in *Regesti*, 1920, II, 121–3. Permission was granted to Claudio Venturini to run a lottery in 1584: *Regesti di bandi*, 1920, II, 127, and there is a further record in 1584 of an 'Editto, col quale si notifica il lotto, ossia ventura, da farsi in Roma, da gioie e danaro per opera di Claudio Venturini.' 1584: *Regesti di bandi* 1920, II, 112. That same year there was another, 'Editto ... col quale si notifica l'elenco dei premi della lotteria da farsi in Roma dal Marchese di Cassano', *Regesti di bandi*, 1920, II, 102. In December 1586, the 'premi della lotteria da farsi in Roma da Mario Sforza, Conte di S. Fiora' was announced, *Regesti di bandi*, 1920, II, 126. This was run under the auspices of the papal treasurer general. Sforza held another lottery the following year while the banker, Ottavio Gratis, held one in piazza di San Lorenzo in Damasceno. In total there were seven separate lotteries held in 1587 by members of Rome's elite. They varied in location. One was held by the Zecca, another on the Via del Pellegrino: *Regesti di bandi* 1920, II, 153. In 1589, a lottery was held on Via dei Banchi, while Giovanni Battista Pisani held another in Piazza Giudea. In the 1590s, they were held in Campo dei Fiori. Although Roman aristocrats were heavily involved in managing lotteries, not all lotteries were run by patricians. In 1588, for example, a 'Lotto di ori e altra roba' was run by maestro Orazio, bottegaio al Corso. In 1589, an edict was issued ordering that the winners of a lottery run by maestro Antonio, sarto a Tor Sanguigna, would be pulled during Lent. See *Regesti di bandi*, 1920, II, 157.

CHAPTER 8

1 Bernardino da Siena, *Prediche volgari sul campo di Siena, 1427*, ed. C. Delcorno, Milan, 1989, II, 1112: 'Prima vediamo de le bugie che s'usa ne le mercantie. Dico che so' molti che pare che eglino abbino giurato di non vendare e non comprare niuna cosa, che almeno non vi si dica su una dozzina di bugie ... Doh, diciamo pur d'uno che vorrà comprare uno paio di scarpette. Egli giogne al calzolaio: – Che vuoi di queste scarpette? – Vuo'ne venti soldi. – A le vagnele, non darò. – Doh, tolle, ch'io ti prometto che elle so' de le perfette da divero (e mente per la gola). – Che ne vuoi tu al meno? – Io non ne vo'meno: a le vagnele, ch'io n'ho potuto avere diciotto soldi. (Hai già uno spergiuro, ché non fu vero.) – Vuo'ne tu quindici? – No: io ti prometto che tu non trovarai migliori scarpette in questa città che queste. – Io non te ne darò più che quindici soldi. (Tu mentirai anco tu.) – Oltre, in buon'ora: da'me diciotto soldi, come io n'ho trovato già parecchie volte. – A le vagnele, io non te ne darò più. – A le vagnele, tu non l'arai. – E poi infine egli le darà, e colui le torrà per diciassette, poi che ognuno arà giurato e spergiurato parecchie volte ...'

2 Bernardino da Siena, 1989, II, 1115: 'Ecci niuno di quegli che vendono gli agli e le cipolle? Che no ne vorranno vendare se non vi si giura su: – Io ne voglio cotanti denari. – Io te ne vo'dare cotanti. – A le vagnele, io non te la darò. – A le vagnele, tu me la darai. – A le vagnele, non darò. – Oimmè, non vedete voi quello che voi fate; mettervi a rinegare Idio per un capo d'aglio!'

3 A. Toaff, *Love, Work and Death: Jewish Life in Medieval Umbria*, London, 1996, 202.

4 A. Zagli, F. Mineccia and A. Giuntini, *Maladetti beccari: storia dei macelli fiorentini dal cinquecento al duemila*, Florence, 2000, 56: vada a colui dove vede più gente e dicagli: – Dammi di qualche buona vitella per quello gentile uomo di Prato – e saragli dato della buona.'

5 M. S. Mazzi, *Prostitute e lenoni nella Firenze del quattrocento*, Milan, 1991, 367.

6 A. Modigliani, 'Taverne e osterie a Roma nel tardo medioevo: tipologia, uso degli

spazi, arredo e distribuzione nella città', in *Taverne, locande e stufe a Roma nel rinascimento*, Rome, 1999, 41: 'tu menti per la gola . . . stronzo che si remasso mezo in corpo de tua matre'.

7 A. Modigliani, *Mercati, botteghe e spazi di commercio a Roma tra medioevo et età moderna*, Rome, 1998, 103.

8 O. Niccoli, *Storie di ogni giorno in una città del seicento*, Rome, 2000, 56: 'il quale . . . gli disse che ne voleva cinque quatrini, e detto putto disse che gli ne voleva dare tre, e poi detto putto ne vidde lì nella mostra un altro pezzo di pegora e disse che gli di[cesse] quel pezzo che era; et lui [il venditore] gli ripose . . . che era de piegora, et che valeva più, dicendo 'quello è di piegora, et questo è di vaccha', ma detto putto replicò, 'ma è di quella vaccha di vostra madre?'

9 P. Ghinzoni, 'Federico III Imperatore a Venezia (7 al 19 Febrajo 1469)', *Archivio veneto*, 37 (1889), 138: 'Alle 21 partì de pallazo venendo per Marzaria cum parechi dela Signoria et vedendo exquisitamente le bothege, spesso domandando el pretio dele merce lui proprio. Benchè domino Dominicho Moro e Zacharia Balbo alle volte dicesse: Sacra Maestà li faremo portare a casa dicte merce, nientemeno a lui pariva pur bono ghiarmare come merchedante, et senza dubio domesticamente da e bono merchadante. Alle Speciarie anchora demorava ghiamando li pretii et alle volte tollendo confeti in mano et manzare publicamente e domesticamente dando alli soi de suo pugno. Volse vedere el Magistero dela Seda. Li Toschani molto equisitamente vedendo assai drapi, spesso ghiamando el pretio. La Signoria diceva a quelli toschani gli portasero a casa le cosse più li piazeva.'

10 For Bartolomeo Bontempelli who was also known as Bartolomeo dal Calice see the frequent mentions of his activities in D. Sogliani, ed., *Le collezioni Gonzaga: il carteggio tra Venezia e Mantova (1563–1587)*, Milan, 2002 and the discussion in R. MacKenney, *Tradesmen and Traders: The World of the Guilds in Venice and Europe, c.1250–c.1650*, London, 1987, 110–11.

11 Archivio di Stato, Venice, Governatori delle pubbliche entrate, busta 495, 11 December 1545, 'Denucia Marchio fante del Officio contra Batista Mercer . . . tien S. Heironymo per insegna.'

12 S. D'Amico, 'Poveri e gruppi marginali nella società milanese cinque-seicentesca', in D. Zardin, ed., *La città e i poveri: Milano e le terre lombarde dal rinascimento all'età spagnola*, Milan, 1995, 281.

13 Most convents used procurators to make their institutional purchases, nuns still seem to have been able to make individual purchases on their own behalf. For example, in the early fifteenth century, Monna Antonia degli Acciaiuoli, 'monicha in San Piero', owed the apothecary shop of Matteo Palmerieri the sum of 1 lire and 3 soldi. See E. Conti, ed., *Matteo Palmieri: ricordi fiscali (1427–1474)*, Rome, 1983, 59. For sixteenth-century book purchases by nuns see P. F. Gehl, 'Libri per donne: le monache clienti del libraio fiorentino Piero Morosi (1588–1607)', in G. Zarri, ed., *Donne, discipline, creanze cristiana dal XV al XVII secolo: studi e testi a stampa*, Rome, 1996, 61–82.

14 A. Astorri, 'Il libro delle senserie di Girolamo di Agostino Manighi (1483–85)', *Archivio storico italiano*, 146 (1993), 389–408.

15 C. Boccato, 'La disciplina delle sensarie nel Ghetto di Venezia', *Giornale economico*, 6 (1974), 27–36.

16 T. Garzoni, *La piazza universale di tutte le professioni del mondo*, ed. P. Cherchi and B. Collina, Turin, 1996, II, 892: 'è commendata la fede, la diligenza, la sollecitudine, la prattica, la prudenza, l'isperienza, l'accortezza, la carità, la bontà, la cortesia . . .'.

17 Garzoni, 1996, II, 892–6.

18 There is a growing literature on domestic service. See D. Romano, 'The Regulation of Domestic Service in Renaissance Venice', *Sixteenth-Century Journal*, 22 (1991), 661–7.

19 *Nuove scelte di vilanelle e altre canzoni inge-*

niose, et belli, cited in D. Romano, *House-craft and Statecraft: Domestic Service in Renaissance Venice, 1400–1600*, Baltimore, 1996, 216. For a comparative discussion see C. Fairchilds, *Domestic Enemies: Servants and their Masters in Old Regime France*, Baltimore, 1990.

20   Quoted in L. Gowing, '"The Freedom of the Streets", Women and Social Space: 1560–1640,' in P. Griffiths and M. S. R. Jenner, eds, *Londinopolis: Essays in the Cultural and Social History of Early Modern London*, Manchester, 2000, 130.

21   R. C. Davis, 'The Geography of Gender in the Renaissance', in J. C. Brown and R. C. Davis, eds, *Gender and Society in Renaissance Italy*, New York, 1998, 19–38, especially p. 22. See also D. Romano, 'Gender and Urban Geography', *Journal of Social History*, 23 (1989), 339–53.

22   F. Moryson, *An Itinerary: Containing His Ten Years Travell through the Twelve Dominions of Germany, Bohmerland, Switzerland, Netherland, Denmark, Poland, Italy, Turkey, France, England, Scotland, Ireland*, Glasgow, 1907, I, 148.

23   This will be discussed in J. Shaw and E. Welch, *Making and Marketing Medicine in Renaissance Florence: The Case of the Speziale al Giglio*, forthcoming.

24   Archivio di Stato, Florence, Libri di commercio e di famiglia 474, 1566.

25   Archivio della Veneranda Fabbrica del Duomo di Milano (AVFDM) Registers 274 and 281.

26   AVFDM, Register 274, f. 238.

27   AVFDM, Register 274, f. 242v.

28   AVFDM, Register 274, f. 137v.

29   AVFDM, Register 274, f. 183.

30   G. Ciapelli, 'Family Memory: Functions, Evolution, Recurrences', in G. Ciapelli and P. L. Rubin, eds, *Art, Memory, and Family in Renaissance Florence*, Cambridge, 2000, 26–38. See also A. Cicchetti and R. Mordenti, *I libri di famigilia in Italia*. I: *filologia e storiografia letteraria*, Rome, 1985.

31   See, for example, the list of loans of goods to friends and relations in Martelli, Ugolino di Niccolò, *Ricordanze dal 1433 al 1483*, ed. F. Pessarossa, Rome, 1989, 102, 127, 137 and 241–2.

32   The costs of supplying the table of the Priors of Florence were recorded on a daily basis throughout the fourteenth and fifteenth centuries. For a sample see C. Mazzi, 'La mensa dei priori di Firenze nel secolo xiv', *Archivio storico italiano*, series v, 20 (1897), 339–43.

33   J. Grubb, 'Memory and Identity: Why Venetians Didn't Keep Ricordanze', *Renaissance Studies*, 8 (1994), 375–87.

34   See, for example, AVFDM, Register 683: Libro di entrate e spese di Signore Paolo Imperiale, 1493–8.

35   Women did keep family accounts once they were widowed. Lucrezia Tornabuoni's *dare e avere* accounts survive for the period following her husband's death in Archivio di Stato, Florence, *Mediceo avanti il principato*, xcix, n. 7: Partite di dare e avere tra Lucrezia Tornabuoni dei Medici e il Banco Medici di Pisa, 1474–7. The many family accounts kept by Strozzi family widows include: Archivio di Stato, Florence, Carte Strozziane, iv series, n. 60: Libro di mona Alexandra donna che fu de Marco Strozzi. Libro debitori e creditori e ricordi di cose domestiche, 1500–6; n. 72: Libretto intitolato Giornale di Mona Francesca, vedova di Nicolo di Carlo Strozzi, 1493–8; nn. 89 and 90: Libro di Albiera di Jacopo di Giunta Binemi e donna gia di Simone Strozzi, 1569–79. For the most famous Strozzi widow, Alessandra Strozzi, see most recently A. Crabb, *The Strozzi of Florence: Widowhood and Family Solidarity in the Renaissance*, Ann Arbor, 2000.

36   T. Tasso, *Discorso della virtù feminile e donnesca*, ed. M. L. Doglia, Palermo, 1997, 56–7: 'Questo che si dice del governo delle città, si verifica parimente nel governo famigliare o della casa, che vogliam chiamarlo, il quael essendo composto d'acquisto e di conservazione, è stato bene instituito he gli uffici suoi si distinguissero, e che l'ufficio dell'acquistare all'uomo e quel del conservare alla donna s'attribuisse. Guerreggia l'uomo per acquistare e l'agri-

coltura esercita e la mercanzia e nella città si adopera . . . ma conserva la donna l'acquistato . . . e così la sua virtù s'impegna dentro la casa, come quella dell'uomo fuori si demonstra.'

37 C. Bec, ed. *Il libro degli affari proprii di casa di Lapo di Giovanni Niccolini de' Sirigatti*, Paris, 1969, 73–4.

38 Bec, 1969, 137.

39 Bec, 1969, 138.

40 C. Yriate, ed. *Livre de Souvenirs de Maso di Bartolomeo*, Paris, 1894, 57, 60 and 87.

41 L. Haas, *The Renaissance Man and his Children*, New York, 1998, 144.

42 J. Kirshner, '"Li emergenti bisogni matrimoniali" in Renaissance Florence' in W. J. Connell, ed., *Society and Individual in Renaissance Florence*, Berkeley, 2000, 79–109.

43 P. Salvadori, ed., *Lucrezia Tornabuoni: Lettere*, Florence, 1993, 60.

44 Y. Maguire, *The Women of the Medici*, London, 1927, 124. The abbess refused any payment but asked for Medici support instead.

45 Maguire, 1927, 121–2.

46 H. Gregory, ed., *Selected Letters of Alessandra Strozzi*, Berkeley, 1997, 35.

47 Archivio di Stato, Florence, Carte Strozziane, IV serie, 72, 1486–99: 'Questo libro sie della Francesca, donna de Ferdinando di Charlo Strozzi e figliuola di Simone Guadagni in su la quale scivero con [. . .] mio afare di debitori e creditori e richordi mi da dalanno incominciano questo dì 8 di febraio 1486 segnato A.' For other examples of a widow's purchases see P. Renee Bernstein, 'In Widow's Habit: Women between Convent and Family in Sixteenth-Century Milan', *Sixteenth-Century Journal*, 25, n. 4 (1994), 787–807.

48 E. Currie, 'The Fashions of the Florentine Court: Wearing, Making and Buying Clothing, 1560–1620', Ph.D. diss., University of Sussex, 2004, 124.

49 C. Collier Frick, *Dressing Renaissance Florence: Families, Fortunes, and Fine Clothing*, Baltimore, 2002, 123.

50 Prato, Archivio di stato, Archivio Datini b. 606, Quaderno di spese di casa compagnia di Firenze. Datini, b. 421: 'Quaderno di casa seg. B. compagnia di Pisa.' Further household accounts are in b. 612, 613 and 618 and b. 212–3. See also Federigo Melis, *Aspetti della vita economica medievale: studi nell'archivio Datini di Prato*, Siena, 1962.

51 Prato, Archivio di stato, Archivio Datini, b. 613, ff. 8–9v.

52 Prato, Archivio di stato, Archivio Datini, 606, f. 99v. Piero di Polo was the launderer. The most expensive items to wash were the *tovaglie* and the *lenzuole*. These were 2 for 1 soldo and 3 for 3 soldi respectively.

53 Melis, 1962, 373–4.

54 Melis, 1962, 374.

55 Prato, Archivio di stato, Archivio Datini, b. 213, f. 11.

56 Prato, Archivio di stato, Archvio Datini, b. 213, f. 10.

57 Prato, Archivio di stato, Archivio Datini, b. 213: Di Francesco di Marcho proprio tenuto per Lionardo . . . nell'anno 1408; f. 10r: '1408 16 Febraio, Sabato: Per iii staia di paniocho chonpero Francesco da uno lavoratore in merchato s. vi lo staio l. una s. xiii. Per 7 staia 1.4 dazo chompero Francesco in merchato da più persone . . . Per 6 staia de spelta compero Francesco da Chaponacco per soldi x lo staio . . . Per ii mazi di menta ad denari iiii l'uno e per iiii mazi de pori ad vi l'una . . . per fare ghobernare al barbiere.'

58 V. Rosati, ed., 'Le lettere di Margarita Datini a Francesco di Marco', *Archivio storico pratese*, 50 (1974), 3–93; 52 (1976), 25–152.

59 Haas, 1998, 144.

60 Francesco di Matteo Castellani, *Ricordanze I: Ricordanza A (1436–1459)*, ed. G. Ciappelli, Florence, 1992 and *Ricordanze II: Quaternuccio e giornale B (1459–1485)*, ed. G. Ciappelli, Florence, 1995.

61 Frick, 2002, 117–19.

62 Castellani, 1992, I, 8.

63 Castellani, 1992, I, 8, n. 20.

64 Castellani, 1992, I, 22.

65   Castellani, 1992, I, 10.

66   Castellani, 1992, I, 64 and 68.

67   See the account drawn up with Mariotto, 'Speziale alla palla' where payment was made partly in cash and partly in kind, in Castellani, 1992, I, 71. In order to gain a true valuation of the grain, it was 'stimata in piaza'.

68   Castellani, 1992, I, 91.

69   Castellani, 1992, I, 10.

70   Castellani, 1995, II, 38 and 92.

71   For payments to the wet nurse of Castellani's son, Niccolò, see Castellani, 1992, I, 113–14. She was paid 20 grossi a month. Her pay was docked when she became pregnant herself as the quality of her milk was thought to have suffered. The same terms were agreed with monna Orsina, the wife of a shoemaker in 1460. See Castellani 1995, II, 136–7.

72   Castellani, 1995, II, 105 and 142.

73   Castellani, 1995, II, 128. Luigi Pulci took Niccolò to the school on his first day since he was good friends with the teacher.

74   Castellani, 1992, I, 77.

75   Castellani, 1992, I, 112.

76   Castellani, 1992, I, 112.

77   Frick, 2002, 117–22.

78   Frick, 2002, 122.

79   Frick, 2002, 131.

80   Castellani, 1992, I, 145 and 1995, II, 36.

81   Castellani, 1992, I, 153.

82   Castellani, 1995, II, 161 and 163.

83   Castellani, 1995, II, 211.

84   Castellani, 1995, II, 69.

85   Castellani, 1992, I, 49 and 75.

86   Castellani, 1992, I, 107 and 112.

87   Castellani, 1992, I, 78.

88   Castellani, 1992, I, 102–3. It is worth noting that Castellani rarely defaulted on payments to his suppliers. When he bought 5 florins worth of high-quality dark red cloth from Franceso Benciardi in November 1444 he promised to pay for the material by the end of January. He made the first payment on 4 February via one of his servants. On the 20th of the month, the vendor's brother came to Castellani's house to collect the final three gold florins. See Castellani, 1992, I, 82.

89   Castellani, 1992, I, 105.

90   Castellani, 1992, I, 142.

91   Castellani, 1992, I, 81.

92   Castellani, 1992, I, 100.

93   Castellani, 1992, I, 101.

94   See Ciappelli's useful discussion in Castellani, 1992, I, 40.

95   Castellani, 1995, II, 27.

96   Castellani, 1995, II, 28.

97   Castellani 1995, II, 58.

98   Castellani, 1995, II 58.

99   Castellani, 1995, II, 53.

100 Castellani, 1992, I, 132.

101 Castellani, 1992, I, 140.

102 Castellani, 1995, II, 65. Manuele 'ebreo' often loaned Castellani money, accepting jewels as pawn pledges in return. In 1451, Castellani sent an emerald and a sapphire over to Manuele via the Captain of the Guards, Giovanni Cafferecci, and received 50 gold florins in return. See Castellani, 1992, I, 146.

103 R. K. Marshall, *The Local Merchants of Prato: Small Entrepreneurs in the Late Medieval Economy*, Baltimore, 1999, 96–7.

104 Castellani, 1992, I, 143–4, 148.

105 Castellani, 1992, I, 51–2 and 1995, II, 60.

106 Castellani, 1992, I, 142–3 and 1995, II, 68.

107 Castellani, 1995, II, 65.

108 Castellani, 1992, I, 131. On this figure see I. Walter, 'Cafferecci, Giovanni', *Dizionario biografico degli italiani*, 16, Rome, 1973, 263–4.

109 Castellani, 1995, II, 38.

110 Castellani, 1995, II, 149.

111 Castellani, 1995, II, 62.

112 Castellani, 1995, II, 91.

113 Castellani, 1995, II, 52.

114 Castellani, 1995, II, 63.

115 Castellani 1992, I, 86.

116 G. Luzzatto, 'Il costo della vita a Venezia nel trecento', in C. M. Cipolla, ed., *Storia dell'economia italiana*, Turin, 1959, 1, 409–24. For an important discussion of the Venetian domestic interior and material culture see P. Fortini Brown, *Private*

Lives in Renaissance Venice: Art, Architecture and the Family, New Haven and London, 2004.

117 L. Lotto, Il libro di spese diverse (1538–1556), ed. P. Zampetti, Venice, 1969. The Priuli volume is in Archivio di Stato, Venice, Archivio Marcello Grimani Giustinian, Donà 171, f. 1: 'Jesus Maria, 1535 a dì primo marzo cunti et spese spenduda per mi Francesco di Prioli fo de messer Jacomo principiado del 1512 adì Marzo che fu dela morte de mio padre fin questo zorno in spesa di bocha, in vestir et in altra cosa come apar in libri . . . d. 4384 l. 4 s. 6.'

118 On the Priuli family see J. Fletcher and R. Mueller, 'Bellini and the Bankers: The Priuli Altarpiece for San Michele in Isola, Venice', in Isda, Venice, Burlington Magazine, 147 (2005), 5–15.

119 Priuli, f. 119: 'a dì primo marzo 1535 . . . Messer Jacopo Marin mio suocero die dar per resto de la mia dotta . . . per saldo di quelo come apar . . . carta 91 . . . d. 1069'.

120 Priuli, f. 126: '1535 . . . magistro Jacomo Adriaticho maistro de Camilo die aver adì 14 Fevrer 1531 che fu el primo dì de quaresima che principio andar ala sua scuola Camilo mio fiolo qual lo (?)aiordo a messer Padre Carolo Retino piovano de San Tomaso per pretio de ducati do correnti come per uno suo conte asegnationi apar mettere per far notta a 7 agosto 1537, die avere per lui medimo per saldo di questo porto . . . d. 10 l.–s.2'.

121 Priuli, f. 15v, '8 Auosto detto 1535 . . . uno libretto de soneti del Burchieloe e del grillo in conto per Camilo . . . s.3; f. 21: 1535 adì 25 settembre . . . per uno libro de carta bona ligado de le epistole de Marco Tulio Cicero per Camilo; f. 43: 1536 a dì 18 luio . . . Per uno Vergilio in stampa d'Aldo vechie per Camilo moi fio . . . l.1'.

122 Priuli, f. 158: '1535 . . . Madona mia madre die dar adì 20 fevrer per conto a lei per spender per el mio andar a Este che ge lassai . . . d. 1 l. 5 s. 16; f. 158v: Madona mia madre a l'incontro die aver adì ultimo fevrer per più speze ha fatto in più sorte in

speze de bocha, in legne et altre speze in casa val . . . d. 1 l. 5 s. 16'.

123 Priuli, f. 145.

124 Priuli, f. 181: '1536 . . . a dì 15 Januer per la mia parte de quatro boletini in 8 copagni a nn. 4561, 4562, 4563, 4564. In el lotto boletini e danari vale et sono . . . l.1 s.11 . . . 1537 adì 15 Marzo per uno bolettini per mità con messer Zuan Bastio in nome ali do compari gobi al n. 4225. Val la mia parte l.1 s.11; f. 181v: Laus deo 1537, Lotto mezi in più volte die aver a dì 27 Settembre per loro medesimi porto avanti per saldo di questo come apar . . . d. 134 l.4 s.5.'

125 Priuli, ff. 23v and 25.

126 Priuli, f. 24v: 'a dì primo novembre 1535 . . . Per l'emosine per l'anema de morti s.8; f. 26v: 21 Novembre detto 1535 . . . Per mandar a tuor el porcho a Martenna, per la boletta a Mestre s.6 et per el datio in questa terra . . . et per la barcha . . . per conto ala pala . . . et per sal quartaruoli . . . et conto al masa porcho in tuto, l.4 s.2; f. 27: a dì 27 Novembre detto 1535 . . . per pietre e polveri de garofali e zafarano et spetie per el porche . . . s.10.'

127 Priuli, f. 29: 'a dì primo Zener 1535 Sabado . . . Per bon' anno a madona mia madre l.6, a Zizilia mia suor l.2.8, a Juana mia suor l.2.8, a Camilo moi fio l.1.4, in tutto d.1 l. 5 s. 16; a dì detto per bon'anno a la nana de Domenego moi fio s.20, a Lugretia s.4, a Paula s.4, a Marco Antonio regazo s.6, in tutto l.1 s.14; a dì detto per bon'anno a Magistro Alezandro Marangoni li de Zizilia s.8 et conto a Agnolin fachin da cha' Marin s.4, in tuto s. 14; a dì detto per bon'anno a dona Orsola nana de Juana intra Zizilia et mi l. 1 s.4.'

128 Priuli, f. 31: '22 Januar detto 1535 . . . Per far metter 12 utii in portego et in le camere s.10 . . . per una sponsa per el portego s.5 . . . Per far meter 4 fiube per candeloti in portego per la festa s.9.'

129 Priuli, f. 2: 'a dì 26 detto Marzo 1535: Per conto a dona Orsola nana per la festa s.12'.

130 Priuli, f. 1v: 'Primo marzo 1535 . . . A Zizilia per confezarse . . . l.1 s.2; f. 35–35v: 8 April

1536: Per confezarse s.24 et l'emosine s. 4; f. 36 . . Per uno oficio de la settimana santa per mi s.16 . . . f. 36: Per uno oficio de la nostra donna per Madona mia madre . . . s.16.' There is some confusion over whether 'oficio' refers to a payment for a mass or for a book of prayers. Given an earlier reference on f. iv, 12 March 1535 to the purchase of 'uno oficio de¹a madona picolo per mi' it seems likely to mean the latter.

131 Priuli, f. 41 '26 Zugno 1536 . . . Per conto ala detta Zizilia per confesarse per el giubileo . . . s.6.'

132 Priuli, f. 39v: '3 Zugno detto 1536: Per conto a Zizilia per andar in Sensa in ducati v; per pagar la Senza a più persone come per uno libretto de memorie del 1536 a par val . . . l.4 s.10.' Priuli also paid 8 soldi, 'per barca per andar in Sensa'.

133 Priuli, f. 6: 'A dì 4 detto Marzo 1535: Ala detta (Zizilia) per spender in Sensa . . . l.3 s.6; f. 40: A dì 4 Zugno detto 1536 . . . Per conto a Zizilia per tenir in borsa per andar a Sensa per spendere l.1.'

134 Priuli, f. 134v: 1535 Messer Polo Marin mio cugnado die avere a dì 14 Marzo per spese facte per mì in Sensa e prima per rassa bianca braza 6¹/₂ a soldi 9 el braza l.2.18.6. Et per rassa festechina braza 5¹/₂ a soldi 13 el braza, l.3.11.6 e per rassa verde braza 1 soldi 15 et per tela per camise braza 6¹/₂ a soldi 11, l. 3.11.6 et per rassa beretina braza a soldi 7 el braza l.3.1 et per una bareta per Camilo s. 24. In tutto val l.15.1.6.

135 Priuli, f. 39v: 'A 3 dì Zugno detto 1536 . . . Per una saliera per tavola de vetro s.5.'

136 Priuli, f. 43: '1536 a dì 18 Luio . . . Per far consar uno par de ochiali a Zizilia mia suor . . . s.3.'

137 Priuli, f. 14: 'a dì 24 detto Luio 1535 . . . Per conto a messer Maphio de Mapleci medego per Zizilia mia mogier scudo uno d'oro'; he returned on August 8 and was again paid a scudo d'oro, f. 15v. During the period of her illness there were also considerable purchases of veal on her behalf.

138 Priuli, f. 61v: 'Primo April 1537, domenega il giorno de Pasqua: dì detto per lemosina in più volte . . . s.4; Dì detto per do para de galine l.3; per marzepane s.12, per zuccero fin s.18, per do coste de tersie s.8, per cunandoli s.7, per zupana s.2, per conto a madona per spender s.36, per barcha per mandar a chiamar compari s.4. In tutto l.7.7 per il parto de Zizilia mia mogier fese una putta a dì 30 di marzo 1537 a hore tre de note vel circha il venere santo venendo il sabato santo la qual fu messo nome Querina et Santa et morite a dì primo del aprile a hore 9 vel il giorno di Pasqua val d.1 l.1 s.34.'

139 Priuli, f. 61v: 'Per spese per la sepultura de mia fia Querina sopradetta. Prima per una scatola grande per meterla dentro s.6, per do torse de l 1¹/₂ l'uno s.36, et terza lira de candele s.12 et per conto al piovano per far aportar largha in giezia de Sant'Antonio et per prete et torzi l.3 in tutto l.5 s. 14; per conto a dona Mara la comara la levo d. 1 s. 11.'

140 Priuli, f. 62: 4 April 1537 '. . . Per uno sedino de indolse per Zizilia . . . l.1 s. 6.' On the role of poultry and other delicacies in pregnancy and confinement see J. M. Musacchio, *The Art and Ritual of Childbirth in Renaissance Italy*, New Haven and London, 1999.

141 Priuli, f. 3v: 'Primo April 1535 . . . Per uno polaruol per il manego de osso per Zizilia per cusir s. 4.'

142 Priuli, f. 141–v.

143 Priuli, f. 164–v.

144 Priuli, f. 8v: 'adì 2 Zugno 1525 . . . Per una quarta e meza de raso bianco per far uno para de zocholi per Zizilia . . . l.2 s. 6. A month later he paid for the 'fatura de v para de zocholi di razo bianco per Zizilia . . . l.1.14 . . . Per fatura de uno para de scarpe de razo bianco per Domenego mio fio . . . s. 8.'

145 Priuli, f. 69v: 'Primo settembre 1537 . . . Per una volpe bianca con su con la testa da portar in mano per Zizilia l.7.10 et per la scatola s. 14 . . . l. 2 s. 4.'

146 Priuli, f. 1: 'Primo Marzo 1535 . . . per una capa de pano de rosa grossa per Marco

Antonio regazo l.4 s.4 et per il comandador per lo incanto s. 1 . . . l. 4 s. 4.'

147 Priuli, f. 64v: 'adì 16 detto Marzo 1537 . . . Per uno letezolo et uno cavazal et uno cusino de piuma per la massera, comprata sopra l'inchanto di sopra gastaldo d.12 et per spesa de comandadori . . . et per el fachin porto a chasa s.2 in tuto d.2 l.–s.11.'

148 Priuli, f. 8: '22 Mazo detto 1535 . . . Per uno fil de perla n.77 non tropo grosa ne iovene et uno balaseta con tre perle su l'incanto di Iudei d. 9 et conto ali savi per lo incanto s. 10 d. 9–l.–s. 10.'

149 Priuli, f. 24v: 'a dì primo Novembre 1535 . . . Per una corda de paternostri ala parisina fatta in fransa d'oro . . . et per lo incanto ali comandadori di sopra gastaldi s.16 et per conto al maser s.4 in tutto d. 11 l. 3 s. 2.'

150 Priuli, f. 10: 'adì 12 Zugno detto 1535 . . . Per oro . . . de far ligar el balasso in pendente per Zizilia . . . et per fatura per ligarlo et far el pendente conto a magistro Lunardo de Piero ioielier per fatura del detto l. 9 . . . in tutto d. 2 l.-s.9.'

151 Priuli, f. 166v: '1536 . . . Francesco Comandador die aver adì 23 settembre per danari mi ha prestato in questo iorno per andar a Este l. 3 . . . adì 26 ottobre per imprestido da lui 5 ducati d'oro . . . adì 18 fevrier per saldo de questo porto analli come apar in questo'.

152 Priuli, f. 124 and 124v.

153 Priuli, f. 183: '1536 . . . Francesco Comandador die dar a dì 19 Fevrer per resto tratto da driedo come apar . . . l. 2 s. 3; dì ditto per haver venduto uno tapedo da tavola per d.13; mi ha datto in questo zorno d.10 resta darmi d.3 . . .'

154 Priuli, f. 154: '1535 . . . Madona Bernardina fiola de Magistro Almoro oreze die dar a dì 22 de Febraro per conto a lei per imprestido sopra una peliza de veludo negro la qual mi ha da commisione de venderla per ducati 22 la qual peliza e fodra de dossi et hola datta a Francesco comandador per venderla val scudi 5 d'oro . . .'

155 Priuli, f. 6: '4 detto Mazo 1535 . . . conto Zizilia in bagatini . . . s.4'

156 Priuli, f. 9v: 'A dì 5 Zugno detto 1535 . . . conto Zizilia mia mogier per portar a Campo San Piero . . . e per spender mosenigi 4 . . . l. 4 s.16.'

157 Priuli, f. 11: '1535 a dì 22 Zugno . . . conto a Zizilia per comprar cordelle per Domenego mio fio, s. 1'.

158 Priuli, f. 58–58v: '2 Fevrer 1536 . . . Per conto a Zizilia per zuogar . . . l.1.' She received a further 12 soldi 'per zuogar' a few days later on 11 February. That same day Priuli paid 4 soldi, 'per barcha per venir la sera da Cha Marin'. He and Cecilia made several trips by boat to Cha' Marin that week, perhaps because one of Cecilia's relatives had just given birth to a baby girl.

159 Priuli, f. 26v.

160 Priuli, f. 28v: 'per barche conto a Marco per vogar mi et Zizilia a cha' Venier per el sposar dela fia de Messr Lunardo Venier'.

161 Priuli, ff. 36v and 18: '1535 a dì 3 Settembre . . . Per barche per Zizilia per andar a Murano . . . s.14.'

162 Priuli, ff. 146v and 166v.

163 Priuli, f. 19: '12 Settembre 1525 . . . Per barcha per veder la festa de i pugni . . . s.4.'

164 Priuli, f. 56v: 'a dì 10 Zener detto 1536 . . . Per tenir a batezemo uno fio de S. Stefano barcharuol el qual fu messo nome Juan Antonio et fisi tenirlo a Camilo mio fio per non poter andar per esser coseglio . . . s.12.' Priuli also acted as godfather to the daughter of Mariso Rigo depentor a Santa Stai on 14 October 1536, f. 50. He only paid 4 soldi on that occasion.

165 Priuli, f. 127v: '1535 . . . a Ser Jacomo Adriaticho die haver per haver insegnatto a più fiol de dona Ruosa barcharuola a leser el libro che così promisi ala detta dona Ruosa per haverla tatto mio fio Domenego quando el nasette chel stava mal et inferma . . . l.3'

166 Priuli, f. 33v: 'Marzo 1536 a dì 12 detto per elemosina conto a dona Ruosa barcharuola l.3. 12 et fu che li ditte la sua vesture mi impegno per avanti in driedo per el maridar de sua fia Paula.' The list of payments paid to dona Ruosa' on behalf of her

husband are listed on f. 146v; the loan of 4 lire to repair the boat seems to have been set against payments made for a range of boat trips, ff. 166–166v: '1536 . . . Stephano barcharuoli die dar a dì 12 agosto danari imprestadi per consar la sua barca l.4.'

CHAPTER 9

1 For Eleanora see L. Chiappini, *Eleanora d'Aragona, prima duchessa di Ferrara*, Rovigo, 1956.

2 There is an increasing literature on the patronage of aristocratic women at court. See S. E. Reiss and D. G. Wilkins, *Beyond Isabella: Secular Women Patrons of Art in Renaissance Italy*, Kirskville, Mo., 2001. See also E. Welch, 'Women as Patrons and Clients in the Courts of Northern Italy', in L. Panizza, ed., *Women in Italian Renaissance Culture and Society*, Oxford, 2000, 18–34. One of the key roles that court women played was ensuring adequate food supplies for their spouse's city. See, for example, the study by B. L. Edelstein, 'Nobildonne napoletane e committenza: Eleanora d'Aragona ed Eleanora di Toledo a confronto', *Quaderni storici*, n. s. 104 (2000), 295–330. For Isabella d'Este's interventions on the Mantuan market in periods of famine see G. Malacarne, *Sulla mensa del principe: alimentazione e banchetti alla corte dei Gonzaga*, Modena, 2000, 92.

3 A. Luzio, *Isabella d'Este e Francesco Gonzaga: promessi sposi*, Milan, 1908, 29: La Vostra Illustrissima Signoria scrive pigliare admiratione del mancamento del vivere in casa. Sia certa quella che si fa tuto quello se po' et non se ge mancha de diligentia . . . La Vostra Excellentia po' havere informatione che'l fu facto l'ordinario su bocche 500 et cum la spesa de la biava per cavali, che Vostra Signoria ne ha più di 650, fu visto ge bisognava per le dicte bocche 500 libre 770 la septimana di ordinario non ponendoli pane et vino che

etiam di questi se ne compra. Posa g'è la resistentia de fori de quella che se spende uno terzo più et a questo se attende che'l non manchi a Vostra Excellentia. Secondo il spenditore de la corte le libre 770 che sono limitate per l'ordinario non se hanno et per questo accade che se ha desagio et molte fiate mancano le robe a la corte.'

4 Malacarne, 2000, 34: 'Vostra Signoria si sapia che gli è stato necessario restare cento nonanta due boche, che hano pan, vino o carne, e boche vintioto de elimosina, setantaquatro cani e cento trenta uni cavallo, cussì limitati; ben perhò c'è mala satisfactione de molti. On courts structures in the sixteenth century see G. Guerzoni, 'Ricadute occupazionali ed impatti economici della committenza artistica delle corti estensi tra quattro e cinquecento', in S. Cavaciocchi, ed., *Economia e arte: secc. XIII–XVIII*, Florence, 2004, 187–230.

5 E. Welch, *Art and Authority in Renaissance Milan*, New Haven, 1995, 210.

6 R. Tamalio, *Federico Gonzaga alla corte di Francesco I di Francia nel carteggio privato con Mantova (1515–1517)*, Paris, 1994, 53.

7 A. Pedrazzoli, 'La Marchesa Isabella d'Este Gonzaga a diporto sul lago di Garda colla sua corte', *Archivio storico lombardo*, 17 (1890), 866–78.

8 G. Porro, 'Preventivo delle spese pel ducato di Milano nel 1476', *Archivio storico lombardo*, anno 5 (1878), 130–4. See also G. Barbieri, 'Gottardo Panigarola mercante e spenditore sforzesco', *Atti e memorie del terzo congresso storico lombardo*, Milan, 1939, 311–26.

9 L. Montalto, *La corte di Alfonso I di Aragona: vesti e gale*, Naples, 1922.

10 Montalto, 1922, 9.

11 G. Malacarne, *Le feste del principe*, Modena, 2002, 242.

12 Malacarne, 2000, 23: 'Isabella Marchionissa Mantuae, etc. Per vigour delle presenti nostre volemo et commettemo alli Rasonati nostri et Maestri de'Conti, che al Spectabile Hieronimo Bressanino nostro

Spenditore, nel saldare delle sue ragioni ogni anno gli accettino et accettare debbano ogni spesa di qualunque sorte et summa de denari che lui ha fatto et farà per bisogno nostro et della nostra Corte per vigore de'mandati overo bollette signate di man proprie d'uno delli infrascritti, cioè li spectabili Zohan Maria Capilupo Scalco, Carlo Ghisi Maestro di Guardaroba, Hieronimo Andrea Sio, Maestro di Stalla et Francesco Cusatio Fattore Generale et filze che sono et saranno signate per loro et successori suoi . . . xv Decembris 1523.'

13 G. Guerzoni, 'From the History of Prices to the Histories of Price: Social Networks and Court Strategies in Sixteenth-Century Italy', in M. O'Malley and E. Welch, eds., *The Material Renaissance*, forthcoming.

14 Welch, 1995, 251.

15 W. Kirkendale, *Emilio Cavalieri, 'gentilhuomo romano': His Life and Letters, His Role as Superintendent of All the Arts at the Medici Court*, Florence, 2001.

16 Malacarne, 2000, 70.

17 C. M. Brown with A. M. Lorenzoni, *Isabella d'Este and Lorenzo da Pavia: Documents for the History of Art and Culture in Renaissance Mantua*, Geneva, 1982.

18 E. Welch, 'The Art of Expenditure: The Court of Paola Malatesta Gonzaga in Fifteenth-Century Mantua', *Renaissance Studies*, 16 (2002), 306–17.

19 Zigliolo was also used by other court women in Ferrara to make purchases on their behalf. In a letter of 28 February 1496, Anna Sforza, the wife of Alfonso d'Este, asked him to buy velvet from Florence for her: Archivio di Stato, Modena, Amministrazione dei Principi 589, Anna Sforza to Girolamo Zuliolo ducali camererio: 'havemo visto lo advixo che ne dati de quelle veludo incarnate ne farite singular piacere a farne venire da Fiorenze o donde vi pare essere meglio fornito. Ma bene havessimo molto carissimo che poi che vuy fati la spexa de mandarlo a tuore fuore che ne facesti venire tanto che ne facesse una

camora cum le maneghe ma che sia tanto bello quanto sia possibile et se cum suportatione gli ne fussi tante che oltra la camora ne facessimo una sbernia riceverisimo grandissimo piacere. Al facto delle facende de me scriviti per che qua da nuy non se raxona del nostro venire et non possemo sapere el quando non stati de scriverne quando sia il tempo. Perchè havemo intexo che Zohanne vostro fratello e ritornato da Franza sapeti gli dessimo comissione che il portassi certi sorti de paternostri et havendoli portati ne fariti singular piacere a manderceli qua et a vuy ne oferimo. Belriguadi xxviii februari 1496.'

20 A. Luzio and R. Renier, 'Il lusso di Isabella d'Este, Marchesa di Mantova: il guardaroba di Isabella d'Este', *Nuova antologia*, series 4, 63 (1896), 453: 'protestandove che non habiati a retornare alcuno indreto, perchè comparate queste cose, s'el ve restasse dinari in mane, spendeteli in qualche cadenella o cosa gallante et nova, et in quello vui judicareti ce habia a gustare. Et se questi dinari non bastaranno, meteteli de li vostri, che subito ve li restituiremo et saremo più contenta de esser vostra debitrice che creditrice, purchè ne portati diverse gallanterie, ma in specie queste sono le cose che volemo . . . cavar de sotto terra qualche cosetta galantissima, che non ce potresti fare cosa più grata.'

21 C. M. Brown, 'Purché la sia cosa che representi antiquità: Isabella d'Este Gonzaga e il mondo greco-romano' *Civiltà mantovano*, 30 (1995), 83: perchè essendo nui de natura appetitose, le cose ne sono più chare quanto più presto le havemo.'

22 Brown, 1982, 79: 'perchè non curamo di spesa a li nostri appetiti'.

23 Malacarne, 2002, 239.

24 Luzio and Renier, 1896c, 267: '. . . Per il nepote del barbiero regio habbemo a questi dì passati una lettera de Vostra Signoria et per essa sei scuffiotti de seta et de oro de nova foggia . . . per tanto pregamo Vostra Signoria se contenta quando qualche nova foggia di abendare la testa li

occorerà, che semo certissimo non man-
carne mai per essere Vostra Signoria fonte
et origine de tucte le belle foggie d'Italia,
de mandarne qualche una bella et che li
piaccia . . .

25 Malacarne, 2002, 243.

26 On Isabella's letter writing see D. Shemek
'In Continuous Expectation: Isabella's
Epistolary Desire', in D. Looney and D.
Shemek, eds, *Phaethon's Children: The Este
Court and its Culture in Early Modern Italy*,
Tempe, Ariz., forthcoming; and 'Isabella
d'Este and the Properties of Persuasion', in
A. Crabb and J. Couchman, eds, *Form and
Persuasion in Early Modern Women's Letters
Across Europe*, Brookfield, Vermont, forth-
coming. Professor Shemek is currently
preparing an edition of Isabella d'Este's
letters for Chicago University Press.

27 A. M. Lorenzoni, 'Contributo allo studio
delle fonti Isabelliane dell'archivio di stato
di Mantova', *Atti e memori dell'accademia
virgiliana di Mantova*, n. s. 47 (1979),
97–135.

28 Brown, 1982, 68–9.

29 Luzio, 1908b, 11.

30 Luzio, 1908b, 30: 'zoye bone et belle per 8
mille ducati, una credenza d'argento de
meglio de 2 mille, puoi scodere quelle
nostre sono in Venesia ne le mani di Francisco Baldi, el balasso che ha Lorenzo in
Firenza, che seranno per conto de 7 mille
ducati e contanti a noy, e 3 mille ducati
portara ley, apresso per il resto insino a li
25 mille . . . La lista de l'altre cose che oltra
il dote vol dare Madama a la Marchesana
so mi che serrà da 8 a 10 mille ducati . . .'

31 Luzio, 1908b, 36: 'scilicet vestes quam-
plures ex serico diversorum colorum et ex
auro et argento et ex utroque egregie lab-
oratas, drapamentaque quamplurima
ornatissima laborata, et cofinos, capsas et
forzerios auratos et non auratos, aliaque
multiplicia ornamenta et donaria diversarum qualitatum et conditionum, pretii
et valoris ducatorum novemillium auri in
totum . . .'

32 E. Welch, 'Between Milan and Naples:

Ippolita Maria Sforza, Duchess of Cal-
abria', in David Abulafia, ed., *The French
Descent into Renaissance Italy (1494–1495)*,
Aldershot, 1995, 123–36.

33 C. Brown, '*Per dare qualche splendore a la
gloriosa città di Mantua: Documents for the
Antiquarian Collection of Isabella d'Este*',
Rome, 2002, 120.

34 Luzio and Renier, 1896b, 312–13: 'Illustrissimo Signore mio patre observandissimo.
Quando io venni a principio in questa
illustrissima casa mi fu deputato de provisione sei mille ducati d'oro l'anno per il
mio vestire et de le mie donne et che
havessi etiam a maritare le doncelle et dare
la provisione a tutti li servitori et donne da
li compagni in fora, cioè dui gentilhuo-
mini et ultra di questo la corte mi faceva
le spese a circa cento bocche. Doppo, per
essere in magiore libertà de acrescere et
sminuire la famiglia a mio modo, conde-
scendendoli etiam volontariamente lo
Illustrissimo Signor mio consorte a per-
suasione di suoi factori, per levarsi in tutto
il peso dalle spalle mi furono deputati dua
millia ducati per le spese, includendoli
etiam le spese de li compagni, li quali me
furono assignati in questo modo: li sei
mille de la provisione sopra il dato de la
macina, mille delle spese sopra una gabella,
et per li altri mille mi fu data la corte et
possessione de Letopaledenao, sì che in
tutto ascendono a la summa de octo mille
ducati. L'è vero che poi per industria mia
et de miei la intrata de dicta corte è
accresciuta circa altri mille ducati et ho de
li avanzi acquistata la corte de Castion
Mantuano et dil Bondenazo per forma che
al presente mi ritrovo havere de entrata
circa due millia et cinquecento ducati
l'anno, ma ho etiam forsi cinquanta
bocche più che non furono deputate. L'è
vero che'l Signore mio mi ha poi dato
alcuni altri loci per mio spasso, come è Sac-
chetta et Porto, ma la intrata non supera la
spesa gran facto, anzi qualche volta se
spende di più, havendoli a tenere reparati,
sì che questo è quanto posso significare alla

Excellentia Vostra per sua satisfactione, in bona gratia di la quale me raccomando sempre. Mantua XVIII Maj 1502.' See also the discussion in Shemek's forthcoming work on, 'Isabella d'Este and the Properties of Persuasion'.

35 Malacarne, 2000, 92 .

36 Malacarne, 2000, 125: 'Io mi trovo haver circa mille et 500 pesi de riso da vendere; et perché io mi penso che sarìa facile ch'el se smaltisse lì in Ferrara o per bisogno della terra o per via di qualche mercatante, ho voluto darne aviso a Vostra Magnificentia et mandarlene la mostra, acciò che le pensarà che il detto riso si possa spazare lì, el si mandi poi a quelle bande, perché quando anche non si ne possa cavare el denaro per quella via, ho designato di mandarlo a Venetia. . . .'

37 For example, in 1512, Isabella made a donation to her husband's cook, Petro Antonio called Mantelina, of the revenues from a local tax belonging to her farm of Letpaludani worth 13.5 ducats. See Malacarne, 2000, 32.

38 Luzio and Renier, 1896b, 314.

39 Archivio di Stato, Mantua, Archivio Gonzaga, b. 2994, f. 5v, n. 19, Isabella d'Este to Francesco II Gonzaga, 12 June 1506: '. . . mi sono maravigliata che volendosi vostra excellentia valere de le nostre zolie mi le habbi rechieste per valuta de mille ducati cum tanto rispecto et scusa perche li bisogni suoi non quelle ch'io ho che tutte sono sue ma voria potermi far zoglia per compiacerla. Se qualche volta ho monstrato renitentia è stato o quando se hano voluto prestar ad altri o si hanno voluto impignare senza ponere ordine a riscoterle che per altro li pari nostri non debeno tenere zoglie se non per una munitione da servirsine ne li bisogni et pero molto voluntieri mando a vostra excellentia quelle che la mi ha rechiesto acciò che in questo importante bisogno di la peste se ne possi servir a modo suo ma non restaro per interesse suo di raccordarli che la pensi de mettere ordine che non solum queste

ma quelle che gia tanto tempo hebe Cesare da Milano siano rescosse. Vostra excellentia scia et quanto tempo e quanto ne furno prestate al conte Philippo Rosso et che se non fusse stata d' inportunità mia quando vostra signoria era fora di casa che anchara seriano tutte in pegno et in periculo di perderle. Restolli una roxetta che mai ho potuto havere se ben e stato da li mei sollicitato non seria male che vostra excellentia gli ne facesse fare ricordo per Bartolomeo perchè forse gli haveria magior rispeco chel non ha a me. Io faccio l'officio mio in persuaderla a tenere la robba sua in casa. Io facci mo il voler suo. El Cusatro consignara a vostra signoria dui zoielli extimati per magistro Zoan Francesco et magistro Niccolo ducati mille quatrocento fiorini . . . Sachette . . . XII Junii 1506.'

40 Luzio and Renier, 1896b, 316: 'che serrà magior la vergogna che'l danno'.

41 Luzio and Renier, 1896b, 315–16; 1908b, 315: 'Io sono sempre disposta ad obedire la Signoria Vostra in omne cosa, ma perchè forsi la non se ricorda che sono in pigno tutte le altre a Venetia, m'è parso significarli che gli sono non solum quelle che me ha datto Vostra Signoria, ma anche quelle ch'io portai a marito et ho comparato io doppo. Il che non dico perchè facia differentia da le sue a le mie, ma perchè la intendi el tutto, per modo ch'io non ho in casa se non quarto zoglieli e el balasso che Vostra Excellentia comparatte quando io era de parto de la prima putta, lo diamante grande, el favorito, et quello che ultimamente la me dette; che quando se impignassero questi io restaria in tutto priva de zoglie da poter portare e me serìa forza ridurmi a vestire de Negro, perchè vestendo de colore e de brocato una mia para senza zoglie serìa calleffata. La Excellentia Vostra può molto ben pensare ch'io non facio questo discorso se non per honore suo et mio.'

42 S. Ferino-Pagden, *La prima donna del mondo. Isabella d'Este: Fürstin und*

Mäzenatin der Renaissance, Vienna, 1994, 74.

43 J. Cartwright, *Isabella d'Este, Marchioness of Mantua, 1474–1539: A Study of the Renaissance*, London, 1904, II, 344.

44 C. Brown, 'Lo insaciabile desiderio nostro de cose antique: New Documents on Isabella d'Este's Collection of Antiquities', in Cecil Clough, ed., *Cultural Aspects of the Renaissance: Essays in Honour of Paul Oskar Kristeller*, Manchester, 1976, 324–53.

45 A. Portioli, *Le corporazioni artiere e l'archivio della Camera di Commercio a Mantova*, Mantua, 1884.

46 Archivio di Stato, Mantua, Archivio Gonzaga, Gride, Register 5f. 17, 1461, 14 March: 'alia Baldezaar dal fontico che tene in capo del portico anti la intrata della chiesa di Sant Andrea, 1459 del mese de novembre: primo braza cinquanta de citanino cremesino in una peza, octo de cremesino de raso braza, trenta, octo de tela de cremesino, dossi cinquecento de varo novi mezani, armelini otanta duy, libre [. . .] trentasey de zucharo fine, scatole tre de confectione minute de più colori, braze due e mezo de citanino verde, rotuli duy de veleti de bonbaci, onze quatro de botoni tondi d'arzento, paro uno de paternostri de corali, uno de paternostri de corali [. . .] una turchina grande ligata in uno anello vale ducati duy, uno anello cum una granata roto extima ducati uno, anello cum una granato roto d'estima ducati uno, turchine trenta disciolte vale ducati tri, vegete due d'oro valer ducati uno, braza uno [. . .] de perpignano, dozene dece de collarini de setta vale ducati l'uno . . .'

47 Welch, 2002, 306–17.

48 Welch, 2002, 314.

49 E. Welch, 'The Gonzaga Go Shopping: Commercial and Cultural Relationships Between Milan and Mantua in the Fifteenth Century', in L. Chiavoni, G. Ferlisi and M. V. Grassi, eds, *Leon Battista Alberti e il quattrocento: studi in onore di Cecil Grayson e Ernst Gombrich*, Florence, 2001, 269–84.

50 Archivio di Stato, Mantua, Archivio Gonzaga, b. 2994, f. 12v n. 26, 12 January 1507, Isabella d'Este to Bernardino Prospero: 'Spectabile amice . . . Per Francisco Cavallaro nostro vi mandiamo uno ligazo de dinari che sono in tutto libre cento setantanove soldi dece sette de nostra moneta mantuana per il montar de gli confeti havuti da magistro Vincentio secunda la notta qui inclusa quali gli dareti, facendo nostra scusa sel in ha portato discunzo et intendereti quanto mo farano la copeta savomea et panpipati chel mi ha mandato ultimamente a cio che gli possiamo remettere gli dinarii . . . XII Januarii mcvii'

51 A. Luzio, 'Isabella d'Este e i Borgia', *Archivio storico lombardo*, anno 41 series 5, I (1914), 469–553, 673–753, anno 42, series 5.2 (1915), 115–67, 412–64.

52 On Eleanora Orsini Del Balzo see A. M. Lorenzoni, 'Tra Francese e Spagnoli: le fortunose vicende di Eleanora Orsini del Balzo, Marchese di Crotone, atraverso carteggi inediti dell' Archivio Gonzaga', in A. M. Lorenzoni and R. Navarrini, eds, *Per Mantua una vita: studi in memoria di Rita Castagna*, Mantua, 1991, 113–39.

53 A. Luzio and R. Renier, *Mantova e Urbino: Isabella d'Este ed Elisabetta Gonzaga nelle relazioni famigliari e nelle vicende politiche (1471–1539)*, Turin and Rome, 1893, 313:

Presento facto per la Serenissima Signoria:
Primo: octo torze de libre octo l'una
Marzapani octo grandi dorati
Scatolette 29 de confecto de più sorte
Pignatte quatro de zenzerverde
Pignatte due sirupo violato
Ciste quatro grande de pesso de diverse sorte
Mazzi dui de candele de cera de l. xx.

54 Brown, 1982, 213: 'andò a vedere gli vetri alla botega de la Serena et per esser quelli excellenti et rari, li vide con tanto suo diletto et piacere che più non potria desiderare, et al presente ha le più belle cose che già mai l'havesse. Il signor Duca di Ferrara vi era stato de poco inanci et vi

lassò de molti ducati. Madama Illustrissima ha anche ella comprato alcuni vasi molto belli.'

55 Archivio di Stato, Mantua, Archivio Gonzaga, b. 410–B, Fascicolo 35: Libretto di spese diverse fatte in Roma et in altri luoghi per i Signori Gonzaga. See also the discussion in Brown, 2002, 289–90.

56 Brown, 2002, 297.

57 Brown, 2002, 299–300.

58 Brown, 2002, 301.

59 On carriages see G. Gozzadini, 'Dell'origine del uso dei cocchi e di due veronesi in particolare', *Atti e memorie della reale deputazione di storia patria per le provincie di romagna*, II (1863), 199–249.

60 Malacarne, 2000, 67: 'Della ambra per hora non curamo di fare quella spesa. Dell'acqua damaschina che voi scrivete non esserni in Venetia, dubitamo che non s'intendiamo insieme, perché di quelle acque si suole haverne in Venetia in ogni tempo; et perché meglio habbia il concetto nostro, sono acque che vengono di Levante et si conservano in zucchette picole coperte di pagia'

61 Welch, 2001, 269–84.

62 See, for example, the published correspondence between Mantua, Bologna, Venice, Florence and other major centres including B. Furlotti, ed., *Le collezioni Gonzaga: il carteggio tra Bologna, Parma, Piacenza e Mantova (1563–1634)*, Milan, 2000 and D. Sogliani, ed., *Le collezioni Gonzaga: il carteggio tra Roma e Mantova (1587–1612)*, Milan, 2001.

63 Malacarne, 2002, 238: che'l ne còmpari una albernia morella cremesina, una negra et un'altra de qualche stranio collore, che siano bellisime.

64 Malacarne, 2002, 238: 'una albernia de leonato scuro, una negra e un'altra de qualche stranio collore che siano bellissime . . .'

65 Luzio, 1896a, 455: 'Desiderando nui avere una bella fuodera de zebellini per una albernia, volemo ne compriati ottanta che siano in tutta excellentia et beleza, se ben

dovessi circar tutta Venetia, et veder de trovarne uno da portare in mane cum l'osso de la testa, se ben costasse dece ducati, che pur sia bello non ce agravarà la spesa. Et ultra di questo volimo ce mandiate otto braza de raso cremesino del più bello se trovi lì a Venetia et sia da parangone, perchè lo volemo per fare dicta albernia, et per Dio usateli la solita diligentia vostra, chè non potresti fare cosa più grata.' On buying silks from the *paragon* in Venice, see Chapter five.

66 C. Zaffanella, 'Isabella d'Este e la modo del suo tempo', *Civiltà mantovana*, 35 (2000), 72.

67 Zaffanella, 2000, 73: 'uno grande paghamento; et questo accade perché questa terra non fu mai pegio fornita de simile tele che la sia adesso, per non essere el viaggio de Fiandra libero come solevo.'

68 Brown, 2002, 276–7.

69 Brown, 2002, 90–1.

70 Brown, 2002, 92.

71 Brown, 1982, 50: '. . . ali quali li ò auti con grandisima dificultate: sono de uno todesco che li astima asai e non li daria per x ducati e per niente non me li voleva imprestare, m'è stato forca lasareli uno pegno per più de xv. So non piacerano tropo ala Signoria Vostra perché io non li aprecio tropo, così so parirà questo medemo, tuta volta, così ala ventura, li ò voluto dare 3 ducati. Per niente non li vole dare, ancora non valeno tanto. E pù ve mando ancora una ganda d'ambra belisima con certi animaleti dentro che so piacerà molto ala Signoria Vostra ma la non é da vendere: é de uno che la stima molto per avere gran piacere de cose rare, ma me l'ò fata inprestare acò che quela la veda. E che potese avere L paternostri d'anbra che tuti avese dentro qualque cosa como questa ganda sariano una cosa ecelente. Et io faco praticha per averene per via de uno mercadante tedesco mio amicissimo'.

72 Archivio di Stato, Mantua, Archivio Gonzaga, b. 2994, n. 73, 9 April 1507, Isabella d'Este to Angelo Tovalia: 'Magistro

Angelo. Havemo facto rispondere al cognato vostro tutti li denari de che vi erevamo debitrice pcr il brocato e veluto qual nì facesti havere li dì passati e d'il officio e diligentia usata per noi in farce servire molto vi ringratiamo. Vero è che quando havessimo saputo che voy ne lo havesti pagato a principio che lo mandasti non l'haverresimo acceptato a questo pretio perchè a dire il vero il veluto haveria possoto esser di assay melior perfectioni. Et semo certe per la fede havimo in vui quando l'havesti veduto non l'haresti consentito che'l nì fussi mandato. Perho accadendovi in l'avenire tuore cosa alchuna per nui haveremo ad charo che non veniati a pagamento se prima non l'haverimo visto et approbata perchè le cose che voleno per la persona nostra desideremo sieno in excellentia et convenienti a nuii sì come anche le pagamo voluntieri et cortesamente et che sì vere quello vi scrivermi dil veluto, vostro cognato qual l'ha visto vi mi potra anchor dare optima chiareza. Siamo a tutti li vostri piacere sempre apparechiati. Mantua, nono Aprilis mdvii.'

73 D. Thornton, *The Scholar in his Study: Ownership and Experience in Renaissance Italy*, New Haven, 1997, 172.

74 Brown, 1982, 33: '. . . pù giorni fa m'à pregato che volese scrivere à la Eccelencia Vostra che quela me volese concedere questa singulare gracia che quela se degnase de fareme avere la trata de qualque cinquecento sachi tra formento e segala e meio e così . . . Averò pù caro a otenere questa gracia per demostrare a questi da Venecia che abia gracia con la Ecelencia Vostra.'

75 See Chapter ten.

76 Archivio di Stato, Mantua, Archivio Gonzaga, b. 2994, filza 19, f. 62, n. 177. This letter will be published in full by D. Shemek in her forthcoming edition of Isabella's correspondence.

77 Luzio and Renier, 1896d, 683: 'Intendemo essere stato portato novamente de Spagna una gran quantità de guanti de Ocagna,

de'quali siamo al bisogno: ma li vorressimo in tutta bontà, et de quelli de Valenza che sono ben zaldi de dentro et se vedono pigati col reverso de fori. Pregamovi ad volere ben examinarli et farli vedere a qualche altra persona et maxime a Spagnoli che se ne intendono et cognoscono la bontà loro et come voleno essere per uso de donna; et essendo al proposito nostro, spendeteli due ducati et mandateceli per el primo ve occorrerà, cum avvisarne a chi doveremo rispondere li dinari.'

78 Archivio di Stato, Mantua, Archivio Gonzaga, b. 2994, filza 19, f. 25, n. 82: 'Magistro Bernardino. Dessimo a Sanzio dece ducati quando andò in Spagna per comprarni tanti guanti de d'Ocagna per uso nostro et noy medessimo essendo a Ferrara gli parlassimo che ne volesse ben servire. Sono molti giorni che'l ritorno e pur adesso nì ha mandati duodece dozene de cossì tristi che se l'havesse cercata tutta Spagna per tuorli tristi non credimo ne havesse ritrovati tanti. Perhò che a Roma, Genova e Firenze senza comparacion sono megliori et quasì che volendo usare diligentia in Ferrara se ne ritrovaria de cossì buoni et forsi megliori. Per il che havimo deliberato remettergleli a fine che' non extimi che habiamo tanto poco iudicio de guanti che reputiamo questi buoni quali haveressimo tenuti per donare alle donzelle nostre et qualche amice ma noi se avergognaressimo darli a persone che amano et loro non li portariano. Piacevi adunque restituirgeli et dirgli che molto male siamo state servite da luy . . . Sachette XVIII Julii 1506.'

79 M. Bourne, 'Out from the Shadow of Isabella: The Artistic Patronage of Francesco II Gonzaga, Fourth Marquis of Mantua', Ph.D. diss., Harvard University, 1997.

80 Luzio and Renier, 1896d, 683: 'Prego Vostra Signoria voglia mandare de li profumi in bona quantità per donar a queste madimiselle . . . et guanti assai, et un albarello di savonetto da mane, che sia

grande per darne a molte et ancor olio, polvere et acque.'

81 Luzio and Renier, 1896d, 683–4: 'venendo in ragionamento de guanti, Sua Maestà me monstrette certi che aveva in mane, et era uno giorno di festa, la dominicha, e disseme erano di guanti che venivano da Vostra Signoria a lei donati per el Signore Marchese suo cugino quando era qua in Francia, e se li aveva conservati che anchora ne aveva uno altro paro e atiò che più li durassero non li portava se non alle feste per qualche tempo, tanto che erano come novi, poi incomenzava a portarli ogni dì ma la sera li cavava e ne metteva poi de altra sorte per farne più massaria, e questo faceva perchè non ebbe mai guanti de sorte che tanto li piacesseno como questi e gli n'era stato mandato una infinitate da diverse persone de Italia e de Spagna, ma questi erano li favoriti dicendo non saper in qual modo fare come fussero finiti . . . '

82 Luzio and Renier, 1896d, 678–9: Mandiamo una scatoletta nela quale sono tre busoletti dil compositione, quel di cristalo col coperto d'oro per la Signora Regina, quelli di corno, l'uno per madama matre dil re, l'altro per la duchessa di Lansone sua sorella, come ci havete raccordato, gli li presentarete in nome nostro con giunta di quelle parole che ve pareranno convenienti. Siamo certe che la gli piacerà, perchè al judicio nostro non facessemo mai la megliore. Et semo contente che dicati alla Regina che molto ne reputamo felici ad essere porta occasione di servire Sua Maestà in cosa che gli gradisca, et che noi sapiamo et possiamo fare, perchè in componer questi odori non cederessimo al miglior perfumero del mondo, e però supplicate Sua Maestà a non cambiare la bottega, ma dandone aviso a tempo che le possiamo servire . . . Siamo contente di fornire la detta regina et madama di la nostra compositione, ma a dirvi il vero non volemo già questa cura per le altre donne. Luzio and Renier, 1908d, 679.

83 Brown, 1982, 193.

84 Brown, 1995, 84.

85 The documentation was first published in C. Brown, 'An Art Auction in Venice in 1506', *L'Arte*, 18–19/20 (1972), 121–36 and then again by Brown and Lorenzoni, 1982. See also the discussion in Welch, 2002, 289–91.

86 Brown, 1982, 173.

87 Brown, 1982, 173.

88 Brown, 1982, 174.

89 Brown, 1982, 177: Et intendendo la Magnificentia Vostra essere da nobilissimo cuore . . . havemo preso animo, per lo grandissimo desiderio che tenemo di havere questa tavola, de pregarla che la voglia per sua cortesia e gentileza darni essa pictura che nui voluntieri gli exbursaremo li dinari suoi cum quello guadagno che lei vorrà. La quale, non solum guadagnarà li dinari ma la persona nostra, con obligo de restarli sempre debitrice et prompta ad gratificata in omne sua occurentia.

90 Brown, 1982, 179.

91 Brown, 1982, 182. Tanto magiore serrà adunque l'obligo nostro quanto magiore è stata la liberalità sua.

92 Brown, 1982, 180.

93 For a useful discussion of the interaction between the art-market and gift exchange in late seventeenth century Italy see G. Warwick, *The Arts of Collecting: Padre Sebastiano Resta and the Market for Drawings in Early Modern Europe*, Cambridge, 2000.

CHAPTER 10

1 C. Brown, *Isabella d'Este and Lorenzo da Pavia. Documents for the History of Art and Culture in Renaissance Mantua*, Geneva, 1982, 29.

2 C. Brown, '*Per dare qualche splendore a la gloriosa città di Mantua': Documents for the Antiquarian Collection of Isabella d'Este*, Rome, 2002, 20.

3 L. Gargan, *Cultura e arte nel Veneto al tempo del Petrarca*, Padua, 1978, 36–9. See

also the discussion in L. Syson and D. Thornton, *Objects of Virtue: Art in Renaissance Italy*, London, 2001, 105.

4 P. Spring, 'The Topographical and Archaeological Study of the Antiquities of the City of Rome, 1420–1447', Ph.D. diss., University of Edinburgh, 1972.

5 R. Lanciani, *Storia dei scavi di Roma e notizie intorno le collezioni di Romane di antichità*, Rome, 1989, I, 30.

6 Lanciani, 1989, I, 77 and 79.

7 Lanciani, 1989, I, 30.

8 Lanciani, 1989, I, 30.

9 M. M. Bullard and N. Rubinstein, 'Lorenzo dei Medici's Acquisition of the "il Sigillo di Nerone"', *Journal of the Warburg and Courtauld Institutes*, 62 (1999), 283–6.

10 S. E. Reiss, 'Widow, Mother, Patron of Art: Alfonsina Orsini de'Medici', in *idem* and D. G. Wilkins, eds, *Beyond Isabella: Secular Women Patrons of Art in Renaissance Italy*, Kirksville, Mo., 2001, 131–2.

11 Lanciani, 1989, I, 213: 'Che sua madre è la più fortunata donna mai fusse, chè li danari che da per dio li fruttono più perchè se li prestassi a usura.

12 Lanciani, 1989, I, 95.

13 Lanciani, 1990, III, 277.

14 Lanciani, 1990, III, 278.

15 Lanciani, 1990, III, 275–6.

16 Lanciani, 1989, I, 120. These arrangements were very common by the 1520s, see *idem*, 1990, III, 275.

17 L. Syson and D. Gordon, *Pisanello: Painter to the Renaissance Court*, London, 2001, 39. For the original document see D. Cordellier, ed., 'Documenti e fonti su Pisanello (circa 1395–1581), *Verona illustrata*, 8 (1995), 160–2, document 74.

18 K. W. Christian, 'The De Rossi Collection of Ancient Sculptures, Leo X, and Raphael', *Journal of the Warburg and Courtauld Institutes*, 65 (2002), 162.

19 M. E. Tittoni, 'La formazione delle collezioni capitoline di antichità fra cultura e politica', in *Il Campidoglio all'epoca di Raffaello*, Milan, 1984, 23–6. It was not only popes who gave antiques to the commune of Rome. In 1546, for example,

Cardinal Alessandro Farnese gave the *Fasti Capitolini*, and a head of Brutus was left to Roman people by Cardinal Rodolfo Pio di Carpi, see Tittoni, 1984, 26.

20 Tittoni, 1984, 23: 'Sixtus IIII pont. Max. ob immensam benignitatem aenaeas insignes statuas priscae excellentiae virtutusique monumentum Romano populo, unde extorte fuere, restituendas condonandasque censuit . . . anno salutis nostre mcccclxxi, xviii kl ianuar.'

21 J. Shearman, *Raphael in Early Modern Sources, 1483–1602*, 2 vols, New Haven, 2003, I, 207–11.

22 R. T. Ridley, 'To Protect the Monuments: The Papal Antiquarian (1534–1870)', *Xenia*, 1 (1992), 117–54.

23 See the extensive and perceptive discussion in P. Findlen, 'Possessing the Past: The Material World of the Italian Renaissance', *American Historical Review*, 103 (1998), 83–114.

24 P. W. Gordon, ed., *Two Renaissance Book Hunters. The Letters of Poggius Bracciolini to Nicolaus De Niccolis*, New York, 1991, 93.

25 Gordan, 1991, 104.

26 Gordan, 1991, 33.

27 Gordon, 1991, 231, n. 11.

28 V. Rossi, *Le indole e gli studi di Giovanni di Cosimo de'Medici: notizie e documenti*, Rome, 1893, 27: 'Egli è vero che m. Enocche ha portato qui certe cose nuove, come vedrete per questo inventario vi mando ed invero da farne più stima per la novità che per la utilità. Lui per insino a qui non ha volute farne copia a persona, imperò dice non vuole avere durate fatiche per altri e non delibera darne copia alcuna, se prima da qualche grande maestro non è remunerato degnamente ed ha oppenione d'averne almanco 200 o 300 fiorini, sì che vedete se volete gettare via tanti denari per cose che la lingua latina può molto bene fare senza esse, che a dirvi l'oppenione di molti dotti uomini che gli ànno visti, da questi quattro infuori che sono segnati con questo segno tutto il resto non vale una frulla. . . . Pur tutta volta starò avisato, se per nessuno se n'arà avere copia, l'abiate

voi pagando solamente chi li copiasse e
così lui m'a promesso . . . Delle medaglie
faro ogni diligentia, ma come per altra vi
dissi, egli ce n'à una carestia meravigliosa
per rispetto di questo monsignore di
Sancto Marco.'

29 R. Weiss, *The Renaissance Discovery of
Classical Antiquity*, Oxford, 1969.

30 Lanciani, 1989, I, 71.

31 Gordon, 1991, 166.

32 L. Fusco and G. Corti, 'Giovanni
Ciampolini (d.1505): A Renaissance Dealer
in Rome and his Collection of Antiquities',
Xenia, 21 (1991), 7–46 and *idem, Lorenzo
de'Medici. Collector of Antiquities*, Cambridge, 2005. Unfortunately this volume
had not appeared before my book went to
press.

33 Fusco and Corti, 1991, 10.

34 Fusco and Corti, 1991, 13.

35 D. Ferrari, ed., *Giulio Romano: repetorio di
fonti documentarie*, Mantua, 1992, I, 81:
'Havemo recevuto la pollice che ni haveti
mandato questi dì circa le teste antique che
ha quello picture lì in Roma, et veduto
quanto la contiene, et il precio che ne
dimanda esso pictore, che sono ottanta
ducati. Benché il si offerto de donarcele,
noi havemo deliberato di volerli ogni
modo, et però volemo che voi l'acettate in
dono in nome nostro, et ce le mandiate più
presto che possiate e volemo che del
primo quartiero che habbiamo diate al
prefato pictor 60 ducati perché havemo
parlato con persone che hanno vedute le
ditte teste, che dicono che sono pagate in
tanto. Ma a lui direte che havemo acettate
le sue teste in dono, che voglia anchor lui
accettar questi dinari in dono, che in dono
gli li diamo.'

36 C. Brown with A. M. Lorenzoni, *Our
Accustomed Discourse on the Antique:
Cesare Gonzaga and Gerolamo Garimberto,
Two Renaissance Collectors of Greco-Roman
Art*, New York, 1993, 193–4.

37 The bibliography on Renaissance gift-
giving is an extensive one. For a summary
see N. Zemon Davies, *The Gift in Six-*
teenth-Century France, Madison, Wi.,
2000.

38 Ferrari, 1992, II, 781.

39 Ferrari, 1992, I, 33–34: 'Giovan Francesco
me scrisse alli dì passati havermi trovato
quelle anticaglie e che costavano x ducati,
io pensandomi che'l tutto fusse con con-
sentimento de Iulio gli ve scrissi che li
doveste dare questi x ducati; hora intendendo che'l parere di Iulio è che non siano
cose troppo excellenti, harei caro, se non
ge li havete dati, che non gli deste, excu-
sandovi di quel modo che vi pare, con dire
che non havete più denari delli mei nelle
mani, o qualche altra cosa che para a voi.
Tanto più che Giulio me ha fatto venire
una sete mirabile d'un cameo, il qual lui
me scrive haver visto et esser cosa extrema-
mente bella, di modo ch'el se potesse
havere a buon mercato, sarei contento
pigliarlo con intentione de non torre
questo anno più cose antiche, salvo se non
venisse qualche gran ventura. E del pretio
e dalla bontà delle cose, Iulio me scrive che
colui di chi glì è, ne domanda cento ducati,
ma che crede che se haveria per 40 o 50, il
che mi pare ancor troppo gran prezzo,
maximamente adesso io ho pochi denari,
però s'el se potesse havere per 25 o 30
ducati vorrei ch'el se pigliasse, non ostando
ancor per un par de ducati de più, parendo
così a Iulio, e questo intendo se non havete
dato li x ducati a Ioan Francisco, perchè
molto più mi piace havere una cosa sola
excellente che haverne 50 de mediocre.
Vorrei el quadro de maestro Antonio da
San Marino, et questo cameo, et il petto
che Iulio me scrive haver trovato per una
testa de marmore che io ho, poi non vorrei
comprare altro per questo anno . . .'

40 Z. H. Klawans, *Imitations and Inventions
of Roman Coins: Renaissance Medals of
Julius Caesar and the Roman Empire*, Santa
Monica, Calif., 1977; and F. Cessi, *Giovanni da Cavino: medaglista padovano del
cinquecento*, Padua, 1969. See also the discussion in Syson and Thornton, 2001,
108–13.

41   Lanciani, 1990, I, 208: 'Die xvi aprilis 1545. Dominicus Rincontro laycus florentinus et Iacobus Barotius de Vignola habitatores in urbe in strata transtiberina subtus sanctum Honufrium promiserunt R. D. Francisco Primaditio clerico bononiensi abbati sancti Martini de Tu . . . fabricare undecim formas nuncupatas . . . pro statua Nilli que reponitur in vividario S. D. N. Pape in loco Belvederis nuncupato, et aliam pro statua Antinoi ibidem positi, et reliquas pro diversis figuris verbo exprimendis per ipsum d. Franciscum. Itaque fabricare promiserunt per totum mensem Augusti proxime futurum in domo Raphaelis de Montelupo. Dictus D. Franciscus promisit Dominico et Iacobo solvere centum scuta auri . . .'

42   On Lafrery see F. Roland, *Un Franc-Comtois, éditeur et marchand d'éditeur et marchand d'éstampes à Rome au xvi siècle: Antoine Lafrery (1512–1577), notice historique*, Paris, 1911 and E. Miller, *Sixteenth-Century Ornament Prints in the Victoria and Albert Museum*, London, 1999.

43   A. H. Allison, 'The Bronzes of Pier Jacopo Alari Bonacolsi, called Antico', *Jahrbuch der Kunsthistorischen Sammlungen in Wien*, 89/90, (1993/4), 38.

44   Allison 1993/4, 268.

45   Allison 1993/4, 42. See also by the same author, 'Antico e Isabella d'Este', *Civiltà mantovana*, 30 (1995), 91–113.

46   Allison 1993/4, 42.

47   Allison 1993/4, 43.

48   Ferrari, 1992, I, 79: 'né restarete per pretio alcuno di torle, et quando anche in qualche parte fussero mutilite, o di naso, orechie, o in altro loco, perciò non restarete di tuorle, perché l'Anticho le acconciarà in modo che starano bene . . .'

49   Allison, 1993/4, 39.

50   Allison, 1993/4, 43.

51   M. Perry, 'Wealth, Art and Display: The Grimani Cameos in Renaissance Venice', *Journal of the Warburg and Courtauld Institutes*, 56 (1993), 273. See *idem*, 'Cardinal Domenico Grimani's Legacy of Ancient Art to Venice', *Journal of the Warburg and Courtauld Insitutes*, 41 (1978), 215–44 and *idem*, 'The *statuario pubblico* of the Venetian Republic', *Saggi e memorie di storia dell'arte*, 8 (1972), 75–150.

52   Perry, 1993, 273.

53   Christian, 2002, 134.

54   D. Thornton, *The Scholar in His Study: Ownership and Experience in Renaissance Italy*, New Haven, 1997, 114, citing Paolo Manuzio, *Lettere volgari*, Venice, 1560, book II, 74. See also V. Mancini, *Antiquari, 'vertuosi' e artisti: saggi sul collezionismo tra Padova e Venezia alla metà del cinquecento*, Padua, 1995.

55   Thornton, 1997, 113.

56   D. Chambers and B. Pullan, eds, *Venice. A Documentary History, 1450–1630*, Oxford, 1992, 429, and M. Schmitter, '"Virtuous Riches": The Bricolage of "cittadini" identities in Early Sixteenth-Century Venice', *Renaissance Quarterly*, 57 (2004), 916–8.

57   Perry, 1993, 271.

58   Perry, 1993, 268–73.

59   B. L. Ullman and P. A. Stadter, *The Public Library of Renaissance Florence*, Padua, 1972.

60   L. Labowsky, *Bessarion's Library and the Biblioteca Marciana: Six Early Inventories*, Rome, 1980.

61   P. Fortini Brown, *Venice and Antiquity*, New Haven, 1996, 145.

62   Gargan, 1978, 45.

63   Perry, 1978, 215.

64   Perry, 1978, 227.

65   P. Findlen, *Possessing Nature: Museums, Collecting, and Scientific Culture in Early Modern Italy*, Berkeley, Calif., 1994, 24.

66   Findlen, 1994, 109.

67   I. Gagliardi, 'Le reliquie dell'Ospedale di Santa Maria della Scala (xiv–xv)', in L. Bellosi, ed., *L'oro di Siena: il tesoro di Santa Maria della Scala*, Milan, 1996, 49. The Hospital officials had the relics valued at 3,000 gold florins. The merchant Pietro di Giunta Torrigiani then donated them to the Scala and was given an annual income of 200 gold florins and a house for himself

and his family in return. See G. Der-ernzini, 'Le reliquie da Constantinopoli a Siena', in the same volume, 67–78, and P. Hetherington, 'A Purchase of Byzantine Relics and reliquaries in Fourteenth-Century Venice', *Arte veneta*, 37 (1983), 9–30.

68 M. Lazzaroni and A. Muñoz, *Filarete: scultore e architetto del secolo xv*, Rome, 1908, 146.

69 *Regesti di bandi, editti, notificazioni e provvedimenti diversi relativi alla città di Roma ed allo stato pontificio*, Rome, 1920, I, 137.

70 M. Ciardini, *I banchieri ebrei in Firenze nel secolo xv e il Monte di Pietà fondato da Girolamo Savonarola*, Borgo San Lorenzo, 1907, 31–2 and E. Castelli, *I banchi feneratizi ebraici nel Mantovano (1386–1808)*, Mantua, 1959, 24.

71 Ciardini, 1907, 52.

72 Ciardini, 1907, 71.

73 *Regesti di bandi*, 1920, I, 20.

74 *Regesti di bandi*, 1920, I, 23.

75 *Regesti di bandi*, 1920, I, 29.

76 For a discussion of the implications of gifts to monasteries in France and the notion of 'sacred pawns', see S. D. White, *Custom, Kinship and Gifts to Saints: The* 'Laudatio Parentum' *in Western France, 1050–1150*, Chapel Hill, 1988.

77 J. Le Goff, *The Birth of Purgatory*, Chicago, 1984.

78 Among the many sixteenth-century writings on this see M. Chemnitz, *Traité des indulgences, contre le décrêt du Concil de Trente. A Génève pour Jacques Chouet*, 1599. See also, K. W. Cameron, *The Pardoner and his Pardons: Indulgences Circulating in England on the Eve of the Reformation with a Historical Introduction*, Hartford, Conn., 1965.

79 Cameron, 1965, 7.

80 N. Paulus, *Indulgences as a Social Factor in the Middle Ages*, New York, 1922.

81 E. Welch, *Art and Authority in Renaissance Milan*, New Haven, 1995, 65.

82 C. Santoro, *I registri dell'uffico di provisione*

e dell'ufficio dei sindaci sotto la dominazione viscontea*, Milan, 1929, I, 15.

83 M. Sanudo, *I diarii di Marino Sanudo*, ed. R. Fulin et al., Venice, 1894, 41, col. 69: 'Il reverendissimo Armelino li ha ditto, si la Signoria vol li farà dare al Papa uno iubileo in tutto il Dominio, con condition la mità di danari vengi a Roma a la fabrica di San Piero e l'altra mità a l'Arsenal . . .'

84 *Regesti di bandi*, 1920, I, 10.

85 A. Mario Rossi, *Lutero e Roma. La fatale scintilla (la lotta intorno alle indulgenze) 1517–1519*, Rome, 1923.

86 Rossi, 1923, 227.

87 J. Pelikan, *The Christian Tradition. A History of the Development of Doctrine: Reformation of Church and Dogma (1300–1700)*, Chicago, 1984, 134.

88 Rossi, 1923, 97.

89 Rossi, 1923, 134–5.

90 Rossi, 1923, 136–7.

91 Paulus, 1922, 29.

92 Rossi, 1923, 139: 'Comprare una Lettera confessionale è sempre un buon affare; infatti, se foste obligati d'andare a Roma o in qualche altro luogo pericoloso, non sareste costretti a mettere i vostari danari alla banca e pagare il 5, il 6, il 10 percento per ritrovarli sicuri a Roma . . . E non volete per un quarto di fiorino ricevere queste Lettere per la cui efficacia, non danaro, ma un'anima divina ed immortale potete ritorvare sicura nella patria celeste?'

93 Rossi, 1923, 131–2.

94 H. Günther, 'I progetti di ricostruzione della basilica di San Pietro negli scritti contemporanei: giustificazioni e scrupoli', in G. Spagnesi, ed., *L'architettura della basilica di San Pietro: storia e costruzione*, Rome, 1997, 144.

95 Günther, 1997, 146.

96 Rossi, 1923, 105–6.

97 Pelikan, 1984, 297.

98 D. Gentilcore, *Healers and Healing in Early Modern Italy*, Manchester, 1998, 117.

99 Gentilcore, 1998, 118.

Bibliography

ARCHIVAL SOURCES

Bologna, Archivio di Stato

Ufficio delle bollette, presentazioni dei forestieri, Scritture diverse, b. 2, 1357–1359

Soprastante ai dazi: introiti per mercanzie entrate in città, b. 92, 1419–1443

Soprastante ai dazi: dazio delle mercanzie e sigillino, stima delle mercanzie, b. 103, I: 1406, II: 1414, III: 1421; b. 103, IV: 1424, V: 1426; b. 105, 1431–1438

Masssarolo dei pegni

b. 16, 1385: Liber massaroli pignoris

b. 17, 1410–1429

Ufficio dell'abbondanza e grascia

Ufficio del pane, 1392–1414

Fornai, 1400

Florence, Archivio di Stato

Magistrato dei pupilli avanti il principato, 190, b. 52: inventory of Alessandro di Francesco Roselli

b. 252, filza d'inventari

Pupilli del principato

b. 2650, f. 5: Francesco di Giusetia, mercaio, 5 January 1551

b. 2647, ff. 438–40: Pierfrancesco di Domenico Biondo già merciaio, 15 July 1571

b. 2742: Filza d'inventari di robe da vedersi all'incanto

b. 3060

Carte Strozziane, IV series, n. 60: Libro di mona Alexandra donna che fu de Marco Strozzi. Libro debitori e creditori e ricordi di cose domestiche, 1500–1506

Carte Strozziane, IV series, n. 72: Libretto intitolato Giornale di Mona Francesca, vedova di Nicolo di Carlo Strozzi, 1493–1498

Carte Strozziane, IV series, n. 89–90: Libro di Albiera di Jacopo di Giunta Binemi e donna gia di Simone Strozzi, 1569–1579

Conventi sopressi, 90 (vaiaio), 132 (speziale)

Fondo Gondi, 35

Libri di commercio e di famiglia:

b. 474, fornaro, 1566

b. 4180: Puccio di Rinaldo di Bernardo Pucci, 1533

b. 5127, 5128, 5130, 5132, 5133: Vignarchi family ledgers

Mediceo avanti il principato XCIX, n. 7: Partite di dare e avere tra Lucrezia Tornabuoni dei Medici e il Banco Medici di Pisa, 1474–1477

Mantua, Archivio di Stato

Archivio Gonzaga,
b. 1469
b. 2994
b. 1502, f. II, cc. 661–664: *Gratie del lotto del banco Dolfin in virtù della parte dell'illustrissimo Collegio de' X et Gionta, sotto di VI settembre M.D.L.XX.*7

Milan, Archivio di Stato

Archivio Sforzesco, Communi 53

Milan, Archivio della veneranda fabbrica del Duomo di Milano

Piazza del Duomo, Spazii 1388–1802
Cartelle 192–204
Fabbrica
Register 11 (1388–1390: Liber incantum qui fiori continguit de drapis, toaliis, mantilibus, sugacapilibus, perlis, botonis, anulis et aliis diversis rebus: 'In principio huius libri adsunt ordinis facti... pro rebus mobilibus parte fabrice oblatus ad publicum incantum vendendis'
Register 22 (1394)
Register 201 (1435–1451)
Register 245 (1457) Liber diversorum patarie ad res
Register 247 (1437–1485)
Register 274 (1483–1487) Registri di amministrazione privati
Register 281 (1490–1491) Hosier's accounts
Register 532 (1400) Registro patariae
Register 533 (1400–1402) Registro patariae
Register 676, (1457–1490) Registro patariae

Register 683, (1493–1498) Libro di entrate e spese di Signore Paolo Imperiale
Heredità 97: Angelo Porro

Prato, Archivio di Stato

Archivio Datini
b. 606, Quaderno di spese di casa compagnia di Firenze
b. 421, Quaderno di casa seg. B. compagnia di Pisa and
b. 613 and 618 and 212–13

Ospedale, Ricordanze

793; 794; 795; 808; 825; 827; 845

Siena, Archivio di Stato

Notarile 1898: Apoteca Giovanni Francesci aurficis, 1528, 26 March

Treviso, Archivio communale

Commune 355: Descrizione case e parrochie di Treviso, 1518–1572

Venice, Archivio di Stato

Arti 354: Merzari/Sensa
Arti 725
Giustizia Vecchia, b. 31, Proclami, 1513–1797
Giustizia Vecchia, b. 49, reg. 79: Registro di costituri per lo notificazione di insegne da porsi sopra i negozi, 1560–1597
Giustizia Vecchia, b. 76, Processi, 1571–1659
Governatori delle pubbliche entrate, b. 495
Procuratori di San Marco, Misti, b. 13, estate sale of Nicolò Sartore, 1464
Procuratori, di San Marco, de supra (chiesa), b. 50
Archivio Marcello Grimani Giustinian, Donà 171

Venice, Biblioteca Marciana

Capitolare antico della Giustizia Vecchia, MS It VII 1572

PRIMARY SOURCES

Agazzari, Giovanni, *Chronica civitatis Placentiae*, ed. Antonio Francesco Villa, Parma, 1862.

Alberti, Leon Battista, *The Family in Renaissance Florence*, trans. Renee Neu Watkins, Columbia, Mo., 1969.

——, *De Re Aedificatoria: On the Art of Building in Ten Books*, trans. Joseph Rykwert, Neil Leach, and Robert Tavernor, Cambridge, Mass., 1988.

Arditi, Bastiano, *Diario di Firenze e di altre parti della cristianità (1574–1579)*, ed. Roberto Cantagalli, Florence, 1970.

Aretino, Pietro, *Tutte le commedie*, ed. Giovanni Battista De Sanctis, Milan, 1968.

——, *Selected Letters*, trans. and ed. George Bull, Harmondsworth, 1976.

Ascheri, Mario, ed., *L'ultimo statuto della republica di Siena (1545)*, Siena, 1993.

Bacchi della Lega, Alberto, ed., *Cronica di Buonaccorso Pitti*, Bologna, 1905.

Barbaro, Francesco, 'On Wifely Duties', in Benjamin Kohl and Ronald G. Witt, eds, *In this Most Earthly Paradise: Italian Humanists on Government and Society*, Manchester, 1978, 189–228.

Bec, Christian, ed., *Il libro degli affari proprii di casa de Lapo di Giovanni Niccolini de' Sirigatti*, Paris, 1969.

Bernardino da Siena, *Prediche volgari sul campo di Siena: 1427*, 2 vols, ed. Carlo Delcorno, Milan, 1989.

——, *Le prediche volgare, campo di Siena, 1427*, ed. Ezio Cantagalli, Siena, 1935.

——, *Le prediche volgare (1425)*, ed. Ciro Cannarozzi, 2 vols, Pistoia, 1934.

Bianchi, Silvana Anna and Rosalba Granuzzo, eds, *Statuti di Verona del 1327*, 2 vols, Rome, 1992.

Bologna, Carlo, ed., *Inventario de' mobili di Francesco di Angelo Gaddi, 1496*, Florence, 1883.

Brown, Clifford M., '*Per dare qualche splendore a la gloriosa città di Mantua': Documents for the Antiquarian Collection of Isabella d'Este*, Rome, 2002.

——, 'Purché la sia cosa che rappresenti antiquità: Isabella d'Este Gonzaga e il mondo greco-romano', *Civiltà mantovano: Isabella d'Este: i luoghi del collezionismo*, 30 (1995), 71–90.

——, '"Lo insaciabile desiderio nostro de cose antique": New Documents on Isabella d'Este's Collection of Antiquities', in Cecil Clough, ed., *Cultural Aspects of the Renaissance: Essays in Honour of Paul Oskar Kristeller*, Manchester, 1976, 324–53.

——, '"Una testa di Platone antica con la punta dil naso di cera": Unpublished Negotiations between Isabella d'Este and Niccolò and Giovanni Bellini', *Art Bulletin*, 51 (1969), 372–7.

——, with Anna Maria Lorenzoni, *Our Accustomed Discourse on the Antique: Cesare Gonzaga and Gerolamo Garimberto, Two Renaissance Collectors of Greco-Roman Art*, New York, 1993.

——, 'Cardinal Sigismondo Gonzaga (1469–1525): An Overlooked Name in the Annals of Collectors of Antiquities', *Xenia*, 21 (1991), 47–58.

——, 'Inventario delli beni dil quondam messer Nicolò Pisavini già aurifice in Mantua, 26 November 1541', *Quaderni del Palazzo Te*, 5 (1986), 75–80.

——, *Isabella d'Este and Lorenzo da Pavia. Documents for the History of Art and Culture in Renaissance Mantua*, Geneva, 1982.

——, 'Isabella d'Este e Giorgio Brognolo nell'anno 1496', *Atti e memorie dell'accademia virgiliana di Mantova*, n. s. 41 (1973), 97–122.

——, 'An Art Auction in Venice in 1506', *L'arte*, 18–19/20 (1972), 126–36.

Caggese, Romolo, ed., *Statuti della repubblica fiorentina*, 2 vols, Florence, 1921, new edition, ed. Piero Gualtieri, Giuliano Pinto, Francesco Salvestrini and Andrea Zorzi, Florence, 1999.

Castellani, Francesco di Matteo, *Ricordanze I: Ricordanze A (1436–1459)*, ed., Giovanni Ciappelli, Florence, 1992.

——, *Ricordanze II. Quaternuccio e giornale B (1459–1485)*, ed. Giovanni Ciappelli, Florence, 1995.

Castignoli, Piero, ed., *Liber daciorum et officiorum communis Placentie (anno MCC-CLXXX): L'appalto delle gabelle e degli uffici in un comune cittadino del dominio visconteo*, Rome, 1975.

Chambers, David and Brian Pullan with Jennifer Fletcher, eds, *Venice: A Documentary History, 1450–1630*, Oxford, 1992.

Chemnitz, Martin, *Traité des indulgences, contre le décrêt du Concil de Trente. A Génève pour Jacques Chouet*, 1599.

Ciasca, Raffaele, ed., *Statuti dell'arte dei medici e speziali*, Florence, 1922.

Commissione Storico-archeologica comunale, *Studi storici sul centro di Firenze*, Florence, 1889.

Conti, Elio, ed., *Matteo Palmieri: ricordi fiscali (1427–1474) con due appendici relative al 1474–1495*, Rome, 1983.

Conway, Melissa, *The 'Diario' of the Printing Press of San Jacopo di Ripoli (1476–1484): Commentary and Transcription*, Florence, 1999.

Coppi, Enrico, ed., *Cronaca fiorentina, 1537–1555*, Florence, 2000.

Corazzini, Giuseppe Odoardo, ed., *Diario fiorentino di Agostino Lapini dal 252 al 1596 ora per la prima volta pubblicato*, Florence, 1900.

Cordellier, Dominique, ed., 'Documenti e fonti su Pisanello (*circa* 1395–1581)', *Verona illustrata*, 8 (1995).

Corsi, Domenico, *Statuti urbanistica medievali di Lucca: gli statuti delle vie e de'pubblici di Lucca nei secoli XII–XIV; curia del fondaco: statuto del 1371*, Venice, 1960.

Coryate, Thomas, *Coryate's Crudities: hastily gobled up in five months travels in France, Savoy, Italy, Rhetia commonly called the Grisons country, Helvetia alias Switzerland, some parts of high Germany and the Netherlands; newly digested in the hungry aire of Odcombe in the county of Somerset, and now dispersed to the nourishment of the travelling members of this kingdome by Thomas Coryate*, Glasgow, 1905.

Coryate, Thomas, *Coryat's Crudities (1611)*, edited and introduced by William M. Schutte, London, 1978.

Croce, Giulio Cesare, *Lamento de poveretti: i quali stanno à casa a piggione, & la convengono pagare. Composta per il Piascentino in Mantova per Benedetto Osanna, stampatore ducale*, 1590.

——, *Chiacciaramenti sopra tutti li traffichi e negoccii che si fanno ogni giorno sù la piazza di Bologna. Composti da Giulio Cesare Croce, opera da ridere. In Bologna per gli heredi del Cochi*, 1625.

D'Arco, Carlo, ed., *Cronaca di Mantova di Andrea Schivenoglia dal MCCCXLV al MCC-CLXXXIV: raccolta di cronisti e doumenti storici lombardi*, Milan, 1857.

Davanzati, Bernardo, *Lezione delle monete di Bernardo Davanzati fiorentino con note scelte dell'autore e di Antonio Maria Salvini*, ed. P. Custodi, Milan, 1804.

Davanzo Poli, Doretta, *I mestieri della moda a Venezia nei sec. XIII–XVIII: documenti*, 2 vols, Mestre, 1986.

Dei, Benedetto, *La cronica dall'anno 1400 all'anno 1500*, ed. R. Barducci, Florence, 1985.

De'Ricci, Giuliano, *Cronica (1532–1606)*, ed. Giuliana Sapori, Milan, 1972.

Di Pasi, Bartolomeo, *Qui comincia la utilissima opera chiamata taripha la qual tracta de ogni sorte de pexi e misure corrispondente per tuto il mondo*, Venice, 1503.

Elmer, Peter, Nick Webb and Roberta Woods, eds, *The Renaissance in Europe: An Anthology*, New Haven and London, 2000.

Ferrari, Daniela, ed., *Giulio Romano: repetorio di fonti documentarie*, 2 vols, Rome, 1992.

Filarete's Treatise on Architecture. Being the

Treatise by Antonio di Piero Averlino, Known as Filarete, 2 vols, trans. and ed. John R. Spencer, New Haven, 1965.

Foucard, Cesare, 'Fonti di storia napoletana dell'archivio di stato di Modena: descrizione della città di e statistica del regno nel 1444', *Archivio storico per le provincie napoletane*, 2 (1877), 725–57.

Franceschini, Adriano, ed., *Artisti a Ferrara in età umanistica e rinascimentale: testimonianze archivistiche*, Parte I: *Dal 1341 al 1471*; Parte II, tomo I: *Dal 1472 al 1492*; Parte II, tomo II: *Dal 1493 al 1516*, Ferrara, 1993–97.

Furlotti, Barbara, ed., *Le collezioni Gonzaga: il carteggio tra Roma e Mantova, (1587–1612)*, Milan, 2003.

——— ed., *Le collezioni Gonzaga: il carteggio tra Bologna*, Parma, Piacenza e Mantua. (1563–1634), Milan, 2000.

Garzoni, Tomaso, *La piazza universale di tutte le professioni del mondo*, ed. Paolo Cherchi and Beatrice Collina, 2 vols, Turin, 1996.

Gregory, Heather, ed., *Selected Letters of Alessandra Strozzi*, Berkeley, 1997.

Gride ducali, provisioni, gratie et ragioni della città di Modena et da osservarsi in essa nuovamente date in luce, Modena, 1575.

Grignani, Maria Antonietta, ed., *Mantova 1430: pareri a Gian Francesco Gonzaga per il governo*, Mantua, 1990.

I cinque libri de gli'avvertimenti, ordini, gride, et editti fatti, et osservati in Milano ne' tempi sospettosi della peste negli anni MDLXXVI et LXXVII . . . Venice, 1579.

Ioly Zorattini, Pier Cesare, ed., *Processi del S. Uffizio di Venezia contro ebrei e giudaizzanti (1561–1570)*, Florence, 1982.

Kohl, Benjamin G. and Ronald G. Witt, with Elizabeth B. Welles, eds, *The Earthly Republic: Italian Humanists on Government and Society*, Philadelphia, 1978.

Gordon, Phyllis W. Goodhart, ed, *Two Renaissance Book Hunters: The Letters of Poggius Bracciolini to Nicolaus De Niccolis*, New York, 1991.

Landucci, Luca, *Diario fiorentino dal 1450 al 1516 di Luca Landucci, continuato da un anonimo fino al 1542*, ed. Iodoco Del Badia, Florence, 1883.

Landy, Michael, *Breakdown*, London, 2001.

Lomazzo, Giovanni Paolo, *Rabisch: Giovan Paolo Lomazzo e i facchini della Val di Blenio*, ed. Dante Isella, Turin, 1993.

Lotto, Lorenzo, *Il libro di spese diverse (1538–1556)*, ed. Pietro Zampetti, Venice, 1969.

Maiocchi, Rodolfo, *Codice diplomatico dell'università di Pavia*, Pavia, 2 vols, 1905–13.

Mancini, Augusto, Umberto Dorini and Eugenio Lazzareschi, eds, *Lo statuto della corte dei mercanti in Lucca del MCCCLXXVI*, Florence, 1927.

Martelli, Ugolino di Niccolò, *Ricordanze dal 1433 al 1483*, ed. Fulvio Pezzarossa, Rome, 1989.

Masi, Gino, ed., *Statutum bladi reipublicae fiorentinae (1348)*, Milan, 1934.

Mazzi, Curzio, ed., *Provvisioni suntuarie fiorentine (29 novembre 1464–29 febbraio 1471)*, Florence, 1908.

Monticolo, Giovanni, ed., *I capitolari delle arti veneziane sottoposte alla Giustizia e poi alla Giustizia Vecchia dalle origini al 1330*, 3 vols, Rome, 1896–1914.

Morandini, Francesca, ed., *Statuti delle arti degli oliandoli e pizzicagnoli e dei beccai di Firenze (1318–1346)*, Florence, 1961.

———, 'Statuti e ordinamenti dell'ufficio dei pupilli et adulti nel periodo della repubblica fiorentina (1388–1535)', *Archivio storico italiano*, 113 (1955), 520–51; 114 (1956), 92–117; 115 (1957), 87–104.

Moryson, Ffynes, *An Itinerary Containing his ten Yeeres Travell through the Twelve Dominions of Germany, Bohmerland, Switzerland, Netherland, Denmark, Poland, Italy, Turkey, France, England, Scotland, Ireland*, Glasgow, 1907.

Nasalli Rocca, Emilio, ed., *Statuti di corporazioni artigiane piacentine*, Milan, 1955.

Natale, Alfio R., ed., *Acta Libertatis Mediolani. I registri n. 5 e n. 6 dell'archivio dell'ufficio degli statuti di Milano (Repubblica Ambrosiana, 1447–1450)*, Milan, 1987.

Newett, M. Margaret, ed., *Canon Pietro Casola's Pilgrimage to Jerusalem in the Year 1494*, Manchester, 1907.

Pandolfi, Vito, ed., *La commedia dell'arte: storia e testo*, 6 vols, Florence, 1957–61.

Prunai, Giulio, ed., *Statuti dei comuni di monastero S. Eugenio (1352), Monteriggioni (1380), e Sovicille (1383)*, Florence, 1961.

Pucci, Antonio, 'Proprietà di mercato vecchio', *Poeti minori del trecento*, ed. Natalino Sapegno, Milan, 1952, 403–10.

Regesti di bandi, editti, notificazioni e provvedimenti diversi relativi alla città di Roma ed allo stato pontificio, 7 vols, Rome, 1920–58.

Renier, Rodolfo, ed., *Strambotti e sonetti dell'Altissimo*, Turin, 1886.

Richards, Kenneth and Laura Richards, eds, *The Commedia dell'Arte: A Documentary History*, Oxford, 1990.

Rosati, Valeria, ed., 'Le lettere di Margherita Datini a Francesco di Marco', *Archivio storico pratese*, 50 (1974), 3–93; 52 (1976), 25–152.

Sabellico, Marc'Antonio, *Del sito di Venezia città (1502)*, ed. G. Meneghetti, Venice, 1957.

Sansovino, Francesco, *Venetia: città nobilissima et singolare, descritta in XIIII libri da M. Francesco Sansovino . . .* Venice, 1581 and 1663.

Santoro, Caterina, ed., *I registri dell'ufficio di provvisione e dell'ufficio dei sindaci sotto la dominazione viscontea*, Milan, 1929.

——, ed., *I registri delle lettere ducali del periodo sforzesco*, Milan, 1961.

Sanudo, Marin, *De origine, situ et magistratibus urbis Venetae, ovvero, la città di Venetia (1493–1530)*, ed. Angela Caracciolo Aricò, Milan, 1980.

——, *I diarii di Marino Sanudo*, ed. Rinaldo Fulin, Federico Stefani, Nicolò Barozzi, Guglielmo Berchet and Marco Allegri, 58 vols, Venice, 1879–1903 (reprinted 1969–70).

Sapori, Giuliana, ed., *Giuliano de'Ricci: cronaca (1532–1606)*, Milan, 1972.

Sartini, Ferdinando, ed., *Statuti dell'arte dei rigattieri e linaioli di Firenze (1296–1340)*, Florence, 1940–8.

Scaruffi, Gasparo, *L'alitinonfo di M. Gasparo Scaruffi Regiano per fare ragione e concordanza d'oro e d'argento che servira in universale tanto per provedere a gli infiniti abusi del tosare et guastare monete, quanto per regolare ogni sorte di pagamenti, et ridure anco tutto il mondo ad una sola moneta*, Reggio per Hercolano Bartoli, 1582.

Sforza, G., 'Autobiografia inedita di Giovanni Antonio Faie speziale lunigianese del secolo XV', *Archivio storico per le provincie parmensi*, n. s. 4 (1904), 129–83.

Shearman, John, ed., *Raphael in Early Modern Sources (1483–1602)*, 2 vols, New Haven and London, 2003.

Sogliani, Daniela, ed., *Le collezioni Gonzaga: il carteggio tra Venezia e Mantova (1563–1587)*, Milan, 2002.

Statuta populi et communis florentiae publica auctoritate collecta castigata et praeposita anno salutis, MCCCXV, 3 vols, Fribourg, 1778–83.

Tassa sopra i prezzi delle robbe nel passagio di N.S., In Roma appresso gli stampatori camerali, 1598, British Library, London, 1897.bb.2(17).

Tasso, Torquato, *Discorso della virtù feminile e donnesca*, ed. Maria Luisa Doglio, Palermo, 1997.

Thomas, Georg Martin, ed., *Capitolare dei visdomini del fontego dei todeschi in Venezia*, Berlin, 1874.

Villani, Giovanni, *Nuova cronica*, 3 vols, ed. Giuseppe Porta, Parma, 1990.

Weil-Garris, Kathleen and John F. d'Amico, eds, *The Renaissance Cardinal's Ideal Palace: A Chapter from Cortesi's 'De cardinalatu'*, Rome, 1980.

Yriate, Charles, ed., *Journal d'un sculpteur Flo-*

rentin au XV siècle: Livre de Souvenirs de Maso di Bartolomeo, dit Masaccio, Paris, 1894.

SECONDARY SOURCES

Adams, Ann Jensen, 'Money and the Regulation of Desire: The Prostitute and the Marketplace in Seventeenth-Century Holland', in Patricia Fumerton and Simon Hunt, eds, Renaissance Culture and the Everyday, Philadelphia, 1999, 229–53.

Adani, Giuseppe, M. Foschi and S. Venturi, eds, Piazze e palazzi pubblici in Emilia Romagna, Milan, 1984.

Adburgham, Alison, Shops and Shopping 1800–1914: Where and in What Manner the Well-Dressed Englishwoman Bought Her Clothes, 2nd edn, London, 1981.

Agnew, Jean-Christophe, Worlds Apart: The Market and the Theatre in Anglo-American Thought, 1550–1750, Cambridge, 1986.

Ago, Renata, 'Il linguaggio del corpo', in Carlo Marco Belfanti and Fabio Guisberti, eds, Storia d'Italia: la moda, 19, Turin, 2003, 117–47.

Ait, Ivana, Tra scienza e mercato: gli speziali a Roma nel tardo medioevo, Rome, 1996.

Albala, Ken, Eating Right in the Renaissance, Berkeley, 2002.

Alberici, C., 'Ambrogio Brambilla', Dizionario biografico degli italiani, Rome, 1971, 13, 729–30.

Allegra, Luciano, ' "Avuto reguardo al maggior prezzo, che dagli ebrei si pagano li viveri": confetti e consumi alimentari nei Ghetti Piemontesi', Zakhor: Rivista di storia degli ebrei d'Italia, 4 (2000), 127–58.

Allerston, Patricia, 'L'abito usato', in Carlo Marco Belfanti and Fabio Guisberti, eds, Storia d'Italia: la moda, 19, Turin, 2003, 561–81.

——, Rags and Riches: The Venetian Second-hand Trade, 1450–1700, New Haven and London, forthcoming

——, The Second-Hand Trade in the Arts in Early Modern Italy', in Marcello Fantoni, Louisa C. Matthew and Sara F. Matthews-Grieco, eds, The Art Market in Italy: Fifteenth to Seventeenth Centuries, Modena, 2003, 301–12.

——, 'Clothing and Early Modern Venetian Society', Continuity and Change, 15 (2000), 367–90.

——, 'Reconstructing the Second-Hand Clothes Trade in Sixteenth- and Seventeenth-Century Venice', Costume, 33 (1999), 46–56.

——, 'Wedding Finery in Sixteenth-Century Venice', in Trevor Dean and Kate Lowe, eds, Marriage in Renaissance Italy, Cambridge, 1998, 25–40.

——, 'The Market in Second-Hand Clothes and Furnishings in Venice, c.1500–c.1650', Ph.D. diss., European University Institute, Florence, 1996. [1996a]

——, 'Le marché d'occasion à Venise aux XIVe–XVII siècles', in Jacques Bottin and Nicole Pellegrin, eds, Echanges et cultures textiles dans l'Europe pré-industrielle: actes du colloque de Rouen, Lille, 1996, 15–29. [1996b]

——, 'L'abito come articolo di scambio – alcune implicazioni', in Anna G. Cavagna and Grazietta Butazzi, eds, Le trame della moda, Rome, 1995, 111–24.

Allison, Ann Hervey, 'The bronzes of Pier Jacopo Alari-Bonacolsi, called Antico', Jahrbuch der Kunsthistorisches Sammlungen in Wien, 89/90 (1993–4), 37–310.

——, 'Antico e Isabella d'Este', Civiltà mantovana, 30 (1995), 91–112.

Anderson, Bruce L. and Anthony J. H. Latham, eds, The Market in History, London, 1986.

Anselmi, Gian Mario and Fulvio Pezzarossa, and Luisa Avellini, eds, La 'memoria' dei mercatores: tendenze ideologiche, ricordanze, artigianato in versi nella Firenze del quattrocento, Bologna, 1980.

Arnade, Peter, Martha Howell and Walter Simons, 'Fertile Spaces: The Productivity of Urban Space in Northern Europe', Journal *of Interdisciplinary History*, 32 (2002), 515–48.

Artusi, Luciano, *Le arti e i mestieri di Firenze*, Rome, 1990.

Astorri, Antonella, ' "Il libro delle senserie" di Girolamo di Agostino Manighi (1483–85)', *Archivio storico italiano*, 146 (1993), 389–408.

——, 'Appunti sull'esercito dello speziale a Firenze nel quattrocento', *Archivio storico italiano*, 147 (1989), 31–62.

Bacchiocchi, Samuele, *From Sabbath to Sunday: A Historical Investigation of the Rise of Sunday Observance in Early Christianity*, Rome, 1977.

Balestracci, Duccio, *The Renaissance in the Fields: Family Memoirs of a Fifteenth-Century Tuscan Peasant*, trans. Paolo Squatriti and Betsy Merideth, University Park, Pa., 1999.

——, 'I libri impegnati al Monte di Pietà senese: una fonte indiritta per la storia dell'alfabetismo nel xv secolo', *Alfabetismo e cultura scritta. Seminario permanente. Notizie*, November, 1982, 14–16.

——, 'Aprovvigionamento e distrubuzione dei prodotti alimentari a Siena nell'epoca comunale: Mulini, mercati e botteghe', *Archeologia medievale*, 8 (1981), 127–54.

Barberi, Sandra, ed., *Il castello di Issogne in Valle D'Aosta: diciotto secoli di storia e quarant'anni di storicismo*, Turin, 1999.

Barbieri, Franco, *La basilica palladiana*, Vicenza, 1968.

Barbieri, Gino, *Origini del capitalismo lombardo: studi e documenti sull'economia milanese del periodo ducale*, Milan, 1961.

——, ed., *Aspetti dell'economia lombarda durante la dominazione visconteo-sforzesca: rassegna di documenti*, Milan, 1958.

——, 'Gottardo Panigarola mercante e spenditore sforzesco', *Atti e memorie del terzo congresso storico lombardo*, Milan, 1939, 311–26.

Barkan, Leonard, *Unearthing the Past: Archae-*

ology and Aesthetics in the Making of Renaissance Culture, New Haven, 1999.

Battara, Pietro, 'Botteghe e pigioni nella Firenze del '500: un censimento industriale e commerciale all'epoca del granducato medico', *Archivio storico italiano*, 95 (1937), 3–28.

Beall, Karen F., *Kaufrufe und Strassenhändler: Eine Bibliographie. (Cries and Itinerant Trades: A Bibliography)*, Hamburg, 1975.

Bec, Christian, 'Une librarie florentine de la fin du xve siècle', *Bibliothèque d'humanisme et renaissance*, 31 (1969), 321–32.

Belfanti, Carlo Marco, 'Maglie e calze', in Carlo Marco Belfanti and Fabio Guisberti, eds, *Storia d'Italia: la moda*, 19 Turin, 2003, 583–625.

——, 'Fashion and Innovation: The Origins of the Italian Hosiery Industry in the Sixteenth and Seventeenth Centuries', *Textile History* (27), 1996, 132–47.

——, 'Le calze a maglia: Moda e innovazione alle origini dell'industria della maglieria (secoli xvi–xviii)', *Società e storia*, 65 (1995), 481–501

——, 'Il dono dell'abito: lusso e consuetudini sociali a Mantova nel Cinquecento: appunti per una ricerca', in Anna Maria Lorenzoni and Roberto Navarrini, eds, *Per Mantova una vita: studi in memoria di Rita Castagna*, Mantua, 1991, 75–81.

——and Fabio Guisberti, eds, *Storia d'Italia: la moda*, 19, Turin, 2003.

Bellettini, Pierangelo, B., Rosaria Campioni, Zita Zanardi, eds, *Una città in piazza: comunicazione e vita quotidiana a Bologna tra cinque e seicento*, Bologna, 2000.

Bellocchi, Lisa, *Le monete di Bologna*, Bologna, 1987.

Bemporad, Dora Liscia, ed., *Il costume nell'età del Rinascimento*, Florence, 1988.

Benadusi, Giovanna, *A Provincial Elite in Early Modern Tuscany: Family and Power in the Creation of the State*, Baltimore, 1996.

Bénézet, Jean Pierre, *Pharmacie et médicament*

en *Méditerranée occidentale (XIII–XVIE siècles)*, Paris, 1999.

Bennet, Bonnie A. and David G. Wilkins, *Donatello*, Oxford, 1984.

Benson, April Lane, *I Shop therefore I Am: Compulsive Buying and the Search for Self*, London, 2000.

Benson, Susan Porter, *Counter Cultures: Saleswomen, Managers and Customers in American Department Stores, 1890–1940*, Urbana, Ill., 1986.

Bernstein, Jane A., *Print Culture and Music in Sixteenth-Century Venice*, Oxford, 2001.

Bernstein, P. Renee, 'In Widow's Habit: Women between Convent and Family in Sixteenth-Century Milan', *Sixteenth-Century Journal*, 25, n. 4 (1994), 787–807.

Bestor, Jane Fair, 'Marriage Transactions in Renaissance Italy and Mauss's Essay on the Gift', *Past and Present*, 164 (1999), 6–46.

Bevilaqua, Mario, *Il Monte dei Cenci: una famiglia romana e il suo insediamento urbano tra medioevo ed età barocca*, Reggio Calabria, 1998.

Bianchi, Maria Luisa, 'Le botteghe fiorentine nel catasto del 1480', *Ricerche storiche*, 30 (2000), 119–70.

——, and Maria Letizia Grossi, 'Botteghe, economia e spazio urbano', in Franco Franceschi and Gloria Fossi, eds, *Arti fiorentine: la grande storia dell'artigianato*. II: *Il Quattrocento*, Florence, 1999, 27–64.

Bistort, Giulio, *Il magistrato alla pompe nella republica di Venezia*, Bologna, 1912.

Bober, Phyllis Pray and Ruth Rubinstein, *Renaissance Artists and Antique Sculpture: A Handbook of Sources*, London, 1986.

Boccato, C., 'La disciplina delle sensarie nel Ghetto di Venezia', *Giornale economico*, 6, November–December 1974, 27–36.

Bocchi, Francesca, ed., *I portici di Bologna e l'edilizia civile medievale*, Bologna, 1990.

Bonfiglio-Dosio, Giorgetta, *Il commercio degli alimentari a Brescia nel primo quattrocento*, Brescia, 1979.

Borsi, Franco, *La capitale a Firenze e l'opera di G. Poggi*, Florence, 1970.

Bortolotti, Maria Pia and Marina Valori, 'Ricerca tra le fonti dell'Archivio di Stato di Milano: Per una storia della confezione pre-industriale', *Archivio storico lombardo*, series 2, 9, anno 118 (1992), 515–27.

Bourne, Molly, 'Out from the Shadow of Isabella: The Artistic Patronage of Francesco II Gonzaga, Fourth Marquis of Mantua', Ph.D. diss., Harvard University, 1997.

Bowlby, Rachel, 'The Ultimate Shopper', *Women: A Cultural Review*, 11 (2000), 109–17.

——, *Just Looking: Consumer Cultures in Dreiser, Gissing and Zola*, London, 1985.

Brackett, John K., 'The Florentine Criminal Underworld: The Underside of the Renaissance', in William J. Connell, ed., *Society and Individual in Renaissance Florence*, Berkeley, 2000, 293–314.

Bravetti, Patrizia, 'Giovanni Aider: L'acesa sociale di un'oste tedesco nella venezia di fine '500', *Annali veneti: società, cultura, istituzioni*, 2 (1985), 85–90.

Brewer, John and Roy Porter, eds, *Consumption and the World of Goods*, London, 1993.

Brown, Alison, 'Lorenzo and Public Opinion in Florence', in Gian Carlo Garfagnini, ed., *Lorenzo il Magnifico e il suo mondo: convegno internazionale di studi (Firenze, 9–13 giugno 1992)*, Florence, 1994, 61–85.

——, and Albinia de la Mare, 'Bartolomeo Scala's Dealings with Booksellers, Scribes and Illuminators, 1459–63', *Journal of the Warburg and Courtauld Institutes*, 39 (1976), 236–45.

Brown, Horatio F., *The Venetian Printing Press: An Historical study*, London, 1891.

Brown, Patricia Fortini, *Private Lives in Renaissance Venice: Art, Architecture and the Family*, New Haven, 2004.

——, 'Behind the Walls: The Material Culture of Venetian Elites', in John Martin and Dennis Romano, eds, *Venice Reconsid-*

ered: *The History and Civilization of an Italian City State*, Baltimore, 2000, 295–338.

——, *Venice and Antiquity: The Venetian Sense of the Past*, New Haven, 1996.

Brucker, Gene, 'Florentine Voices from the Catasto, 1427–1480', *I Tatti Studies: Essays in the Renaissance*, 5 (1993), 11–32.

——, *The Civic World of Early Renaissance Florence*, Princeton, 1977.

Bruni, Annalisa, 'Mobilità sociale e mobilità geografica nella Venezia di fine '500: la parocchia di San Salvador', *Annali veneti: società, cultura, istituzioni*, 2 (1985), 75–83.

Buck-Moss, Susan, *The Dialectics of Seeing: Walter Benjamin and the Arcades Project*, Cambridge, Mass., 1989.

Bulgarelli, Tullio, *Gli avvisi a stampa in Roma nel cinquecento: bibliografia, antologia*, Rome, 1967.

Bullard, Melissa M. and Nicolai Rubinstein, 'Lorenzo de Medici's Acquisition of the *Sigillo di Nerone*', *Journal of the Warburg and Courtauld Institutes*, 62 (1999), 283–6.

Bury, Michael, *The Print in Italy, 1550–1620*, London, 2001.

Calabi, Donatella, *Il mercato e la città: piazze, strade, architettura d'Europa in età moderna*, Venice, 1993.

—— ed., *Fabbriche, piazze, mercati: la città italiana nel rinascimento*, Rome, 1997.

—— and Paola Lanaro, 'Lo spazio delle fiere e dei mercati nella città italiana di età moderna', in Simonetta Cavaciocchi, ed, *Fiere e mercati nella integrazione delle economie Europee, secc. XIII–XVIII*, Prato, 2001, 109–57.

—— eds, *La città italiana e i luoghi degli stranieri: XIV–XVII secolo*, Rome, 1998.

Calabi, Donatella and Paolo Morachiello, *Rialto: le fabbriche e il ponte, 1514–1591*, Turin, 1987.

Camerano, A., 'Donne oneste o meretrici? Incertezza dell'identità fra testamento e diritto di proprietà a Roma', *Quaderni storici*, 99 (1998), 637–66.

Cameron, Kenneth W., *The Pardoner and His Pardons: Indulgences Circulating in England on the Eve of the Reformation with a Historical Introduction*, Hartford, Conn., 1965.

Campbell, Lorne, 'The Art Market in the Southern Netherlands in the Fifteenth Century', *Burlington Magazine* 118 (1976), 195–6.

Camporesi, Piero, *Il palazzo e il cantimbanco Giulio Cesare Croce*, Milan, 1994.

——, *Il pane selvaggio*, Bologna, 1980 (translated as *The Bread of Dreams*, London, 1982).

——, *Il paese della fame*, Bologna, 1978 (translated as *The Land of Hunger*, London, 1966).

——, *La maschera di Bertoldo: G. C. Croce e la letteratura carnevalesca*, Turin, 1976.

——, ed., *Il libro dei vagabondi: lo speculum cerretanorum di Teseo Pini, il vagabondo di Rafaele Frianoro e altri testi di furfanteria*, Turin, 1973.

Campostella, Pietro, *Il Monte di Pietà di Milano*, 3 vols, Milan, 1966–73.

Carnesecchi, Carlo, *Donne e lusso a Firenze nel secolo XVI: Cosimo I e la sua legge suntuaria del 1562*, Florence, 1902.

Carra, Gilberto, 'Speziali e spezierie in Mantova', *Civiltà mantovana*, 12 (1978), 245–75.

——, 'Un tumulto di donne', *Miscellanea fiorentina di erudizione e storia*, 2 (1895), 45–7.

Carrara, Eliana and Sharon Gregory, 'Borghini's Print Purchases from Giunti', *Print Quarterly*, 17 (2000), 3–16.

Carrier, James G., *Gifts and Commodities: Exchange and Western Capitalism since 1700*, London, 1995.

Cartwright, Julia, *Beatrice d'Este, Duchess of Milan: A Study of the Renaissance*, London, 1905.

——, *Isabella d'Este, Marchioness of Mantua, 1474–1539: A Study of the Renaissance*, 2 vols, London, 1903.

Castelli, Enrico, *Storia dell'antichissima fiera delle Grazia dal 1425 ad oggi*, Mantua, 1979.

——, *I banchi feneratizi ebraici nel Mantovano (1386–1808)*, Mantua, 1959.

Castelnuovo, Enrico, ed., *Ambrogio Lorenzetti: il Buon Governo*, Milan, 1995.

Cessi, Francesco, *Giovanni da Cavino: medaglista padovano del cinquecento*, Padua, 1969.

Cessi, Roberto and Annibale Alberti, *Rialto: l'isola, il ponte, il mercato*, Bologna, 1934.

Cherubini, Giovanni, ed., *Storia di Pistoia*. II. *L'età del libero comune: dall'inizio del XII alla metà del XIV secolo*, Florence, 1998.

——, *Il lavoro, la taverna, la strada*, Naples, 1997.

——, *Foires et marchés dans les campagnes italiennes au Moyen Age*, in Charles Desplat, ed., *Foires et marché dans les campagnes de l'Europe médiévale et moderne*, Toulouse, 1996, 71–84.

——, 'Rilegendo Antonio Pucci: Il "mercato vecchio"', in *Cultura e società nell' Italia medievale: studi per Paolo Brezzi*, 2 vols, Rome, 1988, 1, 197–214.

Chiappini, Luciano, *Eleanora d'Aragona, prima duchessa di Ferrara*, Rovigo, 1956.

Chittolini, Giorgio, 'Quasi-città: borghi e terre in area lombarda nel tardo medioevo', *Società e storia*, 47 (1990), 3–26.

——, *La formazione dello stato regionale e le istituzioni del contado: secoli XIV e XV*, Turin, 1979.

Chojnacka, Monica, *Working Women of Early Modern Venice*, Baltimore, 2001.

——, 'Women, Men and Residential Patterns in Early Modern Venice', *Journal of Family History*, 25 (2000), 1–25.

Chojnacki, Stanley, 'Measuring Adulthood: Adolescence and Gender in Renaissance Venice', *Journal of Family History*, 17 (1992), 371–95.

——, 'Political Adulthood in Fifteenth-Century Venice', *American Historical Review*, 91 (1986), 791–810.

——, 'Patrician Women in Early Renaissance Venice', *Studies in the Renaissance*, 21 (1974), 176–203.

Christian, Kathleen Wren, 'The De Rossi Collection of Ancient Sculptures, Leo X, and Raphael', *Journal of the Warburg and Courtauld Institutes*, 65 (2002), 132–200.

Ciappelli, Giovanni, 'Family Memory: Functions, Evolution, Recurrences', in Giovanni Ciapelli and Patricia Rubin, eds, *Art, Memory, and Family in Renaissance Florence*, Cambridge, 2000, 26–38.

—— and Patricia Rubin, eds, *Art, Memory and Family in Renaissance Florence*, Cambridge, 2000.

——, *Carnevale e quaresima: comportamenti sociali e cultura a Firenze nel rinascimento*, Rome, 1997.

Ciardini, Marino, *I banchieri ebrei in Firenze nel secolo XV e il Monte di Pietà fondato da Girolamo Savonarola*, Borgo San Lorenzo, 1907.

Ciasca, Raffaele, *L'arte dei medici e speziali nella storia e nel commercio fiorentino dal secolo XII al XV*, Florence, 1927.

Cicchetti, Angelo and Raul Mordenti, *I libri di famigilia in Italia*, 2 vols, Rome, 1985.

Cipolla, Carlo M., *Before the Industrial Revolution: European Society and Economy, 1000–1700*, London, 1993.

——, *Il governo della moneta a Firenze e a Milano nei secoli XIV–XVI*, Bologna, 1990.

——, *La moneta a Milano nel quattrocento: monetazione argentea e svalutazione secolare*, Rome, 1988.

——, *La moneta a Firenze nel cinquecento*, Bologna, 1987.

——, *Il fiorino e il quattrino: la politica monetaria a Firenze nel trecento*, Bologna, 1982.

——, *Le macchine del tempo: l'orologio e la società (1300–1700)*, Bologna, 1981.

——, *Storia dell'economia italiana: saggi di storia economica*, Turin, 1959.

——, *Money, Prices and Civilization: Fifth to Seventeenth Century*, Princeton, 1956.

——, *Prezzi, salari e teoria dei salari in Lombardia alla fine del cinquecento*, Rome, 1956.

Clunas, Craig, 'Modernity, Global and Local: Consumption and the Rise of the West', *American Historical Review*, 104 (1999), 1497–1511.

Cohen, Elizabeth S., 'Honour and Gender in the Streets of Early Modern Rome', *Journal of Interdisciplinary History*, 22 (1992), 597–625.

——, 'Courtesans and Whores: Words and Behaviour in Roman Streets', *Women's Studies*, 19 (1991), 201–8.

—— and Thomas S. Cohen, *Daily Life in Renaissance Italy*, Westport, Connecticut, 2001.

Cohn, Samuel, *Women in the Streets: Essays on Sex and Power in Renaissance Italy*, Baltimore, 1996.

Concina, Ennio, 'Trasformazioni della struttura urbana attraverso fonti d'archivio. Analasi e restituzione grafica delle fonte locali descrittive per la città di Venezia, in Elisabetta Molteni, ed., *Estimi e catasticazioni, descrittive, cartografia storica, innovazioni catalografiche*, Treviso, 2001.

——, *Fondaci: architettura, arte e mercatura tra Levante, Venezia e Alemagna*, Venice, 1997.

—— Ugo Camerino and Donatella Calabi, eds, *La città degli ebrei: Il ghetto di Venezia: architettura e urbanistica*, Venice, 1991.

Conforti, Claudia, *Giorgio Vasari. Architetto*, Milan, 1993.

Connell, William J., ed., *Society and Individual in Renaissance Florence*, Berkeley, 2000.

Constable, Olivia R., *Housing the Stranger in the Mediterranean World: Lodging, Trade, and Travel in Late Antiquity and the Middle Ages*, Cambridge, 2003.

Corazzol, Gigi, *Livelli stipulati a Venezia nel 1591*, Pisa, 1986.

——, *Fitti e livelli a grano: un aspetto del credito rurale nel Veneto del '500*, Milan, 1979.

Corbin, Alain, *Village Bells: Sound and Meaning in the Nineteenth-Century French Countryside*, New York, 1998.

Cortesi, Santa, *I due testamenti di Fra Sabba da Castiglione*, Faenza, 2000.

Courtright, Nicola, *The Papacy and the Art of Reform in Sixteenth-Century Rome: Gregory XIII's Tower of the Winds in the Vatican*, Cambridge, 2003.

Cowan, Alexander, *Urban Europe, 1500–1700*, London, 1998.

——, 'Love, Honour and the Avogaria di Comun', *Archivio veneto*, series 5, 179 (1995), 5–19.

Cressy, David, *Bonfires and Bells: National Memory and the Protestant Calendar in Elizabethan and Stuart England*, Berkeley, 1989.

Cristallini, Claudio and Marco Noccioli, *I 'Libri delle Case' di Roma: il catasto del Collegio Inglese (1630)*, Rome 1987.

Crouzet-Pavan, Elisabeth, *'Sopra le acque salse': espaces, pouvoir et société à Venise à la fin du Moyen Age*, Rome, 1992.

Currie, Elizabeth, 'The Fashions of the Florentine Court: Wearing, Making and Buying Clothing, 1560–1620', Ph.D., diss., University of Sussex, 2004.

——, 'Prescribing Fashion: Dress, Politics and Gender in Sixteenth-Century Italian Conduct Literature', *Fashion Theory*, 4 (2000), 157–78.

Curtin, Philip D., *Cross-Cultural Trade in World History*, Cambridge, 1984.

Cutini, Clara, 'La disciplina giuridica della fiera di Ognisanti', in *La fiera dei morti di Perugia*, Perugia, 1980, 27–40.

D'Amico, Stefano, 'Poveri e gruppi marginali nella società milanese cinque-seicentesca', in Danilo Zardin, ed., *La città e i poveri. Milano e le terre lombarde dal rinascimento all'età spagnola*, Milan, 1995, 273–90.

Daunton, Martin and Matthew Hilton, eds, *The Politics of Consumption: Material Culture and Citizenship in Europe and America*, Oxford, 2001.

Davies, Martin, 'Two Book Lists of Sweynheym and Pannartz' in *Libri, tipografi, biblioteche: ricerche storice dedicate a Luigi Balsamo*, Florence, 1997, 1, 25–53.

Davies, Robert C., 'The Geography of Gender in the Renaissance', in Judith C. Brown and Robert C. Davis, eds, *Gender and Society in Renaissance Italy*, New York 1998, 19–38.

——, *Shipbuilders of the Venetian Arsenal: Workers and Workplace in the Preindustrial City*, Baltimore, 1991.

Davis, Robert C. and Benjamin Ravid, eds, *The Jews of Early Modern Venice*, Baltimore, 2001.

Day, John, *The Medieval Market Economy*, Oxford, 1987.

Dean, Trevor, ed., *The Towns of Italy in the Later Middle Ages*, Manchester, 2000.

De Certeau, Michel, 'Practices of Space', in Marshall Blonsky, ed., *On Signs*, Baltimore, 1985, 122–45.

——, *The Practice of Everyday Life*, Berkeley, 1984.

Degrassi, Donata, *L'economia artigiana nell'Italia medievale*, Rome, 1996.

De Grazia, Victoria, *Irresistible Empire: America's Advance Through Twentieth-Century Europe*, Cambridge, Mass., 2005.

——, 'American Supermarkets Versus European Small Shops: Or How Transnational Capitalism Crossed Paths with Moral Economy in 1960s Italy', Discussion Paper, Gender Studies Programme Seminar, Robert Schuman Centre for Advanced Studies, European University Institute, 2002.

Della Valentina, Marcello, 'I mestieri del pane a Venezia tra '600 e '700', *Atti del istituto veneto di scienza, lettere ed arti*, 150 (1991–2), 113–217.

De la Mare, Albinia, 'The Library of Francesco Sassetti (1421–1490)', in Cecil H. Clough, ed., *Cultural Aspects of the Italian Renaissance: Essays in Honour of Paul Oskar Kristeller*, Manchester, 1976, 160–201.

——, 'The shop of a Florentine *cartolaio* in 1426', in Berta Maracchi Biagiarelli and Dennis E. Rhodes, eds, *Studi offerti a Roberto Ridolfi*, Florence, 1973, 237–48.

De Luca, G., *Commercio del denaro e crescita economica a Milano tra cinquecento e seicento*, Milan, 1996.

Delumeau, Jean, *Vie économique et sociale de Rome dans la seconde moitié du XVIe siècle*, Paris, 1957–9.

De Maddalena, Aldo, *Moneta e mercato nel '500: la rivoluzione dei prezzi*, Florence, 1973.

De Marchi, Neil, 'The Role of Dutch Auctions and Lotteries in Shaping the Art Market(s) of Seventeenth-Century Holland', *Journal of Economic Behaviour and Organization*, 28 (1995), 203–21.

Derernzini, Giovanna, 'Le reliquie da Con-stantinopoli a Siena', in Luciano Bellosi, ed., *L'oro di Siena: il tesoro di Santa Maria della Scala*, Milan, 1996, 67–78.

Detti, Edoardo, *Firenze scomparsa*, Florence, 1970.

De Vivo, Filippo, 'Dall'imposizione del silenzio alla "Guerra delle Scritture": le pubblicazioni ufficiali durante l'interdetto del 1606–1607', *Studi veneziani*, n. s. 41 (2001), 179–213.

De Vries, Jan, 'Population', in Thomas A. Brady Jr, Heiko A. Oberman and James D. Tracy, eds, *Handbook of European History*, Grand Rapids Mich., 1994, I, 1–50.

——, 'Between Purchasing Power and the World of Goods: Understanding the Household Economy in Early Modern Europe', in J. Brewer and R. Porter, eds, *Consumption and the World of Goods*, London, 1993, 85–132.

——, *European Urbanization, 1500–1800*, London, 1984.

Dewar, David and Vanessa Watson, *Urban Markets: Developing Informal Retailing*, London, 1990.

Dian, Girolamo, *Cenni storici sulla farmacia veneta*, Venice, 1900.

Dittmar, Helga, *The Social Psychology of Material Possessions: To Have is to Be*, Hemel Hempstead, 1992.

Dohroi Rossum, Gerhard, *History of the Hour: Clocks and Modern Temporal Orders*, Chicago, 1996.

Dolcetti, Giovanni, *Le bische e il giuoco d'azzardo a Venezia, 1172–1807*, Venice, 1903.

Edelstein, Bruce L., 'Nobildonne napoletane e committenza: Eleanora d'Aragona ed Eleanora di Toledo a confronto', *Quaderni storici*, n. s. 104 (2000), 295–330.

Edler de Roover, Florence, 'Andrea Bianchi, Florentine Silk Manufacturer and Merchant in the Fifteenth Century', *Studies in Medieval and Renaissance History*, 3 (1966), 223–85.

Eisenblicher, Konrad, ed., *The Premodern Teenager: Youth in Society, 1150–1650*, Toronto, 2002.

Epstein, Stephen R., 'Regional Fairs, Institutional Innovation, and Economic Growth in Late Medieval Europe', *Economic History Review*, 47 (1994), 459–82.

Esch, Arnold, 'Roman Customs Registers, 1470–1480: Items of Interest to Historians of Art and Material Culture', *Journal of the Warburg and Courtauld Institutes*, 58 (1995), 72–87.

——, 'Le importazioni nella Roma del primo Rinascimento (il loro volume secondo i registri doganali romani degli anni 1452–1462)', in Arnold Esch et al., *Aspetti della vita economica e culturale a Roma nel quattrocento*, Rome, 1981, 7–79.

Fairchilds, Cissie, *Domestic Enemies: Servants and Their Masters in Old Regime France*, Baltimore, 1990.

Fanfani, Amintore, *Storia del lavoro in Italia dalla fine del secolo XV agli inizi del XVIII*, Milan, 1943.

——, *Indagine sulla 'rivoluzione dei prezzi'*, Milan, 1940.

Fantoni, Marcello, Louisa C. Matthew and Sara F. Matthews-Grieco, eds, *The Art Market in Italy: Fifteenth to Seventeenth Centuries*, Modena, 2003.

Faroqhi, Suraiya, *Towns and Townsmen of Ottoman Anatolia: Trade, Crafts, and Food Production in an Urban Setting, 1520–1650*, Cambridge, 1984.

Favalier, Sylvia 'Le attività lavorative in una parrochia del centro di Venezia (San Polo–secolo XVI), *Studi veneziani*, n. s. 9 (1985), 187–97.

Ferino-Pagden, Sylvia, *'La prima donna del mondo'. Isabella d'Este. Fürstin und Mäzenatin der Renaissance*, Vienna, 1994.

Ferlisi, Gianfrancesco, 'Sulla quattrocentesca Piazza del Purgo', *Civiltà mantovana*, 36 (2001), 82–107.

Ferraro, Joanne M., *Marriage Wars in Late Renaissance Venice*, Oxford, 2001.

Ferrato, Pietro, *Lettere inedite di donne mantovane dal secolo XV tratte dall'archivio de' Gonzaga in Mantova*, Mantua, 1878.

Ferrone, Siro, *Attori, mercanti, corsari: la commedia dell'arte in Europa tra Cinque and Seicento*, Turin, 1993.

——, ed., *Il teatro del cinquecento: i luoghi, i testi e gli attori*, Florence, 1982.

Findlay, Allan M., Ronan Paddison and John A. Dawson, *Retailing Environments in Developing Countries*, London, 1990.

Findlen, Paula, 'Inventing Nature: Commerce, Art and Science in the Early Modern Cabinet of Curiosities', in Pamela Smith and Paula Findlen, eds, *Merchants and Marvels: Commerce, Science, and Art in Early Modern Europe*, New York, 2002, 297–323.

——, 'Possessing the Past: The Material World of the Italian Renaissance', *American Historical Review*, 103 (1998), 83–114.

——, *Possessing Nature: Museums, Collecting, and Scientific Culture in Early Modern Italy*, Berkeley, 1994.

Finn, Margot, 'Sex and the City: Metropolitan Modernities in English History', *Victorian Studies*, 44 (2001), 25–32.

Firpo, Massimo, *Artisti, gioiellieri, eretici: il mondo di Lorenzo Lotto tra riforma e contrariforma*, Rome, 2001.

Fiumi, Enrico, 'Economia e vita privata dei Fiorentini nelle rilevazioni statistiche di Giovanni Villani', in Carlo M. Cipolla, ed., *Storia dell'economia italiana: saggi di storia economica*, Turin, 1959, 325–60.

Fletcher, Jennifer and Reinhold Mueller, 'Bellini and the Bankers: The Priuli Altarpiece for S. Michele in Isola, Venice', *Burlington Magazine*, 147 (2005), 5–15.

Fontaine, Laurence, *History of Pedlars in Europe*, Cambridge, 1996.

Fornasari, Massimo, *Il 'thesoro' della città: il Monte di Pietà e l'economia bolognese nei secoli XV e XVI*, Bologna, 1993.

Franceschi, Franco, 'La bottega come spazio di sociabilità', in Franco Franceschi and Gloria Fossi, eds, *Arti fiorentine: la grande storia dell'artigianato. II. Il Quattrocento*, Florence, 1999, 65–84.

——, *Oltre il 'Tumulto': I lavoratori fiorentine dell'arte della lana fra tre e quattrocento*, Florence, 1993.

—— and G. Fossi, eds, *Arti fiorentine: la grande storia dell'artigianato. II. Il Quattrocento*, Florence, 1999.

Frangioni, Lucia, *Milano e le sue misure: appunti di metrologia lombarda fra tre e quattrocento*, Naples, 1992.

——, *Milano e le sue strade: costi di trasporto e vie di commercio dei prodotti milanesi alla fine del trecento*, Bologna, 1983.

Fraser, W. Hamish, *The Coming of the Mass Market, 1850–1914*, London, 1981.

Frati, Ludovico, *La vita privata di Bologna dal secolo XIII al XVII*, Bologna, 1900.

Freedman, Paul, *Images of the Medieval Peasant*, Stanford, Calif., 1999.

Frick, Carol Collier, *Dressing Renaissance Florence: Families, Fortunes, and Fine Clothing*, Baltimore, 2002.

Friedland, Roger and A. Robertson, *Beyond the Marketplace: Rethinking Economy and Society*, New York, 1990.

Frommel, Cristopher, L. Stefano Ray and Manfredo Tafuri, eds, *Raffaello architetto*, Milan, 1984.

Frojmovič, Eva, 'Giotto's Allegories of Justice and the Commune in the Palazzo della Ragione in Padua: A Reconstruction', *Journal of the Warburg and Courtauld Institutes*, 59 (1996), 24–47.

Fusco, Laurie and Gino Corti, 'Giovanni Ciampolini (d.1505): a Renaissance Dealer in Rome and his Collection of Antiquities', *Xenia*, 21 (1991), 7–46.

Gabb, Ann, *The Strozzi of Florence: Widowhood and Family Solidarity in the Renaissance*, Ann Arbor, 2000.

Gabrielli, Noemi, *Rappresentazioni sacre e profane nel castello di Issogne e la pittura nella Valle d'Aosta alla fine del quattrocento*, Turin, 1959.

Gagliardi, Isabella, 'Le reliquie dell'ospedale di Santa Maria della Scala (XIV–XV)', in Luciano Bellosi, ed., *L'oro di Siena: il tesoro di Santa Maria della Scala*, Milan, 1996, 49–67.

Gallo, Marzia Cataldi, 'Il commercio degli abti usati a Genova nel XVII secolo', in *Per una storia della moda pronta: problemi e ricerche*, Florence, 1991, 95–106.

Gardner, Carl and Julie Shepherd, *Consuming Passion: The Rise of Retail Culture*, London, 1989.

Gargan, Luciano, *Cultura e arte nel Veneto al tempo del Petrarca*, Padua, 1978.

Garrioch, David, 'House Names, Shop Signs and Social Organisation in Western European Cities, 1500–1900', *Urban History*, 21 (1994), 20–48.

Gay, Hannah, 'Clock Synchrony, Time Distribution, and Electrical Timekeeping in Britain, 1880–1925,' *Past and Present*, 181 (2003), 107–40.

Gazzini, Marina, *Dare et habere: Il mondo di un mercante milanese del quattrocento (con il libro di conti di Donato Ferrario da Pantigliate)*, Milan, 1997.

Geertz, Clifford, 'Suq: The Bazaar Economy in Sefrou', in *idem, Meaning and Order in Moroccan Society: Three Essays in Cultural Analysis*, Cambridge, 1979, 123–244.

Gehl, Paul F., 'Day-by-Day on Credit: Binders and Booksellers in Cinquecento Florence', *La bibliofilia*, 100 (1998), 391–409.

——, 'Credit Sales Strategies in the Late Cinquecento Book Trade', in *Libri, tipografi, biblioteche: ricerche storiche dedicate a Luigi Balsamo*, Florence, 1997, I, 193–206.

——, 'Libri per donne: Le monache clienti del libraio fiorentino Piero Morosi (1588–1607)', in Gabrielle Zarri, ed., *Donne, discipline, creanze cristiana dal XV al XVII secolo: studi e testi a stampa*, Rome, 1996, 61–82.

Gentilcore, David, '"Tutti i modi che adoprano i ceretani per far bezzi": Towards a Database of Italian Charlatans', *Ludica*, 5–6 (2000), 201–15.

——, *Healers and Healing in Early Modern Italy*, Manchester, 1998.

——, ' "Charlatans, Mountebanks and Other Similar People": The Regulation and Role of Itinerant Practitioners in Early Modern Italy', *Social History*, 20 (1995), 297–314.

——, 'All that Pertains to Medicine: Protomedici and Protomedicati in Early Modern Italy', *Medical History*, 38 (1994), 121–42.

Ghetti, Bernardino, 'Gli ebrei e il Monte di Pietà in Recanati nei secoli xv e xvi', *Atti e memorie della reale deputazione di storia patria per le provincie delle marche*, n. s. 9 (1913), 377–434.

Ghinzoni, Paolo, 'Federico III Imperatore a Venezia (7 al 19 Febbraio 1469)', *Archivio veneto*, 37 (1889), 133–44.

Gill, Katherine, 'Women and Performance: The Development of Improvisation by the Sixteenth-Century "Commedia dell'Arte"', *Theatre Journal*, 43 (1991), 59–69.

Gioffré, Domenico, *Il mercato degli schiavi a Genova nel secolo XV*, Genoa, 1971.

Giordano, Louisa, 'Il disegno di una bottega per piazza piccola', *Bollettino della società pavese di storia patria*, n. s. 48 (1996), 181–7.

Goldthwaite, Richard A., 'I prezzi del grano a Firenze dal xiv al xvi secolo', in *idem, Banks, Palaces and Entrepreneurs in Renaissance Florence*, Aldershot, 1995, chapter 6.

——, *Wealth and the Demand For Art in Italy, 1300–1600*, Baltimore, 1993.

——, 'The Empire of Things: Consumer Demand in Renaissance Italy', in Francis W. Kent and Patricia Simons, eds, *Patronage, Art and Society in Renaissance Italy*, Oxford, 1987, 153–75.

——, 'Schools and Teachers of Commercial Arithmetic in Renaissance Florence', *Journal of European Economic History*, 1 (1972), 418–33.

Goldthwaite, Richard A. and Giulio Mandich, *Studi sulla moneta fiorentina: secoli XIII–XVI*, Florence, 1994.

Gowing, Laura, ' "The Freedom of the Streets": Women and Social Space, 1560–1640', in Paul Griffiths and Mark S. R. Jenner, eds, *Londonopolis: Essays in the Cultural and Social History of Early Modern London*, Manchester, 2000, 130–53.

Goy, Richard, *Venice: The City and its Architecture*, London, 1997.

Gozzadini, Giovanni, 'Dell'origine del uso dei cocchi e di due veronesi in particolare', *Atti e memorie della reale deputazione di storia patria per le provincie di romagna*, 2 (1863), 199–249.

Grandi, Antonio, 'Le trasformazioni di Piazza del Duomo nella storia', in A. B. Belgiojoso, A. Grandi, D. Rodella and A. Tosi, eds, *Piazza del Duomo a Milano: storia, problemi, progetti*, Milan 1982, 24–86.

Gravi, A., 'Valori urbani e attività arginali nella Piazza Universale di Tomasso Garzoni', *Richerche storiche*, 20 (1990), 45–73.

Gregson, Nicky and Louise Crewe, *Second-Hand Cultures*, Oxford, 2003.

Griffin, Emnia, 'Sports and Celebrations in English Market Towns, 1600–1750, *Historical Research*, 75 (2002), 188–208.

Grohmann, Alberto, 'Note sulle fiere umbre in età medioevale e moderna', *La fiera dei morti di Perugia: lineamenti storici di un antica tradizione perugina*, Perugia, 1980, 1–25.

——, *Le fiere del regno di Napoli in età aragonese*, Naples, 1969.

Grossi, Maria Letizia 'Le botteghe fiorentine nel catasto del 1427', *Richerche storiche*, 30 (2000), 3–55.

Grubb, James S., *Provincial Families of the Renaissance: Private and Public Life in the Veneto*, Baltimore, 1996.

——, 'Memory and Identity: Why Venetians Didn't Keep "Ricordanze"', *Renaissance Studies*, 8 (1994), 375–87.

Guérin dalle Mese, Jeannine, ed., *Il vestito e la sua immagine: atti del convegno in ommagio a Cesare Vecellio nel quarto centenario della morte*, Belluno, 2002.

——, *L'occhio di Cesare Vecellio: abiti e costume exotici nel '500*, Alessandria, 1988.

Guerzoni, Guido, 'From the History of Prices to the Histories of Price: Social Networks and Court Strategies in Sixteenth-Century

Italy', in M. O. Malley and E. Welch, eds, *The Material Renaissance*, forthcoming.

——, 'Ricadute occupazionali ed impatti economici della committenza aristica delle corti estensi tra quattro e cinquecento', in S. Cavaciocchi, ed., *Economia e arte: secc. XIII–XVIII*, Florence, 2002, 187–230.

Günther, Hubertus, 'I progetti di ricostruzione della basilica di San Pietro negli scritti contemporanei: giustificazioni e scrupoli', in Gianfranco Spagnesi, ed., *L'architettura della basilica di San Pietro: storia e costruzione*, Rome, 1997, 137–48.

Guzzetti, Linda, 'Le donne a Venezia nel XIV secolo: uno studio sulla loro presenza nella società e nella famiglia', *Studi veneti*, n. s. 25 (1998), 15–88.

Haas, Louis, *The Renaissance Man and His Children*, New York, 1998.

Heers, Jacques, *Esclaves et domestiques au Moyen Age dans le monde méditeranéen*, Paris, 1981.

——, *Gênes au xve siècle: Civilisation méditerranéenne, grand capitalisme, et capitalisme populaire*, Paris, 1971.

Heikamp, Detleff, 'Zur Mediceischen Glaskunst, Archivalien, Entwurfs Zeichnungen, Gläser und Scherben', *Mitteilungen des Kunsthistorisches Institutes in Florenz*, 3 (1986), 1–423.

Herlihy, David and C. Klapisch-Zuber, *Tuscans and Their Families: A Study of the Florentine Catasto of 1427*, New Haven, 1985.

Hetherington, Paul, 'A Purchase of Byzantine Relics and Reliquaries in Fourteenth-Century Venice', *Arte veneta*, 37 (1983), 9–30.

Hinton, Jack, 'By Sale. By Gift: Aspects of the Resale and Bequest of Goods in Late Sixteenth-Century Venice', *Journal of Design History*, 15 (2002), 245–62.

Hodges, Richard, *Primitive and Peasant Markets*, Oxford, 1988.

Hohti, Paola, 'The Innkeeper's Goods: The Acquisition and Use of Household Property in Sixteenth-Century Siena', in M. O'Malley and E. Welch, eds, *The Material Renaissance*, forthcoming.

Hollingsworth, Mary, 'Coins, Candlesticks and Cavalli: The Economics of Extravagance', in M. O'Malley and E. Welch, *The Material Renaissance*, forthcoming.

——, *The Cardinal's Hat*, London, 2004.

——, *Patronage in Sixteenth-Century Italy*, London, 1996.

Honig, Elizabeth, 'Desire and the Domestic Economy', *Art Bulletin*, 83 (2001), 294–315.

——, *Painting and the Market in Early Modern Antwerp*, New Haven, 1999.

Hoock, Jochen, Pierre Jeannin and Wolfgang Kaiser, eds, *Ars Mercatoria: Handbücher und Traktate für den Gebrauch des Kaufmanns, 1470–1820*, Paderborn, 3 vols, 1991–2001.

Howard, Deborah, *Venice and The East*, New Haven, 2000.

Hulton, Matthew, 'The Fable of the Sheep, or, Private Virtues, Public Vices: The Consumer Revolution of the Twentieth Century', *Past and Present*, 176 (2002), 222–57.

Hunt, Edwin S. *The Medieval Super-Companies: A Study of the Peruzzi Company of Florence*, Cambridge, 1994.

Jackson, Kenneth T., 'All the World's a Mall: Reflections on the Social and Economic Consequences of the American Shopping Center', *American Historical Review*, 101 (1996), 111–21.

Jacoby, David, 'Venetian Cheese: A Neglected Aspect of Venetian Medieval Trade', in Ellen Kittell and Thomas F. Madden, eds, *Medieval and Renaissance Venice*, Urbana, Ill., 1999, 49–68.

Jardine, Lisa, *Worldly Goods: A New History of the Renaissance*, London, 1998.

Kampen, Natalie Boymel, 'Social Status and Gender in Roman Art: The Case of the Saleswoman', in Norma Broude and Mary Garrard, eds, *Feminism and Art History: Questioning the Litany*, New York, 1982, 63–78.

——, *Image and Status: Roman Working Women in Ostia*, Berlin, 1981.

Katrizky, Margaret A., 'Marketing Medicine:

The Image of the Early Modern Mountebank', *Renaissance Studies*, 15 (2001), 121–53.

——, 'Was Commedia dell'Arte performed by Mountebanks? "Album amicorum" Illustrations and Thomas Platter's Description of 1598', *Theatre Research International*, 23 (1998), 104–26.

——, 'Italian Comedians in Renaissance Prints', *Print Quarterly*, 4 (1987), 236–54.

Kent, Dale, 'Michele del Giogante's House of Memory', in William F. Connell, ed., *Society and Individual in Renaissance Florence*, Berkeley, 2000, 110–36.

Kent, Francis William, 'Be Rather Loved Than Feared: Class Relations in Quattrocento Florence', in William J. Connell, ed., *Society and Individual in Renaissance Florence*, Berkeley, 2000, 13–50.

Kiene, Michael, *Bartolomeo Ammanati*, Milan, 1995.

Killerby, Catherine Kovesi, *Sumptuary Law in Italy, 1200–1500*, Oxford, 2002.

Kirkendale, Warren, *Emilio Cavalieri, 'gentilhuomo romano': His Life and Letters, His Role as Superintendent of All the Arts at the Medici Court*, Florence, 2001.

Kirshner, Julius, ' "Li Emergenti Bisogni Matrimoniali" in Renaissance Florence', in William J. Connell, ed., *Society and Individual in Renaissance Florence*, Berkeley, 2000, 79–109.

Kisch, Bruno, *Scales and Weights: A Historical Outline*, New Haven, 1965.

Kittell, Ellen E. and Thomas F. Madden, eds, *Medieval and Renaissance Venice*, Urbana, Ill., 1999.

Klapisch-Zuber, Christiane, *Women, Family and Ritual in Renaissance Italy*, Chicago, 1987.

Klawans, Zander H., *Imitations and Inventions of Roman Coins: Renaissance Medals of Julius Caesar and the Roman Empire*, Santa Monica, Calif., 1977.

Kline, Naomi, *No Logo: Taking Aim at the Brand Bullies*, New York, 2000.

Kohl, Benjamin, *Padua under the Carrara, 1318–1405*, Baltimore, 1998.

Kowaleski, Maryanne, *Local Markets and Regional Trade in Medieval Exeter*, Cambridge, 1995.

Kowinski, William Severini, *The Malling of America: An Inside Look at the Great Consumer Paradise*, New York, 1985.

Kula, Witold, *Measures and Men*, Princeton, 1986.

Labowsky, Lotte, *Bessarion's Library and the Biblioteca Marciana: Six Early Inventories*, Rome, 1980.

Lambert, Gisèle, *Les premières gravures italiennes, quattrocento-début du cinquecento: inventaire de la collection du département des estampes et de la photographie*, Paris, 1999.

Lanaro, Paola, *I mercati nella repubblica veneta: economie cittadine e stato territoriale (secoli XV–XVIII)*, Venice, 1999.

Lanciani, Rodolfo, *Storia degli scavi di Roma e notizie intorno le collezioni romane di antichità*, Rome, 1989–2002, 7 vols, reprint of original publication of 1902–16.

Lane, Frederic C., *Andrea Barbarigo: Merchant of Venice, 1418–1449*, Baltimore, 1944.

——, and Reinhold C. Mueller, *Money and Banking in Renaissance Venice: Venetian Coins and Monies of Account*, Baltimore, 1985.

Langholm, Odd, *The Merchant in the Confessional: Trade and Price in the Pre-Reformation Penitential Handbooks*, Leiden, 2003.

——, *The Legacy of Scholasticism in Economic Thought: Antecedents of Choice and Power*, Cambridge, 1998.

Latham, Anthony J. H., 'Markets and Development in Africa and Asia', in Bruce L. Anderson and A. J. H. Latham, eds, *The Market in History*, London, 1986, 201–20.

Lazzaroni, Michele and Antonio Muñoz, *Filarete: Scultore e architetto del secolo xv*, Rome, 1908.

Lazzi, Giovanna, 'Abbigliamento e costume nella Firenze dei primi granduchi: fonti e documenti', in Fernando Pasqualone and Paolo Tammetta, eds, *La famiglia e la vita quotidiana in Europa nel '400 al '600: fonti e problemi*, Rome, 1986, 295–320.

Lefebvre, Henri, *The Production of Space*, trans. Donald Nicholson-Smith, Cambridge, Mass., 1991.

Le Goff, Jacques, *The Birth of Purgatory*, Chicago, 1984.

——, Merchant's Time and Church's Time in the Middle Ages', in *idem, Time, Work and Culture in the Middle Ages*, London, 1980, 29–42.

——, Jean Lefort and Perrine Mane, eds, *Les calendriers: leurs enjeux dans l'espace et dans le temps*, Paris, 2002.

Lemire, Beverly, *Dress, Culture and Commerce: The English Clothing Trade Before the Factory, 1600–1800*, Basingstoke, 1997.

Leoni, Aron di Leone, 'Alcuni esempi di quotidiana impreditorialità tra Ferrara, Ancona e Venezia nel XVI secolo', *Zakhor: Rivista di storia degli ebrei d'Italia*, 4 (2000), 57–114.

Leva Pistoi, M., ed., *Costumi a Issogne: aspetti del '400 quotidiano nelle lunette del castello di Issogne*, Aosta, 1985.

Levantini-Pieroni, G., *Lucrezia Tornabuoni, donna di Piero di Cosimo de'Medici: fatto sui documenti dell'archivio mediceo ed altri*, Florence, 1888.

Lincoln, Evelyn, *The Invention of the Renaissance Printmaker*, New Haven and London, 2000.

Lippincott, Kristen, *The Story of Time*, London, 2000.

Lira, Giovanni, 'Il controllo e la repressione degli "oziosi e vagabondi": la legislazione in età spagnola', in Danilo Zardin, ed., *La città e i poveri: Milano e le terre lombarde dal rinascimento all'età spagnola*, Milan, 1995.

——, 'Aspetti dell'applicazione della pena di morte a Milano in epoca spagnola', *Archivio storico lombardo*, anno 115, series 11, 6, (1989), 149–206.

Lombarda, Maria Louisa, 'Abbigliamento e moda a Roma nel secolo XV: fonti documentarie', in Fernando Pasqualone and Paolo Tammetta, eds, *La famiglia e la vita quotidiana in Europa nel '400 al '600: fonti e problemi*, Rome, 1986, 321–41.

Long, Pamela O., 'Invention, Authorship, "Intellectual Property" and the Origin of Patents. Notes towards a Conceptual History', *Technology and Culture*, 32 (1991), 846–84.

Lorenzoni, Anna Maria 'Tra Francesi e Spagnoli: le fortunose vicende di Eleanora Orsini del Balzo, Marchesa di Cortone, attraverso cartegi inediti dell' Archivio Gonzaga', in A. M. Lorenzoni and Roberto Navarrini, eds, *Per Mantova una vita: studi in memoria di Rita Castagna*, Mantua, 1991, 113–39.

——, 'Contributo allo studio delle fonti Isabelliane dell'Archivio di Stato di Mantova', *Atti e memori dell'Accademia Virgiliana di Mantova*, n. s. 47 (1979), 97–135.

Lowe, Kate, *Church and Politics in the Renaissance Italy: The Life and Career of Cardinal Francesco Soderini, 1453–1524*, Cambridge, 1993.

——, 'A Florentine Prelate's Real Estate in Rome Between 1480 and 1524: The Residential and Speculative Properties of Cardinal Francesco Soderini', *Papers of the British School of Rome*, 59 (1991), 259–82.

Lowry, Martin, *The World of Aldus Manutius: Business and Scholarship in Renaissance Venice*, Oxford, 1976.

Luigi, Sibylle, 'The Quarter of Porta Procula: Space and Ritual in Renaisssance Bologna', Ph.D. diss., University of Sussex, 2001.

Luzio, Alessandro, 'Isabella d'Este e i Borgia', *Archivio storico lombardo*, anno 41, series 5, (1914), 469–553; 673–753, anno 42, series 5, 1 (1915), 115–67; 412–64.

——, 'Isabella d'Este di fronte a Giulio II negli ultimi tre anni del suo pontificato', *Archivio storico lombardo*, anno 39, series 4, 17 (1912), 55–144, 393–456.

——, 'Isabella d'Este e Leone x dal Congresso di Bologna alla presa di Milano: 1515–1521', *Archivio storico italiano*, series 5, 40 (1907), 18–97, 44 (1909), 72–128, 45 (1910), 245–302. [1910a]

——, 'La reggenza d'Isabella d'Este durante la

prigonia del marito (1509–10)', *Archivio storico lombardo*, series 4, 14, anno 37 (1910). [1910b]

——, 'Isabella d'Este e Giulio II (1503–1505)', *Rivista d'Italia, lettere, scienze ed arte*, 12 (1909), 837–76.

——, 'Isabella d'Este e il sacco di Roma', *Archivio Storico Lombardo*, series 4, 10, anno 35 (1908), 5–107; 361–425. [1908a]

——, *Isabella d'Este e Francesco Gonzaga: Promessi sposi*, Milan, 1908. [1908b]

——, 'Isabella d'Este ne'primordi del papato di Leone X e il suo viaggio a Roma nel 1514–1515', *Archivio storico lombardo*, series 4, 6, anno 33 (1906), 99–180; 454–89.

——, and Rodolfo Renier, 'Il lusso di Isabella d'Este, Marchesa di Mantova: il guardaroba di Isabella d'Este', *Nuova antologia*, n. s. 4, 63 (1896), 441–69. [1896a]

——, 'Il lusso di Isabella d'Este, Marchesa di Mantova: gioielli e gemme', *Nuova antologia*, n. s. 4, 64 (1896), 294–324. [1896b]

——, Il lusso di Isabella d'Este, Marchesa di Mantova: l'arredo degli appartamenti', *Nuova antologia*, n. s. 4, 65 (1896), 294–324. [1896c]

——, 'Il lusso di Isabella d'Este, Marchesa di Mantova: accessorî e segreti della "toilette"', *Nuova antologia*, n. s. 4, 65 (1896), 666–88. [1896d]

——, *Mantova e Urbino: Isabella d'Este ed Elisabetta Gonzaga nelle relazioni famigliari e nelle vicende politiche (1471–1539)*, Turin and Rome, 1893.

——, 'Delle relazioni di Isabella d'Este Gonzaga con Ludovico e Beatrice d'Este', *Archivio storico lombardo*, anno 17, series 2, 7 (1890), 74–119; 346–99; 619–74.

Luzzatto, Gino, 'Il costo della vita a Venezia nel Trecento', in C. M. Cipolla, ed., *Storia dell'economia italiana*, Turin, 1959, I, 409–24.

——, *Studi di storia economica veneziana*, Padua, 1954.

MacKenney, Richard, 'Public and Private in Renaissance Venice', *Renaissance Studies*, 12, 1998, 110–30.

——, 'The Guilds of Venice: State and Society in the Longue Duree', *Studi veneziani*, n. s. 34 (1997), 15–44.

——, *Tradesmen and Traders: The World of the Guilds in Venice and Europe, c.1250-c.1650*, London, 1987.

Magnussen, Lars, *Mercantilism: The Shaping of an Economic Language*, London, 1994.

Maguire, Yvonne, *The Women of the Medici*, London, 1927.

Maiello, Francesco, *Storia del calendario: la misurazione del tempo, 1450–1800*, Turin, 1994.

Mainoni, Patricia, 'La seta a Milano nel XV secolo: aspetti economici e istituzionali', *Studi storici*, 35 (1994), 871–96.

Maiocchi, Rodolfo, *Codici diplomatico dell'Università di Pavia*, 2 vols, Pavia, 1905.

Malacarne, Giancarlo, *Le feste del principe*, Modena, 2002.

——, *Sulla mensa del principe: alimentazione e banchetti alla corte dei Gonzaga*, Modena, 2000.

Malanima, Paolo, *Il lusso dei contadini: consumi e industrie nelle campagne toscane del sei e settecento*, Bologna, 1990.

Mallett, Michael E., *The Florentine Galleys in the Fifteenth Century*, Oxford, 1967.

Mancini, Donata, 'Storia di uno spazio: La vita economica e sociale di Piazza Maggiore di Bologna del secolo XVI al secolo XVIII', Tesi di Laurea, Università degli studi di Bologna. Faccoltà di Scienze Politiche, 1983/4.

Mancini, Girolamo, 'Il bel San Giovanni', *Rivista d'arte*, 6 (1909), 185–227.

Mancini, Vincenzo, *Antiquari, 'vertuosi' e artisti: saggi sul collezionismo tra Padova e Venezia alla meta del cinquecento*, Padua, 1995.

Marangoni, Giovanni, *Associazioni di mestiere nella repubblica veneta (vittuaria–farmacia–medecina)*, Venice, 1974.

Marchesan, Angelo, *Treviso medievale: istituzioni, usi, costumi, aneddoti, curiosità*, ed. Luciano Gargan, 2 vols, Bologna, 1990.

Marciani, Corrado, 'Il commercio degli schiavi alle fiere di Lanciano nel secolo XVI',

Archivio storico per le provincie napoletane, n. s. 41 (1962), 269–82.

——, 'Il commercio dei cristalli alle fiere di Lanciano nel secolo XVI', *Archivio storico per le provincie Napoletane*, n. s. 39 (1960), 315–24.

——, 'Il commercio librario alle fiere di Lanciano nel' 500', *Rivista storica italiana*, 70 (1958), 421–41.

Marcucci, Roberto, 'La fiera di Senigallia', *Atti e memorie della reale deputazione di storia patria per le provincie delle marche*, n. s. 8 (1912), 247–526.

Marshall, Richard K., *The Local Merchants of Prato: Small Entrepreneurs in the Late Medieval Economy*, Baltimore, 1999.

Martin, John, *Venice's Hidden Enemies: Italian Heretics in a Renaissance City*, Chicago, 1993.

Martines, Lauro, 'The Renaissance and the Birth of a Consumer Society', *Renaissance Quarterly*, 51 (1998), 193–203.

Martini, Angelo, *Manuale di metrologia, ossia misure, pesi e monete in uso attualmente e anticamente presso tutti i popoli*, Turin, 1883.

Masetti Zannini, Gian Ludovico, *Stampatori e librai a Roma nella seconda meta del cinquecento: documenti inediti*, Rome, 1980.

——, 'Ebrei, artisti, oggetti d'arte documenti romani dei secoli XVI e XVII', *Commentari*, 25 (1974), 281–301.

Masschaele, James, *Peasants, Merchants, and Markets: Inland Trade in Medieval England, 1150–1350*, New York, 1997.

Matchette, Ann, 'Unbound Possessions: The Circulation of Used Goods in Florence, c. 1450–1600', Ph.D., University of Sussex, 2005.

Matthew, Louisa C., 'Were There Open Markets for Pictures in Renaissance Venice?', in Marcello Fantoni, Louisa C. Matthew, Sara F. Matthews-Grieco, eds, *The Art Market in Italy: Fifteenth to Seventeenth Centuries*, Modena, 2003, 253–61.

——, '"Vendecolori a Venezia": The Reconstruction of a Profession', *Burlington Magazine*, 144 (2002), 680–6.

Mattozzi, Ivo, 'Il politico e il pane a Venezia (1570–1650): Le tariffe dei calmieri: semplici prontuari o strumenti annonaria', *Studi veneziani*, n. s. 7 (1983), 197–220.

——, 'Crisi, stagnazione e mutamento nello stato veneziano sei-settecentesco: Il caso del commercio e della produzione olearia', *Studi veneziani*, n. s. 4 (1980), 199–276.

Mazzi, Angelo, 'Questioni metrologiche lombarde', *Archivio storico lombardo*, anno 38, series 4, 15 (1911), 5–64.

Mazzi, Curzio, 'La mensa dei priori di Firenze nel secolo XIV', *Archivio storico italiano*, series 5, 20, (1897), 336–68.

Mazzi, Maria Serena, *Prostitute e lenoni nella Firenze del quattrocento*, Milan, 1991.

——and Sergio Raveggi, *Gli uomini e le cose nelle campagne fiorentine*, Florence, 1983.

McArdle, Frank, *Altopascio: A Sudy in Tuscan Rural Society, 1587–1784*, Cambridge, 1978.

McClellan, Andrew, 'Watteau's Enseigne de Gersaint: Gersaint and the Marketing of Art in Eighteenth-Century Paris', *Art Bulletin* 78 (1996), 439–53.

McCracken, Grant, *Culture and Consumption: New Approaches to the Symbolic Character of Consumer Goods and Activities*, Bloomington, Ind., 1988.

McCray, W. Patrick, *Glassmaking in Renaissance Venice: The Fragile Craft*, Aldershot, 1999.

McCullagh, Suzanne Folds and Laura M. Giles, *Italian Drawings Before 1600 in the Art Institute of Chicago*, Chicago, 1997.

McKendrick, Neil, John Brewer and John H. Plumb, eds, *The Birth of a Consumer Society: The Commercialization of Eighteenth-Century England*, London, 1982.

McTighe, Sheila, 'Perfect Deformity, Ideal Beauty, and the "Imaginaire" of Work: The Reception of Annibale Carracci's "Arte di Bologna" in 1646', *Oxford Art Journal*, 16 (1993) 75–91.

Melis, Federigo, *Aspetti della vita economica medievale: studi nell'archivio Datini di Prato*, Siena, 1962.

Menning, Carol Bresnehan, *Charity and State*

in Late Renaissance Italy: The Monte di Pietà of Florence, Ithaca, N.Y., 1993.

Milano, Ernesto and Giulia Luppi, eds, *Libra: la bilancia nei codici Estensi. Immagini e modelli di strumenti di pesatura*, Modena, 1991.

Miller, Daniel, *A Theory of Shopping*, Cambridge, 1998.

Miller, Dwight, *Street Criers and Itinerant Tradesmen in European Prints*, Stanford, Calif., 1970.

Miller, Elizabeth, *Sixteenth-Century Ornament Prints in the Victoria and Albert Museum*, London, 1999.

Miller, Maureen C., 'The Medici Renovation of the Florentine Arcivescovado', *I Tatti Studies: Essays in the Renaissance*, 9 (2001), 89–117.

Miller, Michael B., *The Bon Marché: Bourgeois Culture and the Department Store, 1869–1920*, Princeton, 1981.

Milliot, Vincent, *Les Cris de Paris ou le people travesti. Les représéntations des petits métiers parisiens (XVIE–XVIIIE siècles)*, Paris, 1995.

Mira, Giuseppe, *Le fiere lombarde nei secoli XIV–XVI: prime indagini*, Como, 1955.

Modigliani, Anna, 'Taverne e osterie a Roma nel tardo medioevo: tipologia, uso degli spazi, arredo e distribuzione nella città', in *Taverne, locande e stufe: Roma nel rinascimento*, Rome, 1999, 19–45.

——, *Mercati, botteghe e spazi di commercio a Roma tra medioevo et età moderna*, Rome, 1998.

Mola, Luca, *The Silk Industry of Renaissance Venice*, Baltimore, 2000.

——, *La comunità dei Lucchesi a Venezia: immigrazione e industria della seta nel tardo medioevo*, Venice 1994.

——, Reinhold C. Mueller and Claudio Zanier, eds, *La seta in Italia dal medioevo al seicento: dal baco al drappo*, Venice, 2000.

Molmenti, Pompeo, *La storia di Venezia nella vita privata dalle origini alla caduta della republica*, 3 vols, Bergamo, 1905.

Montalto, Lina, *La corte di Alfonso I di Aragona: vesti e gale*, Naples, 1922.

Montanari, Massimo, *La fame e l'abbondanza: storia dell'alimentazione in Europa*, Rome, 1999.

——, *Alimentazione e cultura nel medioevo*, Rome, 1988.

Montias, John Michael, *Art at Auction in Seventeenth-Century Amsterdam*, Amsterdam, 2002.

Moran, Gerard T., 'Conceptions of Time in Early Modern France: An Approach to the History of Collective Mentalities', *Sixteenth-Century Journal*, 12 (1981), 3–19.

Moretti, Silvia, 'Vicenza: XV–XVII secolo: Tra volontà di riscatto e "normalizzazione"', in Dontella Calabi, ed., *Fabbriche, piazze, mercati: la città italiana nel rinascimento*, Rome, 1997, 224–54.

Moro, Giacomo, 'Insegne librarie e marche tipografiche in un registro veneziano del' 500', *La bibliofilia*, 91 (1989), 51–80.

Morris, Jonathan, *The Political Economy of Shopkeeping in Milan, 1886–1922*, Cambridge, 1993.

Motture, Peta, *Bells and Mortars: A Catalogue of Italian Bronzes in the Victoria and Albert Museum*, London, 2001.

Mueller, Reinhold C., *Money and Banking in Medieval and Renaissance Venice. II. The Venetian Money Market: Banks, Panics, and the Public Debt, 1200–1500*, Baltimore, 1997.

——, 'Effetti della guerra di Chioggia (1378–1381) sulla vita economica e sociale di Venezia', *Ateneo veneto*, n. s. 19 (1981), 27–41.

——, *The Procuratori di San Marco and the Venetian Credit Market*, New York, 1977.

Mui, Lorna and Hoh-cheung Mui, *Shops and Shopkeeping in Eighteenth-Century England*, London, 1989.

Muir, Edward, *Civic Ritual in Renaissance Venice*, Venice, 1981.

Muldrew, Craig, *The Economy of Obligation: The Culture of Credit and Social Relations in Early Modern England*, Basingstoke (1998).

——, 'Credit and the Courts: Debt Litigation in a Seventeenth-Century Urban Community', *Economic History Review*, n. s. 46 (1993), 23–38.

——, ' "Hard Food for Midas": Cash and its

Social Value in Early Modern England', *Past and Present*, 170 (2001), 78–120.

Musacchio, Jacqueline Marie, 'The Medici Sale of 1495 and the Second-Hand Market in Late Fifteenth-Century Florence', in Marcello Fantoni, Louisa C. Matthew and Sara F. Matthews-Grieco, eds, *The Art Market in Italy: Fifteenth to Seventeenth Centuries*, Modena, 2003, 313–24.

——, *The Art and Ritual of Childbirth in Renaissance Italy*, New Haven, 1999.

Muzzarelli, Maria Giuseppina, ed., *Guardaroba medievale: vesti e società dal XIII al XVI secolo*, Bologna, 1999.

——, *Banchi ebraici a Bologna nel XV secolo*, Bologna, 1994.

——, 'Norme di comportamento alimentare nei libri penitenziali', *Quaderni medievali*, 13 (1982), 45–80.

Nada Patrone, Anna Maria, *Il cibo del ricco ed il cibo del povero*, Turin, 1981.

Nardelli, Giuseppe Maria, *Farmacie e farmacisti in Umbria: dagli statuti degli speziali all'ordine*, Perugia, 1998.

Naso, Irma, *Formaggi del medioevo: la 'summa lacticiniorum' di Pantaleone da Confienza*, Turin, 1990.

——, *Una bottega di panni alla fine del trecento. Giovanni Canale di Pinerolo e il suo libro di conti*, Genoa 1985.

Nead, Lynda, *Victorian Babylon: People, Streets and Images in Nineteenth-Century London*, New Haven, 2000.

Nevola, Fabrizio J. D., '"Lieto e trionphante per la città": Experiencing a Mid-Fifteenth Century Imperial Triumph along Siena's Strada Romana', *Renaissance Studies*, 17 (2003), 581–606.

——, '"Per ornato della città": Siena's Strada Romana and Fifteenth-Century Urban Renewal', *Art Bulletin*, 82 (2000), 26–50.

Newett, M. Margaret, 'The Sumptuary Laws of Venice in the Fourteenth and Fifteenth Centuries', in T. F. Tout and J. Tait, eds, *Historical Essays by Members of Owen College, Manchester, Published in Commemoration of its Jubilee*, New York, 1902, 245–78.

Niccoli, Ottavia, 'Rituals of Youth: Love, Play and Violence in Tridentine Bologna', in Konrad Eisenblicher, ed., *The Premodern Teenager: Youth in Society, 1150–1650*, Toronto, 2002, 75–94.

——, *Storie di ogni giorno in una città del seicento*, Rome, 2000.

Novati, Francesco, *Tre postille dantesche. Come Manfredi s'è salvato. La 'squilla di lontano' è quella dell'Ave Maria? La vipera che'l melanese accampa*, Milan, 1898.

Nuovo, Angela, *Il commercio librario a Ferrara tra XV e XVI secolo: la bottega di Domenico Sivieri*, Florence, 1998. [1998a]

——, *Il commercio librario nell'Italia del Rinascimento*, Milan, 1998. [1998b]

——, *Il libro nell'Italia del rinascimento*, Brescia, 1998. [1998c]

Ogborn, Miles, *Spaces of Modernity: London's Geographies, 1680–1780*, New York, 1998.

Olian, Jo Anne, 'Sixteenth-Century Costume Books', *Dress*, 3 (1977), 20–48.

O'Malley, Michelle and Evelyn Welch, eds, *The Material Renaissance*, forthcoming.

Orefice, Gabriella, *Rilievi e memorie dell'antico centro di Firenze, 1885–1895*, Florence, 1986.

Ortalli, Gherardo, ed., *Gioco e giustizia nell'Italia di commune*, Rome, 1993.

Osborne, Peter, 'Modernity is a Qualitative, Not a Chronological Category', *New Left Review*, 192 (1992), 65–84.

Padoan Urban, Lina, *Il bucintoro: La festa e la fiera della 'Sensa' dalle origini alla caduta della Repubblica*, Venice, 1988.

——, 'La festa della "Sensa" nelle arti e nell'iconografia', *Studi veneziani*, 10 (1968), 291–353.

Pagliara, P. N., 'Palazzo Branconio', in C. L. Fommel, S. Ray and M. Tafuri, eds, *Raffaello architetto*, Milan, 1984, 197–204.

Palmer, Richard, 'Pharmacy in the Republic of Venice in the Sixteenth Century', in Andrew Wear, Roger K. French and Iain M. Lonie, eds, *The Medical Renaissance of the Sixteenth Century*, Cambridge, 1985, 100–31.

Palumbo-Fossati, Isabella, 'L'interno della casa dell'artigiano e dell'artista nella Venezia del

Cinquecento', *Studi veneziani*, n. s. 8 (1984), 109–53.

Panciera, Walter, *Fiducia e affari nella società veneziana del settecento*, Padua, 2000.

Panico, Guido, *Il carnefice e la piazza. Crudeltà di stato e violenza popolare a Napoli in età moderna*, Naples, 1985.

Parenti, Giuseppe, *Prime ricerche sulla rivoluzione dei prezzi a Firenze*, Florence, 1939.

Park, Katherine, 'Country Medicine in the City Marketplace: Snakehandlers as Itinerant Healers', *Renaissance Studies*, 15 (2001), 104–20.

Partsch, Susanna, *Profane Buchmalerei der bürgerlichen Gesellschaft im Spätmittelalterlichen Florenz. Der Specchio Umano des Getreidenhändlers Domenico Lenzi*, Worms, 1981.

Paulus, Nikolaus, *Indulgences as a Social Factor in the Middle Ages*, New York, 1922.

Pavanini, Paola, 'Abitazioni popolari e borghesi nella Venezia cinquecentesca', *Studi veneziani*, 5 (1981), 63–126.

Pedralli, Monica, *Novo, grande, coverto e ferrato. Gli inventari di biblioteca e la cultura a Milano nel quattrocento*, Milan, 2002.

Pedrazzoli, A., 'La Marchesa Isabella d'Este Gonzaga a diporto sul Lago di Garda colla sua corte', *Archivio storico lombardo,* anno 17, series 2, 7, (1890), 866–78.

Pelikan, Jaroslav, *The Christian Tradition. A History of the Development of Doctrine: Reformation of Church and Dogma (1300–1700)*, 5 vols, Chicago, 1984.

Perry, Marilyn, 'Wealth, Art and Display: The Grimani Cameos in Renaissance Venice', *Journal of the Warburg and Courtauld Institutes*, 56 (1993), 268–74.

——, 'Cardinal Domenico Grimani's Legacy of Ancient Art to Venice', *Journal of the Warburg and Courtauld Insitutes*, 41 (1978), 215–44.

——, 'The "statuario pubblico" of the Venetian Republic', *Saggi e memorie di storia dell'arte*, 8 (1972), 75–150.

Petrucci, Alfredo, 'Aspetti della vecchia Roma: i venditori ambulanti in una stampa antica', *Capitolium*, 8 (1932), 434–43.

Petrucci, Armando, *Il libro di ricordanze dei Corsini (1362–1457)*, Rome, 1965.

Pezzolo, Luciano, *Il fisco dei veneziani: finanza pubblica ed economia tra XV e XVII secolo*, Verona, 2003.

Piasentini, Stefano, *'Alla luce della luna': i furti a Venezia, 1270–1403*, Venice, 1992.

Pinchera, Valeria, 'Vestire la vita, vestire la morte: abiti per matrimoni e funerali, XIV–XVII secolo', in Carlo Marco Belfanti and Fabio Guisberti, eds, *Storia d'Italia: la moda*, Turin, 19, 2003, 221–59.

Pinelli, Paola, *Le attività molteplici di un caciaiolo pratese alla fine del Trecento*, Florence, 1996.

Pini, Antonio Ivan, 'La fiera d'agosto a Cesena dalla sua istituzione alla definitiva relogamentazione (1380–1509)', *Nuova rivista storica*, 68 (1984), 175–92.

Pinto, Giovanni, *Il libro del biadaiolo: carestie e annona a Firenze della metà del '200 al 1348*, Florence, 1978.

Pirovano, Carlo, *Lotto. Gli affreschi di Trescore*, Milan, 1997.

Pissavino, Paolo, 'I poveri nel pensiero politico italiano tra Cinque e Seicento', in Danilo Zardin, ed., *La citta e i poveri: Milano e le terre lombarde dal rinascimento all'età spagnola*, Milan, 1995, 151–89.

Platt, Verity, 'Shattered Visages: Speaking Statues from the Ancient World', *Apollo*, 158 (2003), 9–14.

Polecritti, Cynthia L., 'In the Shop of the Lord: Bernardino of Siena and Popular Devotion', in Paula Findlen, Michelle M. Fontaine and Duane J. Osheim, eds, *Beyond Florence: The Contours of Medieval and Early Modern Italy*, Stanford, Calif., 2003, 147–59.

Porro, Giulio, 'Preventivo delle spese pel ducato di Milano nel 1476', *Archivio Storico Lombardo*, 5 (1878), 130–4.

Porter, Roy, *Health for Sale: Quackery in England, 1550–1850*, Manchester, 1989.

Portioli, Attilio, *Le corporazioni artiere e*

l'archivio della Camera di Commercio a Mantova, Mantua, 1884.

Postles, David, 'The Marketplace as Space in Early Modern England', *Social History*, 29 (2004), 41–58.

Pullan, Brian, 'The Relief of Prisoners in Sixteenth-Century Venice', *Studi veneziani*, 10 (1968), 221–30.

——, ed., *Crisis and Change in the Venetian Economy in the Sixteenth and Seventeenth Centuries*, London, 1968.

——, 'Wage-Earners and the Venetian Economy 1550–1630', *Economic History Review*, n. s. 16 (1964), 407–26.

Quinlan-McRath, Mary, 'The Villa Farnesina, Time-Telling Conventions and Renaissance Astrological Practice', *Journal of the Warburg and Courtauld Institutes*, 58 (1995), 53–71.

Rabisch. Il grottesco nell'arte del cinquecento: l'accademia della Val di Blenio, Lomazzo e l'ambiente milanese, Milan, 1998.

Randolph, Adrian W. B., *Engaging Symbols: Gender, Politics, and Public Art in Fifteenth-Century Florence*, New Haven, 2002.

Rappaport, Erika D., '"The Halls of Temptation": Gender, Politics and the Construction of the Department Store in Late Victorian London', *Journal of British Studies*, 35 (1996), 58–83.

Ravid, Benjamin, 'Curfew Time in the Ghetto of Venice', in Ellen E. Kittell and Thomas F. Madden, eds, *Medieval and Renaissance Venice*, Urbana, Ill., 1999, 237–75.

——, 'Kosher Bread in Baroque Venice', *Italia. Studi e ricerche sulla storia, la cultura e la letteratura degli ebrei di Italia*, 6 (1987), 20–9.

Redfield, James M., 'The Development of the Market in Archaic Greece', in Bruce L. Anderson and Anthony J. H. Latham, eds, *The Market in History*, London, 1986, 9–28.

Reiss, Athene, *The Sunday Christ: Sabbatarianism in English Medieval Wall Painting*, Oxford, 2000.

Reiss, Sheryl E., 'Widow, Mother, Patron of Art: Alfonsina Orsini de'Medici', in *idem*,

and David G. Wilkins, eds, *Beyond Isabella: Secular Women Patrons of Art in Renaissance Italy*, Kirksville, Mo., 2001, 125–57.

—— and David G. Wilkins, eds, *Beyond Isabella: Secular Women Patrons of Art in Renaissance Italy*, Kirskville, Mo., 2001.

Rendina, Claudio, *Pasquino, statua parlante: quattro secoli di pasquinate*, Rome, 1991.

Revel, Jacques, 'A Capitol City's Privileges: Food Supplies in Early Modern Rome', in Robert Foster and Orest Ranum, eds, *Food and Drink in History*, Baltimore, 1979, 37–49.

Ridley, Ronald T., 'To Protect the Monuments: The Papal Antiquarian (1534–1870)', *Xenia*, 1 (1992), 117–54.

Rinaldi, Rosella, 'Un'inventario di beni dell'anno 1503: Abramo Sforno e la sua attività di prestatore', *Il Carobbio*, 9 (1983), 314–27.

Roberts, Mary L. 'Gender, Consumption and Commodity Culture', *American Historical Review*, 103 (1998), 817–44.

Roland, François, *Un Franc-Comtois, éditeur et marchand d'éditeur et marchand d'éstampes à Rome au XVI siècle: Antoine Lafrery (1512–1577), notice historique*, Paris, 1911.

Romani, Marina, *Una città in forma di palazzo. Potere signorile e forma urbana nella Mantova medievale e moderna*, Mantua, 1995.

Romani, Mario A., 'Il pane quotidiano: approvvigionamenti e consumi alimentari nei ducati padani fra cinque e settecento,' in *La famiglia e la vita quotidiana in Europa nel '400 al '600: fonti e problemi*, Rome, 1986, 343–54.

Romano, Dennis, *Housecraft and Statecraft: Domestic Service in Renaissance Venice, 1400–1600*, Baltimore, 1996.

——, 'The Regulation of Domestic Service in Renaissance Venice', *Sixteenth Century Journal*, 22 (1991), 661–77.

——, 'Gender and the Urban Geography of Renaissance Venice', *Journal of Social History*, 23 (1989), 339–53.

——, *Patricians and Popolani: The Social*

Foundations of the Venetian Renaissance State, Baltimore, 1987.

Romby, Giuseppina Carla and Massismo Tarassi, eds, *Vivere nel contado al tempo di Lorenzo*, Florence, 1992.

Rossi, Mario A., *Lutero e Roma. La fatale scintilla (la lotta intorno alle indulgenze) 1517–1519*, Rome, 1923.

Rossi, Vittorio, *Le indole e gli studi di Giovanni di Cosimo de'Medici: notizie e documenti*, Rome, 1893.

Rouch, M., 'Diffusion orale, fefeuilles volantes, écrits populaires au XVI siecle. Le cas de Giulio Cesare Croce a Bologna', in *Autres Italies. La culture intermediares en Italie: Les auteurs et leur publique*, Talence, 1994, 31–53.

——, *Storia di vita populare nelle canzoni di piazza di G. C. Croce. Fame, fatica e mascherate nel '500*, Bologna, 1982.

Rouse, M. A. and R. H. Rouse, eds, *Cartolai, Illuminators and Printers in Fifteenth-Century Italy: The Evidence of the Ripoli Press*, Los Angeles, 1988.

Saba, Franco, *Il 'valimento del mercimonio' del 1580. Accertamento fiscale e realtà del commercio della città di Milano*, Milan, 1990.

Sapori, Armando, 'Una fiera in Italia alla fine del quattrocento', in *idem, Studi di storia economica (secoli XIII–XIV–XV)* 3 vols, Florence, 1955, I, 443–74.

——, 'Case e botteghe a Firenze nel Trecento', in *idem, Studi di storia economica (secoli XIII–XIV–XV)*, 3 vols, Florence, 1955, I, 305–52.

Sargentson, Carolyn, *Merchants and Luxury Markets: The Marchands Merciers of Eighteenth-Century Paris*, Los Angeles, 1996.

Scarpellini, Emanuela, *Comprare all'Americana: le origini della rivoluzione commerciale in Italia 1945–1971*, Bologna, 2001.

Schama, Simon, *The Embarrassment of Riches: An Interpretation of Dutch Culture in the Golden Age*, New York, 1987.

Scharf, Gian Paolo, 'Fra economia urbana e circuiti intercittadini: il ruolo degli ebrei a Borgo San Sepolcro a metà del quattro-

cento', *Archivio storico italiano*, 156 (1998), 447–77.

Schmitter, Monika, '"Virtuous Riches": The Bricolage of "Cittadini" Identities in Early Sixteenth-Century Venice', *Renaissance Quarterly*, 57 (2004), 908–69.

Schneider, Robert A., 'The Postmodern City from an Early Modern Perspective', *American Historical Review*, 105 (2001), 1668–75.

Sebregondi, Ludovica, 'Clothes and Teenagers: What Young Men Wore in Fifteenth-Century Florence', in Konrad Eisenblicher, ed., *The Premodern Teenager: Youth in Society, 1150–1650*, Toronto, 2002, 27–50.

Segarizzi, Arnaldo, 'Una lotteria di quadri nel secolo XVII', *Nuovo archivio veneto*, n. s. 28, (1914), 172–87.

Sella, Domenico, 'Coping with Famine: The Changing Demography of an Italian Village in the 1590s', *Sixteenth-Century Journal*, 22 (1991), 185–97.

Sframeli, Maria, ed., *Il centro di Firenzo restituito: affreschi e frammenti lapidei nel Museo di San Marco*, Florence, 1989.

Sgarbi, Vincenzo, *Antonio da Crevalcore e la pittura ferrarese del quattrocento a Bologna*, Milan, 1985.

Shammas, Carole, *The Pre-Industrial Consumer in England and America*, Oxford, 1990.

Shaw, James, 'Retail, Monopoly, and Privilege: The Dissolution of the Fishmonger's Guild of Venice, 1599', *Journal of Early Modern History*, 6 (2002), 396–427.

——, and Evelyn Welch, *'Making and Marketing Medicine in Renaissance Florence: The 'Speziale al Giglio' in 1494*, forthcoming.

Shell, Janice and Grazioso Sironi, 'Cecilia Gallerani: Leonardo's Lady with an Ermine', *Artibus et historiae*, 25 (1992), 67–84.

Shemek, Deanna, 'In Continuous Expectation: Isabella's Epistolary Desire', in Dennis Looney and Deanna Shemek, eds, *Phaethon's Children: The Este Court and Its Culture in Early Modern Italy*, Tempe, Ariz., forthcoming.

——, 'Isabella d'Este and the Properties of

Persuasion', in Ann Crabb and Jane Couchman, eds, *Form and Persuasion in Early Modern Women's Letters Across Europe*, Brookfield, Vt., forthcoming.

——, 'Script, Mimicry, and Mediation in Isabella d'Este's Letters', *Rinascimento*, forthcoming.

——, 'Books at Banquet: Commodities, Canon and Culture in Giulio Cesare Croce's "Convito Universale"', *Annalio italianistica*, 16 (1998), 85–101.

Shesgreen, Sean, *Images of the Outcast: The Urban Poor in the Cries of London*, Manchester, 2002.

Sicca, Cinzia, 'Consumption and Trade of Art between Italy and England in the First Half of the Sixteenth Century: The London House of the Bardi and Cavalcanti Company', *Renaissance Studies*, 16 (2002) 163–201.

Simeoni, Luigi, 'L'ufficio dei forestieri a Bologna del secolo XIV al XVI', *Atti e memorie della reale deputazione di storia patria per le provincie di Romagna*, series IV, 25 (1934–5), 71–95.

Simonsohn, Shlomo, *The Jews in the Duchy of Milan*, 4 vols, Jerusalem, 1982–6.

Skinner, Quentin, 'Ambrogio Lorenzetti's Buon Governo Frescoes: Two Old Questions, Two New Answers', *Journal of the Warburg and Courtauld Institutes*, 62 (1999), 1–28.

Smith, Bruce, *The Acoustic World of Early Modern England*, Chicago, 1999.

Smith, Pamela H. and Paula Findlen, eds, *Merchants and Marvels: Commerce, Science and Art in Early Modern Europe*, London, 2002.

Soja, Edward W., *Postmodern Geographies: The Reassertion of Space in Critical Social Theory*, London, 1989.

Solomon, Michael R., Gary Bamossy and Søren Askegaard, eds, *Consumer Behaviour: A European Perspective*, Harlow, 2002.

Spallanzani, Marco, 'A Note on Florentine Banking in the Renaissance: Orders of Payment and Cheques', *Journal of Economic History*, 7 (1978), 145–65.

Spear, Richard E., 'Scrambling for *scudi*: Notes on Painters' Earnings in Early Baroque Rome', *Art Bulletin*, 85 (2003), 310–20.

Spinelli, Marina, *Milano nel quattrocento: la città, la società, il ducato attraverso gli atti dei notai milanesi*, Milan, 1998.

Spring, Peter, 'The Topographical and Archaeological Study of the Antiquities of the City of Rome, 1420–1447', Ph.D. diss., University of Edinburgh, 1972.

Spufford, Margaret, *The Great Reclothing of Rural England*, London, 1984.

Stahl, Allen, *Zecca: The Mint of Venice in the Middle Ages*, Baltimore, 2000.

Stevens, Kevin M. and Paul F. Gehl, 'The Eye of Commerce: Visual Literacy Among the Makers of Books in Italy', in Marcello Fantoni, Louisa C. Matthew and Sara F. Matthews-Grieco, eds, *The Art Market in Italy: Fifteenth to Seventeenth Centuries*, Modena, 2003, 273–81.

Stobart, J., 'Shopping Streets as Social Space: Leisure, Consumerism and Improvement in an Eighteenth-Century County Town', *Urban History*, 25 (1998), 3–21.

Stöckley, Doris, *Le système de l'incanto des galées du marchée à Venise (fin XIIIe-milieu XVe siècles)*, Leiden, 1995.

Stone-Ferrier, Linda, 'Gabriel Metsu's Vegetable Market at Amsterdam: Seventeenth-Century Dutch Market Paintings and Horticulture', *Art Bulletin*, 71 (1989), 427–52.

Styles, John, 'Product Innovation in Early Modern London', *Past and Present*, 168 (2000), 124–69.

Syson, Luke and Dillian Gordon, *Pisanello: Painter to the Renaissance Court*, London, 2001.

Syson, Luke and Dora Thornton, *Objects of Virtue: Art in Renaissance Italy*, London, 2001.

Tacconi, Monica S., 'Appropriating the Instruments of Worship: The 1512 Medici

Restoration and the Florentine Cathedral Choirbooks', *Renaissance Quarterly*, 56 (2003), 333–76.

Tamalio, Raffaele, *Federico Gonzaga alla corte di Francesco I di Francia nel carteggio privato con Mantova (1515–1517)*, Paris, 1994.

Tessari, Roberto, *Commedia dell'arte: la maschera e l'ombra*, Milan, 1981.

Thirsk, Joan, *Economic Policy and Projects: The Development of a Consumer Society in Early Modern England*, Oxford, 1978.

Thompson, Eric P., 'The Moral Economy of the English Crowd in the Eighteenth-Century', *Past and Present*, 50 (1971), 76–131.

Thornton, Dora, *The Scholar in His Study: Ownership and Experience in Renaissance Italy*, New Haven, 1998.

Thornton, Peter, *The Italian Renaissance Interior, 1400–1600*, New York, 1991.

Tittoni, Maria Elisa, 'La formazione delle collezioni capitoline di antichità fra cultura e politica', in *Il campidoglio all'epoca di Raffaello*, Milan, 1984, 23–6.

Toaff, Ariel, *Love, Work and Death: Jewish Life in Medieval Umbria*, London, 1996.

Tognetti, Sergio, 'Problemi di vettovagliamento cittadino e misure di politica annonaria a Firenze nel XV secolo', *Archivio storico italiano*, 157 (1999), 419–52.

——, 'Prezzi e salari nella Firenze tardomedievale: un profilo', *Archivio storico italiano*, 153 (1995), 263–333.

Tristano, Caterina, '"Completus in testu et glosis": Il libro giuridico a Bologna tra XIII e XIV secolo: Il mercato dell'usato', *Nuovi annali della scuola speciale per archivisti e bibliotecari*, 12 (1998), 63–96.

——, 'Prezzo e costo del libro in epoca medievale: presentazione di una ricerca', *Scrittura e civiltà*, 14 (1990), 271–9.

Trivellato, Francesca, *Fondamento dei vetrai: lavoro, technologia e mercato a Venezia tra sei e settecento*, Rome, 2000.

Tucci, Ugo, 'L'alimentazione a bordo delle navi veneziane', *Studi veneziani*, n. s. 13 (1987), 103–46.

——, 'I servizi marittimi veneziani per il pellegrinagio in Terrasanta nel medioevo', *Studi veneziani*, n. s. 9 (1985), 43–66.

——, 'The Psychology of the Venetian Merchant in the Sixteenth-Century', in John Hale, ed., *Renaissance Venice*, London, 1973, 346–78.

——, 'Pesi e misure nella storia della società', *Storia d'Italia: documenti*, 5, Turin, 1973, 581–612.

——, 'Le tariffe veneziane e libri toscani di mercatura', *Studi veneziani*, 10 (1968), 65–108.

Tuliani, Maurizio, 'Il campo di Siena: un mercato cittadino in epoca comunale', *Quaderni medievali*, 46 (1998), 59–100.

——, '*Osti, avventori e malandrini': alberghi, locande e taverne a Siena e nel suo contado tra trecento e quattrocento*, Siena, 1994.

Ullman, Berthold L. and Philip A. Stadter, *The Public Library of Renaissance Florence*, Padua, 1972.

Uzielli, Gustavo, *Le misure lineari medioevali e l'effigie di Christo*, Florence, 1899.

Vallet, Alessandra, *Il miniatore di Giorgio di Challant. L'arte e la vita di un'artista itinerante nella regione alpina occidentale alla fine del medioevo*, Aosta, 1999.

Venturelli, Paola, *Vestire e apparire: il sistema vestimentario femminile nella Milano spagnola (1539–1679)*, Rome, 1999.

——, *Gioielli e gioiellieri Milanesi: storia, arte, moda (1450–1630)*, Milan, 1996.

——, 'Vigegano e la calzatura tra il XIV e il XIX secolo', in *Dalla parte della scarpa: le calzature a Vigevano dal 1400 al 1940*, Vigevano, 1992, 15–48.

Vercellin, Giorgio, 'Mercanti turchi e sensali a Venezia', *Studi veneziani,* n. s. 4 (1980), 45–78.

Verga, Ettore, 'Le leggi suntuarie e la decedenza dell'industria in Milano, 1565–1750', *Archivio storico lombardo*, anno 27, series 3, 13 (1990), 49–266.

Veronese, Alessandra, 'Per la storia della vita materiale degli ebrei nel ducato di Urbino: osservazioni tratte da due inventari di beni del primo quattrocento', *Zakhor. Rivista di storia degli ebrei d'Italia*, 4 (2000), 37–56.

Vigo, Giovanni, 'Real Wages of the Working Class in Italy: Building Workers' Wages (Fourteenth to Eighteenth Century)', *Journal of European Economic History*, 3 (1974), 378–99.

Waldman, Louis Alexander, 'Puligo and Jacopo di Filippo "Fornaciaio": Two Unrecorded Paintings of 1524', *Source: Notes in the History of Art*, 18 (1999) 25–7.

Walker, Jonathan, 'Gambling and Venetian Noblemen *c.*1500–1700', *Past and Present*, 162 (1999), 28–69.

Walsh, Claire, 'The Newness of the Department Store: A View from the Eighteenth Century', in Geoffrey Gossick and Serge Jaumain, eds, *Cathedrals of Consumption: The European Department Store, 1850–1939*, Aldershot, 1999, 46–71.

——, 'Shop Design and the Display of Goods in Eighteenth-Century London', *Journal of Design History*, 8 (1995), 157–76.

Walter, I., 'Cafferecci, Giovanni', in *Dizionario biografico degli italiani*, 16, Rome, 1973, 263–4.

Warwick, Genevieve, *The Arts of Collecting: Padre Sebastiano Resta and the Market for Drawings in Early Modern Europe*, Cambridge, 2000.

Weinstein, Roni, 'Thus Will "Giovanni" Do: Jewish Sub-Culture in Early Modern Italy', in Konrad Eisenblicher, ed., *The Premodern Teenager: Youth in Society, 1150–1650*, Toronto, 2002, 51–74.

Weiss, Bruno and Louis C. Pérez, *Beginnings and Discoveries: Polydore Vergil's 'De inventoribus rerum'*, Nieuwkoop, 1997.

Weiss, Roberto, *The Renaissance Discovery of Classical Antiquity*, Oxford, 1969.

Welch, Evelyn, 'From Retail to Resale: Artistic Value and the Second-Hand Market in Italy (1400–1550)', in Marcello Fantoni, Louisa C. Matthew and Sara F. Matthews-Grieco, eds, *The Art Market in Italy: Fif-teenth to Seventeenth Centuries*, Modena, 2003, 283–300.

——, 'The Art of Expenditure: The Court of Paola Malatesta Gonzaga in Fifteenth-Century Mantua', *Renaissance Studies*, 16 (2002), 306–17.

——, 'Public Magnificence and Private Display: Pontano's '*De Splendore*', *Journal of Design History*, 15 (2002), 211–28.

——, 'The Gonzaga Go Shopping: Commercial and Cultural Relationships Between Milan and Mantua in the Fifteenth Century', in Luca Chiavoni, Gianfranco Ferlisi and Maria V. Grassi, eds, *Leon Battista Alberti e il Quattrocento: studi in onore di Cecil Grayson e Ernst Gombrich*, Florence, 2001, 269–84.

——, 'Women as Patrons and Clients in the Courts of Northern Italy', in L. Panizza, ed., *Women in Italian Renaissance Culture and Society*, Oxford, 2000, 18–34.

——, 'Between Milan and Naples: Ippolita Maria Sforza, Duchess of Calabria', in David Abulafia, ed., *The French Descent into Renaissance Italy (1494–1495)*, Aldershot, 1995, 123–36.

——, *Art and Authority in Renaissance Milan*, New Haven, 1995.

White, Stephen D., *Custom, Kinship and Gifts to Saints: The 'Laudatio Parentum' in Western France, 1050–1150*, Chapel Hill, 1988.

Wilkins, David, 'Donatello's Lost "Dovizia" for the Mercato Vecchio: Wealth and Charity as Florentine Civic Virtues', *Art Bulletin*, 65 (1983), 401–23.

Williams, Rosalind, *Dream Worlds: Mass Consumption in Late Nineteenth-Century France*, Berkeley, 1982.

Witcombe, Christopher L. C. E., *Copyright in the Renaissance: Prints and the 'Privilegio' in Sixteenth-Century Venice and Rome*, Leiden, 2004.

Wood, Merry Wiesner, 'Paltry Peddlars or Essential Merchants? Women in the Distributive Trades in Early Modern Nuremberg', *Sixteenth-Century Journal*, 12, n. 2 (1981), 3–14.

Wrigley, Richard, 'Between the Street and the Salon: Parisian Shop Signs and the Spaces of Professionalism in the Eighteenth and Early Nineteenth Centuries', *Oxford Art Journal*, 21 (1998), 43–68.

Zaffanella, Chiara, 'Isabella d'Este e la modo del suo tempo', *Civiltà mantovana*, 35 (2000), 66–81.

Zaggia, Stefano, 'Imola: 1474–1499. La costruzione della piazza maggiore durante la Signoria Riario', in Donatella Calabi, ed., *Fabbriche, piazze, mercati: la città italiana nel rinascimento*, Rome, 1997, 389–407.

Zagli, Andrea, Francesco Mineccia and Andrea Giuntini, eds, *Maladetti beccari: storia dei macellai fiorentini dal cinquecento al duemila*, Florence, 2000.

Zanelli, Guglielmo, *Traghetti veneziani: la gondola al servizio della città*, Venice, 1997.

Zanetti, Diego, *Problemi alimentari di una economia pre-industriale*, Turin, 1964.

Zanoboni, Maria Paola, 'Frutta e fruttaroli nella Milano Sforzesca', *Archivio storico lombardo*, anno 123, series 12, 4 (1997), 117–51.

——, *Artigiani, imprenditori, mercanti: organizzazione del lavoro e conflitti sociali nella Milano Sforzesco (1450–1476)*, Florence, 1996.

Zardin, Danilo, ed., *La città e i poveri. Milano e le terre lombarde dal rinascimento all'età spagnola*, Milan, 1995.

Zdekauer, Ludovico, *Il gioco d'azzardo nel medioevo italiano*, (reprint) Florence, 1993.

——, 'Per una storia delle fiere di Recanati (1384–1473)', *Atti e memorie della reale deputazione di storia patria per le provincie delle marche*, series 3, 2 (1918), 245–65.

——, *Per la storia del prestito a pegno in Colle Val d'Elsa nel secolo XV*, Castelfiorentino, 1899.

——, 'L'interno d'un banco di pegno nel 1417 con documenti inediti', *Archivio storico italiano*, series 5, 17 (1896) 63–105.

Zemon Davis, Natalie, *The Gift in Sixteenth-Century France*, Madison, Wis., 2000.

Zervas, Diane Finiello, 'The Florentine Braccio da Panno', *Architectura. Zeitschrift für Geschichte der Baukunst, Journal of the History of Architecture*, 9 (1979), 6–10.

Zilocchi, Cesare, *I tormenti della carne: beccai, beccarie, macelli a Piacenza*, Piacenza, 1993.

Zocchi, Daniela, 'Milano: XVI–XVII secolo: il problema dei "siti" e delle piazze', in Donatella Calabi, ed., *Fabbriche, piazze, mercati. La città italiana nel rinascimento*, Milan, 1996, 76–101.

Photograph Credits

Index